Reference Books Bulletin 1992-93

A compilation of evaluations
September 1, 1992, through August 1993

*Prepared by the American Library Association Reference
Books Bulletin Editorial Board*

Edited by Sandy Whiteley and Jane McKeever
Compiled by Caroline Paulison

BOOKLIST Publications
Chicago, 1994

Copyright 1994 by the American Library Association.
Permission to quote any review in full or in part must be obtained
from the Office of Rights and Permissions of the American Library
Association. Permission to quote a review in full will be granted
only to the publisher of the work reviewed.

Library of Congress Catalog Card Number 73-159565

International Standard Book Number 0-8389-5761-7
International Standard Serial Number 8755-0962

Printed in the United States of America

Cover design by Ellen Pettengell

Contents

- v Preface
- vi Reference Books Bulletin Editorial Board
- ix Alumni
- Omnibus Articles
  - 1 1992 Annual Encyclopedia Update
  - 7 Higher Education Directories
  - 12 Consumer Health Information
  - 14 Job and Career Information Sources
  - 17 Native American Reference Sources
  - 21 Business Reference Sources
- Featured Reviews and Reviews
  - 26 Generalities
  - 39 Philosophy, Psychology, Religion
  - 45 Social Sciences
  - 55 Business, Economics
  - 63 Law, Public Administration, Social Problems and Services
  - 76 Education, Communication, Customs
  - 81 Language
  - 89 Science
  - 98 Medicine, Health, Technology, Management
  - 112 Fine Arts, Decorative Arts, Music
  - 120 Performing Arts, Recreation
  - 129 Literature
  - 142 Geography, Biography
  - 156 History
- 166 Index to Type of Material
- 170 Subject Index
- 176 Title Index

Preface

This is the twenty-fifth cumulation of *RBB* reviews. (The first cumulation covered four years, 1956–1960; the following seven covered two years each; the cumulation became an annual publication with the 1974–75 volume.) The reviews were published in twenty-one issues of *Reference Books Bulletin* (a separate publication within *Booklist*) from September 1992 through August 1993. As in previous years, the reviews were published in the name of the Editorial Board, a subcommittee of ALA's Publishing Committee.

The reviews were drafted by Board members or alumni reviewers who are a cross-section of public, academic, and school librarians throughout the U.S. The reviews were then read by other Board members and the chair of the Editorial Board. The editor used the comments of these readers in preparing the reviews for publication.

More than 1,500 sources were considered by the chair and the editor for possible review this year. From these, 456 reviews were published; 18 of them featured reviews of especially important titles. Omnibus reviews, annotated lists of current literature on a particular subject, were published on directories of higher education, consumer health information, job and career information, Native American reference, and business reference sources. The "1992 Annual Encyclopedia Update" was also published as an omnibus article.

The Board continues to review electronic reference sources. Included in this volume are reviews of *Children's Reference Plus, Facts On File News Digest, DISCovering Authors, Gale's Literary Index, Magazine Article Summaries Full Text Elite, Masterplots II, Microsoft Encarta Multimedia Encyclopedia, The Multimedia Encyclopedia of Mammalian Biology,* and *The Oxford English Dictionary.*

Sandy Whiteley and Jane McKeever and their editorial assistants did an outstanding job this year. Jane McKeever was acting editor from December 1, 1992, through May 31, 1993, while Sandy Whiteley was on leave editing a book. Publishing assistants Denise Blank and Caroline Paulison were instrumental in producing our reviews in a timely fashion. Sincere thanks and appreciation go to all the Board members and alumni reviewers who supplied the library community with critical, authoritative, and current reviews. Personally, I wish to thank Richard Johnson and the staff of Milne Library, State University of New York, College at Oneonta, for the support they provided.

Christine Bulson
Chair, Editorial Board, 1992–1993

Reference Books Bulletin
Editorial Board

Christine Bulson, Head of Reference and Associate Librarian, Milne Library, State University of New York, College at Oneonta, Oneonta, New York, Chairperson

Edwina Walker Amorosa, Media Specialist, Kent Center School, Kent, Connecticut

Hampton M. Auld, Branch Manager, Carroll County Public Library, Greenmount, Maryland

Susan Awe, Manager, Arvada Branch, Jefferson County Library System, Arvada, Colorado

Ken Black, Reference Librarian, Rosary College, River Forest, Illinois

Jerry Carbone, Assistant Reference Librarian, Brooks Memorial Library, Brattleboro, Vermont

Ronald Chepesiuk, Head, Special Collections, Dacus Library, Winthrop College, Rock Hill, South Carolina

Ann E. Cohen, Assistant Division Head, Reynolds Information Center, Rochester Public Library, Rochester, New York

Sharon E. Cohen, Assistant Reference Librarian, Bank Street College, New York City, New York

Lesley S. J. Farmer, Library Director, San Domenico School, San Anselmo, California

Elizabeth L. Fraser, Reference/Foundation/ILL Librarian, Kanawha County Public Library, Charleston, West Virginia

John P. Hall, Director of Media Services, Greater Lowell Regional Vocational-Technical School District, Tyngsboro, Massachusetts

Robin Hoelle, Librarian, Badin High School, Hamilton, Ohio

Sarah Sartain Jane, Head of Reference, Fort Meyers/Lee County Public Library, Fort Meyers, Florida

Jane C. Jurgens, Reference Librarian, Ronald Williams Library, Northeastern Illinois University, Chicago, Illinois

Sue Kamm, Associate Librarian, Audio-Visual/Circulation Divisions, Inglewood Public Library, Inglewood, California

Marlene M. Kuhl, Public Services Librarian, Baltimore County Public Library, Reisterstown Area Branch, Reisterstown, Maryland

Marvin Leavy, Reference Services Supervisor, Western Kentucky University, Bowling Green, Kentucky

Marilyn L. Long, High School Librarian, Palma High School, Salinas, California

Carolyn M. Mulac, Assistant Head, Information Center, Chicago Public Library, Chicago, Illinois

Betty Page, Guilford, Connecticut

David N. Pauli, Director, Missoula Public Library, Missoula, Montana

Fannette Thomas, Acting Coordinator of Public Services, Essex Community College, Baltimore, Maryland

Sarah Barbara Watstein, Assistant Director, Virginia Commonwealth University, Richmond, Virginia

A. Virginia Witucke, Central Michigan University, Merrifield Center, Fairfax, Virginia

INTERNS

Rochelle Glantz, Library Media Specialist, Arlington High School, Arlington, Massachusetts

Carol Sue Harless, Media Specialist, DeKalb County School, Decatur, Georgia

Tom Klingler, Head, Reference Department, Bierce Library, The University of Akron, Akron, Ohio

Kathleen M. McBroom, Media Specialist, Fordson Media Center, Dearborn, Michigan

Elizabeth B. Nibley, Reference Librarian, The American University Library, Washington, D.C.

Alumni

James D. Anderson, Associate Dean, School of Communication, Information & Library Studies, Rutgers University, New Brunswick, New Jersey

Hilda Arnold, Drakesboro, Kentucky

Barbara Bibel, Reference Librarian, Oakland Public Library, Oakland, California

Brian E. Coutts, Head, Department of Public Services, Helm-Cravens Library, Western Kentucky University, Bowling Green, Kentucky

Milton H. Crouch, Assistant Director for Reader Services, Bailey/Howe Library, University of Vermont, Burlington, Vermont

Donald G. Davis, Jr., Professor, Graduate School of Library & Information Science, University of Texas at Austin, Austin, Texas

Winifred F. Dean, Business/Social Science Librarian, Cleveland State University Library, Cleveland, Ohio

Carole C. Deily, Reference Librarian, Plano Public Library System, Plano, Texas

Marie Ellis, English and American Literature Bibliographer, History and Humanities Department, University of Georgia Libraries, Athens, Georgia

Jack Forman, Reference/Bibliographic Services Librarian, Mesa College Library, San Diego, California

Charles L. Gilreath, Assistant Director for Public Services, North Carolina State University Public Library, Raleigh, North Carolina

Gary Golden, Director, Camden Arts and Science Library, Rutgers University, Camden, New Jersey

Susan Gooden, Librarian, Concord High School, Wilmington, Delaware

Ruth M. Hadlow, Head, Children's Literature Department, Cleveland Public Library, Cleveland, Ohio

Nancy Huntley, Assistant Director, Lincoln Library, Springfield, Illinois

Vincent J. Jennings, Documents & Map Librarian, Hofstra University Library, Hempstead, New York

Rashelle Karp, Associate Professor, College of Library Science, Clarion University of Pennsylvania, Clarion, Pennsylvania

Martin A. Kesselman, Coordinator of Online and Institutional Services, Library of Science and Medicine, Rutgers University, Piscataway, New Jersey

Donald Krummel, Professor, Graduate School of Library & Information Science, University of Illinois, Urbana, Illinois

John C. Larsen, Baltimore, Maryland

Abbie Vestal Landry, Head of Reference Division, Watson Library, Northwestern State University, Natchitoches, Louisiana

Arthur Lichtenstein, Reference Librarian, Torreyson Library, University of Central Arkansas, Conway, Arkansas

Judith Yankielun Lind, Director, Roseland Free Public Library, Roseland, New Jersey

Josephine McSweeney, Reference Librarian, Pratt Institute Library, Brooklyn, New York

H. Robert Malinowsky, Bibliographer of Science and Engineering, University of Illinois–Chicago Library, Chicago, Illinois

Arthur S. Meyers, Library Director, Hammond Public Library, Hammond, Indiana

Margaret C. Power, Department Head, Reference Librarian, DePaul University Library, Chicago, Illinois

Mary Ellen Quinn, Director of Collection Development, Chicago Public Library, Chicago, Illinois

James R. Rettig, Assistant University Librarian for Reference and Information Services, Earl Gregg Swem Library, College of William and Mary, Williamsburg, Virginia

Stewart P. Schneider, Associate Professor, Graduate School of Library and Information Studies, University of Rhode Island, West Kingston, Rhode Island

Martin D. Sugden, Reference Librarian, Business, Science and Industry Department, Haydon Burns Library, Jacksonville, Florida

David A. Tyckoson, Head, Reference Department, State University of New York–Albany, Albany, New York

Jim Walsh, Government Publications/Microforms, O'Neill Library, Boston College, Boston, Massachussetts

Bobbi Walters, Houston, Texas

Christine A. Whittington, Reference Department, Raymond H. Fogler Library, The University of Maine, Orono, Maine

Wiley J. Williams, Chapel Hill, North Carolina

Raymund F. Wood, Encino, California

Omnibus Reviews

1992 Annual Encyclopedia Update

This was another difficult year for encyclopedia editors, as dramatic events in the former Soviet Union and in Eastern Europe continued through the end of the year. One problem was getting updated maps of these areas to accompany articles, since maps and text should be consistent. Because an encyclopedia is not intended to serve as a current-awareness source like a newspaper, we have not stressed the coverage of the events of late 1991 in our evaluation of these sets, especially since their publication dates vary from January 1 to the end of March.

On the issue of consistency between maps and text, one place where many of these sets fail is in the consistent use of Chinese transliteration systems. The pinyin system has been in use in this country since 1979, but only World Book consistently uses it (Compton's does with a few exceptions.) Many sets use pinyin on maps but Wade-Giles in text (e.g., *Tianjin* on the map of China but *Tientsin* as the entry for the city), and a few sets use Wade-Giles throughout. The Board would like to see all these encyclopedias switch to consistent use of pinyin.

Two encyclopedias for children underwent major structural changes this year. Both *Compton's Encyclopedia* and *The New Book of Knowledge* are eliminating the indexes, which also included brief articles, at the end of each volume. Compton's removed all its "Fact-Indexes" at the ends of volumes in the 1992 set, but the separate index volume still contains many brief articles. *The New Book of Knowledge* will be eliminating its "Dictionary Indexes" over several years. The information in the brief articles will be integrated into the body of the set.

This year these sets incorporate the 1990 U.S. census population figures (except for *New Standard*, which has updated state articles but not all city ones). The statistics the publishers provided us on these changes are a good measure of the relative coverage of American places in encyclopedias. For instance, *The New Book of Knowledge* had to change about 35 city articles; *World Book*, 330 cities; *Funk & Wagnalls*, 1,353; *Collier's*, 1,530; *The New Encyclopaedia Britannica*, 1,800; and *Encyclopedia Americana*, 2,005. Libraries that have not replaced their encyclopedias in several years will find that the inclusion of these new statistics makes this a good year to do so.

Only nine encyclopedias are reviewed here, compared with 11 in our 1991 update [RBB O 1 91]. *Merit Student's Encyclopedia* has ceased publication, and *Children's Britannica*, while still available, was not issued in a revised edition for 1992.

Academic American Encyclopedia. 21v. Lawrence T. Lorimer, editorial director; K. Anne Ranson, editor in chief. Grolier, 1992.

First published in 1980, *Academic American Encyclopedia* is the most recently created general English-language encyclopedia. AAE emphasizes the subjects common to the curriculum of American schools and universities. The encyclopedia's strengths include contemporary events, pop culture, international affairs, and current technology, though more than a third of the work covers the humanities and the arts. AAE's preface indicates that more than 90 percent of the encyclopedia has been written by outside authorities afffiliated with major academic institutions, corporations, and nonprofit organizations. Forty-four new contributors were added to the 1992 edition, including Jefferson W. Tester, professor of chemical engineering at MIT (*Geothermal Energy*), and Louise Bates Ames, associate director of the Gesell Institute of Human Development (*Child Development*). However, many of the most timely new articles such as *Gulf War*, *Cyberspace*, and *Bank of Credit and Commerce International* are unsigned, as are over 25 percent of the articles in the set.

AAE covers a broad spectrum of information through 28,940 concise, factual articles. More than half of them are less than 500 words in length. This format plus excellent tables, graphs, and illustrations makes it ideal for ready-reference questions. The set also includes general overview articles such as the new one *Petroleum* that could serve as a beginning point in student research, identifying key concepts and controversial issues. The editors of AAE identify their audience as upper elementary students through adults. However, a tendency to technical detail, scholarly vocabulary, and lengthy sentences makes some of these articles challenging to even middle school readers. Nearly 40 percent of all articles conclude with a bibliography of one to twelve entries. These include standard and recently published English-language works that should be readily available in most library systems. The bibliographic references are uniform for college and adult audiences. More than 2,000 bibliographies were revised this year, as part of a five-year program to revise all reading lists.

As in the past, approximately one-third of the space is devoted to the handsome illustrations for which AAE is known—photographs, artwork, and maps, three-quarters of which are in full color. Of the 16,900 illustrations, 167 are new this year. The replaced articles *Landscape Architecture* and *Landscape Painting*, for example, have been entirely reillustrated with attractive pictures. *Life-Support Systems* has two new photographs of space suits used in the space program. There are also 93 revised maps documenting the reunification of Germany, the union of two Yemeni states, and other recent changes in world affairs. Page layouts are striking.

AAE's substantial index of over 200,000 entries includes all articles, illustrations, and major map designations, as well as numerous *see* and *see also* references. However, valuable information in fact boxes and tables is frequently ignored in the index. For example, no entry is found for Elias James Corey, the 1990 Nobel Prize winner in chemistry, although he is noted in the list of winners in the article *Nobel Prize*. The 1992 index has been reorganized. Index entries are now arranged in letter-by-letter order, providing an alternative method of searching for subjects as compared with the word-by-word order of the articles themselves. This may improve accessibility to the set's contents by providing another means of approach, but it may also confuse some readers. The index now sets all headings in boldface type while preserving the distinction between article titles and other headings by setting the article titles in capital letters. Within the body of the set, there are also extensive cross-references, both internal and *see also* references, that will help the many encyclopedia users who tend to avoid the index volume.

World events appeared to have triggered most changes in the 1992 AAE. Eighty new articles, including such entries as F-117A *Stealth Fighter*, *High Definition Television*, *Fragile-X Syndrome*, *Language*, and *Thomas, Clarence*, were added to this edition. There are also brief new entries for Nobel Peace Prize winner Aung San Suu Kyi and Edith Cresson, the former prime minister of France. AAE is the only set that has a separate entry for Suu Kyi; *Britannica* and AAE are the only sets with an entry for Cresson. The new entry *Genetic Testing* addresses the ethical aspects of this topic as well as the scientific ones. In addition to these new articles, 50 existing ones were replaced with lengthier, signed entries. These include such subjects as *Breast Feeding*, *Germany*, *Vegetarianism*, and *Fellini, Federico*. Nearly 5,000 existing articles and over 90 maps received major or minor revision. The Gulf War, the dramatic changes in Eastern Europe, and 1990 census data directly impacted the substantial revisions required in 1992. Approximately 17 percent of this edition's articles were revised in some manner, providing an extremely current text.

A slightly modified version of the previous year's edition of AAE is sold in retail stores as *The Grolier International Encyclopedia* and *Barnes & Noble New American Encyclopedia*. A condensed version is sold in supermarkets as *The Grolier Encyclopedia of Knowledge*. AAE is available in several electronic versions. It is online with such services as CompuServe and Prodigy. The CD-ROM version, *The New Grolier Multimedia Encyclopedia*, contains thousands of color pictures, over 250 color maps, plus audio and motion sequences. Additional features include a time line with links to articles and a "knowledge tree" that allows the user to explore additional topics. The set is also available for CD-TV.

Designed to provide quick access to factual information, *Academic American Encyclopedia* is an attractive and easy-to-use reference tool of great value to libraries serving middle school, high school, and adult readers. Its brief entries do not provide the historical depth found in larger sets, but its specific-entry approach makes access easy, and its currency is unsurpassed.

Collier's Encyclopedia. 24v. Lauren S. Bahr, editorial director; Bernard Johnston, editor in chief. Macmillan, 1992.

First published in 1950, *Collier's* is intended to be "a scholarly, systematic, continuously revised summary of the knowledge that is significant to mankind."

Entries range from one paragraph to many pages (e.g., *Architecture* at 74 pages, *United States* at about 100). Although *Collier's* is known for its broad topical approach, there are many short entries; these tend to identify geographic entities, people, specific flora and fauna, and associations. Headings and subheadings are generously used; some longer articles have tables of contents to guide the reader. Most articles are signed. Volume 1 lists 5,000 editors, advisors, and contributors, with identification at time of service. Degrees, titles, and major publications are listed. There are 61 new contributors this year.

Collier's presentation of information is clear and straightforward; articles are aimed at lay readers. Terminology used avoids jargon and pedantry. Some articles are more demanding than others, but this appears to be a function of the technical nature of the material, rather than inappropriate presentation. Periodic instances of non-gender-free language are found; for example, in *Newspaper*, a VDT is described as a "keyboard attached to a television tube on which a reporter can read his story as he writes."

In some entries, glossaries (e.g., *Musical Terms*) or capsule biographies of personalities (e.g., *Musical Theater in America*) are provided. Pronunciation is given for most terms, and the key is printed at the front of each volume. Dates for population are noted; U.S. figures are from the 1990 census. However, population figures for cities in other countries aren't always as current. For instance, the 1971 population is given for Amalfi, Italy.

A 200-page bibliography in the last volume is arranged by broad topics, broken down by form and subject; entries are briefly annotated. *Collier's* policy here is to emphasize current books, readily available, written in English. Sections of the bibliography revised this year include general reference books, chemistry, mathematics, architecture, and sports and games. Some sections need updating. Most of the titles in the education section, for instance, date from the 1960s and 1970s. In recent years, bibliographies have been appended to new and revised articles, but these are still infrequent. This year, none of the new entries has a bibliography. Bibliographies were added to six rewritten or revised articles.

The publisher notes over 14,000 illustrations, 28 percent of which are in color, up from 10 percent in 1988. *Collier's* is moving toward a greater use of color; over 500 attractive color photographs were added this year throughout the set. For example, *Argentina* has 8 new photographs, *Cactus* has 9, and *Eskimo*, 10.

The index in the final volume has 450,000 entries; most entries are identified briefly, e.g., "Detroit Red Wings (hockey team)." The index identifies bibliography entries, illustrations, and maps. Page numbers include page quadrant (*a, b, c,* or *d*). The "Study Guide," also in the last volume, lists under broad topic some of the articles to be found in *Collier's*. For example, under "Modern Philosophers" is a list of 27 people about whom articles are found in the set.

The publisher indicates that this year there are 39 new articles (e.g., *Baker, James*; *Persian Gulf War*; *Marfan's Syndrome*; *Nursing Home*; *King, Stephen*; *Teleology*; *Yeltsin, Boris*; and *Restoration and Conservation*). The lengthiest, *Persian Gulf War*, is 9½ pages and has 9 color photographs and a map. Among the 64 completely rewritten articles are *Columbus, Christopher*; *Germany* (combining both Germanys); *Marsupial*; *Metallurgical Analysis*; *Nervous System*; *Botticelli*; and *Haiti*. Many sections of the USSR entry were rewritten to reflect changes there. The publisher claims over 2,600 "updated or otherwise revised articles." For instance, over 150 entries on German places were revised to reflect the reunification of Germany.

Some articles, however, are in need of revision. For example, *Abortion* was written when the U.S. was moving toward broadened abortion rights, not the opposite. *Audio-Visual Instructional Materials* dates back to the late 1960s and hence doesn't mention video and other new technologies. *Library Research and Reporting* (Louis Shores and Richard Darling, authors) cites superseded editions and gives minimal attention to electronic sources of information. A comparison of volume 17 of the 1992 edition with the same volume in the 1981 set shows new and rewritten articles and new illustrations, but some dated material. For instance, *Newspaper* badly needs revision. It provides extensive historical information, but the section on the contemporary newspaper is out of date. An accompanying photograph, captioned "Modern Newspaper Equipment," shows a manual typewriter and a linotype machine. The entry *Music, History of* also gives good historical treatment but skimps on coverage of modern composers. The accompanying photograph of a synthesizer shows what must have been a very early prototype. *Narcotics, Control of*, contains no mention of cocaine and recent antidrug initiatives.

Collier's Encyclopedia is a large set with extensive historical coverage of many topics, but it is not the first place to turn for information on current subjects. The amount of revision this year is considerably higher than in recent years, and the addition of many new color photographs is improving the set's look; the publisher is encouraged to continue these trends. High school, academic, and public libraries could all benefit from owning *Collier's*.

Compton's Encyclopedia & Fact-Index. 26v. Ed. by Dale Good. Compton's Learning Co., 1992. Previously reviewed [RBB My 15 92]

Compton's, published since 1922, continues to meet the information needs of students at the upper elementary through high school level. *Compton's* completed a radical six-year revision of the text in 1989. Now, for 1992, the set has been completely reset and redesigned and extensively reillustrated.

Articles are arranged alphabetically letter by letter; most of them are not signed. However, for this printing, names of more than 500 contributors were added to articles, bringing the number of signed entries to 1,042. Many of the contributors are affiliated with academic or government institutions; others are writers, teachers, or librarians.

There are 23 new articles in the main text, including *Animal Rights*, *Persian Gulf War*, and *Yeltsin, Boris*. The new entries *Gangs* and *Scouting*, each about a page in length, address topics of interest to children. In addition, around 90 articles have been rewritten, or extensively revised, and more than 900 have been updated. About 120 bibliographies were updated, and three new bibliographies were added. Among articles that have been revised are *Gorbachev, Mikhail* and *Union of Soviet Socialist Republics*. The article on Gorbachev is current through October 1991, when he proposed the economic union of several republics. To the article on the former USSR, the editors have added a brief introductory paragraph noting recent changes and stating that the article deals with the Soviet Union that existed before the changes took place. The articles *Egypt, Iraq, Kuwait,* and *Saudi Arabia* have been updated to show their role in the Persian Gulf War, but not the articles *Israel, Jordan,* or *Syria*. Last year, the Board noted that the Old Slave Mart Museum shown in *South Carolina* had closed; the picture of the museum has been dropped from the rewritten and reillustrated article. The Board also commented on the fact that automation was nearly ignored in *Library*. Though the text in the 1992 printing has not changed, photographs have been added to show library patrons using computers and online catalogs. Revised articles that will be of special interest to children include *Amusement Park* and *Fast Food*.

One major change for 1992 is that the separate indexes at the end of each volume have been dropped. These indexes analyzed the contents of each volume and also contained brief entries for topics not covered in the main alphabetical sequence. They were cumulated in volume 26, *Master Fact-Index*, which has been renamed *Fact-Index*, and now serves as the sole index for the set. *Compton's* is 694 pages shorter because of the elimination of these duplicate indexes. Almost 2,300 new short articles were added to the *Fact-Index*, including *Abscam*, *Electronic Mail*, *Virtual Reality*, *Voguing*, and *Thomas, Clarence*. Entries on a number of people of interest to children, such as Fresh Prince, Whitney Houston, and Fay Vincent, are new. The *Fact-Index* notes the 1991 deaths of Miles Davis, Rajiv Gandhi, and Dr. Seuss. In addition, about 600 entries in the *Fact-Index* had major revision. Also added were 65 new tables, including "Basketball Hall of Fame" and "Major Volcanoes of the World". The list of volcanoes does not show the eruption of Mt. Pinatubo, but it is noted in the Philippines article.

Besides the index, other features that aid access to the set are cross-references, preview boxes that serve as tables of contents for longer articles, and fact-finder boxes that refer the reader to related topics.

By far the greatest amount of change has taken place in the look of the encyclopedia, beginning with its bright, royal-blue binding. The set is now printed on four-color presses, and the entire text has been reset. Running text appears in a new typeface, with ragged-right margins. Captions were reset in a boldface italic type. All tables and sidebars were redesigned. Over 1,000 two-color maps were changed to four-color, and nearly 300 maps were added or revised. There are more than 2,000 new four-color photographs and more than 1,300 new four-color drawings, graphs, and charts. According to the editors, *Compton's* is now about 65 percent four-color, compared to 35 percent in 1991. In addition, about 3,300 pages have been redesigned, including all of the state and Canadian province articles. New illustrations have been provided for many of the articles of interest to children, such as *Circus*, *Doll*, and *Zoo*, and for a number of the science articles, which are *Compton's* traditional area of strength. *Birds*, for example, now has more than 60 color photos, along with numerous four-color illustrations to replace the pictures in the previous edition, which were primarily two-color drawings. Not all the articles have been reillustrated to the same extent. In some cases, such as *Egypt, Ancient* and *Byzantine Empire*, the reillustration consists of replacing the old two-color map with a new four-color one.

Compton's is available in several electronic versions. *Compton's Multi-Media Encyclopedia* combines the text of *Compton's* with illustrations, animation, and sound on a CD-ROM. *Compton's Family Encyclopedia*, another CD-ROM version, offers the same text and illustrations but no animation and less sound. *Compton's Concise Encyclopedia* is available for Data Discman, Sony's hand-held, battery-powered CD-ROM player. A compact disc–interactive version of *Compton's* is under development.

While it led the way in adding graphics to the electronic version, *Compton's* had lagged behind its counterparts in the illustration and design of the print set. Now *Compton's* has taken a major step towards enhancing its visual appeal. There is no question that the set benefits from its new design. The increase in the number of four-color illustrations, the crisper typeface, and the new page layouts give the 1992 printing a much more lively and up-to-date appearance. In the past, the Board has made note of *Compton's* accuracy, concision, and generally adequate updating. This year we can also note its attractive appearance. *Compton's* is recommended for public and elementary and middle school libraries.

Encyclopedia Americana. 30v. Lawrence T. Lorimer, editorial director; Mark Cummings, editor in chief. Grolier, 1992.

Encyclopedia Americana, originally issued between 1829 and 1833, was the first general encyclopedia published in the U.S. Its intended audience is high school and college students and adults. Although international in scope, the set emphasizes subjects for U.S. and Canadian audiences; for example, the entries *New York State Barge Canal System* and *Antietam, Battle of* with detailed maps. The second largest of the sets reviewed here, *Americana* gives a balanced assessment of controversial subjects like homosexuality, sex education, and scientology.

Americana has over 6,500 advisers and contributors, 40 of them new to this edition. A random sampling determined that approximately 36 percent of all articles are signed. A contributors list at the beginning of volume 1 shows affiliations. Most contributors are university faculty; others are government and private industry experts or members of learned organizations. Among the new contributors this year are Barbara S. Okun, Office of Population Research, Princeton University (*United States: Population Growth and Characteristics*) and Elizabeth H. Pleck, Center for Research on Women, Wellesley College (*Roe v. Wade and Doe v. Bolton*).

Pronunciation guides are given for entries within the text. Some specialized articles have a glossary of terms. Many articles contain short bibliographies, most of which cite titles published in the 1980s. There is a limited use of *see* and *see also* references within the text. This moderate usage of cross-references mandates the use of the 353,000-item index to locate appropriate information. Maps and illustrations are also indexed here.

This year, about six percent of the set's approximately 52,000 entries had some revision. There are 21 new entries, 79 replacement articles, 68 articles with major revisions, and 2,986 with minor revisions. Among the new articles this year are several excellent ones under *Banks and Banking*. The new articles *Homelessness*, *Persian Gulf War*, and the rewritten *Canada: Health and Welfare* treat timely topics that will be of interest to students. Biographies are now provided for John Major, Colin Powell, and Clarence Thomas. Replacement articles include *Cold War*, *Warsaw Pact*, *Federal Deposit Insurance Corporation*, and *Savings and Loan Associations*. Among the articles with major revision are AIDS, *Black Americans*, and *Yugoslavia: Yugoslavia after Tito*. Of the 2,986 minor revisions, 415 are updated bibliographies, and more than 2,000 are changes in U.S. population data.

Among the numerous examples of the editors' efforts to keep *Americana* current, the article *Assassination* notes the May 21, 1991, death of Rajiv Gandhi (as does his biography). *Disasters* lists the August 1991 Hurricane Bob and the October 1991 California brushfires. Articles on Czechoslovakia, boxer George Foreman, Supreme Court Justice Thurgood Marshall, and Boris Yeltsin mention events right up to the publisher's deadline of September 1991.

In contrast, many articles demonstrate neglect. For example, *Air Transportation*, which we criticized in our 1989 review as outdated, still has not been revised. As was pointed out in our review last year, the article *Foundations* cites 1967 figures, and *Divorce* gives 1975 and 1976 statistics. *Career Planning* cites salaries from the 1960s. The articles *Automobiles*, *Beer*, and *Crime and Criminology* have old statistical data. The entry *Apprenticeship* states, "The present-day apprentice in American industry can expect $2 an hour." The reunification of Germany is not reflected in all articles. *Potsdam*, for instance, is described as "a city in the German Democratic Republic (East Germany)." Articles on the Philippines, its provinces, and various cities cite census data for 1980, 1975, 1970, and 1960, even though a new census was conducted in 1990. The population for *Nantes* (France) is from 1968, and for *Antung* (China) from 1958. An inconsistent writing style is found in some articles. Susan B. Anthony, for instance, is referred to in her biography as "Miss Anthony" while men are referred to by their surnames.

There are approximately 22,865 photographs, maps, line drawings, and various other illustrations appropriately placed throughout the text. Added this year are 160 new illustrations, including a map of Columbus' voyages and new color photographs for several countries. About 14 percent of the set's illustrations are in color, the lowest proportion among all the sets reviewed here. The editors state that this year they have changed to using coated paper stock throughout the set, which will allow for more extensive use of color in future editions. We hope this change signifies an effort to make improvements in this area. For example, many country articles in *Americana* lack color photographs.

There are also omissions in coverage, such as no biographical articles on such prominent persons as Norman Schwarzkopf and Salman Rushdie. There is an entry for Oral Roberts, but none for Pat Robertson. Only passing references are made to significant black leaders like Ralph Abernathy, Floyd McKissick, and Louis Farrakhan.

This encyclopedia does an excellent job of providing historical coverage of many topics, but there is a problem with keeping articles current. For this historical coverage, *Encyclopedia Americana* remains a useful reference for high school and college students and adults.

Funk & Wagnalls New Encyclopedia. 29v. Leon L. Bram, editorial director; Norma H. Dickey, editor in chief. Funk & Wagnalls, 1992.

Founded in 1876, Funk & Wagnalls first published an encyclopedia in 1912. The present title and a program of continuous semiannual revision date from 1971. The set—designed primarily for junior and senior high school students and the general, nonspecialist adult public—is distributed in the U.S. and Canada through supermarket "book-a-week" programs. In the past, schools and libraries have purchased it directly from the publisher, but a special 1993 school and library edition is being sold by Oxford University Press.

In the spring 1992 printing, volumes 1–27 and the first half of volume 28 contain some 25,000 articles. The latter half of volume 28 is a bibliography of 9,500 annotated entries divided into nearly 1,600 topical reading lists and more than 300 biography reading lists. Volume 29 is the index. Cross-references are provided within and at the ends of articles, but the index should be consulted to find all related entries. It has 130,000 entries and does not include references to illustrations or to the bibliography. F&W does not supply pronunciation for unfamiliar words.

Most entries in F&W are brief (less than a page); a few, however, are fairly long (e.g., *Europe*, 40 pages; *Union of Soviet Socialist Republics*, 52 pages; *United States of America*, 108 pages). While over 900 contributors are identified and their initials are appended to their entries, most of the articles are unsigned and are the work of F&W's editorial staff. More than 3,000 entries conclude with cross-references to the bibliographies in volume 28. Almost every one of these lists contains some books from the 1980s, including some recent titles (e.g., *Atlas of United States Environmental Issues*, 1990; *Cambridge Encyclopedia of Ornithology*, 1991). On the other hand, superseded editions of some works are listed (e.g., the 1983 edition of *The Negro Almanac* instead of the 1989). Works included tend to be popular, rather than scholarly, treatments.

According to the publisher, the fall 1991–spring 1992 revisions added 10 new articles (compared with 24 in 1990–91) and updated more than 2,600 others. Seven of the new entries are biographical (Rachel Field, Saddam Hussein, Helmut Kohl, John Major, Colin Powell, Clarence Thomas, Boris Yeltsin); the other three relate to a national park, a European conference, and the Persian Gulf War. Revised entries are many and varied. A major part of the substantially revised coverage has been in chemistry (*Elements, Chemical; Periodic Law; Chemical Reaction;* and 103 articles on individual chemical elements). There are still the separate entries *Germany, East* and *Germany, West*, but each concludes with a paragraph describing reunification. Maps have been revised to reflect this fact, and 470 entries were updated to remove the East-West designation. Some 25 articles were updated for the Persian Gulf War and other Middle Eastern events (*Air Warfare, Iraq, Kuwait, Palestine Liberation Organization, Saudi Arabia*, etc.). *Computer* was substantially revised, and *Nuclear Energy* was rewritten. The articles on more than 50 U.S. and Canadian national parks were revised and updated. A change of government in Ethiopia, the end of the Angolan civil war, continuation of the U.S. banking crisis, the April cyclone in Bangladesh, Rajiv Ghandi's assassination in India in May, and civil war in Yugoslavia are all duly noted. Also included are the deaths of Miles Davis, Martha Graham, Graham Greene, Rudolf Serkin, Dr. Seuss, and I. B. Singer. Dates for population figures are given; those for the U.S. are from the 1990 census.

This revision continues the pattern of recent years of increasing the number of four-color illustrations by adding 45 new pictures. New color illustrations appear in such articles as *Canada, Kuwait,* and *Guided Missiles*; new black and white ones are included in *Chemical Reaction, Conservative Party* (UK), and *France*. About three-fifths of the set's 9,000 illustrations are in black and white.

Funk & Wagnalls New Encyclopedia, while not as detailed and scholarly as the major multivolume sets, provides clear, up-to-date, worldwide coverage in a readable style well suited for an audience from junior high school upward. While designed primarily for home use, it may be a suitable purchase for libraries, for it gives good value for the price.

The New Book of Knowledge. 21v. Lawrence T. Lorimer, editorial director; Gerry Gabianelli, editor in chief. Grolier, 1992.

The New Book of Knowledge has been an alphabetically arranged encyclopedia since 1966, when Grolier replaced the topically arranged *Book of Knowledge*. This past year, a major five-year revision of the set began. The most notable format change will be the eventual elimination of the "Dictionary Index", which is a separate index in each of the 20 volumes that also includes brief text entries. No new "Dictionary Index" entries were added this year, and existing entries are slowly being integrated into the main body of the text.

The 1,766 contributors to NBK are experts well positioned to be knowledgeable about the subjects they write about or review. Among the 66 contributors new to this edition are Alan Nourse, author of *Teen Guide to AIDS Protection* (*Birth Control*), and Alan Palmer, author of *The Penguin Dictionary of Modern History 1789–1945* (*Balfour, Arthur J.; Bruce, Robert; Chamberlain Family; Macmillan, Harold*). A list of all contributors and their affiliations appears between the text and the "Dictionary Index" in volume 20.

NBK is written primarily for children "both in school and at home" through middle or junior high school. The Dale-Chall readability formula is used to make certain the comprehension level of articles matches the ages at which the topic would appeal to children or be introduced to them in school.

The encyclopedia is organized letter by letter. Many cross-references are included both within and at the ends of articles. About 700 *see* references, including 122 new ones, are also included throughout the set. Unfortunately, some of these references are confusing. For instance, "*Anteaters*. See MAMMALS" appears on the page preceding the new three-page article *Anteaters*. A *see* reference for *Anthrax* appears out of alphabetical order before the article *Anthony, Susan B*.

Volume 21 is an index containing 85,000 entries. It cumulates all the references from the 20 volume indexes and also includes references to all "Dictionary Index" text entries (but doesn't duplicate those entries).

For the 1992 edition, five volumes of NBK were substantially revised (A, B, C, G, and L), compared with only four volumes during the previous three years combined. Seventy-five new articles were added for 1992, including *Amphibians, Arabs,* and *Bible, People in the*. Fifty of these new articles are biographies of such people as Susan B. Anthony, Judy Blume, John Major, and I. M. Pei. Many of these biographies and some of the new narrow topical entries like *Aquaculture, Asbestos,* and *Central Intelligence Agency* used to be in the "Dictionary Index". However, they have been greatly expanded since being moved to the main body of the text. Another 60 text articles were replaced, including *Books, Economics, Georgia, North Carolina,* and *North Dakota*. These three state articles bring the total to seven given in a new format with attractive graphic features. The *Economics* article exemplifies a new feature, namely, the inclusion of biographical profiles of people important to the context of the articles. In this case, five people are profiled: Adam Smith, John Maynard Keynes, Paul Samuelson, Milton Friedman, and John Kenneth Galbraith, several of whom used to be in the "Dictionary Index". Other major articles replaced include *American Literature, Banks and Banking, Germany,* and *Columbus, Christopher*.

Thirty articles were completely updated and substantively rewritten, including *Iraq, Kuwait, Robin Hood, Union of Soviet Socialist Republics,* and *Yugoslavia*. Minor revisions or updates were done for 295 articles, including *Cheerleading, Democracy, Imperialism,* and *Little League Baseball*. Even though *Baltimore* and *Maryland* were among the articles receiving minor revision, errors were noted. The *Baltimore* article states that "Sports fans cheer baseball's Orioles and football's Colts at Memorial Stadium." In fact, the Colts moved to Indianapolis in 1984, and the article *Indianapolis* correctly notes that they play in the Hoosier Dome there. This year, the Orioles started playing in Oriole Park at Camden Yards, their new stadium. In the article *Legislatures*, Bangladesh and Pakistan are noted to be under martial law since 1982 and 1976, respectively, when martial law was lifted in 1986 and 1985. Several entries still refer to West and East Germany. There is no biography of David Souter, who was appointed to the Supreme Court in 1990.

For this edition, 653 new photographs, 180 new works of art, and 27 new maps were added. Most of the new illustrations are in color, as are over 90 percent of the set's pictures. The new graphic features of the past few years and the heavy illustration make NBK a very attractive encyclopedia. The newly illustrated entries *Animals, Books,*

Games, and *Columbus, Christopher* will appeal to children. There are still dated illustrations in such articles as *Paper* and *Reading*.

Special features of NBK, all indexed in the accompanying *Home and School Reading and Study Guides*, include articles on hobbies and leisure activities, literary excerpts, projects and experiments, "wonder questions," and articles of interest to parents. The wonder questions provide excellent explanations; two examples are "How do we get salt?" and "What happens at absolute zero?" This paperback volume also contains a bibliography for parents and teachers that relates NBK articles to the curriculum. Of the more than 5,000 books for young readers listed, over 900 titles are new this year.

The New Book of Knowledge will both satisfy curiosity and encourage further exploration in children. Parents, teachers, librarians, and school-age children up to and in some cases through high school will find it to be a valuable reference resource.

The New Encyclopaedia Britannica. 32v. 15th ed. Robert McHenry, general editor. Encyclopaedia Britannica, 1992.

Britannica was first published in Scotland, 1768–1771. Around 1900 two Americans acquired the rights to the encyclopedia. Currently, the encyclopedia is divided into three parts: a one-volume outline of knowledge, the *Propaedia*; a 12-volume ready-reference set, the *Micropaedia*; and the 17-volume *Macropaedia* with lengthy scholarly articles. There is a superb two-volume index and a yearbook, *Britannica Book of the Year/Britannica World Data* that includes world statistics that first-time purchasers receive free for that year.

This year's *Micropaedia* includes 64,404 articles averaging just under 300 words. These include 282 entirely new articles, 1,434 revised articles, and 1,850 that were updated to include 1990 U.S. census data. One hundred ninety new photographs were added along with 15 drawings and 63 maps. Approximately 40 percent of the new entries are biographies. Examples include James Baker III, Mañuel Noriega, Salman Rushdie, and David Souter. Other new entries describe companies such as Anheuser-Busch and Quaker Oats; places like Ashland, Kentucky; institutions such as the Public Broadcasting System; and such terms as *cha cha* and *sweetener*. Examples of updating are many, ranging from *Abortion*, which now includes discussion of the 1989 *Webster v. Reproductive Health Services*, to *Yeltsin, Boris*, covered through August 1991.

In recent years *Britannica* has made a more concerted effort to update articles rather than relying so heavily on the yearbook. However, more still needs to be done in the *Micropaedia*. The article *Bahrain* was not revised to note that country's role in the Gulf War. In *Sporting Record*, which lists champions in various sports, the most recent entries are for 1987 for events held annually and 1985 for quadrennial events. Numerous bibliographies continue to be out-of-date. The bibliography for explorer LaSalle stops in 1964 despite many recent monographs while that for T. E. Lawrence (of Arabia fame) lists biographies from 1938 and 1977, ignoring several published in the 1980s.

While Britannica has made strides in recent years to increase the number of illustrations, especially in color, the *Micropaedia* is riddled with tiny black-and-white photographs.

The 1992 *Macropaedia* contains 674 signed articles averaging 25 pages in length. These range from three- to four-page articles on cities to 308 pages on the U.S. and 139 pages on the United Kingdom. Biographies make up 14 percent of the entries, cities 11 percent, countries 10 percent, national literatures 4 percent, and geographic regions 3 percent. Africa is slighted in terms of separate entries in the *Macropaedia*. While 26 European countries, 21 Asian countries, and 11 South American countries have entries, only 4 African countries are listed separately. The others are covered in lengthy regional articles. It is hard to see why *Luxembourg* merits independent coverage in the *Macropaedia* and Nigeria does not.

Since encyclopedias are usually static in size, with a new entry meaning the elimination of an old one, entries in the 1992 set were compared with the 1989 one. Since 1989, 29 entries have been added to the *Macropaedia*, and 33 have been deleted. New entries include *Bhutan, Guyana, Madagascar*, and *The Netherlands*. Other notable new entries include those on the Atlantic, Indian, and Pacific Oceans; *Baltic States*; and *Telescopes*. Among articles dropped are several surprising ones: *Education, Higher; Education, Special; Education, Social and Economic Aspects of*; and *Psychology*.

One of the great strengths of the *Macropaedia* has always been its distinguished cast of contributors. The 115 new contributors include 35 Americans, 16 Australians, 11 from the U.K., and others from Canada, New Zealand, Chile, and France.

Some entries in need of updating in the *Macropaedia* include the following: *Alcohol and Drug Consumption*, which includes a world chart with statistics dating from 1971; *Birds*, with a bibliography citing sources principally from the 1950s and 1960s; and *Broadcasting*, which recommends *Techniques of Television Production* (2d ed., 1962) in its bibliography. Despite the rash of new monographs on exploration in recent years, the bibliography for *European Overseas Explorations and Empires* cites nothing since 1969 on exploration. The bibliography in the article on Columbus is short and dated (1967 or older).

On the plus side is the revised article *Australia*, with one black-and-white and 12 color maps, 20 illustrations, a superb commentary, and a lengthy bibliography. Also revised is *Australia and New Zealand, Literatures of*, which is six pages longer than the previous version. Other notable revisions include the articles *European History and Culture; Greek and Roman Civilization, Ancient*; and *Iraq*.

The index with 665,000 references is superb. In checking *Belize*, the index also lists the Spanish equivalent *Belice* and the former colonial name, British Honduras. It refers to an entry in the *Micropaedia*, one in the *Macropaeida*, notes a map in the *Macropaedia*, suggests recent statistical information can be found in the *World Data Annual*, notes its flag is illustrated on plate 2 of *Flag*, and suggests coverage of topics in many other volumes.

This fall Britannica is releasing the *Britannica Electronic Index* on CD-ROM to be used with an IBM PC or compatible computer. This is more than an electronic version of the printed index to the set. Using the search software developed for *Compton's MultiMedia Encyclopedia*, it is possible to search by entry title ("Title Finder") or to do a keyword search ("Idea Search"). "People, Places, and Things" searches subsets of the database. Under "People," for instance, it is possible to get a list of all British writers or French composers discussed in the set. All lists of citations can be printed out. The disc also contains a version of *Webster's Ninth New Collegiate Dictionary*. While the *Electronic Index* must be used with the print set, it does offer enhanced access to it. It is available for $299 or for $99 as a package with the 1992 NEB.

The *Propaedia*, designed as a kind of self-study guide, is scarcely used in libraries. As the twentieth anniversary of the fifteenth edition approaches, it may be an appropriate time to drop it. Time and money spent on updating the many outlines and lists could be more effectively used to update articles in the *Micropaedia* and revise bibliographies. The plates on the human body, missed by most patrons because of their location in the *Propaedia*, could be moved to the *Macropaedia*.

As *Britannica* enters its 225th year, it remains the largest and most scholarly encyclopedia in the English language. Studies have shown that it is the most cited encyclopedia in both academic and popular publications. This authoritative set is suitable for academic, public, and many high school libraries.

New Standard Encyclopedia. 20v. Douglas W. Downey, editor in chief. Standard Educational Corp., 1992.

A moderate-sized set first published in 1910, *New Standard Encyclopedia* is designed for the basic reference use of the general reader from middle school to adult.

Following suggestions on how to use the set, there are listings of editorial board members, contributors, consultants, advisers, and authenticators. Most articles are drafted by editorial staff and are unsigned; authenticators review these entries for accuracy. There are no significant staff changes this year; however, 24 new authenticators were added, and 12 were dropped. Among the new ones are Peter M. Baker of the Laser Institute (*Laser*); Steve Peggs of Fermi National Laboratory (*Particle Accelerator*); and Gerald Strauch of the University of Chicago (*Surgery*).

Most articles are only a few paragraphs in length, though multi-page coverage is given to such topics as *Dress, Motion Pictures*, and *United States*. Writing is concise; in general, vocabulary is accessible to upper elementary students. Pronunciation is provided for foreign and difficult words.

Of the 17,400 articles in the set, 121 are new to this printing; 96 of

ENCYCLOPEDIA SUMMARY CHART 1992

Encyclopedia	Approximate Entries—Excluding Cross-References	Pages	Approximate Illustrations	Consumer Price 1992*	School & Library Price 1992*
Academic American Encyclopedia (21v.)	28,940	9,832	16,930	$775	$599
Collier's Encyclopedia (24v.)	25,000	19,786	14,380	$1,499.50 $1,949.50 w/Home Educational Program	$979
Compton's Encyclopedia and Fact-Index (26v.)	5,234—main text 28,746—Fact–Index	10,591	22,510	$599	$569
Encyclopedia Americana (30v.)	52,000	26,740	22,865	$1,400	$919
Funk & Wagnalls New Encyclopedia (29v.)	25,000	13,024	9,458	$162.81	$295
The New Book of Knowledge (21v.)	8,972	10,572	23,600	$750	$559
The New Encyclopaedia Britannica (32v.)	65,078	32,030	23,617	$1,599	$1,199
New Standard Encyclopedia (20v.)	17,437	11,304	12,000	Determined by independent distributors	$549.95
The World Book Encyclopedia (22v.)	17,500	14,060	29,000	$599-899 depending on choice of binding	$520

* Prices exclude shipping & handling costs

these are found in the volumes covering the letters C and D. Among the new articles are *Carpal Tunnel Syndrome*, *Croatia*, *Cult*, *Domestic Violence*, *Desktop Publishing*, and *Tropical Rain Forest*. All the new articles are less than a page in length, except for *Drug Abuse*, which has two pages of text and a table listing commonly abused drugs, and *Persian Gulf War*, which has four pages of text, several photographs, and a map. More than 50 of the new entries are biographies of such individuals as Jacques D'Amboise, Margaret Drabble, Joshua Gibson, John Major, and Boris Yeltsin. Thirty-six articles were rewritten (e.g., *Computer*, *Folklore*, *Protein*, *Zulus*, and *Degas, Edgar*). *Computer*, for instance, has 22 new color photographs, a glossary of terms, and a bibliography with some titles noted as being for younger readers. Extensive revision occurred in 25 major articles (e.g., *AIDS*, *Dinosaur*, *Germany*, *Radio*, *Surgery*). In addition to the above, over 1,000 articles were updated. New census data was added to all U.S. state articles, and the indexes to state maps were updated to show new population figures. However, entries for some individual cities still list 1980 population. So, for instance, while a table in *Louisiana* lists the population of Lafayette as 94,440, the separate entry *Lafayette* gives it as 81,961.

Updating was generally achieved to date of publication. For example, the article *Union of Soviet Socialist Republics* is prefaced with "As this article was being prepared for the printer, the political situation in the Soviet Union was in a state of flux and the country's future was uncertain. This article describes the Soviet Union as it existed in August, 1991." Also noted are the following: political and economic isolation of Cuba in early 1990s, fighting between Croatians and Serbs in 1991, the bankruptcy of many airlines, and the deaths of Dame Margot Fonteyn and Martha Graham. Not noted were such items as the assassination of Rajiv Gandhi and rebel forces gaining power in Ethiopia. There is still a lack of adequate information on the homeless. *Homelessness* is listed in the index with reference to the article *Vagrancy*.

Two hundred one bibliographies were updated this year. For the most part, bibliographies have titles from the 1980s, with some 1990 ones. Usually a few titles are listed for younger readers. Volume 20, the index, contains 100,000 entries. In addition, the 19 text volumes contain over 13,600 *see* entries and 40,000 cross-references. This extensive cross-referencing system will be of help to students who are reluctant to use an index volume. There are special indexes within the set, for example, "Index to Star Maps," "Index to Breeds of Dogs," "Guide to Reproduction of Paintings."

Revisions were made on 101 maps. Some two-color maps were converted to four-color. Examples are Canada, Germany, and Iran. The effort to update illustrations and to increase the use of four-color is evidenced by the addition of 524 new illustrations (450 of them in color) and the deletion of 469 old ones. Notable among the reillustrated articles are *Dance*, *Drama*, and *Computer*. About two-thirds of the set's illustrations are still black-and-white, and some drab photographs need to be replaced. Some country articles, for instance, lack color.

New Standard Encyclopedia continues to provide basic factual information on a great variety of topics. Within its size limitations, it is a useful reference tool for students and adults.

The World Book Encyclopedia. 22v. William H. Nault, publisher; Robert O. Zeleny, editor in chief. World Book, 1992.

The World Book Encyclopedia was first published in 1917; this year marks its seventy-fifth anniversary. It continues to be an outstanding general encyclopedia with fine illustrations, excellent layout, and up-to-date coverage of a world that is changing rapidly.

World Book's primary objective is to provide information about humanity, the world, and the universe for elementary and secondary school students. It also serves as a general reference source for adults and is popular as a ready-reference tool in libraries. It provides balanced coverage of world events, science, the arts, and other topics.

More than 3,000 experts contribute to the *World Book* as authors, illustrators, authenticators, reviewers, and consultants. Their names appear in the preface to the A volume. Among the new contributors this year are R. Michael Blaese of the National Cancer Institute (*Gene Therapy*) and David A. Deese of Boston College (*Persian Gulf War*). Volume 22 is the index and research guide. The 35-page section, "A Student Guide to Better Writing, Speaking, and Research Skills," at the beginning of this volume, has been extensively revised. It includes information about using online and CD-ROM sources. Many of the 200 reading and study guides that appear in this volume have been updated, too. Most of the sources for scientific and technical articles are from the 1980s and 1990s. Lists for humanities and social science topics contain books with a wider range of publication dates, but most of them contain some titles from the 1980s.

Articles in *World Book* are written at the appropriate vocabulary level for the anticipated reader, so they vary in length and complexity. All technical terms are italicized and defined in the text. An elaborate cross-reference system within the text makes finding related material easy for young users who may not consult the index. More than 1,600 bibliographies, divided by reading level, accompany articles. Eight are new and 350 have been revised for this edition.

This edition of *World Book* contains approximately 17,500 articles. Fifty of these are completely new, 481 have been extensively revised, and more than 2,900 have been partially revised. The new entries include 19 biographies (e.g., of Jim Henson, H. Norman Schwarzkopf, Clarence Thomas, Chris Van Allsburg, Alice Walker). Most of the new topical entries are brief (*Emergency Medical Services*, *Green Party*, and *Zebra Mussel*). However, the new entry *Plate Tectonics* is almost four pages in length and is illustrated with several drawings. *Reproduction, Human*, another new entry, is six pages and illustrated with drawings showing the development of the embryo and the birth of a baby. *Nutrition* is an example of a major revision. It includes all new illustrations, a new bibliography, and revised food groups and charts of recommended dietary allowances. *Earthquake, Evolution*, and *Iraq* are other examples of articles that were extensively revised and reillustrated.

General updating in this set reflects the turbulent world events of the past year. The first printing shows events as of December 1991. The second printing, available in April, contains additional revisions through January 1992. The article on the Soviet Union includes information about the coup and the formation of a transitional government. The second printing covers the demise of the Soviet Union, Gorbachev's resignation, and the independent status of the former republics. The article *Yugoslavia* mentions the ethnic tensions and fighting that continue to plague that country. The ethnic republic boundaries appear on the maps. The end of the Angolan civil war, the beginning of the new Ethiopian government, the disbanding of the Warsaw Pact, as well as the repealing of South Africa's apartheid laws and the lifting of the U.S. sanctions are covered.

Two special features appear in the 1992 *World Book*. One is a section at the beginning of the A volume commemorating the encyclopedia's seventy-fifth anniversary with reprints of old articles to show how much things have changed over the years. For example, a 1917 article about flying machines is reproduced. Articles about Africa show its transition from a continent of colonies to one of independent states. The other special feature is an eight-page foldout section, "The Legacy of Columbus," in the article *Columbus*. It includes maps of the expeditions and information about the changing view of the world as a result of exploration. The biography of Columbus covers both his accomplishments and the current controversies about his impact on the Americas.

World Book is known for its statistical currency. All statistics are reviewed and revised on a regular basis. Sources and dates are provided. Population data for countries of the world include the most recent census figures and, for most countries, a current estimate and a five-year projection. Commodity statistics and economic indicators such as those in the articles *Petroleum*, *Cost of Living*, and *Food Supply* are the latest available.

Outstanding graphics are another *World Book* strength. There are about 29,000 illustrations in the encyclopedia, 80 percent of them in color. Maps, charts, graphs, and time lines help explain material in articles. About 700 new illustrations have been added this year. Sixty-two maps were added or revised to reflect changes in the Soviet Union and Europe. There are new maps in the articles *Persian Gulf War*, *Earthquake*, *Estonia*, *Greece*, *Iraq*, *Latvia*, and *Lithuania*.

The *Information Finder* makes the full text of *The World Book Encyclopedia* and *The World Book Dictionary* available on CD-ROM.

The seventy-fifth anniversary edition of *World Book*, like its predecessors, is an excellent reference source for schools and libraries. It maintains the high standards for currency, accuracy, accessibility, and readability established by the publisher.

Higher Education Directories: An Overview

Choosing the appropriate college or university can be complicated, and librarians are often confronted with the challenge of helping patrons navigate the admissions process. In order to begin, the appropriate facts and figures are needed. Patrons' concerns may range from the geographic location of a school to the size and composition of the student body to cost and admissions difficulty. The assortment of college guides that provide this information is almost as bewildering as the number of institutions offering degree programs. There is no one essential college guide; there are a number of useful books, software packages, and CD-ROM products that vary in terms of purpose, scope, and format.

The print and electronic sources listed below are arranged in four categories: four-year colleges, two-year institutions, graduate study, and lists that rank and rate. To make it easy to locate the CD-ROM guides, they have been marked with the symbol ❖. Regional sources and specialized sources (those that cover education for a specific field or target a specific racial, ethnic, or gender group or the disabled) are not included. Directories of graduate programs leading to professional degrees (D.D.S., M.D., etc.) are also excluded, as are guides to financial aid.

When using these sources several points should be kept in mind. First, changes occur rapidly in higher education—admission standards and requirements are subject to revision, academic programs may be discontinued or added, and course offerings are frequently altered—so college guides in a library must be up-to-date. Second, college guides cannot replace individual college catalogs. Third, when using these sources, it is important to remember that nomenclature and departmental organization vary from one institution to another. Search strategies, especially in electronic guides, should take this into consideration.

FOUR-YEAR COLLEGES

Directories of undergraduate programs give basic statistical and narrative information that allows readers to select colleges for further research. Some of the titles in this section also include information on graduate programs or two-year colleges.

Accredited Institutions of Postsecondary Education. 1991–92 ed. Ed. by William A. Wade. American Council on Education, 1992. annual. $32.50 (P-8268-1211-2).

The lists of institutions and programs in this directory are supplied by accrediting groups recognized by the Council on Postsecondary Accreditation. Entries note professional programs within institutions that have attained specialized accreditation; they do not list all curricula offered. The main body of the directory lists some 5,000 institutions by state. Entries note type of institution, type of student body, branch campuses or affiliate institutions, date of accreditation and accrediting body, levels of degrees offered, and specialized accreditation by 42 professional agencies in 60 fields.

OMNIBUS REVIEWS

American Universities and Colleges. 14th ed. Walter de Gruyter, 1992. $149.95 (0-89925-861-1).

More than 1,900 accredited institutions granting baccalaureate or higher degrees are described in detailed entries based on data derived from questionnaires, catalogs, and Integrated Postsecondary Education Data System (IPEDS) responses. Produced in collaboration with the American Council on Education, the book is in four sections: topical essays on higher education in the U.S.; a list of professional education programs from *Architecture* to *Veterinary Medicine* with the institutions offering them listed by state; colleges listed by state with history, accreditation, admissions and degree requirements, distinctive educational programs, student-life information, etc.; and appendixes that include statistics on doctorates granted by year, an ROTC affiliation list, and an essay on academic regalia and ceremonies.

Barron's Profiles of American Colleges: Descriptions of the Colleges. 19th ed. Barron's, 1992. paper $18.95 (0-8120-4862-8).

First published in 1964, *Barron's* is an irregularly published guide that lists more than 1,500 accredited colleges arranged by state. Beginning the book are special essays on comparing colleges, admissions and financial-aid processes, major selection, and a listing of colleges by competitive levels from most to noncompetitive. College entries provide map coordinates, enrollment and cost data, and SAT and ACT median scores. Entries also provide information on student life and campus environment, programs of study (including degrees and majors), such special options as cooperative education, application deadlines, availability of computer and library services, and admissions contact. An appendix includes a chart for comparison of such issues as selectivity, test scores, enrollment, and costs; guides to religious colleges; ROTC opportunities; and information for international students. For information on the CD-ROM version, see *Profiles of American Colleges* below.

✥ **Beacon**. CD-ROM. Macmillan New Media, 1992. $555 through December 31; $695 thereafter.

Based on three databases from Macmillan and other sources, this new CD-ROM includes information on 3,200 two- and four-year colleges, 1,100 graduate schools, and 900 career paths. The interactive program helps students choose a set of appropriate colleges using more than 200 criteria. After creating this list of schools, they can read a detailed description of each one. More than 2,100 scholarships, grants, and loans can also be accessed. "The Advisor" is an audio feature that gives advice on more than 100 topics. Tips are also provided on preparing an application, visiting a school, and the interview. Requires an IBM-PC or compatible with 640K RAM, headphone jack, MS-DOS 3.1 or higher, CD-ROM drive, and VGA monitor. A hard drive with 3 MB free is recommended.

Chronicle Four-Year College Databook. Chronicle Guidance Publications, 1992. annual. paper $19.99 (1-55631-184-2).

This work and its companions, *Chronicle Two-Year Databook* and *Chronicle Vocational School Manual*, lists 928 majors offered at 2,093 four-year institutions, 980 programs at 2,300 two-year institutions, and 897 programs at 4,192 vocational schools. In the first part of each book, majors are listed alphabetically with the colleges that offer them. The publisher claims this section lists more majors than any comparable directory. Charts that provide standard information on the institutions in a tabular manner make up the second section. An appendix notes accreditation, degrees, and other information for each school. Lists of accrediting agencies conclude each volume.

The College Blue Book. 5v. 23d ed. Macmillan, 1991. biennial. $200/set; $48/v. (0-02-695981-X); v.1: Narrative Descriptions (0-02-695972-0); v.2: Tabular Data (0-02-695973-9); v.3: Degrees Offered (0-02-695974-7); v.4: Occupational Education (0-02-695975-5); v.5: Scholarships, Fellowships, Grants (0-02-695976-3).

First published in 1923, *The College Blue Book* is one of the standard guides. The first four volumes are arranged by state. The first lists almost 3,000 colleges in the U.S. and Canada. State maps introduce each section, and college entries include map coordinates. Narrative descriptions include information on entrance requirements, term system, faculty-student ratios, student-body data, and special programs. Volume 2, *Tabular Data*, includes expected examination scores, percentage accepted, admission plans available, application deadline and fee, required high school units, housing data, library statistics, ROTC opportunities, and athletics. In volume 3, *Degrees Offered*, both campus-specific and standard terms are used n a list of majors and the institutions granting them. Volume 4, *Occupational Education*, includes 7,600 institutions that provide skill training that does not require college. Each entry provides contact information, degrees or certificates granted, veterans' status, accreditation notes, and financial-aid data. Part 2 of the volume lists majors with a list of institutions offering them. See the CD-ROM version below.

✥ **The College Blue Book (CD-ROM).** Macmillan, 1991. $350. [RBB Je 15 92].

This compact disc offers access to four databases: *The College Blue Book*, *Occupational Education*, *Occupational Education State Regulations*, and *Scholarships, Fellowships, Grants and Loans*. Search templates in *The College Blue Book* database allow searching by college name, region, state, city, profile, major, degree, and other criteria. The templates for the other three databases are equally comprehensive, offering users a range of search options. Search criteria utilize either controlled word lists or free text. Hardware requirements include an IBM PC or compatible, MS-DOS 3.1 or higher, 512K free memory, a hard disk with a minimum of 2 MB of free space, and a CD-ROM drive.

The College Comparison Guide. By Kiliaen V. R. Townsend. Agee Publishers; dist. by Publishers Distribution Service, 1992. paper $20 (0-935265-21-X).

Information on 130 selective colleges is presented in tabular form in this new guide. Some of the more than four dozen tables include "Alumni Support per Student," "Colleges Accepting Freshmen in Terms other than Fall," "Percentage of Students Participating in Intramural Sports," and "Availability of Distinctive Sports" (e.g., squash, water polo). Two-page profiles for the 130 schools include an average rating based on five well-known college guides.

The College Handbook. 30th ed. Macmillan, 1992. annual. paper $18.95 (0-87447-431-0, ISSN 0069-5653).

First published in 1941, *The College Handbook* is an official publication of the College Board. It includes information provided by two- and four-year colleges. Section 1 includes guidance on choosing a college, application procedures, paying for college, and major fields of study by discipline. The list of colleges that follows is divided into four-year schools arranged by state, specialized four-year schools, two-year schools by campus environment, and two-year schools by size. Among the factors used for selection are religious affiliation, services to learning-disabled students, ROTC opportunities, and open admissions. The heart of this volume is the college descriptions listed by state. Profiles include first-year admissions requirements and standard data such as degrees given, accreditation, enrollment, the library, and tuition information. Admissions-testing numbers and College Board-membership indicators (if applicable) appear with each entry. See the CD-ROM version below.

College Handbook for Transfer Students. Macmillan, 1992. annual. paper $15.95 (0-87447-435-3).

Essays on choosing the next college, credit transfer, and other topics aimed at community college and returning students begin this book, also compiled by the Collge Board. Descriptions of two- and four-year colleges are arranged by state. Entries include degrees, admissions-testing numbers, transfer statistics, student profiles, financial-aid possibilities, and contact information. See the CD-ROM version below.

Index of Majors and Graduate Degrees, 1993. 15th ed. Macmillan, 1992. paper $16 (0-87447-433-7).

To be used with *The College Handbook*, this book lists 580 majors and the 2,900 institutions that offer them. Institutions with specializations that are not traditional majors also appear. Program degrees from certificates through doctorates and professional degrees are noted. Foreign colleges are included if they are College Board members. A separate section treats special academic options, such as double majors, study abroad, cooperative education, and honors programs.

✥ The College Handbook. CD-ROM. Macmillan New Media, 1992. $129.95.

This new CD-ROM includes information on 2,700 undergraduate schools plus information from *The College Transfer Handbook.* It lets users search over 600 options—such as location, setting, field of study, degreee level, and tuition and fees—to identify institutions that meet their needs and then read the detailed college descriptions. Onscreen help, pull-down menus, and interactive windows aid use. It runs on IBM or compatible PCs with 640K RAM running MS-DOS 3.1 or higher and requires a hard drive with 1.4 MB available and a CD-ROM drive.

Comparative Guide to American Colleges. By James Cass & Max Birnbaum. 15th ed. HarperCollins, 1991. hardcover $40 (0-06-271513-5); paper $20 (0-06-461013-6).

Colleges are arranged here by name and indexed by state, religious affiliation, and selectivity. Among the unique information provided are percentage of college's budget derived from tuition, regulations regarding student conduct (e.g., drinking), the name of the college newspaper so prospective students can request a copy, and information for adult students. The majors index that concludes the book lists only collges that conferred degrees in those fields in 1988–89 and the number of degrees granted.

Directory of Postsecondary Institutions: 4-Year and 2-Year, 1989–1990. v.1. National Center for Education Statistics, 1990. paper $28.

Directory of Postsecondary Instituions: Less than 2-Year, 1989–1990. v.2. National Center for Education Statistics, 1990. paper $20.

Based on information culled from IPEDS reports, this directory lists 10,776 institutions, including ones in such outlying areas as Guam and the U.S. Virgin Islands. Entries are arranged by place. Included are all necessary contact information, various federal identification numbers, form of governance, and highest degree award offered. Accredited institutions are indicated with (H). Each volume ends with a set of tables and a list of changes in the academic world.

HEP Higher Education Directory. 11th ed. Higher Education Publications, 1992. annual. $43 (0-914927-17-5; ISSN 0736-0797).

A continuation of the Department of Education's *Education Directory: Colleges and Universities*, this title lists degree-granting institutions accredited by agencies recognized by the U.S. Secretary of Education, arranged by state. Information provided includes congressional district, county, FICE identification, date established, enrollment, type of student body, affiliation or control, IRS status, highest degree offered, programs offered, accreditation, and administrative and academic officers with personnel classification code. Indexes include one of the administrators and their direct telephone numbers. A prologue includes a list of accrediting agencies, institutional changes, statewide agencies of higher education, higher-education associations, consortia of institutions of higher education, and religious affiliation by denomination.

The Insider's Guide to the Colleges. Comp. by the staff of the Yale Daily News. 19th ed. St. Martin's, 1992. hardcover $26.95 (0-312-08507-9); paper $15.95 (0-312-08224-X).

Providing a snapshot of life at more than 300 colleges in the U.S. and Canada, this title is included because it is representative of directories that rely on the opinions of students for their contents. The editors purport to have selected institutions because of their academic quality or size and geographic diversity. Also included are a cross section of small colleges, technical institutions, and specialty schools strong in the creative and performing arts. Brief sketches arranged by state describe things that would most likely affect sutdents. Every college description is preceded by a statistical profile. Included are undergraduate admissions' telephone numbers, student body composition, number of applicants, percentage accepted, percentage accepted who enroll, and most popular major. Special features include "The College Finder," a rundown on schools according to selected attributes, and "The Changing College Scene," a look at some of the current trends in college life.

Lovejoy's College Guide. 21st ed. By Charles T. Straughn and Barbarasue Lovejoy Straughn. Prentice Hall, 1992. hardcover $40 (0-130554247-2); paper $20 (0-13-524778-0).

Lovejoy's covers 2,500 colleges in four main sections: an introduction, "Career Curricula and Special Programs," profiles of institutions, and a section on intercollegiate sports. The career-curricula section lists nearly 500 majors and the institutions offering them. The third section, the core of *Lovejoy's*, includes full descriptions of four-year institutions. Two-year colleges have full write-ups if room-and-board facilities are available. Information on expenses, degrees, student-faculty ratios, and transfers are presented in capsule form. The narrative portion of each entry includes material on the academic character of each institution, its special programs, foreign students, student life, services and facilities for the disabled, and enrollment and graduation statistics. The fourth section includes information on intercollegiate sports at 52 colleges. *Lovejoy's* is the only college guide that includes this latter information in so much detail.

Peterson's Guide to Four-Year Colleges. 23d ed. Peterson's Guides, 1992. annual. paper $18.95 (1-56079-157-8; ISSN 0894-9336).

Peterson's publishes a wide range of education directories, including regional guides and spcialized graduate guides. Its *Guide to Four-Year Colleges* includes profiles of nearly 2,000 accredited baccalaureate degree-granting instituions in the U.S. and Canada. New this year is "Inside College," a magazine written by college students with information on topics like Greek life and campus safety. "The College Adviser" includes a table of vital statistics, an entrance-difficulty directory, and a cost-range directory. Another section covers the military and higher education. The majors directory lists the 450 most popular undergraduate major fields. "College Profiles & Special Announcements" consists of detailed profiles of colleges arranged alphabetically. The detailed profiles include entering-class data, enrollment patterns, admissions policies, transfer admissions information, graduation requirements, campus life and student services, and contact addresses. In-depth descriptions of more than 800 colleges follow the profiles; the colleges have paid to have them included. *Peterson's College Selection Service* ($165) is a software version for Apple IIs or IBM PCs that guides students through the search and application process. A Macintosh version ($250) contains data on both two-year and four-year colleges. *Peterson's* is also available online with DIALOG, BRS, CompuServe, and Dow Jones News/Retrieval and on CD-ROM (see below).

✥ Peterson's College Database. CD-ROM. SilverPlatter. $595/single user; $995/2–8 users.

This product contains more than 3,400 detailed profiles of colleges; coverage is comparable to that of *Peterson's Guide to Four-Year Colleges* and *Petersn's Guide to Two-Year Colleges*. The database supports searching of over a dozen categories with hundreds of particular institutional characteristics. Users can quickly compare and contrast schools on an impressive number of characteristics. Formulating a search is easy and builds on SilverPlatter search basics. Specialized fields, such as geographic location and control, and limit fields, such as enrollment size or athletics, help to refine searches. Context-sensitive help is available every step of the way. This product is available for either an IBM or compatible system or a Macintosh. Minimum hardware requirements for the IBM PC are 640K of RAM, a 10 MB hard drive, and a CD-ROM drive. Requirements for the Macintosh Plus or greater include 1 MB RAM, a 20 MB hard drive, System 6.0.2 or higher, and a CD-ROM drive.

Profiles of American Colleges on CD-ROM. Laser Resources, 20620 S. Leapwood, Carson, CA 90746. Dec., 1992. $149.

This electronic version of *Barron's Profiles of American Colleges* will be released in late 1992. A beta test version was seen for this review. Options for locating information include browsing through the disc, jumping to a topic from a word, phrase, or symbol that appears on the contents screen, or using the index or search buttons. The index contains all the schools included on the disc and more than 1,500 other topics. The search button allows users to perform a full-text search. Special features are numerous. *Profiles* contains a "Multimedia College Supplement" that provides a map for each college. In addition, a number of colleges have opted to include one or more of the following: full-color photographs, a copy of the current college catalog that is browsable, searchable, and printable, and a printable copy of the application form. Sound and animation clips will be available beginning with the 1993 edition. A brief tutorial and online help screens aid in learning the system. *Profiles* is available for IBM compatible PCs with four MB of RAM, Microsoft Windows, and a CD-ROM drive. In order to view the photos, a VGA card is needed.

The Right College 1992. 6th ed. College Research Group of Concord, Massachusetts. Arco/Prentice Hall, 1991. paper $22.95 (0-13-781758-4).

After a section of essays on choosing and applying to colleges, institutions are grouped by level of competitiveness and indexed by majors and competitive sports. A chart covers "quick data" such as test scores, affiliation, and tuition range. An issues section on job outlooks for new college graduates, racial tensions on campus, and new ways to pay for college also includes articles on preprofessional programs that indicate which schools have the highest placement rates in graduate programs. More than 1,500 four-year colleges are arranged by state. College locations are marked on state maps. For each school there is a box with such data as cost, test scores, and selectivity, followed by text that covers topics in more depth.

The Ultimate College Shopper's Guide. Comp. by Heather Evans and Deidre Sullivan. Addison-Wesley, 1992. paper $12.95 (0-201-60894-4).

A departure from traditional college guides, this book consists of 327 lists arranged by student interests: "Essential Schools for Dead Heads," "Where to Find the Best Dining Hall Food," "Where the Top Companies Recruit the Most," "Schools with the Most Deaf Students." For each list the compilers noted the sources so further information can be obtained. Sources range from *Kiplinger's Personal Finance Magazine* to the Carnegie Foundation for the Advancement of Teaching.

TWO-YEAR INSTITUTIONS

America's community, technical, and junior colleges provide a broad range of educational opportunities for today's students. Remember that some of the directories of four-year colleges treated above also list two-year institutions.

Directory of Postsecondary Institutions: 4-Year and 2-Year, 1989–1990.
Directory of Postsecondary Institutions: Less than 2-Year, 1989–1990.
See *under* Four-Year Colleges above.

American Community, Technical, and Junior Colleges: A Guide. 9th ed. Ed. by Dale Parnell and Jack W. Peltason. Macmillan, 1986. $85 (0-02-904210-0).

Earlier editions of this directory of over 1,500 public, private, and proprietary institutions were entitled *American Junior Colleges*. Arranged by state, descriptions include information on purpose, governance, history, physical plant, and administration. Academic information includes admissions requirements, curricula, faculty, degree requirements, special training facilities and media resources, and student activities. A detailed subject index allows the user to find institutions offering a particular program. This ninth edition is the most recent one.

Chronicle Two-Year College Databook. *See under* Four-Year Colleges above.
A Directory of Public Vocational-Technical Schools and Institutes in the USA. 6th ed. Ed. by Mariliss Johnston. Media Marketing Group, 1992–93. $65 (0-933474-50-4).

This work was created in response to the extraordinary growth in vocational-technical education across the country and to the concomitant need of students to have up-to-date and comprehensive information on these programs. Arranged by state, listings of specific program and course offerings provide the chief administrator's name and telephone number and a description of various statewide programs of vocational education.

Peterson's Guide to Two-Year Colleges. 23d ed. Peterson's Guides, 1992. annual. paper $15.95 (1-56079-158-6) (ISSN 0894-9328).

This title begins with essays on the transfer process and standardized test taking, a chart with at-a-glance institutional statistics, and a majors directory listing associate degree programs at two- and four-year institutions. Then follow profiles of 1,492 colleges arranged by name. A final section has two-page essays on 52 of the aforementioned schools, which are paid for by the schools. This information is also available as *Peterson's College Selection Service* on floppy disk and on *Peterson's College Database* on CD-ROM.

GUIDES TO GRADUATE PROGRAMS

See "Guides to Graduate and Professional Schools" [RBB F 1 87] for a list of specialized directories.

Guide to American Graduate Schools. 6th ed. Ed. by Harold Doughty. Penguin, 1990. paper $16.95 (0-1404-6856-0).

This guide provides information on the general character of more than 900 accredited institutions, graduate- and professional-division requirements and offerings, admissions requirements, financial aid, degree requirements, and fields of study. Institutional entries in the main body are arranged alphabetically with reference to locations. Several indexes facilitate access: by state, by institutional abbreviations, and by fields of study. The latter index provides access to both majors and subfields of study, those of special interest or those sufficiently unusual to justify special notice.

The Official GRE/CGS Directory of Graduate Programs. 4v. 13th ed. Educational Testing Service, 1991. paper $17/v. (v.A: 4463-9378-9; v.B: 0-4463-9380-0; v.C: 0-4463-9382-7; v.D: 0-4463-9384-3) (ISSN 0743-0566).

A service of the Educational Testing Service and the Council of Graduate Schools, this title provides information for more than 800 accredited graduate institutions. It consists of four volumes organized by discipline: volume A covers the natural sciences; volume B, engineering and business; volume C, the social sciences and education; and volume D, the arts, humanities, and other fields. Within each volume, the arrangement is geographic. A list of 50 specific program tables divided among the four volumes is included in the first section. The second section contains institution information presented in tabular form. This allows comparison of institutions based on highest degree offered, average number of degrees awarded annually, faculty size, expenses, student services available, and geographic setting. "Major Fields Offered" lists all areas in which institutions have graduate programs. Narratives in the third section summarize such topics as research affiliations, library holdings, cooperative programs, computer facilities, and institutional resources. A fourth section contains the addresses of each institution. An identical "Index of Programs" concludes each volume.

Peterson's Annual Guides to Graduate Study. 6v. 27th ed. Peterson's Guides, 1992. paper $189.70 (1-56079-188-8; ISSN 0163-6111).

The six volumes in this set are *An Overview*; *Programs in the Biological and Agricultural Sciences*; *Programs in Business, Education, Health and Law*; *Programs in Engineering and Applied Sciences*; *Programs in the Humanities and Social Sciences*; and *Programs in the Physical Sciences and Mathematics*. More than 1,440 accredited institutions in the U.S. and Canada are included. Essays on graduate education, names of accrediting agencies, etc., appear in all six volumes. In the first volume, graduate and professional programs are listed, with the provider institutions and their degree offerings noted. There is also a directory of combined degree programs. The profile section, consisting of entries of varying length, includes general and special program information, such as research facilities, library statistics, application contact data, etc. In the specialized volumes, similarly detailed entries with standard information are arranged by program and then institution name. Institutionally sponsored essays (i.e., advertising) include lists of faculty and their research. This set of guides is also available online with DIALOG and on CD-ROM (see below).

⁌Peterson's GRADLINE. CD-ROM. SilverPlatter. $695/single user; $1,095/2–8 users. annual.

This CD-ROM database from SilverPlatter profiles 28,000 programs offered by 1,500 colleges and universities. Information is comparable to that found in its print equivalent. Within GRADLINE are three types of records: institutional records that provide overall profiles of an institution's graduate offerings, unit records that describe specific graduate programs within an institution, and field-of-study records that describe specific academic disciplines. Searches can be limited to one type of record. GRADLINE supports users who want to find specific programs, those who want to investigate a specific school or field of study, and those who need help determining a field of study. Minimum hardware requirements for the IBM-compatible PC version are 640K RAM, a 10 MB hard drive, MS-DOS 3.1 or higher, and a CD-ROM drive. Requirements for the Macintosh version include Macintosh Plus or greater, 1 MB RAM, a 20 MB hard drive, System 6.0.2 or higher, and a CD-ROM drive.

DIRECTORIES THAT RANK AND RATE

Confronted with a mass of information about colleges, students often ask for information about the quality of programs. Rankings information is obtained by several methods: reputational rankings (what knowledgeable people think about the schools), citation analysis, and faculty productivity studies, for example. Rankings appear in newspapers and popular magazines, books, and college guides, making them difficult to identify. These rankings are inherently subjective, and no complex institution can be described in terms of a single number or symbol, but sources that rank and rate are included here because students continue to seek this information.

The *Gourman Reports*, two companion texts that rate undergraduate, graduate, and professional programs in American and international universities, have been widely criticized. They are, therefore, not included in the following list. An assessment of Gourman is found in David S. Webster's "Jack Gourman's Rankings of Colleges and Universities: A Guide for the Perplexed" RQ (Spring 1986).

Of the sources that rank and rate listed below, some of the more popular ones are out-of-date, and users should be cautioned accordingly. They should also be advised to read the prefatory material in each source which explains the ranking methodology used.

Educational Rankings Annual. Ed. by Lynn C. Hattendorf. Gale, 1992. annual. $130 (0-8103-7989-9).

Containing 2,000 rankings and other lists based on intellectually defensible criteria, this annual is designed to be used in assisting students, parents, and others to find information published in books, newspapers, and magazines about the quality of education at all levels. Entries are arranged in broad categories. Examples include competencies of college faculty, stature of research libraries, college towns, graduate real estate programs, and loan repayment rates. The source of each ranking is provided.

America's Best Colleges, 1993: An Exclusive Survey by the editors of U.S. News & World Report. U.S. News & World Report, 1992. annual. paper $4.95.

This well-known annual college review (also published in a September issue of the magazine) rivals the *Money Guide* described below. "America's best" are listed in five categories: "The Top 25 National Universities," "The 25 Top National Liberal-Arts Colleges," "Top Regional Colleges and Universities," "Top Regional Liberal-Arts Colleges," and "American's Outstanding Specialty Schools." Other sections feature prominent Americans speaking about teachers who changed their lives; information on studying abroad, transferring, and community colleges; "The Best Buys;" a table of entrance exam-scores, acceptance rates, and other key data; and a section on choosing the right school. The directory portion of the survey consists of a state-by-state guide to facts and figures on close to 1,400 American colleges.

America's Lowest Cost Colleges. 2d ed. By Nicholas Roes. NAR Publications, 1991. paper $9.95 (0-89790012-5).

Over 1,000 accredited colleges with no or low tuition are covered here. Entries, arranged by state, include contact information, degrees offered, and two to three descriptive sentences. There is an index by major. The information offered here is modest; much more data would be needed to make an informed decision.

Barron's 300 Best Buys in College Education. 2d ed. By Lucia Solorzano. Barron's, 1992. paper $13.95 (0-8120-4860-1).

This is a guide to 300 myth breakers: schools that break the supposed link between college price and quality. Solorzano has attempted to discover schools where the education dollar goes farther. Data capsules about each school include facts about setting, student-faculty ratio, faculty profile, tuition and fees, financial aid, campus jobs and average earnings, and admissions information. Profiles of the schools address student body, academics, special programs, campus life, cost cutters, rate of return, payoff, and the bottom line. "Quick Lists" to help students target their choices are also provided. These include lists of colleges with 20,000 or more full-time undergraduates, with 1,000 or fewer full-time undergraduates, with tuition and fees of $5,000 or less, with chapters of Phi Beta Kappa, and single-sex colleges. Institutions are arranged by state.

Best Buys in College Education. By Edward Fiske and Joseph M. Michalak. Times Books, 1987. paper $10.95 (0-8129-1701-4).

Entries for more than 200 colleges appear in alphabetical order with a price index and a listing for cooperative education programs. Each entry begins with a quick-data list that gives type, setting, cost, and other standard information. This is followed by an essay on the college that includes the editors' rationale for considering it a best buy.

The Fiske Guide to Colleges. By Edward B. Fiske. Times Books, 1992. annual. paper $16 (0-8129-2024-4; ISSN 1042-7368).

Administrators and students supplied the information for this book on the "best and most interesting" colleges. Listed are 315 selective institutions that were perceived as the "best academically." Geography, public or private status, and institution size were factors in considering institutions for inclusion. Colleges are listed alphabetically. Essays cover academics, student body, housing, food, social life, and extracurricular activities. Beside each entry are such statistics as male-female ratio, SAT/ACT score ranges, and the percentage of students who graduate in five years. Indexed by state and cost. New this year is a section on state schools that provide a quality liberal-arts education.

Money Guide: Best College Buys 1993. Comp. by the editors of *Money*. Time, 1992. annual. paper $3.95.

Aimed to "help you pay no more than you must for an excellent education," *Money Guide* is published as a separate, unnumbered special issue each fall. The most popular sections are "America's 10 Best College Buys" and "*Money*'s Value Rankings." "The State of the State Schools" and "*Money*'s Guide to 1,011 Colleges" give college data. Factors that determine the rankings include faculty strength, library resources, instructional and student-service expenditures, graduation rate, percentage of graduates who go on to earn advanced degrees, and business success of graduates.

Peterson's National College Databank: The College Book of Lists. 5th ed. Peterson's Guides, 1990. paper $19.95 (1-56079-020-2).

Designed to address the questions frequently asked by students and their families: Which colleges cost the least? Which are the hardest to get into? Which have the highest minority enrollment? Which offer women's basketball scholarships? The format is straightforward: colleges are listed under broad subjects. Entries cover basic information about the two- and four-year institutions included.

Public Ivy's: A Guide to America's Best Public Colleges and Universities. By Richard Moll. Penguin Books, 1986. paper $18.95 (0-1400-9384-2).

Sixteen "public ivys" and nine runners-up are analyzed and compared to prestigious private colleges. Chapter-long essays on the first 16 include basic-information charts, first-year student profiles, and statistical data on libraries, faculty, etc. Essays focus on specific topics: academics, libraries and computers, the campus, student life, and school history and tradition. Each of the runners-up is also described with data charts but much less text.

Rugg's Recommendations on the Colleges. 9th ed. Comp. by Frederic Rugg. Rugg's Recommendations, 1992. paper $16.95 (0-9608934-7-4).

More than 600 quality four-year colleges are included here. Students were polled to provide 75 percent of the input; 25 percent of the responses were from secondary-school counselors and college personnel. There are no descriptive entries, just rankings, arranged by standard major (art history, philosophy, etc.) and divided into three groups: most selective, very selective, and selective. A letter code indicates the size of the institution, and the college deemed best is starred. Miscellaneous majors (aerospace, black studies, medical technology, etc.) are not divided into groups but are coded for single-sex or black institutions.

The 200 Most Selective Colleges: The Definitive Guide to America's First-Choice Schools. 2d ed. Arco, 1991. paper $16.95 (0-13-904-2369).

Originally published as *The 300 Most Selective Colleges* in 1989, this is a guide to colleges that purport to maintain selective admissions criteria and challenging programs of study. These include what the editors consider to be America's first-choice colleges—the Big Ten, the Ivy League, and other prestigious institutions. Each school is profiled in depth; profiles are accompanied by an at-a-glance summary of the school's selectivity ranking. Descriptions include test scores, percentage accepted, costs, enrollment, and faculty. Information is also provided on the student body, programs of study, student life, athletics, student employment, foreign students, computer facilities, graduate career data, and prominent alumni.

Sarah Barbara Watstein is Assistant Director for Academic Services at Virginia Commonwealth University and has been a member of the *Reference Books Bulletin* Editorial Board since 1991. Barbara Wurtzel is Reference and Bibliographic Instruction Librarian at Springfield, Massachusetts Technical Community College.

Consumer Health Information: A Selected List of Reference Sources for the Lay User

Health information is always in great demand. People come to the library to learn about their bodies and about illness and its treatment. They want to know more about medications prescribed for them or about the new diet discussed on a talk show. Librarians have an opportunity to educate and to help people participate in their own health care. This list contains general health guides and books about specific health topics written for lay readers within the last five years. I have omitted dictionaries and standard sources that have appeared in previous lists [RBB D 1 88].

GENERAL SOURCES

The American Medical Association Encyclopedia of Medicine. Random, 1989. 1,184p. $39.95 (0-394-56528-2).

This book contains three major sections. "Medicine Today" covers the latest medical advances and gives advice on preventing disease. The A–Z encyclopedia, the largest part of the book, has more than 5,000 entries and 2,200 color illustrations covering anatomy, symptoms, procedures, tests, and drugs. A drug glossary, index, and list of resource organizations complete the work, which is easy to use and provides excellent information.

Columbia University College of Physicians and Surgeons Complete Home Medical Guide. Rev. ed. Crown, 1989. 930p. $39.95 (0-517-57216-8).

This book is organized by broad subject areas; diseases are discussed in chapters on the various organ systems. There are sections on first aid and diagnostic tests, plus a detailed index, glossary, and directory of organizations. The material is current, easy to understand, and well presented.

Consumer Health Information Source Book. 3d ed. By Alan M. Rees and Catherine Hoffman. Oryx, 1990. 210p. $39.50 (0-89774-408-X).

Books, popular magazines, pamphlets, clearinghouses, hotlines, and organizations providing health information are evaluated in this book. It is extremely useful for library collection development, health education, and consumers seeking current resources.

The Mayo Clinic Family Health Book. Morrow, 1990. 1,378p. $40 (0-688-07819-2).

This excellent source includes a color anatomy atlas and colorplates of common skin disorders as well as sections on human development, first aid, fitness, the health care system, tests, drugs, and weights and measures. Diseases are covered by organ system. A detailed index facilitates access. Sony has just announced a CD-ROM version of this book with audio, video, and 500 illustrations. The IBM-PC or compatible version is $99.95; a Macintosh version will be released later this year.

The New Good Housekeeping Family Health and Medical Guide. Rev. ed. Hearst, 1989. 788p. $24.95 (0-688-06164-8).

Introductory material on first aid and a color anatomy atlas are followed by an A–Z encyclopedia of medical terms with brief entries. Separate sections cover family medicine, wellness, senior living, types of practitioners, and tests and procedures. The coverage is less detailed than that of the AMA, Columbia, or Mayo Clinic guides.

Prevention's Giant Book of Health Facts. Rodale, 1991. 608p. $29.95 (0-87857-909-5).

Common ailments and preventive measures as well as alternative treatments such as herbs are covered in this book. It also has an amusing section on such medical oddities as out-of-the-ordinary ailments (stamp-licker's tongue) and death under odd circumstances (falling off a barstool).

The University of California, Berkeley, Wellness Encyclopedia. Houghton, 1991. 541p. $29.95 (0-395-53363-5).

This is just what the title implies, a guidebook for a healthy life-style. It covers diet, exercise, nutrition, safety at home and at work, self-care, using the health care system, and preventing disease. It has a glossary and an index.

ENCYCLOPEDIA YEARBOOKS

The World Book Health and Medical Annual ($24.90, 0-02-944092-0), **The Britannica Medical and Health Annual** ($33.90, 0-85229-570-7), and Collier's **Health and Medical Yearbook** ($20.95, 0-02-944090-2) offer updates on current health and medical topics. All have in-depth feature articles and brief reports on miscellaneous subjects. AIDS, various cancers, smoking, stress, and hospice care are among the topics covered. All the books are nicely illustrated, and all are indexed. *World Book* offers cross-reference tabs to insert in the encyclopedia volumes. These annuals are a good way to update encyclopedia sets.

ALTERNATIVE HEALTH

Alternative Health Care Resources: A Directory and Guide. By Brett Jason Sinclair. Prentice Hall, 1992. $24.95 (0-13-030073-X); paper $12.95 (0-13-156522-2).

This current directory of organizations, publications, and self-help groups providing assistance and information on alternative treatments is useful for referral. The compiler has verified all information. He neither rates nor judges the material.

Alternatives in Healing. By Simon Mills and Steven J. Finando. NAL, 1989. paper $12.95 (0-452-26368-9).

This useful book explains acupuncture, chiropractics, homeopathy, herbalism, osteopathy, naturopathy, and western medicine. It then takes specific conditions and shows the treatment for them in each discipline in side-by-side columns.

Discovering Homeopathy: Medicine in the 21st Century. 2d ed. By Dana Ullman. North Atlantic Books, 1991. paper $12.95 (1-55643-108-2).

A good overview of homeopathy and its place in modern life, this book offers applications for women's health, pediatrics, sports medicine, psychiatry, and AIDS, along with a bibliography and a list of organizations and suppliers.

An Encyclopedia of Natural Medicine. By Michael T. Murray and Joseph E. Pizzorno. Prima; dist. by St. Martin's, 1991. 622p. $28.95 (1-55958-092-5); paper $18.95 (1-55958-091-7).

A good introduction to naturopathy and its use of diet, herbs, and other noninvasive techniques.

SPECIFIC HEALTH AND MEDICAL TOPICS

American Medical Association Handbook of First Aid and Emergency Care. Rev. ed. Random, 1990. paper $8.95 (0-679-72959-3).

With up-to-date information, this book has clear illustrations and instructions that are easy to follow. It includes a section on sports injuries.

The American Society of Plastic and Reconstructive Surgeons' Guide to Cosmetic Surgery. Simon & Schuster, 1992. paper $25 (0-671-76105-6).

This source discusses the different types of plastic surgery, costs, procedures, recovery, and best candidates for surgery. It clearly states what plastic surgery can and cannot accomplish.

The Cancer Sourcebook. Ed. by Frank E. Bair. Omnigraphics, 1990. $75 (1-55888-888-8).

Extensive coverage of all types of cancer is given here—symptoms, diagnosis, treatment, statistics on occurrences worldwide, and risks of carcinogens.

The Columbia University College of Physicians and Surgeons Complete Guide to Pregnancy. Crown, 1988. $24.95 (0-517-570300).

In addition to covering all aspects of pregnancy from planning and choosing a health care provider to getting back in shape after delivery, this book also discusses the role of the father, workplace hazards, and information on infertility and the management of high-risk pregnancy.

The Columbia University College of Physicians and Surgeons Complete Guide to Early Child Care. Crown, 1990. 514p. $32.50 (0-517-57217-6).

Child-care advice is offered on everything from selecting a pediatrician and equipping a baby's room through child development (birth through five years), day-care, and adoption and foster care as well as illness, dentistry, and emotional/psychological problems. Appendixes list resource organizations and poison-control centers.

The Columbia University College of Physicians and Surgeons Complete Home Guide to Mental Health. Holt, 1992. 640p. $35 (0-8050-0724-5).

This is an accessible guide to the diagnosis and treatment of mental illness in adults, adolescents, and children. It includes types of therapists, the use of drugs, eating and sleeping disorders, ethical issues, aging, suicide, and AIDS. An excellent reference source.

The Columbia University School of Public Health Complete Guide to Health and Well Being after 50. Times Books, 1988. $24.95 (0-8129-1325-6).

This guide for older people emphasizes prevention and treatment of physical and emotional problems. It has sound advice on using the health care system, nutrition, immunization, and death and dying (living wills, adjusting to loss, etc.).

The Complete Drug Reference. Consumer Reports. annual. $39.95

This people's PDR, written in lay language, has more information on drugs, their effects, and their interactions with other drugs and foods than the *Physician's Desk Reference* and costs less.

The Complete Foot Book: First Aid for Your Feet. By Donald S. Pritt and Morton Walker. Avery, 1992. paper $12.95 (0-89529-434-6).

Two podiatrists discuss foot care, footwear, and common foot conditions and injuries. They cover calluses, warts, ankle injuries, etc., as well as athletic and occupational problems and foot care for diabetics and pregnant women.

The Encyclopedia of Genetic Disorders and Birth Defects. By James Wynbrandt and Mark D. Ludman. Facts On File, 1991. 426p. $45 (0-8160-1926-6).

Along with complete, up-to-date information on genetic diseases in lay language, this book has statistical tables, referral information for government agencies and resource organizations, and a bibliography.

The Encyclopedia of Phobias, Fears, and Anxieties. By Ronald M. Doctor and Ada P. Kahn. Facts On File, 1989. 487p. $45 (0-8160-1798-0).

Clear information is provided on these relatively common disorders. The book covers the clinical, historical, and cultural aspects of the subject and is useful because it has both the common and medical names for the phobias cross-referenced.

The Essential Guide to Psychiatric Drugs. By Jack M. Gorman. St. Martin's, 1990. $22.95 (0-312-04313-9); paper $14.95 (0-312-06967-7).

The role of drugs in psychiatric treatment is explained, with clear information on the effects and side effects of specific drugs provided. Also covered are withdrawal symptoms, interactions with other drugs and foods, and the use of drugs in elderly and pregnant patients.

The Johns Hopkins Medical Handbook: The 100 Major Medical Disorders of People over the Age of 50. Random/Rebus, 1992. $39.95 (0-929661-04-4).

This outstanding new source has comprehensive, current information on the diagnosis and treatment of the most common illnesses affecting older people. It is arranged, chiefly, by organ systems and ends with a detailed index. Chapters also cover cancer, men's problems, women's problems, and mental health. In addition, there is a directory of medical specialty boards, teaching hospitals, and information and support groups with access by location and by illness.

Medical Tests and Diagnostic Procedures: A Patient's Guide to Just What the Doctor Ordered. By Philip Shtasel. HarperCollins, 1991. 320p. paper $10.95 (0-06-272001-5).

This guide is in two parts. The first is organized by medical specialty, listing the types of assiciated tests and their role in diagnosis. Part 2 covers specific tests and explains how they are administered. Their discomforts and hazards are rated. The book includes laboratory tests, X-rays, ultrasound, magnetic resonance imaging, and biopsies.

The Mount Sinai School of Medicine Complete Book of Nutrition. St. Martin's, 1990. 796p. $35 (0-312-05129-8).

All aspects of human nutrition for various age groups, diseases, and special situations (weight loss, eating disorders) are discussed in this book. It also offers practical advice on shopping, restaurant dining, food storage, and reading labels.

The Mount Sinai Medical Center Family Guide to Dental Health. By Jack Klatell and others. Macmillan, 1991. 304p. $29.95 (0-02-563675-8).

This unique source covers oral anatomy and physiology, the den-

OMNIBUS REVIEWS

tal profession, basic dental care and first aid, oral surgery, endodontics, orthodontics, prosthetics, and implants. It also lists dental schools and professional organizations.

The New A-to-Z of Women's Health: A Concise Encyclopedia. Rev. ed. By Christine Ammer. Facts On File, 1989. 544p. $29.95 (0-8160-2073-6); Hunter House, paper $16.95 (0-89793-089-4).

With current, concise, accessible information on all aspects of women's health, this book considers psychosocial and ethical as well as clinical issues.

The New Our Bodies Ourselves, Updated and Expanded for the 90's. By the Boston Women's Health Collective. Simon & Schuster/Touchstone, 1992. paper $20 (0-671-79176-1).

This classic has been revised to include the latest information on AIDS, birth control, and sexuality.

Organ Transplants: A Patient's Guide. By the Massachusetts General Hospital Transplant Team and H. F. Pizer. Harvard, 1991. $24.95 (0-674-64235-X).

This is a complete guide to the transplant process from the organ donor and the immune system and its suppression through post-treatment adjustment. Heart, lung, kidney, liver, pancreas, and bone-marrow transplants in adults and children are covered.

The Parent's Desk Reference. By Irene Franck and David Brownstone. Prentice Hall, 1991. $29.95 (0-13-649989-9); paper $18 (0-13-650003-X).

With coverage of child raising from conception through college, this encyclopedia includes nutrition, child care, illness and genetic disorders, education, psychology, family law, and social problems. There is a bibliography of books on parenting and one of award-winning children's books as well as a referral list of 2,500 organizations and hotlines.

Symptoms. By Isadore Rosenfield. Bantam, 1990. paper $12.95 (0-553-34902-3).

This brief guide is organized by type of symptom—pain, fever, lumps, etc.—with discussions of what each may mean and the likelihood of it being serious. Charts of points to remember and how to deal with the symptoms are accompanied by clear warnings about getting appropriate medical help.

Who to Call: The Parent's Sourcebook. By Dan Starer. Morrow, 1992. $30 (0-688-10044-9); paper $15 (0-688-11729-5).

This companion to the *Parent's Desk Reference* is a directory of organizations, clubs, government agencies, and hotlines dealing with all aspects of child care—medical, legal, social, recreational, and educational. The introduction explains how to decide who to call and how to organize thoughts to minimize telephone costs.

The Yale University School of Medicine Heart Book. Hearst, 1992. $30 (0-688-09719-7).

This book offers current information on the anatomy and physiology of the heart and the prevention, diagnosis, and treatment of cardiovascular disease in adults and children. Sections on heart disease in various ethnic groups and in women are of special interest.

Your Eyes: A Comprehensive Look at Understanding and Treatment of Vision Problems. By T. L. D'Alonzo. Avanti, 1991. paper $14.95 (0-9629063-5-2).

One of the few books on eye care written for lay readers, this book explains anatomy and physiology, refractive errors, eye diseases, medications, and surgery. Especially useful are sections on children and young adults, sports, environmental eye care, and information on how systemic medications affect the eyes and how eye medications affect the body.

Barbara Bibel is reference librarian for science, business, and sociology at the Oakland, California, Public Library. She was a member of the Reference Books Bulletin *Editorial Board 1988–1992.*

JOB AND CAREER INFORMATION SOURCES

"Career Information Sources" [RBB Ap 1 86] provided substantial annotations for the basic print tools for learning about various occupations. Many of these titles are now available in new editions, as noted below. Since that article, many libraries have expanded the services they offer to job seekers, and new sources—in a variety of formats—are now available to assist individuals in locating employment; these are also discussed here. This article is the result of discussions with more than a dozen librarians and counselors operating career centers. Their expert advice, along with my own work over the years providing career information to the general public, led me to select these resources as some of the most useful, both for job seekers and for builders of career-information collections.

Following a brief listing of guides especially for librarians, three major categories of works are discussed. "Career Exploration" presents tools that provide information about different occupations, which are useful to both career changers and those first entering the labor market. "Identifying Employment Opportunities" focuses on materials for those looking for job leads and openings, once they have chosen an occupation. "Job Search Skills" lists some exemplary guides for career planning, writing résumés, and answering interview questions. I conclude with a list of good video titles. The listed sources, unless otherwise noted, are appropriate for general readers from high school through adult. All works mentioned are listed by title at the end of this article, with full bibliographic information and citations to RBB reviews.

Given the vast outpouring of job and career information, this article does not attempt to be comprehensive, and not every source listed would traditionally be classified as a reference work. Rather, the intent here is to provide information about the variety of tools that have been effective in assisting job seekers to choose a first career, to reenter the labor market, and to locate employment openings. The point is not to have each listed resource in the collection but to have those that can be used most effectively by a library's clientele and that are appropriate for the level of career advice that the library wishes to offer. Some of the tools listed here are appropriate for reference collections or for special career centers; some are universally helpful.

LIBRARIANS' GUIDES. A few books are basic to librarians' work selecting materials and advising patrons because of their excellent organization and/or annotations. In the early 1980s, ALA published two excellent books for public libraries, one on planning job-information services and the other a bibliography of sources. Now both of these have been revised and are scheduled for a spring 1993 release in two volumes under the collective title *Serving Job Seekers and Career Changers*.

Where to Start Career Planning: An Essential Resource Guide for Career Planning & Job Hunting is a bibliography of books, periodicals, and audiovisual materials and is based on sources in Cornell University's Career Planning Library. School media centers may find *Focus on Careers* especially helpful in building their collections, since it integrates good YA fiction with nonfiction and nonprint resources.

CAREER EXPLORATION

U.S. GOVERNMENT SOURCES. The first-choice source for descriptions of duties, requirements, and trends for the 250 most common occupations is the biennial *Occupational Outlook Handbook* (OOH). Many consider this to be the bible of the field, and many other works pattern themselves after this title. Immensely more comprehensive than the OOH is the *Dictionary of Occupational Titles* (DOT), which provides cogent job descriptions for more than 12,000 occupations and is arranged by job categories.

The *Complete Guide for Occupational Exploration* is based on the U.S. Department of Labor's computer data files that were used to prepare the 1991 edition of the DOT. The work organizes more than 12,000 jobs by 12 large interest categories (e.g., artistic, plants and animals, business detail, humanitarian) and by 348 subgroups. Numerous charts, graphs, tables, and worksheets are included to assist an individual (often aided by a counselor) in relating his or her interests, aptitudes, and training to families of occupations.

MULTIVOLUME WORKS. A collection of materials for exploring various occupations would include at least one of the following three multivolume titles. All provide the same type of information as the OOH, but for a greater number of careers. Also, these are established titles that are routinely updated or issued periodically in new editions.

The *Career Information Center* is organized by broad industry in volumes such as *Transportation* and *Administration, Business and Office*. Occupational information is organized into three categories for jobs requiring varying amounts of specialized training or experience (i.e., none, some, or advanced). This work includes extensive lists of recommended titles for further reading and additional resources.

Chronicle Occupational Briefs comes in five binders with four- to eight-page entries for each occupation. Each brief includes a picture, descriptions of work, education and training, employment outlook, and sources of further research. The information for each career is reviewed and updated every four years.

The *Encyclopedia of Careers and Vocational Guidance* includes general articles about choosing a vocation and finding a job. Occupations are grouped by field, and specific job titles are indexed. The entries for various careers cover nature of the work, requirements, advancement opportunities, potential earnings, and sources for additional information.

SINGLE-VOLUME WORKS. Even if libraries already own the multivolume sets above, a few titles are valuable in the career collection because of their unique perspectives. *Great Careers: The Fourth of July Guide to Careers, Internships, & Volunteer Opportunities in the Nonprofit Sector*, written by career guidance professionals at colleges and universities, focuses on meaningful careers, including work with the homeless and the disabled and in labor unions, agriculture, and education. Books of rankings are always popular, as is *The Jobs Rated Almanac Two*, which evaluates 250 jobs based on such various factors as stress, security, income, outlook, and physical demands.

The Encyclopedia of Career Choices for the 1990s: A Guide to Entry Level Jobs is a good basic handbook that covers 42 industries and matches, in a simple fashion, college majors with job opportunities. Career paths that need years of experience are discussed for various industries, and recommended books and periodicals are noted. A volume especially useful for high school libraries is VGM's *Careers Encyclopedia*.

BOOKS IN SERIES. For libraries that need a collection of sources on specific careers, a wide variety of titles is available, including several series. Ten different titles will be available by spring 1993 in Gale's Career Advisor series, which covers such industries as travel and hospitality, marketing and sales, and health care. One example is the *Business and Finance Career Directory*, which includes a dozen or so essays by industry insiders, a section discussing job-search techniques (repeated in each volume), and a directory of companies and opportunities.

The Career Choices for the Nineties series, from Walker, is designed especially for students pursuing a college education, with individual titles geared toward a specific major, such as English, mathematics, history, and psychology. An example title is *Career Choices for Students of English*, which discusses qualifications, breaking into the field, ways to advance, etc.

ELECTRONIC SOURCES. Typically, community colleges, career centers, and other employment counseling sites utilize a computer-based system that allows users to create lists of occupations or colleges based on their skills and interests. One of the most popular of these systems is Discover for Colleges and Adults: A Computer-Based Career Planning and Information System That Supports Mature Decision-Making. Two other examples of popular career-planning software are Modular C-LECT and SIGI Plus.

IDENTIFYING EMPLOYMENT OPPORTUNITIES

Once an individual has selected and prepared for his or her occupation, the library or career center is frequently used to find information about specific job openings or potential employers. Useful to people preparing for job interviews are such business reference sources as annual reports, 10-K files, *Directory of Corporate Affiliations*, S&P Stock Reports, *National Directory of Advertisers*, and *Valueline*. Librarians should also remember to refer patrons, when appropriate, to some of the directories of nonprofit organizations, health-care providers, social-service agencies, educational institutions, and associations.

In addition to print tools, such business-oriented CD-ROM products as *Compact Disclosure* and *Infotrac: General Business Files* are invaluable to the job seeker doing company research. Especially useful is *Business Dateline OnDisc*. This source contains the text of articles from more than 165 national and regional business publications, as well as newspapers and wire services. Some magazines included are *Alabama Business Review*, *Business First-Buffalo*, *Tompkins' Central Illinois*, as well as the *Seattle Times* and the *Washington Post*. This valuable tool is expensive and is also available through online vendor services.

GUIDES TO SOURCES OF EMPLOYMENT LEADS. Templeton's *Help! My Job Interview Is Tomorrow!: How to Use the Library to Research an Employer* is an easy-to-use volume that includes worksheets and helps job seekers save time in searching for employer data.

A recent set of career information guides from Gale is highly recommended for public and academic libraries because, collectively, the three volumes cover the same common occupations listed in the OOH but provide additional and unique information for job seekers. The first title, *Job Hunter's Sourcebook: Where to Find Employment Leads & Other Job Search Resources*, lists sources of classified ads, employer directories, employment agencies and services, and other resources for 155 occupations. The *Professional Careers Sourcebook* includes similar information for 110 careers requiring advanced education and provides lists of professional assocations, publications, grants, standards, and certification agencies. The third title is the *Vocational Careers Sourcebook*, covering 135 occupations such as those in the military, the skilled trades, administrative support positions, and sales.

Three titles by David Lauber include directories of job services, salary surveys, and periodicals in which to find advertisements, etc.: *Professional's Job Finder*, *Government Job Finder*, and *Non-Profits' Job Finder*. These volumes are useful in circulating and reference collections.

EMPLOYER DIRECTORIES. Some reference tools on companies are designed especially for job seekers. An example is another career title from Gale, *Job Seeker's Guide to Private and Public Companies*. Approximately 15,000 employers are profiled in four volumes, each covering a different geographic area of the country. Each entry includes contact information, business description, and application procedures. Another good source is *The Career Guide: Dun's Employment Opportunities Directory*, 1993. More than 5,000 large companies, hospitals, and local governments are included in this annual publication. Profiles provide an overview and history of the employer, opportunities, benefits, and contact names. Enhancing the work are geographic and industrial indexes, as well as indexes by discipline and by employers that offer work-study or internship programs.

Several titles from Peterson's Guides are valuable to those looking for work. *Peterson's Job Opportunities for Engineering, Science, and Computer Graduates*, 1993 describes more than 1,000 employers hiring technical graduates in 1993. *Internships 1993: 50,000 On-the-Job Training Opportunities for Students and Adults* provides solid information on more than 1,500 organizations that offer paid and unpaid internships. Entries include pay, contacts, eligibility, and brief descriptions by former interns.

Some guides to companies are specifically designed for those who have advanced education or experience. The *CPC Annual: A Guide to Employment Opportunities for College Graduates* is where more than 1,000 large employers describe themselves and what kind of employees they are seeking. Occupational, geographic, and special indexes (e.g., "MBA Degrees," "International Employment Offered") provide excellent access to the listings.

GEOGRAPHICALLY BASED GUIDES. Some sources for employment leads to companies are organized geographically. Especially valuable is Bob Adams' *National JobBank* 1992, which lists 11 companies in Wyoming, hundreds in California, and other employers in every state, along with contact names, common job categories, and other brief information. Similar in format to Dun's *Career Guide*, this title includes many more small companies. Bob Adams also publishes a JobBank series for 18 large cities. The main section of each volume, "Where the Jobs Are," lists companies by industry. For the metropolitan areas covered, these books are useful for personnel contact names and brief descriptions of common positions, principle college majors sought, and company benefits.

PERIODICALS AND NEWSPAPERS. Obviously, primary sources of information about job openings are the classified sections of local and national newspapers, but collections can also benefit from some of the other available tools. *Where the Jobs Are: A Comprehensive Directory of 1,200 Journals Listing Career Opportunities* includes a helpful index that links specific occupations to appropriate periodicals. Useful in many collections is a subscription to one of the two weekly newspapers designed especially for professional job seekers. The *National Business Employment Weekly* includes topical articles and compiles advertisements from the four regional editions of the *Wall Street Journal*, while *National Ad Search* reprints help-wanted advertisements for professionals from 75 metropolitan newspapers across the country. Similarly, many libraries would benefit from subscribing to one of the two biweekly sources that list job opportunities with the U.S. government. The *Federal Jobs Digest* includes feature articles and covers openings by agency as well as geographically, and the *Federal Career Opportunities* lists, by agency, available jobs across the country.

SALARY INFORMATION. Many job seekers desire sources of information about wages for various occupations, industries, and locations. An especially helpful source is *American Salaries and Wages Survey*. This work can be used to find salary information for more than 4,500 occupations at different experience levels, in different industries, and in different areas of the country. The bulk of the data is derived from Area Wage Surveys by the U.S. government, but many other sources, such as studies by states and trade associations, are also cited. Included is a list of sources that can be used to locate more recent salary surveys.

JOB-SEARCH SKILLS

Below are listed but a sliver of the massive output of works on personal assessment of skills, job-search techniques, résumés, cover letters, interviewing, etc. Sources such as these should be available, probably in multiple copies, in every library that serves numerous job seekers. This article cannot begin to discuss titles that deal with managing stress, psychological effects of unemployment, methods for presenting a positive image, motivation, and other such topics. Nonetheless, these issues are often crucial to persons seeking employment, and libraries that serve job seekers should provide a selection of these sources, preferably including video materials.

CAREER PLANNING GUIDES. Richard Bolles' *What Color Is Your Parachute? A Practical Manual for Job-Hunters & Career Changers* stays a best-seller year after year because of its solid career-planning guidance, its engaging style and graphics, and its responsiveness to readers' suggestions. Also, librarians should remember that its annotated lists of the best resources for job seekers are updated annually.

While many adult patrons respond well to *What Color Is Your Parachute?* some are less inclined to the self-analysis and the painstaking thoroughness of the Bolles approach. These patrons may prefer the concise and to-the-point approach of *The Very Quick Job Search: Get a Good Job in Less Time* from publisher JIST Works. JIST refers to itself as "The Job Search People" and has developed its own excellent system—explained in this book—of organizing time, creating card files, and developing other skills necessary for successfully seeking employment.

RÉSUMÉS. Dozens of guides are available that provide advice about writing effective résumés. An exemplary title is the *Public Library Association's Guide to Basic Résumé Writing*. Yana Parker has two excellent works on functional résumés: *Damn Good Résumé Guide* and *Résumé Catalog: 200 Damn Good Examples*. Tom Jackson is a popular and prolific author of works on the job market, and software is even available to prepare résumés as outlined in his book *The Perfect Résumé*.

INTERVIEWS. One of the first titles designed to provide tips for the interviewee, and in many ways still the best, is H. Robert Medley's perennial best-seller, *Sweaty Palms: The Neglected Art of Being Interviewed*.

Martin J. Yate has three popular career titles: *Knock 'em Dead: With Great Answers to Tough Interview Questions*; *Cover Letters That Knock 'em Dead*; and *Résumés That Knock 'em Dead*.

VIDEOS

For the visually oriented, video can be engaging and instructive in ways books cannot. For these patrons, a good series of 18 videos is available in the *Video Career Library*. Each title focuses on a group of occupations, such as those in personal services or medicine, and shows approximately a dozen workers actually performing their jobs while a wide variety of information is presented. At the end of each profile, basic data about training, experience, advancement, and future trends are given. Also available from the same producer and distributor is the Emerging Careers Library video series that depicts jobs in such fields as biotechnology and robotics.

The 12-video series *Job Search: How to Find and Keep a Job*, originally produced by the San Diego Office of Education, is a thorough guide to the whole employment process, from knowing your skills to keeping the job. A title that will appeal to many people because of its lively and enjoyable approach is *Wizards of Work*. In this source, Dick Gaither conducts a seminar on how the labor market operates, how to identify your skills, and how to build interview confidence and self-esteem. This seminar utilizes an accompanying workbook, *SkillStalking: How to Eliminate Sneaker Breath & Keep Your Feet out of Your Mouth at Interviews!*

Two other video titles worthy of note include *Interviews, Careers, and the Jitterbug Blues*, which portrays students learning the basics about employer expectations. An abridgement of Peter Lefflsowitz's seminar is available in the video *Interviewing With Confidence: The Complete Guide for Successful Interviewing*.

CITED SOURCES

American Salaries and Wages Survey. Ed. by Arsen J. Darnay. Gale, 1991. $89.50 (0-8103-8042-0).

Business and Finance Career Directory. 2d ed. Ed. by Bradley J. Morgan. Gale, 1992. $29.95 (0-8103-5406-X); paper $17.95 from Visible Ink.

Business Dateline OnDisc. CD-ROM. monthly updates. UMI/Data Courier. $2,950/yr.

Career Choices for Students of English. Rev. ed. Walker, 1990. 166p. paper $8.95 (0-8027-7330-3).

The Career Guide: Dun's Employment Opportunities Directory 1993. Dun's Marketing Services, 1992. 4,100p. $395 (1-56203-121-X).

Career Information Center. 5th ed. 13v. Macmillan, 1993. $210 (0-02-897452-2).

Chronicle Occupational Briefs. Chronicle. monthly. $270.80/initial set; $105.50/yr.

Complete Guide for Occupational Exploration. JIST Works, 1993. 915p. paper $34.95 (1-56370-052-2).

Cover Letters That Knock 'em Dead. By Martin J. Yate. Bob Adams, 1991. 184p. paper $7.95 (1-55850-050-2).

CPC Annual: A Guide to Employment Opportunities for College Graduates. 4v. College Placement Council. annual. $49.95 (ISSN 0749-7474).

Damn Good Résumé Guide. Rev. ed. By Yana Parker. Ten Speed, 1989. paper $6.95 (0-89815-348-4).

Dictionary of Occupational Titles. 4th rev. ed. 2v. U.S. Dept. of Labor, Employment and Training Administration; dist. by Associated Book Publishers, 1991. Reprint editions available from Bernan Press, JIST Works, VGM Career Horizons, and Career Press.

Discover for Colleges and Adults: A Computer-Based Career Planning and Information System That Supports Mature Decision-Making. software. American College Testing Program; dist. by ACT Educational Technology Center, 230 Schilling Circle, Ste. 350, Hunt Valley, MD 21031, 1992.

The Encyclopedia of Career Choices for the 1990s: A Guide to Entry Level Jobs. By Career Associates. Walker, 1991. 862p. $75 (0-8027-1142-1). [RBB D 1 91]

The Encyclopedia of Careers and Vocational Guidance. 8th ed. 4v. Ed. by William E. Hopke. Ferguson, 1990. 2,800p. $129.95 (0-89434-117-0).

Federal Career Opportunities. Federal Research Service. biweekly. $160/yr. (ISSN 1279-2230).
Federal Jobs Digest. Breakthrough Publications. biweekly. $110/yr. (ISSN 0739-1684).
Focus on Careers. By Lynne B. Iglitzin. ABC-Clio, 1991. 200p. $39 (0-87436-588-0).
Government Job Finder. By Daniel Lauber. Planning/Communications, 1992. 366p. paper $14.95 (0-9622019-1-X).
Great Careers: The Fourth of July Guide to Careers, Internships, & Volunteer Opportunities in the Nonprofit Sector. Ed. by Devon C. Smith. Garrett Park Press, 1990. 605p. paper $35 (0-912048-74-3).
The Guide to Basic Resume Writing. By the Public Library Association Job and Career Information Services Committe. VGM Career Books, 1991. 96p. paper $7.95 (0-8442-8123-9).
Help! My Job Interview Is Tomorrow! How to Use the Library to Research an Employer. By Mary Ellen Templeton. Neal-Schuman, 1991. 116p. paper $24.95 (1-55570-089-67-0).
Internships 1993: 50,000 On-the-Job Training Opportunities for Students and Adults. 13th ed. Peterson's Guides, 1992. paper $28.95 (1-56079-149-7).
Interviewing with Confidence: The Complete Guide for Successful Interviewing. video. RMI Media Productions, 1988. 105 min. $69.95.
Inteviews, Careers, and the Jitterbug Blues. video. guide. Beacham, 1988. 29 min. $49.
The JobBank Series. 18 titles. Bob Adams. prices vary.
The Job Hunter's Sourcebook: Where to Find Employment Leads & Other Job Search Resources. Ed. by Michelle LeCompte. Gale, 1991. 1,106p. $49.95 (0-8103-7717-9; ISSN 1053-1874).
Job Search: How to Find and Keep a Job. 12 videos. JIST Works, 1989. $695 (1-56370-005-0); guide, 146p. $12.95 (1-56370-006-9).
Job Seeker's Guide to Private and Public Companies. 4v. Gale, 1992. $350/set; $95/v. (0-8103-7810-8; ISSN 1061-3285). [RBB O 15 92]
The Jobs Rated Almanac Two. Rev. ed. Ed. by Les Krantz. World Almanac, 1992. 352p. $24.95 (0-88687-717-2); paper $15.95 (0-88687-679-6).
Knock 'em Dead: With Great Answers to Tough Interview Questions. Rev. ed. By Martin J. Yate. Bob Adams, 1992. 240p. $19.95 (1-55850-086-3); paper $7.95 (1-55850-053-7).
Modular C-LECT. software. Chronicle. 800-622-7284.
National Ad Search. National Ad Search. weekly. $235/yr. (ISSN 0744-7140).
National Business Employment Weekly. Dow Jones. weekly. $52/10 weeks.
The National JobBank 1992. Bob Adams, 1991. 1,152p. $199.95 (1-55830-075-8).
Non-Profits' Job Finder. By Daniel Lauber. Planning/Commnications, 1992. 212p. paper $13.95 (0-9622019-4-4).
Occupational Outlook Handbook. 1992–93 ed. Bulletin Series #2350. U.S. Dept. of Labor, Bureau of Labor Statistics; dist. by U.S. GPO. 500p. (s/n 029-001-03022-3). Reprint editions available from VGM Career Horizons, $22.95 (0-8442-8700-8) and from JIST Works, $21.95 (1-56370-045-X).
The Perfect Résumé. Rev. ed. By Tom Jackson. Doubleday, 1990. paper $12 (0-385-26745-2).
Peterson's Job Opportunities for Engineering, Science, and Computer Graduates, 1993. Peterson's Guides, 1992. annual. paper $20.95 (1-56079-160-8; ISSN 1048-3411).
Professionals Careers Sourcebook. 2d ed. Ed. by Kathleen M. Savage and Annette Novallo. Gale, 1992. 1,166p. $75 (0-8103-7573-7; ISSN 1045-9863). [RBB Ap 1 90]
Professional's Job Finder. By Daniel Lauber. Planning/Commnications, 1992. 512p. paper $15.95 (0-9622019-2-8).
Résumé Catalog: 200 Damn Good Examples. By Yana Parker. Ten Speed, 1988. 320p. paper $15.95 (0-89815-219-4).
Résumés That Knock 'em Dead. By Martin J. Yate. Bob Adams, 1988. 216p. paper $7.95 (1-55850-955-0).
Serving Job Seekers and Career Changers. 2v. ALA, 1993. $25/set (0-8389-3419-6).
SIGI Plus. Educational Testing Service. 800-257-7444.
SkillStalking: How to Eliminate Sneaker Breath & Keep Your Feet out of Your Mouth at Interviews. Job Search Training Systems, Rd. 1, Dr. 18, CC-12, Nineveh, IN 46164.

Sweaty Palms: The Neglected Art of Being Interviewed. Rev. ed. By H. Anthony Medley. Ten Speed, 1992. 194p. paper $9.95 (0-89815-403-0).
The Very Quick Job Search: Get a Good Job in Less Time. By Michael Farr. JIST Works, 1991. 260p. paper $9.95 (0-942784-72-3).
Video Career Library. Chronicle; dist. by Career Passports, 1319 Spruce St., Boulder, CO 80302, 800-622-7284.
Vocational Careers Sourcebook. Ed. by Kathleen M. Savage and Karen Hill. Gale, 1992. 1,129p. $75 (0-8103-8405-1; ISSN 1060-5630). [RBB Jl 92]
VGM's Careers Encyclopedia. 3d ed. Ed. by Craig Norbuck. VGM Career Books, 1991. 464p. $39.95 (0-8442-8692-3).
What Color Is Your Parachute? A Practical Manual for Job Hunters & Career Changers. By Richard Bolles. Ten Speed, 1992. $18.95 (0-89815-506-1); paper $14.95 (0-89815-492-8).
Where the Jobs Are: A Comprehensive Directory of 1,200 Journals Listing Career Opportunities. By S. Norman Feingold and Glenda Ann Hansard-Winkler. Garrett Park Press, 1989. 110p. paper $15 (0-912048-67-0).
Where to Start Career Planning: An Essential Resource Guide for Career Planning & Job Hunting. 8th ed. By Pamela L. Feodoroff and Carolyn L. Lindquist. Peterson's Guides, 1991. 299p. paper $17.95 (1-56079-056-3).
Wizards of Work. 3 videos. USA Teleproductions, 1992.

Skip Auld manages a regional branch for the Carroll County Public Library in Westminster, Maryland.

NATIVE AMERICAN REFERENCE SOURCES

In 1992, the anniversary of Columbus' landing in the Western Hemisphere was celebrated throughout the world. It also generated a renewed and increased interest in Native Americans—the peoples who had been living in North America and the Western Hemisphere long before Columbus arrived. The U.S. Congress and the president recognized this fact by declaring 1992 as the "Year of the American Indian" and convening the White House Conference on Indian Education. This recognition and renewed interest resulted in an increased publishing agenda (articles, videos, TV series, and books). This omnibus review will focus on the publication of reference materials.

The emphasis here is on the Native Americans of North America as a group. The list will not cover the Indians of Central and South America (e.g., Mayans, Incas, Aztecs), nor will it list publications that cover a specific tribe (e.g., Sioux, Navajo, Shoshone). It concentrates on general reference sources for adults, including electronic media, and also includes a selection of sources for children. This review complements and supplements the special list, "Ethnics in American Society" [RBB Jl 90], which focused on African, Asian, and Hispanic American reference sources.

GUIDES TO THE LITERATURE

American Indian Literatures: An Introduction, Bibliographic Review, and Selected Bibliography. By A. LaVonne Brown Ruoff. Modern Language Association, 1990. 200p. index. paper $19.50 (0-87352-192-7). [RBB Mr 1 91]

As the subtitle suggests, this volume is divided into three parts: part 1 is an introduction to the topic; part 2 is a review of bibliographies, collections, and research guides; and part 3 is a more complete presentation of citations for works discussed in part 2 and also includes journals, films and videos, and Indian authors and their works. Also provided is an index and a chronology of notable American Indian events.

American Indian Reference Books for Children and Young Adults. By Barbara J. Kuipers. Libraries Unlimited, 1991. 190p. indexes. hardcover $32.50 (0-87287-745-0). [RBB N 1 91]

This is an annotated bibliography of 200 entries arranged by

Dewey Decimal classes. The entries are alphabetically arranged within each class. The annotations are thorough in their descriptions. A publishers directory and author-title and subject indexes are included.

American Indian Women: A Guide to Research. By Gretchen M. Bataille and Kathleen M. Sands. Garland, 1991. 423p. index. hardcover $57.00 (0-8240-4799-0).

This guide contains more than 1,500 annotated citations to resources and materials pertaining to American Indian women—a topic that has been ignored in the past. The bibliography is arranged into eight broad subject categories (e.g., *Film and Video*, *Politics and Law*, *Literature and Criticism*, *Autobiography*, *Biography*, and *Interviews*). This arrangement provides the researcher with an organized and thorough starting location. A subject index is included.

Guide to Research on North American Indians. By Arlene Hirschfelder and others. ALA, 1983. 340p. indexes. hardcover $75 (0-8389-0353-3).

This book is "intended to serve as a basic guide to the literature for general readers, students, and scholars interested in the study of American Indians—Native Americans." It is divided into four broad categories: introductory material, history and historical sources, economic and social aspects, and religion, arts, and literature. These four parts are further subdivided into specific topics. For instance, the section on history and historical sources contains chapters on geography and cartography, descriptive narratives, political organization, and federal and state Indian relations. The annotations are detailed and comprehensive. Separate author-title and subject indexes are included.

Native American Checklist. Comp. by Barbara Beaver. Bookpeople, 7900 Edgewater Dr., Oakland, CA 94621, 1992. 20p. paper. free to libraries and schools.

This catalog contains over 900 titles relating to Native Americans. It covers such topics as art, history, literature, religion, travel, and women's studies. Separate sections cover audiovisual materials and children's books.

ENCYCLOPEDIAS

Encyclopedia of Native American Religions: An Introduction. By Arlene Hirschfelder and Paulette Molin. Facts On File, 1992. 367p. illus. index. hardcover $45 (0-8160-2017-5). [RBB My 15 92]

This is the first reference source that focuses specifically on Native American religions. Approximately 1,200 brief, alphabetical entries provide information on beliefs, ceremonies, medicine, rites, and biographies of religious leaders and Christian missionaries. Cross-references and a classified subject index provide additional access points.

Encyclopedia of Native American Tribes. By Carl Waldman. Facts On File, 1988. 293p. bibliog. illus. index. hardcover $35 (0-8160-1421-3). [RBB Mr 15 88].

Concise descriptions on history and culture for more than 150 Indian tribes in the U.S., Canada, and Mexico are presented in this alphabetically arranged encyclopedia. Entries vary in length and include *see* references. A glossary of terms, a classified bibliography, and an index follow the encyclopedic text.

First Americans Series. 8v. Facts On File, 1990–91. 768p. illus. hardcover $18.95/volume.

This set, aimed at grades 5–8, provides an overview of Native American history and culture. Such topics as religion, prehistory, environment, and modern life are discussed. Each volume covers a region of the U.S. that corresponds to the arrangement used in Facts On File's *Atlas of the North American Indian* (see the annotation for this title under "Atlas" below). The eight volumes are *California Indians* (0-8160-2386-7); *Indians of the Arctic and Subarctic* (0-8160-2391-3); *Indians of the Northwest* (0-8160-2389-1); *Indians of the Plains* (0-8160-2387-5); *Indians of the Plateaus and Great Basin* (0-8160-2388-3); *Indians of the Southeast* (0-8160-2390-5); and *Indians of the Southwest* (0-8160-2385-9).

Handbook of North American Indians. 20v. (v.4–11, 15 published). Smithsonian Institution; U.S. Gov. Print. Off., 1978– . index. hardcover. price varies (SI 1.20: vol. no.). [RBB Jl 84]

When complete, this set will give a detailed and comprehensive summary of the prehistory, history, languages, and cultures of the native peoples of Central and North America. To date, nine volumes have been published: *History of Indian-White Relations* (v.4, 1988, $47); *Arctic* (v.5, 1984, $29); *Subarctic* (v.6, 1981, $25); *Northwest Coast* (v.7, 1990, $38); *California* (v.8, 1978, $25); *Southwest* (Pueblo peoples) (v.9, 1979, $23); *Southwest* (non-Pueblo peoples) (v.10, 1983, $25); *Great Basin* (v.11, 1986, $27); and *Northeast* (v.15, 1978, $27).

Reference Encyclopedia of the American Indian. 6th ed. Ed. by Barry T. Klein. Todd, 1993. 679p. hardcover $125 (0-915344-30-0). [RBB Ja 15 91]

This volume is actually a multipurpose resource: encyclopedia, directory, bibliography, and biographical source. Section 1 covers resources for the U.S.; section 2 covers Canadian resources (to a lesser extent than for the U.S.); section 3 contains a bibliography that includes alphabetical and subject listings, plus an index by publisher; and section 4 contains the biographies. There is no overall index to the book. The consolidation and incorporation of a variety of resources on Native Americans here make this a very useful reference volume.

DICTIONARIES

Dictionary of Native American Mythology. By Sam D. Gill and Irene F. Sullivan. ABC-Clio, 1992. 425p. bibliog. illus. index. hardcover $65 (0-87436-621-6).

Past and present rituals, traditions, and myths are meticulously described for more than 100 Native American cultures. Each entry contains the entry word(s), Indian tribe, culture area, cross-references, and bibliographic references. The brief citations in the entries direct the user to the extensive bibliography at the end of the dictionary. The entries range in length from one sentence to several hundred words. An index by tribe, more than 1,000 cross-references, and page headers increase and improve access to the contents of this work. This is a valuable source of information for anyone researching Native American mythology.

Historical Dictionary of North American Archaeology. Ed. by Edward Jelks and Juliet Jelks. Greenwood, 1988. 760p. bibliog. index. hardcover $95 (0-313-24307-7). [RBB S 15 88]

This is an alphabetical listing of more than 1,800 signed entries that vary in length from one sentence to several short paragraphs. These entries provide descriptions for cultures, mounds, ruins, and archaeological sites. Each entry concludes with the source(s) of information, for which full citations can be found in the extensive list of references.

DIRECTORIES

Indian Reservations: A State and Federal Handbook. Comp. by the Confederation of American Indians. McFarland, 1986. 329p. index. hardcover $45 (0-89950-200-8). [RBB My 15 87]

Indian reservations are arranged here alphabetically within state listings. Information on land status, culture, government, climate, tribal economy, transportation, community facilities, recreation, and vital statistics is included in a typical entry. With revised population figures, a new introductory chapter, and an index, this is an updated edition of the U.S. Department of Commerce publication, *Federal and State Indian Reservations and Indian Trust Areas* (1974, U.S. Gov. Print. Off., C 1.8/3: In2).

Native Americans Information Directory. Ed. by Julia C. Furtaw. Gale, 1993. 371p. index. hardcover $69.50 (0-8103-8854-5; ISSN 1063-9632). [RBB Ja 15 93]

Information on approximately 4,500 organizations, agencies, institutions, programs, and publications can be found in this directory. It includes material on American Indians, Alaskan Natives, Native Hawaiians, and Aboriginal Canadians. Its format is similar to

Gale's *Encyclopedia of Associations*, but it is more comprehensive in its listings of Native American information sources.

BIOGRAPHICAL SOURCES

Great North American Indians: Profiles in Life and Leadership. By Frederick J. Dockstader. Van Nostrand, 1977 (o.p.). 386p. bibliog. illus. index. hardcover. (0-442-02148-8). [RSBR O 1 78]

This directory provides comprehensive biographies for 301 famous, and not-so-famous, Native Americans. Arranged alphabetically, it spans more than 400 years of Native American history, from Hiawatha (1525–75) to Jerome R. Tiger (1941–67). The index and separate tribal and chronological listings of individuals provide additional ways to access information. Its thoroughness warrants its inclusion in this list, even though it is out of print.

Native American Women: A Biographical Dictionary. Ed. by Gretchen M. Bataille. Garland, 1993. 352p. bibliog. illus. index. hardcover $40 (0-8240-5267-6).

This new reference profiles more than 200 Native American women born in the U.S. and Canada. It covers both historical and contemporary figures, but the emphasis is on the twentieth century. While some of the profiles are for famous individuals (Pocahontas, Leslie Marmon Silko), many are for women not previously well known. Sketches range in length from a few paragraphs to a few pages; all are signed by one of the 61 contributors; and short bibliographies of primary and secondary works conclude each profile. Appendixes arrange the entry names by area of specialization, decade of birth, state or province of birth, and tribal affiliation.

Portrait Index of North American Indians in Published Collections. By Patrick Frazier. Library of Congress, 1992. 142p. bibliog. illus. index. paper $16 (0-8444-0707-0); U.S. Gov. Print. Off. (LC 1.2: P83/3).

This book identifies and indexes hundreds of pictures, prints, drawings, and lithographs of Native American portraits contained in 75 sources, which are listed at the beginning of the publication. The sources include monographs, multivolume sets, government publications, state historical-society publications, and reprints published between 1835 and 1986. The index is arranged by Indian tribe, with numerous cross-references. Also included is a personal-name index at the end. A National Archives and Records Administration (NARA) pamphlet, *Photographs of Indians in the United States* (NARA, 1985, GS 4.17/7: In2), provides a listing of selected visual materials (microfilms, slides, prints, and negatives) found in various NARA collections.

Who Was Who in Native American History: Indians and Non-Indians from Early Contacts through 1900. By Carl Waldman. Facts On File, 1990. 410p. illus. hardcover $45 (0-8160-1797-2). [RBB S 15 91]

Approximately 1,000 brief biographical sketches are provided for Indians and non-Indians; coverage is split evenly between the two groups. There is no index, but cross-references are used throughout the descriptions. The appendix contains a listing of Native Americans by tribes and a listing of non-Indians by major categories (e.g., explorers, agents, soldiers, painters). *Fighting Men of the Indian Wars*, by Bill O'Neal [RBB Jl 92], is an alternative source of biographical information for non-Indians.

ATLASES

Atlas of American Indian Affairs. By Francis P. Prucha. Univ. of Nebraska, 1990. 191p. bibliog. index. hardcover $47.50 (0-8032-3689-1). [RBB Ap 15 91]

This collection of 109, full-page, black-and-white maps graphically presents the history of Native Americans. The atlas is divided into 10 sections (e.g., "Indian Land Cessions," "Indian Reservations," "The Army and the Indian Frontier"). The 10 sections of maps, which contain almost no text, are followed by an extensive collection of references for the notes.

Atlas of the North American Indian. By Carl Waldman. Facts On File, 1985. 288p. bibliog. illus. index. hardcover $29.95 (0-87196-850-9); paper $17.95 (0-8160-2136-8). [BKL Ja 15 86]

This atlas combines an extensive text, numerous illustrations, and more than 100 two-color, thematic maps (historical, military, cultural, contemporary, and period). The result is a detailed reference source on the history, culture, and locations of Native Americans in North and Central America. The seven chapters provide chronological coverage from ancient civilizations to contemporary times. The appendix provides a series of useful reference lists, such as a chronology of Indian history, major Indian place-names, federal and state Indian reservations, Indian bands in Canada, and a listing of museums, historical societies, reconstructed villages, and archaeological sites.

Children's Atlas of Native Americans. Rand McNally, 1992. 80p. illus. index. hardcover $14.95 (0-528-83494-0).

This atlas is written for children ages 8–12, and it provides an in-depth view of the diverse Native American cultures that once occupied North, Central, and South America. It is arranged geographically: "Peoples of the North," "Tribes of the East," "Great Plains and Western Tribes," and "Central and South American Peoples." The first chapter concentrates on the origins of the Native American and specifically looks at the cliff dwellers and the mound builders of North America and the great civilizations of the Mayans, Aztecs, Toltecs, and Incas. The text, maps, pictures, and illustrations provide a well-balanced presentation.

MAPS

Early Indian Tribes, Culture Areas, and Linguistic Stock. By William Sturtevant. U.S. Geological Survey, Denver, CO 80225, 1967, reprinted 1991. bibliog. $3.10 (1:7,500,000 scale; 19"h x 28"w).

This multicolored map, which is a sheet separate from the *National Atlas of the United States*, shows the geographic extent of major and minor Indian tribes, their culture areas, and 18 linguistic stocks for Alaska and the 48 conterminous states. A brief narrative is printed on the reverse side, along with the Alaska map. A laminated edition, with grommets for hanging, is available for $8.95 from World Eagle, Inc., 64 Washburn Ave., Wellesley, MA 02181.

Quincentennial Map of American Indian History. 2d ed. By George Russell. Thunderbird Enterprises, 8821 N. First St., Phoenix, AZ 85020, 1992. $15. (scale not given; 24"h x 36"w).

This map presents a graphic history of 500 years of the American Indian. The map identifies military forts and dates of activity, major battles and dates, Indian lands and reservations, and state name (48 conterminous states) and date of statehood. The margins contain text that discusses various topics and time periods (e.g., "Broken Treaties," "Trail of Tears," "Spanish Influence," and "Indians Today"). The reservations on the map are numbered and keyed to a chart on the reverse side that provides the reservation name, state, total acreage, tribal lands, total population, and Native American population. The map is accompanied by a pamphlet, *The American Indian Digest*, which provides additional information.

TRAVEL BOOKS

Native America. Ed. by John Gattuso. APA Publications; dist. by Prentice Hall, 1992. 389p. bibliog. illus. index. paper $19.95 (0-13-467119-8).

This guide uses a narrative approach to identify and describe the sites and activities of the Native American. It begins with an overview of the history and culture of Native Americans and includes discussion of American Indian art, Indians and alcohol, and ancestral grounds. The narrative portion of the guide is arranged by region: Great Plains, Northwest, Southwest, and the four winds (northeast, southeast, California, and Oklahoma). *Native America*, one of APA's Insight Guides, concludes with a ready-reference section covering such topics as getting there, travel essentials, getting acquainted, things to do, useful addresses, and emergencies.

OMNIBUS REVIEWS

North American Indian Landmarks: A Traveler's Guide. By George Cantor. Gale, 1993. 409p. bibliog. illus. index. hardcover $34.95 (0-8103-8916-9).

This geographically arranged guide provides information on more than 340 sites in the U.S. and Canada. Included are entries for monuments, museums, parks, battlefields, reservations, and places of birth and burial. Brief narratives outline the history and importance of each site, and information is included about location, hours, fees, and telephone numbers. This work is a sequel to Cantor's *Historic Landmarks of Black America* [RBB S 1 91].

North American Indian Travel Guide. Rev. ed. Ed. by Ralph Shanks and Lisa Shanks. Costano Books, Box 355, Petaluma, CA 94953, 1991. 294p. illus. paper $17.95 (0-930268-11-3).

This is a state-by-state, province-by-province listing of Indian reservations, museums, historic and archaeological sites, burial mounds, tribal events, and rituals. Each listing includes location and basic set of directions, telephone number, and brief description of the place or facility. Introductory material provides information on a variety of categories, such as Indian humor, buying arts and crafts, education, religion, and dances and ceremonies. The book concludes with an alphabetic and descriptive tribal listing.

MISCELLANEOUS COMPENDIUMS

American Indians Today: Answers to Your Questions. 3d ed. Bureau of Indian Affairs, 1991. 36p. bibliog. paper. free from Bureau of Indian Affairs; U.S. Gov. Print. Off. (I 20.2: Am3/2/991).

This pamphlet provides an overview of the role of the federal government and its relationship to Native Americans. Included are general statistics, a map showing federally recognized Indian tribes, and a seven-page, topically arranged bibliography. The pamphlet also includes a series of frequently asked questions about Native Americans (e.g., Who is an Indian? What is a reservation? Are Indians wards of the government?).

Indian Tribes of North America. By John R. Swanton. Smithsonian Institution, Bureau of American Ethnology *Bulletin*, v.145. U.S. Gov. Print. Off., 1953 (o.p.). 726p. bibliog. index. hardcover (SI 2.3: 145).

This classic reference source contains extensive historical information on Indian tribes, their locations, villages, and population. It is arranged by state and then by other countries of North America. Although the original volume is out of print, two reprint editions are available: Smithsonian Institution, 1979 reprint, $35, (0-87474-179-3), and Native American Book Publishers, 1991 reprint, hardcover, $125, (1-878592-17-3); paper, $69, (1-878592-18-1).

Nations within a Nation: Historical Statistics of American Indians. By Paul Stuart. Greenwood, 1987. 251p. bibliog. index. tables. hardcover $45 (0-313-23813-8). [RBB Ja 1 89]

This is a volume of historical statistics on Native American tribes. The scope and purpose are clearly detailed in the introduction. The data are arranged into eight categories: population, land holdings and climate, vital statistics and health, government expenditures, health care and education, employment and income, natural resources and economic development, and relocation, removal, migration, and urbanization. The information is gathered from an extensive collection of government documents and scholarly reports, which are included in a comprehensive bibliography.

Native American Wisdom. Comp. by Kent Nerburn and Louise Mengelkoch. New World Library, 1991. 109p. paper $9.95 (0-931432-78-2).

This book of quotations is arranged into 11 categories (e.g., "The Ways of the Land," "The Ways of Learning," "The Ways of Living," "The Ways of the White Man"). This arrangement makes it a useful resource for all—scholars, teachers, and students. Historical and biographical notes are included. A related title, *Voices of the Winds: Native American Legends* (Facts On File, 1989, hardcover, $27.95; 1992, paper, $14.95), arranges Native American stories and legends by six geographic regions of the U.S.: Northwest, Southwest, Great Plains, Central Region, Southeast, and Northeast.

Trends in Indian Health. U.S. Department of Health and Human Services, Public Health Service, Indian Health Service, 1955–. tables. paper. free from the Indian Health Service; U.S. Gov. Print. Off. (HE 20.9421: year).

This annual compendium "presents tables and charts that describe the Indian Health Service program, and the health status of American Indians and Alaska Natives." Current and historical data are provided, and comparative data to other U.S. population groups are included when appropriate. Previously published under the title, *Indian Health Trends and Services*, it emphasizes general population, natality and mortality numbers, and patient-care and health-care statistics.

SPECIALIZED BIBLIOGRAPHIES

Numerous bibliographies—some annotated and others not—are available that cover a wide range of topics pertaining to Native Americans, individual tribes, and specific traditions and practices. What follows is a selection of a few recently published titles.

American Indian Ghost Dance, 1870 and 1890: An Annotated Bibliography. By Shelley Anne Osterreich. Greenwood, 1991. 96p. indexes. hardcover $37.95 (0-313-27469-X).

This is a short, selective, annotated bibliography on the Indian ghost dance. The annotations for the 110 entries are lengthy and comprehensive and are arranged into seven subject categories. The work provides a good overview on this topic. Separate author and subject indexes are included.

Native American Basketry: An Annotated Bibliography. Comp. by Frank W. Porter. Greenwood, 1988. 249p. index. hardcover $39.95 (0-313-25363-3). [RBB N 1 88]

The 1,000-plus entries are arranged by the major cultural areas of North America. The bibliography provides comprehensive coverage on all aspects of Native American basket making. The annotations are brief, yet concise. An index to authors and subjects is included.

Native American Bibliography Series. Scarecrow, 1980–. (ISSN 1040-9629).

Begun in 1980 with the publication of *Bibliography of the Sioux*, titles in this scholarly series have focused on individual tribes, geographic areas, literature, languages, and collections of documents. Different individuals have authored the volumes; practices have varied regarding the use of annotations. The most recent addition to this series is volume 16, *Yakima, Palouse, Cayeuse, Umatilla, Walla Walla, Wanapum Indians: An Historical Bibliography* by Clifford E. Trafzer (1992, 263p., hardcover, $32.50, 0-8108-2517-1).

ELECTRONIC SOURCES

The American Indian: A Multimedia Encyclopedia. CD-ROM. Facts On File, 1993. $295 (0-8160-2835-4).

A review copy of this CD-ROM product was not available at the time this review was written (the product was released May 1993). It incorporates the contents of four Facts On File Publications: *Atlas of the North American Indian; Voices of the Winds: Native American Legends; Who Was Who in Native American History: Indians and Non-Indians from Early Contacts through 1900;* and *Encyclopedia of Native American Tribes.* It also includes more than 1,000 reproductions of images and maps from NARA publications and documents. The user guide can be downloaded and printed from the CD-ROM. Minimum hardware and software requirements are: IBM or 100-percent compatible with a hard drive, 640 KB RAM, MS-DOS 3.0 or higher, VGA monitor, and a CD-ROM drive with MS-DOS CD-ROM Extensions 2.1 or higher; a mouse is strongly recommended.

Bibliography of Native North Americans on Disc. CD-ROM. ABC-Clio, 1992. annual. $795/yr.

This CD-ROM reference source is based on the Human Relations Area File's *Ethnographic Bibliography of North America* (4th ed., 1975; and *Supplement 1973–1987*, 1990) compiled by Timothy J. O'Leary and M. Marlene Martin. While the print version is in its fourth edition, the product on disc "is the comprehensive fifth edition of the bibliography." The disc contains—and provides convenient access to—more than 60,000 citations (monographs, articles, dissertations, and essays) from the sixteenth century through 1991. Cumulative updates of the CD-ROM will be released annually beginning in 1993. Installation is simple and straightforward. The product uses ABC-Clio's Electronic Library software, which provides "easy-to-follow on-screen instructions." A detailed user's guide and a quick-reference card accompany the CD-ROM. This product will appeal to large libraries, both public and academic. Minimum hardware and software requirements are IBM or 100-percent compatible with a hard drive (20MB minimum), one floppy-disk drive, 512 KB RAM, MS-DOS 3.0 or higher, and a CD-ROM player with MS-DOS CD-ROM Extensions 2.1 or higher.

North American Indians. CD-ROM. Quanta Press, 1313 Fifth St. SE, Minneapolis, MN 55414, 1991. $69.95.

This is a database of text and image (black-and-white and color) on the history of Native Americans. It includes information on leadership, tribal heritage, religion, family life, and customs. The indexing, searching, and retrieval software are contained on the CD-ROM. The installation and searching are easy. The images are high quality and can be downloaded to most desktop publishing systems. The publisher is planning to issue a *North American Indian Wars* CD-ROM in the near future. Minimum hardware and software requirements are IBM or 100-percent compatible with a hard drive, 640 KB RAM (1 MB RAM for SVGA), MS-DOS 2.0 or higher, VGA monitor, and CD-ROM player with MS-DOS CD-ROM Extensions (Macintosh version also available).

Jim Walsh is head of government documents and microforms at Boston College. He was a member of the RBB Editorial Board from 1988 to 1992 and is currently an alumni reviewer. He is the coauthor of *Vital and Health Statistics Series: An Annotated Checklist and Index*, which was the recipient of the GODORT of Michigan Paul W. Thurston Award of 1992.

Business Reference Sources

The titles on U.S. business described here are recommended as core resources for the collections of medium-size libraries. Those that are particularly recommended for small libraries are marked with an asterisk. Some of the sources are listed jointly with similar titles in order to facilitate comparison. Not included are standard reference tools found in almost all libraries, such as the *Encyclopedia of Associations* and the U.S. *County and City Data Book*, although they have great utility as business information sources. Nor are periodical indexes discussed here, though they are an essential tool in libraries providing business reference service. Numerous indexing and abstracting tools are available, in print and electronic formats, with widely varying subscription options, costs, and coverage; they are amply described in "Guides to the Field" listed below. Librarians are urged to use this list as a starting point and to peruse the catalogs of the publishers represented here for further selections.

GUIDES TO THE FIELD

Encyclopedia of Business Information Sources. 9th ed. Ed. by James B. Woy. Gale, 1992. $235 (0-8103-7489-7). [RBB My 15 87]
Directory of Business Information Resources, 1992: Associations, Newsletters, Magazines and Trade Shows. Ed. by Leslie MacKenzie. Grey House, 1992. $135 (0-939300-11-7); paper $110 (0-939300-15-X). [RBB S 15 92]

The Gale encyclopedia provides full bibliographic citations (with prices) to more than 24,000 monographic, electronic, and serial publications. They are categorized in 1,116 business areas, including issues (e.g., air pollution), industries and services, products, activities (e.g., home buying), and investment markets. Along the same lines, the directory provides a current-awareness service with its citations to newsletters, trade magazines, associations, and trade shows for 90 industries. Since the amount of overlap between these two resources is remarkably small, both are highly recommended.

*****Basic Business Library**. 2d ed. Ed. by Bernard S. Schlessinger. Oryx, 1989. 288p. $39.50 (0-89774-451-9). [RBB Je 15 89]

A collection-development resource that focuses on small- to medium-size libraries. The first part of the book annotates 177 business reference sources, including indexes, that are recommended as a core collection for medium-size libraries; the second part annotates the most substantive and practical literature about business librarianship over an 11-year time period; and the third section provides practical essays on various aspects of running a business library or collection. An updated edition of this title is currently in process.

Business Information: How to Find It, How to Use It. 2d ed. By Michael Lavin. Oryx, 1992. 448p. $49.95 (0-89774-556-6); paper $38.50 (0-89774-643-0). [RBB Jl 92]
Handbook of Business Information: A Guide for Librarians, Students, & Researchers. By Diane Wheeler Strauss. Libraries Unlimited, 1988. 500p. $42 (0-87287-607-1). [RBB Je 15 89]

Lavin's *Business Information* identifies more than 1,200 resources that can be used for specific types of business information requests (e.g., "Where can I get information on insider trading?" "What resources track inflation?"). Lavin also explains business concepts, for example, the major indicators of inflation. For the most difficult business reference sources (e.g., *Value Line Investment Survey*), he explains how to read a sample page. The handbook takes an approach similar to Lavin but is not as up-to-date. Novices in the field will still find the second half of the book useful because it provides an overview of major fields of business. Librarians working with large collections have long considered Lorna Daniells' *Business Information Sources* (rev. ed., Univ. of California, 1985) to be the standard guide to the literature. However, it is now dated, and a third edition is not expected until early 1994.

*****Industry and Company Information:** Illustrated Search Strategy & Sources. By Craig A. Hawbaker and Judith M. Nixon. Pierian Press, 1991. $25 (0-87650-287-7).

For the novice business researcher, this title provides a step-by-step guide to researching an industry and a company within an industry. It covers approximately 52 major business resources as it walks the researcher through a specific search for information on the hotel industry, Hilton Hotels (a public company) and Red Roof Hotels (a private company). Librarians who follow the bibliographic instruction units provided will have a good foundation for approaching business reference but will still require other guides for help in deciphering the often cryptic language of business reference sources.

*****Business Information Desk Reference:** Where to Find Answers to Business Questions. By Melvyn N. Freed and Virgil P. Diodata. Macmillan, 1991. 513p. $85 (0-02-910651-6); paper $20 (0-02-897141-8). [RBB Je 15 91]

This recent resource poses questions (categorized into 24 business areas), and then provides the most likely answering tool (print and electronic). Each listed resource is fully described, and the final chapter of the book covers business and trade organizations.

DICTIONARIES AND ENCYCLOPEDIAS

It is difficult to produce a general business dictionary because the field is so large and specialized. This section begins with two general sources and then lists dictionaries that cover a particular specialty, such as insurance or banking.

*****Dictionary of Business and Management**. By Jerry M. Rosenberg. Wiley, 1992. 374p. $39.95 (0-471-57812-6); paper $14.95 (0-471-54536-8). [RBB D 15 92]
*****Dictionary of Business Terms**. By Jack P. Friedman and others. Barron's, 1987. 500p. paper $9.95 (0-8120-3775-8).

Geared toward business proprietors and managers, the *Dictionary of Business Terms* is a useful pocket-size tool that provides 6,000 detailed entries for terminology from the fields of investment, banking, taxes,

OMNIBUS REVIEWS

laws, real estate, management, and computers. The *Dictionary of Business and Management* is written for a general audience and provides 7,500 less-detailed definitions. The 30 fields covered include collective bargaining and labor relations, economics, insurance, business law, accounting, management, research, and marketing. These two works complement each other well—what is not found in one can usually be located in the other.

Encyclopedia of Banking and Finance. 9th ed. By Glenn C. Munn and others. St. James Press, 1991. 1,097p. $115 (1-55862-141-5); paper $49.95. [RBB My 15 91]
*****Dictionary of Banking**. By Jerry M. Rosenberg. Wiley, 1992. 369p. $39.95 (0-471-57435-X); paper $14.95 (0-471-57436-8). [RBB D 15 92]
*****Dictionary of Banking Terms**. By Thomas P. Fitch and others. Barron's, 1990. 698p. paper $9.95 (0-8120-3946-7). [RBB S 1 90]

The standard authority for banking in the U.S. is the hefty, 1,097-page *Encyclopedia of Banking and Finance*. Published since 1924, this ninth edition provides detailed explanations for more than 4,000 topics, including terms, concepts, and historical events. Entries include definitions, examples, statistics (with many charts), citations to laws and regulations, and resources for further information. Although its scholarly style makes it inappropriate as a first stop for novices, it is an essential resource for any public library that serves bankers and business-oriented bank consumers. Less-intimidating resources for novices are such works as the *Dictionary of Banking Terms* or the *Dictionary of Banking*. However, neither of these is comprehensive, and neither provides totally satisfying or complete definitions. For example, Fitch defines ROE as "return on equity," Rosenberg defines it as "rate of exchange," and neither defines ROI ("return on investment," or "rate of interest").

*****Dictionary of Personal Finance.** By Joel G. Siegel and others. Macmillan, 1992. 391p. $70 (0-02-897393-3); paper $20 (0-02-897394-1). [RBB Je 15 92]

In the area of personal finance, this dictionary is a good first choice. Its approach focuses on individuals trying to plan their financial affairs. Provided are jargon-free definitions for 3,500 entries covering the topics of consumer economics; career planning; consumer credit; education financing; personal banking, budgeting, savings, and debts; retirement income; and tax planning. Appropriate even for high-schoolers, it also has appendixes that include annuity and monthly mortgage tables and lists of federal information centers and state government consumer protection offices.

Complete Words of Wall Street: The Professional's Guide to Investment Literacy. By Allan H. Pessin. Business One Irwin, 1991. $49.95 (1-55623-330-2). [RBB News Je 1 91]
*****Dictionary of Finance and Investment Terms**. 3d ed. By John Downes and Jordan E. Goodman. Barron's, 1991. 500p. paper $9.95 (0-8120-4631-5).
*****Dictionary of Investing**. By Jerry M. Rosenberg. Wiley, 1992. 368p. $39.95 (0-471-57433-3); paper $14.95 (0-471-57434-1). [RBB D 15 92]
Wall Street Dictionary. By Robert L. Shook. Prentice-Hall, 1990. paper $14.95 (0-13-950189-4).

For sophisticated or more affluent money managers, resources on investments will be necessary. Dictionaries available range from the professionally oriented, comprehensive, pocket-size, 3,000-entry *Dictionary of Finance and Investment Terms* and the novice-oriented, 7,500-entry *Dictionary of Investing* to such sources for specialized vocabulary as the *Wall Street Dictionary* and *Complete Words of Wall Street*. Although coverage in these resources overlaps, obtaining a complete definition will often involve multiple lookups for the same term. For example, the definition for *Sallie Mae* in Rosenberg's dictionary does not indicate that its bonds are financially backed by the U.S. government; the definition in Pessin does.

Dictionary of Advertising—Direct Mail Terms. By Jane Imber and Betsy Ann Toffler. Barron's, 1987. 500p. paper $9.95 (0-8120-3765-0).
*****Marketing Glossary:** Key Terms, Concepts, and Applications. By Mark N. Clemente. AMACOM, 1992. 470p. $32.95 (0-8144-5030-X). [RBB My 15 92]

The *Marketing Glossary* focuses on terms and concepts needed by people in small businesses, for example, in the areas of advertising, promotion, public relations, direct marketing, market research, and sales. For more detailed coverage of advertising, the *Dictionary of Advertising* is a good choice. Defined are 3,000 key terms used in television, radio, print advertising, and direct-mail campaigns.

*****Dictionary of Insurance**. 7th ed. By Lewis E. Davids. Rowman & Littlefield, 1990. 516p. paper $17.95 (0-8226-3000-1).
*****Dictionary of Insurance Terms**. 2d ed. By Harvey Rubin. Barron's, 1991. 416p. paper $9.95 (0-8120-4632-3).

The lay-oriented, 4,500-entry *Dictionary of Insurance* is very comprehensive. It covers all areas of insurance, including life, health, property, liability, marine, pension, real estate, and municipal and federal regulating agencies. Also provided are addresses of state insurance commissioners and organizations related to the insurance industry. The 300-entry *Dictionary of Insurance Terms* provides more detail, but because the definitions are written for insurance professionals, multiple lookups may be required to understand some entries.

*****Human Resources Glossary:** A Complete Desk Reference for HR Professionals. By William R. Tracey. AMACOM, 1991. 400p. $49.95 (0-8144-5011-3).

Anyone involved in a business that employs more than one person will find this an excellent resource. Everything from professional associations and legislation to marketing and recruitment is covered in this easy-to-read and appropriately detailed 3,000-entry lexicon.

*****Dictionary of Accounting Terms**. By Joel Siegel and Jae Shim. Barron's, 1987. 448p. paper $9.95 (0-8120-3766-9).
*****Encyclopedic Dictionary of Accounting and Finance**. By Joel Siegel and Jae Shim. Prentice-Hall, 1989. 504p. $49.95 (0-13-275801-6). [RBB N 15 89]

The 600-entry *Encyclopedic Dictionary* is written for working professionals. Its definitions include proven techniques, strategies, and approaches to diagnosing and solving accounting and financial problems. Liberally enhanced with charts, computations, checklists, and diagrams, the long entries (averaging 4–6 pages) provide comprehensive coverage of key topics. For shorter entries in a pocketbook format, the *Dictionary of Accounting Terms* provides 2,500 definitions for business managers, accountants, bookkeepers, students, and entrepreneurs. It is enhanced with charts, graphs, and tables.

Dictionary of Real Estate Terms. 2d ed. By Jack P. Friedman and others. Barron's, 1987. 352p. $9.95 (0-8120-3898-3).
St. James Encyclopedia of Mortgage and Real Estate Finance. Ed. by James Newell and others. St. James Press, 1991. 575p. $55 (1-55862-154-7); available in paper as *Encyclopedia of Mortgage and Real Estate Finance*, Probus, 1991, $27.50 (1-55738-123-2). [RBB D 1 91]

The *St. James Encyclopedia*, oriented toward people with some business experience, provides more than 2,000 clearly written entries ranging from drawings of arcadian architecture to detailed explanations of the Federal Housing Administration. For pocketbook-size coverage, the *Dictionary of Real Estate Terms* provides shorter, but amply illustrated, definitions for first-time home buyers, real estate investors, and veteran brokers.

*****Dictionary of Computer Terms**. By Douglas Downing and Michael Covington. Barron's, 1989. 288p. paper $8.95 (0-8120-4152-6).
Computer Glossary: The Complete Illustrated Desk Reference. 6th ed. By Alan Freedman. AMACOM, 1993. 574p. $36.95 (0-8144-5104-7); paper $24.95 (0-8144-7801-8); paper and computer disk $39.95 (0-8144-7809-3). [RBB Jl 91]

Since computers have become a necessity in businesses, people require business-oriented (not computer-hacker–oriented) computer glossaries. These titles are two such resources; for example, bar codes are defined in terms of their use in grocery stores. The 5,300-entry *Computer Glossary* is the more general of the two and is available in a paper-and-disk combination that allows the text to be loaded onto a personal computer and accessed electronically. The *Dictionary of Computer Terms* is narrower in focus and, for the terms it includes, is often more detailed.

HANDBOOKS, MANUALS, AND STATISTICS

*Standard Industrial Classification Manual 1987. Govt. Print. Off., 1991. $24 (0-16-004329-8; S/N 041-001-00314-2).

This title is crucial in business information retrieval because industries and corporations are often classified in business reference sources according to its hierarchical numbering system. Online searching and access to comparative data are facilitated by utilizing SIC numbers.

*The Business One Irwin Business and Investment Almanac, 1993. Ed. by Sumner N. Levine. Business One Irwin, 1992. annual. $75 (1-55623-723-5).

Among the many sources providing financial statistics, this title is indispensable. A first choice for all libraries, the almanac defines investment and financial terms and concepts; supplies bibliographies of general business reference sources and source documents for business statistics; and provides summary graphs, charts, statistics, and narrative for numerous aspects of the American and foreign markets. Everything from a listing of America's most-admired corporations to consumer price indexes can be found here.

*Finance and Investment Handbook. 3d ed. By John Downes and Jordan E. Goodman. Barron's, 1990. 1,152p. $29.95 (0-8120-6188-8).

This handbook defines 3,000 investment terms, explains in great detail how to read annual reports and financial pages, describes 30 major personal investment vehicles (e.g., annuities, option contracts), and provides information on various market indexes. Since it provides details not in the *Business One Almanac*, it is recommended as an additional reference purchase.

*Security Analysis. 5th ed. By Sidney J. Cottle and others. McGraw-Hill, 1988. $59.95 (0-07-013235-6).

The choices that people make regarding investments are often based upon analysis of a company's current and future financial strength. This excellent resource explains the ways in which companies' securities are analyzed. People who are having trouble understanding the value of various pieces of information provided in investment advisory services will find the explanations here of great help.

Thorndike Encyclopedia of Banking & Financial Tables. Warren, Gorham and Lamont. annual. $125 for base volume and annual supplement; supplement $86/yr.

Businesspeople require detailed information about interest rates and future and present values of money. This annual publication provides this type of information in tables that include 20- and 30-year computations of loans and amortization, interest and annuity, income interest rates, mortgage rates and yields, savings-withdrawal interest rates, and equity growth rates. Also provided are historical performance comparisons between various equity instruments (e.g., money markets versus certificates of deposit) and state-by-state analyses of interest-rate ceilings, bad-check laws, and taxation rates. A lengthy glossary of banking and financial terminology concludes the volume. Although some of these tables can be obtained inexpensively from many trade publishers, the versatility of this resource makes it a good one-volume choice.

*Almanac of Business & Industrial Financial Ratios. 20th ed. By Leo Troy. Prentice-Hall, 1991. paper $49.95 (0-13-026451-2).
*RMA Annual Statement Studies, 1992. Robert Morris Associates, 1650 Market St., Ste. 2300, Philadelphia, PA 19107, 1992. annual. 900p. $99.50 (0-936742-56-9; ISSN 0080-3340).

Both titles are summaries of financial ratios within selected SIC categories. Financial ratios are numbers that are calculated from a company's balance sheets and income statements in order to allow comparisons to other companies and to an industry. For example, these allow comparisons in terms of net worth, percentage of sales that goes to employee fringe benefits, or percentage of net income that is held as retained earnings. These comparisons are used to determine if a business is performing as well as it should, to evaluate areas within a business that need attention, and to gauge the creditworthiness of a company applying for a loan. The almanac describes the significance of various ratios; it is easy to read and is probably a first choice for small libraries. The RMA *Annual Statement Studies* is more detailed in certain areas and presents the calculations used to compute each financial ratio.

*Business Rankings Annual, 1993. By Brooklyn Business Library Staff. Gale, 1993. annual. $155 (0-8103-5347-4).
Market Share Reporter, 1993. 3d ed. Ed. by Arsen J. Darnay and Marlita A. Reddy. Gale, 1993. annual. $170 (0-8103-8184-2; ISSN 1052-9578). [RBB Ja 1 91]

These are good sources for patrons who are interested in business rankings. *Business Rankings Annual* is a compilation of answers to frequently asked questions at the Brooklyn Public Library Business Library. It includes international lists of the 10 largest, biggest, best performing, and other superlatives. These range from A (the 10 largest accounting firms in the U.S.) to Z (the most actively traded shares on the Zurich exchange). For 449 SIC categories, *Market Share Reporter* provides lists of companies, geographic regions, and commodities that have captured the largest share of their market. Coverage exceeds 5,600 companies, 1,500 brands, and 2,900 facilities. One can learn from this source that lawn-and-garden retail sales are highest for flower gardening, followed by vegetable gardening, herb gardening, and berry growing; or that portable phones have captured 50 percent of all cellular phone sales, followed by transportable phones and mobile phones, respectively.

DIRECTORIES

In addition to the directories listed here, titles providing information about companies are discussed in the following section of this article, "Investment Resources." But directories produced for investors emphasize publicly held corporations. Some of the titles discussed here should be considered for purchase—even if the investment sources are owned—because they cover both public and privately held corporations. Also, directories are listed here that focus on the products or services of various companies, making them indispensable for ready-reference questions.

Ward's Business Directory of U.S. Private and Public Companies, 1993. 4v. Gale, 1993. annual. $1,150 (0-8103-7566-4; ISSN 1048-0707). [RBB Ag 91]

Provides alphabetic (by company name), geographic, and ranked access to more than 135,000 U.S. companies. Information includes telephone numbers and addresses; total sales, gross billings, operating revenues, or assets; number of employees; founding date; type of company (i.e., subsidiary, private, public); ticker symbol; import/export designation; immediate parent; primary SIC code; description of the business or products manufactured; and up to five executive officers. Also provided are rankings by sales, number of employees, and revenue per employee. This directory is available on CD-ROM along with the *World Business Directory* for $1,995.

Million Dollar Directory Series, 1993: America's Leading Public & Private Companies. 5v. Dun & Bradstreet, 1993. annual. $1,225 (0-56203-125-2; ISSN 0734-2861).

This series provides alphabetic (by company name), geographic, and primary and secondary SIC code access to approximately 160,000 public and privately held companies. For each listed company, D&B provides the same information as Ward's, with the addition of more executive officers, principal bank, accounting firm, and state of incorporation. Compared with Ward's, D&B includes more companies but does not have ranking information. Also, the *Million Dollar Directory* must be leased via an agreement that stipulates that the previous year's volumes be returned when the current year is received. The lack of historical information resulting from the lease agreement is a drawback.

*Hoover's Handbook of American Business, 1993. Reference Press; dist. by Publishers Group West, 1992. 640p. annual. $34.95 (1-878753-05-3; ISSN 1055-7202). [RBB Mr 1 91]

This title is especially helpful for libraries with severely limited budgets. It provides readable profiles of approximately 500 private and public corporations. The information for each company includes history, officers, address and telephone number, 10-year financial data, and brand names. A unique feature not available in other directories is the list of key competitors for each company. It is also available as an electronic book for the Sony Discman at $39.95. It will be appreciated by business novices, people who just like to read about business, students, and librarians doing general business ready reference.

Standard & Poor's Register of Corporations, Directors, and Executives. annual with quarterly supplements. $575/yr.

Standard & Poor's is one of the companies discussed in "Investment Resources" (below), since its products provide coverage of publicly traded corporations. However, this standard directory is not included in any of the library packages available from the company. The *Register* provides brief biographical data on the officers and directors of more than 55,000 corporations and also includes a "who owns whom" directory that identifies subsidiaries, divisions, and affiliates. This source is also available on CD-ROM and online.

International Directory of Company Histories. 2d ed. 7v. St. James; dist. by Gale, 1992–93. $135/v. (0-8103-9870-2). [RBB S 1 90]

Provided here are detailed histories (3–4 pages in length) of more than 1,000 large companies in 36 industries. Especially helpful features are lists of subsidiaries and recommendations for further reading about the companies. This directory uses a less-popularized approach than Hoover's but is, nonetheless, a general-interest resource for businesspeople and laypersons.

*****Everybody's Business:** A Field Guide to Four Hundred Leading Companies in America. By Milton Moskowitz and others. Doubleday, 1990. $49.95 (0-385-26547-6); paper $22.50 (0-385-41629-6).

This almanac of curious facts is a popular and often irreverent look at 400 U.S. companies. The facts presented here range from market rankings, sales/profits, and address information to reviews of a company's ethics and the inclusion of interesting pictures from various pivotal events in a company's history.

*****Thomas' Register of American Manufacturers, 1993**. 83d ed. 26v. Thomas Publishing, 1993. annual. $240/yr.
Brands and Their Companies. 10th ed. 2v. Gale, 1992. $355. (0-8103-7542-7).
Companies and Their Brands. 10th ed. 2v. Gale, 1992. $355. (0-8103-7541-9).
Sweet's Catalog File: General Building and Renovation. McGraw-Hill/Sweet's Group. annual. $329/yr. (ISSN 0743-4049).
MacRae's Blue Book, 1993. 100th ed. 2v. Business Research Publications; dist. by Manufacturers' News, 1633 Central St., Evanston IL 60201. annual. $145 (0-8991-0215-8).

These are directories to the products of companies. The most well known is *Thomas' Register*, whose familiar oversize multivolume format provides alphabetic (by company name), geographic, product/service, and brand-name access to the addresses and telephone numbers of more than 145,000 public and privately held manufacturing companies in the U.S. It is also available online through Dialog and on CD-ROM. Gale's *Brands and Their Companies* and *Companies and Their Brands* provide information on more than 255,000 consumer brands from approximately 47,000 U.S. manufacturers and importers. For libraries serving the building and construction industries, *Sweet's Catalog File* provides indispensable detailed alphabetic (by company name), product/service, and brand-name access to more than 2,000 manufacturers in the construction industry. Other sets of *Sweet's*, which can be ordered separately, cover products for homebuilding and remodeling and industrial construction. Finally, *MacRae's Blue Book* provides alphabetic (by company name), product, and brand-name access to more than 50,000 original-equipment manufacturers.

INVESTMENT RESOURCES

In the field of investment advisory services, four names stand out: Moody's, Morningstar, Standard & Poor's, and Value Line. Each provides competing services whose purpose is to help individuals and institutions make investment decisions. An array of reference materials is available from these companies; only a small number are mentioned here. The formats of these services range from sophisticated statistical electronic databases to printed loose-leaf newsletters. The content ranges from ratings of an individual company's stocks and bonds to profiles of industries; the prices range from reasonably priced library packages to very expensive services. Librarians should remember that many of the resources from these publishers are available in online files from various vendors, as well as on CD-ROM. Increasingly, accessing these sources in electronic formats is becoming the preferred method because it is more efficient, online files are more up-to-date (many of the print services are quarterly), and, in many cases, more cost effective than the expensive print products.

Value Line Investment Survey. Value Line Publishing, 711 Third Ave., New York, NY 10017. weekly. $525/yr. (ISSN 0042-2401).

This loose-leaf service provides investment advice on 1,700 commonly traded stocks. It ranks stocks on two different measures: probable price performance in the future and a stock's risk in terms of its price stability and the company's financial strength. Three sections are included in each weekly issue. "Ratings and Reports" provides industry analyses and one-page company reports that include stock ratings, historical information about performance, and estimates of a company's future performance. "Summary and Index" provides an index to the weekly issues, as well as summary and comparison charts (e.g., the highest-yielding stocks). "Selection and Opinion" includes newsletter-type articles. Although it is difficult to decipher (the user's guide is a necessity), *Value Line* is considered by many to be the Cadillac of investment advisory services. It is a first choice for libraries that need the detailed information that this source provides on a limited number of companies.

Morningstar Mutual Funds. Morningstar, 53 W. Jackson Blvd., Ste. 460, Chicago, IL 60604. biweekly. $395/yr.

This relative newcomer has become an indispensable rating service for mutual funds. Similar in format to *Value Line*, it rates approximately 1,500 funds on the basis of their performance, risk, and return to investors and provides detailed historical and forecasting information. Since many small investors use mutual funds as a preferred investment vehicle, this source is a first choice for libraries.

Standard & Poor's Bond Guide. monthly. $185/yr. (ISSN 0277-3988).
Standard & Poor's Stock Guide. weekly. $124/yr. (ISSN 0737-4135).
Standard & Poor's Outlook. weekly. $280/yr. (ISSN 0030-7246).

Among the wide variety of products available from Standard & Poor's (25 Broadway, New York, NY 10004), these three titles might be the first choices of a library. The *Bond Guide* provides ratings and historical and current price information for more than 6,000 debt instruments. The *Stock Guide* provides similar information covering 5,300 stocks. The *Outlook* is an investment newsletter that discusses developments affecting stock performance and makes recommendations on when to buy, hold, and sell. These three titles are included in most of the bundles of services offered by Standard & Poor's for libraries. One of the least-expensive bundles, available for libraries with materials budgets less than $25,000, is the Investor's Package for Libraries. For $615 per year, a library receives the above titles plus three additional sources: *Current Market Perspectives* provides four-year historical stock information for approximately 1,500 companies, the *Stock Market Encyclopedia* includes balance-sheet information for approximately 750 companies, and *Trends and Projections* offers statistical data on the state of the economy. More expensive packages are available, ranging in price to $2,180 per year for the Complete Library Reference Shelf #2. This includes all the above plus three different publications covering business statistics, dividends, and mutual funds; a current-awareness periodical; and *Standard & Poor's Corporation Records*, the daily loose-leaf service providing detailed financial information covering 12,000 companies, which is priced separately at $2,785 per year. *Corporation Records* is also available online and in CD-ROM format.

Moody's Bank and Finance Manual. annual. $1,395/yr.; $765/yr. with library package (ISSN 0545-0152).
Moody's Industrial Manual. annual. $1,395/yr.; $765/yr. with library package (ISSN 0545-0217).
Moody's Public Utility Manual. annual. $1,250/yr.; $730/yr. with library package (ISSN 0545-0241).
Moody's Transportation Manual. annual. $1,150/yr.; $655 with library package (ISSN 0545-025X).

Moody's Investor's Service (99 Church St., New York, NY 10007) produces resources that can be compared with Standard & Poor's products. These include such titles as *Moody's Handbook of Common Stocks* (quarterly, $225/yr., ISSN 0027-0830) and *Moody's Bond Record* (monthly, $280/yr., ISSN 0148-1878). However, Moody's is best known for its excellent manuals, which provide detailed descriptive and financial data on corporations and units of government. Each subcription includes the annual volume as well as weekly or semi-weekly News Reports. The manuals listed above are generally the most commonly used, but four additional titles are also available: *Moody's Municipal and Government Manual*, *Moody's International Manual*, *Moody's Over the Counter Industrial Manual*, and *Moody's Over the Counter Unlisted Manual*. Libraries that need and can afford comprehensive information on more than 10,000 public companies should consider *Moody's Company Data* on CD-ROM. Prices range from $2,500 to $5000, depending upon the frequency of updates and other services owned by the library.

Moody's also packages some of its services in bundles, and libraries that purchase any of them are eligible to acquire additional titles at substantial discounts. Moody's Reference Library Package is the least expensive, at $475 per year, and is available for libraries with annual book budgets of less than $15,000. This package includes *Moody's Industry Review*, two handbooks covering stocks, and an annual publication on dividends. The four manuals listed above are included in Moody's Special Library Service for $1,895 per year. This package includes, in addition, the titles from the Reference Library Package, several sources covering bonds, and some of the Moody's manuals.

Hulbert Guide to Financial Newsletters. 5th ed. By Mark Hulbert. Dearborn, 1993. paper $27.95 (0-7931-0619-2).

Investment advisory newsletters come in a variety of formats ranging from one-page mimeographed sheets to slick loose-leaf services; all try to predict the markets. Since these newsletters are numerous and generally expensive, libraries typically do not subscribe. Evaluative information about various newsletters is provided by the *Hulbert Guide*, which tracks the performance, over a series of years, of approximately 100 well-known investment newsletters.

SMALL BUSINESS

People who operate small businesses, as well as those who wish to do so, are frequently major patrons for library reference services. Several types of tools are especially helpful for them, ranging from references that list opportunities to those with do-it-yourself information. This section describes a few key titles.

*****How to Set Up Your Own Small Business.** 2v. By Max Fallek. American Institute of Small Business, 7515 Wayzata Blvd., Ste. 201, Minneapolis, MN 55426, 1993. $149.95 (0-939069-43-1).

A readable introduction to the basics of all aspects of setting up a new business. Included are chapters on market research, sales forecasting, site selection, financing, advertising, purchasing, bookkeeping, accounting, selling, insurance, use of computers, writing the business plan, and franchising. This is a good general resource for people just getting started.

How to Write a Business Plan. 4th ed. By Mike McKeever. Nolo Press, 1992. paper $19.95 (0-87337-184-4).
Legal Guide for Starting & Running a Small Business. By Fred S. Steingold. Nolo Press, 1992. paper $19.95 (0-87337-174-7).
Trademark: How to Name Your Business and Product. By Stephen Elias and Kate McGrath. Nolo Press, 1992. paper $29.95 (0-87337-157-7).

Many of the publishers represented in this article publish resources designed to guide businesspeople through business law. Resources from Nolo Press are particularly noteworthy, since Nolo publishes exclusively in the area of self-help; the above titles are representative. All of Nolo's excellent books are written by practicing attorneys or other legal professionals and oriented toward nonlawyers.

*****Franchise Opportunities Handbook.** 22d ed. Comp. by U.S. Department of Commerce, Minority Business Development Agency. Sterling, 1992. 320p. paper $12.95 (0-8069-8619-0). [RBB D 15 83]
*****Franchise Annual, 1993.** Info Press, P.O. Box 550, Lewistown, NY 14092, 1992. annual. 250p. $45 (0-685-56480-0). [RBB Ag 87]
*****Source Book of Franchise Opportunities, 1993.** By Robert E. Bond. Business One Irwin, 1992. annual. $34.95 (1-55623-899-1). [RBB D 15 85]

Many small business people are franchise owners, and the purchase of a franchise is often a first option for entering business. The above titles provide information about franchises, how much money is required for an initial investment, and address and telephone-number information. Although they overlap, a great deal of unique information can be found in each one. The *Franchise Opportunities Handbook* provides lists of U.S. franchises, information about government help that might be available for small-business owners, the types of assistance that the franchisor offers for franchisees, and recommended readings. *Franchise Annual* includes U.S., Canadian, and overseas franchises. It provides less descriptive information than the other two titles but includes royalty fees that must be paid to the franchisor, and so presents a more realistic estimate of initial investment dollars. The *Source Book* covers U.S. and Canadian opportunities and indicates whether prior industry experience is helpful for specific franchises. Also, it provides the most detailed descriptive information; for example, whether passive ownership is allowed and the average number of employees per franchise.

MAJOR PUBLISHERS OF HOW-TO BUSINESS MATERIALS

AMACOM, American Management Association, 135 W. 50th St. New York, NY 10020. Publishes everything from books for novices to how-to resources for established business owners.
Barron's Educational Services, P.O. Box 8040, 250 Wireless Blvd., Hauppauge, NY 11788. Its publishing focus is on "quick mastery" of business concepts in various areas, as well as on reference titles.
Dearborn Trade, 520 N. Dearborn St., Chicago, IL 60610-4354. Publishes trade reference and how-to resources in the areas of manufacturing, administration, entrepreneurship, personal finance, and investment.
NTC Business Books, 4255 W. Touhy Ave., Lincolnwood, IL 60646-1975. Focuses on advertising, marketing, and advertising media.
Probus Publishing, 1925 N. Clybourn Ave., Ste. 401, Chicago, IL 60614. Publishes books on financial markets, such as options, stocks, banking, and health care.
Self Counsel Press Inc., 1704 State St., Bellingham, Washington 98225. Publishes practical, step-by-step guides to all aspects of business planning, operations, and management.
Upstart Publishing Company, 12 Portland St., Dover, NH 03820. Publishes start-up guides for specific types of businesses.
Wiley, 605 Third Ave., New York, NY 10158-0012. Publications include professional resources (e.g., for practicing accountants), resources for novices, reference titles, and educational materials and textbooks.

Rashelle S. Karp is associate professor in the College of Communication, Computer/Information Science, and Library Science at Clarion University of Pennsylvania.

Featured Reviews & Reviews

GENERALITIES

Computer Dictionary. 4th ed. By Donald D. Spencer. Camelot Publishing, P.O. Box 1357, Ormond Beach, FL 32175, 1993. 459p. paper $24.95 (0-89218-239-3).
004'.03 Computers—Dictionaries || Electronic data processing—Dictionaries [CIP] 92-34432

Illustrated Computer Graphics Dictionary. By Donald D. Spencer. Camelot Publishing, 1993. 305p. illus. paper $24.95 (0-89218-117-6).
006.6'03 Computer graphics—Dictionaries [CIP] 91-9433

Because computer technology and its associated jargon change so quickly, the new edition of Spencer's classic *Computer Dictionary* is welcome news. With more than 5,800 short entries, the coverage is almost doubled compared with that of the 1987 version. Entries range from *Hollerith tabulating machine* and *geek* to *data* and *IEEE 696/S-100*. Defined are terms from allied fields, including brand names, as well as those from electronic research. Most entries are a couple of lines in length, which lead to cursory, dense definitions. A few cross-references aid the reader. A positive new feature is an appendix with 74 line drawings of computer pioneers.

Spencer has now issued the timely *Illustrated Computer Graphics Dictionary*. He includes more than 2,100 entries and almost 500 illustrations for terms that range from neophyte usage to expert levels. Entries range from one line to one-third page; most are brief. Some definitions are for general computer terms, such as *monitor* and *save*. Some standard words associated with graphics, such as *scripting* and *extension*, are omitted. While most entries are accurate, some are misleading, especially for terminology from other disciplines. For example, the definition for *genre art* is "the casual representation of everyday life and surroundings," rather than stylized artwork of standard subjects such as sports or mysteries. Also, the long explanation of *fractals* is confusing. Illustrations are usually clear and well done; they certainly enhance the readability of the text.

Both titles are apparently available only in paperback, which will limit their durability. However, terms change quickly enough so that binding is not much of an issue. The *Illustrated Computer Graphics Dictionary* will join Spencer's *Computer Dictionary* as a standard quick-reference tool in public libraries and other collections used by nonspecialists.

Macmillan Encyclopedia of Computers. 2v. Ed. by Gary G. Bitter. Macmillan, 1992. 1,080p. bibliog. illus. index. hardcover $150 (0-02-897045-4).
004'.03 Computers—Encyclopedias [CIP] 91-45339

The purpose of this well-written and interesting encyclopedia is to "provide an authoritative comprehensive work on all aspects of computers." The more than 200 articles range in length from biographies of 500 words to broad topics like *Ethics and Computers* and *Education, Computers in* with over 5,000 words. Volume 1 opens with an alphabetical list of the articles; a detailed index concludes volume 2. Adequate *see* and *see also* references aid access.

The topics covered can be classified as biographical, technical, historical, or pertaining to applications of computers in various areas. Biographical entries include current people such as Dan Bricklin, Bill Gates, and Steven Jobs as well as historical figures like George Boole and Herman Hollerith. Examples of technical topics covered include *Binary Numbers*, *Data Compression and Fractuals*, *Hypertext*, *Robotics*, and *Supercomputers*. Important programming languages are covered in entries like COBOL and *Pascal*. There are no entries for specific software packages, but they are discussed in general articles like *Spreadsheets*, *Word Processing*, and *Games, Computer*. Among the historical topics are *Cards*, *Jacquard and Hollerith*, and *History of Computing*. Articles can be found on the use of computers in such fields as banking, insurance, politics, religion, retailing, the arts, and sports. Entries are provided on applications of current interest, such as *Desktop Publishing*, *Multimedia*, and *Voice Mail*. There is even the entry *Careers in Computing*. Liberal use is made of charts, graphs, photographs, and diagrams to assist in understanding entries. All of the articles are signed by the academicians or professionals in the computer field who wrote them; their credentials are listed in volume 1. Entries are written in nontechnical language that most laypeople will be able to comprehend with a little effort.

The entry *Decision Making* is a good example of the coverage of this encyclopedia. It begins with a general introductory section that gives a conceptual framework for the topic. Four categories of decision making—rule based, model based, classical, and decision processes—are then described in several paragraphs each. Drawings of a decision table and decision tree illustrate the concepts. The article concludes with a discussion of the importance of decision making and the place of computing and artificial intelligence in this process. A list of nine references is provided for additional information. Every article concludes with a list of references or a list for further reading, and some contain both.

Volume 2 concludes with 32 pages of appendixes listing computing associations and manufacturers of peripherals, mainframes, computer components, personal computers, and supercomputers. Short company descriptions and addresses are given for most of the manufacturers.

This encyclopedia offers the reader an excellent introduction to the world of computers, and the brief bibliographies at the ends of entries will lead to more detailed information. Good current dictionaries briefly define computer terms (Spencer's *Computer Dictionary* and *Microsoft Press Computer Dictionary* are two examples). The *McGraw-Hill Encyclopedia of Electronics and Computers* [RBB O 1 88] is a spin-off of the previous edition of the *McGraw-Hill Encyclopedia of Science and Technology* and is written at a more technical level than the set under review. Even in a rapidly changing field like computing, the *Macmillan Encyclopedia of Computers* will be a standard work for some time to come. Academic and large public libraries should consider purchase; high schools will find it useful too.

Reference Sources for Small and Medium-sized Libraries. 5th ed. Ed. by Jovian P. Lang. ALA, 1992. 317p. index. paper $35 (0-8389-3406-4).
011'.02 Reference books—Bibliography || Small libraries—Book lists [CIP] 92-10007

This new edition of a well-established work continues its tradition of providing descriptions of reference materials appropriate for public libraries as well as for college and large secondary school libraries. It contains a total of 1,974 entries, 186 more than the fourth edition [RBB F 1 85]. The scope, similar to the fourth edition's, includes "reference materials for children and young adults as well as adults; sources in other formats, such as microforms and databases, online, and CD-ROM, are added; and out-of-print sources considered to be basic reference sources are listed." The cutoff date is 1990, with new editions bearing a 1991 date "included in some cases." The work is compiled by an ad hoc subcommittee of the Reference Sources Committee of ALA's Reference and Adult Services Division.

Divided into chapters by discipline and subdivided by form or more specific subject, the work is generally arranged by major divisions of the Dewey Decimal Classification. Each chapter lists the committee member(s) responsible for its compilation, along with a brief introduction discussing reference works in that discipline. Many of the subdivisions carry useful introductions, too, such as the "Energy and Environment" subdivision of "Science and Technology," which states that such material "virtually died off during the early to mid-eighties, when federal funding was scarce." Each entry lists author, title, publisher, date of publication, pagination, and price (or out-of-print designation). ISBN or ISSN is also supplied when available for books and serials; SuDoc numbers and stock numbers are included for government publications. A notation is made if the work is available online, on CD-ROM, or on tape, although connect time and/or subscription prices are not given.

The annotations accompanying each entry are mainly descriptive, but often include some critical commentary when appropriate. Phrases like "beautifully executed," "very attractive," or "must acquisition" are sprinkled throughout this work, making it a somewhat more opinionated acquisitions tool than, for example, *Guide to Reference Books*, though this work does not have the latter's extraordinary breadth of subject matter. The annotations are typically anywhere from 20 to 100 words in length. A J or a Y ends entries that are useful for children or young adults, respectively. The volume concludes with an author-title index. The arrangement of the book combined with a good number of cross-references make it relatively easy to find appropriate subject areas. Many chapters have greater specificity than in previous editions. "Literature," for example, now has a section on specific genres. The "Computer Science" subdivision of the "Science and Technology" chapter has grown from 12 entries with no subdivisions to 24 entries with 5 subdivisions.

Virtually all libraries, regardless of size, will find the annotations in this work quite helpful; for public libraries this title remains a virtual requirement.

Newbery and Caldecott Medalists and Honor Book Winners: Bibliographies and Resource Material through 1991. 2d ed. By Muriel W. Brown and Rita Schoch Foudray. Neal-Schuman, 1992. 511p. bibliog. index. hardcover $59.95 (1-55570-118-3).

011'.62 Children's literature, American—Awards ∥ Children's literature, American—Illustrations—Awards ∥ Illustrated books, Children's—U.S.—Bibliography ∥ Bibliography—Best books—Children's literature ∥ Caldecott medal books—Bibliography [CIP] 92-14324

Newbery and Caldecott Medal and Honor Books in Other Media. By Paulette Bochnig Sharkey. Neal-Schuman, 1992. 142p. bibliog. index. hardcover $29.95 (1-55570-119-1).

028.1'62 Newbery medal books—Study and teaching—Audio-visual aids—Catalogs ∥ Caldecott medal books—Study and teaching—Audio-visual aids—Catalogs ∥ Children's books, Illustrated—Study and teaching—Audio-visual aids—Catalogs ∥ Children's literature—Study and teaching—Audio-visual aids—Catalogs ∥ Nonbook materials—Catalogs [CIP] 92-15391

These two volumes update a 1982 directory of Caldecott and Newbery Award winners.

In the first volume, coverage has been expanded to include 327 individual authors and illustrators. The medalists and honorees are arranged in alphabetical order. Each entry includes the recipient's name and dates, award(s), a bibliography of his or her published works, a listing of pertinent library collections, and a bibliography of background readings. Other features include separate chronological lists of award-winning books through 1992 and updated bibliographies of collections and background readings. A combined author-illustrator-title index is also provided.

Two features included in the first edition have been discontinued: exhibitions are no longer listed, nor are media versions of award-winning books. This latter information is now available in *Newbery and Caldecott Medal and Honor Books in Other Media*, edited by librarian and author Sharkey. The increase in licensing of media rights for award-winning books over the last decade prompted the publication of a separate directory with a comprehensive listing of nonprint versions. The selections are arranged in reverse chronological order and include Newbery books from 1992 through 1922 and Caldecott selections from 1992 through 1938. Entries provide a bibliographic reference to the first edition of each book and then list subsequent media interpretations in formats such as audio- and videotapes, bookmarks, calendars, dolls, recordings, software, etc. Brief product descriptions, information on reviews, major awards, and producers or distributors are also provided.

Additional features include a bibliography of media related to Newbery and Caldecott books in general, media selections about Newbery and Caldecott authors and illustrators, a bibliography of resources (including reference books, databases, journals, and review services), a directory of producers and distributors, and a list of selections by media format. There is also a complete index.

Both of these books will be helpful for researchers and librarians in public and school libraries and in academic libraries where children's literature is studied.

Children's Reference Plus: Complete Bibliographic, Review, and Qualitative Information on Books, Reference Books, Serials, Cassettes, Software, and Videos for Children and Young Adults. Bowker, 1992. CD-ROM. annual. $595

011.62 Children's literature—Indexes—Software ∥ Children's literature—Book reviews—Indexes—Software ∥ Children's mass media—Indexes—Software [BKL]

Using *Children's Reference Plus* is like sitting down with a stack of reference books and magazines to check prices, publishers, and reviews or to compile a bibliography on a topic. Included are all the children's titles listed in *Books in Print*; *Books Out-of-Print*; *El-Hi Textbooks*; *Fiction, Folklore, Fantasy & Poetry for Children, 1876–1985*; *Ulrich's International Periodicals Directory*; *Bowker's Complete Video Directory*; and *Words on Cassette*. Reviews of children's books from *Booklist*, *Publishers Weekly*, *Library Journal*, *School Library Journal*, and *Kirkus* appear in full. While this selection of reviews is essentially a subset of Bowker's *Books in Print with Book Reviews Plus* (another CD-ROM title), *Children's Reference Plus* provides access to many additional evaluative sources. One of the best features of the product is the inclusion of the text of reviews, annotations, and plot summaries from 24 well-known Bowker publications such as *Best Books for Children*, *Books for the Gifted Child*, *Primaryplots*, *More Notes from a Different Drummer*, *School Librarian's Sourcebook*, and *High/Low Handbook*. Even assuming that a library can afford to keep all of these titles current, having them in one database is a tremendous convenience.

HARDWARE, SOFTWARE, AND INSTALLATION. *Children's Reference Plus* runs on IBM PCs and compatible computers with 640K RAM, a hard disk with 4MB of free space, a monochrome or color monitor, and a CD-ROM drive running under Microsoft extensions. The data on the disc is accessed using Bowker's Plus software, which is also used in *Books in Print Plus* [RBB Je 15 87] and *Library Reference Plus* [RBB Ag 92]. Libraries operating another *Plus* product on their computers will still need to load the software for *Children's Reference Plus*, which comes on two 5¼- or one 3-inch floppy disk.

SEARCHING AND DISPLAYING. This CD-ROM product provides a variety of options for accessing the information. Users can apply up to 18 fielded search criteria and can use free-text terms to search the critical review material. The information from the source directories can be searched by title, name (author or contributor), subject, keyword, publisher, price, grade level, audience, status code (active, out-of-print, etc.), LC number, special index (presence of illustrations, annotations, or reviews), series title, language, year published, and ISBN. Videos can also be searched by color, awards received, UPC number, and rating; and serials can be searched by country, Dewey number, ISSN, and CD-ROM or online availability. Not all searches can be done in all databases. For instance, awards information is not available for the records taken from *Ulrich's International Periodicals Directory*.

Two basic means of retrieving the information are provided: browse and search. In the former mode, the user selects one of 20 indexes and then scrolls through the alphabetic list. A "jump" feature allows the user to move through this information quickly. Users can view citations attached to a heading and also can save terms for later use as a search statement. In the search mode, a workspace opens where the user enters a two-character abbreviation for the search category (e.g., *ti* for title, *su* for subject), an operator (e.g., = or), and the word or phrase to be searched. If a two-character abbreviation is not entered, the program automatically defaults to the keyword index. Truncation of the end of search terms is possible, and the

Boolean operators AND, OR, and ANDNOT can be used for all searches. Also, the adjacency operators, NEAR and WITH, can be used to search full-text reviews. The number of citations retrieved is posted in the workspace, and then additional windows can be opened to display increasing amounts of information about selected citations. Users highlight items of interest with the ENTER key, and function keys are pressed to display brief citations, full bibliographic records, critical material when available, and information about the publisher or producer. Pressing ESCAPE moves the user back to the previous stage of the search, and the screen display includes prompts to retrieve help when needed.

The product can be used for a variety of types of searches. For instance, if a user remembers only partial information about a work, it is possible to locate the full record in a matter of seconds. A search for the keyword *ozone* and the publisher *Watts* produced citations to four different books. Using the keyword *witch* and the name *Jones* produced three records, all with reviews, for *Witch Week* by Diana Jones. This product can readily be used to compile special lists or bibliographies for various educational purposes. A search for Spanish-language videos for a juvenile audience yielded 47 records. Seventy items—including books, videos, and audiotapes—about Martin Luther King, Jr. were quickly identified. Users can move from the bibliographic records to the text of reviews, and items can be saved, deleted, annotated, and edited to meet the user's purposes.

OTHER FEATURES. Within the program are several helpful options. Orders may be printed, sent electronically to a chosen vendor, or saved to a disk for future consideration. The colorful screens are attractive, and users can define specialized formats for display or printing. Passwords can be established to restrict access to the features of the programs. A loose-leaf user's guide gives complete instructions for installation and use. Technical support is offered through a toll-free number that is staffed during business hours.

EVALUATION. This unique product increases access to the information found in standard works that are heavily used by children's librarians and educators. A novice can quickly learn to search this product through the help provided within the program. However, expertise requires complete familiarity with the information in the user's guide in order to know such specifics as which fields are available in which databases, dates when different language codes were used, or which abbreviation is used by which source to indicate juvenile material. In the printed guide, Bowker recommends browsing the indexes to locate the appropriate headings, and this was found be essential for many types of searches. For instance, pseudonyms do not cross-reference to the author's name, and subjects must be entered exactly in the approved form of heading. Nevertheless, the Board found *Children's Reference Plus* easy to use and capable of retrieving records in a variety of ways not possible in print sources. Hopefully, Bowker will adopt standard data elements and terminology in its printed directories, as this will make an even better CD-ROM product in the future. This is the kind of one-stop program that every library serving young people would like to have.

Recommended Reference Books in Paperback. 2d ed. Ed. by Andrew L. March. Libraries Unlimited, 1992. 263p. indexes. hardcover $37.50 (1-56308-067-2).

011'.73 Bibliography—Best books—Reference books ‖ Bibliography—Best books—Paperbacks ‖ Reference books—Bibliography ‖ Paperbacks—Bibliography [CIP] 92-15875

Librarians seeking sources of inexpensive reference tools, either for their own collections or to recommend for home use, will find this second edition of *Recommended Reference Books in Paperback* useful. It is a complete revision and update of the first edition, and more than 75 percent of the entries are for titles published from 1987 to the present. The editor annotates nearly 1,000 works in 37 broad categories from general reference to subjects ranging from agriculture to zoology. Sixty-two percent of the titles cost less than $15, and 98 percent cost less than $40. Some government documents and free publications are also listed.

Each entry includes author, title, imprint, collation, series, price, LC card number, ISBN, and an annotation. If the title was reviewed in *American Reference Books Annual*, that fact is noted with a reference to the review. No other reviews are cited. Annotations are evaluative and especially useful. Frequently a work is compared to similar sources, and the history of the edition is noted. For instance, the entry for the abridged edition of *Bulfinch's Mythology* relates the purpose of the original three volumes, briefly explains what the cited edition includes, and notes that the full text is available in paperback with a different imprint. Separate author-title and suject indexes refer to the numbered entries.

This compilation is not intended to provide a comprehensive listing of paperback reference works. All the entries are for recommended titles, having been "selected for their quality, availability, and economy," and an effort was made to provide a "selection over a broad range of topics." Users will find many topics omitted (e.g., Islam, autograph collecting) without knowing whether the subject was viewed as too specialized or whether the available titles were thought to be substandard; other evaluative methods will need to be used in these instances. *Recommended Reference Books in Paperback* identifies and evaluates both hard-to-find inexpensive tools, as well as paperback editions of standard reference works. It will be valuable in a wide variety of libraries, particularly in these days of tight budgets.

More Exciting, Funny, Scary, Short, Different, and Sad Books Kids Like about Animals, Science, Sports, Families, Songs and Other Things. Ed. by Frances Laverne Carroll and Mary Meacham. ALA, 1992. 192p. indexes. paper $15 (0-8389-0585-4).

011.62 Children's literature—Bibliography ‖ Bibliography—Best books—Children's literature ‖ Children—Books and reading [CIP] 92-11588

More is the key word to this updated version of a bibliography first published in 1983. Not intended as a buying guide, it is a readers' adviser for children in grades 2 through early junior high school and those librarians, teachers, and parents who hear requests, in the words of young readers, for an "exciting," "funny," "scary," or "short" book.

Arranged by category, each section contains an average of 4–12 titles submitted by children's librarians. About 75 percent of them were published since 1983. Categories in the new edition reflect today's requests, and about 75 percent of the headings are new. For example, the first edition had four pages of "I want a short book" titles; the new edition has 11 pages of "I want a skinny book" titles. Libraries owning the earlier edition will still find use for it for access to older works. Titles in this edition include such well-loved stories as *Ben and Me* and *Johnny Tremain* as well as newer titles like *Number the Stars* under the chapter titled "I Want a Story with History in It." Good books and authors are repeated in several categories, when appropriate. For instance, Gary Paulsen's *Hatchet* is listed in three chapters: "I Don't Like to Read, But I Have to Do a Book Report," "I Want a Book about Kids," and "I Want an Adventure Story."

Books in each category are arranged alphabetically by title with brief annotations written for the young reader that are also useful for booktalks. Some chapters like "Do You Have Any Scary Books?" are subdivided into "Funny and a Little Scary" and "Scary" lists to encompass narrower aspects of specific requests. An author-title and a subject index offer additional access.

Recommended for children's libraries, whether they be public or school, this paperback is affordable and will meet many requests with a diversity of reading resources.

Sensitive Issues: An Annotated Guide to Children's Literature K–6. By Timothy V. Rasinski and Cindy S. Gillespie. Oryx, 1992. 277p. index. paper $29.95 (0-89774-777-1).

011.62 Children's literature—Bibliography ‖ Social problems in literature—Bibliography ‖ Children—Life skills guides—Bibliography ‖ Social problems—Bibliography ‖ Children—Books and reading [CIP] 92-18682

With the continuing interest in the literature-based curriculum in the elementary school, this annotated guide to children's literature for grades K–6 will be welcomed by library media specialists, teachers, and parents. Featuring titles published since 1975, the guide focuses on problems facing children in their everyday lives and how they can be used as a basis for study by student groups.

The first chapter suggests a variety of activities, such as guided listening and art, for using children's literature to deal with issues. The remainder of the book consists of eight chapters, each devoted to a sensitive issue: divorce, substance abuse, death and dying, nontraditional home environments, child abuse, prejudice and cultural differences, moving, and illness and disability. Each chapter includes an alphabetical listing of 25 to 30 titles, with some chapters divided into fiction and nonfiction. Each entry includes grade-level information (suggested levels for independent reading and levels for reading aloud), bibliographic information, a summary of the book, a critique, and activities that can be used to heighten students' understanding and appreciation of the text. Suggested activities include topics for discussion groups, role plays, art projects, writing assignments, and other common classroom techniques. The author has some creative and ingenious suggestions, such as a search of classified advertisements for jobs that a fictional mother would like. A directory of publishers and an index of subjects, authors, and titles complete the book. Most of the books listed were in print at the time of publication.

The Best of Bookfinder [RBB Ag 92] also describes books dealing with problems facing children. However, it does not include suggested activities as does *Sensitive Issues*.

Many professionals will agree with this statement in the preface: "By identifying high-quality literature, sorted by theme or issue, and providing summaries and suggested approaches for teaching, this book goes a long way in helping teachers and librarians choose materials and methods that are meaningful to their students and that will encourage them to become proficient lifelong readers."

Books for You: A Booklist for Senior High Students. 11th ed. Ed. by Shirley Wurth. National Council of Teachers of English, 1992. 259p. indexes. paper $16.95 (0-8141-03650).

011.62'5 Young adult literature—Bibliography || High school students—Books and reading || High school libraries—Book lists || Bibliography—Best books—Young adult literature [CIP] 92-26206

NCTE publishes an ongoing series of book lists, each updated in a four-year rotation, that is compiled by a committee of teachers and librarians. The intent is to include books published in a wide variety of subjects since the last edition that are recommended for teachers and students. This eleventh edition of *Books for You* annotates nearly 800 fiction and nonfiction titles, grouped into 32 sections, that are geared to the interests of senior high school students.

Each section is numbered, with books arranged alphabetically by author within a section, and each title is assigned an accession number. The pages are clearly laid out and easily read. The listed titles cover a wide range of interest and reading levels, although recommended grade levels are not included. Entries provide publication data, with the exception of noting whether an item is a reprint or is in hardcover or paperback. Annotations of 500 to 1,000 words give the flavor of the book's content rather than a summary. Because the annotations are written by several people, they tend to be erratic, some revealing more about the books than others. The volume contains a directory of publishers and indexes by author, title, and subject.

Best Books for Senior High Readers [RBB F 1 92] lists more than 10,000 titles from a wider time span. It has briefer annotations but provides references to reviews of books. *Books for You* provides valuable assistance to teachers, librarians, and students who wish to connect with a good book, especially in those high schools and public libraries that do not own *Best Books for Senior High Readers*.

A Reference Guide to Afro-American Publications and Editors, 1827–1946. By Vilma Raskin Potter. Iowa State Univ., 1993. 104p. bibliog. indexes. hardcover $21.95 (0-8138-0677-1).

015.73034'08996073 Afro-American periodicals—Bibliography || Brown, Warren Henry—Checklist of Negro newspapers in the United States (1827–1946) || Indexes [CIP] 91-17167

This collection of indexes is based on Warren Henry Brown's checklist of nearly 500 African American publications, which the Lincoln University School of Journalism published in 1946 as *Checklist of Negro Newspapers in the United States (1827–1946)*. Compiled by Potter, professor emeritus at California State University at Los Angeles, this guide seeks to build on Brown's pioneering work by providing additional and important information on the role of the black press in American history.

The guide is divided into an introduction and three chapters. The introduction discusses the scope, form, content, and usefulness of Brown's checklist, pointing out that Brown's form is "inconsistent" and his method of identifying editors of African American newspapers is "careless." Potter concludes that Brown's contribution is largely archival. "It is a heroic piece of work; but the alphabetical format limits its usefulness as a research tool," she explains.

Chapter 1, titled "An Enduring Commitment," provides specific direction on how the lists could be used to study various aspects of American culture. The chapter includes information on Brown's life and work as a scholar, black women journalists, early researchers of the African American press, a further discussion of Brown's checklist, information on what the early African American press printed, and one example of a "research model" that discusses Robert Kerlin's study of the responses of the African American press to the events of 1919.

Chapter 2 reprints Brown's checklist. The list includes the name of the newspaper, where copies of the publication are filed, and the location and date of founding. The third chapter, "Additional Compilations," updates Brown's checklist by providing three indexes. The first is arranged alphabetically by state, and then alphabetically by the name of the newspaper. The second provides essentially the same information but is arranged by year of publication. The third is an index of editors of the newspapers. In addition to the name of the newspaper, its location and inclusive dates of operation are provided in these indexes. But unlike Brown's checklist, no effort is made to provide current information on the location of extant copies of the newspapers.

The author also provides three supplementary lists. The first is a list of weekly African American newspapers from Brown's Ph.D. dissertation upon which he built his major checklist. The next two lists—one of editors and one of additional newspaper titles—are derived from a pamphlet by George Gore, *Negro Journalism: An Essay on the History and Present Conditions of the Negro Press*, written in 1922 while Gore was studying journalism at DePauw University. Potter includes no other information about Gore.

The book concludes with a list of references to sources used by the author in compiling the index. There is no general index to the compilation, a feature that could have enhanced its usability. While the author's prose style and the guide's format make this reference work difficult to use, scholars in a wide range of areas, especially journalism, African American studies, women's history, and American studies, will still find it useful.

CD-ROM 1992: An Annotated Bibliography of Resources. By Jennifer Langlois. Meckler, 1992. 298p. index. hardcover $45 (0-88736-861-1).

016.0253'0285 CD-ROM—Bibliography || Libraries—Automation—Bibliography [CIP] 93-30427

CD-ROM has become an established information storage and retrieval technology and has become an integral part of many libraries throughout the world. CD-ROM 1992 is a bibliography of books, articles, and other materials discussing the use of CD-ROM technology in libraries. Entries are divided into 44 categories, covering such topics as acquisitions, document delivery, networks, reference services, and use studies. Most entries are annotated and range in time from the beginning of CD-ROM in the early 1980s through 1991. A subject index and a list of acronyms are also provided.

Several things about this book are misleading. The title, CD-ROM 1992, implies that either all of the materials included were published in 1992 or that this is the first in an annual series of CD-ROM bibliographies. In fact, no entries from 1992 are included, and there is no indication as to future publication plans. Some of the chapter headings may also lead users astray. The chapters "Circulation" and "Interlibrary Loan" are not related to the lending of CD-ROM disks to either patrons or other libraries but discuss using CD-ROM–based circulation and interlibrary loan systems. The chapters "Software," "Theses," and "Video" each contain but a single entry.

The annotations are informative but repetitive, with virtually every entry beginning with the phrase "Article discusses . . ." or "Article describes. . . ." Most of the sources selected for inclusion in this work may also be found by searching Library Literature, ERIC, and/or LISA databases. The databases have the advantage that information retrieved will be more current, and searches may be customized to the users' own interests. This work is not recommended for librarians needing up-to-date information, but it might be useful for library-science students researching the evolution of CD-ROM technologies for library operations.

GENERALITIES

National Trade and Professional Associations of the United States, 1993. 28th ed. Ed. by John J. Russell and others. Columbia Books, 1993. 637p. indexes. paper $65 (1-880873-00-1; ISSN 0734-354X).

060 Trade and professional associations—U.S.—Directories ‖ Trade-unions—U.S.—Directories [BKL]

This annual directory, published since 1966, lists information on 7,300 national membership organizations throughout the U.S. The scope of the work has not changed since we reviewed the fifteenth edition [RSBR Ap 15 81]. Included are trade associations; labor unions; professional, scientific, or technical societies; and "other national organizations composed of groups united for a common purpose." Excluded are organizations that serve only as accreditation bodies. A companion publication, *State and Regional Associations of the United States* [RBB S 1 89] provides directory listings for major groups functioning on a state or regional level.

Arranged alphabetically, the directory lists each organization's address and telephone and fax numbers, identifies the executive officer or contact, and provides information on the organization's origins and aims, budget level, staff and membership size, membership fees or dues, periodic publications, and future meetings and convention schedule, with projected attendance. Cross-references trace associations through name changes, mergers, etc. Five indexes provide access by subject, location, budget level, acronym, and personal name of the association contact. A useful and unique feature added since our last review is a special appendix that lists more than 400 association-management firms. For each company, complete contact information is provided, as well as a roster of client associations.

NTPA is a carefully edited, standard reference used daily by librarians, businesses, and professional organizations. The only similar source is Gale's *Encyclopedia of Associations* (EA). With more than 23,000 listings, that work covers many other types of organizations as well as professional and trade groups. Its descriptions in each entry are lengthier than NTPA's, although the latter is more consistent in the data it provides, such as budget range and size of staff. The Gale title is also a more expensive multivolume set. For libraries that do not need (or cannot afford) the more comprehensive scope of EA, NTPA is clearly an alternative.

If a library subscribes to *Encyclopedia of Associations*, should it also consider purchasing *National Trade and Professional Associations*? In an effort to answer this question, the Board compared a sample of listings between the two sources. Based on the results, more than 95 percent of the 1993 NTPA entries can also be located in the 1993 edition of EA. Groups unique to NTPA included the National Society of Newspaper Columnists (Louisville, Kentucky) and Women Construction Owners and Executives (Beltsville, Maryland). However, in comparing contact information for a sample of 50 entries located in both sources, different addresses or telephone numbers were given for 10 organizations (20 percent). We were able to contact nine of these organizations by telephone, and found that NTPA was accurate for six of these listings, EA had correct information in two cases, and both sources were incorrect in one instance. The EA listings with inaccurate contact information were also checked in the online version, but the addresses and telephone numbers found there were the same as in the print volumes.

NTPA's listings are updated and confirmed every year, and the publisher claims that the directory "contains more complete and up-to-date information than can be secured anywhere." The source is easy to use, and its multiple indexes and appendix facilitate various methods of accessing association information that are not possible in other print sources. NTPA continues to be a reasonably priced, excellent reference source for trade, labor, and professional groups. It is also recommended for any library that needs comprehensive coverage and the most current information about these national organizations.

Gale Directory of Databases. v.1: Online Databases; v.2: CD-ROM, Diskette, Magnetic Tape, Handheld, and Batch Access Database Products. 2v. Ed. by Kathleen Young Marcaccio. Gale, Jan. 1993– . semiannual. 2,300p. indexes. paper. $280/yr. (0-8103-5746-1); v.1 only: $199/yr. (0-8103-8458-2); v.2 only: $119/yr. (0-8103-8439-6) (ISSN 1066-8934).

025 Data bases—Directories ‖ Information storage and retrieval systems—Directories ‖ Information services—Directories ‖ Machine-readable bibliographic data—Directories [OCLC] 92-565

This top-of-the-line directory is well designed and executed. Either volume will be appreciated on its own; together they are a formidable gateway to the electronic information environment. The publisher's press release tells no lie when it boasts that the best features of three former reference sources—*Directory of Online Databases* [RBB S 1 84], *Directory of Portable Databases* [RBB My 1 90], and *Computer-Readable Databases* [RBB My 15 89]—were combined and enhanced to create this new product. All three of *Gale Directory of Databases*' antecedents were well received by the Board when they made their original appearance. It is not surprising that their progeny is top notch.

The first volume, covering online databases, provides information for more than 5,400 databases worldwide, ranging from *A-V Online* (New Mexico) to *ZVEI Electro/Electronics Buyer's Guide* (Germany). Volume 2 profiles more than 3,000 database products offered in portable format (CD-ROM, diskette, magnetic tape, hand-held) and through batch-processing services. Both volumes have three descriptive sections and three indexes. Together, they contain contact and descriptive information on more than 8,000 databases, 3,100 database producers, 800 on-line services, and 760 vendors and distributors of database products.

The entries in volume 1, alphabetically arranged by name of database, are crammed with information including address, telephone and fax numbers, contact person, database type, coverage, language, and alternate formats. In all, each database has 20 different descriptive elements. Database type may be one or more of 12 classifications such as bibliographic, full-text, image, statistical, and bulletin board. A typical entry, *Legal Resource Index*, notes that it "contains more than 512,000 citations, with selected abstracts, to articles published in more than 800 key law journals, bar association publications, and legal newspapers." Per-hour price, price of online and offline prints, time span, updating schedule, and alternate formats are also listed. New entries are indicated by a star symbol, and a triangle indicates substantial revision. Overall layout is very kind to the eyes, with generous use of boldface headings and white space. The prefatory material offers a detailed, user-friendly sample entry.

The remainder of volume 1 consists of two descriptive sections, one on database producers and another for online services. Both sections provide contact information and a list of the names of databases produced by, or available through, the various companies. Three separate indexes—geographic by producer, subject, and master—are keyed to the main body of the work by entry numbers. The subject index is quite detailed. For example, there are more than 10 sections for energy-related databases alone (e.g. solar, wind, thermal, policy, research, resources, industry). The master index, covering all three sections of volume 1, is an alphabetical arrangement of database names, keywords in database names, acronyms, former names, etc.

Volume 2, *CD-ROM, Diskette, Magnetic Tape, Handheld, and Batch Access Database Products*, mirrors the first volume in terms of overall appearance, arrangement, construction of entries, and indexes. Listed are 1,321 CD-ROM products, 676 on diskette, 584 on magnetic tape, 39 hand-held, and 389 available via batch access.

Gale plans to publish replacement issues with new entries and revisions each six months; the annual price of $280 includes both the January and July editions of the two volumes. The directory is available online through Data-Star, ORBIT, and Questel and is planned for Dialog by the end of 1993. A compact disc version is planned for late 1993, which also will contain selected information from two other Gale products, *Information Industry Directory* and *Telecommunications Directory*; the tentative price for a single-user CD-ROM is $800, and a network version will be available for $1,200.

Although expensive, the *Gale Directory of Databases* is a must purchase for any academic library or large public library serious about providing its community with access to electronic information resources. Libraries not extensively engaged in electronic information retrieval will value it as a high-quality encyclopedia of the electronic-information environment.

CD-ROM Periodical Index: A Guide to Abstracted, Indexed, and Fulltext Periodicals on CD-ROM. By Pat Ensor and Steve Hardin. Meckler, 1992. 420p. indexes. hardcover $65 (0-88736-803-4).

025.04 Periodicals—Abstracts—Data bases—Directories || Periodicals—Indexes—Data bases—Directories || Periodicals—Data bases—Directories || CD-ROM industry—Directories [CIP] 92-6948

Described here are 77 CD-ROMs that index, abstract, or contain the full text of serials or books. Each entry notes the publisher, price, years covered, and search software and capabilities (e.g., keyword, Boolean, proximity searching). In the case of a database available from more than one publisher, such as *Medline*, information is given on all versions. This is followed by a list of the serials or books on the disc. Twenty-eight of the CD-ROMs contain full text, usually of a newspaper, a single periodical, or a book. Examples are the *Chicago Tribune*, the *British Medical Journal*, and the *Thomas Register*. The remaining titles index or abstract a large number of periodicals. The list of journals indexed on the MLA *Bibliography* disc, for instance, goes on for 27 pages.

The second half of the book is an index to all the titles listed in the 77 product entries. Here one learns, for instance, that *Harper's Magazine* is available on 13 different CD-ROM indexes and is full text on one of them.

This book covers only a fraction of the CD-ROM products available but does include the popular titles from Wilson, Information Access, EBSCO, DIALOG, UMI, and Silver Platter that overlap in coverage. While *Ulrich's International Periodicals Directory* notes CD-ROM indexing of journals, it doesn't list as many indexes nor does it distinguish print indexes from CD-ROM ones. Libraries owning more than one periodical index on CD-ROM will find CD-ROM *Periodical Index* useful to help the patron who is looking for indexing of a specific magazine. Libraries trying to select an index for purchase will find it provides a useful way to compare coverage. —*Sandy Whiteley*

Tapping the Government Grapevine: The User-Friendly Guide to U.S. Government Information Sources. 2d ed. By Judith Schiek Robinson. Oryx, 1993. 228p. bibliog. illus. index. paper $34.50 (0-89774-712-7).

025.17′34 Government publications—U.S.—Information services [OCLC] 92-40201

This informative guide to accessing government information first appeared in 1988. The new edition incorporates material about recent developments, notably the advent of CD-ROM as a major medium of dissemination. Various types of federal government information searches are discussed, such as legislation and regulations, statistics, patents, scientific reports, Freedom of Information Act requests, and National Archives material.

The text is helpfully illustrated with "search tip" boxes, time-saving finding charts, and reproductions of sample pages and screens. One typical chart lists a number of sources for tracing legislative histories and the status of bills, indicating what access points (subject heading, bill or law number, etc.) apply in each case. The lists of further reading at the end of each chapter have been updated and now include such recent key titles as the 1991 GPO/2001 report. Brief coverage of nonfederal documents is provided in the chapter on reference sources, and the chapter on foreign and international documents by Karen Smith has been updated. Sets of exercise questions have been added at the end of each chapter, with answers in an appendix at the back. The chapter on the administration of government-documents collections has been dropped.

Somewhat confusingly, information about ordering from the National Technical Information Service still appears under the heading "Monthly Catalog" (and now the index does not refer to these pages), and information about the *National Trade Data Bank* CD-ROM is found in a section headed "Labor." The section on federal mapping might have mentioned the U.S. Geological Survey's *Maps for America*. But what matters is that this concise, well-designed guide to many mystifying realms of government information has now been brought up-to-date and is available in paperback at a reasonable price. It is a most useful acquisition for high school, public, and academic libraries.

Best Books for Public Libraries: The 10,000 Top Fiction and Nonfiction Titles. Ed. by Steven Arozena. Bowker, 1992. 840p. indexes. hardcover $75 (0-8352-3073-2).

025.2′1874 Public libraries—U.S.—Book lists || Bibliography—Best books—English imprints [CIP] 92-18410

The editor describes *Best Books for Public Libraries* as "designed to give librarians a current, single-volume guide to the top critically acclaimed books suitable for general readers." Covering more than 6,000 nonfiction and 4,000 fiction titles published between 1965 and early 1992, the book lists those receiving positive reviews from two or three of the primary sources librarians use for collection development (*Atlantic*, *Booklist*, *Choice*, *Christian Science Monitor*, *Library Journal*, *National Review*, *New Republic*, *New York Review of Books*, *New York Times Book Review*, *New Yorker*, *Newsweek*, *Publishers Weekly*, *Saturday Review*, *Time*, and *Times Literary Supplement*). The entries include a note for those titles receiving starred reviews, those receiving major awards, and those appearing on year-end "best" lists. The volume excludes scholarly materials, reference titles, and children's books.

Nonfiction titles are arranged alphabetically by author within Dewey Decimal Classification numbers; fiction titles appear alphabetically by author within 15 broad genres that are defined in the preface. Each record contains standard bibliographic information (taken from OCLC records, when possible), price, review citations, and Dewey number for nonfiction. A brief annotation is provided, sometimes being a direct quotation from a reviewing source. The type is clear and easy to read. Three indexes—by author, title, and subject—comprise 30 percent of the book.

Because Arozena's selection criteria relied upon positive reviews in recent sources, the list of titles is seriously affected by publishing trends and reviewing practices. Some subjects are underrepresented (non-Christian religions), whereas others are overrepresented (more books on baseball than other sports). In some subjects, the bulk of citations are to biographies instead of how-to information. Thus, this new work will not compete with such standard tools for collection development as the *Public Library Catalog* and the *Fiction Catalog*, both Wilson. For instance, no editions of the works of classic authors (Shakespeare, Poe, etc.) are included in *Best Books*; only two works by Mortimer Adler are listed, whereas ten appear in the ninth edition of *Public Library Catalog*; and five titles by Eudora Welty appear, compared to nine in the twelfth edition of the *Fiction Catalog*. While substantial duplication exists for some topics and authors, *Best Books* lists works not found in the Wilson catalogs, including supplements to the most recent editions. For instance, *Best Books* lists five titles on Nicaragua and five by Derek Walcott, whereas the *Public Library Catalog* includes, respectively, one and three of these titles.

Best Books for Public Libraries has some useful features: citations to the major book-reviewing publications in one volume, genre lists of noteworthy fiction titles, and citations for some critically acclaimed books that are in addition to those listed in the standard tools. It is recommended for purchase by those libraries needing a supplementary source for this type of information.

Online Inc.'s Top 500 Library Microcomputer Software Application Programs. Online Inc./Eight Bit Books, 1992. 350p. index. paper $44.95 (0-910965-09-9).

025.3′028 On-line data processing—Library applications || Computer software—Directories || Microcomputers—Programming—Directories || Library Science—Computer programs—Catalogs [OCLC]

This volume offers a unique compilation of library microcomputer software based on the online database *Buyer's Guide to Micro Software*, also known as *Soft*, available as file 237 on Dialog and on BRS in the file called *Soft*. All records have been derived directly from the online source with no significant alterations. According to the foreword, the following types of software are selected for incorporation into the *Buyer's Guide* database: microcomputer business and professional software, programs rated "good" by the technical press, best-sellers, packages from major producers (regardless of reviews), and professional specialties. This volume represents that portion of the *Soft* database that is important for libraries.

Karl Beiser, an authority on library systems, provides an excellent 10-page introductory essay addressing issues surrounding the selection of software for libraries. The work is divided into two major parts. "Library-Specific Software" duplicates all the records in *Soft* that deal with library applications. "Library-Related and/or Support Software" includes listings for programs selected by Beiser. In both parts of the book, software packages are arranged alphabetically under broad subject categories, such as *Cataloging*, *Serials*, *Graphics*, and *Virus Protection*. Two appendixes provide an alphabetical product-name index and a directory of software producers.

Each software listing contains the following information: version, release date, cost (with admonition to check with vendors before purchase), application, producer, description, operating environment, hardware requirements, and other software that works with the package. Product descriptions are informative and include special features; for example, Central Point Backup works well with Novell Netware and IBM-PC LAN software. Where applicable, bibliographic citations and a line or two from critical reviews are provided. Reviews are from such periodicals as *Infoworld*, PC *Magazine*, and *MacUser*.

The records are current as of the August 1992 update to the online database, which, in turn, is updated monthly. A list of search terms is provided in the introductory material for those libraries having access to Dialog or BRS. For these institutions, a quarterly update can be produced at a relatively low cost (the update from August 1992 through the first week in January 1993 produced 14 records). Although the foreword indicates that all library-specific packages in part 1 can be searched using the descriptor *library applications*, programs like Gofer are not retrievable this way, which brings up some correctable editorial problems with this work. Research Assistant, which appears to be one program with two entries in the index, turns out to be two entirely different products. Many page numbers in the index are incorrect. Fifteen entries are duplicated, which is acceptable since they fit in more than one category, but it reduces the total number of products below 500, suggesting a new title for the work is in order.

The concept behind this volume is good. It contains more library-specific software, is easier to use, and is more up-to-date than Elsevier's *Software Catalog: Microcomputers*, 1990. However, any print directory of this kind will be quickly outdated; therefore, libraries with online access will benefit from the *Soft* database. The print volume will be useful to other libraries when its problems are corrected.

The Contemporary Thesaurus of Social Science Terms and Synonyms: A Guide for Natural Language Computer Searching. Ed. by Sara D. Knapp. Oryx, 1993. 424p. hardcover $95 (0-89774-595-7).
025.4'9300285 Social sciences—Bibliography—Data bases ‖ Social sciences—Terminology ‖ Online bibliographic searching [CIP] 92-32899

Perhaps motivated by advice from F. W. Lancaster that "the most significant cause of recall failure in a natural language system is the inability of the searcher to think of all possible approaches to retrieval," Knapp has compiled this thesaurus of more than 6,000 concepts in the social sciences, together with equivalent, narrower, and related terms. Knapp, coordinator of the computer-search service at the State University of New York at Albany, is the author of a number of books and articles on online searching.

The body of the thesaurus consists of entries for each concept, listed alphabetically by a keyword or phrase (e.g., *adolescence, adolescent behavior*). Lists for each concept of related terms and synonyms range in length from a few lines to more than a column (e.g., *phobias*). Pages are well laid out, with three columns, readable type, and scope headings at the top left and top right of each two-page spread. Entries are displayed in hanging-indent format, with the heading itself set off in boldface type. Cross-references from alternative terms abound, including references from inverted forms so that access is provided via most keywords in multiword headings. Homographs are distinguished with qualifiers, for example, *depression* (*economic*), *depression* (*psychology*).

Entries do not use the standard format mandated for information-retrieval thesauruses by the recently revised National Information Standards Institute standard for thesauruses (nearing final approval and publication). Instead, they resemble the format of an alphabetically arranged dictionary-type thesaurus. This is appropriate since the intended audience includes end-user searchers who are usually comfortable with this arrangement.

The typical entry begins with the headword and equivalent terms, with alternative endings indicated for possible truncation. For instance, *homosexuality* begins "Homosexual(ity,ism). Lesbian(ism). Homoerotic(ism). Homoerotism. Homogenitality. Gay(ness). Tribade." Next come suggested term combinations, for example,

"*Choose from*: same sex *with*: orientation(s), preference, relationship." *Consider also* prefaces a list of suggested related terms, and references to related entries are indicated by *see also*. Within each section of the entry, terms are arranged in conceptual order, with closely related terms next to each other, rather than alphabetically. Some entries consist of long lists of narrower terms. For example, *phobias* includes a long list of particular phobias, and *North American native cultural groups* includes a list of Native American tribes.

Prefatory material includes two essays, "Basics of Computer Searching" and "Natural Language Searching," which will be very helpful for novice searchers who want a brief overview of how electronic search systems work and how to use them effectively. Appendixes are also useful: a list of "system features used in natural language searching in popular online and CD-ROM systems"; a guide to British spellings; and methods for "defining large subsets" in order to focus searches in databases that use category descriptors. The volume concludes with a lengthy list of dictionaries, thesauruses, and indexes that were used as sources for terms and a form for readers to suggest additional terms for future editions.

It is ironic that this thesaurus for online searching must be published in a print format, rather than an electronic one. A current challenge is to design and install more open and hospitable search systems that would welcome the addition of a wide variety of search thesauruses and search aids. A user should be able to search this thesaurus electronically and add the terms it suggests directly to a search, without rekeying. Soon users should be able to do just this.

The book quotes Lancaster as saying that "The searcher in a natural language system needs a thesaurus, or similar aid, just as much as the searcher in the controlled vocabulary system—perhaps even more so." This thesaurus admirably fills that bill for searchers of social science databases. It is designed specifically for searchers, not for indexers, and it should be very helpful for its intended audience of both librarians and end users. Academic and large public libraries that provide or encourage electronic information retrieval will want this helpful aid.

A Library, Media, and Archival Preservation Glossary. By John N. DePew and C. Lee Jones. ABC-Clio, 1992. 192p. bibliog. hardcover $59 (0-87436-576-7).
025.84 Audio-visual materials—Conservation and restoration—Dictionaries ‖ Archival materials—Conservation and restoration—Dictionaries [OCLC]

This dictionary provides definitions of approximately 1,500 terms for techniques used in conserving and preserving books, microforms, maps, and other media. Written by a library science educator (DePew) and a director of a micrographic preservation service (Jones), it is meant to serve as a companion to DePew's *Library, Media, and Archival Preservation Handbook* (ABC-Clio, 1991).

Definitions are, for the most part, brief (averaging about 5–10 lines in length). Citations to the sources of the definitions are provided. Sampling indicates that about half of the definitions have been culled from other authoritative sources (including 55 books, journal articles, and technical reports); half were provided by the authors. Historically significant words such as *parchment* and *vellum* can be found in other library science dictionaries (e.g., Harrod's *Librarian's Dictionary*, ALA *Glossary of Library and Information Science*), but most of the terms included here are largely absent from other standard dictionaries of librarianship. Some terms (e.g., ASTM, *halon*, NAB) might also be found in discipline-specific or acronym dictionaries, but one would have to look in several sources rather than just one.

The definitions are comprehensible to the nonspecialist, and the selection of terms to be defined includes many recent words as well as terms covering nonbook materials, including photographic processes. Words in a definition that are defined elsewhere in the book are in capital letters, although the authors sometimes capitalize phrases that are actually two (or more) separate listings. The user does not know in advance whether to look up the phrase in its entirety or to look up individual words (e.g., under *acid*, one finds "ALUM-ROSIN SIZING" but must look up both *alum* and then *rosin size*). One other peculiarity in terms of access is that in many cases there are no references from abbreviations or acronyms to the spelled-out form. For instance, there is no reference from DEZ to *diethyl zinc* or from PVA to *polyvinyl acetate*; however, for Hz, EF, and ADC references are provided. This inconsistency could cause unwary users to miss some definitions. Included also are terms associated with computer preservation areas (e.g., CD-ROM, *laser disc*), building and insurance issues (*flashing, expediting expense*), and the publishing industry (*quire, beater*).

This dictionary is unique in its focus, and the authors' provision of definitions for terms not covered elsewhere (about half of the entries) makes it one from which future sources in the field will draw. It will be quite useful for library school educators and students. Academic libraries serving either of these audiences should purchase this book, and large public libraries involved in preservation projects might also consider purchase.

Unlocking the Files of the FBI: A Guide to Its Records and Classification System. By Gerald K. Haines and David A. Langbart. Scholarly Resources, 1993. 336p. index. hardcover $60 (0-8420-2338-0).
026'.3530074 U.S. Federal Bureau of Investigation—Archives ‖ Law enforcement—U.S.—Archival resources [CIP] 92-16728

Haines, CIA historian, author, and member of a National Archives FBI task force, and Langbart, a National Archives and Records Administration (NARA) archivist, have pulled off an information heist with this first comprehensive guide to the content, organization, location, and access to the records of the U.S. Federal Bureau of Investigation. In 1980–81, by court order, experts from NARA systematically analyzed the FBI's records and record-keeping practices and made recommendations for retention and destruction of central and field-office files. Reviews were also conducted in 1986 and 1991 with future reviews to occur at five-year intervals. Ultimately, about 20 percent of all records will be transferred to NARA. The purpose of *Unlocking the Files of the* FBI is to provide researchers with a profile of the records.

A detailed introduction apprises the researcher of the history of the bureau's recordkeeping from 1909 to the present and explains how to use the guide. The FBI's Central Records System utilizes a classification scheme to organize its files, with each category of records derived from a specific law. This same arrangement is used in the book, and entries appear for the 278 classifications, such as "Kidnapping," "Ethics in Government Act of 1978," "Toxic Waste Matters," and "Hostage Taking—Terrorism."

Each entry provides the classification number, title, background on when the category was established and changes over time, description of typical files, notes of unusual cases (e.g., in "Espionage," files on Errol Flynn and the Duke of Windsor), suggested research potential, the quantity of records, the date span, the location (central bureau or field office), and the NARA/FBI Task Force recommendations concerning retention or disposal. Each classification includes a statement about accessing the records; generally a researcher is advised to file a Freedom of Information Act request. The notes about related records are especially useful because many investigations are categorized in alternative classifications. For example, "Classification 49—Destruction or Overthrow of the Government" is handled mostly under "100—Domestic Security," "105—Counterintelligence," and "176—Antitrust Law." Forty-three classifications are labeled "obsolete," and information concerning 19 of the most recent were not available but were due for inclusion in the 1991 NARA update.

Approximately 100 specialized indexes maintained by the FBI, from the general index to the Witness Protection Program Index, have been kept on 3-by-5-inch cards at the central office and at the field offices, which the authors describe in a separate section. A section called "Special Files" includes descriptions of high-interest files, such as J. Edgar Hoover's Official (O & C) File, Electronic Surveillance Files, and Japanese Activities in the United States. Twelve appendixes cover such topics as abbreviations and symbols, locations of foreign and field offices, and various matters pertaining to the Freedom of Information Act. A detailed name-subject index provides a key to the wealth of information in this volume.

Haines and Langbart have added value to the information gathered by the NARA/FBI Task Force by pointing out the research potential of the records. For example, social historians will note the shift in emphasis over the years in cases classified in the "Involuntary Servitude and Slavery" category. Early cases concentrated on chain gangs and Jim Crow laws; in the 1940s and 1950s, focus was on exploitation of black tenant farmers; and in the 1960s and 1970s, Latin American workers in the U.S. were emphasized. Any reader or student interested in what the FBI does will treasure this guide; however, its price will preclude purchase for the merely curious. *Unlocking the Files of the* FBI will be most valuable to serious researchers, and it is recommended for academic and large public libraries.

Play, Learn, and Grow: An Annotated Guide to the Best Books and Materials for Very Young Children. By James L. Thomas. Bowker, 1992. 439p. indexes. hardcover $27 (0-8352-3019-8).
028.1'62 Bibliography—Best books—Children's literature ‖ Preschool children—Books and reading ‖ Children's literature—Bibliography ‖ Audio-visual materials—Catalogs [CIP] 92-15458

Joining the family of distinguished Bowker books on children's literature is this extensive guide to the selection of print and non-print materials for infants, toddlers, preschoolers, and kindergarteners. More than 1,000 titles were chosen, graded, and ranked as to purchase priority by an impressive panel of 64 librarians and early childhood education specialists. This group considered approximately 5,000 materials in different formats, choosing such classics as Wanda Gag's *Millions of Cats* and more recent books and media. The audience for this work is wide, including educators, child-care professionals, librarians, students, and parents.

The book opens with a concise and informative paper by Frances Smardo Dowd on the role of the adult in emergent literacy development in children. Two briefer papers provide an introduction to the book and a review of how materials may be chosen to support and encourage children's development. Quite often patrons can be confused as to how "preschoolers" differ from "kindergarteners," and it might have helped if the essays had discussed how the compilers of this book define these terms.

Each numbered entry is listed alphabetically by title. Each entry includes bibliographic information, cost, and a category descriptor, similar to a genre type. The eight category designations are *Concept/Counting/Alphabet, Folklore/Folk Tales/Fairy Tales, Informational, Periodicals, Participation and Manipulative, Poetry/Nursery Rhymes/Songs, Story,* and *Wordless*. Titles are suggested for one age or a range of ages, such as T,P,K—toddlers, preschoolers, and kindergarteners. Entries also include a descriptive and evaluative annotation, a purchase priority (first, second, or third), and citations to reviews and awards where applicable. The book concludes with five indexes: name, subject, age/category, age/purchase priority, and format. These indexes are very useful, enabling the reader to locate such materials as a list of periodicals for preschoolers in the age/category index or a list of software in the format index.

This book is not a comprehensive volume for library collection development. Some favorite children's authors are missing, and the selection policy is not given in enough detail to explain their absence. For instance, the Berenstains, Dick Bruna, Jeannette Caines, Karla Kuskin, and Sara Bonnet Stein are not included. And what should be said to the parent or kindergartener wishing a chapter book such as Averill's *Cat Club* or a "hard" book such as volumes by Edward Ardizzone? Also missing is that pioneer of mood or concept books, Alvin Tresselt. Finally, in this age of multiculturalism, only two books in Spanish are included and none in French.

Compared to this new title, *The Elementary School Library Collection* (18th ed. [RBB Je 1 92]), *Best Books for Children* (4th ed. [RBB D 15 90]), and the *Children's Catalog* (16th ed., Wilson, 1991) are more comprehensive listings that will continue to be used for book selection for older preschoolers and kindergarteners. However, *Play, Learn, and Grow* is uniquely geared toward advising caregivers of young children about the best materials to enhance literacy development. This impressive reference source is recommended for public and school libraries and for those academic libraries dealing with young children's literature.

Children's Book Awards International: A Directory of Awards and Winners, from Inception through 1990. By Laura Smith. McFarland, 1992. 649p. indexes. hardcover $75 (0-89950-686-0).
028.1'62 Children's literature—Awards—Directories ‖ Young adult literature—Awards—Directories ‖ Children's literature—Illustrations—Awards—Directories ‖ Young adult literature—Illustrations—Awards—Directories ‖ Bibliography—Best books—Young adult literature [CIP] 91-50940

This directory lists 424 awards that were or are being given for the writing and illustrating of children's and young adult literature in 45 countries and the winners of these awards. It includes awards given as early as 1922 (*John Newbery Award*) through 1990.

Organized alphabetically, the 11,157 entries are arranged by country, from *Argentina* to *Yugoslavia*, and then by award name. For each award is given the sponsoring organization with contact information, the date of the award's inception, what constitutes the award (cash, certificate, etc.), and eligibility. A chronological list of award recipients follows, with the title of the book (in English, if available) and publication information.

Four indexes follow the detailed awards listings: authors, awards and sponsors, illustrators, and titles. The title index is confusing. First, titles are alphabetized under initial articles such as *The*. Second, although titles of books are given in the directory first in English and then, if appropriate, in the language in which they were published, the title index lists them only in the language of publication, not in English translation.

More detailed information on the two best-known American prizes is available in *Newbery and Caldecott Medalists and Honor Book Winners* (2d ed. [RBB N 1 92]). *Children's Literature Awards and Winners: A Directory of Prizes, Authors, and Illustrators* (2d ed.) lists winners of 211 awards in English-speaking countries through 1987 or 1988. Academic libraries supporting programs of study in children's literature and large public libraries needing international coverage of awards should consider purchase of *Children's Book Awards International*.

Reference Books for Children. 4th ed. By Carolyn Sue Peterson and Ann D. Fenton. Scarecrow, 1992. 399p. indexes. hardcover $39.50 (0-8108-2543-0).
028.1'62 Children's reference books—Bibliography || Libraries, Children's—Book lists || School libraries—Book lists [CIP] 92-14234

This annotated bibliography lists more than 1,000 titles that can be used for or with young people, grades K–12. Last published in 1981, it is intended to be used as a buying guide by librarians who work with young people.

General reference books are listed (e.g., evaluation sources, encyclopedias, and the like), and then subject-specific tools under more than 50 specific topics. Bibliographic citations include price and ISBN and are followed by one- to three-sentence content summaries. These annotations do not note the differences between editions of a book; an older edition of a reference book may suffice in some libraries. In the introduction, the authors give detailed criteria for reference-book selection. Author-title and subject indexes aid access.

This bibliography is current only as of June 1990. This means that many superseded editions are listed and that the many good reference books published in 1991 are missing. Some annotations are also unreliable. Those for general encyclopedias, for instance, do not reflect the current state of these sets.

This bibliography is a useful checklist for selection, both for public and school libraries, but librarians will need to use it with reviews from professional journals to find books published after the middle of 1990.

The Treasury of the Encyclopaedia Britannica: More Than Two Centuries of Facts, Curiosities, and Discoveries from the Most Distinguished Reference Work of All Time. Ed. by Clifton Fadiman. Viking, 1992. 698p. illus. index. hardcover $35 until January 1, 1993; $40 thereafter (0-670-83568-4).
031 [CIP] 92-54069

This anthology of excerpts from *Britannica* shows the development of the encyclopedia as it mirrored the growth of knowledge over more than 200 years. The first section reprints 200 extracts with brief introductory remarks telling why they were selected. They show that early editions were full of practical information, for example, how to get rid of bedbugs and how to cure baldness with burdock roots and red onions. Those editions also reflected the defective knowledge of the day. *California* is described in the first edition (1768–1783) as being in the West Indies, and "it is uncertain whether it be a peninsula or an island." *Plantership*, in the second edition (1778–1783), counseled humane treatment of slaves. Other material is surprisingly modern. While we think of anorexia and bulimia as modern maladies, the third edition (1788–1797) contained articles on them. *Britannica* first had an article on television in the 1929 set. Black-and-white illustrations from early editions add interest to this section.

The second part reprints articles from later editions, when entries were signed by outside contributors. Here material has been selected because the author is famous (e.g., John Muir on Yosemite, Henry Ford on mass production, W. E. B. DuBois on black literature, Trotsky on Lenin). Appendixes reproduce the article *Encyclopedias* from the current *Britannica* and a dialect poem by Eugene Field, "The Cyclopeedy," which hearkens back to the day when encyclopedias were sold on the subscription plan.

Public and academic libraries will want to consider this interesting volume for their circulating collections. Browsing in it provides a glimpse of the history of this esteemed reference source. —*Sandy Whiteley*

The Information Please Kids' Almanac. By Alice Siegel and Margo McLoone Basta. Houghton, 1992. 361p. illus. index. paper $7.95 (0-395-58801-4).
031 Almanacs, children's [OCLC] 92-28037

Children's almanacs tend to be selective rather than comprehensive in their coverage. This is a compendium of information on everything from animals to disasters, sports, and war. Among the other titles by these authors are *The Kids' World Almanac of Records and Facts* (1985) and *The Second Kids' World Almanac of Records and Facts* (1987). While similar in format, *Information Please* has all new text.

Interesting topics include the nine orders and three triads of angles; how to talk in secret languages (eggy-peggy, pig latin, skimono jive); symbolism of colors around the world; and sports superstitions. Also included are things typically found in an almanac, such as a metric-system chart with conversions, Roman numerals, and a time-zone chart. Black-and-white drawings are found on every page, and a brief index is provided.

The World Almanac's InfoPedia [RBB D 1 90] is larger and offers more substance and complete listings. For example, the *InfoPedia* list of the states notes capital, area in square miles/kilometers, and population estimate. *Kids' Almanac* offers capital and one bit of trivia and illustrations of only 9 of the 50 state seals. *InfoPedia* also contains a section with a mini–world atlas and flags of the world in color. *The Macmillan Book of Fascinating Facts: An Almanac for Kids* (1989) is also larger and more expensive.

Full of facts and trivia, *Kids' Almanac* is fun to browse, but *The World Almanac's InfoPedia* is the more useful reference tool and more like almanacs geared for adults. Considering the price, libraries may still want to consider *The Information Please Kids' Almanac* for their circulating collections.

Microsoft Encarta Multimedia Encyclopedia. CD-ROM. Microsoft Corp., 1993. $395/single user; $249/educator special price.
031 Encyclopedias and dictionaries—Software [BKL]

Microsoft Encarta takes full advantage of the multimedia capabilities of an enhanced PC. You will need quite a sophisticated setup to use this new encyclopedia. Using all the capabilities of *Encarta* requires, at a minimum, a multimedia PC (386SX or higher processor), 2 MB of RAM, a 30 MB hard disk, a CD-ROM drive, an audio board, a mouse, a VGA or better display, Windows 3.1, and MSCDEX 2.2 or later. Based on what I learned doing this review, I would recommend a 486-25 or better processor, a Super VGA display and card, and 4 MB or better of RAM. If you are willing to settle for just text and graphics (a waste of the program), it is possible to operate without the sound board.

The above requirements are just the beginning, as I found out when I tried to use the program. Just any sound board won't do—it must be one of the newer MPC-compatible boards (i.e., one such as Sound Blaster Pro). Also, the CD-ROM drive should meet MPC standards, with CD-DA outputs, sustained 150/second transfer rate, and a maximum seek time of one second using no more than 40 percent of the CPU's processing power. The faster the CD-ROM drive, the better the performance. I have a medium speed drive (325ms) and some of the screen rewriting/display times were painfully slow. I was able to compare the screen quality with a lower-end SVGA display and a high-end NEC multisynch monitor. The difference is striking—the difference between looking at an obvious computer-screen illustration and looking at near-photographic quality. If you have the equipment, this is without doubt the best graphics and sound encyclopedia that I have reviewed to date. If your equipment is less than optimum, the installation program will carefully point out any lacks in your system during the setup process.

Encarta is based on *Funk & Wagnalls New Encyclopedia*, although the text part of the product occupies only a small amount of the CD-ROM storage space. The thousands of images, animations, interactive charts, and seven hours of sound that Microsoft has added take up the rest of the space. Installation is done through Windows and will probably be very easy for most users. I had considerable trouble getting the program to run on two different machines and was fortunate enough to have a Microsoft programmer come out and figure out that the problem was a bad disc—a benefit of living in Microsoft's geographic vicinity. I also learned that the install program would not recognize a compressed disk that I was running on my home machine. However, a new CD-ROM that Microsoft sent immediately installed perfectly on a noncompressed disk and was used for this review.

Documentation with *Encarta* is contained in two simple, well-illustrated, small manuals—a 38-page "Getting Started" booklet and a 4l-page reference guide. Actually, a four-page, glossy help card, which could be put out by the work station, contains all the information a user would need to work with the encyclopedia. The main user interface is through the Main Window, divided into several smaller windows. One window contains the Article Frame, a textual description of the item of interest. A second frame shows the Category (groups of such common entries as *Transportation*, *Physics*, *Astronomy and Space Science*, *Earth Science*, etc.). A third window contains the Gallery Frame, an illustration related to the article being viewed. Small icons, such as a camera, filmstrip, and earphone, indicate further related screens or sound bites. There is also a top menu bar that allows the user to search for keywords, skip into an atlas or time-line section, or just browse alphabetically through the encyclopedia.

I began the session for this review by looking up *Irving Berlin*. After clicking on Find on the menu line and typing in his name in the small window that appeared, another part of the screen provided six listings of the places in the encyclopedia where *Berlin* appeared. These were an entry specifically for him, a World War II bibliography, and the topics *Musical*, *Song*, *American Music*, and *Folklore*. Clicking on the *Berlin* entry brought up the article frame and an illustration of a guitar and trumpet. Since there was a sound-bit icon, I clicked on this and was treated to 22 seconds of Ethel Merman singing "Alexander's Ragtime Band." I found the sound quality particularly striking since I have my system hooked up to two 15-inch three-way speakers.

I was curious about the *Folklore* entry, so I clicked on this and was taken to the appropriate article at the spot where Irving Berlin's name was mentioned. I found this process more helpful than the usual way where programs simply highlight word occurrences but start at the beginning of an article. Within a text display the user can click on Outline and see a brief listing of major points of each article. Within each article, cross-references (or terms perhaps better labeled *hyperlinks*) are highlighted and can be accessed directly by clicking on them.

Each window and icon is arranged in such a user-friendly manner that prolonged browsing is almost inevitable. The user can always move forward or backward, or even bring up a Topic Tracker to get a list of the last 40 topics viewed. The program as a whole might have been designed to serve as a one-stop shopping center for term-paper writing, if one can accept the premise that using one source constitutes research. There is even a guide to writing a research paper using *Encarta* in the reference pamphlet. I found it very easy to mark passages in text and copy them to the Clipboard in Windows, later pasting them into a word-processing document. Animations are cleverly done. For example, when illustrating the principles of flight, a plane rotates in accordance with text display describing the effects of aileron, rudder, and yoke.

Even the Atlas is fun to use. This choice opens with a picture of the globe (that can be rotated), contains a Zoom-In option, a Place-Finder option, and a Pronunciation option (you can actually hear some of the place-names pronounced). There are so many other nice features of this system that it would take more than this short review to cover them all.

Encarta is the third CD-ROM encyclopedia that I have reviewed, beginning with Grolier's *Academic American*, followed by *Compton's* (Windows version). While it's probably unfair to make a direct comparison between the three CD-ROM products given the time elapsed between each review, nevertheless I did feel as if in *Encarta* I was working with the mature version of a technology that has been evolving over the past several years. I can highly recommend it for school and public libraries. Also, librarians who may have some trepidation about exploring the Windows environment should be reassured. Using *Encarta* as a multimedia learning tool (leaving aside fancier operations, such as copying and pasting text to a word processor) is simple, intuitive, and does not require a sophisticated Windows expert. —*Charles Anderson*

Factfinder. Comp. by Theodore Rowland-Entwistle and Jean Cooke. Kingfisher Books, 1992. 278p. illus. index. maps. hardcover $16.95 (1-85697-835-4); paper $12.95 (1-85697-803-6).
031 Children's encyclopedias and dictionaries [CIP] 92-53118

Factfinder is an easy-to-use, lavishly illustrated compendium of facts and figures on a variety of topics for preteens. Divided into 13 subject areas—"The Universe," "Planet Earth," "World Atlas," "Countries of the World," "History," "The Human Body," "Animals," "Plants," "Science," "Transportation," "Communication," "Arts and Entertainment," and "Sports"—it provides concise information supplemented with appropriate illustrations.

Subject sections vary in length from 12 to 32 pages; the shortest is "Communication," the longest, "History" and "Science." Due to the different kinds of information, subjects may be presented in different ways. However, each section begins with a brief introduction of the topic and includes a time line of events and a glossary, if appropriate. All of the sections contain a wealth of full-color illustrations and photographs, as well as tables, graphs, and charts. The majority of the illustrations are vivid and eye-catching. A few, particularly the portraits, appear dark and grainy. However, this slight deficiency is more than outweighed by the number of really fine drawings that illustrate the inner workings of the human body or the parts of a camera, for example.

Information in *Factfinder* is current through the early part of 1992. Tables of sports results include the 1991 World Series and the 1992 Super Bowl. The world atlas shows an up-to-date configuration for the former Soviet Union. Much of the information, of course, will remain useful and valid long past the publication date.

An alphabetical index of subjects and names completes this work. Not all entries are indexed. If a term is not listed, the reader is instructed to consult the tables and glossaries within the general subject area. *See* references guide the user to the correct term.

Though no grade or age level is indicated, *Factfinder* would appear to be most useful for children in the upper elementary grades through middle school. It could certainly be used by adults looking for brief information on a variety of subjects. Similar in style and content to a good almanac, *Factfinder* would be useful in school and public libraries.

From Archetype to Zeitgeist: Powerful Ideas for Powerful Thinking. By Herbert Kohl. Little, Brown, 1992. 246p. bibliog. index. hardcover $19.95 (0-316-50138-7).
031 Encyclopedias and dictionaries [CIP] 91-37658

The noted educator who wrote this book describes it as a guide to the language of ideas. As a teacher he has observed that high school students and college freshmen often lack the vocabulary and training to think critically and to communicate complex ideas and concepts. He solicited suggestions for "powerful" words and ideas to include here from teaching faculty, students, and colleagues. He reports his methodology in "How This Guide Was Made" at the end of the volume.

The work is divided into 11 categories such as "The Arts," "Literature," "Religion," "Economics," and "Political Science." Unlike a standard dictionary, the 247 entries are arranged alphabetically within these categories. Since the entries are drawn from actual experience in coursework, the emphasis is on concepts (*Ockham's razor*), foreign terms (*qua*), common prefixes (*meta-*), and other words and phrases that students must master in order to talk about ideas. Each entry is highlighted in boldface in the wide margin, with variant pronunciations, part of speech, and a simple derivation below it. The majority of words are Greek or Latin in origin, with such exceptions as the Arabic *algorithm*. Definitions are as short as two sentences (*parasitism*) or as long as 2½ pages (*psychoanalysis*).

As a result of the categorical arrangement of the work, the "Complete Word List" serves as an index, with many cross-references. Also, within the text, words and phrases that appear elsewhere as main entries are italicized. There are a few simple line drawings scattered throughout the text. The "Pronunciation Guide" at the beginning of the work is helpful, but it would be more valuable if the occurence of sounds in words were italicized. The bibliography consists of works the author has consulted, including dictionaries, subject-area resources, and standard handbooks of English usage.

Libraries owning the five-volume *Dictionary of the History of Ideas* (Scribner, 1973–74) and E. D. Hirsch's *Dictionary of Cultural Literacy* [RBB Ap 1 89] will use *Archetype* as an enrichment tool. Entries in *Archetype* are more clearly defined for high school students and college freshmen than those in the *Dictionary of the History of Ideas* and longer than those in *The Dictionary of Cultural Literacy*; however, both of these titles contain many more entries.

Kohl states that he hopes to add more volumes in the future to cover the many ideas he omitted in this eclectic guide. Meanwhile the present volume serves as a handy tool to augment other sources and to generate thought and class discussion on important ideas. High school, undergraduate, and public libraries will all want to consider purchase.

My First Encyclopedia. By Carol Watson. Dorling Kindersley; dist. by Houghton, 1993. 80p. illus. index. hardcover $16.95 (1-56458-214-0).
031 Children's encyclopedias and dictionaries [CIP] 92-53477

Young World: A Child's First Encyclopedia. 6v. Random, 1992. illus. indexes. hardcover $10/v.
031 Children's encyclopedias and dictionaries [BKL]

These two attractively illustrated titles for young children are both compilations from British-based publishing houses. *My First Encyclopedia*, from Dorling Kindersley, is an oversize one-volume source that introduces a great variety of information geared to the interests and curiosity of the young child, preschool to beginning reader. *Young World* was originally published in 1992 in Great Britain by Kingfisher Books of Grisewood & Dempsey. It is a series of six volumes (each 125 pages) designed to encourage children, ages four to eight, to find facts for themselves on a wide range of topics. Neither title is as comprehensive as those encyclopedic sources designed for readers age seven and up. Rather, both of these new works present selected and concise information, in an organized sequence and accessible through an index, that can introduce young children to fact-finding.

My First Encyclopedia is thematically arranged. It starts with a look at the human body and then explores such topics as families, pets, jobs, plants, animals, geography, and travel. A prefatory note explains that the sequence of topics in the book parallels a child's development, beginning with everyday experiences and then topics related to exploration of the wider world. The earlier pages are addressed to the young reader; later pages have a more impersonal instructional style of writing. This arrangement is intended to be useful for children first learning to read. As with other Dorling Kindersley publications, such as the books in the Eyewitness Visual Dictionary series, there is a strong visual appeal, with much use of color photography, and the pages are easily read.

Each of the six compact-sized volumes of *Young World* concentrates on a special theme. The included materials were checked by experienced educational advisors and teachers. Vocabulary is simple and yet not pedestrian. Volume 1 covers *All Kinds of Animals* (0-679-83697-7). Volume 2, *How Things Are Made* (0-679-83695-0), examines the natural and mechanical processes that produce such objects as clothes, food, timber products, coins, and skyscrapers. Volume 3, *My Body* (0-679-84160-1), handles the topic of reproduction particularly well. Volume 4, *On the Move* (0-679-83694-2), introduces various kinds of transportation on land, air, sea, and space. Volume 5 covers *Our Planet Earth* (0-679-83696-9), and Volume 6 explains the world of *Plants* (0-679-84161-X).

Both *My First Encyclopedia* and *Young World* present accurate introductory information on many subjects. Because of the larger size of the latter title, it offers more systematic coverage of its topics. For instance, the only reference to *cactus* in *My First Encyclopedia* occurs in the section "In the Desert," with the entry focusing on how a saguaro cactus grows slowly, can live more than 200 years, and can "grow taller than a house." The index to the *Plants* volume of *Young World* has four references for *cactus*. These explain that the cactus stores water in its stems and leaves to survive, that it is a plant that scratches, and that it can be attacked by mealy bugs. However, *My First Encyclopedia* presents many unique tidbits, such as in the entries *camper van*, *librarian*, and *plankton*. Both titles are balanced in their representations of gender roles and depictions of a variety of ethnic peoples.

While not necessarily an essential purchase, *My First Encyclopedia* is an excellent browsing volume and is very reasonably priced. It is an eye-appealing compilation of facts that will be entertaining learning. It is recommended for libraries and media centers that serve preschool children. The volumes in *Young World* can each stand on their own. However, together, the set resembles an encyclopedic source and offers a good starting point for the learning and discovery of the young child. However, the publisher is not offering the option of ordering *Young World* as a set; each volume must be purchased separately. The total price of $60 (more if the sturdiest binding is ordered) for six small volumes will be prohibitive for many collections.

Webster's II New Riverside Desk Reference: Home and Office Edition. Houghton, 1992. 471p. index. tables. hardcover $7.95 (0-395-59520-7).
031 Encyclopedias and dictionaries [CIP] 91-41366

This reference book is well organized with logical groupings of information and clearly printed charts and narratives. The pages are about one-fourth larger than those in *The World Almanac and Book of Facts* and *Information Please Almanac*, so the print is slightly larger and somewhat less cramped. However, *Webster's II* has only about half the number of pages of either almanac.

Webster's II is, in fact, selected pages from *Information Please Almanac*, reproduced exactly from the 1992 edition of this source, also published by Houghton Mifflin. Chosen for inclusion in *Webster's II* are portions of the subjects of the calendar and holidays, U.S. information (statistics, geography, states and cities, and history and government), world information (statistics, geography, United Nations, and countries), business, education, weather, travel, etc. The sections of *Information Please Almanac* not included in *Webster's II* include sports, headline history, major events of the year, astronomy and space, people, first aid, health and nutrition, environment, atlas, and the year in pictures.

Since no material was found in *Webster's II* that is not also in *Information Please Almanac*, it is recommended that libraries purchase the latter and get nearly twice the information for the same price.

The Guinness Book of Records 1492: The World Five Hundred Years Ago. Ed. by Deborah Manley and Geoffrey Scammell. Facts On File, 1992. 192p. bibliog. illus. index. hardcover $24.95 (0-8160-2772-2).
031.02 Curiosities and wonders || World records || Civilization [CIP] 91-58588

Records of firsts intrigue the public for many reasons, and Guinness has responded with books on an annual basis. This book provides a periscope on the time of Columbus' voyages. The introduction states it "sets the records broken by Columbus alongside other quantifiable achievements, worldwide, over a period of about one hundred years from *c.* 1450." While most of the records are from the time period noted, a number have no relationship to the Columbian encounter (e.g., highest mountains, noisiest animals, bloodiest ancient battles). Some readers might find the additional facts of interest, but these do not strengthen the book's value as a reference source on the world at the time of Columbus.

Editor Manley is a world traveler and previously wrote *The Nile: A Traveller's Anthology*. Editorial consultant Scammell teaches history at Cambridge University and is the author of books on the maritime age. The work is arranged in chapters by subject, such as "Exploration and Discovery," "Buildings and Structures," and "Religion and Popular Belief." Each chapter is further divided (e.g., *Fortifications*, *The Garden*, and *Canals and Dams*). The three-column layout contains boldface headings for each achievement (e.g., largest mosque, largest Turkish mosque, largest mosque in India, largest pillared mosque). The first is then described in a brief paragraph with essential facts and dates. The many color illustrations add to the visual appeal of this work. A list of further reading and an accurate, though somewhat cursory, index are included.

With attractive endpapers and fascinating illustrations, this book will be enjoyed by many people. It is not, however, a source in which readers will seek specific information. It is instead a browsing item for readers in public and high school libraries who enjoy records of achievements or world facts and might be better placed in the circulating collection.

Webster's New World Encyclopedia. Prentice Hall, 1992. 1,230p. illus. maps. tables. hardcover $75 (0-13-947482-X).
032 Encyclopedias and dictionaries [CIP] 91-43020

Although the title is new, this one-volume encyclopedia is based on a standard British work first published in 1948, *Hutchinsons's Twentieth Century Encyclopedia*. The sixth edition, entitled *The New Hutchinson 20th Century Encyclopedia*, was the most recent to be reviewed by the Board [RSBR Ap 1 79], which noted its heavy British emphasis. Now Prentice Hall has prepared an extensively revised and Americanized version of the ninth edition published in 1990. The publisher indicates that more than 11,000 of the entries in *Webster's New World Encyclopedia* were written especially for this edition. In addition, the spelling throughout is American, and measurements are given first in those units commonly used in the U.S. and then in metric equivalents.

Particularly notable are the encyclopedia's currency and its broad scope, with topics treated ranging from historical events to popular culture. Entries for U.S. states and cities use 1990 census figures, and a number of articles refer to events from late 1991 or early 1992. For instance, George Bush's trade mission to Japan is included, as is the winner of the 1992 Super Bowl. However, death dates of individuals who died in 1991 are provided inconsistently. While the deaths of Margot Fonteyn, Graham Greene, and Edwin Land are noted, those of Peggy Ashcroft, John Tower, and Angus Wilson are not.

The more than 25,000 entries are arranged alphabetically, letter by letter. Page layouts feature an attractive mixture of text and illustrations, but the typeface used for the text is unusually small. Although the numerous illustrations may attract younger readers, the level of the text is most appropriate for high school students through adults. An excellent system of cross-references guides the user to related entries. Most of the entries are fairly brief, generally fewer than 100 words. Articles for countries are more substantial, consisting of a narrative covering government and history and a box with a picture of the flag, a small area map, basic statistics, and other information in tabular form. Articles on the major performing arts and on national literatures also tend to be longer than the norm.

The encyclopedia is illustrated with more than 2,500 photographs and drawings, many in color. A number of the illustrations help explain technological or biological processes, such as paper making and acid rain. Also supplementing the text are numerous maps, tables, diagrams, and charts. However, users will miss many of these because they do not appear on the same page as the entry, and the entries provide no references to illustrations. For example, the World War II chronology is two pages after the article it complements, while the feather diagram appears on the verso of the page with the Feather entry.

In general, this work provides excellent coverage of contemporary health concerns (e.g., AZT, *Alzheimer's Disease*, *The Pill*) and of recent technological innovations (e.g., CD-ROM, *Cellular Phone*, *Laptop Computer*). Therefore, it is surprising that no entries for chronic fatigue syndrome, high-definition television, or hypertext are included. Federal government agencies and individual Supreme Court decisions are also well represented, as are sports celebrities, film stars, and writers. However, some contemporary figures, such as Magic Johnson, Larry McMurtry, and Ted Turner, are lacking.

This encyclopedia is flawed by an imbalance in the amount of treatment accorded certain topics. For instance, *Gulf War* is considerably more extensive than the narrative entry in World War II (excluding the chronological chart), which is so cursory that it does not even explain the origins of that war. The inadequate *Supreme Court* entry names only the chief justice, not the associate justices. Although the seven newest justices, including Clarence Thomas, are treated in separate entries, the two with the most seniority (Byron White and Harry Blackmun) are not. The 15-line entry for *United Nations* is particularly insufficient and contrasts sharply with the nearby 27-line article *Unification Church* ("Moonies"). Although most entries appear to be accurate, a striking exception is the diagram of a baseball field, which mislabels home plate as "houseplate."

Of the five one-volume encyclopedias published in the last 4 years, this work is closest in format and number of entries to the *Cambridge Encyclopedia*. While *Webster's New World Encyclopedia* is more successful in masking its British origins, and although its numerous illustrations make it more visually appealing, the aforementioned flaws diminish its value. However, its currency and breadth make it an attractive candidate for home purchase. Libraries in the market for a new one-volume encyclopedia may want to consider purchase.

Magazines for Libraries. 7th ed. By Bill Katz and Linda Sternberg Katz. Bowker, 1992. 1,212p. indexes. hardcover $139.95 (0-8352-3166-6; ISSN 0000-0914).
[050.25 Perioicals—Direcotories || Periodical Selection BKL] 86-640971

The well-known team of periodical reviewers, Bill and Linda Katz, have compiled a new edition of this useful work. Assisted by 153 consultants, more than 40 percent of them new to this edition, they have surveyed over 70,000 periodicals and selected "the best and most useful for the average elementary or secondary school, public, academic, or special library." As with past editions, this edition has undergone significant revision. There has been a slight increase in the number of entries from 6,521 to 6,665. The publisher states that 20 percent of the titles are new to this edition and the remaining 80 percent have all had their annotations rewritten. Approximately three-quarters of the contributors are academic librarians.

Although the organization of the book remains unchanged, several sections have been expanded. Of the 145 alphabetically arranged subject categories, nine are new to this volume. They include *Aquaculture*, *Classroom Magazines*, *College and Alumni*, *Comic Books*, *Food and Wine*, *Hospitality/Restaurant*, *Music Reviews*, *New Age*, and *Women: Feminist and Special Interest*. Within each subject category, entries are arranged alphabetically by title. Sources of microform and reprint copies and online and CD-ROM access are listed for each periodical. Each entry has an indication of audience or type-of-library level. Critical annotations address writing style, format, coverage of material, and audience appeal.

In the past, the Board criticized this book for its lack of coverage of microform materials and electronic indexes. The editors are to be congratulated for adding this information in this edition. In future editions, the editors might address the lack of uniformity in annotations. For example, the annotations for the *Chronicle of Higher Education* and *Poultry Science* note that they contain classified job advertising, but those for *American Libraries*, *Library Journal*, and *Aviation Week & Space Technology* do not.

There is nothing comparable to *Magazines for Libraries*. *Magazines for Young People* [RBB S 15 91] is an abridged version, covering some 1,300 titles. A valuable tool for collection development, *Magazines for Libraries* should be considered by academic and public libraries. Libraries owning the previous edition may wish to retain it for reference on periodicals not covered in the new one.

Magazine Article Summaries Full Text Elite on CD-ROM. Version 3.41. EBSCO, 1992. monthly. 2 discs. $3,199/yr.
031 Periodicals—Abstracts [BKL]

Originally released in late 1991, the current version of *Magazine Article Summaries Full Text Elite on CD-ROM* (version 3.41) provides keyword and subject-heading access to abstracts of articles from 382 general-interest periodicals. This product includes the full text of 90 of these magazines, as well as text from *Magill Book Reviews*. The indexed journals were selected as the most popular in high schools and public libraries, based on subscriber surveys, and range from *House Beautiful* to *Ebony* and from *Scientific American* to *Bon Appetit*. Also covered are the *New York Times* and some academic journals such as *American Political Science Review* and *Journal of the American Medical Associa-*

tion. Among the 90 magazines available full text are the three major news weeklies plus such titles as *Prevention, FDA Consumer, Forbes, Runner's World, Money, Popular Photography, Sports Illustrated, Rolling Stone,* and *Harvard Health Letter.*

A subscription consists of a current disc with the most recent 18 months of covered articles and a disc with older data. The list of included magazines indicates the dates coverage began for each title. For some, the back file begins with 1984, while other titles were added to the database since then. Subscription options are available for updates monthly, quarterly, or on an academic-year basis. Also, another version of the database is available that provides full text for 60 titles, rather than the 90 included in the elite version reviewed here.

HARDWARE AND SOFTWARE. Hardware requirements do not include anything unusual—PC XT/AT or compatible; 640K RAM (2 MB recommended); floppy-disk drive; 10 MB hard disk; and a CD-ROM player. The software requires MS DOS 3.3 or higher and Microsoft CD-ROM Extensions 2.1 or higher.

SEARCHING AND DISPLAYING. To check on the currency of the database, I used *Clinton* as a search term. In the November 1992 disc, I found the most recent articles were dated October 19, 1992. This is reasonable updating for a CD-ROM product. The results of a search are displayed in a hit-list format, with the parts of the citation clearly labeled as *subject, title,* and *source.* The list indicates if full text is available, which is accessed by pressing the F7 key. If a local library has input its journals-holding list, a note indicating the article is available in hard copy is also displayed. The user can move the cursor down to a particular citation in the list and press ENTER to see an abstract. Adding highlighting to the location of the cursor would improve the user interface a bit.

The appearance of the initial search screen is clean and intuitive, with a simple "Query Profile" that asks the user to type up to three lines of terms. These lines are labeled FIND [A] AND [B] AND [C] for a Boolean search. Entering terms in this part of the screen searches only the citation fields (abstract, title, source, and subject heading). Entering text in three more lines lower down on the screen will cause a search in the full-text portion of the database, as well as in the citation information. For simple, one-term searches, particularly when a term is relatively new, the full-text approach probably will yield better results. For example, I did a search on *nanotechnology* and found 16 hits in the citation portion and a total of 21 hits when the full-text fields were included.

A number of ways are available to access the information in this database. Besides single subject or keywords, one can search multiword terms in proximity to each other, with the user controlling the distance between terms. The searcher can also use right-hand multicharacter or internal single-character truncation. The context-sensitive help screens are clear and easily followed.

INSTALLATION. Simple installation consists of typing the CD-ROM drive letter and the word *install.* My only objection to the process is that after installation finishes, one is informed that modifications have been made to the system files, and the computer must be rebooted to use the program. On principle, I do not think it is good programming practice to automatically modify the AUTOEXEC.BAT and/or CONFIG.SYS files without offering the user an option to do this manually. In this case, the only change is to increase the FILES= parameter in the CONFIG.SYS file, so no harm is done. However, some problems can be caused by install programs that take this approach.

OTHER FEATURES. After installation, a rather simpleminded security system allows the librarian access to administrative functions. Any library would be well advised to take the further step of adding a password to this process. Once logged on at an administrative level, staff can customize such things as maximum print size, prevent exit to DOS, lock the CD-ROM drive, and choose colors for the display. A nice feature of the product is that it provides statistics on system use, such as average queries per search, average hits per query, and number of queries performed.

SUPPORT AND DOCUMENTATION. Technical support personnel were knowledgable when I called about several problems encountered. All these problems, by the way, stemmed from inaccuracies in the otherwise well written manuals furnished with the program. According to EBSCO personnel, they are in the process of sending revised manuals to users.

CONCLUSION. All in all, this is an extremely well designed product that is easy to use and that provides coverage of the most popular magazine titles in high school and public libraries, as well as in some collections serving beginning college students. In these markets, *Magazine Article Summaries* provides serious competition for versions of CD-ROM periodical indexes from Information Access, Wilson-Line, and University Microfilms. —*Charles Anderson*, deputy librarian, King County Library System, Seattle, Washington.

The Encyclopedia of the British Press, 1422–1992. Ed. by Dennis Griffiths. St. Martin's, 1992. 694p. bibliog. illus. hardcover $79.95 (0-312-08633-4).

072'.09 Press—Great Britain—Encyclopedias ‖ Journalism—Great Britain—Encyclopedias ‖ Journalists—Great Britain—Biography [CIP] 92-29118

This authoritative compilation provides valuable information on British newspapers and press associations, as well as important journalists, editors, printers, and others in British journalism. Editor Griffiths, a former production director of Express Newspapers, has more than 40 years' experience working for newspapers. Contributors include not only newspaper professionals but archivists and librarians for such important institutions as St. Bride Printing Library and the British Newspaper Library.

The encyclopedia begins with a series of six essays, chronicling the history of the British press from the sixteenth and seventeenth centuries, the period "conventionally regarded as heralding the independent press." Other essays cover the eighteenth century, "a great age in the development of the British press" that saw "qualitative and quantitative growth and a diversification of type with the foundation of the first dailies, the first provincial papers and the first Sunday newspapers," and the period from 1861 to 1918, the so-called Golden Age of the British press.

The entries that follow the essays are arranged in alphabetical order. Entries for people cover a wide range of individuals, including newspaper giants and members of dynasties as well as obscure but interesting characters in the history of British journalism, such as Charles Westacott, who used his paper as a means for blackmail. Many of the entries contain citations to the works consulted in their preparation. The entries for the biographies and newspaper histories are followed by a chronology of the British press, circulation statistics for both national and regional newspapers, a list of women editors, and a list of Fleet Street editors. Short histories follow on such important newspaper organizations as the Associated Press, the Audit Bureau of Circulations, and the National Union of Journalists. The encyclopedia ends with a comprehensive bibliography arranged by subject.

The book's format is attractive and the information provided, interesting. Journalists, press historians, and librarians seeking information on the British press will find this encyclopedia a handy, useful, and easy-to-use addition to the literature.

The New York Public Library Book of Twentieth-Century American Quotations. Ed. by Stephen Donadio and others. Warner, 1992. 622p. indexes. hardcover $24.95 (0-446-51639-2).

081 Quotations, American [CIP] 91-50395

The latest entry in the New York Public Library Reference series is a collection of quotations notable for its sheer variety. Many different kinds of quotations are included, such as advertising, campaign, and political slogans, as well as state mottos, speeches, and sermons. This array of material is divided into 40 major topics, for example, *War and Peace, Nature,* and *Social Issues.* About half of these topics are further subdivided; for example, *Nature* is divided into *Evolution, Flora, Fauna, Weather,* etc.

Topics and subtopics are arranged alphabetically, and all are listed in the table of contents. Quotations appear in alphabetical order by personal name under most topic (and subtopic) headings. In addition to speakers' (or writers') names, printed sources are given, an important feature in any quotation dictionary. Considerable cross-referencing is used, necessary when the arrangement is thematic.

The work concludes with both subject and author indexes. They include an L or R with a page number, referring to the right or left side of the two-column pages. Another useful feature of the subject index is that it contains keyword listings in context. However, the subject index is broad and, for quotes that do not contain unique terms, users will need to read the appropriate section of the main body of the work to find the entries. For example, a quote from Marian Anderson, "As long as you keep a person down, some part of you has to be down there to hold him down, so it means you cannot soar as you otherwise might," is not indexed under any of its terms. The user could find it by reading the pages on "Discrimination and Racism," being directed there either from the headings list in the table of contents or by looking up *discrimination* or *racism* in the subject index.

With approximately 9,000 quotations from twentieth-century America, the coverage here is, at least proportionally, as good as that of *Bartlett's*, whose latest edition offers, more or less, the wisdom of the ages in 22,000 quotations. As for an accurate representation of this century, note that only approximately 16 percent of the people quoted in this new work are women. Several Englishmen, such as Leslie Stephen and Robert Burchfield, are also included here. Among the selections to be found are more than 20 entire documents. These include Dr. Martin Luther King, Jr.'s "I Have a Dream" speech, Alcoholics Anonymous' "12 Steps," and William Faulkner's Nobel Prize acceptance speech.

All in all, the many points of access offered by this quotation compendium make it a useful addition to the quotation shelf.

The New Quotable Woman. Rev. ed. Ed. by Elaine Partnow. Facts On File, 1992. 714p. indexes. hardcover $40 (0-8160-2134-1).
082'.082 Women—Quotations || Quotations, English [CIP] 91-25960

The Beacon Book of Quotations by Women. Comp. by Rosalie Maggio. Beacon, 1992. 336p. indexes. hardcover $25 (0-8070-6764-4)
082'.082 Quotations, English || Women—Quotations [CIP] 92-4697

The chief drawback of the flood of quotation books being published now is that many of them do not give printed sources for the words they quote. Here are two collections of quotations by women that help the librarian by giving sources.

Partnow's collection enables us to continue the "flight through women's history." It is an updated version of her *Quotable Woman, from Eve to 1799* (Facts On File, 1985) and *The Quotable Woman, 1800–1981* (Facts On File, 1982). More than one-third of the quotations from those volumes have been deleted; material on 150 contemporary women has been updated, 450 women have been added, and the book has been supplemented with about 2,000 new quotations.

More than 2,500 women are represented here by over 15,000 quotations in an arrangement similar to the earlier volumes. Women quoted are presented in chronological order according to the year of their birth, from Eve to Tracy Chapman, then alphabetically within each year. Each woman has been given a number that is used in the biographical and subject indexes. The biographical index briefly identifies each woman (e.g., "*Geyer, Georgia Anne* (1935–) Am. columnist, author, educator"). The subject index now includes approximately 4,000 classifications and subclassifications and abundant cross-references. Two new indexes have been added. In the occupation index, women are listed by career. The notes to this section include an outline of the categories within which occupations are divided. An index of nationality and ethnicity provides access by nation of birth. Women of color have, additionally, been arranged according to their race and/or ethnic background within the context of their nation of birth. The criteria used in selecting new material is much the same as stated in the preface to the first edition: women were chosen because of their reputation, quotability, and availability of their work.

The Beacon Book of Quotations by Women is arranged by 800 subjects, from *Absence* to *Writing*, and is indexed by personal name. *See also* references are provided for most subject headings. The more than 5,000 quotations are from 1,500 women ranging in time from Sappho to the present, but the emphasis is on twentieth-century writers. There is little overlap between this book and *The New Quotable Woman*. In her introduction, Maggio, author of *The Dictionary of Bias-Free Usage* [RBB O 15 91], gives some hints on adapting sexist quotations.

Two other recent collections, *The Last Word: A Treasury of Women's Quotations* by Carolyn Warner and *Write to the Heart: Quotes by Women Writers* by Amber Coverdale Sumrall [BKL Ag 92], are arranged by broad topics and do not give any sources for the quotations. There is surprisingly little overlap among the quotations selected for these four books.

The New Quotable Woman deserves a place on academic and public library shelves, even those that already hold its two predecessors. *The Beacon Book of Quotations by Women*, with its largely unique material, is an excellent companion volume and is also recommended for libraries.

PHILOSOPHY, PSYCHOLOGY, RELIGION

Dictionary of Mysticism and the Esoteric Traditions. Rev. ed. By Nevill Drury. ABC-Clio, 1992. 328p. bibliog. illus. hardcover $49.50 (0-87436-699-2); paper Avery Publishing $14.95 (1-85327-075-X).
133'.03 Occultism—Encyclopedias || Mysticism—Encyclopedias [OCLC] 92-23484

Drury is an internationally known authority on mysticism and the paranormal. He has written several books, including *Vision Quest* and *The Gods of Rebirth*. This volume is a revision of his 1985 *Dictionary of Mysticism and the Occult*. It has been thoroughly revised, and a bibliography and black-and-white illustrations have been added.

Nearly 3,000 entries appear here, ranging from one sentence to one-half page. Information is matter-of-fact and to the point. The book's scope is wide, including information on symbols, herbs, mythology, religious terms, movements, legends, astrology, and more. There is very little coverage of Christian mysticism, and what there is tends to be of people like Rasputin, rather than of important Christian mystics such as St. Teresa of Avila. The identification of people, particularly contemporary mystics, psychics, occultists, and researchers, is a strength of the book. Illustrations include historical drawings and contemporary paintings and photographs.

The one-page selected bibliography of 44 titles is a good starting point for people who wish to pursue further information. However, it does not include similar books such as Gale's *Encyclopedia of Occultism and Parapsychology* [RBB S 1 91], which is much larger and more expensive, or *Harper's Encyclopedia of Mystical and Paranormal Experiences* [RBB O 1 91], which is similar in size and price. The *Dictionary of Mysticism and the Esoteric Traditions* will be useful in reference departments of academic and public libraries that need additional sources on this topic. It will be particularly helpful for ready reference or telephone reference.

The Encyclopedia of Ghosts and Spirits. By Rosemary Ellen Guiley. Facts On File, 1992. 384p. bibliog. illus. index. hardcover $40 (0-8160-2140-6).
133.1'03 Ghosts || Spirits || Parapsychology [CIP] 91-37427

Guiley, author of *The Encyclopedia of Witches and Witchcraft*, has created an encyclopedia of disembodied spirits or ghosts. She covers a wide-ranging variety and number of psychical researchers, places, types of ghosts, festivals, mediums, and even spiritualists' unions. More specifically, expected entries are found here—*Houdini, Harry; Levitation; Banshee; Whisht Hounds;* and *Tower of London*—as well as such lesser-known topics as *Herne the Hunter; Institut Metapsychique International; Little Bastard, Curse of the;* and *Podmore, Frank*. The alphabetically arranged entries range from three pages to a couple sentences. Many include a "Further Reading" list, and cross-references are plentiful, such as "Halloween see All Hallows Eve." Seventy black-and-white illustrations enhance the work, which already is fascinating reading. The index will further aid information seekers.

Works similar to this one include *Dictionary of Ghost Lore* by Peter Haining (Prentice-Hall, 1984) and *Encyclopedia of Ghosts* by Daniel Cohen (Dorset Press, 1984, 1990), but as popular as this subject is, an additional source is always welcome. *The Encyclopedia of Ghosts and Spirits* is an informative book and a good read. If questions on paranormal phenomena, especially those with a an international flavor, are frequent, this title will prove useful in public libraries.

PHILOSOPHY, PSYCHOLOGY, RELIGION

Encyclopedia of Learning and Memory. Ed. by Larry R. Squire. Macmillan, 1992. 678p. bibliog. illus. index. hardcover $105 (0-02-897408-5).
153.1'03 Learning, Psychology of—Encyclopedias ‖ Memory—Encyclopedias ‖ Learning in animals—Encyclopedias ‖ Animal memory—Encyclopedias ‖ Neuropsychology—Encyclopedias [CIP] 92-15964

This single volume is a tremendous compendium of psychological and biological research on learning and memory. It is an authoritative and scholarly work. Editor Squire is a professor of psychiatry at the University of California at San Diego and is a well-known researcher in the area of amnesia. The other contributors are primarily academics as well.

Each of the 189 alphabetically arranged articles is signed and followed by a list of references. Entries vary in length from 500 to 2,000 words. Longer entries such as *Invertebrate Learning* and *Long-Term Potentiation* are subdivided into shorter articles. The types of analyses in the essays range from general treatments of topics like *Dementia* or *Drugs and Memory* to detailed discussions of specific processes such as *Protein Synthesis in Long-Term Memory in Vertebrates*. While the focus of the work is on human memory and learning, essential current research on animals is also covered. Included as well are biographies of individuals who made important contributions, such as Pavlov, William James, and Edward Thorndike.

The encyclopedia includes many illustrations, diagrams, and photographs that are especially useful in clarifying biological and anatomical information. The bibliographies vary widely in the number of references; some contributors cite more than 30 references, and others list only a few for similar-length articles. Most lists include current items, many from 1990 and a few from 1991. Cross-references appear as blind entries and within articles to related text. There is a detailed index that also contains *see* and *see also* references.

The emphasis is on experimental research rather than clinical or psychosocial considerations. There is, of course, a biography of Freud, and *Amnesia, Functional* does discuss memory disorders that are not biologically instigated. But a clinician will not find any information on the uses of reminiscence with the aged or extensive discussion of post-traumatic stress disorder, and the general reader will look in vain for references to *déjà vu* in the index. *Natural Settings, Memory in* mentions that only recently has there been systematic study of the operation of memory in everyday life.

The potential readership is identified as students, teachers, journalists, and members of the educated public. While some articles are informative and appropriate for a general reader, such as *Tip-of-the-Tongue Phenomenon* or *Alzheimer's Disease*, many of the entries assume a sophisticated readership. For the most part, the level of writing and subject matter seem to be most suitable for professionals or advanced students. This volume will be an essential source for academic reference collections, and large public libraries will also want this survey of current knowledge about the process of acquiring and storing information.

Encyclopedia of Ethics. 2v. Ed. by Lawrence C. Becker and Charlotte B. Becker. Garland, 1992. 1,462p. bibliog. index. hardcover $150 (0-8153-0403-X).
170'.3 Ethics—Encyclopedias [CIP] 91-4978

Addressed to scholars and students of philosophical ethics, this two-volume encyclopedia is actually quite broad in scope, encompassing the history and theory of ethics as well as the relation of ethics to other fields of study. The 435 signed articles by 267 international scholars focus primarily on topics (e.g., *Common Good, Humility, Social Contract*) and personalities (e.g. *Cicero, William of Ockham*), including even a few living ethicists such as John Rawls. Entries are found on practical applications of ethics such as *Legal Ethics* and *Nursing Ethics* and on ethics in non-Western traditions such as *Buddhist Ethics*. Ethical issues of current interest such as *Animals, Treatment of* and *Academic Ethics* are also treated.

The double-column articles range in length from 500 to 9,000 words. Readers may be confused by the sequence of the articles, since they follow a letter-by-letter alphabetical plan. Thus *Mo Tzu* appears after *Motives*.

Many of the articles are excellent and provide the reader with a balanced overview of the topic under consideration, including historical background and a summary of the current discussion. Quite helpful is a 13-part, multiauthor series of articles on the history of ethics from the pre-Socratics to today. However, as with any collection involving so many contributors, the reader will find articles uneven in quality. For example, while the helpful article *Virtue* traces the concept historically, beginning with Aristotle, the article *Conscience* largely focuses on Thomas Aquinas and does not examine the concept among the Greeks, nor does it discuss the impact of Freud's views on contemporary discussions of conscience. And the reader may puzzle at the curiously brief article on Martin Heidegger (less than one page) compared with nine pages on feminist ethics. Likewise, while most articles are balanced, an occasional one may strike the reader more as an apologia than what would be expected in an encyclopedia (e.g., *Homosexuality*).

Two helpful features are the brief but current bibliographies at the end of each article and an index of all authors mentioned in the 435 bibliographies. A fairly comprehensive index to the articles (which is alphabetized word by word, not letter by letter like the text) is also included.

The four-volume *Encyclopedia of Bioethics* (Macmillan, 1984) covers that aspect of ethics in greater depth than can the set under review. Academic libraries and medium-size to large public libraries should purchase the *Encyclopedia of Ethics*. It will prove to be useful to scholars and university students but is also accessible to the general reader.

Great Thinkers of the Western World: The Major Ideas and Classic Works of More than 100 Outstanding Western Philosophers, Physical and Social Scientists, Psychologists, Religious Writers, and Theologians. Ed. by Ian P. McGreal. HarperCollins, 1992. 572p. bibliog. hardcover $40 (0-06-270026-X).
190 Philosophy ‖ Theology ‖ Science [CIP] 91-38362

This guide to 116 selected authors in the fields of the social and physical sciences, psychology, religion, and philosophy spans the ancient Greeks to the first half of the twentieth century. These people are well known, and most can be easily located in other sources. The guide is arranged chronologically by the birthdate of the writer. Each entry contains birth and death dates, a list of the author's major ideas, an essay of three to five pages, and a short annotated list of secondary sources.

The format of *Great Thinkers* is identical to the earlier *Masterpieces of World Philosophy* [Ja 15 91]. There is substantial overlap between the two sources in the field of philosophy. Early and modern philosophers such as Plato, Parmenides, Zeno of Elea, Marcus Aurelius, Descartes, and Henri Bergson are duplicated in both volumes. Despite these duplications, *Great Thinkers* may prove a useful companion volume to *Masterpieces* because the former includes biographical sketches on harder-to-find physical scientists such as Gregor Johann Mendel, James Clerk Maxwell, Dimitri Ivanovich Mendeleev, Max Planck, and Charles Sanders Pierce. A bibliography of works by the thinkers and an index of their names conclude the volume.

Its readable essays that are accessible to the layperson make *Great Thinkers of the Western World* suitable for public and small college libraries that don't own the Magill sets like *World Philosophy*, on which it is modeled.

Religious Information Sources: A Worldwide Guide. By J. Gordon Melton and Michael A. Köszegi. Garland, 1992. 569p. indexes. hardcover $75 (0-8153-0859-0).
016.2 Religion—Bibliography ‖ Religion—Information services [CIP] 91-47697

Attempting "to provide in one volume broad coverage of the major sources of information in religion," this book is intended to serve a broad spectrum of users ranging from scholars "to anyone seeking information about religion." While coverage is worldwide, North America receives the major emphasis, and most materials are in English. Melton, director of the Institute for the Study of American Religion, is the compiler of numerous reference works on American religion, most notably *The Encyclopedia of American Religions* (3d ed., 1989).

The guide is organized into four main sections, each of which includes numerous subdivisions, and proceeds from general and theoretical considerations on religion through the religions of the world (grouped according to geographic areas) to a section devoted to Christianity. This latter section accounts for more than half the 2,527 entries in the guide, reflecting the fact that "the greatest number of sources in religious studies relate primarily to Christianity." The final section covers the often-neglected areas of esoteric, New Age, and occult religion.

Sources include both print and microform and electronic material. Reference books in each section or subdivision are listed under such headings as "Encyclopedias and Dictionaries," "Biographical Materials," "Directories," and "Atlases." A particularly valuable feature of the guide is the inclusion of lists of professional associations, research and resource centers, and archival collections. For example, in the subsection "Women and Religion" are listed the American Women's Clergy Association, the Women's Studies in Religion Program at Harvard, and *Women Religious History Sources: A Guide to Repositories in the United States*.

Most entries are not annotated, leaving the user to infer from the title and length of the work some idea of its scope and content. The list of 23 Bible atlases omits *Harper's Atlas of the Bible* (1987), generally regarded as the outstanding recent work in this category.

Title, author, subject, and organizations indexes facilitate access to the guide. Errors were noted in three of the four indexes. Ferm's *Encyclopedia of Religion* is listed twice in the title index, separated by four intervening entries. The author index includes a listing for Thomas P. Slavens, but the entry cited, *The Shelf List of the Union Theological Seminary Library*, does not list him as an author. The author index gives 2518 as the entry number for Melton's *Magic, Witchcraft, and Paganism in America*, whereas the correct number is 2519. The organizations index includes three references to the Institute for the Study of American Religion, the first of which is erroneous. The final page of the table of contents is blank. Examination of the text shows that the missing page included 20 main or subheadings.

While *Religious Information Sources* suffers from a degree of careless editing, its coverage of a wide variety of subjects relating to religion will make it a useful addition to academic and large public library collections.

Dictionary of Cults, Sects, Religions and the Occult. By George A. Mather and Larry A. Nichols. Zondervan, 1993. 384p. bibliog. illus. hardcover (0-310-53100-4).
200'.3 Religions—Dictionaries || Cults—Dictionaries || Sects—Dictionaries || Occultism—Dictionaries [CIP] 92-36212

Two Christian ministers compiled this volume of information about selected cults and religions. Their purpose was "to account for a small portion of the story of religions . . . particularly in twentieth-century America." Recognizing that they could not be all-inclusive, the authors write about the best-known world religions as well as sects and cults chosen because they are the "most interesting, popular, and influential" in the U.S. and because information is available about them. Comparisons with Christian principles or practices are found in many articles, making this most useful to people already well versed in more traditional theology.

Arrangement is strictly alphabetical, with names of groups (*Sikhism, Zoroastrianism*) interfiled with founders (*Ali, Mirza Husayn; King, George*), sacred writings (*Koran, Bhagavad Gita*), practices (*hajj, exorcism*), as well as historical periods, symbols, and clothing. Many entries are merely a sentence or two for identification and refer the user to longer articles where history, beliefs, terms, and individuals are more fully explained. As expected, the traditional religions have the most text, with *Christianity* the longest article at 14 pages, *Judaism* at 11 pages, and *Islam* at 7 pages. *Satanism* (9 pages) and *Jehovah's Witnesses* and *Mormonism* (13 pages each) are the only other lengthy articles. Sources are quoted in many articles, often from the late 1980s and some as recent as 1992. A bibliography at the end of the book is topically arranged and includes titles that have not been footnoted in the text. Consider, for example, the 1½ pages of citations on "Gay Theology" when there is not a single dictionary entry related to the topic.

Coverage, while understandably limited, just is not comprehensive enough. Included, of course, are *Eckankar, The Forum* (EST), *People's Temple*, and *Church of Armageddon* (*Love Family*). Not found here are Quakers, dervish, Jainism, Confucianism, Shakers, Jews for Jesus, or Mennonites. Lots of editing errors and poor cross-references make this work far less useful than it could have been. Someone looking for Black Muslims or the Nation of Islam will not find the information because no cross-references are included to *World Community of Ali Islam in the West*, which discusses these groups. There is no listing for Pentecostal or Assemblies of God, although both are covered under *Oneness Pentecostalism*. There are many blind cross-references. When referred to *Reformation*, it just says "see *Christianity*." A note under *Islam* says that the "similar motifs between Shi'ites and the RCJCLDS [Reorganized Church of Jesus Christ of Latter-Day Saints] are remarkable." However, no similarities are described. Spelling errors are also noticeable, for example, "B'nai Berith," "supremicist," "Hail Selassie."

The foreword briefly discusses the challenges posed by religious pluralism in today's society. It states that the Christian community must acquire basic information about various "unconventional religious organizations" and that the comparative analyses to "traditional Christian teachings" are provided in order to "equip Christian believers with the material they will need in the continuing struggle." This frame of reference is evidenced in many ways in the text of the book. For example, an excerpt from a Black Mass, in the entry *satanism*, includes this warning: "It should be noted that what follows is highly offensive and blasphemous. Sensitive readers beware."

This dictionary should be considered only by specialized, comprehensive collections. Other titles provide better reference information. The third edition of J. Gordon Melton's *Encyclopedia of American Religions* [RBB S 1 89] covers far more cults, sects, and major religious traditions than the work under review. Also available are good sources covering specific aspects, such as *Dictionary of Mysticism and the Esoteric Tradition* [RBB D 15 92], *New Age Encyclopedia* [RBB S 15 90], and the *Encyclopedia of Occultism and Parapsychology* [RBB S 1 91].

The Anchor Bible Dictionary. 6v. Ed. by David Noel Freedman and others. Doubleday, 1992. bibliog. illus. maps. hardcover $360 (0-385-19351-3).
220.3 Bible—Dictionaries [CIP] 91-8385

The Anchor Bible Dictionary (ABD) represents the most comprehensive collection of scholarly articles on biblical studies since *The Interpreter's Dictionary of the Bible* (IDB) (1962; supplementary volume, 1976) and will no doubt be the foremost reference work in its field for many years to come. (See RBB [D 1 89] for a review of IDB and other reference works on the Bible.) Editor-in-chief Freedman has authored numerous religious works, serves as general editor of the ongoing Anchor Bible Commentary series, and was a consultant on IDB. Freedman and his coeditors gathered some of the leading biblical scholars in the world to contribute to this work. The six-volume set boasts nearly 1,000 contributors of varying religious and scholastic backgrounds. The 6,200 entries include every proper name mentioned in the Bible, whether person or place; all versions of the Bible; methodologies of biblical scholarship; and "hundreds of entries on various historical and archaeological subjects." The primary focus of ABD is on topics before the fourth century A.D.

The set opens with the list of contributors and an introduction, followed by an eight-page user's guide that clearly spells out the scope of the work and the components of an entry. The editors make clear that this work is aimed at "the educated reader" and that "it assumes that the reader has a general understanding of and interest in modern biblical scholarship." Following this is a 27-page listing of abbreviations, which is reproduced at the front of each volume in the set.

Each entry in this alphabetically arranged work includes a heading; a qualifying tag (e.g., "person," "place," or a map reference number); a transliteration providing the original biblical form of the word with an indication of whether it is Aramaic, Greek, Hebrew, or Latin; any variations on the spelling of the heading; and any derivatives (e.g., "Aaronites" after the heading *Aaron*). The text of entries varies in length, from a single line for letters of the alphabet (*Beta* is simply defined as "the second letter of the Greek alphabet") to just under 75 pages for the entry *Languages*. All but single-line entries are signed.

Articles have up-to-date bibliographies, ranging from a few citations to hundreds. The bibliographies feature the seminal works in the field and greatly enhance the reference value of this set. Many longer entries are subdivided, with each section written by a different scholar and with a separate bibliography. For example, the

PHILOSOPHY, PSYCHOLOGY, RELIGION

47-page entry *Righteousness* is subdivided into four articles: "Old Testament," "Early Judaism," "Greco-Roman World," and "New Testament." Most of the longer entries feature an outline at the beginning that lists the major topics to be covered. Such entries have boldface-type subdivisions throughout the article, making it relatively easy for the reader to scan to an area of interest. It would greatly aid the reader, however, if page numbers were given in the beginning outline.

The ABD is clearly of value to institutions with an interest in religious studies, but it has appeal for a much wider audience as well. Because of its broad scope, historians and those with an interest in classical studies will find it invaluable. The article *Mesopotamia, History of*, for example, is 63 pages, with five separate articles. Of course, those interested in biblical scholarship will not be disappointed. Such entries as *Computers and Biblical Studies*, *Poststructural Analysis*, or *Statistical Research on the Bible* provide excellent overviews of recent techniques.

It is in the area of archeology that ABD is particularly strong, as it takes advantage of the plethora of recent scholarship and excavations in this field. The entry *Jericho*, for example, was just over four pages in length in IBD but is 18 pages here, four of which are devoted to drawings of plans with another two pages featuring a chronological chart. *David, City of* was barely one page in IDB but is more than 16 pages here, boasting a bibliography of more than 100 entries—with more than 30 citations dated from the 1980s. The set also reflects recent scholarship regarding the Dead Sea Scroll manuscripts and the Nag Hammadi codices.

The paucity of illustrations may be viewed as a possible area of weakness in ABD, a fact that the editors acknowledge in the user's guide, stating that considerations of space and costs resulted in providing only those illustrations "essential to the comprehension of our articles." All illustrations are black and white, with the majority appearing within the archeological articles. Presently, an index to the set is lacking; it is scheduled to be published in the summer of 1993. Cross-references within articles are noted in small capital letters. Nevertheless, an index will certainly be a welcome addition, as the work is arranged primarily by broad topic rather than specific entry. Virtually every entry for an animal, for example, has a *see* reference to the 57-page article *Zoology*, with no indication of on what page within that article the given animal appears.

ABD should be considered for purchase by every public and academic library, regardless of size. It is the finest collection of articles available in one place on a topic of wide appeal. Just as appealing is its price; at $360 for six volumes, this work constitutes a real bargain. The introduction states that "every generation needs its own Dictionary of the Bible." The editors have admirably fulfilled this task.

Religious Radio and Television in the United States, 1921–1991: The Programs and Personalities. By Hal Erickson. McFarland, 1992. 228p. bibliog. index. hardcover $39.95 (0-89950-658-5).
261.5'2 Radio in religion—U.S.—Dictionaries ∥ Television in religion—U.S.—Dictionaries [CIP] 92-50304

"Religious broadcasting, now 70 years in existence, has grown from being merely an appendage of commercial broadcasting to a major, multimillion-dollar industry in its own right." This new encyclopedic listing of programs and personalities is the result of the author's efforts to trace the history of inspirational broadcasting. He compiled the work by viewing videotapes, listening to radio broadcasts, and conducting research in religious archives. The resulting compendium of information does not purport to be comprehensive. Rather, the scope is confined to those stars and programs in the U.S. that have had national influence.

The book's introduction is an informative history of religious broadcasting, which is further developed in the entries. The 400 numbered profiles are arranged alphabetically with names of persons and programs interfiled. Entries range in length from one sentence to several pages; more detailed information is provided for those personalities and broadcasts that have had the greatest influence. Thus, the types of data provided vary widely; for example, sometimes birth dates for individuals are included, other times not. A description may be as general as the one sentence for "Know the Truth": "a well-circulated 15-minute filmed television program of the late 1950s, designed to explain Catholicism to non-Catholics."

The entries aim for objectivity, but the author does relate interesting anecdotes and points out quirks, foibles, and stereotypical aspects of programs and personalities. For instance, the entry for "Light of the World" begins: "In 1940, most of the radio community thought that NBC and General Mills were a little gone in the head to attempt a daily program serializing the stories of the Old Testament, but no one was laughing and everyone was backslapping when they heard the results." No citations to sources are provided within the entries, but the work does conclude with a bibliography.

Religious Radio and Television in the United States, 1921–1991 is a unique and entertaining work that will be welcome in libraries serving patrons with religious or communications interests.

Encyclopedia of Heresies and Heretics. By Chas S. Clifton. ABC-Clio, 1992. 160p. bibliog. illus. index. hardcover $50 (0-87436-600-3).
273'.03 Heresies, Christian—Encyclopedias [OCLC] 92-29996

A work listing "heretics, organized heresies, and schools of thought or key ideas that were judged heretical," the *Encyclopedia of Heresies and Heretics* provides an alphabetically arranged overview of the key heretical movements and individuals from roughly the time of Jesus' crucifixion to the sixteenth century. Not counting cross-references, the work features 127 entries ranging from *Abelard, Peter* to *Wycliffe, John*. Entries vary in length from just over 50 words (*Concorezanes*) to close to 5,000 words (*Albigenses, Albigensians; Gnostics;* and *Witchcraft*). A few illustrations—primarily reproductions of woodcuts or other artwork—are scattered throughout the volume; a 10-page subject index completes the work.

Clifton, a free-lance writer who has been a contributing editor to the journal *Gnosis* and editor of a recently released volume on witchcraft entitled *The Modern Craft Movement* (1992), has written a work clearly intended for the general reader and not the scholar. His well-written introduction provides a survey of the various heretical movements throughout the history of the Christian church up to the time of Luther, at which point "the line between heresy and reform grows faint." (It is odd, however, that an entry is not devoted to Luther himself.) The entries are written in a manner that assumes virtually no knowledge of the subject matter. For example, in the *Tanchelm* entry, the author parenthetically defines the Holy Roman Empire as "chiefly a German empire" and Flanders as "an area chiefly within present-day Belgium." The use of bibliographies at the end of entries is also omitted "in order to keep the text uncluttered and more accessible to the casual or nonspecialized reader." Unfortunately, this makes the work of limited value to those trying to find additional information on a given subject. Such users must instead scan through the 58 items of the unannotated bibliography in the back of the volume.

Most entries in the book under review may be found in such larger works as the *New Catholic Encyclopedia* or the *Encyclopedia of Religion*, both of which also feature more extensive bibliographies. The specificity of subject matter in the *Encyclopedia of Heresies and Heretics* duplicates information already available in many libraries, and the lack of bibliographies limits the work's usefulness as a first-choice source. Nevertheless, it is a unique volume that high school, public, and academic libraries that cater to clients interested in church history may wish to consider as a secondary source of information.

Contemporary Religions: A World Guide. By Ian Harris and others. Longman; dist. by Gale, 1992. 512p. index. hardcover $175 (0-582-08695-7).
291'.03 Religions—Encyclopedias [BKL]

Four editors and 52 other contributors—primarily U.K.-based scholars of religious studies—present a work that gives readers an idea of the multitude of religious groups and movements in the world today. Strictly historical topics are avoided, which means such movements as Jim Jones' People's Temple are not included. The work is arranged in three parts. Part 1, "Major Religious Traditions," offers seven lengthy essays designed to "allow the reader to contextualize particular group entries within the framework of their religious tradition." The essays cover such topics as "Contemporary Judaism," "Hinduism," and "New Religious Movements." Part 3, "Country-by-Country Summary," features essays ranging from 44 words (*Monaco*) to more than 1,500 (*Russia and Successor States to the Soviet Union*). These articles discuss the state of religion in 169 countries and their territories. The work concludes with a 13-page glossary and an index of personal names.

The largest portion of the book is part 2, "Religious Groups and Movements," which features approximately 900 articles on various topics dealing with contemporary religion. The entries include specific churches (*Society of Friends [Quakers]*), movements (*Jihad Organization*), organizations (*Soka Gakkai*), and survey-type articles (*Native American Religions*). The length of these entries varies greatly. Some are borderline *see* references offering brief identifications (e.g., "*Nihangs*. A warrior subgroup of Khalsa Sikhs"); others range from 100 to more than 2,000 words (*Orthodox Church [Byzantine tradition]*). A sampling of articles found that approximately 35 percent fall into what could be called the Judeo-Christian tradition, and just under 30 percent do not fit neatly into any large, worldwide religious tradition. The latter include such entries as *Dadu Panthis* and *Pan-Indianism*.

The preface is correct in stating that this work represents "an unprecedented attempt at producing a contemporary world guide" on religious groups. Yet despite the abundance of material within *Contemporary Religions*, the work has several flaws—primarily editorial. Why, for example, does the entry on the Orthodox Church command a length almost twice that of most other entries? Why is the *Zen* entry some 500 words while an article on a specific Roman Catholic order, *Benedictines*, is more than 800? There are two entries titled *Sikhism* (*Sikh Panth*)—one after the other.

These quibbles are minor, however, compared with the number of blind, misleading, circuitous, or nonexistent cross-references. Given that cross-references are indicated by boldface type in an entry, the Board discovered numerous mistakes. *Baptists*, for example, mentions in boldface *American Baptist Churches*, but there is no such entry. The *United States* article in part 3 uses boldface type for the names of several Jewish organizations that, in turn, refer to other articles. For example, *United Synagogue of America* appears in boldface in the essay; when turning to that entry in part 2 one merely finds a *see* reference to *Conservative Judaism*.

The glossary presents its own set of problems. Simply called a "glossary of religious terms" in the preface, it features such "terms" as *Martin Buber* (under the letter M) and *John Paul II*. No distinction is made in the book as to whether a term in boldface appears in part 2 or in the glossary. For instance, *Theravada Buddhism* in part 2 mentions *Mahayana* in boldface; the latter appears in the glossary rather than in part 2. Yet, *Brazil* in part 3 mentions liberation theology—a term in the glossary—without placing it in boldface type. Some entries in the glossary, such as *Ghehenna*, which is defined simply as "the place of after-life punishment," fail to indicate from which religious tradition the term originates.

Perhaps the most frustrating aspect of this work is the complete lack of bibliographies anywhere. Many of the religions will be unfamiliar to most readers, and anyone wishing to do further research will be disappointed.

Works similar to the title under review, such as *Dictionary of Comparative Religions* (Scribner, 1970) or *Abingdon Dictionary of Living Religions* (Abingdon, 1981), are becoming dated and do not cover as many groups as the present volume. The *Encyclopedia of World Faiths* [RBB Ag 88] has more of a broad-entry approach. Libraries interested solely in American religions are better off with Melton's *Encyclopedia of American Religions* [RBB S 1 89], and a work written for general readers that provides international coverage of 34 religions and movements is available in the inexpensive volume *The Spiritual Seeker's Guide* [RBB N 1 92]. Even though *Contemporary Religions* represents a considerable effort at listing many religions around the world, the Board cannot recommend it because of its numerous editorial flaws.

The Spiritual Seeker's Guide: The Complete Source for Religions and Spiritual Groups of the World. By Steven S. Sadler. Allwon Publishing, 3000 Redhill Ave., Costa Mesa, CA 92626, 1992. 391p. bibliog. illus. index. paper $12.95 (1-880741-28-8).
291 Religions ‖ Religions—Directories [CIP] 91-77865

The Spiritual Seeker's Guide covers 34 religions and movements. The introduction explains the author's purpose: to "provide an unbiased synopsis of the world's spiritual teachings." He chose to include "those teachings which are currently active and accessible, and has omitted other groups which are relatively small, isolated, or did not want to be listed." He participated as fully as he was allowed in each of the religions and submitted the chapter to the group for its approval before publication. A disclaimer in the introduction states that many of the organizations included are considered cults by more mainline religious groups.

Each entry summarizes the basic tenets of a religion or movement in two to four pages, defining important words in the text. The entries end with a short bibliography of primary source material that gives only authors and titles and a list of addresses for further information. The book is divided into five main sections: "Eastern Religions" (Hinduism, Buddhism, Jainism, and others); "Western Religions" (Judaism, Islam, and Christianity, including Jehovah's Witnesses and the Unification Church); "Spiritual Paths" (druidism, wiccan, cabalism, freemasonry, and others); "Metaphysical Teachings" (Baha'i, Alcoholics Anonymous, crystals, channeling, etc.); and "Masters and Movements" (swamis, babas, maharishis, gurus, and yogis). A final chapter, "Where to Go from Here," gives some suggestions on developing one's spiritual life. A "Hindu Supplement" gives further information on that religion. A detailed index concludes the book, and there is an insert of black-and-white photographs of prominent religious leaders.

A few editorial inconsistencies were found. Most notable is the lack of distinction in the section on Christianity between apostle and disciple (Paul was not a disciple, nor is Mary Magdalene considered a disciple in most Christian teachings) in contrast to meticulous definitions in other entries. Also disturbing is a line in the section on sacred substances: "wine is imbibed in the Holy Eucharist to commune with the Lord Jesus in a Holy Sacrament."

The inclusion of Alcoholics Anonymous as a spiritual path is applauded, as that is the primary tool of recovery in 12-step programs. The 12 steps should have been explained before the 12 traditions, though, as they are what the program is based on, nor is the spiritual aspect of the program emphasized as it should be in a work of this nature.

On the whole, this is an impressively informative and objective work. For the information it provides on less well known religions, it will be useful in school libraries that study religions, and public libraries will find it helpful for ready-reference questions.

Brewer's Book of Myth and Legend. Ed. by J. C. Cooper. Cassell; dist. by Sterling, 1992. 310p. hardcover $21.95 (0-304-34084-7).
291.1'3 Mythology—Dictionaries ‖ Legends—Dictionaries [OCLC] 92-12599

According to its editor, who has published other works on symbolism and folk literature, this compilation seeks to incorporate the relevant entries from *Brewer's Dictionary of Phrase and Fable* with new material treating myths and legends of Eastern, Far Eastern, African, and other cultures that Brewer neglected. Its more than 4,000 alphabetically arranged entries focus on mythological places and beings, animals and plants associated with myths and legends, and common mythological themes. In addition, it devotes a smattering of articles to fictional characters (e.g., *Pinocchio*, *Uncle Remus*) and to twentieth-century phenomena (e.g., *Bermuda Triangle*, *Loch Ness monster*).

Although most entries are approximately one paragraph in length, some extend to several columns. Pronunciation is indicated when appropriate. Cross-references are numerous, but, unfortunately, they are not provided consistently. For example, only two of the 20 names of swords in the entry *sword* actually appear with a cross-reference in their appropriate alphabetical sequence.

A comparison of the entries on a 45-page sample of this work with the latest edition of *Brewer's Dictionary of Phrase and Fable* [RBB Mr 1 90] revealed that only five entries (including *Fortune Islands*, *kingfisher*, and *woodpecker*) were actually new. All of the other entries were extracted verbatim from the parent work except for 17 that had been augmented with new material. In general, the entries most frequently expanded were those dealing with animals in myth and legend (e.g., *cock*, *frog*, *lamb*, *owl*, *whale*).

For many libraries that own a recent edition of *Brewer's Dictionary of Phrase and Fable* and a good, general mythological dictionary, such as *The Facts On File Encyclopedia of World Mythology and Legend* [RBB F 15

PHILOSOPHY, PSYCHOLOGY, RELIGION

89], the small amount of additional information in this work will not be sufficient to justify its purchase.

Greek and Roman Mythology A to Z: A Young Reader's Companion. By Kathleen N. Daly. Facts On File, 1992. 132p. bibliog. illus. index. hardcover $19.95 (0-8160-2151-1).
292.1'3 Mythology, Classical—Encyclopedias, Juvenile [CIP] 91-43037

From the author of *Norse Mythology* A *to* Z [RBB S 1 91] comes this new work focusing on Greek and Roman myths. Many of the 400 alphabetically arranged entries are for characters (*Electra, Mars*) but also include places (*Athens, Troy*), important literary and scholarly works (*The Aeneid, The Golden Bough*), and mythical terminology (*Bacchanalia, Underworld*). Some entries are brief, providing one or two sentences of description (*Centaurus, Chione*), but most entries are one or two paragraphs in length. Some entries provide important lists, for example, *Olympian Gods* shows the Greek and Roman names, along with the attributes of the deities. For major characters, two or more pages usually are subdivided to discuss the various myths or stories. For instance, four pages are devoted to *Heracles* (Hercules) with subheadings for his childhood, as a young hero, the 12 labors, his exploits, the centaur, and his death.

More than 40 illustrations complement the text; the work includes an essay introducing the subject, a selected bibliography, and an index. Abundant cross-references to related entries are shown by small-capital letters. The book generally includes entries for the names of both the Greek and Roman god or goddess, indexing both, and the entries provide cross-references. Oddly, this is not the case for Ulysses; he is named in the *Odysseus* entry but does not appear in the index or in the main alphabetic sequence.

Greek and Roman Mythology A *to* Z is an effective basic reference source, providing an introduction to classical mythology. It is recommended for purchase by school and public libraries serving students in the middle grades and up.

The Blackwell Dictionary of Judaica. By Dan Cohn=Sherbok. Blackwell, 1992. 597p. hardcover $74.95 (0-631-16615-7); paper $24.95 (0-631-18728-6).
296'.03 Judaism—Dictionaries || Jews—History—Dictionaries || Jews—Biography—Dictionaries [OCLC] 91-38052

More than 7,000 entries in this dictionary provide brief information about Jewish history, civilization, and religion. The intent of the author, a teacher of Jewish studies in England, was to provide a single-volume dictionary for students and general readers that "could serve as first point of entry into the world of Judaica." The entries are one paragraph in length and cover the Judaic aspects of people, organizations, places, and concepts. Entries for Yiddish, Hebrew, and Aramaic terms are spelled out as Sephardic transliterations. Approximately 50 percent of the entries are for people and include birth and death dates and highlights of their lives. Entries for places describe their Jewish population, Jewish history, or significance in modern Jewish life. All the dictionary's entry words begin with a capital letter, making it difficult to differentiate between proper names and other types of words.

The volume begins with a two-page chronological table detailing the history of the Jews from 1900 B.C. through 1948 (the founding of the State of Israel) and maps of the ancient Near East and ancient Israel. This historical focus dominates the dictionary in a variety of ways. For the most part, detailed information in the entries is no more recent than the 1940s. For instance, although the dictionary states that both New York City and Tel Aviv are now major centers of Jewish life, the Jewish population of New York City is given for 1940, and the last historical fact for Tel Aviv is 1949. Furthermore, important post-1948 developments are often missing. For example, Jerusalem's history is detailed up through the second destruction of the temple in the first century; Golan Heights and the West Bank are not mentioned. Nor does the work include the intifada or Gorbachev. The definition for Nazism does not discuss the current Nazi parties in the U.S., and the definition for Zionism covers its history only through 1948.

Although the information provided in *The Blackwell Dictionary of Judaica* is accurate, it is dated. Had Cohn-Sherbok included information from more recent history, this work could have been a valuable resource. Public and academic libraries are better served by other standard reference sources, such as *The New Standard Jewish Encyclopedia* (7th ed. [RBB Ja 1 93]), *Encyclopedia Judaica* (1972), and *The Encyclopedia of Judaism* [RBB Mr 1 90].

Islam in North America: A Sourcebook. Ed. by Michael A. Köszegi and J. Gordon Melton. Garland, 1992. 414p. index. hardcover $59 (0-8153-0918-X).
297.0973 Islam—North America—Handbooks, manuals, etc. || Islam—U.S.—Handbooks, manuals, etc. [CIP] 92-17794

This sourcebook is the eighth volume in Garland's Religious Information Systems series, under the general editorship of Melton of the Institute for the Study of American Religion. Earlier volumes in the series have included *Religious Information Sources* [RBB D 1 92] and the *Encyclopedic Handbook of Cults in America* [RBB D 15 86]. This new title will be beneficial for research in an emerging subfield of Islamic studies—American Islam— by providing an interesting mix of articles, bibliographies, and directories on all aspects of the topic. The information for this source was culled from the holdings of the American Religions Collection of the University of California Library, which has one of the largest collections of materials on American Islam in the U.S.

The sourcebook begins with an informative preface and introduction and a bibliography of the major reference sources on Islam. The bulk of the work consists of eight chapters. "Islam in North America: The First Wave" includes three essays and a bibliography that cover the colonial period through the nineteenth century. "Islam in North America: The Second Wave" contains four articles and a bibliography devoted to Muslims who migrated from the Middle East to the U.S. during the twentieth century up to 1970. This same pattern of articles and bibliographies continues through the next four chapters, which focus on Islamic sectarian movements, Afro-American Islam, the Sufis, and the encounter of Islam with Christianity.

The articles included in these chapters are a mix of original essays written for the volume, including reports of research as in "A Survey of Arab-Muslims in the United States and Canada"; reprints of rare historical documents as exhibited by Muhammad Alexander Russell Webb's 1893 address, "The Spirit of Islam"; and reprints of recent significant articles, some in full and some excerpted, such as Lawrence H. Mamiya's 1982 "From Black Muslim to Bilalian: The Evolution of a Movement." The bibliographies list important sources drawn from a variety of disciplines, including historical, religious, anthropological, and sociological studies. Annotations are used infrequently. Collectively, a total of 1,294 citations are included for books, pamphlets, periodical titles, dissertations, and journal articles. A directory of Islamic organizations and centers in North America and a list of nonprint Islamic sources comprise the final two chapters of the work.

The book concludes with an index that lists names of authors and titles of periodicals that appear in the bibliographies. Disappointingly, no indexing is included for the material in the articles or the directory listings. This lack creates frustration and problems for the user. For instance, the article by Mamiya listed above includes substantial information on Louis Farrakhan, but the only items shown in the index for Farrakhan are references to four works he authored. The Albanian American Islamic Society is not included in the index, and its address can be located only by going to the directory chapter, then to the subsection listing mosques, which is organized by state, and then to the Wisconsin listings.

Despite its inadequate indexing, *Islam in North America* is a timely guide that will assist researchers engaged in Islamic studies and members of the public who seek information on Islam in North America. Because of its unique subject matter, this work is recommended for purchase by research and academic libraries building Muslim collections and public libraries serving American Muslim communities.

Islam and Islamic Groups: A Worldwide Reference Guide. Ed. by Farzana Shaikh. Longman; dist. by Gale, 1992. 316p. bibliog. index. hardcover $155 (0-582-09146-2).
297.65 Islam and state || World politics—1989- || Islam [OCLC]

The introduction states that this work is the "first comprehensive worldwide survey of the current status of Islamic political groups."

It is, indeed, a major reference tool that offers a country-by-country survey—from Afghanistan to Yugoslavia—of political activity by Muslim communities. The need for such a work is shown in the current interest in Islamic fundamentalism (or revivalism), the global spread of Islamic militancy, and the adherence to Islam as a political ideology by one-fifth of the world's population.

The editor and 10 additional contributors are British academics, researchers, or regional editors of *Keesing's Record of World Events*. In compiling this volume, they used a variety of sources: international press reports, investigations by human rights organizations, proscribed publications of opposition groups, information supplied by international Muslim bodies, and traditional academic research. Because information on radical political groups is difficult to verify, the editor alerts the reader that observations about semiclandestine groups must be regarded as tentative, rather than authoritative. The text is careful in its use of language when discussing militant organizations and events, such as "reports indicated possible links." Nonpolitical Muslim missionary groups are also included.

The work is arranged alphabetically by country name, with profiles varying in length from one page (Brazil, Nepal) to six or more (Indonesia, Pakistan). Each country entry begins with an objectively written survey, focusing on the Islamic presence in the particular land during the twentieth century. The entries also note the distribution of Muslims along sectarian and ethnic lines, salient Islamic issues, and involvement of major Islamic organizations. Groups that are listed separately following the narrative are noted in bold. Information is current; for example, a May 8, 1992, law in Afghanistan. Following the survey is a list of major Islamic organizations in the country. Each of these entries usually includes the date of founding, background (e.g., assistance from the CIA, the role of Saudi Arabia), leadership, membership, aims, publications, and affiliated organizations. The information is often brief but ranges up to an extended paragraph, such as for Hamas in Israel.

The book also contains information on international organizations, although not for the League of Arab States or Arab League. A two-page glossary, a bibliography of 10 titles, and an accurate index conclude the book. Information on the Muslim Brotherhood (or Brethren) in Egypt and the World Muslim League is consistent with *The Cambridge Encyclopedia of the Middle East and North America* (1988). While the work under review is unique in its international coverage, more North American organizations are listed in *Islam in North America: A Sourcebook* [RBB Ap 15 93]. *Islam and Islamic Groups* will be of major value for academic, large public, and special libraries.

The Gods and Symbols of Ancient Mexico and the Maya: An Illustrated Dictionary of Mesoamerican Religion. By Mary Miller and Karl Taube. Thames and Hudson; dist. by Norton, 1993. 216p. bibliog. illus. index. hardcover $34.95 (0-500-05068-6).

299.792 Indians of Mexico—Religion and mythology—Dictionaries ‖ Mayas—Religion and mythology—Dictionaries [BKL] 92-80338

This new dictionary is a foray into a world as fascinating as ancient Egypt, but not nearly as well known. One reason for this lack of popularity might be the difficulty encountered when trying to read the names of dieties and places, with consonants and letter patterns that often are strange to native English speakers. The reader's guide at the front of this book gives a short explanation of pronunciation. Since many of the words are very complicated, it is easy to stumble. Frequently, books about Mesoamericans do not tell the reader how to pronounce these foreign terms, so this new work is valuable if only for the guide.

The introduction is lengthy and scholarly, explaining the development of the religions of the area. The authors give a brief history of the different Mesoamerican civilizations, explaining the rise and fall of each, and how one may have influenced the others. The subject index appears between the introduction and the body of the dictionary. It organizes the entry words related to various topics and lists them under such headings as *Gods and Goddesses*, *Flora and Fauna*, *Sacred Places*, *Symbols*, *Natural Phenomena*, *Concepts*, and *Ritual Practices*. This is helpful to the user who wants information but does not know what terms apply.

The major portion of the work is the alphabetical dictionary section of approximately 300 terms. Most entries are between one-half column and one column in length, but some are more extensive; for example, *Calendar* is six pages with several illustrations and a chart of day names in Mayan and Aztec. The entries give etymologies where available, definitions, and commentary when appropriate. Abundant cross-references are shown in small capital letters. Throughout this section, pages are divided into two columns; one column of each spread is devoted to illustrations.

Following the dictionary entries is a bibliographic essay that provides a critical commentary about many of the sources used by the authors and available to the researcher. This helps the reader place much of the information in perspective since primary source material is scant. Full bibliographic citations to a range of materials conclude this section.

Some drawbacks to the book were noted. All the illustrations are in black and white. While this keeps the cost low, the brilliant colors used by these civilizations are as much a part of their religion as the symbols themselves. There is no index to the introduction or to the bibliographic essay. With such a wealth of material, many users will not want to read it all to find the one or two pieces of information needed.

On the whole, *The Gods and Symbols of Ancient Mexico and the Maya* is a marvelous addition to the religion section of any library. There is a need in most libraries for a reference on Mesoamerican religions, and this work nicely fills that need, especially at an affordable price.

SOCIAL SCIENCES

The Blackwell Dictionary of Twentieth-Century Social Thought. Ed. by William Outhwaite and Tom Bottomore. Blackwell, 1993. 720p. index. hardcover $49.95 (0-631-15262-8).

300'.3 Social sciences—History—20th century—Encyclopedias ‖ Philosophy—History—20th century—Encyclopedias ‖ Civilization, Modern—20th century—Encyclopedias [CIP] 92-20837

Widely published in sociology and Marxism, Outhwaite and Bottomore, both of the University of Sussex, edit here "a reliable and comprehensive overview of the main themes of social thought" of the twentieth century. The articles were commissioned from more than 200 scholars, mostly British and European but also from other countries, including the U.S. The scope of the work includes major and influential concepts, methods, and movements from the social sciences, philosophy, political science, culture, and the natural sciences. The result is an economical, compact, and broad-ranging success.

The entries can be categorized into three main types: major concepts of social thought (*Morality*, *Crime and Deviance*, *Self-Management*), principal schools of thought and movements (*Durkheim School*, *Feminism*, *Keynesianism*), and important institutions and organizations (*Market*, *Military*, *State*). Short biographical entries for 83 major social thinkers are reserved for an appendix. Cross-references are noted in small-capital letters within the text, and *see* references file in the main alphabetical arrangement. Each entry ends with a short list of further readings; a lengthy bibliography appears in the rear of the book. A comprehensive general index promises easy access to concepts, schools, and thinkers.

Articles range in length from 500 to more than 2,500 words, with the longer ones devoted to individual social science disciplines or principal schools of thought. These typically include cross-references to related articles that elaborate on specific concepts. The entries consistently focus on a concept and its definition, its history and development, and its impact on twentieth-century thought. The four-page article *Anthropology* is representative. Following a brief definition is a discussion of how the field has fragmented into social and biological branches. The reader learns that the emphasis on comparative frameworks for mapping human variation is both the unifying element of the discipline and the basis for its impact on modern thought. The article summarizes the development of key concepts in various areas of anthropological investigation and concludes by noting the shift from documenting historical patterns toward an emphasis on practical applications.

With such a breadth of contributors, the quality of writing necessarily varies. In the work's first entry, *Action and Agency*, one reads that, "Aristotle, in his *Nichomachean Ethics*, saw the rationality of an action as lying in the conclusion which leads from intentions or norms and from assessments of the situation and of the available means to immediate consequences in terms of action." This is not writing that is easily digested. Many of the entries presume a basic familiarity with philosophy, political science, and social theory.

Compared with this new work, the revised edition of *The Harper Dictionary of Modern Thought* [RBB S 1 88] generally provides shorter definitions for a larger number of concepts drawn from a wider range of fields, such as computer science, music, linguistics, and electoral politics. *The Blackwell Dictionary of Twentieth-Century Social Thought* provides lengthier treatments for a smaller universe of ideas. This dictionary is appropriate for college students and faculty, as well as sophisticated public library readers. In a small library with a tight budget, it might substitute for a raft of specialized dictionaries in the social sciences, especially where a twentieth-century focus is desired. In the large academic library, it will prove an important, unique addition, providing a summary and contemporary context for most major concepts in philosophy, economics, and political science.

Encyclopedia of American Social History. 3v. Ed. by Mary Kupiec Cayton and others. Scribner, 1993. bibliog. index. maps. tables. hardcover $320 (0-684-19246-2).

301'.0973 U.S.—Social conditions—Encyclopedias || U.S.—Social life and customs—Encyclopedias || Social history—Encyclopedias [CIP] 92-10577

Social history has been variously defined as the history of everyday life or history "from the bottom up." Professor Cayton and her colleagues Elliot J. Gorn and Peter W. Williams are all scholars affiliated with Miami University of Ohio. Together with 171 contributors from many fields, including history, geography, sociology, anthropology, gender studies, literature, and religion, they have compiled the *Encyclopedia of American Social History*.

The set's 180 essays are arranged in 14 sections. These sections include "Periods of Social Change," with essays covering the period prior to the arrival of Europeans through the 1980s, and "Methods and Contexts," with essays on oral history, Marxism, and feminist approaches to social history, among others. Other sections cover ethnic and racial subcultures, regions of the U.S., labor, aspects of popular culture and recreation (sports, music, television), family history, social problems, science and technology, and education and literacy. Among the more interesting essays are those on sexual orientation, the suburbs, clothing and personal adornment, household labor, and peace movements. The average essay is approximately 12 pages in length. Articles on geographic topics are illustrated with black-and-white maps and those citing statistical information with tables. The approach of the essays varies depending upon the author, and some are rather scholarly in style.

Each essay is accompanied by a bibliography of one to four pages. Most cite monographs, although a few mention periodicals and one includes musical recordings. Citations in the bibliographies note only author, title, and date of publication. Researchers may find the lack of complete bibliographic citations a hindrance. Organization of the bibliographies follows the format of the essays (e.g., time periods, subjects) or is alphabetical. At the end of each essay are frequent *see also* references.

To assist users in locating the appropriate essay, volume 1 contains an overall listing of all essays in the set and volumes 2 and 3 each have two contents sections: one listing the articles in the volume and the second listing articles in the other two volumes.

Rounding out the set is an 11-page list of contributors and a detailed index. The contributors section provides information on affiliation, scholarly publications, and the title of the essay contributed by the author. The 92-page index contains a few *see* references. Index references are to page number and either the left or right column of text.

This unique work is in the scholarly tradition of other titles in the Scribner's American Civilization Series, such as the *Encyclopedia of the American Religious Experience* [RBB My 15 88] and the *Encyclopedia of the American Judicial System* [RBB N 15 87]. The *Encyclopedia of American Social History* is recommended for academic and, where appropriate, public and high school libraries.

Reverse Symbolism Dictionary: Symbols Listed by Subject. Comp. by Steven Olderr. McFarland, 1992. 181p. bibliog. hardcover $29.95 (0-89950-561-9).

302.2'22 Symbolism—Dictionaries || Emblems—Dictionaries [CIP] 90-53517

This reverse dictionary of symbols lists the thing or idea to be symbolized first, followed by a list of symbols. The stated purpose is to help "the person looking for a symbol to use in his own creation." This slim volume is not comprehensive and does not claim to be, but it does cover many popular common symbols or emblems. It is based on and complementary to another book by Olderr, *Symbolism: A Comprehensive Dictionary* (1986).

Some of the ideas and things included are Jesus Christ, anger, New Year, childbirth, winter, and Rome. The subjects are listed alphabetically, with many *see also* references. Some concepts have only one symbol ("nirvana—lotus") while the discussion for *Jesus Christ* covers three pages. In this latter example, the symbols are subdivided with such headings as "Last Supper of Christ" and "Nativity of Christ." There are no illustrations to show what the symbols look like. A short, annotated bibliography included in the foreword lists additional sources on symbolism.

The *Reverse Symbolism Dictionary* will help students, researchers, and writers discover how ideas and things have been represented or symbolized and will suggest words they can use to represent something else in writing. It is a possible purchase for academic and public libraries.

Dictionary of Symbolism. By Hans Biedermann. Tr. by James Hulbert. Facts On File, 1992. 592p. bibliog. illus. indexes. hardcover $45 (0-8160-2593-2).

302.23 Signs and symbols—Dictionaries [OCLC] 91-44933

The *Dictionary of Symbolism* is a scholarly work intended to acquaint the reader with significant cultural symbols throughout the history of civilization. The work was originally published in German in 1989, as *Knaurs Lexikon der Symbole*, and, with this first English edition, the title has now been translated into 18 languages. Biedermann concentrates on the meanings of images for various cultures. He attempts to avoid Eurocentrism and includes symbols from the traditions of Asia, Africa, and the Americas.

More than 500 entries, arranged alphabetically, focus on legends, mythical figures, animals, objects, natural phenomena, conditions, psychological states, events, designs, and images. Some entries receive considerable textual attention, while others are dispatched in a paragraph. Each entry discusses the origins, variant meanings, and power of the symbol. For example, the entry *golem* discusses Mary Shelley's *Frankenstein*, the golem of Jewish myth, and the Christian Adam "before his soul was breathed into him." *Calumet* links the native American peace pipe to sacred pipes in Central Europe and to the medical caduceus, the messenger's staff in classical western tradition. Biedermann links entries together in a variety of ways. Words in an entry that have a separate listing are in small-capital letters; and *see also* references to related articles appear at the end of entries, where appropriate. The author specifies the origin of some terms, but not all. Especially useful is a detailed index that is arranged by name of the symbol, with related entries and page numbers listed below each one.

The dictionary is illustrated in black and white with more than 600 depictions of the symbols from works appearing through history. While some symbols have no pictorial representations in the book, the entry *rat*, for example, has two: an English woodcut, 1650, depicting rat catchers, and an 1846 children's book illustration of rat tails as symbolic of confusion. All the illustrations are reproduced together at the back of the book in a unique 35-page "Pictorial Index" that refers the user to the page in the text where the image is discussed. Also included is an extensive bibliography, much of it German in origin, that represents works from Europe, Africa, Asia, classical antiquity, the occult, and most recognized religions.

Libraries owning Cirlot's *Dictionary of Symbols* (1971) will notice content similarities between the two works. However, The *Dictionary of Symbolism* includes such recent, and perhaps controversial, symbols as *unidentified flying objects* and names of such individuals as *Xanthippe* that have cultural and psychological connotations for today. In addition to this type of dictionary, libraries may want to own a reference work such as Liungman's *Dictionary of Symbols* (ABC-CLIO, 1991), an excellent dictionary of ideograms and signs from many cultures, especially useful for graphic designers and artists. The *Dictionary of Symbolism* is an asset to those libraries focusing on literature, psychology, orientalism, mythology, the classics, or civilization in general.

Lesbian Sources: A Bibliography of Periodical Articles, 1970–1990. By Linda Garber. Garland, 1993. hardcover $75 (0-8153-0782-9).
016.305489664 Lesbianism—Bibliography ‖ Lesbianism—Periodicals—Bibliography ‖ Lesbians—Bibliography [CIP] 92-21941

Lesbianism: An Annotated Bibliography and Guide to the Literature, 1976–1991. By Dolores J. Maggiore. Scarecrow, 1992. 265p. bibliog. indexes. hardcover $32.50 (0-8108-2617-8).
016.30367663 Lesbianism—U.S.—Bibliography [CIP] 92-34699

Maggiore's bibliography is an update of her earlier work, *Lesbianism: An Annotated Bibliography and Guide to the Literature, 1976–1986* (Scarecrow, 1988; see "Reference Materials for or about Gays and Lesbians" [RBB Je 1 88]). Maggiore is a social worker who maintains a private practice in psychotherapy serving the gay and lesbian community. Her bibliographies are intended "to introduce the professional to the world of the lesbian and to invite this professional to interact with the information in a way as to benefit both the worker and the lesbian client."

While compiling the initial volume, Maggiore located 300 items. Entries for these are repeated in the update, along with 200 additional articles, dissertations, and books. She omitted foreign publications, works on religion or spirituality, and highly specialized works. Such new areas as lesbian battering have been added, and family issues have been expanded. Prefatory materials include a 1992 introduction and reprints of the literature-review essays from the original volume.

The bibliography is divided into five topical chapters: "The Individual Lesbian," "Minorities within a Minority," "Lesbian Families," "Oppression," and "Health." The sources listed are drawn from the fields of social work, the social and behaviorial sciences, health, law, and feminist social analysis. Many types of researchers will find materials of interest listed here, for instance, "Bibliography: Lesbian Health" and "Gay and Lesbian Youth." However, the primary emphasis is on works useful to the helping professions, such as "The Lesbian Illness Support Group" and "Lesbians in Therapy." Complete bibliographic citations are provided for each entry; annotations are one paragraph in length and are generally descriptive. A few annotations are critical, such as the first one on page 95 where Maggiore warns the reader that this is "a good example of a study to beware of."

Lesbian Sources is a unique resource providing a subject approach to the journal literature. It includes 3,500 index entries for nonfiction articles by and about lesbians that appeared in periodicals having a national or international distribution. Approximately 60 journals dealing with lesbians, feminism, and women are indexed in full. Also included are articles that deal with lesbianism from more mainstream publications, such as *Saturday Review*, *New Statesmen*, *Time*, *JAMA*, and *Social Work*. The coverage deliberately excludes archival materials, titles that were included in Clare Potter's *Lesbian Periodical Index* [RBB Je 1 86], and the local community papers included in the Women's Herstory Microfilm Collection.

The book is topically arranged by more than 100 subject categories ranging from *Abuse*, *Monogamy*, and *Body Image* to *Parenting*, *Legislation*, and *Youth*. Topics are listed alphabetically; these headings are in boldface print and underlined. No running heads are provided on the pages, which would have been a helpful feature. Citations contain the author, title of the article, journal title in italics, volume, issue, date, and page numbers. While most entries are not annotated, they are frequently enhanced with a brief note specifying the subject or identifying a person when this information is not apparent from the title of the article.

This work does not contain any supplemental indexes; however, a variety of mechanisms are employed to assist the user in accessing the information. The table of contents is 16 pages and approximates a subject index by including cross-references and topical subdivisions. For instance, *History* is broken down by time periods. *Media* exemplifies the extensive cross-referencing with its *see also* citations to *Art*; *Censorship*; *Film and Video*; *Mass Media*; *Periodicals: Lesbian/Feminist/Gay*; *Photography*; *Publishing*; *Radio*; *Television*. If an article has more than one author, the citation is repeated under both names. If the article is about more than one person, each individual is listed as a subject and the citation is repeated. This system enables the user to locate an article reporting an interview with Rita Arauz about AIDS education in Nicaragua under *Acquired Immune Deficiency Syndrome*, *Lesbians around the World—Nicaragua*, and under her name in *Interviews*.

The Atlas of Endangered Animals. By Steve Pollock. Facts On File, 1993. 64p. illus. indexes. hardcover $16.95 (0-8160-2856-7).
591.52'9 Endangered species—Juvenile literature ‖ Wildlife conservation—Juvenile literature [CIP]

The Atlas of Endangered Places. By Steve Pollock. Facts On File, 1993. 64p. illus. indexes. hardcover $16.95 (0-8160-2857-5).
304.2'8 Man—Influence on nature—Juvenile literature ‖ Man—Influence on nature—Maps—Juvenile literature ‖ Pollution—Juvenile literature ‖ Pollution—Maps—Juvenile literature [CIP] 92-20388

These companion books, by the same author, originated in Great Britain. They provide specific information for the middle school student on selected endangered animals and places around the world. Both books share the same format: an introduction that summarizes the main issues and a page of instructions that shows the symbols used to designate characteristics of the endangered animals and places. These pages are followed by the body of each book, consisting of maps and text for each region of the world. Full-page maps for each region also include a small inset indicating the place's position on the planet, a compass, the scale, and latitude and longitude lines. Color photographs illustrate the various entries of places or animals for each region. Each book concludes with a brief glossary and further information, a map index, and an index of endangered places or animals.

A typical section is the four pages devoted to Central America and the Caribbean in the *Animals* volume. A brief introduction mentions the main habitats and environmental risks of the region. Eight animals have entries, ranging from one to three paragraphs in length, and each is accompanied by a photograph. An example of the use of the symbol boxes noted above is the entry *Cuban Crocodile*, which includes four symbols: a visual silhouette of the animal; an E for *endangered*; a hunter designating the overhunted status of the animal; and a cut tree signifying habitat destruction.

These inexpensive books have sturdy bindings, attractive printfaces, and interesting photographs. Much information is packed into each page without the appearance of clutter. Additionally, maps seem to have adequate gutters, although many of these are printed vertically so that the books have to be rotated to read them. One impressive feature is the inclusion of such current events as the resulting damage from the Gulf War and the correct maps and labels for the former Soviet Union. *The Atlas of Endangered Places* also presents the young reader with 23 specific symbol designations that provide analysis of various problems, such as the difference between *deforestation* and *tropical forest destruction*.

The major criticism of these books is that the criteria for selection of endangered animals and places are not spelled out. Nor is it anywhere noted that although the books are limited to approximately 90 animals and 60 places, there are many more endangered places and animals than are included here. There is a danger that a young reader might think that the featured entries are the only ones endangered rather than viewing them as selected examples. Another point is that these books, presumably for American readers, seem to slight U.S. aspects of the problem of endangered animals and places. Few endangered American animals, places, parks, agencies, and refuges are included. While one might argue that it is good to view the U.S. equally with other regions, a bibliography plus notes in the introduction might have directed students to additional pertinent information about their own country. Only one factual error was noted: in the *Places* volume, Love Canal is said to be in New York City.

These new atlases are well written in a noncondescending style.

SOCIAL SCIENCES

The attractive format and information provided make them fun to read. However, because of the limited coverage noted above, they should not be regarded as primary references. School and public libraries may wish to consider them as supplementary purchases for young readers.

Atlas of the 1990 Census. By Mark T. Mattson. Macmillan, 1992. 168p. charts. tables. hardcover $90 (0-02-897302-X).
304.6'0973 U.S.—Census, 21st, 1990—Maps || U.S.—Population—Maps [CIP] 92-24006

This work is organized into six sections containing maps that graphically depict the statistical results of the 1990 census of population and housing. Population includes density, age, sex, death and birth rates, etc. Information about households depicts families, marital status, female-headed, nonfamily, etc. The section on housing provides data about median value, sales, rent or own, etc. Race and ethnicity data cover immigration and African, Hispanic, Asian, and native Americans. Per capita income, manufacturing, transportation, retail, wholesale, service, and agriculture are covered in the section on the economy. The school-age population is depicted in the final part on education.

Each section starts with a single-page summary of the data. This is followed by a national map of the 1980 census data, a map showing percentage of change from 1980 to 1990, and one of the 1990 census results. Regional data in graph form and specific statistics for each state are listed. Data are then presented for each of five regions of the country in maps that use color and shading to depict the statistics by county. The lists on these regional pages give statistics for major cities and the 10 counties with the most population. Throughout the book, the major cities for each region and the colors used on the regional map are consistent. Concluding the volume are maps naming the counties in each region, a metro fact finder that lists cities by size (not alphabetically) and then breaks down population by ethnicity and age, and a glossary of terms used in the census.

Two problems were noted. The graph on page 125 for native Americans by region is the same as the graph on page 101 for African Americans by region. On page 144, it is not clearly labeled which line is for constant dollars and which is for current dollars. Otherwise, this is an excellent statistical reference source for libraries. Although it is not as exhaustive as the actual census reports from which it is derived, it has the numbers most users need for their reports, and it has the further advantages of being visually pleasing and easy to use. The atlas is recommended for purchase by academic and public libraries and by those high school and special libraries that need statistical references.

UpClose 1990 Census Sourcebook. v.4: West. UpClose Publishing, P.O. Box 1147, El Granada, CA 94018, 1992. 687p. indexes. tables. paper $250 (1-56410-018-9).
304.6021 Demography—U.S.—Statistics || Housing—U.S.—Statistics || U.S.—Economic conditions—Statistics || U.S.—Census, 21st, 1990 || U.S.—Population—Statistics [OCLC]

As the results from the 1990 decennial census of population and housing are compiled, the U.S. Bureau of the Census, as in the past, is distributing and selling this statistical information in a variety of formats: computer tapes, printed publications, microfiche, and CD-ROM. However, it is the computer tapes (i.e., Summary Tape Files [STF]) that are the basis for all census reports. Utilizing STF1A ("100-percent" questions—questions that everyone answered regardless of the questionnaire form) and STF3A ("sample" questions—questions that were answered only by those households that received the long- form questionnaire), UpClose Publishing produced its *Census Sourcebook* series. The set consists of a national volume and four regional volumes (*Northeast*, *South*, *Midwest*, and *West*).

Volume 4, *West*, was the only one seen for this review. It consists primarily of statistics, arranged in two parts: demographic summary tables and profile tables. The demographic summary table section is arranged alphabetically by state (13 in the West), then alphabetically by county within each state, then by place (city, town, Census Designated Place [CDP]) within each county. A demographic summary table of the 63 Metropolitan Statistical Areas (MSAs) in the West concludes this section. For each geographic place, the tables provide population and housing characteristics for 50 different variables (e.g., sex, age, race, households, income, employment, and education). The data are clearly laid out, which makes it easy to locate and read the information.

The profile tables section consists of a one-page statistical summary for each geographic area selected for inclusion. Each profile includes information about 281 variables—demographic, housing, income, employment, educational attainment, commuting to work, etc. These profiles are arranged alphabetically by name of the place (counties, cities, towns, etc.), regardless of state, which makes it inconvenient and time-consuming when locating data for a number of places in one state. Also, only counties with a population of 100,000-plus and cities with a population of 25,000-plus are included. As a result, the profiles section includes no counties in Wyoming and only three Wyoming cities (Cheyenne, Casper, and Laramie). Indexes by place, county, and MSA provide alternate access to both sections of tables.

The *UpClose 1990 Census Sourcebook* provides a convenient selection of data, except when the county, city, or town is excluded due to its small population. The user must remember that the sourcebook series is, as its goal states, only a selection of the data most frequently asked for. All of the data in each sourcebook, plus additional information, can be found in the various printed reports, CD-ROMs, and other products from the U.S. Bureau of the Census. The sourcebook, by itself, is not sufficient to answer many 1990 census questions, and the $250-per-volume price makes this an expensive and luxurious purchase for most libraries.

Senior Citizen Services: How to Find and Contact 15,000 Providers. 4v. Ed. by Charles B. Montney and Jolen Marya Gedridge. Gale, 1993. 1,150p. index. hardcover $99/set (0-8103-8319-5); $29.95/v. (Northeastern States, 0-8103-8320-9; Southern and Mid-Atlantic States, 0-8103-8321-7; Midwestern States, 0-8103-8322-5; Western States, 0-8103-8323-3) (ISSN 1065-9226).
305.'2 Aged—Services for—Directories [BKL]

Connecting "older Americans and their caregivers to government agencies, nonprofit organizations, and companies that offer free or low-cost services to the elderly," this four-volume set lists some 15,000 entities. Volumes are organized geographically and may be ordered separately. Each is arranged in the same manner and includes the same introductory and prefatory material.

A summary of the Older Americans Act of 1965 (OAA) begins each volume. This act initiated the Aging Network, a system of organizations and services for older Americans. The act also established federal, state, and local structures to deliver these services and promote the interests of this growing segment of the population. The four types of services described in the OAA—in-home, community based, access, and institutional—are the focus of *Senior Citizen Services*.

Within each regional volume, separate chapters are included for each state. These are arranged into two sections. A geographic-service index starts the chapter, listing cities and counties alphabetically, with types of service (nutrition, recreation, transportation) listed under each place name. Entry, rather than page, numbers are given. If a particular agency offers several services, the entry number is repeated under each heading. The instructions clearly state that listings for both the city and the county of residence need to be checked when searching for services.

The second section of each chapter presents the directory entries. Starting with listings for the state unit on aging and then area agencies on aging, the service providers in the state are listed alphabetically by city or by town (these are also arranged alphabetically). The organization's name is printed in boldface type, with an entry number highlighted in a box to its left. Address, telephone and fax numbers, director, area served, days and hours open, and services provided are given. These descriptions are brief: rarely is information included about costs or eligibility; services are described in short phrases (e.g., "friendly visiting," "health care services," etc.); and "area served" includes no finer detail than the names of cities or counties. At the end of each regional volume is an organization and agency index in which services in all of the states in a region are listed alphabetically, followed by entry number.

In smaller communities, the lack of details in the directory listings may not be problematic because the number of agencies listed is small enough that the person seeking service will not have to make an unmanageable number of inquiries. In large cities, many programs are limited to particular neighborhoods, but this information is not included. Thus, one is confronted by 80 index entries for places offering congregate meals in New York City and 81 for recreational programs in the Bronx, without any additional information about geographic limitations of the programs. In the prefatory material the book states "there may be restrictions based on the senior's income or place of residence" and advises all users to telephone the appropriate area agency on aging as the first step in locating the services they need.

Even though this new directory does not provide in-depth information about the listed programs, in most cases adequate data are included to get a person started in a search for services. This reasonably priced and well-organized resource is recommended for public libraries and others with an interest in services for the aging. The directory is also available on disk and magnetic-tape formats. Libraries with extremely limited budgets may want to opt for one regional volume, but the price for the full set is a better buy. In making the decision about which volumes to buy, librarians might want to consider that it is frequently the children of seniors who are looking for services for their parents, and in today's mobile society, they often reside elsewhere.

Developments and Research on Aging: An International Handbook. Ed. by Erdman B. Palmore. Greenwood, 1993. 456p. bibliog. index. hardcover $79.95 (0-313-27785-0).
305.26 Gerontology—Cross-cultural studies [CIP] 92-25737

This is a revised edition of Palmore's *International Handbook on Aging*, published by Greenwood in 1980 [RSBR Jl 15 81]. Information on programs and research in gerontology in various countries is given in 25 chapters, arranged alphabetically by country. Each chapter was written by an expert on gerontology in that country. Contributors and their addresses, which usually identify professional affiliations, are listed. Palmore is professor emeritus of medical sociology at Duke University.

Articles cover such information as "unique features of the country; the growth of gerontology; roles and status of the aged; problems of the aged; programs for the aged; research in biomedical, psychological, and social science aspects of the aging; and information sources on aging." Articles vary in length. Many include charts and tables, and each has a bibliography. There is also a general bibliography for the book, an index, and an appendix ("International Directory of Gerontological and Geriatric Associations").

This work aspires to promote the internationalization of the growing field of gerontology by making information available from a variety of countries. Eleven countries are included that were not in the original work. However, several countries included in *International Handbook on Aging* are omitted here, due to problems in obtaining information. Countries included are both large and small, highly urbanized and less so, represent various economic systems, have high and low proportions of aged citizens, and high and low birth and death rates. Latin America is represented by Argentina, Brazil, and Costa Rica; Asia by China, Japan, India, and Taiwan; and Africa by Egypt and South Africa. The article "USSR Nations" covers the former Soviet Union; other articles are on the advanced countries of Europe and North America as well as Australia and Israel.

When gerontology first began as a science, most work came from the U.S. and a few European countries. Historically, countries with programs and research have tended to have a high proportion of aged and be urbanized and industrialized. However, developing countries with fewer resources will soon be challenged by growing numbers of aged citizens. The information in this well-done book will be useful to those who are in any way concerned with gerontology and related studies. It is recommended for professional, academic, and large public libraries.

The European Women's Almanac. Ed. by Paula Snyder. Columbia, 1992. 399p. tables. hardcover $35 (0-231-08064-6).
305.4'094 Women—Europe—Handbooks, manuals, etc. [CIP] 92-13451

The 26 countries covered in this new almanac are listed in alphabetical order. The information provided for each country includes an introductory snapshot and a short description of the country's political and cultural status. The bulk of information is a reference section, providing both statistics and narrative commentary about the status and rights of women. The data are organized into such topics as immigration and residence, health care, parental benefits, child care, state benefits, employment, politics, and education. The final sections of the entries include complete citations for the sources of the statistics, letters from women in the country, and addresses for the major organizations concerned with women's rights or benefits. The book concludes with 24 comparative tables that rank countries on various measures of population, health, and life-style trends. Finland, for example, is shown with the highest proportion of women in the national government, while Malta has the lowest.

The book covers standard demographic statistics, such as population by sex and age, labor-force participation rate, women's earnings as a percentage of men's, women's representation in higher education, etc. Some data make historical comparisons possible, such as for Portugal, where the birth rate per 1,000 population has declined from 23.8 in 1960 to 11.9 in 1988 and where the infant mortality rate has declined from 77.5 per 1,000 live births to 13.1 in the same time period. Also included are succinct descriptions of laws and benefits that pertain to women, children, and families. In Luxembourg, for instance, public funding for child care increased by 235 percent between 1985 and 1990, while in Poland, in 1991, only 12 percent of couples used contraceptives, contributing to the high rate of abortion, which is free. Important milestones in the progress of women's rights are also noted, such as the election of Mary Robinson as Ireland's first female president in 1990.

The European Women's Almanac is published at a moment of both profound crisis and transmutation in the rights and status of women in Europe. The book does not include profiles of the newly independent Baltic states or other countries from the former Soviet Union. One entry is devoted to Germany, but many of the statistics cover either East or West Germany before reunification. Since the author compiled data from a wide variety of available sources, the amount of information for each country varies. In some cases, desired statistics simply do not exist, a fact that is particularly true of Eastern European communities. These shortcomings notwithstanding, the almanac succeeds as a single source of information on European women. Many public and academic libraries will want to own this resource.

Black Americans: A Statistical Sourcebook, 1993. Ed. by Alfred N. Garwood. Numbers & Concepts, 2525 Arapahoe Ave., Ste. E4-221, Boulder, CO 80302, 1993. annual. 364p. index. tables. hardcover $49.95 (0-929960-13-0); paper $39.95 (0-929960-12-2); (ISSN 1048-7992).
305.8'96073 Afro-Americans—Statistics [BKL]

Hispanic Americans: A Statistical Sourcebook, 1993. Ed. by Alfred N. Garwood. Numbers & Concepts, 1993. annual. 264p. index. tables. hardcover $49.95 (0-929960-15-7); paper $39.95 (0-929960-14-9); (ISSN 1056-6992).
305.868 Hispanic Americans—Statistics [BKL]

These 1993 editions of annual handbooks compile statistical data on two important segments of the U.S. population into compact, easily utilized tables that facilitate identification of trends in the minorities' development and comparison of their status with the white population and with the total population. The volumes are "not intended to serve any cause or advance any point of view but to serve as a reportorial resource, providing access to federal government information." *Black Americans* was first issued in 1990, while *Hispanic Americans* began publication in 1991.

The data come mostly from the U.S. Bureau of the Census. If *Statistical Abstract of the United States* is cited as the source, the original reference has been checked for additional information, and SA's citation (if it is not the bureau) is listed as well. Each table includes sources (with SuDocs Classification Number), notes, and explanation of the units used. A glossary and key-term index provide additional help in interpreting and using these references.

Hispanic Americans reports statistics on the ethnic or cultural group for which the federal government gathers separate data; for its purposes, Hispanic persons are those who say they are Hispanic (or Spanish, Latino, etc.). Generally, the overwhelming majority of persons who identify themselves as Hispanic also identify themselves as white. B*lack Americans* compiles statistics on persons who say they are black, Negro, or Afro-American in federal government surveys. The editor uses the term *black* "because it is the word currently used by the federal government in gathering data" and indicates that changes in federal usage will be reflected in future editions.

In both works, several chapters of tables cover demographics, social characteristics, household and family charactersitics, education (preprimary through high school, postsecondary and education attainment), government and elections, labor force, employment and unemployment, earnings and income, and poverty and wealth. A final chapter, "Special Topics," provides data on AIDS, health-insurance coverage, victimization rates for personal crimes, selected characteristics of farms and farm operators, summary of results of the 1988–89 consumer expenditure survey, and selected characteristics of occupied housing units. Most tables include recent data—1990, 1991, 1992. Many of those concerned with education (high school completion, enrollment in schools of medicine, etc.) provide figures from the 1970s and the 1980s. Also covered in B*lack Americans'* "Special Topics" are Social Security benefits and beneficiaries, black-owned firms by major industry group, black-owned firms by state, and housing affordability. More tables in this title than in H*ispanic Americans* allow comparisons from the 1970s and the 1980s; a few trace dates from earlier years.

Although the data included in both these volumes can be located elsewhere, the convenience of having so much information on a specific group offered in concise, logically arranged tables makes each sourcebook a boon. The editor's solicitation for suggestions for inclusion or improvement in future editions indicates an ongoing desire to produce a useful reference source.

50 Fabulous Places to Raise Your Family. By Lee Rosenberg and Saralee Rosenberg. Career Press, 1993. 320p. index. paper $17.95 (1-56414-034-2).
306'.0973 Quality of life—U.S. || Family life surveys—U.S. || Metropolitian areas—U.S. || Social indicators—U.S. [CIP] 92-39518

This new title seeks to help people find a place to live that has excellent schools, a low crime rate, reasonably priced housing, ample employment opportunities, and low taxes—all within a 15-minute commute. It does not rank the communities it profiles. Rather, the authors present guidelines to assist readers in making their own choices based on personal preferences for type of climate, scenery, size, etc. Introductory chapters discuss how to find a new hometown, including worksheets on developing priorities; planning and budgeting for relocating; evaluating schools; conducting an out-of-town job search; and the physical move to the new location. While the book contains no quantitative rankings, the introductory materials list 15 factors that were used to select the communities to be profiled. These range from a strong economic outlook to plentiful recreation and cultural activities and community services and programs (libraries are *not* mentioned). Approximately one-half of the communities included have less than 100,000 population.

The meat of the book is the section providing the profiles, which are each five pages in length. The 50 communities analyzed are in 30 states, arranged alphabetically by state and by city within each state. Each examination begins with a snapshot that lists the local population, the county and its population, the closest metropolitan areas and the distance from each, the median housing price, the average household income, and a summary of the best reasons to live there. An outline map of the state locates the community in relation to the state capital and other important cities. The profile discusses such topics as physical features, real estate, living costs, taxes, job and business opportunities, education, medical care, community life, sports, entertainment, annual events, the environment, and transportation options. The information in each of these sections is concise but very useful. For example, under real estate, the authors provide an overview of the market, including what houses look like; give prices for starter homes, trade-ups, and luxury homes; summarize rental costs for apartments, houses, and condos; discuss "great neighborhoods"; and suggest other nearby areas to consider. Also included in the profiles are climate tables and a list of addresses for local groups and publications. A box entitled "What Every Resident Knows" gives tidbits of information unique to the community. For instance, in the Fountain Hills, Arizona, Thanksgiving Day Parade, children dress up their pets and march together. There are some minor typographical errors, but factual data seem accurate.

Because the authors were selective in their choice of cities to analyze, this book does not replace either *The Livable Cities Almanac* [RBB Je 1 92] or *Places Rated Almanac* [RBB S 1 85]. Even though this new book includes data about few large cities, 50 *Fabulous Places to Raise Your Family* will be a welcome low-cost addition to public library collections and could find a home in high school and academic libraries to assist recent graduates moving to their first home and job.

Oxford Illustrated Encyclopedia of Peoples and Cultures. Ed. by Richard Hoggart. Oxford, 1992. 392p. illus. hardcover $49.95 (0-19-869139-4).
306.097 Geography—Dictionaries [OCLC]

This seventh volume in the *Oxford Illustrated Encyclopedia* series "explains how and why people throughout the world live as they do" and also covers the major political and economic systems that are influential in today's global village. More than 2,200 brief entries cover the important ideas and institutions active in society, the major problems facing various countries, as well as ethnic, religious, and cultural groups. The focus of the work is contemporary but with a historical perspective showing impacts on current trends.

The entries in the main portion of the book are in an alphabetic sequence and range in length from a few sentences to more than 500 words. Numerous cross-references are denoted by asterisks. Entries are provided for important concepts from a wide range of subjects. All major world religions are covered, as well as a variety of peoples (e.g., *Cherokee, Ibo, Palestinians,* etc.). Economic, political, and legal ideas and institutions are discussed in such entries as *Balance of Power, Co-operative, Military-Industrial Complex* and *International Court of Justice*. International organizations, such as the *Arab League* and the *Council of Europe,* are profiled, and entries are included for a vast array of terms from philosophy (*Idealism*), education (*Literacy*), and the social sciences (*Psychosexual Development*). A limited number of biographical entries are included for important historical figures whose ideas continue to be influential, such as M*uhammed*, *Plato*, and *Marx*.

As with all volumes in the series, the book is written in nontechnical language and provides concise, informative explanations. Enhancing the work are attractive color and black-and-white photographs, charts, graphs, and diagrams. For example, a full page is devoted to diagrams of the playing fields for various versions of football; small maps depict the countries hosting the most refugees; and an organizational chart of the United Nations is included. Following the main encyclopedic sequence is another A–Z arrangement covering "Countries of the World." Each country profile includes basic economic, political, and demographic facts, as well as a paragraph of narrative description. These are relatively current, with many statistics from the late 1980s; facts in some narratives are as recent as 1992.

The *Oxford Illustrated Encyclopedia of Peoples and Cultures* is a necessary purchase for libraries owning other volumes in the set. While the multivolume *Encyclopedia of World Cultures* [RBB Jl 91] offers more indepth coverage, the Oxford title is an effective one-volume resource for high school, public, and small academic libraries that cannot afford the larger work.

Statistical Handbook on the American Family. Ed. by Bruce A. Chadwick and Tim B. Heaton. Oryx, 1992. 295p. charts. index. tables. hardcover $59.50 (0-89774-687-2).
306.85'0973 Family—U.S.—Statistics || U.S.—Statistics, Vital [CIP] 91-44175

This is volume 4 in Oryx's series of statistical handbooks. Earlier volumes treated aging Americans (1986) and Hispanics and women [RBB My 1 91].

The sources used in this volume include government documents, Gallup polls, professional journals, research studies, and national databases. For example, information comes from the National Survey of Families and Households (1987–1988), the General Social Survey of the National Opinion Research Center (1972–1991), and the 1982 and 1988 National Surveys of Family Growth. The sources for data for each table are given in a 15-page list at the back of the volume. The book's index is complete and contains *see* and *see also* references.

The main body of the work is divided into nine categories—marriage, quality of marriage and family life, divorce, children, sexual attitudes and behavior and contraceptive use, living arrangements and kinship ties, working women, family violence, and elderly families. Each main topic is further divided into two to five subtopics. At the beginning of each section is a page or two introducing the charts and tables that follow. The majority of the information is in graphic form, but the introductions provide valuable summaries and trends. In addition to tables, pie and bar charts and graphs are used to display data.

The subjects of the tables are wide-ranging, from "Frequency of Contact with Brothers and Sisters during Past Year for Different Age Groups" and "Living Arrangements of Persons 65 and Older" to "Would You Marry Someone with Less Education" and "Frequency That Parents Yell at Their Children of Different Ages, for White, Blacks, and Hispanics." The format is attractive, and the statistical data is easy to read.

The preface states, "The combination of previously unpublished materials along with the compilation of family data from a wide array of published materials provides a rich cache of information regarding the status of contemporary American families." This book provides solid statistics, particularly from the 1950s through the 1980s. Although some of the information is available in such standards as the *Statistical Abstract of the United States*, the handbook also provides heretofore elusive information. Used with electronic databases for post-1988 statistics, it will meet many of the information needs of public library patrons and high school and college students for statistical data on the American family.

Charts, Graphs & Stats Index: 1988–1991. Ed. by Robert Skapura. Highsmith Press, W5527 Highway 106, P.O. Box 800, Fort Atkinson, WI 53538-0800, 1992. 285p. index. hardcover $42 (0-917846-09-5; ISSN 1060-1465).

310 Charts, diagrams, etc. Indexes || [BKL] 91-7869

This index to quantitative information presented graphically in major news stories comes from the compiler of *The Cover Story Index* [RBB N 1 90]. It lists periodical articles that contain graphs, charts, diagrams and maps displaying statistics. Covering the 1988–91 issues of *Black Enterprise, Bulletin of the Atomic Scientists, Business Week, FDA Consumer, Ms., Newsweek, Scholastic Update, Time*, and *U.S. News & World Report*, it provides information relevant for the student, researcher, or reference librarian.

Each entry includes the title as it appeared in the original article, a description if the title is not clear or needs further elaboration (such as the sex of a survey's responders), the date or date range of the quantitative information, the name of the periodical, the issue date, and the page number. For example, under the subject heading *Jobs* one finds the entry "Struggling to bounce back. Nonfarm payrolls (in millions of workers). 1989–1991. *Business Week* Dec. 23, 1991 p.25." Subject headings are arranged from *Abortion* to *Yugoslavia*. Entries under each subject heading are arranged chronologically in reverse order to allow for easier access to recent information. There are more than a dozen entries under such headings as *North Atlantic Treaty Organization, Unemployment*, and *Older Americans* and only one each for *Kidney Stones, Birth Order*, and *Ergonomics*. A simple "User's Guide" allows preteens through adult patrons to use this book effectively without assistance.

A list of the subject headings appears at the back of the book, but *see* and *see also* references are found only in the main body of the work, making this list less functional. It is useful for seeking subdivision information for headings like AIDS that have many. Geographic subdivisions for topics like *Nuclear Weapons* or *Population* are also noted here.

Skapura notes in his introduction the impact on other publications of the high-quality graphics in *USA Today*; it is unfortunate, therefore, that he didn't index that newspaper. High school, college, and public libraries will find this index useful for locating current statistics and other information presented in graphic form.

International Marketing Data and Statistics, 1993. 17th ed. Euromonitor Publications; dist. by Gale, 1993. 652p. index. hardcover $300 (0-86338-462-5; ISSN 0308-2938).

310 Economic history—1971- || Marketing—Statistics || Commerce—Statistics [OCLC]

The seventeenth edition of this work is packed with useful statistical data for more than 153 countries in the Americas, Asia, Africa, and Oceania. Europe and the Commonwealth of Independent States are covered in a companion volume, *European Marketing Data and Statistics*.

The data, divided into 24 subject areas, are from various national and international sources and are current to 1990 or 1991. Some of the subjects covered are economic indicators, finance and banking, defense, retailing, consumer expenditure patterns, literacy and education, communications, tourism and travel, and cultural indicators. While tables do not list the specific source of the data, the editors state they were "drawn largely from OECD sources" or "mainly drawn from the UN, UNESCO and national statistical offices." A more than 70-page directory of sources gives names and addresses for national and international organizations and various libraries and their publications used as sources in this work.

The first section provides information on more than 153 countries: present head of state, ruling party, population, area, language, currency, and major cities with their population. This is followed by several paragraphs detailing an important highlight, major resources, manufacturing, and other general economic information. This is useful for a snapshot of the country. The tables of data arranged by subject follow. Tables of vital statistics, population, civil aviation, employment, exchange rates, agricultural output, and railways contain data going back to 1977. For other subjects, such as demographic breakdown by age and sex, government expenditure, production of selected metals, and conservation, only the most current year is available. For some countries under some subjects, there are no data available.

The work concludes with a section of regional comparisons (e.g., external trade, energy, consumer spending, agriculture, automotive) and a subject index to the tables. Much, but not all, of the data in this book is available in various publications found in libraries, for example, *Statistical Abstract of the United States, UNESCO Statistical Yearbook, United Nations Statistical Yearbook, National Accounts Statistics: Main Aggregates and Detailed Tables by the United Nations, World Tables by the World Bank*, and many OECD publications. However, this work pulls together this data and other proprietary Euromonitor data into one easy-to-use reference tool. It is also a good source for time-series data in certain subject areas. Large business collections should consider adding it to their collections.

Census Snapshot for All U.S. Places, 1990. Toucan Valley Publications, 142 N. Milpitas Blvd., Ste. 260, Milpitas, CA 95035, 1992. 582p. tables. paper $48 (0-9634017-0-X).

317.94 U.S.—Population—Statistics || Income—U.S.—Statistics || Housing—U.S.—Statistics [CIP]

Census Snapshot is not intended to be an all-inclusive reference source for the 1990 Census of Population data. The publishers state clearly in the introduction that the purpose of this one-volume statistical source is "to provide limited but most sought after data for the entire U.S." With a few exceptions, it does just that. The arrangement is simple and straightforward—alphabetical by state and then by place within each state. Each entry includes the following information: two-letter abbreviation for the state; place name or census designation (e.g., city, town, village, borough, or census-designated place); county location; total population; breakdown of the population, shown as percentages, by race (white, black, American Indian, Asian/Pacific Islander, and other), Hispanic origin, and age (under 6, 6–17, 18–64, and over 64); land area; median household income; and median home value.

The introduction states that this volume provides "the most commonly used Census data for all 23,435 places in the U.S." This does not mean that it covers every place in the U.S. *Census Snapshot* omits the census-place designation of minor civil divisions (MCD), which eliminates many New England towns from the tables. Also, the boroughs of New York City are not listed individually. Military installations are included; Indian reservations are not. For comparison and reference purposes, it would have been useful to include the same entry information for the entire state and maybe for each county.

The price, the layout, and the one-volume format make the *Census Snapshot, 1990* a useful ready-reference source for basic 1990 census data. The user must keep in mind, however, that the data are limited, as the publishers clearly indicate, and the coverage is not comprehensive for some states.

Dictionary of Politics: Selected American and Foreign Political and Legal Terms. 7th ed. By Walter John Raymond. Brunswick, 1992. 760p. maps. charts. hardcover $60 (1-55618-008-X).
320'.03 Political science—Dictionaries [CIP] 92-14215

This is the seventh edition of a work last published in 1978. Many of the shortcomings noted in a review of that edition in the 1979 *American Reference Books Annual* have not been significantly overcome in this 1992 version. For example, in that review definitions were often termed "casual" and occasionally "careless." A casual tone can still be discerned.

This large volume is a cornucopia of alphabetically listed entries for events, slogans, legislative and executive practices, doctrines, and the like in the political sphere; there are no biographical entries. Coverage is international. Very recent developments are included (e.g., the Ross Perot grassroots upsurge and the Los Angeles riots in 1992). Cross-references are extensively and usefully employed.

Many definitions are informal and often idiosyncratic. B*igger bang for the dollar* sticks out as lacking the alliteration that most readers would expect. Forms of entry headings such as W*e are not animals* and W*e shall continue* are not useful, since it is unlikely anyone would think to look up something under those words. Some concepts appear unexpectedly, for example, *science* (which merits one full paragraph whereas *political science* gets only one sentence). A list of terms defined on a page picked at random will convey the tenor of the work: *majority president, majority rule, Make love not war, Make the world safe for democracy, Make war on poverty—not people, mala fide, maladministration, malapportionment, Malayan Emergency, male chauvinist pig, malfeasance, malinchismo, Malta Conference, Malthusian Law, malum in se,* and *malum prohibitum*. Seven of these sixteen terms are not defined but are cross-referenced to other entries.

The best part of the dictionary may be the 107 appendixes that cover almost 200 pages. These range from major American and international documents to organization charts and lists of various officials, maps, and tables of governmental information.

If a library is now well stocked with general political dictionaries, it can forgo purchase of this one. The *HarperCollins Dictionary of American Government and Politics* [RBB My 1 92] has superior coverage for U.S. terms. Graham Evans' *Dictionary of World Politics* [RBB Mr 15 91] is another preferable source. Jack Plano's series of frequently updated specialized dictionaries are also more useful for the reference rooms of public and academic libraries.

The Oxford Companion to Politics of the World. Ed. by Joel Krieger and others. Oxford, 1993. 1,088p. bibliog. index. hardcover $49.95 (0-19-505934-4).
320'.03 Political science—Encyclopedias || World politics—Encyclopedias [CIP] 92-25043

This new work focuses on such broad themes and topics as the social basis of politics, national and international organizations and institutions, law, foreign policy, economic and social policy, links between international and domestic issues, and the politics of change. The companion accomplishes its goals through 650 entries by 500 scholars from more than 40 countries. These articles vary from short, factual pieces to essays of more than 4,000 words. In addition to articles on virtually every country in the world and approximately 100 persons who, according to the editor, "played exceptionally significant roles in contemporary political life," the work features 21 major analytical essays addressing such topics as ethnicity, gender and politics, war, and race and racism. Finally, the companion includes three long, interpretive essays on comparative politics, international politics, and comparative law.

One of the strengths of this work is its coverage of the conflicts and issues that are headlines in the news, both today as well as in the recent past. For instance, in the three pages devoted to *Yugoslavia*, one can learn the history of the country, the ideology of the competing factions, and pertinent facts about the current crisis, including events as recent as the initiation of the Serbian assault on Bosnia-Herzegovina in April–May 1992. In the two and one-half pages of *Liberation Theology*, the reader not only learns of the concepts, writings, and key individuals, but also of its relationships with the Vatican as well as with the politics of Latin American countries over the last three decades.

Articles are arranged alphabetically, with blind entries referring the user from the terms not used to those that are. For example, a reader seeking information on abortion is referred to *Reproductive Politics*, and on Abdel Nasser to N*asser, Gamal Abdel*. Many articles include *see also* references, and starred terms within articles alert the reader to other topics; for instance, in *Cabinet Government* there are references to *Commonwealth* and *France*.

Each entry is signed, and most include brief lists of bibliographic citations to monographs or important periodical articles. Contributors, with their credentials, are listed in the front of the book. Information is current through fall 1992. Although there are exceptions, coverage—particularly of individuals—is concentrated on post–World War II. The work is not illustrated but does include six black-and-white maps of world regions that show country boundaries and capital cities. A comprehensive index lists names, concepts, and subjects.

While the scope of the companion is broad, there are some omissions. Eleanor Roosevelt is mentioned only in passing within the article on her husband. Excluded are articles on broadcasting (particularly television), telecommunications, advertising, and the computer revolution (although that topic is implied in *Technology Transfer*). The politics of sport—specifically of the Olympic Games—is another issue not discussed. Included are articles on Buddhism, Hinduism, Islam, and the Roman Catholic Church that deal with the political effects of the adherents' beliefs, but the work omits specific papers on Judaism or Christianity. Jewish issues are treated in *Antisemitism, Arab-Israeli Conflict, Holocaust,* and *Israel,* but there is no analysis of the Jewish lobby's effects on U.S. politics or on international relations.

These omissions, however, do not detract from this useful work, which would have grown beyond one volume if all possible topics were included. As it is, the companion will be consulted for authoritative information on international issues and organizations, domestic conflicts in countries around the globe, forms of government and institutions, historical events, and biographical sketches of persons important in international affairs. *The Oxford Companion to Politics of the World*, at a very reasonable price, will be welcome in public and academic libraries.

The Washington Almanac: A Guide to Federal Policy. By Lawrence J. Haas. Holt, 1992. 653p. index. hardcover $50 (0-8050-1761-5).
320'.6 U.S.—Politics and government—1989– || Political planning—U.S. || U.S.—Economic policy—1981– || U.S.—Social Policy—1980– [CIP] 91-37577

Compiled by a longtime Washington reporter, *The Washington Almanac* is to serve as a "one-stop guide to policymaking in the nation's capital." Haas covers 23 areas of public interest and describes for each the major power figures inside the Beltway, basing his profiles on extensive interviewing and reading of news sources. These 23 areas are arranged in five major sections: "American Society" (e.g., health, civil rights), "Leading Actors" (e.g., farmers, states and cities), "The Economy" (e.g., taxes), "The Nation of Tomorrow" (e.g., energy, telecommunications), and "America and the World" (e.g., defense). This arrangement is of little consequence, and the index will help the baffled reader.

The key questions to ask are (1) how accurate are Haas' selections of key players on these issues, and (2) how valuable to the novice will this source be? The first question is easier to answer. For each topic, Haas supplies a brief essay on recent developments, then provides thumbnail sketches and addresses and telephone numbers for key individuals from the Executive Branch, Congress and its staff, and the private sector (i.e., the heads of special-interest groups based in Washington). For example, under "The Poor" he profiles the assistant secretary for children and families and the commissioner in the Administration for Children, Youth, and Families, both in the Health and Human Services Department. We also find Senators Daniel Moynihan and Jay Rockefeller, Congressmen George Miller, Tom Downey, and Leon Panetta and two staff members of the House Ways and Means Committee. From the private sector, Haas picks the executive directors of the Center on Budget and Policy Priorities, the Children's Defense Fund, the Food Research and Action Center, and the Committee for Economic Development. He also treats two scholars from the Urban Institute and the American Enterprise Institute for Public Policy Research. Haas warns the reader that policy-makers whose influence spans many issues, such as the president, are not profiled.

How accurate is Haas in his depictions? In checking the biographical details of the political figures with the *Almanac of American Politics* and the *United States Government Manual*, no discrepancies were found in executive or legislative branch biographies and official appointments. Checking the private sector's movers and shakers was more difficult. Most of the chief officers of unions, public interest groups, or associations are not sketched in other convenient sources. Whether another analyst, equally in the know, would have selected the same people is the most difficult question to answer.

The strength of the almanac lies in the breezy characterizations in the sketches of these policy shapers. Haas speaks as one who is familiar with the salient issues. The work will be most helpful to experienced political activists. *The Washington Almanac* is recommended for public and academic library consideration.

The Right Guide: A Guide to Conservative and Right-of-Center Organizations. Ed. by Derk Arend Wilcox and others. Economics America, 612 Church St., Ann Arbor, MI 48104, 1993. 444p. index. hardcover $74.95 (0-914169-01-7; ISSN 1064-7414).

320.52'06 Conservatism—Societies, etc. || Right and left (Political science)—Societies, etc. [BKL] 92-3456

This is the only "comprehensive and independent source of information on the organizations that are developing the conservative agenda," claim the editors in the preface to *The Right Guide*, a directory of more than 2,500 groups and publications in the U.S. and abroad. The book admirably achieves its purpose of providing information about the organizations and people producing the ideas and advancing right-oriented public policy and scholarship today.

The largest section of the work is "Profiles," which lists 500 organizations alphabetically by their official name. Each entry includes the group's mission, accomplishments, publications, availability of internships, key personnel, and contact information. Organizations listed range from the well-known Heritage Foundation (150 employees) and the Hoover Institution on War, Revolution, and Peace (250 employees) to Quality Education Inc. (one employee), whose mission is "freedom from Damn Yankees and other oppressive governments." "Features" is a section that gives a more detailed look at 30 of these groups, such as Consumers' Research Inc., "the only consumer-oriented magazine that analyzes and reports on issues with an appreciation of free markets and an understanding of economic principles."

While most profiles include only a paragraph or two of narrative description, the entries are not merely puff pieces. For example, the book states that the Ronald Reagan Presidential Foundation's mission "has, to date, been preoccupied with obtaining funds for itself." The information provided in half-page profiles is often substantial. For instance, the reader can learn that the Heartland Institute, founded in 1984, produces more free-market research and delivers it to more legislators and journalists than any other state-based research organization in the U.S. It is credited with major influence in deregulating taxicabs in Chicago and defeating mandated health insurance in Wisconsin. The organization produces conferences, seminars, videotapes, and more than 30 publications a year and sponsors the Madison Group, a national organization concerned with public policy.

Other sections of the book include addresses for right-wing organizations in 98 countries of the world; addresses for more than 600 periodicals offered by organizations listed in the "Profiles" section; names and addresses for conservative campus newspapers; and lists of organizations that are now defunct or whose current address or status is unknown. Two means of access to the directory listings are provided. Every significant word in the names of organizations and of publications is included in the keyword index. A profile subject index lists the organizations under 34 topics, such as *Right to Work, Traditional Values,* and *Race/Nationality-Based*.

A major strength of *The Right Guide* is its inclusion of many influential organizations that are not listed in other standard directories of associations, research centers, or publishers. This new work is recommended for academic and public libraries needing information about groups and publications of the political right.

Amnesty International: The 1992 Report on Human Rights around the World. Hunter House, 1992. annual. 320p. illus. maps. hardcover $24.95 (0-89793-110-6); paper $15 (0-89793-109-2).

323.49 Civil rights—Periodicals || Political prisoners—Periodicals || Human rights—Periodicals [OCLC]

As in previous annual reports of this human rights watchdog organization, the main body of the book is a country-by-country summary and analysis of human rights violations during the previous year. The report covers investigations Amnesty International (AI) made in 143 countries during 1991. Each entry includes a one-paragraph summary and a narrative analysis (from one-quarter page to three pages in length, though the size of the analysis represents "no basis of comparison of the extent and depth of concern to Amnesty International"). The analysis consists of documentation resulting from on-site AI investigations as well as a statement regarding any action the government took in response to AI's findings.

The report begins with six short essays discussing AI's work. The first, "Getting Away with Murder," highlights how, despite the monumental changes that have transformed the world during the past two years, human rights abuses are as prevalent as ever. "Taking On New Challenges" describes how AI has broadened its concerns about human rights by extending its investigations to opposition political groups that practice torture or engage in arbitrary attacks on civilians for terror value. Other essays show how AI campaigns in 1991 have made a difference in freeing prisoners or changing government policies in such countries as Malawi, Turkey, South Korea, Morocco, and Egypt; how its world-wide opposition to the death penalty has resulted in a decrease of official executions of prisoners; and how AI has helped secure the rights of refugees throughout the world.

Appendixes include a table of AI visits in 1991, AI office addresses throughout the world, and a table describing relevant international human rights treaties. The report lacks an index, which makes it difficult for readers to highlight particular groups of people who are targets of abuses.

For the first time, AI has made this annual report available to the general public. This offers libraries an opportunity to offer an authoritative and inexpensive report on a major international problem from an organization that has been generally recognized to be a fair and impartial investigator of human rights violations. Strongly recommended for academic, public, and high school libraries.

Handbook of Campaign Spending: Money in the 1990 Congressional Races. By Sara Fritz and Dwight Morris. Congressional Quarterly, 1992. 567p. index. tables. hardcover $105 (0-87187-735-X).

324.7'8 Campaign funds—U.S.—Handbooks, manuals, etc. || U.S. Congress—Elections, 1990—Handbook, manuals, etc. [CIP] 92-8597

Open Secrets: The Encyclopedia of Congressional Money and Politics. 2d ed. By Larry Makinson. Congressional Quarterly, 1992. 1,339p. charts. index. tables. hardcover $136 (0-87187-689-2).

324.7'8 Campaign funds—U.S. || Political action committees—U.S. || U.S. Congress—Elections, 1990 [CIP] 92-5802

These two books show how campaign funds are spent and where they come from.

A simple bar graph in the *Annual Report 1990* of the Federal Election Commission indicates that median receipts and disbursements for incumbent Senate Republican candidates in the 1990 elections were about $2 million each. To see how this money was spent, one could consult the commission's *Combined Federal/State Disclosure Directory* to find addresses of federal and state agencies that provide campaign and personal financial reports. A federal government document, FEC *Reports on Financial Activity: Final Report: U.S. Senate and House Campaigns,* provides some summary statistics on receipts and expenditures of individual congressional campaigns.

None of these documents provides the extent of detail (nor the moralizing) that do Fritz and Morris in the *Handbook of Campaign Spending.* Not a spin-off of a government document, the handbook is the first comprehensive study of congressional campaign spending. With support from the *Los Angeles Times*, these journalists analyzed 437,753 expenditures reported to the FEC by 972 candidates for the 1990 elections. They crunched the data into 220 categories such as direct mail, travel, and rent and output it in a clear, well-organized format.

In a prefatory statement, the authors set the tone for the work. They proclaim the electoral process as distorted, seeing politicians as power-mad spenders consumed by the "urge to build a political empire." They conclude that the presence of large amounts of easy money causes exorbitant spending; rising campaign costs are not to blame. Introductory chapters provide interesting and readable text on such matters as fund-raising, television expenditures, and the phenomenon of exorbitant incumbent spending. Numerous tables list top spenders in various categories: meals, flowers, cellular phone bills. The authors disprove several myths. They reveal, for example, that individual donations exceeded PAC donations in the 1990 campaign. And expenditures for television time were much lower than proclaimed by the candidates themselves.

To their credit, the authors limit their preaching on reform to one chapter. What follows is the meat of the book: a page on the Senate races in each state followed by a page on each House district race. In these pages, we see individual campaign expenses in each of eight categories: overhead, fund-raising, polling, advertising, other campaign activity, gifts/entertainment, donations, and unitemized expenses. Each page also includes text explaining the financial and political environment of the particular contest. Here we learn which candidate used campaign money to buy a pig for the local food bank, who was frugal enough to have his wife cater his PAC fundraisers, and who spent $17,000 on a Potomac River cruise for his constituents.

Handbook of Campaign Spending makes FEC spending data conveniently available to the public for the first time. It informs on individual politicians' behavior. More important, though, is its broader study of the American election phenomenon. It allows us "to study the full impact that special-interest money is having on American democracy." For this last reason, this well-prepared, thorough, and entertaining book should be considered by all academic and public libraries.

Two hundred pages longer than the first edition (1990), *Open Secrets* is the definitive encyclopedia of contributions to the 1990 congressional election. It details political action committee (PAC) and, for the first time, individual contributions to each member of Congress and sorts and ranks these monies by numerous criteria. Names of persons who made individual contributions are not listed; rather, the companies where these persons work are. More than 3,200 PACs, every member of Congress, and over $260 million in contributions are analyzed.

To find that Eli Lilly & Company was the top contributor ($55,700) to members of the Senate Labor and Human Resources Committee seems puzzling until one sees that biomedical research falls under the jurisdiction of the committee. Reported in a chart of the "Biggest Contributors to Senators," Shearson Lehman Hutton's contribution to Bill Bradley of $71,800 makes sense when the reader is informed that he chairs the International Debt subcommittee of the Senate Finance Committee. The careful reader might question the data when this same contribution is reported as $72,300 in Bradley's two-page profile later in the book. (Such an apparent error does little damage to an informative book.)

A project of the Center for Responsive Politics, *Open Secrets* results from extensive research in the files of the FEC's Public Records Office. The current edition follows the same five-part organization as the first. Beginning the book are short essays on subjects such as the top 100 PACs by dollars donated. PACs are then surveyed by industry group, reporting which sectors the money came from and what elected officials received the money. Each House and Senate committee is profiled, revealing total contributions to committee members and charting industry category and sector contributions to the committee members. "Member Profiles," by far the book's largest section, gives a two-page profile of every member of Congress' receipts, including company/PAC names and dollar amounts.

The *Almanac of Federal* PACs (Amward Publications, 1990) gives brief PAC profiles and summary contributions but names no companies and analyzes no committees or PAC sectors. *Public Interest Profiles, 1992–1993* (Congressional Quarterly, 1992) makes the best companion piece to *Open Secrets*. It gives extensive textual profiles of the PACs, discussing at length their purpose, operations, effectiveness, and political orientation. *Open Secrets* will be useful in public and academic libraries. Smaller libraries unable to afford a copy will want to consider its spin-off, *The Cash Constituents of Congress*. It provides an overview of campaign financing but does not include profiles of every member of Congress. It is available from CQ in paper for $30.95 (0-87187-690-6).

An Atlas of World Political Flashpoints: A Sourcebook of Geopolitical Crisis. By Ewan W. Anderson. Facts On File, 1993. 243p. bibliog. hardcover $40 (0-8160-2885-0).
327.1'01 Geopolitics—Maps ‖ Boundary disputes—Maps ‖ World politics—1985–1995—Maps [CIP] 92-30193

This novel sourcebook of the 80 most volatile global hot spots covers boundary disputes between nations and ethnic struggles within them. The entries have been sketched by Anderson, a senior lecturer at Durham University (U.K.), who specializes in geopolitics. In a thoughtful introduction, he distinguishes actual or potential political crises as either geographic (physical), strategic (struggles over defensive position), sociocultural, or over economic resources. These distinctions, however, are not further developed in the work.

Alphabetically listed, the crisis regions are briefly sketched in one or two pages each; thus, the treatments are pithy and cursory. Included in each sketch are a description of the area, a few paragraphs of history, a summary of the current situation, a black-and-white line map, and a few references. Many of the conflicts would be unknown to all but specialists (e.g., Bab-el-Mandeb, Cabinda, the Hatay, Kosovo, Mururoa Atoll, the Ogaden, Rockall, Spitzbergen, Tacna, and the Tunbs Islands).

In terms of the geographic range of flashpoints, only mainland Australia escapes Anderson's eye. However, the only North American dispute he includes is Panama. Some might think that ethnic tensions in Canada or even in the U.S. are as volatile as many that are covered. The description of the Ogaden slights current anarchy in Somalia, even though the book was written in 1992. Anderson's sketch of the cleavages ravaging the former Yugoslavia (the Alps-Adriatic Region) is timely; it mentions the Serbian shelling of Sarajevo.

While the approach in this work is original, its utility is uncertain. The entries are similar in length to what one would expect in a general encyclopedia's treatment of the areas and conflicts in question. However, in comparing the coverage of 10 areas to 1992 encyclopedia sources, it was found that the *Atlas of World Political Flashpoints* included more information about current tensions. The flashpoints are most densely packed in the Middle East and Eastern Europe. One might say that the book could be of greatest benefit to the prospective tourist or retireee as a directory of places best *not* to visit and certainly *not* in which to retire. More seriously, academic libraries and large public libraries might want to consider for purchase this affordable, basic sourcebook.

Spies and Provocateurs: A Worldwide Encyclopedia of Persons Conducting Espionage and Covert Action, 1946–1991. By Wendell L. Minnick. McFarland, 1992. 310p. bibliog. index. hardcover $45 (0-89950-746-8).
327.1'2 [B] Intelligence officers—Biography ‖ Spies—Biography ‖ Agents provocateurs—Biography [CIP] 92-50312

The author has used autobiographies and secondary sources to prepare brief biographical information on 725 spies. Individual entries provide information on an agent's major espionage activity and its consequences for the espionage systems and countries involved. Most of the entries conclude with references to the sources used by the author, including reference works, books, journal articles, and newspaper reports.

A brief glossary contains special vocabulary and initialisms for agencies (RCMP, SSD, STB, etc.). Another useful feature is a chronology of significant events in espionage taking place between 1946 and September 6, 1991. The index is helpful but is not used to full advantage. For example, there are no subject entries for *assassins*, *political coups*, or *sabotage*.

This collective biography contains more agents than does Ronald Payne's *Who's Who in Espionage* (1984), but Payne provides much more complete and interesting information for the agents he selected to include. WWIE covers a longer time period, primarily the twentieth century. Payne gives good, brief coverage of the major intelligence systems, such as the CIA, and includes helpful background information on such subjects as *Blackmail and Entrapment, Counter-Espionage,* and *Interrogation*. His glossary, entitled "Spytalk," is also more informative, serving to define the spy's vocabulary. Both works provide a good bibliography. WWIE does not include a chronology. Funds permitting, the sheer number of agents included in *Spies and Provocateurs* makes this new work a necessary supplement to Payne.

Directory of Russian MPs: People's Deputies of the Supreme Soviet of Russia-Russian Federation. Ed. by Martin McCauley. Longman; dist. by Gale, 1992. 326p. hardcover $260 (0-582-09647-2).
328.47'092 [B] Legislators—Russia (Federation)—Biography ‖ Russia (Federation)—Officials and employees—Directories [OCLC] 93-121409

The members of the First Congress of People's Deputies of the Russian Federation who convened their meeting in May 1990 were riding a wave of change that was sweeping across the Soviet Union. Key players in the Russian political drama have been the members of the Russian parliament, the Supreme Soviet—252 delegates selected from the larger Congress of People's Deputies who carry on many of the functions of government between sessions of congress. This directory provides biographical information about each of these deputies as of April 1992.

Each of the entries provides the deputy's office address, telephone number, hometown, list of parliamentary posts held, and text of approximately 500 words. The text details the votes that led to the deputy's election and provides information regarding personal, educational, professional, and political backgrounds. Two final paragraphs outline the issues important during the deputy's election campaign and the significant actions that the deputy has supported or opposed in the first through the fourth sessions of the congress. No sources are given for this information.

Introducing the entire work is a 20-page essay that provides both an excellent background of the structure of the Russian legislative body and a detailed history of the sessions of the congress from its first meeting on May 16, 1990, through early April 1992. In addition, introductory matter contains a list of national territorial subdivisions in the Russia-Russian Federation; a list of MPs by name, nationality, and constituency; listings of various committees, subcommittees, and other subgroups of the Supreme Soviet; and a glossary of terms.

Given the enormous changes in the former Soviet Union in the recent past, the need for up-to-date information on this area of the world is obvious. This is an excellent source for reference collections serving the serious researcher. At $260, however, it will be an acquisition only for large or specialized collections.

Election Results Directory: A Complete Listing of State and Federal Legislative and Executive Branch Officials. National Conference of State Legislatures, 1993. 282p. index. paper $35 (1-55516-741-1).
328.730025 U.S.—Congress—Directories ‖ Legislators—U.S.—States—Directories [OCLC]

After every biennial federal and state congressional election, reference librarians are hard-pressed for several months to locate or to document for patrons the names of newly elected (or reelected) senators and representatives. Who in the early winter of 1993 could find a handy tool naming the new members of the 103d U.S. Congress or specifying which party now controls the House or Senate in Iowa? To the rescue comes the *Election Results Directory,* issued in January by the staff of the National Conference of State Legislatures. In it one can find the answers to questions such as these earlier than usual, for it supplies exactly what its subtitle promises.

The work is prefaced by an overview of the 1992 elections in 50 state legislatures. The inroads made by Republicans, women, and minorities are reported, and the impact of decennial redistricting upon the 1992 races is suggested. While Democrats suffered a net loss of 150 seats nationwide, they still control both chambers in 25 states and one chamber in eight more. This section closes with a table showing the legislative makeup and gubernatorial control by party in all of the states.

The directory itself begins with a list of the present members of the U.S. Senate and House of Representatives, respectively. Presented alphabetically by state, each member's party affiliation, district, and gender are identified. The list is particularly useful for establishing the 114 new members of Congress and the 13 new senators (they are marked by asterisks).

The bulk of the directory furnishes for each state its primary executive-branch officials and all current members of its senate and general assembly (or house of representatives) endorsed by the voters in 1992. In addition to the same data as their national counterparts, the home addresses (without telephone numbers) of these 7,424 legislators are given. A few basic facts about each state's political (i.e., congressional) environment also appear.

The final list is of elected officials and legislators in Guam, Puerto Rico, District of Columbia, North Mariana Islands, and U.S. Virgin Islands. An appendix chart reports the legislative calendars for the 50 states. No maps of legislative districts are included, so a user needs to know their district numbers if looking for the names of their representatives. A name index of all individuals posted in the directory ends the volume. Would you believe that there are more than 80 Smiths in the state legislatures?

This tool is the earliest published source for the November general-election results. As such, it will be of value in any library that feels the need to field queries on election winners as promptly as possible after these contests. Thus, the Board hopes that this new, inexpensive source will become a regular biennial product.

BUSINESS, ECONOMICS

Link's International Dictionary of Business Economics. By Albert N. Link. Probus Publishing, 1992. 328p. hardcover $45 (1-55738-495-9); paper $24.95 (1-55738-505-X).
330'.03 Economics—Dictionaries ‖ Business—Dictionaries [BKL]

Link, a professor at the University of North Carolina at Greensboro, is the author of numerous scholarly books and articles and serves as consultant to government agencies and major corporations. He designed this dictionary for professionals who occasionally need to refresh their memory regarding an economics term used in business. The book defines approximately 2,200 terms, phrases, and statistical methods. Throughout the work are frequent uses of *see* and *see also* references. Although some acronyms are cross-referenced (e.g., "GATT See General Agreement on Tariffs and Trade"), many others (e.g., CPI, GDP) are not. A basic understanding of statistics is helpful for the user, as statistical formulas are frequently used within entry definitions. No charts, graphs, or diagrams appear as illustrations in any of the definitions. A useful feature of this book is the citation of significant court cases when relevant. Definitions are succinct, averaging only three or four sentences in length. As with many specialized dictionaries, there are no pronunciation or word-origin keys.

An abundance of business dictionaries is available in libraries. Two recent works, *A Lexicon of Economics* [RBB Je 1 92] and the *HarperCollins Dictionary of Economics* [RBB My 15 91], are useful for comparison. The first title has approximately 800 entries; the second, 1,700. Each makes appropriate use of a variety of illustrations to support entry definitions. In general, each requires less knowledge of statistics. A random comparison of entries in the three works showed little duplication. *Link's International Dictionary of Business Economics* is a useful reference work for academic, public, and specialized libraries serving a business clientele that need an up-to-date dictionary on this topic.

Economic Indicators Handbook: Time Series, Conversions, Documentation. Comp. by Arsen J. Darnay. Gale, 1992. 1,056p. index. tables. hardcover $145 (0-8103-8400-0).

BUSINESS, ECONOMICS

330.973 Economic indicators—U.S. ‖ U.S.—Economic conditions [CIP] 92-13545

Gross domestic product, leading economic indicators, consumer price index—these are terms we hear on the evening news and read in our daily newspapers. They are statistical series used to measure the health of the U.S. economy. Here Darnay, the compiler of such business reference sources as Manufacturing USA [RBB Je 15 90], provides 805 tables for 267 series. The tables are almost all based on U.S. government sources, usually the Commerce or Labor departments. Most tables are current as of 1991. Some give monthly data for the past 20 years, others for 50 years, and some go back more than 100 years. Most series are given in two forms: in actual dollars and converted to constant dollars.

Each statistical series is introduced by an explanation of the tables, which is accessible to laypeople. Brief bibliographies are often provided for further reading. Among the tables in the gross national product and gross domestic product series are "Change in Business Inventories" and "Net Exports of Goods and Services." Also given are business-cycle indicators (composite indexes of leading, coincident, and lagging indicators) and such cyclic indicators as unemployment. The consumer price index is presented for the average U.S. city and then for 27 specific cities. For each city are listed figures for food, housing, apparel, transportation, medical care, and entertainment. Producer price indexes are given for a range of businesses from farm products to machinery and equipment. The final chapter provides selected stock-market indexes. A keyword index completes the volume.

Libraries with large government-publications collections will be able to pull together some of the information presented here. However, having data provided for these series since their inceptions in one volume is extremely handy. Academic and large public libraries will find Economic Indicators Handbook a worthy addition to their business collections. —Sandy Whiteley

Dictionary of United States Economic History. By James S. Olson and Susan Wladaver-Morgan. Greenwood, 1992. 667p. bibliog. index. hardcover $85 (0-313-26532-1).

330.973'003 U.S.—Economic conditions—Dictionaries [CIP] 91-32193

Two historians have compiled a basic source on 1,300 topics in American economic history. It covers prominent businesspeople and labor leaders, corporations and government agencies, officials and organizations, and events and legal matters. Asterisks note cross-references to related articles. References to books or articles for further reading follow each entry.

Entries are usually one paragraph in length, although American Revolution and Women receive more extended treatment. The entries Drake, Francis, and American Samoa don't seem to be relevant to the topic. The rather short article New Deal is supplemented by many other entries located through the index. The time period covered begins with acts of the British Parliament before the Revolutionary War and ends with the entries Supply-Side Economics and Trickle-Down Theory. There is no separate entry on the recent problem of the federal debt; the articles on H. Ross Perot and the recession of 1991 do not note it. The entry Funding the National Debt refers to the beginning of the nation; Reaganomics mentions the federal deficit. While biographical entries make up almost half the book, Boston Tea Party, Dollar Diplomacy, Hoovervilles, and Whip Inflation Now are examples of other subjects covered. The 20-page chronology of U.S. economic history, the selected bibliography, and the accurate index add to the reference value of the work.

Information on many topics found here—for example, Rachel Carson, Eugene Debs, Louisiana Purchase, and the National Grange—is in other readily available sources, such as general encyclopedias. Scribner's three-volume Encyclopedia of American Economic History has lengthy articles on broad topics rather than the specific entries found here. As a brief information source, the Dictionary of United States Economic History may be useful in public and academic libraries.

Markets of the U.S. for Business Planners: Historical and Current Profiles of 183 U.S. Urban Economies by Major Section and Industry, with Maps, Graphics, and Commentary. 2v. Ed. by Thomas F. Conroy. Omnigraphics, 1992. charts. index. maps. tables. hardcover $185 (1-55888-313-4).

330.973'009173 U.S.—Economic conditions—1981—Statistics ‖ Income—U.S.—Statistics ‖ Industrial surveys—U.S. ‖ Market surveys—U.S. [CIP] 92-5430

The purpose of this compilation of economic and demographic data is to "provide business people with an easy way to evaluate and compare opportunities in different locations."

The 183 locations, arranged from Bangor, Maine, in the east to Honolulu, Hawaii, are economic areas as defined by the Bureau of Economic Analysis (BEA), the federal government's principal analytical and forecasting agency. For each community, the following information is provided: a map of the market area (which includes surrounding counties), an analytical summary that discusses the economic base and growth rate of the area's economy, and a bar chart that shows the contribution of various parts of the economy in 1969 and 1988. Other bar charts show the most important industries and the most dynamic ones. These are followed by five tables of personal income: income history, real annual change, annual percentage change, index of change from 1969, and measure of importance. Included on each table are population data and the 77 major industries that generated the personal income, including services, retail trade, and government.

Concluding the volume are an index that lists the 183 market areas alphabetically and an appendix that contains tables of county growth rates listed numerically by BEA areas. In general, the information in Markets is presented in an easy-to-read format.

Data in this set were taken from the BEA's Personal Income and Earnings Database. This information is not available in any government publication in exactly the same form, although BEA's Local Area Personal Income, 1984–89 has somewhat similar tables. Covering every county, urban and rural, Markets of the U.S. will be welcomed by business planners, corporate librarians, business-school students, and market researchers.

American Directory of Organized Labor: Unions, Locals, Agreements, and Employers. Ed. by Cynthia Russell Spomer. Gale, 1992. 1,638p. indexes. hardcover $275 (0-8103-8360-8).

331.88'025 Trade-unions—U.S.—Directories [CIP] 92-2803

Gale has issued a hefty new directory that sketches the composition of 230 major international unions and approximately 40,000 local affiliates across the U.S. The editor compiled the information through questionnaire surveys of major unions and a review of the annual reports filed by labor organizations with the U.S. Department of Labor.

The directory is divided into four sections. "Parent Unions" focuses on the national level, giving basic historical and structural data, key officials' names (it does not specify the positions of the officials), finances, and major collective bargaining agreements. Much of this data can be found in the Encyclopedia of Associations and, for historical treatments, in Fink's Labor Unions (1977). Another feature of the work under review lies in "Regional, State, and Local Unions," containing more than 39,000 brief directory entries. These are arranged alphabetically by parent union, then by state, and by city within state. For example, the American Postal Workers Union is represented by some 2,000 local units in this section, while the Coliseum Usher and Usherette Association has only one local, in Bath, Ohio.

Two shorter sections complete the directory. "Selected Bargaining Agreements," organized alphabetically by name of the parent union, lists major labor contracts and, for each, the number of workers covered, and the dates when a contract became effective and when it is to expire. Some of the listings also specify key provisions in the contract. Finally, a listing of these agreements is arranged by employer name.

The final 929 pages of the volume consist of four index listings: by industry, by geographic location, by name of AFL-CIO affiliate, and by master name and keyword. These indexes have several problems. For instance, in the geographic index the entries begin with the full name of the labor organization, followed by address information. The user has to scan several lines to decipher that the alphabetic sequence is by city name, which is shown in italics toward the end of each entry. Despite the 497 pages in the master-name and keyword index, users may have difficulty locating entries for local unions by common names or when the parent organization is not known. For example, New York State United Teachers (entry 3960) is not indexed under any of its terms; it appears in the index alphabetically under A as American Federation of Teachers, New York State United Teachers. Local 100A of the United Food and Commercial Workers (entry 33236) is known locally as the Beef Boners and Sausage Makers Union, but this descriptive name is not included in the directory nor its indexes. In addition, listings for some labor organizations, including the United Federation of Teachers and the Motion Picture Studio Mechanics, could not be found.

The closest rival to this directory is the biennial *Directory of U.S. Labor Organizations* (Bureau of National Affairs), but that work provides only headquarters data. The cost of the *American Directory of Organized Labor* ($275) far exceeds that of the BNA publication and, despite the criticisms mentioned, if information on organized labor is of importance to a library's clientele, then there is no present substitute for this new Gale directory.

The New Palgrave Dictionary of Money and Finance. 3v. Ed. by Peter Newman and others. Stockton Press, 1992. 860p. bibliog. hardcover $595 (1-56159-041-X).
332'.03 Finance—Dictionaries [OCLC] 92-28016

With the 1987 publication of *The New Palgrave: A Dictionary of Economics*, Macmillan U.K. and Stockton Press produced the landmark encyclopedia of economics for the twentieth century. This new work, intended as a companion set, concentrates on the theory and applications of money and finance. It is a scholarly work, covering both the mathematical principles behind the concepts as well as the results of their actual use in today's economy.

The dictionary's 1,008 entries are arranged alphabetically within three volumes. The essays are intended to be authoritative for each topic, ranging in length from a single paragraph to dozens of pages, and each is signed. The vast majority of the 803 contributors are academics, representing universities and research centers throughout the world. Other authors are associated with major institutions in the banking and finance industries, such as the Federal Reserve or the Bank of Israel. Approximately 80 percent of the more than 1,000 essays were commissioned specifically for this work. The entries reflect the international flavor of the contributors, providing articles as diverse as *Hong Kong Stock Exchange* and *Islamic Banking*. While the dictionary provides descriptions of systems throughout the world, it tends to concentrate on topics of interest to British and American readers.

In general, the theoretical articles are much more difficult for the layperson to comprehend than those on applied topics. However, even the theoretical entries usually begin with a brief summary that can be of use to the general reader. A large number of the entries require an understanding of differential calculus and advanced mathematics to fully comprehend the subject matter. The entries *Cost of Capital* and *International Finance* rely heavily on high-level mathematical skills. In contrast, other entries (e.g., *Credit Unions*, *Discount Rate*) use more common terminology and familiar examples so that they can be understood by a layperson.

Each entry contains a bibliography, varying in length according to the specificity of the topic. Cited materials range from classic works to papers published as recently as 1990. Each of the longer entries is followed by five to ten references to other essays. This system of cross-referencing is intended to replace a traditional index. Other than the alphabetical list of entries and cross-references, the only method of identifying an article is through the subject classification system, included as an appendix, that places each entry into a hierarchical scheme. Such a classification may be useful to the knowledgeable reader but will be difficult for those without a specialized background.

The New Palgrave Dictionary of Money and Finance is clearly a landmark publication. It presents the economic information that affects our daily lives, with each entry written by one of the foremost experts in the field. However, because of its reliance on advanced mathematics and economic theory, much of the information will not be accessible to the general reader. While this work will be a welcome addition to the reference collections of libraries supporting business and economic research, it will not be as useful in the general public library. Librarians considering this work should have a clear understanding of their user population before making a positive selection.

Dictionary of Banking. By Jerry M. Rosenberg. Wiley, 1992. 369p. hardcover $39.95 (0-471-57435-X); paper $14.95 (0-471-57436-8).
332.1'03 Banks and banking—Dictionaries [CIP] 92-7419

Dictionary of Investing. By Jerry M. Rosenberg. Wiley, 1992. 368p. hardcover $39.95 (0-471-57433-3); paper $14.95 (0-471-57434-1).
332.6'03 Investments—Dictionaries [CIP] 92-6357

Dictionary of Business and Management. By Jerry M. Rosenberg. Wiley, 1992. 374p. hardcover $39.95 (0-471-57812-6); paper $14.95 (0-471-54536-8).
330'.03 Business—Dictionaries ‖ Management—Dictionaries [CIP] 92-7977

These three dictionaries have been updated to reflect the importance of the global perspective that has affected all fields of business and finance in recent years. Their purpose is to help businesses in an international environment to be aware of accepted meanings, to enhance the process of sharing information, and to assist in stabilizing terminology. Rosenberg is also the compiler of the *McGraw-Hill Dictionary of Business Acronyms, Initials, and Abbreviations* and similar titles [RBB Ja 1 92].

Dictionary of Banking, first published in 1985, includes terminology from more than 39 fields of banking, such as brokerage, computer systems, financial management, mortgages, personal finance, public finance, and trusts. The *Dictionary of Investing*, a revision of the 1986 *Investor's Dictionary*, covers securities, banks, commodity markets, and insurance, plus 19 other areas. The *Dictionary of Business and Management*, first published in 1979 and revised in 1983, seeks to include terms from 33 fields, including accounting, administration, collective bargaining, personnel, and public policy.

More than 7,500 entries are listed in each dictionary. The entries in all three contain general and specialized information for both the experienced user and the newcomer. Where several meanings are given for an entry, these are arranged with the definition that has the widest use given first, progressing to more specific usages. Entries are arranged with compound terms listed under their most distinctive component and are alphabetized word by word up to the first comma to establish clusters of related terms. Slang terms as well as common acronyms and abbreviations are defined. Terms such as *cats and dogs* (highly speculative stocks) and *bed and breakfast deals* (short selling abuses) make the *Dictionary of Investing* a browser's delight. Typical entries range from one-sentence definitions to essay-like explanations, such as *savings industry bill* (*Dictionary of Banking*), which takes up one-half page. Syllabication and pronunciation are not given.

As in the earlier editions, several special appendixes are included in the *Dictionary of Business and Management*, with the most useful being the "Foreign Exchange" list. Others include a table of equivalents of area, capacity, etc.; a simple interest table; and the years in which a given amount will double at several rates of interest.

The amount of overlap between the more specialized *Dictionary of Banking* and *Dictionary of Investing* with the more general *Dictionary of Business and Management* is slight. Since each volume is available in paperback, most public and academic libraries can afford to purchase all three to maintain current awareness of the new terminology in these fields.

Who Owns Corporate America: A Comprehensive Listing of More than 75,000 Officers, Directors, and 10% Principal Stockholders and Their Holdings of Securities Issued by U.S. Public Companies. Ed. by Catherine M. Ehr. Taft Group; dist. by Gale, 1992. 1,716p. index. paper $275 (1-879784-36-X; ISSN 1061-1258).
[BKL] 92-3818

This new volume is the first printed source to arrange Securities and Exchange Commission (SEC) major stockholder data alphabetically by the last name of the stockholder. This arrangement enables nonprofit organizations, researchers, sales professionals, and other wealth-watcher professions to match a major wealth indicator to lists of current or prospective donors and to more accurately target funding appeals.

All of the information in this directory is derived from the *CDA/Spectrum Insider* database available online through Dialog. The 75,600 individuals listed are officers, directors, 10-percent principal stockholders, and other "insiders," as registered on the SEC's approved lists, which are updated quarterly. The data in the volume are current as of the May 1992, SEC filings and cover approximately

BUSINESS, ECONOMICS

4,000 publicly held companies. Each entry provides the following: the inside holder's full name; issuing company and its stock exchange symbol; number of shares; date; type of security (i.e., common, preferred, or class A); insider's relationships to the company and with the listed security (i.e., direct, indirect, or market maker); and the market value of the number of shares held.

The only index is the "Security Name Index," which lists the stockholders by the name of the securities company. After the stockholder's name is a code (in parentheses) showing the person's relationship to the issuing company. For its high price, a hardcover would help this volume last through hard use. Although relatively expensive, *Who Owns Corporate America* is a unique and valuable print resource that, hopefully, will be updated regularly. Business, public, and academic libraries will want to make this new reference work available to researchers, nonprofit organizations, and college development offices.

A Dictionary of Environmental Quotations. Comp. by Barbara K. Rodes and Rice Odell. Simon & Schuster, 1992. 355p. indexes. hardcover $35 (0-13-210576-4).
333.7 Nature—Quotations, maxims, etc.—Dictionaries ‖ Ecology—Quotations, maxims, etc.—Dictionaries [OCLC] 92-3055

A Dictionary of Quotations from Shakespeare: A Topical Guide to Over 3,000 Great Passages from the Plays, Sonnets, and Narrative Poems. By Margaret Miner and Hugh Rawson. Dutton, 1992. 368p. hardcover $25 (0-525-93451-0).
822.3'3 Shakespeare, William—Indexes ‖ Shakespeare, William—Quotations ‖ Quotations, English—Indexes [OCLC] 92-1354

Webster's II New Riverside Desk Quotations. By James B Simpson. Houghton, 1992. 420p. indexes. hardcover $8.95 (0-395-62024-4).
082 Quotations, English [CIP] 91-43811

One of this triad of quotation books is devoted to a topic previously untreated in a volume by itself. One covers a writer whose words are quoted more than any other source except the Bible. One is a spin-off of an earlier title. All three deserve consideration for that portion of the reference collection where there is always room for just one more book, provided, of course, the indexing is adequate.

A *Dictionary of Environmental Quotations* is a unique and timely offering of more than 3,700 quotations organized into 143 categories from *Acid Rain* to *Zoos*. Within each, the quotations are presented in chronological order. This provides a kind of overview of a particular concern throughout the ages (or at least through the last few decades). Each quotation includes the name of the author (when known), title of publication or occasion, and date (sometimes this may be an approximation). All manner of sources has been used for this compendium: slogans, the press, broadcast media, congressional hearings. Authors of the quotations include presidents, philosophers, poets, and politicians.

Two indexes are appended: one by author and one by subject. Both refer to the numbered categories and the numbered quotations within them, rather than to page numbers. A *Dictionary of Environmental Quotations* is a fine reference work, in which only a keyword index is lacking.

A topical guide to over 3,000 quotations, A *Dictionary of Quotations from Shakespeare* includes passages not only from the plays, but also from the sonnets and narrative poems. The quotations are grouped under more than 400 categories (e.g., *Abstinence*, *Money*, *Youth*). Act, scene or verse, and beginning line are provided for each passage. Almost half of the quotations are further annotated with the name of the speaker, the context, historical references, etc. This is an important feature since Shakespeare is all too often quoted inappropriately and out of context. There are abundant cross-references throughout and an ample keyword index.

A *Dictionary of Quotations from Shakespeare* compares favorably with *The Quotable Shakespeare: A Topical Dictionary* (1988), compiled by Charles DeLoach. Both books are topically arranged. However, DeLoach collected roughly twice as many quotations as Miner and Rawson. Although none of the quotations selected by DeLoach is set in context, character and title indexes are provided in addition to the topical index. Shakespeare scholars take note: DeLoach uses *The Riverside Shakespeare*, and Miner and Rawson use the Signet Classic editions.

A *Dictionary of Shakespeare Quotations* is an easy-to-use, well-planned collection of quotations of practical use to contemporary writers and speakers. Although it does not include as many quotations as *The Quotable Shakespeare*, its strength lies in its extensive cross-references and contextual settings and explanations.

The third and last title, *Webster's II New Riverside Desk Quotations*, is a smaller version of *Simpson's Contemporary Quotations* (1988). The emphasis is on contemporary wit and wisdom from the 1950s to 1987. More than 6,000 quotations (compared with nearly 10,000 in the parent volume) are topically arranged. Although a quick glance at the detailed table of contents allows for fairly easy access to particular topics, there are indexes by personal name and by subjects and key lines.

This book is intended for home use and is printed on cheap paper that will not have a long life. Libraries owning the parent volume will not want *Webster's II*, but it is an inexpensive collection for libraries on limited budgets.

The Big Outside: A Descriptive Inventory of the Big Wilderness Areas of the United States. Rev. ed. By Dave Foreman and Howie Wolke. Crown/Harmony, 1992. 499p. bibliog. index. maps. tables. paper $16 (0-517-58737-8).
333.78'2 Wilderness—U.S. [OCLC] 92-2272

Mountains, deserts, swampland, and forests are all part of this inventory of 385 wilderness areas in the 48 contiguous states that was first published in 1989. Wilderness areas are defined as roadless or inaccessible to all motor vehicles. Areas of over 100,000 acres in the West are organized by state and then by region. Areas of over 50,000 acres east of the Rockies are grouped by geographic region (e.g., Southeast, North Central) and then by either bioregion (swamp, forest) or geographic location within the state.

Each entry begins with an introductory discussion that includes the history of the area's wilderness, an ecological description, threats to the ecology, preservation efforts, and active conservation groups. Maps accompany each state and region. Entries for specific wilderness areas include the name and acreage of the area and its ownership or administrative agency listed on a table, followed by a detailed description of the terrain and its wildlife. A status report outlines the ecological importance and uniqueness of the area and past and possible future threats to the land and wildlife as a result of activities such as logging, mining, and tourism. Specific conservation recommendations are made; it is in this section that the strong conservationist bias becomes a bit strident. The authors are highly critical of governmental action, or lack thereof, in preserving the wilderness.

Essays on wilderness camping, a review of other wilderness inventories, and a description of specific ecological threats and their impact are included. Several appendixes conclude the work: wilderness areas ranked by size; acreage by state; national, regional, and state conservation groups (including addresses and telephone numbers); research notes; a bibliography; and Robert Marshall's (founder of the Wilderness Society) 1927 and 1936 inventories, which are the touchstones for this work. Comparison of existing acreage with that from Marshall's lists is noted when appropriate. The index lists the wilderness areas and some personal names.

This is an enlightening, well-researched, and beautifully written book that will be useful to conservationists, wilderness campers, and readers with a special interest in the subject of wilderness preservation.

Water Quality and Availability: A Reference Handbook. By E. Willard Miller and Ruby M. Miller. ABC-Clio, 1992. 430p. bibliog. index. hardcover $39.50 (0-87436-647-X).
333.91'00973 Water quality—U.S. ‖ Water-supply—U.S. [OCLC] 92-33057

Written out of concern for the environment, this title in the Contemporary World Issues series deals with a variety of topics relating to water, which, according to the authors, is our most fundamental resource. References are made to international organizations and problems, but the focus of the book is the U.S. water supply and its preservation. The book is divided into six sections. The first part deals with the history of water use and contamination in the U.S., and the second contains chronologies of several aspects of water use and abuse. Part 3 describes laws and regulations, part 4 lists national and international organizations that deal with water issues, part 5 is an extensive annotated bibliography, and part 6 is an annotated mediagraphy. The last three sections will be most helpful to readers looking for detailed information on the topic.

A glossary and short appendix containing four pertinent maps are included. Information in the text is made accessible by the use of guide phrases at the top of each page. The index does not add to the book's usefulness as a research tool because it contains mostly authors and titles found in the bibliography. Searching for a topic in the index will not yield much more information than skimming the text.

The handbook's greatest value is to the informed user who is looking for an organization or additional material on a water-related issue. The best place for this volume would be in a public library or in the private library of an environmental activist, to be used as a quick-reference source.

Guide to the National Wildlife Refuges. Rev. ed. By Laura Riley and William Riley. Macmillan/Collier, 1992. 684p. index. paper $16 (0-02-063660-1).
333.95'0973 Wildlife refuges—U.S.—Guidebooks [CIP] 92-19254

The Rileys sent questionnaires and talked to more than 200 refuge managers to produce this updated version of their 1979 guidebook of the same name. They have included 100 new refuges, deleted a few that have closed, and revised many entries, calling attention to wildlife species not previously mentioned. The 485 refuges listed in this new version are arranged by state within regions of the country, making it more useful than the first edition for travelers who want to explore more than one wildlife habitat in a geographic area.

The table of contents reflects the regional arrangement of the book: Northeast and Mid-Atlantic states, Southeast, Great Lakes, Hawaiian and Pacific Islands, and Alaska. Each of these regional sections opens with an introduction that characterizes the area and discusses the most prevalent forms of wildlife. Also described are features that affect the ambience of the place: large metropolitan areas nearby, swamps, superhighways, oil storage tanks, etc. As a result, anyone planning a visit to one of these refuges will have a good sense of what to expect. This introductory material concludes with a list of birds of special interest that are commonly found in the area, with the names of the refuges where they may be viewed and the best season in which to see them.

The listings for specific refuges contain an even more detailed description of the wildlife to be found there, ranging in length from short paragraphs to two and one-half pages. The authors, founding trustees of the Raptor Trust and directors of the National Wildlife Refuge Association, obviously love their work, for their descriptions are filled with the excitement of discovery. Each contains highlights: how to get there, hours open, what to see, what to do, where to stay, weather to expect, points of interest nearby, and an address to contact for more information. Some entries contain cautionary information such as what to take ("extra water," "good tires") and what to wear for "extremely variable temperature," and "ferocious biting insects . . . including ticks with Lyme disease."

A final section, "Refuges of the Future," briefly describes those areas in the planning stages. The book concludes with an index that can be used to find the location of specific wild creatures inhabiting more than one region. *Guide to the National Wildlife Refuges* is a unique purchase for any library, there being no other current comprehensive sourcebook like it. Its true usefulness, however, will be on the road with the traveler, in glove compartment or backpack.

American Wholesalers and Distributors Directory. Gale, 1992. 1,450p. biennial. hardcover $150 (0-8103-8248-2; ISSN 1061-2114).
338 Wholesale trade—U.S.—Directories [OCLC] 92-3850

As its straightforward, descriptive title implies, this is a directory of approximately 18,000 companies in the U.S. that act as wholesalers or distributors for a variety of products. Those products belong to 69 Standard Industrial Classification (SIC) categories that encompass both consumer goods (e.g., confectionery, furniture, toys) and industrial goods (e.g., construction and mining machinery, industrial supplies, scrap and waste materials).

The 18,000 companies are listed alphabetically by company name in the directory section. There each of the unnumbered entries lists, in varying degrees of completeness, address, telephone and fax numbers, "primary" and "additional" SIC numbers, year of establishment, estimated annual sales, number of employees, chief officers, and product line. The elements most likely to be omitted are product line, estimated annual sales, and company officers. The information presented about each company is similar to that given in *Ward's Business Directory*, also from Gale. Comparison of the two directories reveals that all but about a third of the companies listed in *American Wholesalers and Distributors Directory* are also listed in *Ward's*; however, in *Ward's* nothing distinguishes them as wholesalers or distributors rather than as, say, manufacturers.

The directory's geographic index lists the companies by state and by city within each state section. Scaled-down entries in this index list only company name, address, telephone and fax numbers, and primary industry, without that industry's SIC number. The second index, by SIC codes, ranks the companies active within each code by estimated sales, rounded off to the nearest $100,000.

This directory, by virtue of its 6,000 or so unique listings, supplements *Ward's* and other business directories. In comprehensive business reference collections, it can help manufacturers identify additional wholesale customers or distributors for their products, just as it can help retailers identify potential new suppliers.

The Government Directory of Addresses and Telephone Numbers: Your Comprehensive Guide to Federal, State, County, and Local Government Offices in the United States. Omnigraphics, 1992. 1,290p. maps. hardcover $89 (1-55888-799-7; ISSN 1062-1466).
338 U.S.—Politics and government—Directories || State governments—U.S.—Directories || Local government—U.S.—Directories || U.S.—Politics and government—Telephone directories || State governments—U.S.—Telephone directories [OCLC] 92-645925

This directory supplies addresses and detailed telephone listings for government agencies, with separate sections for federal, state, and local levels; over 100,000 offices are covered. Names of officeholders are provided only in the case of legislators and chief executive officers.

The federal section provides far more telephone numbers than the *United States Government Manual* and the *Official Congressional Directory*, both for the Beltway and for regional offices. For the Census Bureau, for instance, the headquarters listings are comparable in depth of detail to the bureau's own "Telephone Contacts" list (except that state data centers are not included in the directory under review), and several numbers are furnished for each of the bureau's regional offices. The list for members of Congress includes committee assignments and a detailed staff breakdown (without staff names); a separate subsection gives several telephone numbers for offices in the home states. There are separate subsections for congressional committees, giving committee and subcommittee membership and staff telephone numbers. A set of 60 half-page maps shows the service-area boundaries for the regional offices of various federal executive-branch agencies and for the Court of Appeals.

The state government section of the directory has separate subsections, arranged by state, for the executive and legislative branches; the latter includes listings for standing committee chairs. A keyword index is found at the end of both the federal and state sections. The local government section is divided into subsections for counties (by state) and cities (arranged alphabetically by city name); separate subsections are appended, with brief listings, for counties with populations under 25,000 and municipalities under 15,000. Introducing each of the directory's three main sections are a few pages of quick-reference listings.

A list of state delegations in Congress places Representative José Serrano incorrectly in New York's seventeenth district rather than the eighteenth, where the name given is that of his predecessor, Robert Garcia; however, the seventeenth's actual representative at the time of publication, Ted Weiss, does appear in the other House listings. The name information for elective offices is in some cases now obsolete, but, otherwise, this directory will be a convenient one-stop source for the major levels of government wherever specific telephone-number information is called for.

Harris Manufacturers Directory, 1993: National Edition. 2v. Ed. by Richard M. Fein and Frances L. Carlsen. Harris Publishing Co., 2057 Aurora Rd., Twinsburg, OH 44087, 1993. 3,512p. hardcover $395 (1-55600-049-9; ISSN 1061-2076).

BUSINESS, ECONOMICS

338 Manufactures—Directories ‖ U.S.—Manufactures—Directories [BKL] 92-3860

Harris is a publisher of state manufacturers directories. It seems to have combed its files for large companies to create the *Harris Manufacturers Directory*, which provides information on 37,645 publicly- and privately-held manufacturing establishments that employ at least 100 workers. Other firms that provide value-added services to manufacturing are also included. These firms fall into such categories as steel service centers, research and laboratory testing areas, and vocational rehabilitation centers.

The sources consulted to compile these volumes were association lists, buying guides, state and local departments of economic development, and local chambers of commerce. Company listings have been verified by telephone and mail within the last six months.

The two volumes are divided into six sections. The "Statistical Section" in volume 1 includes summary data by SIC code. Within each SIC code are listed the number of establishments and total number of employees for all of the firms listed in the directory. Also in this volume is the alphabetical listing of companies. Each of the 37,645 entries is sequentially numbered in order to make cross-referencing easier when searching other sections. Each company entry may have up to 18 data elements, such as address, telephone and fax numbers, number of employees, plant size (in square feet), primary and secondary SIC, headquarters, parent company and locality listing, estimated annual sales, computer make and model, product description, and principal officers. Most entries do not include all of these data elements. When sales figures are not available, they are estimated on the basis of the annual average sales per employee for the firm's SIC category, which is multiplied by the total number of employees at the firm.

Sections in volume 2 arrange the firms by state and city; by four-digit SIC designations with company name, city, state, and number of employees by class size; by ranking (largest manufacturing establishments are listed in rank order for the nation, then by each state giving the top companies); and by 4,000 product and manufacturing service categories.

For small libraries needing only regional information, Harris offers five regional editions of this book (Northeast, Southeast, Midwest, Southwest, Western) at prices ranging from $99 to $159. The *Harris Manufacturers Directory* is also offered on diskette or CD-ROM as the *Harris Selectory*.

If the need in a library for a manufacturers directory is just product and company-address information, then it may do well by purchasing the more economical *Thomas Register of Manufacturers* (20-plus volumes), which lists 152,000 U.S. companies, 112,000 trademark names, and more than 2,000 supply catalogs—all for $225. But where shelf space is a concern and the need is for company information beyond product, address, and telephone number, the *Harris Manufacturers Directory* is an excellent choice.

World Business Directory. 4v. Ed. by Meghan A. O'Meara and Kimberley A. Peterson. Gale, 1992. indexes. hardcover $395 (0-8103-7715-2; ISSN 1062-1172).

338 Business enterprises—Directories ‖ International business enterprises—Directories [OCLC] 92-655171

More than 200 World Trade Centers around the globe provide information, assistance, and facilities to support exporting and importing by member companies. Membership lists of these centers have been used as one of the sources for this first edition of *World Business Directory*, which lists over 100,000 companies in 190 countries, including the U.S. Selected because of their interest in international trade, the entries include major multinational businesses and small- and medium-size companies affiliated with World Trade Centers. Also listed are chambers of commerce, consulates, clubs, and WTC Network members.

Volumes 1–3 are geographically arranged from *Afghanistan* to *Zimbabwe*. Within each country, entries are alphabetical by company name. Full listings include address; telephone, fax, and telex numbers; names of executive officers; basic financial data; number of employees; year founded; products traded; parent company; WTC Network Code; company type; and fiscal year end. The information is in English, although the introductory pages are in French, Spanish, and German as well. Data come from WTC questionnaires, chambers of commerce, trade officials, annual reports, and telephone interviews. However, not all entries have full information. Under *Turkey*, for example, more than half the entries do not tell the nature of the business or merely list "exporting." Volume 4 consists of 3 indexes that provide access by specific product, by 95 different industries, and alphabetically by company name. All three indexes note the country along with company name, so it is possible to find companies that make knitted apparel in Algeria or companies in the automotive industry in Mexico. The information is also available in other formats—including customized lists on magnetic tape or floppy disk and mailing labels.

Dun's *Principal International Businesses* is an annual publication that is similar in coverage. It is, however, twice as expensive and is only leased, not sold.

Because some countries have few entries and because not all entries have full information, those interested in specific parts of the world or in a limited range of products may want to examine a copy of *World Business Directory* before purchasing. It will be valuable for those exploring international markets, locating potential trading partners, or seeking job opportunities around the world

Environmental Industries Marketplace: A Guide to U.S. Companies Providing Environmental Regulatory Compliance Products and Services. Ed. by Karen Napoleone Meech. Gale, 1992. 779p. hardcover $175 (0-8103-8569-4; ISSN 1061-2122).

338 U.S.—Industries—Directories ‖ Environmental protection—Directories [BKL] 92-3851

This is a name, subject, and geographic guide to "nearly 11,000 companies in the United States that provide environmentally effective products or services in compliance with federal and state regulations."

Each citation in the main alphabetic listing is numbered consecutively and contains the address, telephone and/or fax number, and a brief description of the product or service the company provides. The subject index lists the companies under 69 subject headings, from *Acid Rain* to *Water Pollution*. There are nine subject headings for specific types of recycling—battery, liquids, plastic, etc. The companies are also listed by geographic location (by state and by city).

The usefulness of such a list in either a public or an academic library is doubtful. There is little information given about the companies' services and products. Too many entries have as their entire description "Provides services to the environmental industry." Library patrons may find the geographic index useful if they are seeking employment with an environmental company. Others will have to use other company directories to supplement the information found here. Specialized titles such as the *Indoor Air Quality Directory* [RBB O 1 92] provide more detailed information about parts of this market.

Contemporary Entrepreneurs: Profiles of Entrepreneurs and the Businesses They Started, Representing 74 Companies in 30 Industries. Ed. by Craig E. Aronoff and John L. Ward. Omnigraphics, 1992. 477p. bibliog. index. hardcover $85 (1-55888-315-0).

338'.04 [B] Businessmen—U.S.—Biography ‖ Business enterprises—U.S.—History [CIP] 91-7637

Entrepreneurs are highly regarded in the U.S. Included here are 74 biographical profiles of entrepreneurs chosen from the mid-1970s and 1980s. The entries are arranged alphabetically and include both factual data (company name, address, telephone number, founding date, current revenues, number of employees, etc.) as well as five to seven pages of text. The essays follow a standard format with such sections as "Founders," "Business Origin," "Business Growth," "Business Obstacles," "Keys to Success," "Future Vision," and "Entrepreneurial Lessons." A short bibliography on the entrepreneur and company follows each entry. Each profile is signed by the compiler, most of whom appear to be free-lance writers. An index provides access by personal and corporate name, geographic location, type of business, and subject headings such as *family in businesses* and *women in business*. The 74 entries represent 36 industries, evenly divided between manufacturing and service. However, 16 profiles come from the computer industry, which comes as no surprise with the explosion of activity in this field during the 1980s. Of course, Steven Jobs, former Apple computer guru and current NeXT Computer CEO, is profiled in this book, along with Raymond Kurzweil, Debbi Fields of cookie fame, and film and record producer David Geffen. Industries covered range from a winery to the Home Shopping Network. The purpose of *Contem-*

porary Entrepreneurs is to give students a starting place for case studies, investors a place to find information on areas of economic growth, and other entrepreneurs the inspiration and vision for their particular pursuits. The work's primary usefulness will be in a college library, though much of the information in each biography could be assembled from a search in the standard periodical sources listed in the bibliographies provided at the end of each entry.

European Business Services Directory. Ed. by Michael B. Huellmantel. Gale, 1992. 1,374p. indexes. hardcover $275 (0-8103-7916-3; ISSN 1063-5718).

338.4 Business enterprises—Europe—Directories ‖ Europe—Commerce—Directories [OCLC] 92-24125

An associate editor of Gale's *Encyclopedia of Associations*, Huellmantel has produced in *European Business Services Directory* a first-of-its-kind directory. Entries for approximately 20,000 European service companies appear in 16 sections such as *Accounting, Advertising and Marketing, Computer Services, Insurance, Legal Services, Real Estate,* and *Translation and Interpretation*. Companies are arranged by service, then by country and city. The format is similar to other Gale directories. The typical entry includes sequential entry number, company address, annual sales, services offered, geographic scope, language capabilities, principal officers, and related companies. Entries seldom include data in all possible entry points.

The directory devotes the most space to Western Europe. The states of the former Soviet Union, Turkey, Greece, and Eastern European nations do appear; in most sections England, France, and Germany dominate. In the *Accounting* section, the single entries for Croatia and Austria pale in comparison to the 2,341 under England (exclusive of Northern Ireland, Scotland, and Wales).

Geographic and company-name indexes provide easy access to the service-listings section, which is the bulk of the book. The geographic index is arranged from *Albania* to *Yugoslavia* and is subarranged by city. The introduction and user's guide are each presented in English, German, and French.

Compiled from questionnaire responses, input from trade organizations, and related Gale databases, *European Business Services Directory* is the product of an extensive research undertaking. Nevertheless, the volume's comprehensiveness is difficult to judge. *Associated British Ports* (water transportation, U.K.) appears, though its parent, Associated British Ports Holdings PLC, a real-estate concern, does not. Hagemeyer N.V. (marketing research, the Netherlands) appears in *Moody's International Manual* but not *European Business Services Directory*. The *Folksam Group* (insurance, Sweden) appears in both works.

This work will be useful for large and affluent public libraries with a significant demand for directory information on the European service sector. Academic libraries collecting extensively in international business, libraries of corporations with significant international dealings, and individual recruiters, consultants, and marketers looking to tap the European market will want to consider purchase. This is probably the only directory available that includes 355 shipping and transportation companies in England, 90 engineering and related technical-services companies in Sweden, and 125 advertising and marketing companies in Denmark, all between the same two covers.

Job Seeker's Guide to Private and Public Companies. 4v. Ed. by Charity Anne Dorgan and Jennifer Mast. Gale, 1992. indexes. hardcover $350; $95/v. (0-8103-7810-8; ISSN 1061-3285).

Job hunting—United States—Directories ‖ Business enterprises—United States—Directories ‖ Corporations—United States—Directories [BKL]

This directory of over 15,000 companies is yet another of Gale's career titles. Divided into four volumes by region, it is meant to enable job seekers to pinpoint potential employers in a particular geographic area or industry.

Each regional volume is arranged by state and then by city. Supplementary material includes an industry index (by industry name, not SIC code) and a cumulative corporate-name index that is repeated in each volume. Each entry includes basic company data, such as telephone, fax, and toll-free numbers; founding date; if it is publicly or privately held; a business description; major products or services; parent company or subsidiaries (if relevant); corporate officers; sales for a recent year; and number of employees. If the company is included on a media ranking (e.g., *Fortune* 500), that is noted. The name of the human-resources contact and information on application procedures conclude the entry.

The companies included were selected by editors scanning the pages of *Ward's Business Directory* and *Business Rankings Annual* to find the largest companies, best small companies, fastest-growing companies, and the most valuable companies. This process has resulted in uneven coverage. For instance, despite the existence of many communities with large IBM operations, the one in White Plains, New York, is the only one listed in the set. Though the arrangement by place is intended to be helpful to people seeking jobs in the local area, it is sometimes misleading. For example, Berkshire Hathaway, with headquarters in Omaha, is listed as having 14,000 employees. In fact, few of these jobs are in Omaha. Most of them are in subsidiary companies around the country. Some information is already dated. For example, NCNB merged last year with C & S Sovran to become NationsBank. This work includes entries for the two former banks only. The entry for Pan American World Airways states that "this company is reported to be out of business."

Most of the information in this work can be found in *Ward's Business Directory*. *Job Seeker's Guide* does provide some unique information, namely the human-resources contact and application procedures. *Job Seekers Guide*, while attempting to compile information also found in the *Directory of Corporate Affiliations*, *S & P Register of Corporations*, the *Standard Directory of Advertisers*, and the *Million Dollar Directory*, does not consistently provide information of the quality of those other works. It is worth quick-and-dirty exploring, but job seekers would be well advised to check other sources before proceeding to contact employers. This set, or perhaps the volume covering the local region, should be considered by public and academic libraries.

Corporate Eponymy: A Biographical Dictionary of the Persons behind the Names of Major American, British, European and Asian Businesses. By Adrian Room. McFarland, 1992. 280p. bibliog. hardcover $35 (0-89950-679-8).

338.7'4 Businessmen—Biography—Dictionaries ‖ Industrialists—Biography—Dictionaries ‖ Business names—Dictionaries ‖ Eponyms—Dictionaries [CIP] 92-53502

This biographical dictionary aims to give users insight into the people behind such business names as Wimpy, Procter & Gamble, and Bacardi. The emphasis here is on identifying people who are difficult to locate in standard reference sources. Compiler Room finds it "interesting to see who these business people were, where and when they lived, and how... they came to give their name to a particular product or service." Users may find it fascinating and read the book cover to cover.

Only personal names are included; therefore, *Matsushita* is included while *Hitachi*, a place name, is not. In addition to surnames, abbreviations or initials, such as J & B, KP, or *Bejam*, are identified. Names are listed in a strict alphabetical arrangement, where K-Mart falls between *Kimberly-Clark* and *Knight-Ridder*. Entries are short; just several sentences giving the basic information on who, where, when, and how businesses were named. The emphasis is on the English-speaking world, but continental European and Asian names are sometimes featured (e.g., Braun of Germany and Honda of Japan). A concise description of the product or service for which the firm or company is best known is given for each entry. *See* references are used throughout, for example, "J. M. *Dent* see Dent." A short selected bibliography completes the book.

Corporate Eponymy is a worthwhile addition to any business collection and will intrigue many who happen to pick it up.

Directory of European Business. Comp. by Cambridge Market Intelligence. Bowker-Saur, 1992. 512p. index. tables. hardcover $195 (0-86291-617-8).

338.7'4 Europe—Commerce—Directories ‖ Europe—Industries—Directories ‖ Business enterprises—Europe—Directories [OCLC] 92-30040

This unique new directory provides coverage of 4,000 leading business-service companies, organizations, governmental agencies, and top manufacturing companies in 35 countries in Western and Eastern Europe. It is an invaluable resource that will help anyone who wants to understand the business environment and the importance of Europe in today's world. Its currency is demonstrated especially by the information included about the

Commonwealth of Independent States, Croatia, and Germany. The information was collected and compiled by Cambridge Market Intelligence in London.

The book is organized alphabetically by country, with each chapter discussing the business environment and then listing services, organizations, leading companies, government agencies, and sources for business information. For each country, the following information is given in the section on business conditions: a summary of the political system and government; an economic overview, including recent policy and performance; a description of the business culture; the principle cities; banking and business hours and currency; the tax system and trade regulations; business incentives; accounting standards; sources of finance; and selected other information.

The business-services section of each profile lists personal names, contact information, activities, and languages for accountants, advertising agencies, banks, insurance companies, law firms, management consultants, and companies specializing in market research, public relations, and venture capital. The section on leading companies provides net world-sales figures, and the entry for each company generally includes contact information, names of executives, personnel turnover, number of employees, activities, parent, subsidiaries, and year founded. A detailed table of contents and a comprehensive index enhance access to the information in this easy-to-use resource.

While other international directories provide more data about markets, a wider variety of statistics about countries, or a lengthier list of companies, none is as comprehensive in scope as this compilation. Also, this new directory includes personal names of contacts, which are frequently lacking in other sources. Called a "first edition," the directory will hopefully be regularly updated, as this type of information quickly becomes outdated. Strong business collections will need a copy of the *Directory of European Business*, as well as public libraries that serve patrons interested in international trade.

European Business Rankings: Lists of Companies, Products, Services and Activities Compiled from a Variety of Published Sources. Comp. by Oksana Newman and Allan Foster. Gale, 1992. 450p. bibliog. index. tables. hardcover $140 (1-873477-00-7).
338.7'094 Corporations—Europe—Rankings || Corporations—Rankings || Europe—Commerce || Europe—Industries || Europe—Economic conditions—1945– [BKL]

Newman and Foster, who are affiliated with the Library and Information Service of the Manchester Business School in England, have compiled an interesting new work similar to Gale's *Business Rankings Annual*, which covers mostly U.S. companies. *European Business Rankings* is a collection of rankings taken from periodicals, newspapers, financial services, directories, and statistical annuals. The 2,260 consecutively numbered entries generally list the top 10 companies, products, services, or activities in Europe. The authors state that most of the data were taken from 1991 publications.

An excellent preface repeated in English, French, and German explains the purpose and organization of the book. An abbreviations list precedes the outline of contents, which lists the subject headings under which the rankings are arranged. Cross-references appear in this outline wherever appropriate.

A typical entry begins with a title and a description of the ranking method. This is frequently followed by remarks concerning data and sources and then the number of companies listed in the original source. For example, in entry 643, "Most Profitable Scottish Companies," 10 firms are ranked by percentage profit. It notes that 100 companies were ranked in the original source, and a complete bibliographic citation is provided for that source. Assisting users is a comprehensive index that lists all companies, products, and persons. Rounding out this volume is a bibliography citing the 216 sources from which the ranking lists were obtained. Complete bibliographic information is provided, including address, telephone and fax numbers, ISSN, frequency, and price. Only 10 of the citations are to U.S. publications, so the average public library won't own many of them.

There are several sources that cite world statistics and provide ranking information, for example, *The Economist Book of Vital World Statistics* (1990), *The New Book of World Rankings* (1991), and *The World in Figures*, (1988). However, these books rank countries, not specific companies, while *European Business Rankings* does both. The growing interest in global markets makes this book an appropriate consideration for business libraries needing European marketing information. Rankings such as "Europe's Leading Business Schools," "Best Hotels in Geneva," and "Highest AIDS and HIV Positive Reported Cases in Western Europe" will make it of interest to a wider readership as well.

Mexico Company Handbook, 1992: Data on Major Listed Companies. IMF Editora; dist. by Reference Service Press, 1992. 178p. indexes. tables. paper $29.95 (1-878753-11-8).
[BKL] 91-25624

The U.S.-Mexico Trade Pages: Your Single Source for Transborder Business. By Kara Kent. Global Source, 1730 K St. NW, Ste. 304, Washington, DC 20006, 1992. 329p. paper $39.95 (0-9633670-0-5).
382'.09730720294 U.S.—Commerce—Information services—Directories || Mexico—Commerce—Information services—Directories [OCLC] 92-238942

Anyone with an interest in Mexican business or finance will find both of these volumes useful for their valuable information and their easy-to-use formats.

The fourth edition of *Mexico Company Handbook* is "a comprehensive reference manual for the international investment and business community, particularly for financial analysts, as well as money managers, investors and representatives of the securities industry, government entities and the financial press." In addition to fundamental information about Mexico's demographics, geography, and economy, profiles of major public companies, brokerage houses, and mutual funds are included. Financial data are provided in U.S. dollars for easy comparison. Investment opportunities, regulations, and Mexican *bolsas* (stock exchanges) are described, as well as Mexican taxation and accounting practices. Insights into Mexican patents, trademarks, and arbitration are offered. This edition has been updated to provide an overview of Mexico's economic developments in 1991, and five-year tables allow the reader to study trends.

The *U.S.-Mexico Trade Pages* is primarily a directory of information resources for transborder trade but also offers pointers on buying, selling, and investing in Mexico and provides a profile of imports and exports between U.S. states and Mexican states. Directories included cover government resources, trade associations, and a variety of professional services (e.g., consulting, advertising, law, banking, accounting, insurance, travel). Explanatory material is in Spanish and English. The bibliography of books, magazines, special reports, and databases should be useful to anyone developing a collection in this area, and the chapter on transborder communication offers practical advice on time differences, business hours, and correspondence via telephone, fax, and mail. Commonly used abbreviations, forms of address, and holidays are listed.

The books complement each other nicely, and both are recommended for any collection that serves patrons with a commercial interest in Mexico.

Directory of Multinationals. 2v. 4th ed. By John M. Stopford. Stockton Press, 1992. tables. hardcover $600 (1-56159-053-3).
338.8'8 International business enterprises—Directories [BKL]

The title *Directory of Multinationals* is somewhat misleading, as the 428 firms profiled are strictly manufacturing companies. Despite the omission of banking, insurance, retailing, engineering, and other service companies, as well as family-controlled holding companies, this specialized directory will be useful in large business collections.

The editor has included only those manufacturing corporations with consolidated sales of more than $1 billion and "significant international operations," (i.e., a value for foreign sales of at least $500 million). Entries are arranged alphabetically by the name of the parent company and include the company's address, a summary of its business, a list of its directors, an outline of its structure, a list of its products (including brand names, where applicable), a brief history, and a description of the company's current situation, major shareholders, and principle subsidiaries and affiliates, listed alphabetically by country.

In addition, each profile includes a five-year summary in order "to provide a clear and precise indication of the company's financial performance over the period from 1987 to 1991." These accounts are the consolidated figures of the group, although in some cases they refer only to the parent company. The currency used for each table is clearly noted. A table ranks the companies profiled in descending order of foreign sales (in U.S. dollars), including the percentage of each company's total sales that are foreign.

Although many subsidiaries have the same name as the parent company, some do not. For these, it would be useful to have a name index to assist users in locating data. Geographic, product and/or SIC, and brand-name indexes would also be helpful.

Most business librarians will find such publications as Dun & Bradstreet's *Principal International Businesses*, *Moody's International Manual*, or *Ward's International Business Directory* adequate. Except for *Moody's*, however, none provides similar in-depth financial information to the *Directory of Multinationals*. Given the cost and the limited scope of the title under review, it is most suitable for large business collections in public and academic libraries or those concentrating on international operations.

World Class Business: A Guide to the 100 Most Powerful Global Corporations. By Philip Mattera. Holt, 1992. 763p. bibliog. index. hardcover $50 (0-8050-1681-3).

338.8'8 International business enterprises—Handbooks, manuals, etc. [CIP] 91-45585

Reminiscent of business sources such as *Hoover's Handbook of World Business, 1992* [RBB Ja 1 92] and *The Global Marketplace: 102 of the Most Influential Companies Outside America* (1987), this new book presents information on 100 businesses, selected by the author as the most important enterprises controlling the destiny of the global economy. A variety of criteria were used to select the companies, beginning with size and extent of international activity. Also, the author attempted to present a diversified list in terms of industry and geography, to represent Third World multinationals, and to include some companies not yet in the top tier of international business but clearly on the way up (e.g., Apple Computer). The resulting list of companies includes 43 based in the U.S., 16 in Japan, and 32 in European countries.

Business researcher and author Mattera, who also wrote *Inside U.S. Business* [RBB Ap 1 91], has prepared this new work with the general reader in mind, avoiding unnecessary business jargon and detailed financial analysis. For each company, he has tried to provide an overall understanding of its background, its main areas of operation, its current competitive position, and its labor and environmental records, while also providing some basic information on each firm. Special pains were taken to identify joint ventures, to focus on the investments in Eastern Europe, and to examine environmental and health issues related to each company. Mattera compiled the company data from corporate reports and from information supplied by citizens groups, research centers, and labor organizations.

Entries are arranged alphabetically by company name and include sections on history, operations, executives, labor relations, and environmental and health records. Also supplied are several charts and tables presenting a geographic breakdown of revenues and operating income (e.g., for Mitsubishi, revenue in yen and by percentage for Japan, Europe, and "Elsewhere"). Entries conclude with a brief bibliography.

World Class Business does not do as much ranking as *Hoover's Handbook* (covering 165 companies), and it does not approach *Hoover's* in terms of graphic presentation. It does provide more thoughtful analysis. Compared with *International Directory of Company Histories* (St. James Press, 1990), it is more succinct and obviously more up-to-date but considerably less comprehensive. The Board compared the Nissan entries from *Global Marketplace* and *World Class Business*. The former source includes more than six pages of text and a map of Japanese car plants in the U.S. The latter includes slightly less text and somewhat more financial data. Both are well written and readable.

In today's economic environment, it is virtually impossible to have too many up-to-date international business sources. *World Class Business* is a recommended purchase for medium-size to large public libraries and any academic library supporting business research.

LAW, PUBLIC ADMINISTRATION, SOCIAL PROBLEMS AND SERVICES

Martindale-Hubbell Bar Register of Preeminent Lawyers. 76th ed. Martindale-Hubbell, 1992. annual. n.p. hardcover $129.95 (1-56160-047-4; ISSN 1051-5518).

340.025 Lawyers—Directories [OCLC] 90-33543

Eight thousand prestigious lawyers and law firms in the U.S. and Canada are listed in the seventy-sixth edition of the *Bar Register*, a spin-off of the 17-volume *Martindale-Hubbell Law Directory*, which lists 800,000 lawyers and firms. The *Bar Register* serves as a guide to the "most highly regarded members of the legal profession." Firms and attorneys are chosen for inclusion on the recommendation of their colleagues. Four new specialty areas have been added to this edition, bringing the number of legal disciplines covered to 22. The new areas are commercial, insurance defense, personal injury, and probate and estate-planning law.

Following the "General Practice" section, specialty areas are listed alphabetically. Within each field, firms are arranged by state and then city. Each firm entry includes address, telephone and fax numbers, rating from the *Martindale-Hubbell Law Directory*, a list of the firm's partners and associates, and representative clients. Entries do not contain the biographies of individual attorneys from the parent set. The information in the *Bar Register* can also be accessed through Martindale-Hubbell on CD-ROM and online via NEXUS/LEXUS service.

Libraries that can't afford the full *Martindale-Hubbell* and that need a national directory of lawyers have several options. *Law Firms Yellow Book: Who's Who in the Management of U.S. Law Firms* [RBB D 15 91] covers 557 major firms but lists only administrative staff, not all partners and associates. *The American Bar* (2v., Foster-Long, $250), with 4,000 firms and 90,000 attorneys, is arranged by place and has an index by type of practice. The *Bar Register of Preeminent Lawyers* is a less expensive option that lists attorneys on a selective basis.

International Organizations: A Dictionary and Directory. 3d ed. By Giuseppe Schiavone. St. Martin's, 1992. 338p. indexes. tables. hardcover $75 (0-312-09143-5).

341.2'025 International agencies—Dictionaries ‖ International agencies—Directories [CIP] 92-38142

Schiavone, an Italian scholar and specialist on multilateral cooperation, has updated this overview of international organizations to reflect developments up to early 1992. The first edition of this title was positively evaluated here [RBB D 1 84] because of the clarity and objectivity of the writing and its presentation of directory information in an accessible format. This third edition, maintaining the scope and arrangement of the original, profiles more than 200 organizations in which national states are associated in a common purpose.

The book is divided into two major parts—the dictionary and the directory—and approximately 100 organizations are profiled in each section. Entries are listed under the organization's name in English; numerous *see* references direct the reader to the entry from the name in other languages, as well as from acronyms. The dictionary is the largest portion of the book and provides organizational descriptions ranging in length from one column to more than five pages. The directory, on the other hand, has brief entries, most no longer than 8–10 lines of a column, that provide contact information and a succinct description. The only explanation of why the book is divided into these two major parts, or why a particular organization is listed in one section or the other, is found on the dust jacket: the organizations in the directory are those "with largely technical and administrative tasks." Included in the directory section are listings for such groups as *Pacific Basin Economic Council*, *International Rubber Study Group*, and the *European Civil Aviation Conference*.

The lengthy entries in the dictionary section profile such organizations as *African Development Bank*, *Entente Council*, *Latin American Integration Association*, and *Organization of the Islamic Conference*. The United Nations and its various agencies and conferences take up a total of

44 pages and include an entry as recent as the Earth Summit held in June 1992, under *United Nations Conference on Environment and Development* (UNCED). Each entry includes a narrative on the aims of the organization, membership criteria, member countries, number of meetings held regularly, committees and projects, and affiliated agencies. A short history is given that explains such organizational developments as changes in goals and objectives, governance structure, legal mandates, and relationships with other international bodies. Each profile ends with the name of the current chief official, the headquarters address (often with fax numbers), and a list of the most pertinent publications. Some entries also include a short list of bibliographic references.

Other features of the book include a 22-page introduction that reviews the development of international organizations and discusses challenges faced in the post–Cold War era. Membership charts for the major international and regional organizations are provided, and several indexes list organizations by name, year of founding, acronym, and interest area (e.g., commodities, energy).

Contact information for the groups profiled here can be found in many other sources, such as the *International Organizations* volumes of *Encyclopedia of Associations*. Compared with typical directories, Schiavone's dictionary entries provide lengthier analyses of a group's history, governance, and current objectives. These profiles are comparable to those found in the "International Organizations" section of the *Europa World Yearbook*, and many libraries that subscribe to this source will not need the duplicative coverage. However, Schiavone's profiles frequently include some unique information about an organization, as well as his objective commentary about problems and successes. This work will be useful in academic libraries that support programs in international relations and political science, as well as in large public libraries where this type of information is often requested.

Chronology and Fact Book of the United Nations, 1941–1991. 8th ed. By Kumiko Matsuura and others. Oceana Publications, 1992. 598p. tables. hardcover $75 (0-379-21200-5; ISSN 0066-4340).
341.23 United Nations—History [OCLC]

Matsuura and his coauthors have produced this revised edition at an appropriate time. As the preface notes, the end of the Cold War and events in such areas as Cambodia, Kuwait, and Yugoslavia have revitalized the role of the United Nations. The chronology brings this role into perspective against the background of the last 50 years of international history. Based on the presentation of events in the quarterly journal *United Nations Chronicle*, the chronology may be studied as a mirror of how the U.N. presents its activities to the public.

Events were selected for inclusion on the basis of anticipated reader interest and a desire to be comprehensive. Specifically, activities of specialized U.N. agencies are not reported, and limited references are made to decisions of U.N. expert groups and commissions. Those decisions are usually reflected through coverage of the General Assembly. Events of recent years and particularly Security Council activity are emphasized. Generally, individuals are identified by position title, not personal name.

The chronology is arranged in three chapters, a 220-page listing of events, 47 pages of tables, and 321 pages of documents. Page layout is especially well designed for the chronology section, with dates on the left, ample white space, and a key label in all capitals (e.g., CYPRUS, HUMAN RIGHTS, MIDDLE EAST) preceding several sentences of text. For example, the entry for February 9, 1990, is "CUBA: Security Council considers a complaint by Cuba about an 'armed attack' by the USA on 31 January on a Panama-registered merchant ship manned by Cuban nationals: meeting adjourns without a draft resolution having been tabled," and for January 1–4, 1980, "IRAN: Secretary-General visits Iran in connection with the detention of US diplomatic personnel in the US Embassy."

The 14 tables include membership with date of admission and assessment percentage (as of May 22, 1992), Security Council membership 1946–91, and U.N. peacekeeping operations. The most recent peacekeeping operation given is the U.N. Protection Force in Yugoslavia (giving headquarters, duration, and function—"To create the conditions of peace and security required for the negotiation of an overall settlement of the Yugoslav crisis within the framework of the European Community's Conference on Yugoslavia." The nine documents include the Charter of the United Nations, the rules for the International Court of Justice, the General Assembly rules and procedures, and the U.N. staff regulations. Although there is no subject index, the table of contents lists all of the tables and documents.

Much of the information presented here is available elsewhere. However, the chronology format provides an added value well worth the price. This source is a valuable complement to such standard U.N. references as *Encyclopedia of the United Nations and International Agreements* (2d ed. [RBB F 15 91]), *Yearbook of the United Nations* [RSBR Mr 15 75], and *Annual Review of United Nations Affairs* [RSBR O 1 77]. The chronology is recommended for all academic and large public libraries. Subscribers to the *Annual Review* will receive it as part of their subscription since the chronology is considered a supplement.

Who's Who in the United Nations and Related Agencies. 2d ed. Ed. by Stanley R. Greenfield. Omnigraphics, 1992. 850p. indexes. hardcover $185 (1-55888-762-8).
341.23'092 [B] United Nations—Biography ‖ International agencies—Biography [CIP] 92-28304

A directory of this type has been long overdue, as it has been more than 15 years since the appearance of the first edition of this work. The first edition was also edited by Greenfield. He states in his preface here that this directory "presents brief biographies of the men and women who led the UN Secretariat and the Specialized Agencies and Related Organizations during the year 1991." The work also contains many of the ambassadors to the UN and its agencies in New York, Geneva, and Vienna. Altogether, the volume gives biographical entries for some 3,000 persons.

After the prefatory material, which clearly spells out the criteria for inclusion in this work, the volume begins with a six-page table of abbreviations and acronyms used, a sample entry, and two appendixes outlining the restructuring of the secretariat and new appointments of senior secretariat officials made in March 1992 by the new secretary-general. The entries proper, arranged alphabetically, are typical who's who–type entries, listing such things as current position within the UN (including telephone and fax numbers), birthdate, marital status, career positions, education, professional interests, publications, awards, and current residence. The work concludes with an abundance of helpful material, including an abridged *United Nations System of Organizations*; a list of member states; a list of permanent missions to the UN in New York, Geneva, and Vienna; and a list of UN depository libraries. Two indexes conclude the work: an index by organization, which lists organizations such as the International Monetary Fund or UNESCO and all entrants affiliated with them, and an index by nationality, which lists entrants by country.

A random sampling of more than 100 names in this work revealed that fewer than 10 percent are also listed in *The International Who's Who, 1992–93*, indicating that this volume contains many entrants who may not be easy to find in other sources. Although the price is on the high side, this is a unique work that is essential for libraries that deal in any way with international relations. The Board hopes, however, that newer editions of this work will appear with greater frequency.

Tuttle Guide to the Single European Market: A Comprehensive Handbook. By Richard Owen and Michael Dynes. Tuttle, 1992. 352p. bibliog. index. paper $15.95 (0-8048-1815-0).
341.24'22 Europe 1992—Handbooks, manuals, etc. [CIP] 92-22219

Owen and Dynes, both affiliated with *Times* of London, have extensive reporting experience on economics and international relations. They state in the introduction to this interesting book that the coming single European market will bring major changes in the way business is conducted. People and firms who are well informed could prosper, while the uninformed could suffer economically.

With 18 essays examining the history, economic and political policies, specific accomplishments, future proposals, and problem areas in the single European market, this book is similar in style to a *Reference Shelf* publication and is thus not intended for ready reference. Some of the diverse topics covered include trade, financial and monetary policies, telecommunications, tariffs, environmental and consumer laws, industrial standards, the professions, and foreign policy. One interesting fact found in this book: in the future there will not only be a common European monetary unit and passport but also a common college degree entitled IB (International Baccalaureate).

As this is an British publication, there is some emphasis upon British concerns, for example, the lack of study of foreign languages in Britain. However, adequate attention is focused upon U.S. interests. At the end of most chapters is a "Checklist of Changes" outlining forthcoming events. The book is very up-to-date, with mention of the June 1992 Danish rejection of the Maastricht Treaty and coverage of the Yugoslavian crisis.

Among the 16 appendixes are a glossary of EC terms, lists of summits, texts of declarations, and summaries of treaties. Also included are a short bibliography and a list of U.K. contacts with addresses and telephone numbers, which includes information centers and consultants.

The *European Communities Encyclopedia and Directory* [RBB F 1 92] has addresses of contacts worldwide (not just British) and also has essays that cover similar topics but is much more expensive. *The New Europe: An A to Z Compendium on the European Community* [RBB Jl 91] defines more than 2,000 terms. The *Tuttle Guide* is an inexpensive publication that academic and public libraries may find useful for the circulating collection, especially if they don't own *The European Communities Encyclopedia*.

The Evolving Constitution: How the Supreme Court Has Ruled on Issues from Abortion to Zoning. By Jethro K. Lieberman. Random, 1992. 752p. bibliog. hardcover $26 (0-679-40530-5).
342.73'02 U.S.—Constitutional law—Encyclopedias || U.S. Supreme Court [CIP] 92-16590

Author of several books on constitutional law and professor at the New York Law School, Lieberman offers in this title an effective, new type of constitutional reference for the nonspecialist. In an alphabetic arrangement of more than 1,000 short essays, the work focuses on the constitutional nature of the topic under discussion, the Supreme Court's treatment of the issue, and the ruling's effect on subsequent interpretations of the Constitution. Several cases may be discussed in the same entry if they illustrate the evolution of the constitutional issue. Included are essays on topics considered by the Court, legal concepts, common terms with legal meanings, significant clauses of the Constitution, and major cases. A typical entry is *Freedom of Religion*, wherein Lieberman establishes the constitutional foundation of the issue, provides a historical narrative of how the Court has ruled on the issue, and reports on the latest developments. In doing so, he takes the reader from the First Amendment's free-exercise clause to a 1940 case against a proselytizing Jehovah's Witness to the 1990 Oregon peyote case—in three concise pages that maintain a tight focus on the constitutional nature of the issues and the Supreme Court's effects on everyday life.

The book is a convenient reference tool; for example, *Separation of Powers* is treated in two succinct pages, with Truman's wartime seizure of the steel mills given as an illustration of executive-branch encroachment. The work's arrangement is efficient, and the book is easy to use. *See* references are filed in the main alphabet, *see also* references appear at the end of entries, and terms within the text of an essay that have their own entry are cross-referenced through the use of small capital letters. For example, in *Separation of Powers*, "Steel Seizure Case" is cross-referenced to the essay where the 1952 *Youngstown Sheet & Tube Co. v. Sawyer* case is discussed. The names of the Court's cases are entered in italics, and superscripted numbers are used to refer the reader to the book's "Table of Cases" where more than 2,000 Supreme Court decisions are listed, including those as recent as the 1991–92 term. "Table of Cases" lists the case name, citation to *United States Reports*, date, vote, justice writing the majority opinion, names of dissenting justices, and the number of pages in the decision.

Lieberman avoids footnotes, and endnotes are used for occasional secondary comments, as well as for bibliographic citations to materials other than Supreme Court decisions. While a topical index is purposefully omitted, an assortment of other items has been added to make this work a coherent whole. Included are introductory essays on the nature of the Constitution, constitutional interpretation, and the Supreme Court's procedures of hearing and deciding cases, as well as instructions for using the book. The appendixes provide the text of the Constitution; a concordance to all significant words in the Constitution; biographical sketches of all Supreme Court justices, along with a time chart showing which justices served during each term of the court; and a list of suggested further readings.

Many good reference tools for the Supreme Court are available, for instance, *The Oxford Companion to the Supreme Court of the United States* [RBB D 1 92]), as are textbooks and anthologies on the Constitution. However, no other convenient reference compilation aimed at general readers has the specific focus of *The Evolving Constitution*. It will not only be consulted for information on legal decisions and interpretations, but its treatment of everyday issues—from abortion to censorship and from hate speech to students' rights—make it an effective tool for students researching topics for speeches and papers. This very affordable and effective encyclopedic source has a place on the reference shelf of any high school, public, or academic library.

Primer on Sexual Harassment. By Barbara Lindemann and David D. Kadue. BNA Books, 1992. 302p. index. paper $38 (0-87179-764-X).
344.73'014133 Sexual harassment of women—Law and legislation—U.S. || Sex discrimination in employment—Law and legislation—U.S. [CIP] 92-25748

Over the last few years, an increased amount of attention has been directed toward the problem of sexual harassment in the workplace, and many libraries have received numerous inquiries about the subject. Both employers and employees have questions about what laws are applicable and how problems can be solved. A new source of help is the *Primer on Sexual Harassment*, which is aimed especially at human resource professionals. It provides guidance on preventing harassment, investigating complaints, and avoiding liability. While the work is designed to be used by employers, the information will be valuable to employees as well.

In nontechnical language, the book explains that two major legal theories govern the realm of sexual harassment: "quid pro quo" and "hostile environment." Presented in detail are examples of such incidents involving females and males, with the identification of legal cases that pertain to the issues. A review is made of the claims of third parties in matters of sexual harassment. Retaliation is discussed in some detail, as well as other adverse employment decisions. Applicable state and federal regulations and codes are thoroughly considered.

The latter half of the text presents guidance on various aspects of the topic, such as elements of an effective corporate policy and internal company procedures for investigations and corrective actions. Also discussed is the role of the enforcement agency when an official complaint is filed. Clear explanations are provided about a number of legal matters, for instance, defense strategies, evidence, remedies, and settlement. Several appendixes enhance the effectiveness of the work: the EEOC guidelines on sexual harassment, a sample antiharassment policy with suggested methods for the evaluation of its effectiveness, and a summary of the Civil Rights Act of 1991. The work concludes with a table of cases and a detailed subject index.

The *Primer on Sexual Harassment* is an effective tool that explains a wide variety of technical matters in nonlegal language. It is most appropriate for library collections that serve business, since it is geared for managers who are confronted with the problem. But representatives of employee organizations and individuals in need of information on the topic will also benefit from the book's understandable explanations of the legal environment and its advice about handling complaints and litigation. It is recommended for purchase consideration by public libraries and by academic libraries that do not collect the legal sources that cover this topic.

Legal Resource Directory: A Guide to Free or Inexpensive Assistance for Low Income Families, with Special Sections for Prisoners. By Anthony J. Bosoni. McFarland, 1992. 148p. index. paper $29.95 (0-89950-737-9).
344.73'03258 Legal aid—U.S.—Directories || Legal assistance to prisoners—U.S.—Directories [CIP] 92-50301

This directory provides a state-by-state listing of more than 1,700 organizations that provide free or inexpensive legal advice to low-income families. Three separate sections cover civil and criminal law offices, projects opposing capital punishment, and national CURE (Citizens United for the Rehabilitation of Errants) chapters. National, state, and local organizations are represented. The information is brief, providing only address and telephone numbers. Author and inmate Bosoni includes instructions for prisoners seeking legal aid and lists programs offering assistance to inmates. While some of this information can be extracted from such references as the *Encyclopedia of Associations* and its regional directories, the *Legal Resource Directory* is useful for its particular audience.

Legal Issues and Older Adults. By Linda Josephson Millman. ABC-Clio, 1992. 273p. bibliog. index. hardcover $45 (0-87436-594-5).
346.7301'3 Aged—Legal status, laws, etc.—U.S. [CIP] 92-31475

The aging of the U.S. population has created a need for information geared toward older adults. With the publication of this new volume, ABC-Clio's Choices and Challenges: An Older Adult Reference series has now issued nine titles designed to address this need. The latest volume deals with legal issues and provides basic background on eight common areas of law in which seniors might have reason to seek guidance.

The first section of the book is divided into eight chapters that cover legal services, personal autonomy, income security, health care, housing, consumerism, family law, and estate planning. Each chapter begins with a list of basic facts that apply to the main topic. This is followed by a brief introductory overview of the topic. The chapter then expands on the facts and on the introduction. For example, the basics and the introduction to the income-security chapter present facts about Social Security, SSI, private pensions, and age-discrimination laws. The body of the chapter expands on this by explaining what Social Security is, who is eligible, how to file for benefits, and how to appeal a decision. The same detailed discussion is provided for other topics covered by the book. The information is clearly written, logically organized, and easily understood. The use of large print is a distinct advantage for older users.

The second section of the book is a two-part resource list. A directory of organizations is topically arranged according to the chapter headings in the first section of the book. It also includes a general category covering such organizations as AARP, Gray Panthers, and the ABA. Nonprofit, for-profit, government, and professional agencies are represented. Each entry contains the group's address, telephone number, contact name, service description, and publications.

The second part of the resource section is a list of reference materials (print and nonprint) that supplement the information in part 1. Print materials are subdivided into loose-leaf services, books, booklets, pamphlets, and articles. With the exception of the loose-leaf services, all titles are annotated, and bibliographic information is provided. Nonprint sources include electronic databases, software, and audiovisual material (film, video, and slides). Format, source, and cost are provided for software and length, date, cost, and/or rental fee for audiovisual material. The entries are indexed by topic and by title. This section also includes a glossary of terms.

The information and format of the book are similar to that in *Your Legal Right in Later Life* (AARP, 1989). The latter title does not include a resources section, but it does discuss federal income tax law and nursing-home rights, neither of which are covered in the work under review. The strength of *Legal Issues and Older Adults* lies in its clarity of presentation of information emphasizing the older adult's options and means of legal recourse in specific situations. Its organization and ease of use make it a valuable resource for older adults and their advocates and for library reference desks.

The Oxford Companion to the Supreme Court of the United States. Ed. by Kermit L. Hall and others. Oxford, 1992. 1,028p. bibliog. illus. index. hardcover $49.95 thereafter (0-19-505835-6).
347.73'26 U.S. Supreme Court—Encyclopedias [CIP] 92-3863

This convenient and authoritative guide to the Supreme Court succeeds well in accomplishing its goal of providing a political, economic, cultural, and legal history of the Court and, by extension, of the very country itself. In more than 1,000 entries, about 300 contributors interpret the Court to the layperson, providing historical context, evaluation, and explanation of its decisions and procedures. The contributors explain the Court's influence on American life and vice versa. While the editors are all professors of law, browsing through the list of contributors reveals professors of history, political science, and government as well as librarians, justices, attorneys, and archivists.

Entries are of several types. Biographies treat every justice, every nominee, and many prominent lawyers who argued before the Court. Sheldon Novick's entry on Oliver Wendell Holmes is a masterpiece of interpretation, pointing out Holmes' chief theories and influences on the Court. Conceptual entries define ideas. The entry *Double Jeopardy*, for example, provides historical context, relevant cases, and the importance of the idea to the court. Institutional entries treat such matters as the clerks of the justices and the office of chief justice. Entries on the physical surroundings of the Court highlight its location. Longer entries end with brief bibliographies of nontechnical literature.

The more than 400 entries on Court decisions include a U.S. *Reports* citation, date argued, date decided, and chief spokesman; each entry discusses the impact of the case on American life. Interpretive entries treat substantive topics such as abortion and procedural topics such as the insanity defense. *History of the Court* is a four-part chronological essay. Other historical entries treat such broad subjects as slavery and race and racism—again, always with the interpretive approach that explains the effect of the issue on the Court as well as the Court's effect on the issue. Vocabulary entries provide definitions for basic terms like *writ of mandamus* and such famous phrases as *separate but equal*.

The companion is thoroughly cross-referenced. Any topic that has its own entry is marked by an asterisk in the text. *See* and *see also* references are plentiful; for example, the entry *Flag Burning* leads to several important cases and to the entry *Symbolic Speech*. In a project of this scope, there is always room to quibble. For example, *McCulloch v. Maryland* is fundamental to the discussion in *State Regulation of Commerce*, but the entry for the case itself does not refer to the broader entry.

The companion concludes with case-name and topical indexes as well as extensive appendixes, including the succession of justices, vacancies, appointing presidents, Senate votes of confirmation and rejection, length of service of each justice, and trivia and traditions of the Court. About 100 black-and-white photographs add interest.

The companion is a unique work. It covers landmark cases and biographies—as do *Congressional Quarterly's Guide to the U.S. Supreme Court*, second edition [RBB My 1 90], and Facts On File's *Reference Guide to the United States Supreme Court* (1986)—but is in a handy A-Z arrangement and lacks the long essays of those two books. It complements but does not replace them.

The Oxford Companion to the Supreme Court of the United States belongs in every library, high school and up, and on the shelf of the practitioner and the teacher. It will prove to be the standard reference work on the Supreme Court.

How to Research the Supreme Court. By Fenton S. Martin and Robert U. Goehlert. Congressional Quarterly, 1992. 140p. bibliog. indexes. hardcover $22.95 (0-87187-697-3); paper $13.95 (0-87187-633-7).
016.34773'26 U.S. Supreme Court—Bibliography [CIP] 91-46903

This selective annotated bibliography is divided into three sections. The first covers secondary sources on the Supreme Court such as biographical directories, legal and historical encyclopedias, and newspapers as well as finding aids (indexes, bibliographies). Relevant CD products and online databases are included. The second section deals with primary sources (digests of Court decisions, official government publications) and related guides and finding aids. The final section consists of a selective unannotated bibliography on the Supreme Court, with a separate subsection of entries for individual justices (up through Clarence Thomas). There are three brief appendixes: a chronology of Supreme Court nominations, thumbnail biographies of the justices (limited to the basic dates), and a glossary of common legal terms; author and title indexes conclude the book. Suggestions on developing a research strategy are offered in the introduction.

The compilers, librarians at Indiana University, have produced a concise, up-to-date research guide that will be useful wherever the Supreme Court is studied. The annotations and other explanatory materials are informative and to the point and will be especially helpful to the novice researcher unfamiliar with the complexities of federal legal sources. Various finding aids and sources for the different elements of a legislative history are conveniently listed in one place. There are a few omissions. Project Hermes, which in early 1991 made the full text of Supreme Court opinions available to federal depository libraries within eight hours of release, is not discussed. The selected list of newsmagazines in the first section includes The National Review and The New Republic, but not The Nation. Only one of the several competing CD versions of the U.S. Government Printing Office Monthly Catalog is mentioned. But these are minor oversights; this guide will be a timely and valuable addition to academic and law library collections.

Federal Regional Yellow Book: Who's Who in the Federal Government's Departments, Agencies, Courts, Military Installations and Service Academies outside of Washington, DC. Monitor, winter 1993. semiannual. 1,324p. indexes. maps. paper $165/yr. (ISSN 1061-3153).

351 Administrative agencies—U.S.—Directories || Executive departments—U.S.—Directories || U.S.—Officials and employees—Directories [OCLC] 92-3930

From the publisher of such directories as the Municipal Yellow Book [RBB N 1 91] and the Law Firms Yellow Book [RBB D 15 91] comes this new who's who in the federal government *outside* of Washington, D.C. It is intended as a companion publication to the Federal Yellow Book, which lists government departments and staff in the capital city and which, until this year, also included some information about regional offices. The Federal Regional Yellow Book, to be issued semiannually, expands the scope of the regional office listings that appeared in the Federal Yellow Book in the past.

Listed in this new title are 20,000 individuals located in more than 8,000 regional offices throughout the country. Coverage extends to federal departments and their subdivisions, independent agencies (National Mediation Board, Tennessee Valley Authority), military installations and service academies (Air Force Academy, 58 locations of the U.S. Army Corps of Engineers), U.S. courts, and congressional support agencies (Government Accounting Office, Government Printing Office).

Federal departments and the agencies within them are listed first, followed by the independent agencies and then by the courts. Many of the sections are further subdivided into specific operations or programs of the departments. Within each category, directory information is presented alphabetically by state. Provided for each entry are an address, telephone and fax numbers, and the names of key staff along with their direct telephone numbers. The arrangement of the work is indicated in the contents pages that open each section, and additional access points are provided by three separate indexes—geographic, personal name, and subject.

Many directories of federal agencies exist, and frequently regional office addresses are included. Less often provided are the personal names of regional staff. The Federal Staff Directory (semiannual, Congressional Staff Directory Ltd.) does include the names and addresses for the heads of regional agencies and departments within them; the names of staff further down in the bureaucracy are usually not included. In comparison, the Federal Regional Yellow Book provides the names, job titles, and telephone numbers for 15 staff below the level of regional administrator of the Immigration and Naturalization Service, Northern Region, located in Fort Snelling, Minnesota; for 22 individuals working at the Bettis Atomic Power Laboratory in West Mifflin, Pennsylvania; and for 11 staff in the San Francisco regional office of the Small Business Administration, plus the names and addresses for the directors of eight district SBA offices in that region. For specialized collections and large libraries that need such extensive listings, the Federal Regional Yellow Book will be a useful tool.

The Presidency A to Z: A Ready Reference Encyclopedia. Ed. by Michael Nelson. Congressional Quarterly, 1992. 574p. illus. index. hardcover $100 (0-87187-667-1).

353.03'13 Presidents—U.S.—Encyclopedias || Presidents—U.S.—Biography [CIP] 92-20360

This second volume in Congressional Quarterly's Encyclopedia of the American Government series is similar in nature to the first volume, Congress A to Z [RBB Mr 1 89], in that it provides brief articles in nontechnical language outlining an important branch of American government. The third volume of the series, The Supreme Court A to Z, is planned for spring 1993 publication.

The work includes biographical entries on all of the presidents and vice presidents as well as some first ladies and such topical entries as Ethics, Interest Groups and the Presidency, and Public Opinion and the Presidency, plus articles on each of the cabinet departments and other executive departments. The specific powers associated with the office of the president are also covered in such articles as Appointment and Removal Power, Economic Powers, and Treaty Power. Entries are relatively brief, with most no longer than three or four pages; the longest article, Elections Chronology, is nine pages in length. Following the entries are several appendixes, including a summary of presidential elections and a list of all cabinet members under each president. The work concludes with a selected bibliography and an index.

This book succeeds in being, as its preface describes, a "ready-reference encyclopedia that offers quick answers to your questions about the presidency and the individuals who have served in it." As such, it complements CQ's other work on the presidency, Congressional Quarterly's Guide to the Presidency [RBB My 1 90], which offers greater detail on most of the same issues but is not arranged in an A–Z fashion. Indeed, the preface acknowledges that the larger work, which was also edited by Nelson, was "the impetus for the current volume" and refers readers to it for more extensive articles. The Presidency A to Z features more up-to-date material, however, as evidenced by the Persian Gulf War entry and references to the Clarence Thomas hearings and appointment. The work is well illustrated, featuring black-and-white photographs or drawings on virtually every page.

Although this volume was clearly designed for the high school student and other general readers, the lack of bibliographies can, at times, be a drawback. Of the 301 entries in the work, only 15 have bibliographies. The selected bibliography, which concludes the book, is not annotated or divided by topic in any way. The article Historians' Ratings of the Presidents refers to numerous polls of historians but provides no exact citations. Readers interested in the mention of a series of January 1992 Washington Post articles by Woodward and Broder within the Quayle, Dan entry will be frustrated, as the entry has no bibliography and the articles are not cited in the selected bibliography.

High school and public libraries requiring an easy-to-access, well-written work on the presidency or those libraries that found the Guide to the Presidency somewhat heavy going for their patrons will certainly want to consider this work. Academic libraries will probably be satisfied with the Guide, which, although $80 more, also features almost 1,000 more pages and more extensive bibliographies.

International Military and Defense Encyclopedia. 6v. Ed. by Trevor N. Dupuy. Brassey's, 1993. bibliog. charts. illus. index. tables. hardcover $1,250 (0-02-881011-2).

355'.003 Military art and science—Encyclopedias [CIP] 92-33750

This important new subject encyclopedia is the result of years of careful preparation by respected scholar Dupuy, author of such reference sources as the one-volume Encyclopedia of Military History from 3500 B.C. to the Present (Harper, 1993) and editor of the Almanac of World Military Power (1970–   ), and Brassey's, one of the world's leading publishers on military affairs. The emphasis of the set is on events and developments since the end of World War II, but important events and leaders prior to this period (e.g., Crimean War, Genghis Khan) are included.

The six-volume set contains 785 articles written by historians and military and defense professionals, many having participated in combat operations. Contributors represent 38 different countries, the majority from the U.S., the U.K., and Germany. There are approximately 600 illustrations in the set, including charts and graphs as well as quality halftone illustrations. Entries are well written, and all but the shortest have topical divisions, helping to outline the essay-length entries. For example, Ethnicity and the Armed Forces is divided into "Recruitment," "Ethnic Relations within the Armed Forces," "Coups d'Etat," and "Relations between Society and the Armed Forces." Most entries end with *see also* references and a brief bibliography. Many users will appreciate locating citations to official government and U.N. publications, including publications of the U.S. Army Intelligence and Threat Analysis Center, U.N. War Crimes Commission, and several USSR publications.

A few gaps in coverage were noted. The four major submarine entries contain too little information on the early technical development of the weapon or information on individuals closely associated with their technical development and tactical possibilities (e.g., Karl Doenitz). However, much excellent information on antisubmarine technology, silencing, and detection is presented. The article *Ammunition* has information on search-and-destroy armor-piercing shells but omits more abhorrent projectiles, such as tactical nuclear (including neutron) and proximity-fused tungsten shell (COFRAM).

Biographical coverage is perforce selective; omitting such important individuals as Nathanael Greene and Nathan Bedford Forrest will be considered a serious oversight by U.S. users. Canadians will wonder at not finding Andrew George Latta McNaughton, an important soldier, military leader, and diplomat. However, most important eighteenth-, nineteenth-, and twentieth-century military leaders one expects to find are included. An example of a most satisfying biographical article is *Sun Tzu*, a sound appreciation of both the ancient Chinese military theorist, his influence, and his modern commentators and translators.

A useful feature of the encyclopedia is a list in volume 1 of all articles arranged in 17 broad subject areas, such as *Aerospace Forces and Warfare*, *Combat Theory and Operations*, *Armed Forces and Society*, and *Manpower and Personnel*. According to the preface, there are a total of nearly 25,000 index terms. Index references are to page numbers, an annoying feature in a multivolume set containing 2,984 consecutively numbered pages. The next printing or edition should include page notations on the spine of each volume.

To locate the information contained in this work would require searching military histories, general encyclopedias, military handbooks, technical reports, and official goverment documents issued by nations having major military and defense organizations. The technical information in the set will become dated, and there is no indication that supplements are to be issued. However, most of the topics included will remain useful to the general reader for many years. Libraries providing reference service to users interested in defense topics should consider this a necessary purchase.

International Affairs Directory of Organizations: The ACCESS Resource Guide. Ed. by Bruce Seymore. ABC-Clio, 1992. 326p. bibliog. index. hardcover $75 (0-87436-686-0).

355.02'0285 War—Information services—Directories || Peace—Information services—Directories || Security, International—Information services—Directories [OCLC] 92-32969

This aptly named directory was prepared by ACCESS, a security information service founded in 1985, in Washington, D.C. It is an update of a 1988 edition listing organizations involved in international affairs, especially in global security concerns. In the introduction, Seymore gives an overview of these organizations. The 865 profiled groups are engaged in research and analysis, advocacy (i.e., public-interest groups), citizen diplomacy, and information dissemination, in that order of frequency. Most are small in staff and in funding, are headquartered in the capitals of North American and European countries, and see as their primary audience other specialists and government officials. Government agencies are excluded from the directory.

In terms of geopolitical focus, the Middle East ranks first among the organizations, followed by the former USSR and East Asia. Issues cover economic, environmental, and human rights concerns as well as traditional foreign policy issues and military containment efforts. Seymore states that arms control and disarmament are less represented in this edition than in the 1988 edition (no doubt due to the demise of the Soviet Union).

In part 1, organizations are briefly profiled alphabetically by the country in which they are headquartered, leading off with the U.S. with 407 entries. The main fields of information supplied (and confirmed by the organizations themselves) are founding date, address, telephone and fax numbers, director's name, purpose, publications, subject specialties, staff size, primary audiences, and affiliations. There are six indexes in part 2. Groups are indexed by name, by 23 major topics, by product or services offered (e.g., speakers bureaus, computer databases, curriculum materials), by state in the U.S., by name of individuals within the entries, and by name of serial publications issued. This indexing is a most useful feature. Additionally, a "Guide to Guides" lists 227 reference works and periodicals that could be of value to anyone studying international affairs. Altogether, the work is an enormous corpus of information.

The directory that this work most closely resembles in mission is the *Yearbook of International Organizations* (K. G. Saur), a far more expensive annual publication. The depth of detail in the directory under review is no match for that found in the yearbook's exhaustive list of governmental and nongovernmental agencies. Even so, some organizations listed in the *International Affairs Directory* were not found in a recent edition of the *Yearbook*. Libraries that can not afford the *Yearbook* might profitably turn to this work.

Warriors' Words: A Quotation Book from Sesostris III to Schwarzkopf, 1871 B.C. to A.D. 1991. By Peter G. Tsouras. Arms & Armour; dist. by Sterling, 1992. 534p. bibliog. index. hardcover $29.95 (1-85409-088-7).

355'.003 Military art and science—Quotations, maxims, etc. [BKL]

This specialized compilation includes quotations from more than 250 military personalities who represent almost 4,000 years of military history. Unlike Trevor Royle's *Dictionary of Military Quotations* (Simon & Schuster, 1989), this source quotes only those who have "exercised the profession of arms." While some individuals—Napoleon Bonaparte, Douglas MacArthur, Julius Caesar—are routinely found in such sources as Bartlett's *Familiar Quotations*, other more obscure choices such as Zhuge Liang and Saladin are included here. Quoted individuals are further identified in a biographical index of sources that provides brief summaries of military careers.

The quotations are divided into approximately 350 subject areas. These do not include any proper names or names of particular battles or campaigns. Standard headings such as *Bravery* and *Loyalty* appear, as well as the concepts *Strike Weakness*, *Economy of Force*, and *River Defence*. The topic *War* is divided into 12 subheadings. For each quotation, the entry lists author, title, date of the source, and, when appropriate, translator; pagination is not included. Complete publication details appear in a select bibliography in the back of the book.

Quoted individuals are futher identified in a biographical index of sources that provides brief summaries of military careers. This index—the only one included in the work—also provides references to the page numbers where quotations from the individual can be found.

Warriors' Words was compiled to assist and enlighten military professionals and enthusiasts, and the book should be included in collections that serve these clienteles. It is alo appropriate for libraries that extensively colloct quotation books.

African American Generals and Flag Officers: Biographies of Over 120 Blacks in the United States Military. By Walter L. Hawkins. McFarland, 1993. 264p. illus. index. hardcover $25.95 (0-89950-774-3).

355'.0089 [B] Afro-American generals—Biography || Afro-American admirals—Biography || U.S.—Armed Forces—Biography || U.S.—Armed Forces—Afro-Americans || U.S.—History, Military [CIP] 92-50886

The title of this work clearly describes its focus: biographies of African American officers who have attained the rank in the armed forces of general or its naval equivalent. Generals of the Army and Air Reserves as well as the National Guard are included. Each entry consists of biographical and career information with awards and decorations noted. Most are accompanied by a black-and-white photograph.

While the focus is on the post–World War II military, a chronology traces significant events in black military history from Crispus Attucks to the 1991 assignment of Brigadier General Clara Leach Adams-Ender as commanding general of Fort Belvoir. The appended matter includes a list of firsts in the military and lists of the officers by birth states and college attended. No list of published sources of information is included, although there is passing mention to a Department of Defense publication, *Black Americans in Defense of Our Nation* (1985), in some of the entries. The acknowledgement notes assistance from various branches of the military.

In school and public libraries where such information is needed, this will be a handy reference. *Who's Who among African Americans*, for example, does not list many of the men and women included here.

The Harper Encyclopedia of Military Biography. By Trevor N. Dupuy and others. HarperCollins, 1992. 834p. bibliog. hardcover $65 (0-06-270015-4).

355'.0092 [B] Military biography—Dictionaries [CIP] 89-46526

This book is intended to be a companion to Dupuy's *Encyclopedia of Military History* (Harper, 1986), which will be issued in 1993 in a fourth edition as *The Harper Encyclopedia of Military History*. Together with 32 contributors, the editors have developed a biographical dictionary of approximately 3,000 entries that ranges in time from Alexander the Great to Norman Schwarzkopf. It complements Spiller's three-volume *Dictionary of American Military Biography* (Greenwood, 1984) and offers more entries than another one-volume dictionary, *Who's Who in Military History from 1453 to the Present Day* (Morrow, 1976) by Keegan and Wheatcroft. Spiller provides much better coverage for American military leaders but is not as current as Dupuy. Keegan and Wheatcroft has excellent illustrations and provides more interesting coverage of the greatest military leaders.

Entries in the new work consist of a subject's name followed by alternative spellings (an important aid to identifying military leaders associated with Asia and the Middle East), biographical information, and a summary of military contributions. The entries serve to give the facts, and generally no attempt is made to make them interesting reading. However, the longer entries end with paragraphs evaluating the subject's character, abilities, and contributions. Douglas MacArthur's summary paragraph states in part, "MacArthur was egotistical and always controversial, so much so that his arrogance somewhat overshadows his military brilliance; nevertheless he was one of the greatest generals of World War II and of history." Some entries are as brief as two sentences; others such as *Napoleon* are two pages.

Most entries are signed and give bibliographic citations to important published sources, usually autobiographies and secondary sources (including the *Dictionary of American Biography* and the *Dictionary of National Biography*). The absence of any subject indexing detracts from the reference value of the work. Indexing that would identify leaders with geographic areas and conflicts would be helpful. Facts are important, however, and this work is a necessary purchase for libraries having the companion volume on military history cited above.

The Soldier's Chronology. By James W. Atkinson. Garland, 1993. 602p. bibliog. hardcover $93 (0-8153-0813-2).
355'.00973 U.S.—Armed Forces—History—Chronology || U.S.—Armed Forces—Military life—History—Chronology [CIP] 92-16454

Military history is a broad field covering events, technology, social conditions, and artifacts. Organizing this material is not easy. *The Soldier's Chronology* is a new reference work that focuses on the history of enlisted soldiers and noncommissioned officers in the U.S. military from 1775 to 1991. It explains the conditions affecting the lives of soldiers on active duty and the changes that occurred as the armed services evolved. The book will interest historians as well as museum curators and artifact collectors.

This work is organized chronologically and divided into four major sections: "The Iron Armies," covering the years 7,000 B.C.–1774 A.D.; "The Blue Army," 1775–1901; "The Brown Army," 1902–56; and "The Green Army," 1957–91. Each section begins with an essay summarizing the history of the period. Chronological entries by year or by specific date follow. These entries range in length from one line to several paragraphs and provide information on such topics as pay scales, mosquito netting being adopted for barracks beds in June 1884, and Christmas dinner at Valley Forge, December 25, 1777: "a soggy firecake, carrion beef (if available) and creek water." These are things that most military history books overlook. This source includes coverage of the Persian Gulf War and important international events affecting the U.S., such as the dissolution of the Soviet Union and China joining a nuclear nonproliferation treaty. The book concludes with a glossary of military terms and an extensive bibliography of books and periodicals.

The Soldier's Chronology fills a gap in military-history reference by providing detailed coverage of American soldiers' daily lives. Older books, such as *American Army Life* by John Elting (Scribner, 1982) and *Almanac of Liberty* by Benjamin F. Schimmer (Macmillan, 1974), provide illustrated overviews of major events, but they are less current and less extensive in their coverage. Evans E. Kerrigan's books—*American Badges and Insignia* (Viking, 1967) and *American War Medals and Decorations* (Viking, 1971)—provide coverage of only one aspect of military life. *The Soldier's Chronology* is more complete. Unfortunately, it lacks a subject index and illustrations of the clothing, insignia, and equipment listed. These would facilitate access and clarify the explanations. This book belongs in specialized military-history collections and academic libraries.

The Atomic Bomb: An Annotated Bibliography. By Hans G. Graetzer and Larry M. Browning. Salem Press, 1992. 168p. index. hardcover $40 (0-89356-677-2).
016.3558'25119 Atomic bomb—Bibliography [CIP] 92-29628

The Nuclear Present: A Guide to Recent Books on Nuclear War, Weapons, the Peace Movement, and Related Issues, with a Chronology of Nuclear Events, 1789–1991. By Grant Burns. Scarecrow, 1992. 633p. indexes. hardcover $69.50 (0-8108-2619-4).
016.3271'74 Nuclear arms control—Bibliography || Nuclear weapons—Bibliography || Nuclear warfare—Bibliography || Nuclear industry—Bibliography [CIP] 92-32440

While there is some overlap between these two new titles, they will appeal to different audiences. *The Atomic Bomb* is aimed at high school and college students, adult discussion groups, and nonspecialists. This annotated bibliography of English-language materials delivers a simple overview of the development of atomic weapons inside and outside of the U.S., testing, Hiroshima and Nagasaki, the H-bomb, and the peace movement. Included are chapters on videocassettes, documentaries, movies, and the literature of the bomb. The latter lists well-known novels and works of science fiction, but no short stories. Excluded are the history of the cold war and international relations, scientific works, and general studies of military strategy. The introduction does provide a quick overview of the nuclear arms race, 1940–90, and concludes with a three-page chronology of important events.

Entries are arranged in 10 topical chapters. The authors indicate that all books and media should be available through college or public libraries. Highly recommended works are identified in the annotations. The work concludes with an index listing authors and titles of the bibliography entries, as well as selected names of important persons, places, and events that appear in the annotated listings.

The Nuclear Present also is a topically arranged, annotated bibliography. It lists works published between 1984 and 1991, providing an update to *The Atomic Papers*, which RBB favorably reviewed [RBB Ap 15 85]. Burns, a reference librarian at the University of Michigan at Flint, explodes with concern about the control of nuclear weapons, terrorists, and the consequences of ignorance. While these concerns are detailed in the introduction to this new title, Burns maintains objectivity in the bibliography by including works on all sides of the nuclear debate.

The scope of *The Nuclear Present* is broad, although fiction is not included. It lists not only books and documents on nuclear weapons, testing, the arms race, proliferation, and strategic defense, but also titles on ethical and religious issues as well as peace and disarmament. The chapter on nuclear weapons and nuclear war is subdivided into sections on such topics as history, legal considerations, civil defense, behind the scenes at the bomb factories, spies, and the Cuban missile crisis.

Also provided is an annotated list of magazines, journals, and newsletters the reader should consult regularly. The final chapter, "A Nuclear Chronology," is 108 pages in length and provides an annotated listing of events from 1789 through 1991. Access to the information in the book is enhanced by four indexes: author-editor, title, subject, and a separate index for the chronology. Another feature is a list of publishers and distributors that includes well-known trade publishers, small presses, foreign and university presses, and government agencies.

More than three times as many entries appear in *The Nuclear Present* as in *The Atomic Bomb*. However, many of the listings in the former title will be of primary interest to academic researchers, and some of its reports and documents may be difficult to obtain. Unlike Graetzer and Browning, Burns does not include works on the history of nuclear fission or biographies of nuclear scientists. *The Atomic Bomb* will be a welcome bibliography for general readers and beginning researchers who want a general overview of standard works. *The Nuclear Present* will appeal to college students and others who want to be better informed on nuclear weapons and peace issues.

Assistance & Benefits Information Directory: Volume 1: Programs. Ed. by Kay Gill. Omnigraphics, 1992. indexes. hardcover $95 (1-55888-423-8).

Assistance & Benefits Information Directory: Volume 2: Publications. Ed. by Mary Emanoil. Omnigraphics, 1992. indexes. hardcover $75 (1-55888-756-3); $155/2v. set (1-55888-797-0).
361'.0025 Economic assistance, Domestic—U.S.—Directories || Economic assistance, Domestic—U.S.—States—Directories [CIP] 92-7645

Published in two hefty volumes, the *Assistance & Benefits Information Directory* (ABID) details more than 2,000 federal, state, and association or organization financial-assistance programs, as well as 1,200 related supporting publications. With coverage geared toward the needs of individuals and families, the set addresses six major areas: "Cultural Affairs"; "Education"; "Employment, Labor, and Training"; "Health and Social Services"; "Housing and Home Energy"; and "Law, Justice, and Legal Services."

Program entries in volume 1 typically include agency address, application information, eligibility requirements, award amounts, and the like. The work invites comparison with the GPO's *Catalog of Federal Domestic Assistance* (CFDA) in the federal programs portions. In the area of support for the arts, for example, CFDA lists 23 federal programs and ABID lists 38. But one suspects a bit of padding here. Where CFDA gives a single entry under *Promotion of the Arts—Theater*, ABID gives three different entries for theater fellowships, all with similar requirements, the same telephone number, and all referring to the NEA Theater Program. ABID then proceeds to describe 185 state programs and 20 association or organization programs in support of the arts, coverage that would not be found in CFDA. Unfortunately, much of the data on state programs is limited, but addresses, contacts, and telephone numbers are nearly always included. Concluding volume 1 are four program indexes (federal programs, state programs, organizations, and combined) and extensive appendixes listing regional offices for federal and state program entries. The indexes and the volume's simple arrangement by broad area of assistance make for easy use.

Volume 2 is essentially a huge supporting bibliography to the listings in volume 1, listing brochures and pamphlets that explain the assistance programs. It follows the same arrangement and has indexes analogous to those in volume 1, in addition to such special indexes as "Women's Publications" and "Youth Publications."

ABID does not attempt to be a more efficient version of CFDA; Omnigraphics' *Government Assistance Almanac* ($84) does that. Both CFDA and *Government Assistance Almanac* treat programs in all subject areas available to businesses and organizations as well as to individuals. *Government Giveaways for Entrepreneurs* (1988) and *The Guide to State and Federal Resources for Economic Development* (1986) both differ in scope. ABID is the only directory that goes to the state level (and even county and local levels in its appendixes) to describe support programs in areas most pertinent to individuals.

For libraries needing comprehensive coverage of benefit programs in all 50 states, *Assistance & Benefits Information Directory* has no competition. Although the two volumes are available separately, one should think hard before skipping volume 2. Its listings include addresses and telephone numbers that allow the user to obtain the publications.

Who's Who in the Peace Corps. Ed. by Cheryl Klein Lacoff. Reference Press International, P.O. Box 4126, Greenwich, CT 06830-0126, 1993. 724p. indexes. hardcover $95 (1-879583-03-8); paper $75 (1-879583-02-X) (ISSN 1065-8459).
361.6'025 Peace Corps (U.S.)—Directories [BKL]

The thirtieth anniversary of the Peace Corps was in 1991. Since 1961 more than 130,000 volunteers have served in various nations around the world. This new directory, in its first edition, provides current biographical information on approximately 50,000 active and returned Peace Corps volunteers and staff.

The main section of the directory is an alphabetical listing of these individuals. The amount of biographical information included for volunteers varies based on responses to the questionnaire surveys that were used to compile the directory. In all cases, country of service and current residential address are listed. While these shorter entries predominate, the complete descriptions include country and years of service; specialties; languages; education; current occupation; achievements; publications; such vital statistics as birth date, spouse, and children; and current residential address and telephone number. Women listed by their married name are often cross-referenced by their maiden name.

Also included is a list of the names of deceased volunteers and staff. Another section of the work is a directory of national and regional organizations that serve returned Peace Corps volunteers. Again, the amount of information included for different groups varies, but, in all cases, an address and name of a contact person are listed.

Three separate indexes are provided. "Geographic Index—U.S." lists volunteers by the current city and state of residence; "Geographic Index—Foreign" lists volunteers by the current country of residence, other than the U.S.; and a "Country of Service Index" is also included. More than 100 countries have hosted Peace Corps volunteers. The majority of these nations are in Africa, South America, and Asia. Poland is the only Eastern European country listed as having current volunteers, although in 1992, volunteers were sent to Russia and several other former Soviet republics.

Less than half of all former and current staff and volunteers are listed; it is hoped that in future editions this percentage will increase. The editor states that the objectives of *Who's Who in the Peace Corps* are to help returned volunteers stay in touch, to familiarize them with the organizations available to serve them, and to inform future volunteers. For these purposes, the book is primarily recommended to large libraries. However, because of its value in locating people with language or country specialties, it can be used by libraries, museums, businesses, and civic groups as a referral source in finding former volunteers for speeches, background information, or other research purposes.

Fund Raiser's Guide to Religious Philanthropy. 6th ed. Ed. by Bernard Jankowski. Taft Group; dist. by Gale, 1993. 335p. indexes. paper $129 (1-879784-45-9; ISSN 1042-0053).
361.75 Endowments—U.S. Directories || Church charities—U.S.—Directories [OCLCL]

The Taft Group, one of the large publishers of grant information, has released the sixth edition of this directory, profiling 417 private foundations and corporate contributors to religious organizations. The entries, arranged alphabetically by corporate name, follow the typical Taft pattern. Included for each foundation are contact name and address, telephone and fax numbers, denominational preference, geographic limits, grant types, types of recipients, application procedures, publications, names of officers and directors, brief financial data, and a list of major grants. Provided for each organization is a brief analysis of the percentage of giving to various programs of religiously affiliated groups. Possibly one negative feature of the guide is the inclusion of foundations that preselect their grantees and are not open for applications from others.

To assist users in targeting funding sources, the directory includes eight different indexes, with access points for locations, denominations, types of grants (e.g., general support, endowment), and types of recipients (e.g., aged missions, shelters). One of the indexes is an alphabetical list of the names of foundation staff, trustees, and directors appearing in the book. A detailed table of contents, showing the page numbers for different sections of the indexes, will help patrons organize their search.

Because the profiles in the *Fund Raiser's Guide* are focused on religious philanthropy, they are not necessarily as long as those in the *Foundation Reporter* (Taft Group, 1991), in which more than 100 of the same organizations are also listed. Most of the foundations profiled in the work under review are also listed in the *Foundation Directory* (14th ed., Foundation Center, 1992). The latter source provides similar directory information, although it lacks the analysis of religious giving and omits a list of sample grants. A work focusing on religious philanthropy is the *National Guide to Funding in Religion* (Foundation Center, 1990). It is priced comparably to the Taft directory and covers more corporate and private giving programs with its list of 2,800 funding sources. The material in the *Fund Raiser's Guide to Religious Philanthropy* is current, accurate, and presented in a straightforward manner. It is a good secondary purchase for libraries serving religious organizations actively seeking funding and for strong grantsmanship collections.

Social Work Almanac. By Leon Ginsberg. NASW Press, 750 First St., Ste. 700, Washington, DC 20002-4241, 1992. 215p. bibliog. charts. index. tables. paper $29.95 (0-87101-196-4).
361.973 Social service—U.S.—Statistics || U.S.—Population—Statistics [OCLC] 92-31194

This compilation of data from the 1990 census, other government sources, and national social welfare agencies is a successor to *Face of the Nation, 1987*, a supplement to the eighteenth edition of the *Encyclopedia of Social Work*, which was favorably reviewed here [RBB Ap 1 87].

The foreword states that no single compendium of social work data exists for social work students and practitioners. The introduction notes that the primary source of the data here is government documents (especially the *Statistical Abstract of the United States*), *World Almanac*, *Universal Almanac*, and an annual publication on entitlement programs published by the U.S. House Ways and Means Committee.

The work is divided into nine chapters, ranging from "Basic Demographic Data" to specifics—"Crime and Delinquency," "Mental Illness," "Older Adults," and "Social Welfare, Economic Assistance, Housing, and Homelessness." The format is a section of background text followed by tables of data. Included are some gross state and metropolitan area figures, many pre-1990 statistics (1986 mental health data is noted as the best available), growth projections for the number of older adults, the impact of the deinstitutionalization of the mentally ill, and an explanation of the great number of social welfare programs. Easy access is ensured by detailed contents and list of tables at the beginning of the book and an index at the end.

The *Social Work Almanac* includes national data used in the social work field. While most libraries have the statistical sources that were used in compiling the book, this work will be useful in tracking national trends in the areas noted. However, most users want data for individual states, so the *Social Work Almanac* is not essential for libraries that need to make hard selection choices.

Native Americans Information Directory. Ed. by Julia C. Furtaw and Kimberly Burton Faulkner. Gale, 1992. 500p. bibliog. index. hardcover $69.50 (0-8103-8854-5; ISSN 1063-9632).
361.997 Indians of North America—Societies, etc. || Hawaiians—Societies, etc. || Indians of North America—Bibliography || Hawaiians—Bibliography [BKL]

The *Native Americans Information Directory* provides information on approximately 4,500 organizations, agencies, institutions, programs, services, and publications that pertain to native Americans, their life, and their culture. The directory is similar to Gale's parent volume, *Encyclopedia of Associations*, and its two specialized minority directories, *Black Americans Information Directory, 1990–1991* and *Hispanic Americans Information Directory, 1990–1991* [RBB Ja 15 90].

The directory is divided into five parts. Each of the first four parts covers a specific group (American Indians, Alaskan natives, native Hawaiians, and aboriginal Canadians) and includes descriptive entries on tribal communities. The last section contains material of a general nature on native Americans. All five sections provide listings for national, regional, state or provincial, and local organizations; federal, state or provincial, and local government agencies; library and museum collections; research centers; education programs, scholarships, and fellowships; and print and broadcast media, publishers, and videos. A master name and keyword index provides access to the entries in all five sections. A major omission is the lack of information about federal Indian reservations.

Similar information, except for native Hawaiians, can be found in the *Reference Encyclopedia of the American Indian* [RBB Ja 15 91]. It does include Indian reservations, plus a biographical section on living native Americans. In a broader work, although now somewhat dated, *Minority Organizations: A National Directory* (3d ed. [RBB My 15 88]), information is included for approximately 2,100 American Indian and Alaskan native organizations and for 1,100 Asian and Pacific Islander organizations. Unfortunately, all of the desired information is not contained in any one source.

The *Native Americans Information Directory*, in spite of its Indian reservation omission, provides a wealth of information. Its arrangement by native American group makes locating specific information extremely efficient. Also, it is one of the few sources that lists grant and scholarship opportunities specifically for native Americans. If a library owns Gale's directories on Hispanics and African Americans, the *Native Americans Information Directory* will complement the collection. However, if a library acquires current editions of the *Reference Encyclopedia of the American Indian*, the acquisition of the *Native Americans Information Directory* would be duplicative except for native Hawaiians. Libraries that collect heavily in the area of native Americans would want to acquire both publications.

The AIDS Directory: An Essential Guide to the 1500 Leaders in Research, Services, Policy, Advocacy, and Funding. Buraff Publications, 1350 Connecticut Ave. NW, Ste. 100, Washington, DC 20036, 1993. 814p. indexes. paper $250 (1-882594-00-2; ISSN 1065-6162).
362 AIDS (disease)—Directories [BLK]

The publisher of this compilation specializes in producing information sources for business, legal, and human resource professionals. Among its titles is the biweekly newsletter *AIDS Policy & Law*, begun in 1986. This new directory grew out of the company's ongoing activities in keeping abreast of AIDS-related developments. The book is intended to assist "health care professionals, community leaders, local governments, and the general public" tap into the networks combatting the disease.

The major portion of the directory is the section providing descriptive profiles of 1,500 national, regional, and international organizations dealing with aspects of AIDS/HIV. These were selected as the "leaders" in the field from the more than 20,000 organizations currently serving the AIDS community. The book's goal is to comprehensively cover state and national entities, medical research facilities, and regional service organizations that support community-based initiatives. It does not attempt to list all the strictly local groups working on the disease. The scope of the directory is broad. In addition to listings for government agencies, profiles are included for such organizations as Harvard AIDS Institute, National Minority AIDS Council, Berkeley Free Clinic, Iowa Center for AIDS, Pen Pal, Hospice of Chattanooga, and AIDS Coalition to Unleash Power (ACT UP). Approximately 250 of the directory's entries are for foundations and grant-making organizations.

The profiles, arranged alphabetically by name of the organization, include contact person, address and telephone number, mission statement, type of organization, type of services provided, focus areas, publications, and names of officers, directors, and staff. Additional helpful information is included when appropriate. For instance, "notes" are used to relate that services are available in particular foreign languages at a clinic, that an agency received a specific amount in funding for its AIDS programs, or that the organization operates an electronic bulletin board. The profiles for funding organizations typically list the groups that have been financially supported, including the amount and a short phrase describing the purpose of the grant. Most frequently, the grant's financial data cover 1991, although 1992 figures are given in some instances.

Extensive cross-referencing through 10 indexes allows the user multiple access points to the organizational entries. Different indexes are provided for the entities by name, location, type (clinic, state agency), services offered (lobbying, meals), and focus areas (bisexuals, Haitians). Also included are indexes for organizations that issue publications, for those that receive financial support (with the index entry giving the name of the donor and the amount), and an alphabetical list of the personal names of staff and and officers that appear in the entries. For those searching for funding sources, two indexes are of special interest. One is an alphabetical list of grant-making organizations, and the second is an index to the type of support offered (seed money, publications, clinical trials). This indexing system and the list of terms used are explained in the prefatory material. Also included there are additional instructions for using the book, names of congressional committees that consider AIDS-related legislation, a summary of available federal funding programs, a brief guide to major publications that focus on the disease, and a list of state and national hotline numbers.

The *AIDS Directory* succeeds as a one-volume reference for advocates, specialists, and professionals who need to connect with others in the field. Community organizations and local government agencies that either offer or are planning AIDS-related services will find it useful for identifying programs and funding opportunities. These advantages of the directory recommend it to university, health, and large public libraries. The drawback is its price, which will be prohibitive for many collections serving the general public. These libraries might remain satisfied with the 900 listings in the directory section of the reasonably priced *AIDS Information Sourcebook* (3d ed., Oryx, 1991).

Alternative Health Care Resources: A Directory and Guide. By Brett Jason Sinclair. Parker/Simon & Schuster, 1992. 498p. index. hardcover $24.95 (0-13-030073-X); paper $12.95 (0-13-156522-2).
362.1'025 Alternative medicine—U.S.—Directories || Alternative medicine—Information services—U.S. [OCLC] 92-28096

As dissatisfaction with the current medical system and a desire to take an active part in disease prevention and treatment increase, interest in alternative health care is growing. This directory provides access to this broad field.

The compiler has obtained information on approximately 400 organizations, publications, and self-help groups that provide assistance and information on a variety of conditions and health-related topics. He personally contacted all the sources included in the directory and read at least six issues of each publication listed. The book neither rates nor offers opinions on the material provided but presents an opportunity for users to find the different options available to help make informed health-care decisions.

Entries are arranged alphabetically by subject and, within each heading, alphabetically by name. The approximately 100 subjects included here demonstrate the diversity of alternative health care; for example, AIDS, Cancer, Environmental Illness, Homeopathy, Lifestyle, Mind-Body Connection, Oriental Healing and Exercise, and Seasonal Affective Disorder. The American Holistic Veterinary Medical Association and the International Veterinary Acupuncture Society offer alternative care for animals. Each entry includes address, telephone and fax numbers, contact person, and background information on the source and services offered. Cross-references to entries offering related information are provided. A cumulative alphabetical index facilitates access.

Since the Holistic Resources Directory has not been issued since 1988, Alternative Health Care Resources is the only current directory in this field. It is easy to use, objective, and reasonably priced. This book will meet a growing demand for information on alternative health care. It is a good addition to all public and academic library collections.

AIDS Crisis in America. By Mary Ellen Hombs. ABC-Clio, 1992. 280p. bibliog. index. hardcover $39.50 (0-87436-648-8).
362.1'969792 AIDS (Disease)—U.S.—Epidemiology || AIDS (Disease)—Government policy—U.S. || AIDS (Disease)—U.S.—Bibliography [OCLC] 92-48841

Dictionary of Aids-Related Terminology. Ed. by Jeffrey T. Huber. Neal-Schuman, 1993. 176p. hardcover $39.95 (1-55570-117-5).
616.97'92 AIDS (Disease)—Dictionaries—Juvenile literature [OCLC] 92-31265

The number of books published on the topic of AIDS has steadily increased over the past few years. Some have been written out of anguish, anger, and hope that what is printed will give comfort; others are compilations, documenting the history of this tragic disease; and still others are reference books guiding individuals through the maze of publications, organizations, and terminology. These two new references are reasonably priced and clearly written for the layperson.

AIDS Crisis in America, a title from the Contemporary World Issues series, presents a variety of information about the available resources on the subject. The introduction provides a good historical overview, including public policy issues. This is followed by a chronology documenting the major discoveries, events, and personalities from 1970 through July 1992. Included is a brief section of biographical sketches of AIDS researchers and prominent individuals who have died or been diagnosed as HIV positive. The rest of this guide consists of numerous useful statistics, glossaries, directory information, and bibliographies. All the sections are designed to provide quick, up-to-date data that one can consult easily. Entries in the bibliography are annotated, and all directory entries have brief descriptions of facilities, including major publications produced by the listed organizations. Compared with the AIDS Information Sourcebook (3d ed., Oryx, 1991), this guide is more general, providing highlights or key sources rather than detailed information or extensive lists.

AIDS Crisis in America has several glossaries throughout the text, plus detailed definitions of the term AIDS itself. However, for those who want a good source of definitions of AIDS-related and safe-sex terms, one should consult the Dictionary of AIDS-Related Terminology. This excellent work not only includes terms related to AIDS, diseases, and medications, but also includes organizational names and personal names of researchers, making it an encyclopedic dictionary. It is arranged in alphabetical order, letter by letter, with numerous cross-references from acronyms, abbreviations, and alternate spellings to the accepted entry. Any serious researcher or layperson not familiar with the terminology of AIDS will want this dictionary at hand.

Since research on AIDS and its terminology, medications, and organizations are evolving, these books will have to be considered for revision on a periodic basis until, hopefully, AIDS books become obsolete. Aids Crisis in America and the Dictionary of AIDS-Related Terminology should be considered for purchase by all libraries serving general readers, from the teen years through adult.

Register of North American Hospitals, 1993. Ed. by Natalie Axelrod and others. American Preeminent Registry, 510 Old Bridge Turnpike, South River, NJ 08882, 1992. 746p. indexes. paper $97.95 (0-9633783-0-9; ISSN 1062-7340).
362.11 Hospitals—U.S.—Directories || Hospitals—Canada—Directories [BKL] 92-2835

The premier edition of the Register of North American Hospitals is a quick-reference source for locating addresses and telephone numbers of more than 9,000 hospitals in the U.S. and Canada. Arrangement is by dictionary format—alphabetical by state or province and then by city, with the first and last city mentioned on the page appearing as headers. Each entry includes the hospital name, address, telephone number, number of beds, and names of the chief administrator and chief medical administrator. In the U.S. section, a summary page is included for each state and provides the following: a state map; names of the governor, U.S. senators, and U.S. representatives; area and zip codes; and numbers of hospitals and beds. These summaries and maps are omitted for the Canadian provinces.

Alternating between white and grey shading makes each entry stand out for ease of reading. However, the highlighting proves frustrating if the user must search to find the beginning of each city's section. It would have been helpful if the city name appeared ahead of the hospital listings, rather than just being included in the hospital addresses. A more serious flaw is the treatment of some hospital groups or conglomerates. For example, United Health Services is a major health-care provider with two member hospitals: Binghamton General Hospital, Binghamton, New York, and C. S. Wilson Memorial Hospital, Johnson City, New York. There is no mention in the register of U.H.S. or United Health Services or its primary facility, C. S. Wilson Memorial Hospital. Only Binghamton General Hospital appears. In this respect, it appears that not all hospitals for the stated localities have been included. Additionally, geographic coverage is for Canada, the U.S., Puerto Rico, and the Virgin Islands. The U.S. territories and possessions in the Pacific Ocean have been excluded.

The Register of North American Hospitals, 1993 was designed as a marketing tool for direct-mail campaigns, and it is fine as far as it goes. It will adequately fill the need for many directory-assistance inquiries, and it covers Canadian hospitals that are not found easily in other directories. But it is not as comprehensive nor as statistically complete for U.S. hospitals as the American Hospital Association's publication, AHA Guide to the Health Care Field, although it costs one-half as much. Libraries requiring detailed information for hospitals in the U.S. and all of its territories and possessions must continue to rely upon the more expensive AHA Guide, which provides in-patient data, newborn data, accreditation, affiliation listings, specialized services, and more.

The National Housing Directory for People with Disabilities, 1993. Grey House, 1993. 1,429p. index. paper $180 (0-939300-13-3).
362.4'0973 Handicapped—Housing—U.S.—Directories || Handicapped—Institutional care—U.S.—Directories [BKL]

From the publisher of The Complete Directory for People with Disabilities [RBB Ja 15 92] comes this one-volume directory—of nearly 1,500 pages—listing thousands of special housing options for the disabled. Information presented was current as of September 1992 and was collected from housing departments, mental health agencies, case managers, and referral agencies throughout the country.

The primary arrangement of this source is alphabetically by state, with a final chapter on U.S. government and national organizations that deal with housing issues. The directory includes five different types of sources: 900 agencies that have responsibilities for housing for the disabled; 6,500 referral agencies; 3,700 intensive- and intermediate-care facilities, such as rehabilitation hospitals and skilled-nursing facilities; 7,500 licensed group homes; and 3,200 independent-living facilities, including supervised apartments. All entries include contact information, but the length of annotations varies. Generally, brief information is included about programs offered, disabilities served, accessibility of facilities, and number of beds, clients, or units.

The only index is by entry name. Another index by "disabilities served" would have given the directory a useful access point. The information is also available in a computerized version that can be merged with most database software programs. This format could make this directory a powerful tool if it were mounted on a library's electronic network of resource and referral information.

This directory is a unique source of more than 20,000 nationwide entries to help people with physical and mental disabilities—and the professionals who serve them—find suitable housing. While relatively expensive, it should be considered for purchase by large public and medical libraries.

Caregiving of Older Adults. By Louise G. Fradkin and Angela Heath. ABC-Clio, 1992. 260p. bibliog. index. hardcover $45 (0-87436-671-2).
362.6 Aged—Care—U.S. || Caregivers—Services for—U.S. || Adult children—Services for—U.S. [OCLC] 92-34591

Child Care Crisis: A Reference Handbook. By Diane Lindsey Reeves. ABC-Clio, 1992. 170p. bibliog. index. hardcover $39.50 (0-87436-645-3).
362.712 Child care services—U.S. || Child care services—Government policy—U.S. [OCLC] 92-38144

The "sandwich generation" is caught between the needs of aging parents and dependent children. These books provide resources that will help people deal with both issues.

Caregiving of Older Adults is in ABC-Clio's Choices and Challenges series. Essays, augmented by case studies, discuss challenges to caregivers of the elderly and how to understand care receivers. Finding support systems, such as meals programs and adult day care, and planning for financial and legal issues, such as powers of attorney and living wills, are also treated. Such safety and welfare issues as age-proofing the house and housing options, including nursing homes, are covered as well. The last third of the book is an extensive annotated list of resources, including organizations and print and nonprint materials, followed by a glossary and index. Another volume in this series, *Final Choices: Making End-of-Life Decisions*, is an extension of *Caregiving* and includes in its resources section state-by-state funeral and cemetery regulatory information.

Child Care Crisis: A Reference Handbook is in ABC-Clio's Contemporary World Issues series. Like others in the series, it begins with a chronology of child-care issues and a series of biographical sketches of important people in the field (e.g., Berry Brazelton, Burton White). This is followed by essays on child-care options, defining quality child care, and the role of government. Almost two-thirds of the book is a resource directory, with annotated lists of organizations and print and other media resources. A state-by-state directory of child-care regulatory agencies, a glossary, and an index conclude the book.

These titles are valuable additions to these two helpful series. Academic libraries will want them for student research papers; public libraries will find them useful as sources for information and referral. —*Sandy Whiteley*

Caring for Kids with Special Needs: Residential Treatment Programs for Children and Adolescents. Peterson's Guides, 1993. 482p. charts. illus. index. hardcover $89.95 (0-56079-168-3).
362.7'32 Children—Institutional care—U.S.—Directories || Group homes for children—U.S.—Directories || Teenagers—Institutional care—U.S.—Directories || Group homes for teenagers—U.S.—Directories [CIP] 92-36346

This one-volume resource provides 817 brief profiles and 35 detailed descriptions of residential treatment programs for children and adolescents, ages 8–18. The guide purports to provide a list of facilities in both the U.S. and Canada. However, no Canadian listings were identified in the book. The range of facilities profiled is wide: drug and alcohol rehabilitation centers, psychiatric hospitals, residential schools, acute-care facilities, general hospitals, and wilderness programs and camps. While the variety of problems addressed at these facilities is broad, severe mental retardation is beyond the scope of the volume.

The work opens with a quick-reference chart of the programs included. It is organized geographically and provides the facility name, address, page number, type, security, admission policy, ages, gender, and disorders treated. The major portion of the book, "Program Profiles," presents the facilities alphabetically by name. The amount of information included for each facility varies, depending on responses received to a survey by the publisher. All entries include contact information and brief descriptions of the type of facility and type of disorders treated. Fuller profiles also briefly cover such topics as staff, facilities, educational offerings, costs, and additional services. A third directory section provides more detailed descriptions of 35 facilities, which were also included in the profiles. The volume concludes with a glossary, a brief list of resources for more information, and an alphabetical index of facility names.

The process used for finding a particular facility can be confusing. The reference chart is listed geographically, followed by the actual profiles listed alphabetically, and then more detail for several facilities is presented in another section. Thus, the user utilizes three different sections to gather needed information. Another flaw is the variant ways some facilities are listed in the different sections of the book. For example, in the "Quick Reference Chart," the North American Wilderness Academy is listed with a page reference of 275. On page 275, the user is directed to look on page 400 for a more detailed description. However, the facility on page 400 is listed with a different name, the Academy, which the description states is affiliated with the North American Wilderness Academy. No reference is made in the chart or in the profile to this alternate name. Nor will the user be able to find the Academy in the index. Also, "disorders treated" in the quick-reference chart uses nine broad categories, such as "learning disabilities" and "psychosocial disorders." Without additional indexing, the user has to read the profiles to discover which facilities have special programs for the hearing impaired or for children with a history of arson. Another objection is to the word *kids* in the book's title, which seems inappropriate for the subject matter.

Other directories exist that list programs for children and adolescents with special needs, and these typically provide better access to the listings of facilities that serve particular difficulties. For instance, the geographically arranged *Directory of Residential Facilities for Emotionally Handicapped Children and Youth* [RBB Jl 1 88] covers approximately 1,000 facilities and includes a "Specialized Programs Index." The biennial *Directory for Exceptional Children* (12th ed., Porter Sargent, 1990) is organized into sections covering various conditions such as speech impairment, mental retardation, and social maladjustment; it provides brief listings for more than 3,000 facilities offering day care, summer programs, and residential treatment (see RBB [Je 15 87] for a review of the 11th edition). In these directories, as well as in the work under review, the amount of information provided on each facility is only useful as a preliminary step in researching suitable programs for a given individual, and additional details will be needed.

Loving Journeys Guide to Adoption. By Elaine L. Walker. Loving Journeys, P.O. Box 755, Peterborough, NH 03458, 1992. 394p. index. maps. tables. paper $24.95 (0-9633642-0-0).
362.7'34 Adoption—U.S.—Handbooks, manuals, etc. || Adoption agencies—Directories || Intercountry adoption [CIP] 92-93516

This book consists of two parts, the first with 14 chapters of background information about the adoption process, and the second providing a directory of adoption agencies and services.

Chapters in part 1 are especially helpful for dealing with such issues as the age of the child, agency versus private adoption, international alternatives, choosing an attorney, and adoption of special-needs children. Other chapters deal with the adoption process itself, covering such issues as deciding, waiting, paperwork, adjustment difficulties after placement, and talking with the child about his or her birth parents.

Part 2 provides separate lists of public and private agencies, each arranged alphabetically by state. A few paragraphs of description are given for the agencies that responded to a questionnaire. Apparently, many agencies did not answer the author's survey, and, for these, only name, address, and telephone number are listed. Characteristics and requirements of the U.S. agencies are compared in chart form in separate chapters covering infant programs and children programs. International adoptions are highlighted in separate sections for each of six areas of the world. For each country, a brief summary of adoption information is provided: numbers of children and infants available, restrictions, estimated range of costs, etc. Also listed are adoption attorneys, support groups, and newspapers that take adoption ads. The volume concludes with a name and subject index.

Other recent books on this subject include *Encyclopedia of Adoption* [RBB F 15 92], *CWLA's Guide to Adoption Agencies* [RBB S 1 89], and *The Adoption Directory* [RBB F 1 90]. *Encyclopedia of Adoption* is rich in background information, but it lacks directory listings. Both the CWLA and *The Adoption Directory* excel in directory information but lack background articles. Libraries that bought the *Encyclopedia of Adoption* and either the CWLA or *The Adoption Directory* will not need to add *Loving Journeys* to the reference collection. However, this new title makes a unique contribution by discussing such recent trends and issues as private adoption, adoption by single parents and unmarried couples, and the controversy over transracial adoption. The work is written for persons considering adoption alternatives, and it serves this audience well by telling both how to adopt and where to get help. Public libraries already owning adequate reference tools on the topic should consider adding *Loving Journeys* to the circulating collection.

Women's Information Directory: A Guide to Organizations, Agencies, Institutions, Programs, Publications, Services, and Other Resources concerned with Women in the United States. Ed. by Shawn Brennan. Gale, 1993. 700p. index. hardcover $75 (0-8103-8422-1; ISSN 1063-0554).
362.83 Women's institutes || Women's studies || Abused women || Women—Services for—U.S.—Directories [OCLC]

The objective of this directory is to serve as a one-stop source of information about and for women, listing organizations and agencies, programs, library collections, museums, higher education, awards, women-owned businesses and consulting organizations, publications, videos, and electronic resources. The volume is organized in the standard format for Gale directories: topical sections listing the various types of resources. A group of consultants reviewed the book's scope and contents.

More than 10,000 entries are included. Each lists address, telephone number, chief officer, and description. Some include historical, publishing, services, and membership information. One reason for the large number of entries is the inclusion of many local programs, such as agencies offering services to battered women and women's studies programs in individual institutions.

Entries were compiled from other Gale sources, directories, governmental publications, and organizational sources. Some sections may indicate a bias; for instance, the list of booksellers was provided largely by *Feminist Bookstore News* in San Francisco. In the section listing publishers, some have issued only one title and, sometimes, not within the last two years.

A name and subject index is extensive and provides access to entries by such topics as *abortion, pay equity, lesbians,* and *breast cancer.* However, perhaps because the index looks computer generated, coverage is uneven. Particularly for organizations with national headquarters and local chapters, entries are misleading. For one thing, the chapter listings take a disproportionate amount of space, both in the main section as well as the index (e.g., local YWCAs and La Leche). Second, some chapters are omitted, such as the activist San Francisco Bay Girl Scout Council, without apparent reason. Third, some of these associated groups are separated because of inconsistencies in the form of name used in the listings (again, Girl Scouts Gateway Council is relatively far from the entry Girl Scouts of the United States of America, Stamford Council). More careful manual editing could have cleared up these details.

With its wide range of sources, this volume should be useful in many types of libraries. It is a convenient compilation, especially for readers with information needs about displaced-homemaker programs, agencies working on family-violence problems, and other topics where directories are sometimes hard to locate. Librarians will still have to wait, though, for the definitive women's information directory.

Health Care State Rankings, 1993: Health Care in the 50 United States. Ed. by Kathleen O'Leary Morgan and others. Morgan Quitno Corp., P.O. Box 1656, Lawrence, KS 66044, 1993. annual. 456p. index. tables. paper $43.95 (0-9625531-4-X; ISSN 1065-1403).
363 Health status indicators—U.S.—States—Statistics || Medical care—U.S.—States—Statistics [BKL] 92-374

This reference annual is the lead volume in a new series designed to provide statistical information on a state-by-state basis. It presents a wide variety of American health-care data in a no-frills, straightforward manner.

The health-care field is divided into seven major categories— "Births and Reproductive Health," "Deaths," "Facilities," "Finance," "Incidence of Disease," "Personnel," and "Physical Fitness." More than 450 charts and tables rank states on specific items pertaining to each of these categories. "Births and Reproductive Health" concerns itself with everything from specific types of births (low birth weight, live births, vaginal and caesarian deliveries) and legal abortions to specific and marital-status age groups (teenage mothers, unmarried women, women ages 35–49). "Deaths" covers similar items—infant mortality, neonatal deaths, deaths by specific diseases (AIDS, various cancers, cerebrovascular, pulmonary, etc.), as well as suicides and complications during pregnancy and childbirth. Racial comparisons are made in all categories throughout these two major sections.

"Facilities" comprises the smallest section in the guide. Hospital types include federal, psychiatric, and general nongovernment not-for-profits and their counterparts, the for-profits. Beds, admissions, average stays as well as certified nursing care, nursing home populations, and pharmacy data are covered. Conversely, "Finance" is the largest section. A huge variety of data on insurance coverage, HMOs, health-care payments, and expenditures for hospitals, health programs, and disabled benefits are provided. One of the more interesting and unusual sections is "Incidence of Disease." In this category, estimated new cases of various cancers are predicted. Data are found on reported cases of AIDS, meningitis, chicken pox, encephalitis, venereal disease, and more. "Personnel" provides data on physicians (age, specialties) and nurses, medical school graduates, and pharmacists. The last section, "Physical Fitness," includes data on alcohol, wine, and beer consumption; smokers; overweight adults; sedentary and active life-styles; and seat belt use.

Sources and dates are cited on all tables. Although at first glance many of the statistics seem dated (1989, 1990), they were, in fact, the most current statistics available at publication time. While most of this information can be found elsewhere, in government reports such as *Health, United States* and *Statistical Abstract of the* U.S. and almanacs, the convenience of having everything in one easy-to-use volume far outweighs the alternative—searching through numerous sources. Individual state reports can be purchased separately.

The Indoor Air Quality Directory: Commerical Residential, Industrial. IAQ Publications, 4520 East-West Hwy., Ste. 610, Bethesda, MD 20814, 1992. 375p. indexes. paper $75 (0-933003-1-8; ISSN 1062-0621).
338.7613637392 Air pollution control industry—U.S.—Directories || Indoor air pollution || Air quality management—Bibliography—Peridocials [BKL] 92-4508

The quality of indoor air has increasingly become a major concern in offices and homes. Buildings are better sealed; outside ventilation is sometimes impossible; synthetic materials emit gases; and chemical cleaners, pesticides, and personal-care products contaminate the air. As a result, there are more firms devoted to improving indoor air quality.

The indoor air pollutants stressed in this unique directory are asbestos, combustible products, electromagnetic fields, environmental tobacco smoke, lead, microbials, radon, and volatile organic compounds. There are basically three ways to eliminate these pollutants—removal, ventilation, or air cleaning. The first three sections list firms and organizations that specialize in the elimination of these pollutants. The first section lists service firms alphabetically by name, giving all pertinent directory information, followed by an index by state. The second section lists product manufacturers and distributors with an index by product; the third lists support services with an index by service. The remainder of the book lists supporting materials: workshops and courses that stress indoor air quality; federal government agencies, state agencies, professional associations, and publications; and a glossary. Indexes include advertisers, personal names, and companies.

This highly specialized directory is arranged in an easy-to-use format. The indexing is good, and the information is as accurate and up-to-date as the returned questionnaires could provide. Advertising throughout the book does not distract significantly from the directory information.

Business and technical libraries involved in air-quality research will need this directory. Research and public libraries will find it a useful source of information on air quality for reference collections.

Education for the Earth: A Guide to Top Environmental Studies Programs. Peterson's Guides, 1993. 175p. bibliog. indexes. paper $10.95 (1-56079-164-0).
363.7071 Environmental sciences—Study and teaching (Higher)—U.S. ǁ Environmental sciences—Vocational guidance [CIP] 92-33025

This specialized Peterson's guide lists more than 100 colleges and universities that offer programs in environmental studies. The book was published in cooperation with the Alliance for Environmental Education, an association of more than 240 business, labor, health, educational, and environmental organizations. Representatives from the alliance formed an advisory board that prepared minimum selection criteria for the programs to be included in the book. More than 400 programs were evaluated in order to choose the ones profiled here.

"Career Watch 2000" consists of five essays discussing environmental careers in business, government, nonprofit organizations, and educational institutions. "Program Profiles" comprises the bulk of the book. Five different sections—"Environmental Engineering and Design," "Environmental Health," "Environmental Science," "Environmental Studies," and "Natural Resources Management"—give one-page descriptions of each institution. The entries follow the same basic format of the larger Peterson's guides, containing specific facts about the school and the program, including areas of major concentration. The profiles include a brief summary of the most likely employment results for the graduating students, and some entries name employers that have recently recruited on campus. The guide provides a glossary, bibliography, geographic index, and an index to the listed colleges and universities. It does not contain information on special scholarships or sources of funding.

For the price ($10.95), this small guide is a convenient ready-reference source that will supplement the larger *Peterson's Guide to Four Year Colleges*. The more comprehensive source does list all these colleges and universities but does not contain descriptive summaries of these specific programs.

The Green Encyclopedia. By Irene Franck and David Brownstone. Prentice Hall, 1992. 512p. bibliog. illus. hardcover $35 (0-13-365685-3); paper $20 (0-13-365677-2).
363.7003 Environmental protection—Encyclopedias ǁ Nature conservation—Encyclopedias ǁ Environmental law—Encyclopedias ǁ Environmental protection—Directories ǁ Nature conservation—Directories [CIP] 92-12240

Described as a "comprehensive guide to the issues, dangers, endangered species and endangered places, environmental disasters, people, philosophies, works, laws and treaties that most concern environmentally minded people," this is a source for all ages, from the middle school child to his grandparent, and for the activist to the ordinary citizen. Franck and Brownstone are prolific compilers of popular reference works, including *The Parent's Desk Reference* [RBB Ag 91].

Among the more than 1,000 entries are brief biographies of famous environmentalists, specific animals, organizations and government agencies, specific pesticides, and parks and wildlife preserves. Coverage is international, including the 1984 Bhopal disaster and the Bikini evacuation in 1946. Each entry is succinctly written, with internal cross-references in small capital letters. For example, the 350-word entry *Ecosystem* lists 15 cross-references, including *Food Chain, Nitrogen Cycle, Ecological Succession,* and *Realms and Ecosystem Diversity*. The most useful features of this book are the lists of concerned organizations and governmental agencies following many entries. For example, the entry *Glen Canyon Dam* provides a telephone number for Earth First! and notes its circulating movie on the dam. In addition, the Friends of the River and the National Parks and Conservation Association are listed with their telephone numbers. Separately boxed "Information and Action Guides" with extensive lists of organizations follow major issues. In addition to providing telephone numbers, these list publications from the organizations.

A "Special Information Section" in the last quarter of the book gives more sources of detailed information on animal rights and ecotourism. There are also lists of endangered and threatened animals and plants, toxic chemicals, Biosphere Reserves and World Natural Heritage Sites, superfund sites, and key U.S. laws on the environment. "The Green Bookshelf," another appendix, is an excellent source for collection development, and the "Environmental Alphabet" assists in chasing down the various acronyms and abbreviations associated with these topics.

The Encyclopedia of Environmental Studies [RBB Ja 15 92] is similar in terms of the topics covered but is not as oriented to action as is *The Green Encyclopedia* with its lists of contacts. A good inexpensive source for the public or school library, *The Green Encyclopedia* answers the question "Where can I find someone who is concerned about . . .?"

The McGraw-Hill Recycling Handbook. Ed. by Herbert F. Lund. McGraw-Hill, 1993. illus. index. hardcover $84.50 (0-07-039096-7).
363.72'82 Recycling (Waste, etc.) ǁ Recycling (Waste, etc.)—U.S. [CIP] 92-18267

This comprehensive, user-friendly handbook is a valuable addition to the growing literature on the important environmental topic of recycling. Practical in its format and content, the handbook provides up-to-date information for individuals responsible for developing recycling programs and operations. The handbook is divided into 35 chapters, each written by an expert in the recycling field. For example, "Separation and Collection Systems Performance Monitoring" was written by Abbie Page McMillen, president of McMillen Environmental, Inc., while "Batteries" is a collaborative effort of Ann Patchak Adams, project leader at Roy F. Weston, Inc., and C. Kenna Amos, former technical director at Weston. Editor Lund is a recycling consultant and a former recycling manager for the city of Hollywood, Florida.

The first chapter, "Recycling Overview and Growth," puts recycling in context, provides definitions, and explains the importance and varieties of recycling options. Twelve of the chapters examine the many recyclable materials—from batteries, tires, and construction and demolition debris to yard waste, household hazardous waste, and scrap metal and steel cans. Other chapters deal in depth with many aspects of recycling, including processing equipment, training personnel and managers, and quality control monitoring for recyclable materials. The last chapter provides case histories for a variety of locations, ranging from a small rural county to a medium-size suburban community to a large urban community. Each chapter contains features reflecting the background of the contributing editor. Some contain summaries or references; others, appendixes or glossaries.

The book also contains three useful appendixes: a glossary of recycling terms; a list of abbreviations; and "Recycling Information and Sources," which provides listings for relevant federal and state agencies, periodicals, and sources for solid-waste information. Numerous easy-to-understand illustrations depict the technology used for recycling management, including processing equipment, drop-off stations, and material-recovery facilities.

There is not much difference in the scope of this handbook and two other recent titles, *Recycling in America* (ABC-Clio, 1992) and *Recycling Sourcebook* (Gale, 1992) [both RBB Fe 1 93]. However, *The McGraw-Hill Recycling Handbook* is directed toward those responsible for planning and implementing recycling operations and has more detailed practical instructions. It is strongly recommended for purchase by any library building a collection on recycling. If a library can afford it, it should buy all three titles and have the most complete reference information on recycling. If it can buy only one, then it should select this new volume.

Recycling in America: A Reference Handbook. By Debi Kimball. ABC-Clio, 1992. 240p. bibliog. index. hardcover $39.50 (0-87436-663-1).
363.72'82 Recycling (Waste, etc.)—U.S. ‖ Recycling (Waste,etc.)—Law and legislation—U.S. ‖ Recycling (Waste, etc.)—Bibliography [CIP] 92-29984

Recycling Sourcebook: A Guide to Recyclable Materials, Case Studies, Organizations, Agencies, and Publications. Ed. by Thomas J. Cichonski and Karen Hill. Gale, 1992. 600p. bibliog. index. hardcover $75 (0-8103-8855-3; ISSN 1064-4938).
363.72'82 Recycling (Waste, etc.)—U.S.—Sources—Directories ‖ Recycling industry—U.S.—Sources—Directories ‖ Refuse and refuse disposal—U.S.—Directories [BKL]

With recycling now an established part of the American environmental landscape, *Recycling in America* and *Recycling Sourcebook* are two new sources that provide librarians and patrons with access to state-of-the-art information on almost anything one wants or needs to know about this hot trend but doesn't know where to look.

Recycling in America is divided into seven chapters, beginning with "Recycling: a State of Flux," which includes short summaries of such topics as curbside recycling, new technologies, and changes in the industry. Included next are a chronology of significant dates and biographies of important people in recycling history. "Facts and Data" discusses various commodities (e.g., glass, plastic, paper, and aluminum), explaining how the products are made, collected, and recycled. The discussion of legal requirements, arranged alphabetically by state, includes the author's narrative description of major features of applicable laws, followed by complete citations to the statutes and regulations. This chapter also includes several useful tables and figures on such topics as tax incentives for recycling and recycling grants and loans. The entries in "Directory of State, Federal, and Private Recycling Organizations" include the organization's contact information and a brief description of the organization's programs. The final chapter, "Reference Materials," includes annotated entries for books, brochures, journals, curriculum guides, articles, videos, and databases. The volume concludes with a useful glossary of recycling terms, a list of acronyms, and an index.

Unlike *Recycling in America* (the work of a single author), *Recycling Sourcebook* is the result of the collaboration of editors who compiled this volume by culling information from other Gale publications, soliciting written materials from several experts on recycling, and conducting additional research. Part 1 of the sourcebook consists of 28 essays, some reprinted from other sources, on current trends and practices. These articles provide information on 13 types of recyclable materials and case studies of recycling programs in urban and rural communities, workplaces, homes, and other institutions. Part 2 provides information on approximately 3,000 recycling organizations, agencies, and publications. This part is subdivided into 16 sections, with categories for different types of organizations and agencies, media, databases, businesses, and funding sources. Part 3 includes a glossary and an appendix listing more than 350 products evaluated by Scientific Certification Systems (formerly Green Cross) as either reusable or made from recycled materials. The volume concludes with an index listing subject terms and names of all the organizations, publications, and other entities that appeared in both the essay and directory sections of the book.

Understandably, both volumes under review cover some of the same subject matter, but there are differences in each book's scope and content. *Recycling Sourcebook* is clearly the larger and more comprehensive work in format, length, and number of entries; *Recycling in America*, however, provides some information that the larger volume does not. For example, by looking up the references under *motor oil* in the index to *Recycling Sourcebook*, the user can locate directory information for one research center and one regional collection facility; citations to five books, two directories, and one periodical; brief references to used oil in two essays; and one essay specifically on the topic "Motor Oil Recycling," with a list of sources for suggested reading. The index to *Recycling in America* uses the term *oil disposal*, and, by checking these references, the user is provided with some very brief facts about the environmental problem caused by motor oil; learns of a 1976 patent for a method of reclaiming used oil; is given one bibliographic citation to a free brochure; and is directed to the laws of 18 states that address motor oil.

A wide variety of users—students, environmental activists, consumers, business executives, and workplace task forces—will find both of these guides useful. *Recycling Sourcebook* is the more comprehensive of the two works and is recommended for purchase consideration by all high school, public, and academic libraries. *Recycling in America* supplements the sourcebook by providing citations to state recycling laws and is recommended for libraries needing additional materials on the subject.

Register of North American Insurance Companies, 1993.
American Preeminent Registry, 510 Old Bridge Turnpike, South River, NJ 08882, 1992. paper $125 (0-9633783-1-7; ISSN 1066-6486).
368'.0065 Insurance companies—U.S.—Registers ‖ Insurance companies—Canada—Registers [BKL]

This new reference tool offers basic information about U.S. and Canadian insurance companies and about workers' compensation regulations in the U.S. and in Canada. Section 1 lists nearly 5,000 companies alphabetically and provides, for each entry, the company's address, telephone number, and lines of insurance offered. Fax numbers and toll-free telephone numbers are included where applicable. The directory information was compiled by the publisher's in-house research department. Companies are not evaluated or ranked.

Section 2 offers state-by-state highlights of workers' compensation laws, including statute or code citations in most instances and the appropriate address to write for complete information. The summaries of these laws were prepared by Joan E. Smith, a practicing attorney in the San Francisco area. These highlights are written in nonlegal language so that the information is readily understandable to nonspecialists. However, lack of adequate editing is apparent in this section, which contains errors in punctuation and grammar.

The entry for each state in section 2 lists its time zone, area code, and first three digits of its zip codes. Also included is a brief directory of relevant state officials (governor, U.S. senators, and key personnel in the Department of Insurance). Canadian workers' compensation highlights are presented but without the agency addresses and key personnel.

Libraries that subscribe to insurance-rating services that include directories (e.g., those from the A. M. Best Company) and to publications including workers' compensation information (e.g., Martindale-Hubbel's *Digest of State Laws*) probably do not need to add this volume to their collections. This directory, however, provides the convenience of listing all the Blue Cross/Blue Shield entries in one spot, and areas that serve a Canadian population will find this premier edition useful.

EDUCATION, COMMUNICATION, CUSTOMS

Multicultural Projects Index: Things to Make and Do to Celebrate Festivals, Cultures, and Holidays around the World. By Mary Anne Pilger. Libraries Unlimited, 1992. 200p. bibliog. hardcover $35 (0-87287-867-8).
016.370'19'6 Intercultural education—Activity programs—Indexes ‖ Festivals—Indexes ‖ Handicraft—Indexes ‖ Games—Indexes [CIP] 92-13731

From *Achilles costume* to *Zuni mask*, this index presents over 15,000 projects relating to multicultural handicrafts, foods, games, and activities. The aim is to enable educators to assist children of all ages in creating projects reflecting the varying cultures of our world. Subject headings are followed by a description of the project, then a number in brackets that correlates to the list of books indexed at the back of the book, and, finally, page numbers where the project will be found in that book. For example, under *Navajo Indians—musical instruments*, we find that there is an article on making a drum rattle on pages 54–5 of book #468. The subject headings are quite encompassing, covering all imaginable holidays, countries, and ethnic groups around the world. The list of books indexed contains 1,161 sources, as recent as 1990 and as far back as 1950. The availability of sources that old is questionable. Nevertheless, the majority of the books do have more recent publication dates. Not all the books listed in the back of this volume are indexed here, as there are two "cousin" publications by the same author (*Crafts Index for Young People* [$42.50, 1-56308-002-8] and *Holidays and Special Days Project Index for Young People* [$29.50, 0-87287-998-4]) that use the same resource list.

With the emphasis on the study and awareness of multiculturalism in schools today, this index is a valuable tool from which educators can choose projects to be incorporated into the curriculum. *Multicultural Projects Index* will be a useful resource for elementary and middle school libraries and for public libraries' children's collections where students need a resource from which to choose a school project. In whichever facility this index is housed, it is suggested that those books that are available in the library be highlighted for easy access.

How to Pick a Perfect Private School. By Harlow G. Unger. Facts On File, 1993. 218p. index. hardcover $21.95 (0-8160-2753-6).
371'.02 Private schools—U.S. || School, Choice of—U.S. [OCLC] 92-24176

This book purports to be a vital resource for parents in the process of choosing a private school, grades K–12, for their child. The examples in the text are mostly schools in the northeastern U.S.; however, an appendix lists more than 900 member schools of the National Association of Independent Schools.

This work begins with a detailed discussion of public versus private school education followed by several chapters discussing a variety of criteria to be used in the decision-making process. The chapter "Defining Your Children's Needs" provides a cursory discussion of a topic that plays an important role in this decision-making process. An assumption is made in this chapter that every parent knows the normal levels of development for children. Bibliographic references to books on child development by Piaget and others would be worthwhile for parents at this point.

The chapter describing different types of schools (nondenominational day schools, Roman Catholic schools, boarding schools, military schools, coed versus single-sex schools) is somewhat confusing. The format for the discussion of each type of school varies greatly. There are eight standards discussed in a separate chapter on evaluating schools, which include accreditation, educational philosophy/goals, educational results, faculty quality, academic strength, physical plant, and school personality.

The final steps in the selection process include a chapter on evaluating the schools on paper, which utilizes the eight basic standards discussed earlier, and the final phase—a visit to the school. The author at this point recommends that the reader use *Peterson's Guide to Independent Secondary Schools* as a guide to this process. However, that work covers only secondary schools. *The Handbook of Private Schools*, a Sargent Handbook title, covering grades K–12, would seem to be more complementary to this book than Peterson.

Appendix A provides an evaluation form to be used during the decision-making process. Appendix B provides the list of more than 900 schools, subdivided into five listings, by state and city, foreign members, five-day boarding schools, junior boarding schools, and military boarding schools. The final appendix provides a list of financial-aid resources.

This text might be a helpful resource for a public library reference section when used in conjunction with a handbook containing detailed descriptions of the private schools. However, many libraries will want to put it in the circulating collection.

Wilderness U: Opportunities for Outdoor Education in the U.S. & Abroad. By Bill McMillon. Chicago Review Press, 1992. 281p. bibliog. illus. indexes. paper $12.95 (1-55652-158-8).
371.3'8 Outdoor education || Nature study || Environmental education || Wilderness survival—Study and teaching || Vacations [CIP] 92-19616.

Learning and adventure travel vacations are now booming; this volume will help people select the appropriate program for their needs. *Wilderness U* is a unique compilation of opportunities for enjoying and learning about nature and the outdoors in nontraditional ways while (in many cases) earning college credits for the experience. Programs listed run the gamut from free one-day workshops to year-long programs costing thousands of dollars. They are sponsored by universities, museums and nature centers, clubs and organizations, and tour agencies and lodges. While most are based in the U.S., some are Canadian and others worldwide in scope. Listings include such well-known organizations as Elderhostel, the Cornell Laboratory of Ornithology, various Audubon groups, and the National Outdoor Leadership School but also range to Sail North in Canada, the Slapton Ley Field Centre in England, and Explorama Tours in Peru. Most programs are for adults, but some will accept children, and a few are specifically designed for family participation.

Entries in the directory section are arranged by type of sponsor (e.g., college and university programs). All provide address, telephone number, and a description, which may be as short as three lines or up to 1½ pages, occasionally with a black-and-white photograph. Cost is usually mentioned (e.g., "workshops last between 2 and 8 days and cost between $200 and $800"). A few miscellaneous organizations (for nature photography, rock climbing, etc.) are not given descriptions. A second section, "Vignettes," provides 11 articles by program participants describing their personal experiences. Programs are indexed by subject (e.g., *Geology, Rain Forests, Birds*) and region (*Asia, Mexico, Rocky Mountains*). Three organizations are indexed as *Women Only*; a note says that other organizations offer some of their programs exclusively for women. There is no index of all the organizations in one alphabet. A brief appendix lists books and periodicals for further reading and information. The author has written several other books, including *Volunteer Vacations*.

Wilderness U is a helpful and fascinating guide to unusual opportunities for learning about the natural world first-hand. Whether patrons are looking for college credit or not, this book will appeal to a large audience in academic and public libraries.

Encyclopedia of Early Childhood Education. Ed. by Leslie R. Williams and Doris Pronin Fromberg. Garland, 1992. 518p. bibliog. charts. index. hardcover $95 (0-8240-4626-9).
372.21'03 Early childhood education—U.S.—Encyclopedias [OCLC] 92-4579

This comprehensive work contains approximately 200 articles concerning all aspects of early childhood education (from birth through age 8) written by eminent specialists in the field. It is intended not only for researchers but for students, parents of young children, and administrators. It encompasses the study of early childhood with all its diverse movements and influences. Until now, these issues were scattered through many classics such as Evelyn Weber's *The Kindergarten: Its Encounter with Educational Thought in America* (1969), *Handbook of Research in Early Childhood* (1982), edited by Bernard Spodek, and the ongoing series edited by Lillian Katz, *Current Topics in Early Childhood Education*.

The book is not alphabetically arranged like a traditional encyclopedia. It is divided into six chapters: the historical and philosophical background of early childhood education; sociocultural, political, and economic influences; perspectives on children; varied curricula programs; and perspectives on educators. Each chapter begins with an outline of topics to be addressed and an introductory essay that summarizes current and past thought. The signed entries are arranged thematically. The volume opens with a list of 23 specialists comprising the editorial board and a list of contributors with their affiliations. A combined name and subject index follows the text, and cross-references are provided as needed. A few articles, such as "The Froebelian Kindergarten," are reprinted from *The International Encyclopedia of Education*.

Entries are scholarly but readable. Statistics and charts accompany some entries; for instance, a chart shows teacher certification requirements for early childhood education in the 50 states. The references given at the end of each entry range from older to very recent books, journal articles, and reports. They provide research results on practices like all-day kindergarten, home-based day care, and holding children (especially boys) back a year to begin kindergarten at age six. Up-to-date topics are included, for example, the article *AIDS and Children* and references to whole language. Many entries were written by scholars who have produced enduring works, such as Beatrice Cullinan, Dorothy Strickland, and Bernard Spodek.

Several small flaws mar this otherwise excellent and unique resource, largely centering around lack of accessability. For example, there are no instructions for use that alert the user to the organization of topics within a chapter according to the outline preceding it. In the index, substantial treatment of a topic is not distinguished from simple mention of it; this could have been rectified by boldface numerals or some other device. There are 30 page references under *Head Start*, for instance. While the contributors are given with their affiliations, there is no corresponding list of entries written by each of these specialists. Some authors of entries are not listed either as contributors or editors. See, for example, the entry *Child Abuse* written by L. R. Mitchell.

Problems of access aside, this is a comprehensive and valuable contribution to the field of early childhood education. It should find a place in all libraries that support the study and practice of education. Public libraries ought to consider making it available to daycare providers. This book provides astute selection of topics with accurate and clearly written entries by recognized authorities on an issue of great interest.

The American Curriculum: A Documentary History. Ed. by George Willis and others. Greenwood, 1993. 425p. bibliog. index. tables. hardcover $65 (0-313-26730-8).

375'.00973 Education—U.S.—Curricula—History [CIP] 92-29468

The field of curriculum studies is devoted to examining how decisions are made about what schools teach. Only recently has this academic discipline begun to study the history of what has been taught in American schools and the reasons for the selection of the curriculum. Many of the documents and reports essential for this study are not readily available outside of archives and large research libraries. This new volume increases access to the historical record of the development of the U.S. curriculum by printing a sampling of primary source materials.

Thirty-six documents are reprinted here, mostly in excerpted form, ranging from the seventeenth through the twentieth centuries. The emphasis is on the more recent era, however, and 26 of the sources are dated later than 1900. Articles are arranged in chronological order, beginning with "The Rules and Course of Study of Harvard College, 1642" and concluding with "A Nation at Risk: The Imperative for Educational Reform, 1983." The entry for each excerpted document begins with a one- to two-page introduction by the compilers that gives the historical context for the reading, cites the original source in full, and briefly discusses its significance and its relation to other documents in the volume. The scope of the work is broad, encompassing sources that address elementary through higher education. A diversity of materials is included, such as reports of national studies, explanations of curriculum principles, and documents outlining specific courses of study.

The educators who compiled this work selected documents for inclusion because they influenced subsequent curriculum history, are representative of prevailing practices or ideas at the time, or exemplify important but unusual practices. For instance, "Cardinal Principles of Secondary Education, 1918," from a report commissioned by the National Education Association, is cited as an influential document; it contributed to the expansion of school curricula from covering only academic subjects to encompassing such other life areas as citizenship, health, and vocational preparation. Benjamin Franklin's advocacy of practical studies in his "Proposals Relating to the Education of Youth in Pennsylvania, 1749" was not influential at the time, yet it exemplified the utilitarian justification for curriculum decisions that would become popular in a later time period. A five-page selected bibliography concludes the body of the book, which is well indexed.

Academic libraries supporting teacher education and school-district libraries should seriously consider purchasing *The American Curriculum*. While one could argue endlessly about what really belongs in a collection of primary documents, the variety and importance of the selections in this volume make it a useful and convenient, although not inexpensive, source.

Student Contact Book: How to Find Low-Cost, Expert Information on Today's Issues for: Term Papers, Debates, Research Projects and More! Ed. by Annette Novallo and others. Gale, 1993. 525p. index. paper $29.95 (0-8103-8876-6; ISSN 1066-2413).

378 Research—Handbooks, manuals, etc. ‖ Associations, institutions, etc.—Directories ‖ Report writing—Sources ‖ Information services—Directories ‖ Debates and debating—Sources [BKL]

The editors of this work pulled information from other Gale publications (*Encyclopedia of Associations, Research Centers Directory,* etc.) to produce a directory of more than 800 organizations that provide free or inexpensive (under $25) information. All of the listed government agencies, information clearinghouses, research centers, and nonprofit organizations responded to a prepublication survey, so students' information requests should be honored. The book was developed with the assistance of an advisory board in order to match the content to the curricula and popular interests of students from junior high through the junior college level.

Approximately 150 topics are grouped in 10 broad subject chapters, such as "Careers and Work," "Arts and Entertainment," and "Science and Environment." Each chapter opens with a list of the specific subjects covered, references to related topics found elsewhere in the book, and suggestions for research projects. For instance, "Government and Public Affairs" covers 25 topics ranging from *Censorship* and *Elections* to *Gun Control* and *Rape*. Sample research questions are provided for the listed subjects, for example, "Prison reform—are more cells the answer?"

The chapters are divided into two major sections: the first provides information about organizations, and the second lists directories of people. Each of the 800 organizational entries consists of a brief description and area(s) of expertise, free informational items, information available for a fee (and the price), and complete addresses and telephone and fax numbers. The lists of pertinent biographical directories are intended so that students can identify experts in various fields. More than 200 current sources (who's whos, membership lists, etc.) are those readily available in most reference collections and were selected from Gale's *Directories in Print*. Each entry includes title, publisher, frequency, and a brief annotation of content.

A special section, "How to Contact Organizations and People," provides information-gathering tips, sample contact letters, and a script for a telephone interview. The book's complete index will be helpful to students who have identified research topics. The broad subject-chapter format also lends itself to browsing, although "Beliefs, Cults, and Sects" lumps together such diverse organizations as the Federation of Islamic Associations and the Greek Orthodox Archdiocese with Haunt Hunters and the MENSA Pagan/Occult/Witchcraft Special Interest Group.

Many libraries will already own the basic sources that provide the directory information available in this title. While not an essential purchase, *Student Contact Book* will be useful for beginning researchers in identifying topics and tracking down additional low-cost resources.

Which MBA? A Critical Guide to the World's Best Programmes. 4th ed. By George Bickerstaffe. Economist Intelligence Unit, 215 Park Ave. South, New York, NY 10003, 1992. 441p. index. tables. paper $85 (0-85058-648-8).

378.1'553 Master of business administration degree—Directories ‖ Business education—Directories [BKL]

The Economist Intelligence Unit, a well-known research agency, consulting firm, and publisher in the U.K., has produced another useful reference book with this new edition of *Which MBA?* The MBA degree is one of the most popular and sought-after business qualifications. Some 800 business schools in the U.S. and Europe produce approximately 100,000 MBA graduates each year, while the rest of the world contributes approximately 5,000. Thus, there is much interest in business degrees and a growing trend of international education. Included in this work are 102 schools, with selection based upon international reputation, nationality mix of faculty and students, and quality of programs. Represented are 48 European, 44 North American, and 10 schools from other regions.

The first 66 pages consist of eight chapters that detail the history of the MBA degree, the various types of programs, how to select and get into a school, and how to find a job after graduation. These short chapters would be useful tools for anyone considering attending a business school. The bulk of the text consists of a directory, divided into three sections that cover business schools in Europe, North America, and the rest of the world, respectively. Opening the directory section is a "Key Comparative Data" table, allowing users to determine, for each school, the average number of years of work experience and average GMAT scores of entering students; numbers of company recruiting visits and average starting salaries of graduates; and percentages of faculty and students not from the home country. Each section on a region of the world begins with a list of schools featured and additional tables that summarize entry requirements, class characteristics, and fees and costs. This last is given in the currencies of the various countries (e.g., dollars, pounds, lira, francs, etc.).

Within each section, entries are alphabetical by school name (e.g., *Sheffield, Stirling, Strathclyde*) and are two to three pages in length. A typical entry presents address, location, telephone number, type of school, and descriptions of the facilities and activities. Also included is information on admission requirements, procedures, and fees; the numbers of persons enrolled, including ratio of men to women, age range, and proportion of foreign students; and the course of study, describing the program, teaching methods, and duration. Approximately 500 alumni from many of these schools returned evaluation surveys to the publisher, and selected remarks are included within the entries as well. Some of these comments are critical, such as "Help in finding a job after qualification could be improved."

Although the amount of information provided in the directory entries is fairly uniform, some slight inconsistencies result from the variances in reports obtained from the schools. For example, for "nationality of class," some schools list the proportion of "international" or "overseas" students, while others give percentages of various nationalities. Also, there are a few references to European terms that would be unfamiliar to people from other regions, such as the IELTS test required for admission to several British schools.

A number of references are available that provide coverage of business schools, but generally the focus is on the U.S. Some titles, such as *Barron's Guide to Graduate Business Schools* (8th ed., Barron's, 1992), include entries for a few dozen programs in Canada and a comparable number for other areas of the world. *Which MBA?*—while substantially more expensive—is an appropriate purchase for public and academic libraries that need additional international listings of business schools and for libraries that maintain a comprehensive collection of directories describing selected U.S. business schools.

Fund Your Way through College: Uncovering 1,100 Great Opportunities in Undergraduate Financial Aid. By Debra M. Kirby and Christa Brelin. Visible Ink Press/Gale, 1992. 454p. index. paper $19.95 (0-8103-9422-7).
378.30973 Student aid—U.S. ‖ Scholarships—U.S. ‖ Student loans funds—U.S. [OCLC]

In this work, students will uncover funding opportunities available to U.S. and Canadian students for study throughout the world. Included are scholarships and grants that do not require repayment; loans that require repayment either monetarily or through service; internships and work-study programs that provide training, work experience, and monetary compensation; and awards and prizes recognizing excellence in a particular field. *Fund Your Way* also includes a broad representation of government-backed awards at the national and state levels, along with a representative sampling of narrowly focused awards.

The funding opportunities are arranged alphabetically by the name of the sponsoring organization and are indexed by name of scholarship, grant, or loan and sponsoring organization. A type of subject access is provided by the "Vocational Pathfinder," which arranges the awards under broad fields of study and notes the award type and limitations by residence or special affiliation (e.g., employer, military, minority). However, the lack of true subject indexing means the student looking for scholarships awarded to caddies or Lutherans or residents of Marin County will have to skim through the entire book. The entries for the awards include eligibility requirements, funds available, deadlines, and other details. Sidebars are sprinkled throughout the book with helpful rankings ("Most Affordable Colleges for Out-of-State Students," "Colleges with Most Winners of Harry S Truman Scholarships"); sources are provided for this data.

This guide does not list awards given by specific colleges. It is complemented by the College Board's *College Cost Book*, which is a guide to current costs and financial aid at 3,200 schools. *Fund Your Way* does not supersede any of the other financial aid guides, but libraries needing another inexpensive scholarship source will want to consider purchase.

The Complete Guide to College Visits. By Janet Spencer and Sandra Maleson. Citadel, 1993. 610p. index. paper $19.95 (0-8065-1320-9).
378.73 College, Choice of—U.S. ‖ Universities and colleges—U.S.—Guidebooks ‖ Universities and colleges—U.S.—Maps [CIP] 92-39839

Complete is a misnomer for this guide; it covers only 251 colleges out of the thousands in the U.S. Only 41 states have entries (omitted are Alaska, Arkansas, Hawaii, Montana, Nevada, North Dakota, Oklahoma, South Dakota, and Wyoming). The guide stresses private colleges and is skewed toward the East Coast (New York has 29 institutions listed, Massachusetts 25, Pennsylvania 16). Only California, with 25 schools listed, has as many as the east. The Naval Academy in Maryland and the Military Academy in New York are listed, but not the Air Force Academy in Colorado.

The introduction explains that this guide is for parents and students planning college visits. It assumes that the user has already investigated things like curriculum, acceptance criteria, and price. Arranged by state, sections begin with a map showing the colleges mentioned and a mileage matrix of the distances between colleges and major cities. The entry for a college begins with a calendar of the typical school year. The address and telephone number of the admissions office is given, followed by information about tours, interviews, class visits, overnight dorm accomodations, and directions on getting to the campus by car, bus, plane, etc. The entry ends with information about off-campus accomodations and tourist attractions. The reader is sometimes referred to information in another college's entry if the two are in close proximity. A final section has regional maps and mileage matrixes to facilitate planning trips to several states in an area. There is also an index of colleges. There is no mention of selection criteria for the schools included in this guide or of the methods for collecting and verifying information.

The four-volume *How to Get to the College of Your Choice: By Road, Plane or Train* [RBB O 1 92] provides similar information on many more colleges. For example, volume 1 covers 179 colleges in the Northeast. However, it is also almost four times as expensive as *The Complete Guide to College Visits*. Depending on the kind of colleges students in the community attend, this new book may be a useful addition to a public library and possibly a high school guidance center or library.

The Official Guide to U.S. Stamps: 1993 Edition. Triumph Books, 1992. 344p. illus. tables. hardcover $34.95 (1-880141-42-6).
382.2 Postage stamps—U.S.—Catalogs [BKL]

Previously titled *The Postal Service Guide to U.S. Stamps*, this work is a comprehensive reference on U.S. stamps. As an introduction to stamp collecting, it includes definitions of terms, notes significant stamp details, and lists organizations, publications, and resources.

Chronologically listed and in full color, stamps issued from 1847 through 1991 comprise the bulk of the book. The largest section covers commemorative, definitive, and special stamps. Other types of stamps are listed in separate sections: airmail and special delivery; registration, certified mail, and postage due; official and penalty mail; parcel post and special handling stamps; stamped envelopes and postal cards; souvenir pages; and American commemorative panels. Each entry includes a color illustration; *Scott's Catalog* number; denomination; description; first day of issue; prices for single unused and used stamps; number of stamps in a plate block, line pair, or plate-number coil and their current values; first-day cover price; and quantity issued.

Scott's Standard Postage Catalogue offers illustrations of the stamps in black and white and does not note first day of issue or quantity of stamps issued. Geared for the more advanced stamp collector, it does list perforation size, watermarks, and whether the stamp was typographed, engraved, embossed, or from photogravure. While *Scott's* is the indisputable classic work, the full-color representation of the stamps, focus, and handy format of *The Official Guide to U.S. Stamps* merit a place for this volume in all popular collections.

EDUCATION, COMMUNICATION, CUSTOMS

Importers Manual USA: The Single Source Reference Encyclopedia for Importing to the United States. 1993 ed. Ed. by Edward G. Hinkelman. World Trade Press, 265 Summit Ave., San Rafael, CA 94901, 1992. 920p. bibliog. charts. illus. index. hardcover $87 (0-9631864-1-8; ISSN 1065-5158).
382.5'068 Imports—U.S.—Handbooks, manuals, etc. [BKL]

The purpose of this new resource is to provide an overview of the field of importing for businesspeople who would like to import goods but have never done so before. It is also intended to assist people in small businesses who import goods but wish to increase their knowledge about the process. The work is organized into five major sections plus three indexes, all of which are marked with tabs.

A section of 60 "Info-Lists" begins the volume. It provides capsulized information on such topics as 18 reasons to go into importing, 30 easy-to-import products, the top 50 suppliers of U.S. imports, 24 questions to ask about your competition, and 10 tips for negotiating. Some of these lists might be used effectively as skeleton lecture formats for business professors or seminar leaders.

"International Law" provides useful how-to information regarding safe travel in other countries, international sales contracts, and contract laws in other countries. "International Banking" shows users how to get information about foreign banks and also covers such topics as documentary credits, uniform rules for collections, and foreign-exchange dealing. Along with the text in these sections are reproductions of such items as a 1983 pamphlet from the International Chamber of Commerce and a 1987 pamphlet from the Swiss Bank.

The section "U.S. Customs Entry" is a reprint of *Importing to the United States* (U.S. Customs Service, 1991) that has been enhanced with cross-references to other sections of the work under review. "Packing, Shipping and Insurance" gives detailed information, provided by Hapag-Lloyd Shipping Lines, on securing and packing containers. The data on marine insurance and ocean cargo were provided by the Insurance Company of North America.

One hundred thirty-five product groups are arranged alphabetically in the "Commodity Index." Provided for each is an overview of regulatory requirements, pertinent publications, addresses for the governmental regulating agencies, and a list of principal exporting countries. SIC and harmonized commodity-description coding system numbers are not provided, but U.S. Customs Classification information is included. A "Country Index" provides economic, trade, travel, banking, and product-source information for the top 100 countries that export to the U.S. The volume concludes with a well-constructed and detailed general index.

The information provided in *Importers Manual USA* is useful and often reprinted from unquestionably authoritative sources. It will assist small businesses that are novices at importing, and some of the material will be of interest to college and university students and faculty. It is recommended for academic libraries and large public libraries. The publicity indicates that the title is to be produced annually, but, unless substantial changes are made to the content, it would not need to be purchased every year.

The Almanac of Anniversaries. By Kim Long. ABC-Clio, 1992. 240p. bibliog. index. hardcover $40 (0-87436-675-5).
394.2 Anniversaries—Calendars [OCLC] 92-28945

Long's latest compilation will allow social directors, history teachers, and greeting-card producers to plan celebrations of significant anniversaries from 1993 through 2001. It also enables cultural historians and the merely curious to view past events in interesting, thought-provoking clusters. What was it about the year 1921 that produced the first successful demonstration of aerial bombardment, the introduction of drive-in food service at Royce Hailey's Pig Stand in Dallas, the first experiments with insulin treatment of diabetes, the lie detector, the first Miss America contest, Eskimo Pies, independent Ireland, Prokofiev's *The Love for Three Oranges*, *Barron's Weekly*, and *The Sheik* (starring Rudolph Valentino)?

For each of the nine years to come, *The Almanac of Anniversaries* provides information about people, places, products, and events that will reach the "biggie" anniversaries: 25, 50, 75, 100, 150, and so forth through 500. There are birthdays, deaths, first performances (music, television, movies, and drama), premier editions (newspapers, magazines, and books), foundings (colleges, museums, zoos, and major businesses), inventions, and historical events. The emphasis is on the U.S., but people and events elsewhere are included if they are deemed important to our collective memory. Some items such as birth dates and foundings are just listed; events are described in two or three sentences.

The bibliography lists works used in compiling the almanac and does not purport to be comprehensive. It features some subject-specific sources that might interest someone doing research in a particular field, such as Krug's *Salient Dates in American Education* (1966) and DuVall's *Domestic Technology: A Chronology of Developments* (1988). The extensive index includes every name, institution, creation, and event from the entries. Place-names are indexed when appropriate, such as cross-referencing Annapolis, Maryland, and the opening of the U.S. Naval Academy. Anyone who has spent time seeking the proper Latin term for the twenty-fifth anniversary (quartocentennial) will appreciate the "Anniversary Glossary" provided.

The book's format is visually appealing, making use of boxes and milestone stars to cluster related events, but some confusion occurs when listings for one anniversary spill over to the page where the next begins. For example, it's difficult to know which anniversary the Peach Bowl will celebrate in 1993—the twenty-fifth or the fiftieth.

The Almanac of Anniversaries will be fun to browse, helpful for historical research, and useful to those looking for a cause for celebration.

Festival Europe! Fairs & Celebrations throughout Europe. By Margaret M. Johnson. Mustang Publishing, 1992. 236p. maps. paper $10.95 (0-914457-41-1).
394.2/694 Festivals—Europe ‖ Fairs—Europe ‖ Europe—Social life and customs ‖ Europe—Description and travel—Guidebooks [OCLC] 90-50867

Festival Europe! describes festivals—both well known and not so well known—in Western Europe and Greece.

Arrangement is by country or group of countries (e.g., Benelux countries). For each is provided an introduction to the festival life of the area followed by a calendar of festivals arranged from May through October. Specific dates are not given for events, so the book's usefulness is not limited to one year. Festival descriptions in the calendar sections are brief, rarely more than 100 words. The calendars are often followed by a brief summary of out-of-season events and by essays highlighting festivals. For example, for England, maypoles and mop fairs are featured. For Italy, two festivals—the Calcio Storica and the Palio of Siena—are compared. An outline map of Europe faces the table of contents, and outline maps of each country or country group precede the text. Locations of festivals are sometimes shown on the maps.

The strength of *Festival Europe!* is the variety of celebrations described. Its weaknesses are its awkward arrangement and lack of an index. France is divided into five regions, each with its own calendar of events and three with their own off-season summaries and summarizing essays. There is no indication of this arrangement in the table of contents. The book needs an alphabetical index by town and name of event.

Festival Europe! will be used by prospective travelers and school report writers who want more information than is available in general reference books. Libraries serving these populations should consider purchase, but most will probably put it in the circulating collection.

The Dictionary of Sacred and Magical Plants. By Christian Rätsch. Tr. by John Baker. ABC-Clio, 1992. 235p. bibliog. illus. index. hardcover $49.50 (0-87436-716-6).
398'.368 Plants—Folklore—Dictionaries ‖ Psychotropic plants—Dictionaries ‖ Ethnobotany—Dictionaries ‖ Medicinal plants—Dictionaries [OCLC] 92-29983

According to Rätsch, "Magic . . . entails a conscious attempt to modify a constantly changing world in order to achieve a particular end." Every culture has had magicians who learn to harness normally invisible powers to either serve or harm their communities. Through knowledge and performance of the proper rituals, plants are transformed into the tools of magic. With this anthropological perspective, *The Dictionary of Sacred and Magical Plants* explores the cultural uses of a select group of pharmacologically active substances. The book has been expanded and revised since its original 1988 publication as *Lexikon der Zauberplanzen aus ethnologischer Sicht*.

A detailed introduction provides a preliminary classification of the plants to be discussed, an overview of who might use them, and how such plants might be employed in rituals of knowledge. The majority of the book is an alphabetical listing, by common name, of approximately 135 substances, most of which are plants, but also includes such mind-altering mixtures as *beer* and *wine*. Entries range from common items found in U.S. kitchens (*ginger, garlic*) to unfamiliar plants grown only in other parts of the world (*mwamfi, tulasi*). Each entry provides the common and botanical names of the plant or substance, a description of the magical or sacred uses of the substance in different cultures, and the pharmacology of the substance. Entries conclude with citations to literature, which are keyed to the lengthy bibliography of English- and German-language works at the back of the book. Many entries include illustrations, and some are supplemented by charts, usually showing various species of the plant. The work concludes with a cross-index from botanical name to the common name used in the entry and a brief glossary.

The Dictionary of Sacred and Magical Plants contains no recipes or directions for making charms; it will not replace any titles dealing with herbal therapies. A detailed index would have increased its reference usefulness. However, the dictionary is a scholarly work that will be consulted in public libraries where there is a demand for such material by informed laypeople, as well as in academic libraries supporting studies in anthropology, ethnology, botany, medicine, and pharmacology.

The Concise Oxford Dictionary of Proverbs. 2d ed. By John Simpson. Oxford, 1992. 316p. bibliog. index. hardcover $22.95 (0-19-866177-0).

398.9'2103 Proverbs, English ‖ Proverbs, American [CIP] 91-39366

This dictionary was first published in 1982. Simpson, the author of both editions, is also coeditor of *The Oxford English Dictionary*. He notes that the proverb serves as a commentary on life and is now used to spice up ordinary discourse, especially in newspapers and magazines. Proverbs also pepper the speech of candidates for public office. Many of them in this collection seem quaint and unfamiliar, but a careful perusal reveals that they are similar to ones we know well.

This volume is very similar to the first edition, which contained 1,000 proverbs known principally in the twentieth century in Great Britain and America. The second edition has 90 proverbs that did not appear in the first. The bibliography of sources consulted remains the same with the addition of one new entry that relates to research in early French proverbs. Some of the 90 additional proverbs have been spawned in the political-cultural milieu of the U.S., for example, "What goes around comes around" and "If it ain't broke, don't fix it." These additions are included because they are now common in Great Britain.

The proverbs are arranged by the first significant word: "If you can't beat them, join them" is alphabetized under the word *beat*. The history of each proverb (its earliest known occurence in English literature) is given followed by selected examples of usage up to the present with dates and works cited. Many proverbs in English have French, Greek, and Latin origins. If the proverb exists in other languages, that is noted before the quotations, all of which have been rechecked for this edition.

There are ample cross-references to main and related entries. The most visible new feature of this edition is the "Thematic Index." Proverbs are listed under such themes as *Tact* ("Different strokes for different folks") or *Emergency* ("Any port in a storm"). This index would have been more valuable if the themes assigned to each proverb had been noted at the end of each entry, enabling the reader to select other proverbs on similar themes.

Libraries owning recent larger works, such as *Modern Proverbs and Proverbial Sayings* (1989), with five times more entries, or *The Dictionary of American Proverbs* (1992), may want *The Concise Oxford* for portability and conciseness. At half the cost of the above works, it will also serve as a valuable reference for libraries that do not own the first edition.

The Joys of Hebrew. By Lewis Glinert. Oxford, 1992. 224p. hardcover $22 (0-19-507424-6).

398.9'924 Proverbs, Hebrew—Dictionaries ‖ Proverbs, Jewish—Dictionaries ‖ Bible, O.T.—Quotations—Dictionaries ‖ Rabbinical literature—Quotations, maxims, etc.—Dictionaries ‖ Jews—Folklore—Dictionaries [OCLC] 92-28624

This dictionary includes approximately 600 of the "best-known, most loved Hebrew words and phrases in the English-speaking world." Arranged alphabetically, entries include both the Ashkenazi (northern European) and Sephardic (Mediterranean/Mideastern) spellings, a definition, and illustrations of use, which often include excerpts from the Bible, Talmud, Psalms, or sayings of famous rabbis or Jewish humorists and writers. Included are religious words (e.g., *Kaddish*: "A prayer customarily recited by mourners"), words for Jewish holidays (*Tu Bi-shvat*: "New Year for Trees, a kind of Arbor Day"), words from everyday Jewish life (*tefilin*: "small black leather boxes containing biblical verses on parchment"), Israeli words (*ozeret*: "cleaning woman"), and traditional Jewish sayings (*chutzpah*: "breathtaking cheek"). The book begins with a popular history of the Hebrew language and concludes with an alphabetical list of approximately 60 familiar biblical names in English, with Sephardic/Israeli Hebrew and Ashkenazi Hebrew forms and pronunciations.

This is a unique resource. Unlike many Hebrew-English dictionaries, it lists words transliterated into the Roman alphabet, rather than in the Hebrew alphabet. This is quite appropriate for its intended audience: English-speaking people who have encountered a Hebrew term in print or speech, "those who feel a sentimental attachment to Jewish life," people planning a trip to Israel, or speakers planning speeches for Jewish audiences. It is not a dictionary in the purest sense of the word. For example, parts of speech are not given. Instead, it provides an entertaining and informative discourse about Hebrew terms, many of which do not have exact English translations and which must be described in a way that will project a specific nuance. Glinert is not afraid to insert his own opinions. For example, in the entry *ikvot meschicha* ("the prelude to the messiah"), he says: "I wonder how long we can avoid some madman blowing up the world." This informality, although at times seemingly irrelevant, often helps to convey a nuance better than might a strict definition. For example, the description of *mesirut nefesh* ("self-sacrifice") indicates the seriousness of the phrase when it states that the "inmates of Bergen Belsen who contrived to retain their humanity represent *mesirut nefesh*." Conversely, the entry *meshuga* ("crazy") captures the humorous rather than clinical connotation of the word.

This is not a scholarly resource, though Glinert is the author of *The Grammar of Modern Hebrew* and has at least two BBC documentaries on language to his credit. It will probably be appreciated as much in the circulating collection as in reference. This delightfully entertaining book is recommended for academic libraries; it will also be of value in public libraries serving diverse populations.

LANGUAGE

An Encyclopedic Dictionary of Language and Languages. By David Crystal. Blackwell, 1992. 428p. illus. hardcover $29.95 (0-631-17652-7).

410'.3 Language and languages—Dictionaries ‖ Linguistics—Dictionaries [OCLC] 92-34195

Crystal, a professional fellow of the University College of North Wales, has written extensively in the field of linguistics, language acquisition, prosody, style, and grammar. He prepared the *Encyclopedic Dictionary of Language and Languages* (EDLL) to "combine the convenience of an alphabetical dictionary with the general range of a thematic encyclopedia." The latter, of course, is his *Cambridge Encyclopedia of Language* (CEL) [RBB Je 15 88]. In this new work, he adds terms from linguistics, but the emphasis is on language.

EDLL is arranged alphabetically, letter by letter, with cross-references to key concepts in capital letters at the end of each entry, which creates a "cats cradle" effect, leading the reader back and forth through a fascinating body of knowledge on language. In addition, words and phrases in boldface type within each entry highlight important ideas that lead to more entries. The author assumes a certain sophistication on the part of the reader; pronunciation is provided only where deemed necesary, excluding words like *implicature* and *glottochronology*. British spelling is preferred, although U.S. spelling is mentioned in some entries, for example, "*centre* (UK) or *center* (US)."

Highly useful are the entries for countries, which include the population in 1990 and official languages, lingua francas, and dialects spoken by small percentages of the population. One nice feature is the ease with which extinct languages such as Anatolian can be identified quickly. In CEL, the reader must dig into eight appendixes before locating that information. In addition to entries for language families, grammatical terms, and diacritics, names of such individuals as Edward Sapir are included, with cross-references to their contributions. Acronyms and abbreviations are treated in alphabetical order with cross-references to the full wording. Enhancing the dictionary are illustrations such as a depiction of the runic alphabet and six different ways to notate intonation.

Crystal mined the thematically arranged CEL for important terms and concepts, organized the information alphabetically, and made the data eminently more accessible in this new work. Public and academic libraries that can afford both the richly rewarding CEL and the more practical EDLL should purchase both. If a library can purchase only one, prefer the CEL.

The Oxford Companion to the English Language. Ed. by Tom McArthur. Oxford, 1992. 1,184p. index. hardcover $45 (0-19-214183-X).
420 English language ‖ English language—Grammar ‖ English language—Rhetoric ‖ English language—Style [OCLC]

Written to serve as an "interim report on the nature and use of the English language," this book is difficult to characterize. It combines some of the features of a dictionary, a style manual, and a usage guide. It attempts to provide a distillation of scholarship on the varieties of the increasingly global English language. Entries cover grammar, literary terms, linguistic terms, and subjects like sexist language and child language acquisition. There are entries for every nation where a significant part of the population speaks English as well as for dialects. The coverage of American English is extensive. (The fascinating entry *American English and British English* describes the systematic ways they differ.) Entries are provided for all major dictionaries and for people like Noah Webster who have influenced the language.

Entry arrangement is alphabetical, but entries can also be accessed from a very sophisticated system of cross-referencing. At the first level, cross-references lead to closely related words or phrases. For example, *Legalese* is cross-referenced to *Jargon, Law French, Legal Usage,* and *Register.* At the second level, the cross-reference system leads users to 22 broad linguistic "themes" where long lists of additional references can be found. For example, *Legalese* is cross-referenced to the themes *Style* and *Usage.* At the entry for *Style* are listed more than 500 other entries, such as *Analogy, Boilerplate, Stream of Consciousness,* and *Technospeak.* Theme listings allow users to formulate reading plans or to draw up their own lists of terms within a field of study. The 22 themes used are based upon Murray's (editor, *Oxford English Dictionary*, 1933) description of a "circle of the English language." However, *The Oxford Companion* has extended Murray's original concept of a nucleus that branches out into a few related circles of words to one with 22 related circles.

The approximately 5,000 entries range from the brief (e.g., *Comic Relief* is one sentence) to the lengthy (more than five pages for *Suffix*). Many entries also include references for further research and dates for a sense's use (when appropriate); all are signed by one of the more than 90 contributors. A few are accompanied by illustrations. For example, *Great Vowel Shift* has a chart that shows the change in pronunciation of vowels from Middle English.

The development of this scholarly reference was truly a labor of love. Linguists, students, and even trivia buffs will find it useful. The entries for linguistics terms are fairly technical, but most entries are accessible to the educated layperson. This book will ably serve as a companion to English-language dictionaries. Academic libraries serving departments of English and lingustics should purchase; public libraries will want to consider it too.

The Fifth Directory of Periodicals: Publishing Articles on American and English Language and Literature, Criticism and Theory, Film, American Studies, Poetry and Fiction. By Richard G. Barlow. Ohio Univ./Swallow Press, 1992. index. 349p. hardcover $49.95 (0-8040-0958-9); paper $19.95 (0-8040-0962-7) (ISSN 0070-6094).
016.4205 English philology—Periodicals—Directories [OCLC] 65-9218

This publication "is intended to serve scholars in the humanities as a reference guide to a number of scholarly journals to which they may submit manuscripts for publication." Given that *The Fourth Directory* appeared in 1974, this revised and expanded *Fifth Directory of Periodicals* is long overdue. The work is divided into six sections: literature journals, criticism and theory journals, film journals, language and linguisitics journals, American studies, and fiction and poetry journals. Each section is arranged alphabetically by journal title. Entries consist of name, editorial address, price, founding year, major field(s) of interest, manuscript submission information, payment, where the journal is indexed, and copyright and reprinting policy. Entries are marked with an asterisk if the journal is a member of the Council of Editors of Learned Journals. Oddly, the name of the editor of the periodical is not given within the entries.

Information within most entries was furnished by the editors of the periodicals, although there is no notation in those cases where the annotations had to be compiled by the editor of the directory. Ample data are provided to give a potential contributor information on whether or not the journal is suitable for his or her manuscript. A few errors were noted: *Romanic Review* is mistakenly called *Romantic Review*, and *Ironwood* is listed although it ceased publication two years ago. Also, the alphabetization ignores the articles *a* and *the* so that *Studies in Weird Fiction* appears before *Studies in the Age of Chaucer* and other titles beginning with *Studies in the.*

The eight-page introduction gives several tips on submitting articles and is written with the "beginning scholar" in mind. The volume concludes with an index, arranged by subject heading, including both personal names and broad topics (e.g., *Renaissance Studies, Rhetoric and Writing*). Although this is a useful feature, the Board questions why there is not also a title index. When looking for the entry on a known title, the reader must turn to the front of the volume to scan the alphabetical list of journals under each of six sections.

The Fifth Directory of Periodicals, listing 611 journals, has a limited scope; the emphasis is on established journals that publish scholarly and critical articles. Specialized periodicals such as alumni magazines, state historical society bulletins, and undergraduate literary magazines restricted to on-campus contributors are not included. Authors of creative works will continue to consult the *International Directory of Little Magazines and Small Presses* for publications interested in contemporary writing. The work with which *The Fifth Directory* most closely competes is the MLA *Directory of Periodicals*, which is updated regularly, includes editorial descriptions, and provides submission requirements. Although the MLA *Directory*, at $115, costs over twice as much as *The Fifth Directory*, the 1990–91 edition contains entries for 3,225 journals. Of the 661 journals in *The Fifth Directory*, all but 80 also appear in the MLA *Directory.*

The Fifth Directory is still likely to appeal to many scholars. The MLA *Directory* lacks any subject approach, and its sheer bulk may be intimidating to all but the most seasoned veterans of the "publish or perish" game. *The Fifth Directory* clearly takes a more user-friendly approach. All academic libraries should certainly consider *The Fifth Directory of Periodicals*, even if they already own the MLA *Directory.* The relatively low price of this volume will also make it an appealing purchase for many public libraries.

The Oxford English Dictionary: Second Edition on Compact Disc. Oxford, 1992. $895.
421.3 English language—Dictionaries ‖ English language—Etymology [BKL]

The first *Oxford English Dictionary: On Compact Disc* [RBB D 1 88] was based on the 1933 edition of the OED. This new version is derived from the second edition published in 20 volumes in 1989. Thus, it incorporates all of the material in the supplements to the OED while also adding approximately 5,000 new words and meanings. It provides access not only to the approximately 290,000 headwords in the OED2, but also to all of the 616,500 word forms contained in the entries, their definitions, and the 2.4 million quotations used to illustrate their usage. The version under review is for use with an IBM PC, but a Macintosh version is scheduled for release in early 1993.

HARDWARE, SOFTWARE, AND INSTALLATION. The OED2 on Compact Disc requires considerably more in the way of both hardware and software than did its predecessor. Minimum system requirements include an IBM PC or compatible with an 80386 processor, DOS version 3.0 or higher, 2 MB RAM (4 MB is recommended), 1 MB free hard-disk space, Microsoft CD-ROM extensions 2.0 or higher, Windows 3.0 or higher, a VGA monitor, and a CD drive. Although installation of the software is relatively simple, it requires an additional step to load six special fonts to allow the various elements of the dictionary entries to display properly.

SEARCHING AND DISPLAYING. Like its predecessor, the OED2 on Compact Disc is contained on a single disc, but, unlike the earlier version, it operates under the Windows environment and requires the use of a mouse. Thus, users must be familiar with Windows' basic features and operating techniques in order to search the OED disc. For the occasional and general user, the easiest way to search is to click on the SEARCH option in the menu bar. This displays a list of the five components of each dictionary entry that can be searched: word, text (searches the entire dictionary), etymology, definition, or quotation. (A significant improvement in this version is the use of search terminology that reflects more common usage, for example, *word* is used instead of *lemma* and *definition* instead of *sense*.) Some of these types of searches offer additional options. For example, a basic word search will find headwords only, but the user also can choose to search the word as a variant form or phrase, to limit the search to a specific date or range of dates or to a part of speech, or to search in the phonetic or Greek alphabets. A quotation search allows the user to search by date, author, title, text, or by a combination of any or all of these components. For instance, a user can quickly determine that for the period 1980–90 the OED2 includes 17 quotations from *Newsweek* and 43 from *Time*.

When the user clicks on the type of search desired, both a search window and a list window appear. The search window includes a box or boxes in which the items to be searched can be typed, while the list window provides an alphabetical display of all the words, names, or titles within the category being searched. A user interested in locating words derived from the Aztec language could initiate an etymology search by typing *Aztec* in the language box of the search window or by activating the list window and selecting the word *Aztec* from the language list. The system also provides a mechanism for selecting multiple items from a list. Because of the inconsistencies in the use of abbreviations and in citing languages, authors, and works that occurred during the many years of compiling the OED, the list windows should be consulted when conducting searches on parts of the dictionary in which such variations might appear. For example, a check of the author list reveals that Lewis Carroll is cited six different ways.

Once a search has been run, a summary of the matching records appears in a results window, which posts the total number of results and a truncated list of the matches. The results window also provides options for how the results list is to be displayed (i.e., list only, list and text, or text only). When an entry from the results window is selected for viewing, a display window opens in which a variety of colors, different typography, and underlining are used to distinguish parts of the entry. For instance, variant forms display in green, definitions in black, quotations in blue, and work titles in italics. Colors and fonts can be changed to suit individual preferences. Options at the bottom of the display window provide ways to move efficiently to other entries in the results list or to other words in the OED2.

A major enhancement in this version is the ability to conduct both wild-card and proximity searches, thus permitting searching by parts of a word or of a phrase. These are powerful and flexible options that allow the dictionary entries to be explored in ways previously inaccessible. A question mark can be substituted for a single character in a word, while an asterisk can be used to represent single or multiple characters within a word or at the beginning or end of a word, providing the ability to truncate words. Thus, the question about words ending with -gry that periodically makes the rounds of reference departments can be answered quite easily by entering a search for *gry as both a word search and a variant-form search. The results of this search yielded not only *angry* and *hungry*, but also obsolete terms like *nangry* and *pedagry*. In addition, an asterisk preceded and followed by a space can be used to represent an entire word. This is useful when searching a phrase that contains common words that would slow the search or for searching a phrase or quotation when one is uncertain of all the words. Wild-card searches typically take longer than others to complete (the *gry search took approximately 10 minutes).

Another innovation is the ability to conduct proximity searches, which allow the user to search words separated by up to 32 other words by using the number sign (#) and the number of possible intervening words. Thus, a researcher trying to locate a source other than Coleridge for an allusion to having an albatross around one's neck could conduct a quotation search for *albatross #2 neck* and locate two results.

For more sophisticated users, the OED2 offers the capability to perform more complex searches by using a prescribed query language to construct search statements. These searches allow the use of Boolean operators and permit combined searches of different components of an entry. Query statements require a precise format with components that specify the field to be searched, the type of search within that field, the term(s) to be searched, and a file name to which the results are to be saved. For example, *ent df=(fear)* or *df=(dread) into (phobia.ent)* produces a file of all entries that are defined with the terms *fear* or *dread*.

DOCUMENTATION. The OED2 on Compact Disc is accompanied by a copy of "A User's Guide to the *Oxford English Dictionary*," a 71-page booklet that explains all the elements of a typical dictionary entry, and a 123-page CD-ROM user's manual. Since no instructions for using the system appear on the primary screens, careful study of the user's manual is necessary to gain an overview of the system's capabilities and idiosyncrasies. Although help screens are available throughout the system, the user's manual, with its greater detail and sample screens, is a more efficient means of solving problems. Fortunately, the manual is well indexed, and most sections are well organized and clearly written. An exception is the chapter on using query language, which is murky and poorly organized. For example, one has to read seven pages into the chapter before finding instructions on how to activate a search once the query statement is keyed in. Although the user's manual includes some basic information about Windows procedures, novices will probably need to consult the "Windows User's Guide" as well.

PRINTING. A major flaw of the OED2 on Compact Disc is its failure to provide menu options for printing directly from the OED. Since the previous CD offered a variety of printing options, this omission is difficult to understand. Although a sophisticated user of Windows can overcome this obstacle by moving into other Windows applications, the procedures involved are cumbersome. For example, to print an entire screen, one can press the ALT and PRINT SCREEN keys, minimize the OED screen, open up the word-processing application (i.e., Write), go to the EDIT option, select PASTE, go to the FILE option, and select PRINT. Printing the entire screen has the advantage of preserving the differences in fonts, special alphabets, etc. However, the user can also copy an entry or part of an entry through a nine-step process. Printing all the results to a query requires an even more circuitous route because it involves choosing the OUTPUT TO TEXT option to create a file before moving into the word-processing application. While these methods may be acceptable to individual owners of the OED2 on Compact Disc who are working with their own computers, they present a number of complications for libraries. In addition to being time consuming and require considerable Windows expertise, they require that libraries provide access to the word-processing applications in Windows rather than restricting users to certain databases. Most libraries will be reluctant to do this since they cannot afford a work station configured to accommodate a number of databases to be monopolized by individuals who simply want to use its word-processing capabilities.

CONCLUSION. While this version is far superior to the first compact-disc version of the OED in content, searching capabilities, and access speed, its lack of a straightforward print option is a step backward. Restoring this ability should be Oxford's first priority in the next version.

The Board's assessment of the first OED on compact disc as "a complicated, sophisticated system that requires patience and perseverance to search with precision and effectiveness" remains true of this version. However, because of its significantly greater coverage and its enhanced searching mechanisms, the OED2 system offers benefits that are well worth the effort required to master the system. Its primary users will undoubtedly be scholars, students, and librarians in academic or research institutions, but libraries that were unable to afford the $2,500 printed version of the second edition of the OED may consider the CD-ROM version a practical alternative.

The American Heritage Dictionary of the English Language. 3d ed. Houghton, 1992. 2,140p. illus. hardcover $39.95 (0-395-44895-6).

423 English language—Dictionaries [CIP] 92-851

With this third edition, *The American Heritage Dictionary* (AHD) has reverted back to the large format (8½ by 11 inches) of the first edition published in 1969. (The second edition, designated the "second college edition," released in 1982 was the size of a desk dictionary.) The new AHD provides approximately 200,000 main entries, compared with 155,000 in the first edition and 145,000 in the second. This makes it larger than standard college/desk dictionaries but smaller than unabridged ones. About 16,000 entries are new to this edition. Sampling indicates that it is up-to-date through late 1990. For example, CD-ROM and *Paz, Octavio* (the 1990 Nobel Prize winner for literature) are listed, but *ecotourism* is not.

Abbreviations, acronyms, people, and places are all in the A–Z main text. (In the second college edition, biographical and geographic entries were in separate sections at the end.) Population figures from the 1980 census, rather than the 1990 one, are given for U.S. places. Meanings of a word are ordered so that the one most often sought is first, not the oldest one. Etymologies appear for more than 30,500 entries. These do not use abbreviations or symbols, nor do they give a date of earliest use. In addition, there are 400 word histories, entertaining paragraphs that tell how words interact with history and culture.

Five hundred usage notes, also in paragraph form, deal with grammar, diction, and pronunciation. They go into detail on the appropriate use of a word (e.g., *Jew* as a demeaning term in certain situations but not in others, *materialize* as a verb meaning "to appear suddenly") and seem to indicate that the dictionary leans more toward a prescriptive rather than a descriptive approach. Many entries use labels to indicate subject areas, archaic or obsolete terms, regionalisms, and dialect usage. So, for instance, the word *ain't* is labeled "Non-standard," and several meanings of *screw* are labeled "Vulgar Slang." The "Usage Panel," unique to this dictionary, remains a central feature of this edition. Among the 173 members are such people as Roger Angell, Barbara Taylor Bradford, John Kenneth Galbraith, and Susan Sontag. They responded to questions about disputed usage, and their views are noted in many of the usage notes. For example, only 11 percent approved the use of *holocaust* in talking about AIDS.

More than 900 synonym notes list and discriminate among synonyms. In many of the synonym notes and in some of the regular entries are illustrative examples. Some of these were made up by the editors; approximately 4,000 of them are quotations from famous people. New to this edition are more than 100 regional notes. For instance, under *tonic* is a note that this is the word used by Bostonians for the beverage that people in the Northeast call *soda* and the rest of the country calls *pop*.

Also unique to the AHD is the use of black-and-white photographs as illustrations. There are 4,000 photographs and line drawings in the outside margins of pages. Especially noteworthy are the many photographs of famous people and pieces of art. Special tables (e.g., a currency table, a table of books of the Bible) are located close to their main entries and are cross-referenced from related entries. Front and back matter includes short essays on the history of the English language, the use of notes in the dictionary, the mathematics of language, and Indo-European languages (including an excellent chart of the Indo-European family of languages); an appendix defines and gives examples of derivatives for approximately 400 Indo-European roots. Some of this material is reprinted from previous editions, and some of it is new.

Definitions in the AHD are easy to understand (they do not require lookups of words used in the definitions, and they do not use the word being defined in the definition), and the illustrative quotes are relevant and helpful. The volume is thumb indexed, and the pictures are unmatched by other dictionaries. A larger typeface is used for entry words than in previous editions, and the overall effect is a dictionary that is attractive and easy to read. This new edition of *The American Heritage Dictionary* is a highly recommended resource for all libraries, high school and up.

British English for American Readers: A Dictionary of the Language, Customs, and Places of British Life and Literature. By David Grote. Greenwood, 1992. 728p. bibliog. hardcover $85 (0-313-27851-2).

423 English language—Great Britain—Dictionaries || Great Britain—Civilization—Dictionaries || English literature—Dictionaries [CIP] 91-45575

This book is introduced—and justified—by an Oscar Wilde quotation: "The English have everything in common with the Americans—except language." While reading British authors, viewing films based on the novels of E. M. Forster or Thomas Hardy, or watching PBS's "Masterpiece Theatre", we often have to rely on contextual clues to help us guess the meaning of words like *dingle* (a small hollow among hills), *tuck* (candies and such sent from home to children at boarding school), *bursary* (a scholarship or grant), or *neeps* (turnips).

Here is a book to answer questions about British terms. *British English for American Readers* has entries in one alphabet for words in these categories: titles, ranks, and honors; widely used words not part of the typical American vocabulary; words used differently in America and Britain; customs, terminology, and activities of daily life not shared by Americans; governmental organizations; political and legal customs and methods; communities and places often used in literary works; foods and common commercial products; common animals and plants not found in the same form in America; and social practices that differ from modern American practice. The entry *Battersea* tells a good deal about this area near the Thames; *tea* and *cheese* describe the many varieties of each and the customs associated with these foods; BBC gives a short history of this famous organization. Author Grote, a magazine editor, points out that he is not British and therefore knows which British terms need explanation. *British English* places emphasis on place-names, especially in London. Terms from other parts of the British Empire, especially India, are included. An asterisk in the text of an entry indicates a word that has its own entry. Seven appendixes explain more mysteries of British life, including money and values, reigns and historic dates, class structure, calendar of holidays and festivals, military ranks, and honors and initials.

British English, A to Zed, by Norman Schur (Facts On File, 1989), covers much the same ground as *British English for American Readers*, but each book has many unique terms and features. The title under review has unusually broad coverage, including elements found in guidebooks, almanacs, gazetteers, and history and sociology books. On the other hand, *A to Zed* has a list of automotive terms, cricket terms, and information on British punctuation and style. It includes occasional quotations by way of illustrating word meanings. A smaller library owning *A to Zed* could bypass purchase of *British English*, but libraries could certainly use both books.

Eminently browsable, *British English* provides the type of pleasure found by dipping into *Brewer's Dictionary of Phrase and Fable* or *Benét's Reader's Encyclopedia*, where one learns something for the pure fun of it. *British English* is appropriate for all public libraries and for libraries in educational institutions from high school through graduate school.

Webster's New World Dictionary for Young Adults. Ed. by Jonathan L. Goldman and Andrew N. Sparks. Prentice Hall Press, 1992. 1,040p. illus. hardcover $18 (0-13-945734-8).

423 English language—Dictionaries, Juvenile [CIP] 92-3061

This dictionary is the successor to *Webster's New World Dictionary for Young Readers*, originally published in 1978. Compared with its predecessor, the volume under review is a new work, with a different format, updated definitions, and more than 2,700 entirely new dictionary entries. It is designed for children ages 11–14, grades 6–9. The school editions, distributed by Silver Burdett & Ginn by Modern Curriculum Press, have different covers but are otherwise the same as the volume under review.

Assembled by the team of lexicographers that created the third college edition of *Webster's New World Dictionary*, this new work was compiled with the assistance of an advisory board of education specialists. A computerized database of vocabulary from 16,000 compositions written by students was checked to ensure that the dictionary included words used by today's young adults. A total of 47,500 words and phrases appear here, with main entries for approximately 28,500 words and 2,100 idioms. Included are more than 400 biographical entries and 1,200 geographic entries, which are current and reflect recent changes in Europe, Asia, and Africa. Definitions are included for new words and idioms such as *dork*, *streetwise*, and *T cell*.

Entries include syllabication, pronunciation, part of speech, and definitions. Some entries also include cross-references, examples of use in sentences, synonyms, and word histories. The book includes features to indicate variant spellings and homographs and also provides usage labels (e.g., *obsolete*, *informal*). The definitions provide meanings of words as they are commonly used, and they are written in appropriate language for the age range of the intended audience. Pronunciation guides for vowels are inside the front cover and appear in an abbreviated form in a colored box on each page. A "Word Finder Table" of consonant and vowel sounds is inside the back cover. The "Guide to the Use of the Dictionary," found in the opening pages, provides clear explanations of the book's features.

The illustrations are appropriate for the intended users, and the type size, margins, use of guide words, and general look of each page give this dictionary a form that will be accepted by the emerging elementary scholar and open the door to the adult dictionaries. *Webster's New World Dictionary for Young Adults* is a recommended purchase for libraries serving middle school students. It will find use among young adults, both in libraries and in homes.

Roget's International Thesaurus. 5th ed. Ed. by Robert L. Chapman. HarperCollins, 1992. 1,141p. index. thumb-indexed $18.95 (0-06-270014-6); plain $17.95 (0-06-270046-4).
423'.1 English language—Synonyms and antonyms [CIP] 92-7615

The fifth edition of the classic *Roget's International Thesaurus* includes more than 325,000 words and phrases (up from 250,000 in the fourth edition) grouped according to ideas into 15 classes and further subdivided into 1,073 major categories. In this completely revised and reorganized edition, 31 new major categories have been added, including such topics as substance abuse and computer science, in order to make this resource more reflective of modern society. Within the 1,073 major categories, ideas are further broken down into paragraphs, each of which reflects more discrete connotative or part-of-speech groupings. In an effort to more clearly distinguish between groups of synonyms within a paragraph, synomyms that are closest in meaning to each other are "offered in clusters that are set off with semicolons," which indicate changes in sense or application. Also, foreign and technical terms are identified by labels in angle brackets (e.g., *starets* <Russian>; *Animalia* <zoology>).

Also helpful are the use of boldface for synonyms most often used for the idea being represented; lists of words that fit within a category but do not have synomyms (e.g., a list of phobias is found under *phobias by name*; a list of various football plays can be found under *football plays and calls*); *see* references to the number at which a listed synonym can be found as a headword; and the inclusion of quotations (referenced to a person but not to a source) that refer to a guideword or category. The comprehensive index refers back to category and paragraph, allowing the reader to zero in to the right spot on the page.

Since the thesaurus is arranged topically, it stands quite apart from other thesauruses that are arranged alphabetically. Other differences are also noted. In terms of sheer number of synonyms provided, *Roget's* has more than either *Webster's New Dictionary of Synomyms* (Merriam-Webster, 1984) or the *Random House Thesaurus College Edition* (Random, 1984). However, both *Webster's* and *Random House* provide antonyms, and *Webster's* also provides contrasting and analogous words. Additionally, unlike *Roget's*, which does not define guidewords or synonyms, both *Webster's* and *Random House* provide some definitions. *Random House* uses guidewords in sentences, and *Webster's* provides explanatory paragraphs in which major synonyms are clearly differentiated in terms of their connotations. Both *Webster's* and *Roget's* also provide quotations that help to clarify or expand the nuances of listed words.

Finally, in terms of ease of use, although the alphabetically arranged sources require less page turning, *Roget's* idea-based groupings facilitate creative generation of synonyms as well as easier browsing (once one has found the correct classified area).

The fifth edition of *Roget's* is a handsome product whose larger print and uncluttered pages are unintimidating. For junior high or high school, public, and academic libraries, the sheer number of words presented in *Roget's* makes it clearly a first purchase. However, since it seems to be geared toward people who know the English language, it should probably sit next to *Webster's New Dictionary of Synonyms*, whose clear distinctions between fewer words make it a first purchase for nonnative speakers as well as less-sophisticated or younger writers. And, as *Roget's* urges, all thesauruses should be used in conjunction with a good dictionary in order to ensure that a selected synonym, which may be unfamiliar to the user, is appropriate.

Roget's 21st Century Thesaurus in Dictionary Form: The Essential Reference for Home, School, or Office. Ed. by Barbara Ann Kipfer. Dell, 1992. 978p. index. hardcover $18 (0-440-50386-8).
423'.1 English language—Synonyms and antonyms [CIP] 91-37916

Like *Webster*, the name *Roget* is in the public domain and is used by many different publishers. *Roget's 21st Century Thesaurus* is approximately the same physical size as the new fifth edition of *Roget's International Thesaurus* [RBB O 1 92], but—unlike the traditional classified order of that work—it employs a hybrid arrangement. The bulk of *Roget's 21st* is in dictionary order like the *Random House Thesaurus College Edition* and *Webster's New Dictionary of Synonyms*, but it also has a "Concept Index" that groups together main-entry words that share the same idea or property. This index has 10 broad concepts (e.g., actions, life forms, qualities) divided into 837 more specific topics.

Users of *Roget's 21st* who look up one of the 17,000 main entries in the A–Z section will find a short definition of the word, a lengthy list of alphabetically arranged undifferentiated synonyms, and cross-references to the "Concept Index," located at the back of the volume. At each numbered concept in this index, lists of related main-entry terms can be found. Users can then turn to each of these main entries to find other synonyms for the first word that have different nuances. For the user who will take the time to search each main entry referenced by the "Concept Index," this resource is a gem. For the person who wants to quickly narrow down a search for synonyms, the classified approach provided by *Roget's International* may be preferred.

Although the synonyms listed in both titles necessarily overlap, each has unique words and groupings. For example, *Roget's International* provides synonyms for *ear* as a body part; *Roget's 21st* does not. Through its "Concept Index," *Roget's 21st* provides such related colorful words for the main-entry *abase* as *crucify* and *nettle*; *Roget's International* provides synonyms that fall under the general senses of *humility* and *promotion/demotion*. *Roget's International* provides a list of types of guns within the synonym lists for *arms*; *Roget's 21st* does not. Both titles seem to be equally up-to-date. For example, they include such modern concepts as *significant other*, such slang as *get down* and *gnarly*, and such scientific terms as *genetic*.

For people who want immediate access to specific words, *Roget's International* is probably going to continue as a first choice. For example, words and phrases such as *significant other*, RNA, and *all of a sudden* can be directly accessed through the alphabetical index at the back of *Roget's International*; they are not direct access points in the A–Z section of *Roget's 21st*. Conversely, people who wish to browse will appreciate *Roget's 21st*'s "Concept Index," which provides access to words that may be less closely related to the original lookup. *Roget's 21st* claims approximately 38 percent more words (450,000 to *Roget's International's* 325,000). The preface of *Roget's 21st* indicates that it uses fewer abbreviations and symbols than other recent thesauruses. Indeed, the only abbreviation used is for part of speech; an asterisk is employed to denote nonstandard usage. *Roget's International* uses 43 abbreviations to denote foreign or technical words; this information isn't found in *Roget's 21st*. *Roget's 21st* provides brief definitions for all main entries; *Roget's International* occasionally provides quotations that help to define a word. Neither thesaurus provides antonyms.

The preface of *Roget's 21st* states that classified editions of *Roget's* bury synonyms and that "all to often, the right word remains elusive." For those who dislike a classified approach to word finding, this may be true; for others, *Roget's 21st's* approach may cause the pitfall that it claims to eliminate. Ultimately, a writer's first choice of a thesaurus will depend upon personal preference. But since both of these inexpensive titles are exceptional, academic and public libraries should purchase both of them. Depending upon the student body, high school librarians might also consider acquiring both.

The Oxford Thesaurus: American Edition. By Laurence Urdang. Oxford, 1992. 1,005p. index. hardcover $19.95 (0-19-507354-1).
423'.1 English language—U.S.—Synonyms and antonyms ‖ Americanisms—Dictionaries [CIP] 91-3938

Compiled by Laurence Urdang (an editor of *The Random House Dictionary of the English Language*), this thesaurus contains 650,000 words. The main A–Z section presents headwords selected on the basis of their frequency of use in the language and, for the most part, they represent basic forms of a word (i.e., *live* is a headword, but *living* and *livable* are not). Entries include part-of-speech designations followed by numbered synonym lists. Each numbered list groups synonyms by sense and is illustrated by an example sentence. Within numbered lists, synonyms that have their own main entries are marked with a symbol and, where appropriate, usage and dialect labels are provided. Within a sequence of numbered senses, more commonly used words are listed first, followed by less commonly used or more colorful words (e.g., the first synonym listed for *fracture* is *break*; the last two are *rift* and *cleave*). Spellings of words are those preferred by American writers, with frequently used American variants also indicated.

This is a straightforward and easy-to-use resource. The instructions for use are a model of clarity, and the index is especially well designed; it includes phrases as well as plural and tense forms, and its referencing system leads users directly to appropriate numbered senses within main entries. In terms of number of words included, *Oxford* compares favorably with *Roget's International Thesaurus* (5th ed. [RBB O 1 92]), the major difference being that *Roget's* employs a classified rather than alphabetical approach. Access to specific words in the two books overlaps but does not entirely duplicate. For example, the index to *Oxford* includes *infirmary* (*Roget's* doesn't); the index to *Roget's* includes *infix* (*Oxford* doesn't). *Oxford's* illustrative sentences will help nonnative speakers select appropriate synonyms from lists (a problem when undifferentiated synonyms are presented). Having this thesaurus in a library lessens (but probably does not eliminate) the need for *Webster's Dictionary of Synonyms*, which presents fewer words but thoroughly defines subtle differences in meaning. *Oxford* also compares favorably to *Roget's 21st Century Thesaurus in Dictionary Form* [RBB O 15 92], which leads to more synonyms with the use of its "Concept Index" and gives brief definitions but lacks example sentences. The typeface in *Oxford* is smaller than that used in these other two new thesauruses.

The Oxford Thesaurus is highly recommended for all large public and academic libraries (even those with the other three titles mentioned above), and small libraries might also seriously consider purchase.

Random House Word Menu. By Stephen Glazier. Random, 1992. 977p. index. hardcover $22 (0-679-40030-3).
423'.1 English language—Glossaries, vocabularies, etc. ‖ English language—Synonyms and antonyms ‖ English language—Terms and phrases ‖ Vocabulary [OCLC] 92-13539

In order to fully appreciate the true value of this unusual reference work, the user needs to know why Glazier compiled it. The late writer Glazier made lists of words to enrich his fiction, then created a classification system for his words that reflects modern usage and modern slang. The result is a system that enables the user to begin searching for appropriate words to express an idea by selecting from a menu of seven subject areas: *Nature, Science and Technology, Domestic Life, Institutions, Arts and Leisure, Language,* and *The Human Condition.* Each of these parts contains three or four chapters; these are divided into 134 categories and 300 subcategories. The volume serves as a reverse dictionary when the user knows a meaning but cannot think of the appropriate word or phrase. In this respect it differs from a dictionary of synonyms or a thesaurus in which the user knows a word and seeks a better word or more words to express an idea, although it can serve this function too.

Word Menu is not illustrated, but it is jam-packed with information. The detailed table of contents is broken down by chapters, categories, and subcategories; the appropriate headings also appear at the top of each page. A detailed 120-page index serves as an alternative entry point into the book. Not given are pronunciations, etymologies, or usage notes as in a dictionary. However, this truly innovative approach to organizing vocabulary allows the work to function as a simple dictionary where a brief definition is all that is needed. For example, under *Science and Technology: Transportation: Railroads: Parts, Practices, Argot,* the word *ferrophiliac* is defined as "amateur lover of railroading." One way this book differs from traditional thesauruses is in its provision of proper names. For instance, under *Trees* (in the section *Living Things: Plants*) are listed several hundred specific trees from *acacia* to *yew*. So it serves as a glossary in many areas, as well as a book of lists, an almanac, a grammar book, a book of days, and a handbook of slang. And unlike a visual dictionary, which has a scope limited to words that can be shown in pictures, the *Word Menu* has lists of words for intangibles such as *smells, heaven,* and *truth*. A word or phrase may appear more than once, for example, *booby hatch* appears in *Mental Disturbances* and later in *Ships and Boats*. There are no cross-references between the two, but both entries appear in the index.

The true value of this work will be to help the writer think of words to use in creative writing. Crossword-puzzle buffs and browsers will savor it too. A big book, it contains a rich collection of verbal comestibles, reflecting the menu metaphor of the title, and will be a welcome addition in high school, public, and academic libraries.

The word *menu* also conjures up the idea of computers. It seems appropriate, therefore, that Microlytics has produced an electronic version of *Word Menu* on CD-ROM. According to literature from the company, the CD-ROM version is available for IBM PC and compatibles and as a desk accessory for Apple computers.

The Macmillan Visual Dictionary. Macmillan, 1992. 862p. illus. index. hardcover $40 through January 1, 1993; $45 thereafter (0-02-528160-7).
423'.1 Picture dictionaries, English ‖ Handbooks, vade-mecums, etc. [OCLC] 91-34460

Recently a number of visual dictionaries have been published that rely on illustrations and accompanying labels to portray technical terms as well as more ordinary words. The purpose of these works is to enable readers to find the name of an object that they can identify visually. *The Oxford-Duden Pictorial English Dictionary* (1981) is a good example of this type of dictionary. Dorling Kindersley has published a number of single-topic dictionaries such as *The Visual Dictionary of Ships and Sailing* [RBB F 1 92]. *The Macmillan Visual Dictionary* was compiled by the same people who produced *The Facts On File Visual Dictionary* (1986). It is arranged in the same way, with 28 classification groups, such as "Astronomy," "Vegetable Kingdom," and "Symbols," covering more than 600 subjects and identifying 25,000 terms. The major difference between the two books is that Facts On File used black-and-white drawings and the Macmillan book has all new art, employing 3,500 full-color illustrations. While most of the objects identified are the same in both books, Macmillan has some unique items that could only be shown with color, for example, its drawings of precious and semiprecious stones. Some cutaway pictures are employed. Everything is carefully labeled with dotted lines indicating the exact part named. While Facts On File uses both British and American terms in its labels, the Macmillan dictionary uses American English.

The book concludes with an index to all the terms used on the pictures. Words in boldface type refer to the title of an illustration. While this book is targeted at adults, with pictures of fuse boxes and navigation devices, it will be fascinating to children as well. Though its conventional illustrations lack the dramatic appeal of the Dorling Kindersley works with their innovative layouts, *The Macmillan Visual Dictionary* covers far more topics. It will be useful for those learning English as a second language and for anyone looking for the name of a whatchamacallit, though libraries owning *The Facts On File Visual Dictionary* will have to decide if the addition of color makes purchase necessary.

The Oxford Dictionary of Modern Slang. By John Ayto and John Simpson. Oxford, 1992. 299p. hardcover $22.50 (0-19-866181-9).
427'.09 English language—Slang—Dictionaries [OCLC] 93-108616

The slang of the twentieth century included in the 20-volume *Oxford English Dictionary* (2d ed., Oxford, 1989) is presented here, along with another 500 or more words from the OED's unpublished files. British, American, and Australian slang is emphasized. Each entry includes the date the word first appeared in print, its origin, and an illustrative quotation. One will not only find such words as *homeboy* and *tubular* here, but also *twenty-three skiddoo* and *peachy-keen*. Readers will also find a number of words unprintable in a family newspaper.

Readers needing further information about a particular word may wish to consult the OED. Those looking for words culled from the unpublished files usually will have to be content with the information provided here. However, many of the contemporary words included can also be found in *The Oxford Dictionary of New Words* [RBB F1592] with more illustrative quotations. Collections already owning that source and other twentieth-century slang dictionaries (e.g., Partridge's *Dictionary of Slang and Unconventional English* in one or more of its various editions) may wish to pass on this new title. On the other hand, any collection lacking the full OED will find *The Oxford Dictionary of Modern Slang* a necessity. Its modest price will be an attraction for ready-reference collections even if the full OED is owned.

Whistlin' Dixie: A Dictionary of Southern Expressions. By Robert Hendrickson. Facts On File, Jan. 1993. 272p. hardcover $24.95 (0-8160-2110-4).
427'.975 English language—Southern States—Terms and phrases ‖ English language—Southern States—Dictionaries ‖ Southern States—Popular culture—Dictionaries ‖ Americanisms—Southern States—Dictionaries [CIP] 91-47861

This is volume 1 of the projected five-volume Facts On File Dictionary of American Regional Expressions series. The next volume, covering the West, is due to be published at the end of 1993. The compiler is a free-lance writer whose earlier works include *The Facts On File Encyclopedia of Word and Phrase Origins* (1987) and *American Literary Anecdotes* (1990).

Hendrickson traveled "from Baltimore to Key West, from Charleston to Houston" over a period of seven years to gather material for this book. The terms come from fiction, scholarly works, newspapers, magazines, and Southern correspondents. The lengthy introduction is a solid overview of the dialects that make up "South Mouth": Mountain (or Hill), Virginia Tidewater, South Carolina Low Country, General Southern Lowland, East Texas, Charleston, Baltimore, New Orleans, Cajun, Creole, Gumbo, Conch, and Gullah. The alphabetically arranged entries that follow include examples from each. The definitions and word histories range from one to several sentences.

A disturbing feature is the unevenness of documentation. Many entries have none—such as *fallacy*, which is listed as a Southern term for mistake or error with no allusion to any peculiarly Southern usage. Some sources are cited, but not enough for the serious researcher or the reference librarian. *Afromobile* is accurately defined as an early 1900s Palm Beach vehicle consisting of a two-seated wicker chair in the front and a bicycle in the back pedaled by a black man; the entry includes the assertion that this was "the only vehicle permitted in the city." Cassidy's *Dictionary of American Regional English* (1985–) states that only bicycles and afromobiles were permitted in the city and provides four sources for the material. *Heroes of America* is defined as a "secret organization, also called the Red Strings, formed in North and South Carolina after the Civil War." It actually flourished in the Carolinas and Virginia as early as 1863 and supported the Union. More consistent pronunciation guidance would be helpful. *Zouave* and *unaker* are two Southern words not used by us-all.

Hendrickson's stated goal, however, was to create "a book for the general reader that is fun to read yet reliable." He has produced an entertaining and educational work that has humor (the definition of Southern gentleman is worth the price of the book), some bawdiness (see *boody, easy rider,* and *horsing*), and the ability to stimulate thought and discussion. How many of us know that drawing out the word *bad* to *baaad* to describe someone or something good dates from eighteenth-century slavery? Or that *Land of Abstractions* is a nineteenth-century nickname for the state of Virginia due to its abundance of political thinkers? One could spend "the whole enduring day" looking for descriptive phrases better than "he couldn't hit the ground if he fell," "she could talk a cat down out of a tree," and "courting fool."

Libraries will want this volume for amateur philologists and students of Southern culture. Only the first two volumes (covering through H) of Cassidy's *Dictionary of American Regional English* have been published. That much more scholarly work has maps that show the distribution of terms. In spite of its protracted publishing schedule, academic and large public libraries will also want to have it on hand to answer the questions *Whistlin' Dixie* will raise.

Dictionary of the American West. By Winfred Blevins. Facts On File, 1993. 497p. bibliog. illus. hardcover $35 (0-8160-2031-0).
427'.978 English language—Dialects—West (U.S.)—Dictionaries ‖ West (U.S.)—Popular culture—Dictionaries ‖ Americanisms—West (U.S.)—Dictionaries [OCLC] 92-4336

This work contains approximately 3,500 entries, providing definitions for 5,000 words and terms pertaining to the American West over the last 200 years. In the introduction, Blevins explains that his objective was to include "women, Indians, Mormons, Hispanics, blacks, French-Canadians, mountain men, half-breeds, immigrants, missionaries, and everyone else" who had been excluded from previous dictionaries of the West. Coverage extends, for example, to the *coureurs de bois* (fur traders) of French Canada, who had their own terminology (*plew, bourgeois, voyageur*). Definitions for several Mormon words are included (*stake, ward, sealing*), and coverage extends to native American expressions (*sun dance, kachina, sand painting*).

Most definitions are a few sentences in length, but longer explanations are occasionally provided. For instance, *branding* covers more than one page, including a long quotation from Stewart Edward White's *Arizona Nights*. Another example is the entry *yarn*, which gives in full a typical tale, exaggerating the size and ferocity of western mosquitoes. Some etymologies are given (e.g., *brujo, chaparral, churro*). Also, some disputed word origins are discussed, such as those of *dogie, greaser*, and *gringo*. French-derived words are also listed with their original meanings, such as *Coeur d'Alene* and *nez percé*. Many definitions include cross-references, indicated by small capital letters.

A few entries are disappointing. *Mal de vache* is defined as "diarrhea ... thought to be caused by alkali water or by the change to an all-meat diet." A non-French reader might wonder if *vache* refers to the water or to the meat. Pronunciation is frequently given, especially for non-English words. The author does not make use of accents in the text. Thus, he stumbles over the word *albondiga* (meatball), which he assumes to be Spanish. It is actually Hispanicized Arabic, from *al-búnduqa*, meaning "little ball," and it requires a diacritical mark in order to be pronounced correctly.

The introduction acknowledges the author's dependence on earlier compilations, notably *Western Words* by Ramon Adams (1968), *Southwestern Vocabulary* by Cornelius Smith (1985), and *Dictionary of the Old West* by Peter Watts (1977). Blevins criticizes previous works as unsatisfactory, chiefly because of regional or ethnic limitations. However, he overstates his case by giving examples of words he claims were excluded from other books when, in fact, some of them do appear. Blevins seldom cites sources for the definitions, and when he does so, it is usually Adams; however, Watts, in the work mentioned above, usually cites at least one authority for each definition and often two or three. The book under review concludes with two brief lists containing suggestions for further reading. Some of the sources cited are not specific to the topic, such as standard English dictionaries, a religious encyclopedia, and a field guide to flowers.

In summary, despite some disappointments, this dictionary of western words is more complete than any of its predecessors and is written in a free-and-easy style, sometimes with interesting quotations. It will find a place in large public and academic libraries. Small public libraries that already own the other three works listed above might find these earlier compilations adequate for their readership.

Children's Writer's Word Book. By Alijandra Mogilner. Writer's Digest, 1992. 354p. bibliog. hardcover $19.95 (0-89879-511-7).

428.1 English language—Glossaries, vocabularies, etc. || Children's literature—Authorship || Children—Books and reading || Children—Language || Vocabulary [CIP] 92-17778

Promoted as a desk reference for authors of children's literature, this book provides lists of specific words known to children in each grade (kindergarten through sixth grade), a thesaurus of words with synonyms annotated by reading level, advice on word usage in writing for children, and writing samples. Additionally, guidelines are given for sentence length, word usage, and theme at each reading level. After an introduction that contains instructions on using the book, an alphabetical list of the words with their grade levels follows. Each grade's list is preceded by a brief discussion of child development principles and typical curriculum content. A bibliography of 27 items concludes the book. Omitted was mention of any of the professional books that provide bibliographies of graded reading, such as *The Elementary School Library Collection* (18th ed., 1992); *The Children's Catalog* (16th ed., 1991); and *Beyond Picture Books: A Guide to First Readers* (1989).

In the introduction to *Beyond Picture Books*, the compilers, Barbara Barstow and Judith Riggle, note that assigning readability is controversial. The widely available formulas of Fry and Spache do not take into consideration children's cultural differences in language, sophistication, or the conceptual difficulty of information. At best, the *Children's Writer's Word Book* provides possible word choices rather than definitive ones in the tricky task of combining creativity with appropriateness for children. Hopefully, all who use this work will have been exposed to E. B. White's words on writing for children found in *The Writer's Chapbook*: "Anyone who writes down to children is simply wasting his time. You have to write up, not down. Children are demanding.... They love words that give them a hard time, provided they are in a context that absorbs their attention." Onions to Writer's Digest Books for giving us an incomplete and emasculated view of the complexity and mystery of writing for children.

The Kingfisher Book of Words: A–Z Guide to Quotations, Proverbs, Origins, Usage, and Idioms. By George Beal. Kingfisher Books, 95 Madison Ave., New York, NY 10016, 1992. 200p. illus. hardcover $10.95 (1-85697-805-2).

428.1 Vocabulary—Juvenile literature || English language—Usage—Juvenile literature [OCLC] 92-53105

The Kingfisher Children's Encyclopedia. Ed. by John Paton. Kingfisher, 1992. 816p. illus. indexes. maps. hardcover $29.95 (1-85697-800-1).

031 Children's encyclopedias and dictionaries [CIP] 92-4785

The Kingfisher Illustrated Encyclopedia of Animals: From Aardvark to Zorille—and 2,000 Other Animals. Ed. by Michael Chinery. Kingfisher, 1992. 379p. illus. index. hardcover $19.95 (1-85697-801-X).

591.03 Animals—Encyclopedias, Juvenile [OCLC] 92-53113

The Random House Library of Knowledge First Encyclopedia. By Brian Williams and Brenda Williams. Random, 1992. 189p. illus. indexes. hardcover $18 (0-679-83059-6).

031 Children's encyclopedias and dictionaries [CIP] 91-32817

Kingfisher, an imprint of British publisher Grisewood & Dempsey, used to license its books to U.S. publishers but has recently opened an American office. Of the following Kingfisher books, three have been published here by them; the fourth has been licensed to Random House. All have been adapted for the American market.

The Kingfisher Book of Words, for children ages 9 and up, portrays the fun of words. Within each of the six chapters (covering modern quotations, proverbs, idioms, roots, origins, and English usage), entries are alphabetically arranged. Each of the chapters begins with an explanation of the concept, as well as directions on how to use the chapter. Differences between American and British meanings of words are pointed out. This book is a useful resource for the elementary school library or classroom. Students will require adult assistance in using it, but it would be a worthy purchase for teaching about the complexities of the English language.

The Kingfisher Children's Encyclopedia, for children ages 7–12, is a revised one-volume edition of a four-volume encyclopedia first published in this country as the *Doubleday Children's Encyclopedia* [RBB D 15 90]. The more than 1,300 entries, arranged alphabetically, range in length from as few as 20 words to more than 600. The text is easy to read, and cross-references are noted in small capitals. The entries are surrounded by more than 2,000 full-color illustrations, including diagrams, photos, cutaways, and maps. Each page contains many helpful features for the young researcher. Next to each heading is one of 16 subject symbols, which aids when browsing for entries relating to a specific subject. For instance, all entries about transportation show an airplane in a small box next to the entry. Special-feature entries on two-page spreads treat such topics as *Dance* and *Middle Ages*. Fact panels providing details on historical dates or statistics accompany some entries. Practical application through hands-on activities can be found in "See It Yourself" panels. The subject index lists main entries in boldface type followed by related entries in lighter type, with illustrations shown in italics. Following the main index is a classified index with the entries listed under the 16 subjects noted by symbols in the text. Information here appears to be current, noting the unification of Germany and the breakup of the Soviet Union.

This encyclopedia purports to provide information on every subject that children need to know about; however, one volume cannot be totally comprehensive. Yet compared with the *Random House Children's Encyclopedia* [RBB O 15 91], it does cover such topics as individual U.S. states and the Declaration of Independence, which *Random House* (also British in origin) does not. The text is clearly written, but younger children may need some assistance in using the index. This inexpensive, appealing encyclopedia is a fine purchase for both media centers and the children's department of public libraries.

Arranged from *Aardvark* to *Zorille*, over 2,000 animals are presented for upper elementary children in *The Kingfisher Illustrated Encyclopedia of Animals*. Entries describe animal-name origins, geographic location, size, habitat, behavior, and order, family, and species. The more than 1,000 color drawings and photographs provide the reader with an excellent visual image of the animal. Colored panels throughout the book provide information on animal behavior, such as "Camouflage" and "Migration." A glossary is found after the animal listings, as well as an index of animals by both common and scientific names. An index of alternative names concludes the volume. This book surpasses the *Macmillan Animal Encyclopedia* [RBB Ja 1 92] and its similar counterparts, *The Animal Atlas* and *Children's Animal Atlas* [RBB May 15 92], even though the introduction lacks a detailed explanation on utilizing the volume. Worth consideration for media centers and libraries as an initial resource on animals around the world.

The Random House Library of Knowledge First Encyclopedia, also a Kingfisher product, is aimed at the same age level as *The Kingfisher Children's Encyclopedia*; however, it has only about one-third the number of entries and less than one-quarter the number of pages. It appears to have no relationship to the other encyclopedia; it does not repeat any of the art or text. Encyclopedia conventions utilized include guide words, cross-references, and an index. Special features in colored panels include "Life Story" (to call attention to biographies in the book), "Did You Know That" (to elaborate on nearby entries), and "Find Out for Yourself" (to describe activities the reader can do). The 300 color illustrations are all drawings; no photographs are used. The text is succinct, but at best provides an outline of a topic. This book is suitable for family use and the circulating collection in school and public libraries; its reference use is limited.

SCIENCE

Today's Science on File: News Digest with Index. v.1. Facts On File, Sept. 1992– . monthly. index. paper $185/yr. (ISSN 1059-9274).
016.5 Science—Periodicals—Indexes [BKL] 91-2480

Facts On File adds to its list of news-digest indexes by introducing this series, which focuses on science articles of popular interest including advancements in technology, medicine, and the environment. The monthly subscription service is intended for junior high and high school students, but the articles in the two reviewed issues are geared to a lower reading level and could easily be used for research by intermediate-grade students. The editors have culled the information from more than 25 general and science periodicals. A year's subscription consists of 12 monthly issues, each 24 pages in length and numbered consecutively, a monthly cumulative index, and a binder. Four extra "teacher copies" of each issue are included.

The index, which includes a glossary, is arranged by subjects, which are capitalized in boldface print, making them easily identifiable, and a brief description of the article (not the title) with issue date and page(s). Articles listed under more than one subject are identified by a different description each time, which is misleading to users. As in other Facts On File news digests, index pages are a different color from the articles.

The articles are no more than three pages in length, with most less than two. Each one begins with an overview of the topic so that the reader is given the necessary background information. The longer articles are accompanied by black-and-white photographs or illustrations, and many include current suggested readings in books and magazines. In a subject area where currency is so vital, this source will provide students, middle school through lower-level high school, with up-to-date information in a readable, attractive format.

The Henry Holt Handbook of Current Science & Technology: A Sourcebook of Facts and Analysis Covering the Most Important Events in Science and Technology. By Bryan Bunch. Holt, 1992. 689p. index. hardcover $50 (0-8050-1829-8).
500 Science ‖ Technology [CIP] 92-6119

At first glance, this book appears to be just another *Advances in . . .* , *Progress on . . .* , or *Yearbook of . . .* type of book: interesting but not really that useful for reference. However, upon further scrutiny, it is full of general information on science and technology, as well as the latest developments for 1990 and 1991. For the general reader, it presents well-written articles on a wide variety of topics in astronomy, space, chemistry, earth sciences, environment, life sciences, mathematics, physics, and technology that have been in the sci-tech news. (Medicine is not covered.) In fact, one could easily read it all the way through as nonfiction.

The book is arranged the same for each broad subject area. First is a statement about the state of the subject in 1990–91. Next is a timetable or chronology of events pertinent to the subject, followed by the main article and subarticles that speak of developments in 1990 and 1991. For the reader who is not sci-tech literate, the article may contain set-off background material, where a particular development is historically described in a screened box so that the main article can be better understood. Included with the articles are tables, charts, and lists of useful data and references to further reading in newspapers and such journals as *Science*.

It is this material that makes this a useful reference handbook. Some 85 tables, charts, and chronologies cover such things as astronomical record holders (the largest, the farthest, the brightest), a list of major accomplishments of satellites and space probes, a chronology of earthquakes with magnitude and deaths, a list of volcanoes, a timetable for dioxin as a pollutant, a list of major indoor air pollutants, a table of major taxons, and a list of members of the National Inventors Hall of Fame. The appendixes include a bibliography with difficulty level indicated, obituaries of scientists and engineers for 1990 and 1991, and units of measure. There is a detailed index.

This is not a book that would be purchased in place of such excellent one-volume encyclopedias as the *McGraw-Hill Concise Encyclopedia of Science and Technology*. It will serve, however, as a companion to such encyclopedias, updating with the newest developments on a particular topic. This handbook is recommended for public, high school, and undergraduate libraries, especially those that have not been able to purchase new editions of more comprehensive and expensive encyclopedias.

The New Book of Popular Science. 6v. Grolier, 1992. bibliog. charts. illus. index. maps. tables. hardcover $219 (0-7172-1218-1).
500 Science—Popular works ‖ Technology—Popular works ‖ Natural history—Popular works [CIP] 91-38365

The last edition of *The New Book of Popular Science* was published in 1990 [RBB S 1 90]. Still organized in six volumes with a separate paperback index that duplicates the index in volume 6, the set is a standard in junior and senior high libraries. Volumes are thematic, with astronomy and math in volume 1; energy, environment, and the earth in volume 2; physical science and biology in volume 3; plants and animals in volume 4; mammals (including humans) in volume 5; and technology and the index in volume 6. Articles, which average about six pages, are signed, and a four-page list identifying contributors is found in volume 1. Few contributors have changed since 1990. Selected readings are found at the end of each volume. They have been slightly updated and are current.

Revision in this edition focused on the astronomy and space-science articles in volume 1. Among the new articles are *Uranus*, *Collapsed and Failed Stars*, and *The Early Sky Watchers*. Some new and appealing short articles are complete on two-page spreads, including *Dressing for Space* and *How Safe Is Space?* Rewritten articles include *Quasars and Energetic Galaxies* and *The Search for Extraterrestrial Life*. *Eyes on the Sky* describes defects in the Hubble Space Telescope. Another article notes a 1990 *Columbia* mission, and charts are updated to include new Nobel Prize winners and spaceflights through 1991.

Throughout the rest of the set, articles have been revised to note the growing rabies epidemic, the nuclear fusion debate, and other current news. Also noticeable in this edition is the extra attention to color in illustrations. Of the 216 new photographs, 168 are in color, as are most charts and diagrams now.

Writing, as usual, is clear, with many terms italicized and defined in the text. While the amount of revision this year is much higher than it was in 1990, libraries owning that set may find there is not enough updated material to justify replacing their set so soon. Libraries owning an earlier edition will want to consider purchase of this attractive set.

Science and Technology Desk Reference: 1,500 Answers to Frequently-Asked or Difficult-to-Answer Questions. Ed. by the Carnegie Library of Pittsburgh, Science and Technology Department. Gale, 1993. 575p. bibliog. illus. index. hardcover $39.95 (0-8103-8884-7).
500.02 Science—Handbooks, manuals, etc. ‖ Technology—Handbooks, manuals, etc. [OCLC]

Many libraries accumulate a special rolodex or vertical file, or maintain a computer database, of frequent or difficult questions they have answered. Following the success of the *New York Public Library Desk Reference* [RBB N 1 89], the Science and Technology Department of the Carnegie Library of Pittsburgh has stepped forward to share its treasure trove of information. The *Science and Technology Desk Reference* is an eclectic mix of questions and answers divided into 20 broad subject categories.

The 1,500 numbered entries are arranged into chapters covering such topics as "The Animal World"; "Bridges, Buildings, Etc."; "Food and Nutrition"; and "The Plant World." Within each chapter, the subject is further broken down. For instance, in "Weather and Climate," information is organized into sections covering air phenomena; snow, rain, hail, etc.; temperature; weather prediction; and wind. Each entry consists of the question, answer, and source(s). The diversity of the information provided in this desk reference is marked, although it does not include highly specialized or technical data. Questions range from "Which foods originated in the New World?" and "Why do cats' eyes shine in the dark?" to "How is Pascal's triangle used?" and "What is the fog index formula?"

Typically, answers are short, ranging from one sentence to a few paragraphs in length, although some extend to a couple of pages (e.g., the chart of terms for juvenile animals, the list of constellations and what they represent). The information can be specific, as in the answer to "How large is a googol?" While the response is "the number 1 followed by 100 zeros," this entry expands by discussing the origin of the term and the definition for a googolplex, and then providing a table showing other very large numbers. Answers can also be summaries of information on complex topics, for instance, the response to the question "How is nuclear waste stored?" Numerous charts, tables, and illustrations are included to help explain answers, as in the response to "Which biological events occurred during the geologic time divisions?"

Many of the sources cited for answers are commonly owned references, such as general and scientific encyclopedias, handbooks, dictionaries, almanacs, and other compendia, as well as popular monographs. Not infrequently, however, answers were found in periodical literature (e.g., *Cornell Animal Health Newsletter*, *Nature*, *Pennsylvania Woodland News*) or in such specialized tools as *Essentials of Dermatology*, *Egg Science and Technology*, and *The BOCA National Building Code*. Complete citations are provided to periodical articles on the page where the answer is printed; abbreviated information is shown there for monographs and multivolume works, with all imprint details included in a bibliography in the rear of the book.

In the subject index, where question numbers are used to refer to the body of the text, information on Melvin Calvin, for instance, can be found by name and under *Nobel prize winners* and *photosynthesis*. Generally, the index works well, but it may be that a thorough browsing of the book will better prepare staff to use it most effectively. For example, the question about googols is indexed under *googol and googolplex*, but not under *numbers*. However, familiarity with the "Mathematics, Numbers, and Computers" chapter would help the user recall that it contains information about large numbers. Also, the index does not include references to the 16-page chronology, listing highlights of inventions and discoveries, that opens the text.

The *Science and Technology Desk Reference* is a low-cost and easy-to-use compilation with answers for many common inquiries, as well as for some questions that are difficult and unusual. Small libraries will want this tool because they may not own all the resources cited, and large libraries will find it useful in eliminating some time-consuming searches in numerous references. It is recommended for high school, public, and academic library collections.

Academic Press Dictionary of Science and Technology. Ed. by Christopher Morris. Academic Press, 1992. 2,432p. illus. hardcover $115 (0-12-200400-0).
503 Science—Dictionaries || Technology—Dictionaries [CIP] 90-29032

Several excellent science and technology dictionaries and desk encyclopedias have been published in the last four years, including McGraw-Hill's *Dictionary of Scientific and Technical Terms* (4th ed. [RBB Je 1 89]), *Chambers Science and Technical Dictionary* (Cambridge, 1988), *Van Nostrand's Scientific Encyclopedia* (7th ed. [RBB My 1 89]), and the *McGraw-Hill Concise Encyclopedia of Science and Technology* (2d ed. [RBB S 15 89]). All have had favorable reviews, and each, to some extent, provides definitions of unique terms and has varying methods of presenting the information. Since Academic Press is a major publisher of science and technology information, it is only natural that it would produce its own one-volume reference tool.

This large 2,432-page dictionary has a place on all reference shelves, even if the aforementioned titles are owned. This outstanding work covers 124 fields of science and technology from acoustical engineering to cartography, graphic arts, microbiology, organic chemistry, radiology, and zoology. Each of the fields has a brief "window" essay, written by an authority, defining the field, presenting some historical facts, and indicating its current emphases and applications.

The dictionary is easy to use with as few complicated instructions as possible. Entries are listed alphabetically letter by letter. There are entries for single words and compound words, abbreviations and acronyms, proper names, and geographic terms. Brief biographical entries include years of birth and death (if applicable). Pronunciation is given for terms where the spoken form of the word may be in question. Each entry has one of the 124 scientific fields assigned to it to further help in understanding the definition. Also included for some entries are etymology, variant spellings, and plural forms of the word. There is a generous use of cross-referencing.

The definitions are concise and written on a professional level but can be understood by high school users as well. Illustrations are usually crisp and clear; 24 pages are in full color. Appendixes include symbols and units, fundamental physical constants, measurement conversions, the periodic table, atomic weights of the elements, Solar System data, a geologic timetable, classification of organisms, and a chronology of modern science, including an entry for 1992.

Comparing the Academic Press volume with those from McGraw-Hill, Van Nostrand, and Cambridge, the work under review provides the most comprehensive coverage of terminology, with more than 125,000 entries produced over four years through the efforts of more than 400 experts. Terms were gleaned from specialized encyclopedias, dictionaries, and glossaries; textbooks and professional books; and journals and scientific periodicals. The *Academic Press Dictionary of Science and Technology* captures the terminology of today and gives modern definitions. This dictionary is highly recommended for all public, academic, and high school libraries.

The Concise Illustrated Dictionary of Science and Technology. By Stan Gibilisco. TAB, 1993. 520p. illus. hardcover $36.95 (0-8306-4152-1); paper $24.95 (0-8306-4153-X).
503 Science—Dictionaries || Technology—Dictionaries [CIP] 92-22545

With such outstanding dictionaries as the *Academic Press Dictionary of Science and Technology* [RBB Ja 15 93], one might wonder why *The Concise Illustrated Dictionary of Science and Technology* was published. The overriding reasons are audience and affordability. This dictionary is intended for students at the junior and senior high school level and, in that context, it is an excellent dictionary. It includes more than 5,000 terms that students will encounter in their reading, such as *pie graph, greenhouse effect, integrated circuit, power plant, creationism*, and *group therapy*. The definitions are nonthreatening and easy to follow and include the most common terms from astronomy, chemistry, earth science, engineering, life science, mathematics, and physics. A few biographical entries are included, and some common abbreviations are entered in the main alphabet.

There is ample use of *see* and *see also* references, and several tables and charts are included as appendixes, such as animal classification, geologic time, Morse code, primate family tree, and trigonometric identities. The word *Concise* in the title is well suited, but the word *Illustrated* may not be as appropriate. Illustrations average only one per page, but they are well drawn, clear, and always near the word being defined. This is a recommended dictionary for any school library and would be appropriate for small public and home libraries. It is not intended to replace any of the scholarly works published by Academic Press, Van Nostrand Reinhold, or McGraw-Hill.

McGraw-Hill Encyclopedia of Science & Technology. 20v. 7th ed. Ed. by Sybil P. Parker. McGraw-Hill, 1992. bibliog. illus. index. hardcover $1,900 (0-07-909206-3).
503 Science—Encyclopedias || Technology—Encyclopedias [CIP] 91-36349

The only general-purpose, multivolume scientific encyclopedia for adults currently on the market, the *McGraw-Hill Encyclopedia of Science & Technology* has been published regularly for over 30 years. Previous editions have generally been reviewed favorably by RBB [RBB S 15 87]. The current one is similar in format and style to earlier versions and will be very familiar to users of any previous edition.

Parker remains the editor in chief, as she has for the past two editions. Some additions have been made in the editorial staff, bringing new personnel into the project for the first time in 10 years. Approximately 7 percent of the 3,000 contributors are new to this edition. While most of the contributors are academics, the editors have also made an effort to recruit writers from industry. The encyclopedia is international in scope, with articles written by scientists from around the world. Twenty-one Nobel Prize winners contributed to the set.

The objective of the seventh edition remains the same as the previous six: to offer up-to-date, authoritative, and comprehensive coverage of each of the disciplines in science and engineering. To meet this goal, the editors have tried to keep up with the constant changes in scientific knowledge. The encyclopedia continues to be a work *of* science and not *about* science. It contains articles on theoretical, applied, and experimental scientific research but specifically excludes material of a purely historical, biographical, or sociological nature. Similarly, the encyclopedia concentrates only on well-established scientific theory and applications. It does not contain information on subjects not considered to be in the mainstream of the scientific establishment, such as creationism, astrology, or New Age science. While avoiding these topics maintains the scientific integrity of the work, it also excludes some subjects of great interest to readers. For example, the "cold fusion" debate, which made headlines worldwide as a potential advancement in the field of physics, is completely ignored here.

The main body of the seventh edition contains approximately 7,500 entries. A random sample of entries from the sixth and seventh editions reveals the extent of revision of the set. Approximately 4 percent of the articles studied are new to the seventh edition. Each of these articles is a lengthy review of a topic of current interest, such as *Aircraft Design* and *Chaos*. Six percent of the articles in the sample have been significantly lengthened and revised. Once again, these articles tend to be topics of current interest, such as *Optical Recording* and *Optical Communications*.

To make room for the newer and longer articles, approximately 10 percent of the entries have been significantly shortened. These articles tend to discuss technologies of the past (*Airships*), areas in which little change has occurred (*Butter* and *Chlorine*), or topics that are no longer being heavily investigated (*Oil Shale*). Although it is unfortunate that the editors must drop some previous material, the choices made for reductions appear to be sound. Readers interested in older technologies or scientific concepts can refer to the previous editions of the encyclopedia. In addition to these reductions, approximately 200 entries have been dropped entirely from the seventh edition. It appears that relevant material from these entries has been incorporated into related articles. For example, material formerly contained in the entry *Terrestrial Frozen Water* is now combined with related material in the article *Ice*. Once again, entries that have been eliminated represent topics not of current emphasis in the sciences.

Many of the articles have been revised to include recent information but have not changed significantly in length. Some entries, such as *Agricultural Soil and Crop Practices*, have been updated to incorporate new procedures while at the same time eliminating older material. Others, such as *Nuclear Power*, received only minor revisions reflecting changes in government regulations regarding power plants. Approximately 15 percent of all the entries in the encyclopedia received such revision.

Finally, the bibliographies of many otherwise unrevised articles have been updated. Over 18 percent of all of the entries received such treatment, with the latest dates of publication in the updated bibliographies ranging from 1987 to 1990. In most cases, the bibliographic references are to texts, reference works, and standard reviews of the topic. Some bibliographies contain journal article citations, but only when books do not adequately cover the field.

More than 13,000 illustrations are used to supplement the text of the entries. The vast majority consist of two-color tables, charts, and drawings or black-and-white photographs. They are helpful to the reader, although not extremely attractive. The editors have made an attempt to vary the background colors of the illustrations, but this is done only from volume to volume, so that all illustrations within any one volume use the same color scheme. A few full-color plates are included within each volume but not in sufficient number to greatly enhance the overall appearance of the work. The editors state that over 1,900 illustrations have been revised or added to the seventh edition. From the sample of articles examined, no changes in illustrations were noted except in cases where an article had received a significant amount of revision. Even many articles that did receive significant revisions have not received any update in illustration. One noticeable physical change in the set's format is the reduction in size of the typeface. Although it is large enough to be readable without discomfort, it is slightly smaller than that used in the sixth edition.

Readers of this work will require a significant knowledge of the sciences to be able to fully comprehend entries. Many require a high-level knowledge of calculus and other advanced mathematical skills, such as the ability to read partial differential equations. Most of the chemistry articles rely heavily on chemical equations and structures. Electronics articles use circuit diagrams, and nearly every entry of any significance requires the reader to interpret at least one chart or diagram. High-school students and the nonscientific layperson may be able to understand parts of an entry, but complete comprehension will be limited to persons with a college science background.

Three indexes are included in this encyclopedia. A standard alphabetical index of over 160,000 terms refers readers to all articles with information of interest. In cases where the topic is a separate article in the encyclopedia, the index entry is marked with an asterisk. In addition, the set also contains a topical index and a study guide. The topical index lists all of the article titles related to a certain broad subject area, such as *Immunology*, *Psychiatry*, or *Theoretical Physics*. The study guide provides outlines of major scientific fields, such as chemistry, biology, or physics. Within each outline, entries on related topics are listed together. For example, by using the "Geosciences" study guide it is possible to identify that glaciology, seismology, and volcanology are all branches of geophysics and that the set contains separate articles on each of these topics. In general, the study guides are more detailed and more useful to the reader than the topical index.

This work remains one of the standard sources for scientific and technical information. Since almost two-thirds of the entries have received no textual changes (other than their bibliographies) since the sixth edition, some libraries that already own that edition may not need to invest in this one. However, the rapid pace of change in science and technology has resulted in significant revision of many articles. Any library serving college-level science students or practicing scientists should consider this work. High school libraries serving advanced science students will want to consider replacing the sixth edition too.

Nature Projects On File: Experiments, Demonstrations, and Projects for School and Home. By the Diagram Group. Facts On File, 1992. charts. illus. index. tables. loose-leaf $145 (0-8160-2705-6).
508 Natural history—Experiments ‖ Environmental protection—Experiments ‖ Natural history—Study and teaching—Activity programs ‖ Science projects [CIP] 91-40846

Similar in purpose and format to *Science Experiments On File* [RBB Je 1 89], *Nature Projects On File* contains "interesting, challenging, inexpensive, fun experiments covering a wide range of biological and environmental topics" for students in grades 4 to 12. The 74 experiments can be used by students independently or by teachers to supplement classroom texts. These easy projects are simply explained, enabling children to do many of them at home with minimum adult supervision. Following the table of contents, an introduction, and safety guidelines, the projects are organized into eight sections: earth, weather, animals, plants, ecology, population, energy, and environmental quality. For each project there is a brief introduction, the time and materials needed, a reminder about safety precautions, and step-by-step instructions for conducting the experiment. An appendix lists the appropriate grade level for each experiment, but this information would be more useful within the project itself. The projects are enhanced by line drawings and include data tables on which students record their findings. Students are encouraged to photocopy the data tables before doing so. Each project concludes with analysis questions and instructs students to compare their findings with the author's in the "Our Findings" section near the back of the volume. The pollution section includes experiments that measure residues from cigarette smoke (under adult supervision), corrosion caused by acid rain, and pollution in streams and rivers. The plant projects demonstrate how seeds are dispersed by humans and how to determine the age of trees, for example. A section of identification charts precedes the appendixes and contains simple line drawings of worms, snails, and insects; animals found in ponds; cloud types; and mushrooms and toadstools. Appendixes identify the grade level of each project, list those projects that require adult supervision, state which projects can be done by individuals or by two or more persons, and list those that can be completed in one hour or less. An index refers users to section and project numbers. Browsing through the projects makes even an adult reviewer curious about their outcomes. For instance, in building and observing a worm farm, what really happens to the separate soil layers? Incidentally, after this project is completed, students are instructed to "carefully return the worms by taking your worm farm outside and gently shaking out the contents onto soft ground." *Nature Projects On File* will be popular with teachers, students, and parents and is highly recommended for public and middle and high school libraries.

The Way Nature Works. Macmillan, 1992. 359p. illus. index. hardcover $35 (0-02-508110-1).
508 Natural history—Encyclopedia || Science—Encyclopedias [CIP] 92-12283

The Way Nature Works is a fascinating foray into the variety of earth and biological sciences. It is divided into nine sections: "Shaping the Planet" (plate tectonics, volcanoes, mountains, ice ages, water bodies, etc.); "The Power of the Atmosphere" (weather, seasons, ozone, etc.); "Evolution and Adaptation" (DNA, planets, animals, etc.); "Reproducing to Survive"; "The Search for Food"; "Movement and Shelter"; "Attack and Defense"; "Senses and Communication"; and "The Living Environments" (ecosystems, pollution, etc.).

Individual topics are treated on two facing pages, introduced in a single boldface paragraph. More specific text follows and takes up about one-third of the total page space. Large, lifelike illustrations, accompanied by additional narrative, occupy the remaining space. The explanations are easy to follow and refer to numbered or lettered parts of the diagrams. Unfamiliar terms are in italics and are defined in the text. At the bottom of each page are "Connections" to related topics with their page numbers. The first page of each chapter lists, in order, the specific topics to be covered. Some also have such helpful charts as the geologic time scale, the Beaufort Wind Scale, and the classification of plants and animals.

A few problems are noted in this otherwise beautiful work. First, because the larger illustrations for each topic cross the binding, some of the detail is lost and the effect is distorted. Measurements are given in customary units with the metric equivalent in parenthesis. While a four-page glossary is included, the reader must rely on contextual definitions for many of the scientific terms. No pronounciation guide is provided either in the text or the glossary. The index is extensive but not exhaustive, and a few editing and proofreading errors were noted.

On the whole, *The Way Nature Works* is an excellent addition to the science reference collection for its unique and comprehensive treatment of the natural world and the beauty of its design. For science students in the sixth to ninth grades, it will be popular as a browsing book and useful for the clarity of its explanations. Its low cost makes it affordable for school and public libraries.

Who's Who in Science and Engineering, 1992–1993. Reed Publishing, 1992. 1,084p. indexes. hardcover $199 (0-8379-5751-6).
509 Scientists—U.S.—Biography || Scientists—Canada—Biography || Engineers—U.S.—Biography || Engineers—Canada—Biography [BKL] 92-80582

This work is the first from Marquis Who's Who that is designed to cover science and engineering. Like the other publications in this famous series, each entry provides highlights from the life of the biographee. Standard information for each person includes current address, birth date and place, family members, education, and a complete career history. Additional information provided when relevant includes awards received, publications, military service, association memberships, and significant professional achievements. The directory also provides material that may be interesting to readers but which is not directly relevant to the scientific careers of the subjects, including religion, political affiliation, and community service.

This volume includes 22,000 living scientists from 70 nations. A sample of entries reveals that about 80 percent of them are from the U.S. While the majority of the entries are for researchers and practitioners in the hard sciences, a few noteworthy individuals from the social sciences and humanities are also included. Entries are arranged alphabetically by name, with indexes by discipline and geographic location. An appendix lists recent major award winners in the sciences.

The primary competition to this work comes from *American Men and Women of Science* (AMWS), published by Bowker, another division of Reed Publishing, which also owns Marquis Who's Who. The current edition includes over 120,000 scientists and engineers, over five times the number in *Who's Who in Science and Engineering* (WWSE). AMWS provides virtually the same biographical information as WWSE, except for some details of personal information. The subject areas and geographic coverage are also quite similar. Both concentrate on U.S. scientists in the hard sciences but include distinguished persons from other nations and notable researchers in other fields. Both sources contain an index by discipline, although only WWSE has a geographic index.

The result of comparing these two works is a surprising lack of overlap between them. In a study of random names selected from WWSE, less than one-third of them appeared in AMWS, despite the fact that it is much larger. There also appears to be no distinct pattern as to why persons were omitted from one source or another. From the sample studied, WWSE appears to include a slightly higher percentage of women and foreign scientists and more science educators, whereas AMWS seems to concentrate more on practicing scientists. The long-standing reputation of AMWS as the primary source for scientific biography will be difficult to change, but the Board's study shows that WWSE contains a significant amount of information not found in AMWS. At $199, WWSE is slightly more than one-fourth the price of AMWS.

The differences between these two works make recommendations difficult. Those libraries that require comprehensive biographical coverage of scientists will want to purchase both titles. Libraries that have been purchasing AMWS for years may wish to continue that subscription to maintain consistency in their collection. However, those that do not frequently receive requests for this type of information could save some money by switching to WWSE. Unfortunately, neither work provides a clear advantage over the other.

The Numbers You Need. By Nigel J. Hopkins and others. Gale, 1992. 354p. bibliog. charts. illus. index. tables. hardcover $29.95 (0-8103-8373-X).
513'.0212 Mathematics [CIP] 92-4305

Practical handbooks such as this one are often only as good as their indexing and table of contents. In this case, both are very good and the result is an easy-to-use, well-organized source of all manner of numerical information and, most important, *how* to interpret it. At home, work, and play we are often faced with many kinds of statistics and formulas that might require searching through mathematics textbooks for explanation (often without success). Here in a single compact volume can be found everything from windchill factors and card-game odds to kitchen calculations and sports scoring.

The information is organized in nine chapters devoted to themes such as health, gambling, weather, and sports. Each of these chapters is further subdivided. For example, the sports chapter is divided according to sport, and the weather chapter includes subsections on temperature scales, pollution, earthquakes, etc. Following the main body of text are three appendixes with further explanations of units of measurement, money matters (e.g., compound interest, present value), and the use of tables, graphs, and statistics. Also included are suggestions for further reading, grouped by chapter. Finally, a carefully prepared index allows easy access to the myriad concepts found in the book.

The closest comparable source is Mary Blocksma's *Reading the Numbers* (Viking, 1989). Her entries are presented in a straight alphabetical arrangement and receive a more narrative treatment than in *The Numbers You Need*. There is also a detailed index as well as a bibliography of sources for further reading. A quick check, however, finds a number of items in *Reading the Numbers* that are not found in *The Numbers You Need*: Roman numerals, sandpaper grades, and time zones. Blocksma's explanation of Social Security numbers here actually tells what (that is, where) those first three digits stand for. *Reading the Numbers*, however, lacks one of the best features of *The Numbers You Need*: a perpetual calendar.

All in all, *The Numbers You Need* is a concise, crisply packaged quantity of information. It would be a welcome addition to general reference collections or home libraries (even those owning *Reading the Numbers*). After all, any reference librarian knows that there is at least one other place (remember the *World Almanac*?) where a perpetual calendar and explanation of Roman numerals may be found. For home users, a paperback edition is available as *Go Figure* in Gale's Visible Ink line ($16.95, 0-8103-9424-3).

Religious Holidays and Calendars: An Encyclopaedic Handbook. By Aidan Kelly and others. Omnigraphics, 1993. 150p. bibliog. indexes. tables. hardcover $60 (1-55888-348-7).

529'.3 Calendars—History || Fasts and feasts [OCLC] 92-41189

This handbook combines information on the history of lunar and solar calendars with encyclopedic entries for the holidays of major and minor religious groups. Covered are numerous holy days from such world religions as Buddhism, Christianity, Judaism, Hinduism, and Islam. Also included are entries for less widely observed occasions, for example, *Volunteers of America Founder's Day* and *Parsi Remembrance of the Departed*, which is celebrated by the Persian sect of Zoroastrianism. Although the scope of the work is broad, it does not attempt to include all the saints' days of the Roman Catholic and Orthodox traditions.

The first part of the book, "The History of Calendars," consists of five essays designed to assist the reader in understanding the origin of religious holidays, the evolution of calendars, and various rules set by different societies for measuring time and designating special days. These essays discuss and explain both Eastern and Western traditions, the ancient calendars of Egypt and Rome, and calendar reforms in the modern era. Many tables are included, such as one for the Baha'i calendar that gives the names of special events, corresponding dates in the Western calendar, and the name of each month's first day.

The largest part of the book presents approximately 300 entries in alphabetical order ranging in length from one sentence to more than one page. Each entry contains the name of the holiday, the date on which it is celebrated, and a brief discussion of its history and current practice. Words from other languages are translated or explained, and, occasionally, entries end with *see also* references. Included in the main alphabetic sequence are *see* references that direct the reader to the correct form of the entry. For example, a cross-reference is included from *Water Drawing Festival* to *Omizutori Matsuri*, where one can find information about this two-week period of meditation observed by Buddhists in Nara, Japan.

Following the dictionary portion of the book is a bibliography of more than 100 sources that were used in preparing the introductory essays and entries. Three indexes are included. One gives a monthly index of holidays covered in the book; a second is organized by name of religion with a list of the associated holidays for each. Also provided is a master index of all persons, holidays, events, and terms mentioned in the book.

While this work does not claim to be comprehensive, it was somewhat disappointing to find only scant mention of animism, Shintoism, and Chinese folk religions. It seems curious, in the limited space of 150 pages, to find that *Abbey Fair*, a local monastic fair celebrated by the Abbey of Regina Laudis in Bethlehem, Connecticut, is given lengthier coverage than the national week-long holiday *Kwanza*. The lengthiest entries are devoted to commonplace information about the major holidays of Christians, such as *Christmas* and *Easter*, whereas further explanation would have improved the entries for some of the observances of nonwestern faiths, for instance, the Hindu *Pooram*.

Still, the scope of this book is unique in its coverage of not only holidays of both major and minor religions, but in relating them to the religious influence in the evolution of various calendars. The text of *Religious Holidays and Calendars* is carefully worded to give the reader instant identification of the religion associated with a holiday. The thoughtful essays are a valuable aid in providing a context for the observances of unfamiliar religions, as well as a reference tool on the major calendars of the world. This convenient compilation should be given purchase consideration by high school, public, and undergraduate libraries.

The Economist Desk Companion: How to Measure, Convert, Calculate and Define Practically Anything. Holt, 1992. 272p. index. tables. hardcover $40 (0-8050-2380-1).

530.81 Weights and measures—Tables || Metric system || Mensuration—Conversion tables [OCLC] 92-53161

This work was "developed from" the 1980 *World Measurement Guide* [RBB D 15 83]. It updates, revises, and expands the coverage of the previous volume. Both works were prepared by staff of the well-known British financial paper and are especially intended for those engaged in business, technical communications, and international commerce. The companion is "designed to provide quick, accessible information on every area of international measurement." While the coverage is international, the emphasis is on U.S., U.K., and metric measurements, and U.S. readers will notice a British slant to the work.

The book is organized into four parts plus an alphabetical index to assist in accessing the information. Part 1 is an introduction to the metric, English, and American systems of measurement. This short section includes definitions and various tables for converting time, velocity, length, mass, capacity, volume, etc.

The second, and largest, part lists definitions, special measurements, formulas, and calculations for 24 subject categories, such as agriculture, fishing and forestry, chemistry, food and drink, health, iron and steel, mineral alloys, sound and music, transport, and weapons. Much information is included in these well-organized sections. For instance, the five pages devoted to "Energy" begin with a section of measures that provide conversions between various energy and power units (e.g., calorie, therm, horsepower, kilowatt, BTU) as well as tables of energy equivalents and contents for various fuels. This is followed by subsections specifically covering oil, natural gas, coal, and electricity; these provide definitions of terms, tables, and other useful facts. For example, the conversion of one barrel of oil into 158.987 liters and 42 U.S. gallons is given, as are tables that classify coal by fixed carbon and by heat content.

Part 3 consists of 72 pages of conversion tables. It begins with four pages summarizing formulas for the conversion of various items (e.g., to convert BTU's to watts, multiply by 0.2930171). This is followed by detailed tables for length, area, volume, weight, pressure, and temperature and then for measures specific to nine industries, such as engineering, finance, and iron and steel. Some of these conversions are miles to kilometers, grams to ounces, tonnes to U.K. and U.S. bushels, plant spacing (square or rectangular), joules to foot pounds-force, measurement of alcoholic strength by density, and centimeters of water to kilopascals.

Part 4 consists of appendixes that provide a table of common abbreviations and symbols, rough conversions of metric to U.S. and U.K. imperial measures, and a history of measurements for the U.K. that begins with 410 A.D. Also included is an alphabetically arranged, 18-page table of 2,100 local units of measurement, with metric equivalents, for both industrialized and Third World countries. This section is both unique and interesting. One can easily determine that a *cuadra* in Spain equals 125.4 meters, while that same unit of measurement in Uruguay equals only 85.9 meters. In Brunei, Malaysia, and Singapore, one *bhara* is equivalent to 181.4 kilograms in all three countries.

Many of the basic conversions, formulas, and definitions provided by this work are also in such sources as the *Information Please Almanac* or the *World Almanac*. *Conversion Factors*, by James L. Cook (Oxford, 1991), includes hundreds of different conversions. However, these sources lack information about local measurements throughout the world and do not have the business emphasis of *The Economist Desk Companion*. Any library that receives questions about how to convert one measurement to another that cannot be answered with almanac sources will want to consider purchasing this handy compilation.

Minerals of the World. By Walter Schumann. Sterling, 1992. 224p. illus. index. hardcover $19.95 (0-8069-8570-4).

549 Minerals—Handbooks, manuals, etc. || Minerals—Identification—Handbooks, manuals, etc. [OCLC] 91-42362

Over 500 of the most collectible minerals are represented in full-color photographs in this field guide, which was originally published in Germany under the title *Mineralien aus aller Welt* in 1990. Schumann has also written *Gemstones of the World* (Sterling, 1977) and *Minerals and Rocks* (Chatto & Windus, 1978). He states that while there are more than 3,000 known minerals with many variations, this title includes only those found in abundance and typically of interest to collectors.

The introduction explains the identification system in which minerals are organized based on measurable properties that include streak or powder color, Mohs' hardness, and specific gravity. External shapes of minerals are briefly discussed, and structure of minerals, crystal systems, twinning in crystals, and mineral aggregates are detailed. Another section describes luster, tenacity, magnetism, florescence, and other mineral characteristics.

Designed to be a manual to identify minerals based upon observational information, the body of the text is arranged by streak color or the inherent color when the mineral is pulverized—white and colorless, green, grey and black, etc. Approximately four minerals are detailed on each two-page spread. The left-hand page contains bar charts noting the streak, Mohs' hardness, and specific gravity or relative density for each mineral. The text, also on the left-hand pages, is brief in keeping with the field-guide approach and notes aggregates, minerals accompanied by, location, and similar minerals. Photographs on right-hand pages are not examples of museum-quality minerals but rather samples that a typical collector might encounter. Those that have been enlarged to show detail have notations in the form of a ratio. A glossary and index complete the work.

A Field Guide to Rocks and Minerals, fourth edition, in the Peterson Field Guide series (Houghton, 1976) provides drawings of the crystal structure for individual rocks and minerals. However, the illustrations are contained in a section of plates apart from the text in the center of the book, and many are in black and white. The Audubon Society Field Guide to North American Rocks and Minerals by Charles W. Chesterman (Knopf, 1978) contains full-color illustrations of the minerals arranged by color, comprising the first half of the title, while the descriptions and scientific information follow. Not a field guide, The Encyclopedia of Gemstones and Minerals [RBB Mr 15 92] is arranged alphabetically and presents information in a form that allows for the study of minerals within the context of nature rather than as collectibles.

Minerals of the World offers wider coverage, side-by-side presentation of full-color photography and complementing text, and easy identification of minerals based on observational information. It will be a useful handbook for the hobbiest or naturalist and a valuable addition for most libraries.

An Illustrated Guide to Rocks & Minerals. By Michael O'Donoghue. Smithmark, 1992. 192p. bibliog. illus. index. hardcover $24.98 (0-8317-6389-2).
552 Mineralogy || Rocks [OCLC]

O'Donoghue was a curator of earth sciences, technology, and industry at the British Library. He has authored numerous books, including Encyclopedia of Minerals and Gemstones (1976), and edits the Gemmological Newsletter. He created An Illustrated Guide to Rocks & Minerals as an introduction to the major rock and mineral species and as an inspiration for further field investigation. Included are 200 beautifully photographed specimens in full color from various natural history and mineralogical museums. These photographs capture the great beauty found in geologic activity and are the major strength of this work, which resembles a coffee-table book inasmuch as the pictures sometimes encompass more space on the page than does the text.

The book is divided into three main parts. Part 1 details the igneous, metamorphic, and sedimentary classifications of rocks. Part 2 is the largest section, containing discussions of mineral chemistry, crystals, minerals' value to man, and identification as well as the descriptions of specific minerals. Typical entries for each mineral are one page in length and include a photograph, chemical composition, hardness, specific gravity, refractive index, mode of occurrence in nature, and localities. The 96 minerals treated are listed according to the Natural History Museum's (London, England) Chemical Index of Minerals, which first lists the elements and then the various compounds. Part 3 includes a selected listing of major deposits (10 in the United States and 29 located internationally); names of museums in Canada, Czechoslovakia, Germany, Poland, the U.K., the U.S., and the Commonwealth of Independent States; and a bibliography, glossary, and index.

An Illustrated Guide to Rocks and Minerals is not a comprehensive field guide or a prospecting manual. While it may serve as an introduction to major species and may have superb photographs, patrons will be better served by other titles in the reference collection. The Encyclopedia of Gemstones and Minerals by Martin Holden [RBB Mr 15 92] more successfully provides a source of nonspecialist information, and Walter Schumann's Minerals of the World [RBB S 1 92] is a more useful and comprehensive handbook for the identification of 500 minerals.

Gemology: An Annotated Bibliography. 2v. By John Sinkankas. Scarecrow, 1993. 1,216p. index. hardcover $179.50 (0-8108-2652-6).
016.5538 Gems—Bibliography || Precious stones—Bibliography [CIP] 92-42847

This is destined to become a classic, since the name Sinkankas is synomous with gemology. His book Gem Cutting is still used as an authoritative text, and his Gemstones of North America, with its outstanding watercolor illustrations painted by the author, has been the reference source of choice on gems. Beginning in the 1940s, he began collecting books on gems and gemology until he amassed a collection of more than 14,000 volumes, many dating to the sixteenth and seventeenth centuries. This collection has formed the nucleus of the library at the Gemological Institute of America in Santa Monica, California, and has provided the information for this monumental work.

This is no ordinary bibliography. Each of its 7,500 entries is described in detail as if it were a rare book, providing numbered and unnumbered pagination, signatures, decoration, description of the cover, notes on paper quality, and other descriptive information. For current materials, a suggested price is given, and reviews of major works are also noted.

The work is arranged by author and then chronologically by title. For some authors, a brief biographical sketch is given. The books themselves are not only bibliographically described but also include a descriptive annotation that indicates their worthiness or, in some cases, unworthiness. Included are books, journals, articles, pamphlets, auction catalogs, technical papers of the U.S. and other governments, treatises, reprints, publicity booklets, sales catalogs, and other materials that contain information about gems. Materials cover cultural aspects of gems, including their ornamental and decorative use; technological aspects including mining, extracting, processing, cutting, marketing, and evaluation; and scientific aspects. Books in all languages are included; however, English is the most prevalent, with European languages next.

There are many illustrations, most of them title pages from books in the bibliography. The index is somewhat misleading, titled "Index of Entries," when actually it is a subject index. There is no other comparable book, making this a mandatory purchase for geology libraries, academic and large public libraries where there is interest in the subject, and personal libraries of gemologists.

Rand McNally Picture Atlas of Prehistoric Life. By Robert Muir Wood. Rand McNally, 1992. 64p. illus. index. hardcover $16.95 (0-528-83525-4).
560 Animal, Fossil—Juvenile literature || Plants, Fossil—Juvenile literature [CIP] 92-5761

The development of life on Earth is presented in 26 double-page spreads, each colorfully depicting a different era. Despite Atlas in the title, illustrations and text dominate in this work. Small maps are used to illustrate points made in the text (e.g., the distribution of the animals discussed, or the pattern of wind movements).

An introduction explains why Earth, alone among the planets, hosts life and depicts extant animals that originated at different time periods. Brief chapters explain such topics as evolution, fossil formation, and the reconstruction of dinosaur skeletons, as well as the ages of fish, reptiles, and mammals. One or more paragraphs of basic information are typographically prominent on each subject, with paragraphs offering greater detail in smaller print and less prominently positioned. Each chapter includes a geologic time scale, highlighted to show the era under discussion. The book concludes with a brief glossary and a topical index.

Both the author and illustrator Tim Hayward of the Picture Atlas have previous experience with children's science books, including material about prehistoric animals. In this volume, scientific explanations are consistent with those found in adult publications (e.g., asteroids as the probable cause of dinosaurs' extinction). Some of the explanations in this work are unique for a children's book, for example, the genetic code's role in evolution and the movement of tectonic plates altering climates and landscapes, necessitating adaptation by animals. The book addresses other questions not often asked in juvenile literature about prehistoric life, such as why Ireland has no snakes and what we can expect in the way of future evolution. Since children are usually fascinated by prehistoric animals, this work could prove useful in arousing their interest in other scientific matters.

As a reference tool, *The Macmillan Illustrated Encyclopedia of Dinosaurs and Prehistoric Life* [RBB Mr 15 89], discussing 600 species of animals, treats the subject in greater detail than does the work under review. However, the profuse illustrations, text arrangement, and clarity of scientific explanations make the *Picture Atlas of Prehistoric Life* usable at many levels of interest and reading ability. This reasonably priced *Picture Atlas* is recommended for the circulating collections of all elementary school libraries and public libraries needing additional material on the subject.

The Cambridge Encyclopedia of Human Evolution. Ed. by Steve Jones and others. Cambridge, 1992. 506p. bibliog. charts. illus. index. hardcover $95 (0-521-32370-3).
573.2 Human evolution—Encyclopedias [OCLC] 92-18037

What makes us human? *The Cambridge Encyclopedia of Human Evolution* draws on the expertise of more than 70 scholars to answer this question, placing modern humans in evolutionary perspective. Divided into 10 parts, such as patterns of primate evolution, the primate fossil record, and early human behavior and ecology, this book resembles a textbook more than an encyclopedia. Each part is further subdivided into such topics as classification of primates, evolution of apes, and how bones reveal diet.

Articles average three to five pages in length and include a variety of black-and-white photographs, graphs, and drawings. Each article is signed by a leading academic in the field. *See* references are used at the end of each article to connect related articles within the volume; however, no references exist to outside sources or primary literature. The volume also provides three appendixes: select biographical information on historical figures, a geologic time scale, and a world map of relevant research sites. The encyclopedia ends with a useful glossary, an excellent list of further readings, and a strong index.

Many library reference collections will already include Milner's *Encyclopedia of Evolution* [RBB Ja 1 91] and *The Encyclopedia of Human Evolution and Prehistory*, edited by Tattersall [RBB Fe 1 89]. Both these volumes approach the topic of human evolution with brief articles presented in alphabetical order. They provide quicker access and often unique information on such concepts as aggregation dispersal or on methodology, such as cladistics. In contrast, *The Cambridge Encyclopedia* covers human ecology through broad topical articles. Topically, this new encyclopedia seems stronger on most behavior issues and provides more extensive attention to the evolution and ecology of relevant living primates, such as lemurs and monkeys. In addition, it is more up-to-date on such controversies as "Mitochondrial Eve." The academic approach and article length of *The Cambridge Encyclopedia of Human Evolution* will appeal most to university and research libraries.

The Great Book of the Sea: A Complete Guide to Marine Life. By Francesco Guerrini. Running Press/Courage, 1993. 280p. illus. index. maps. hardcover $29.98 (1-56138-270-1).
574.92 Marine fauna ‖ Marine biology [OCLC] 92-54935

This comprehensive guide to marine life was orginally published in Italy in 1988. Author Guerrini is director of the Museum of Natural History in Naples, Italy. The introduction discusses the marine environment; adaptation as related to osmoregulation, feeding habits, visual organs and luminescense, sound, balancing, coloration and mimicry, colony formation, and symbiosis; the benthros, plankton, and nekton; pollution; zoogeography; and fishing methods and regulations.

Invertebrates are covered in a 26-page section; 160 pages are devoted to fish, including well-known and lesser-known kinds. A small section on reptiles covers sea turtles, the yellow-bellied sea snake, and the estuarine crocodile. The 20-page portion on birds includes penguins, tropic birds, brown booby, frigate bird, common gull, and puffin. Prefacing the discussion of each bird is a brief fact section covering such items as order, family, length, weight, and distribution. The final 28-page section of the volume concentrates on mammals—whales, seals, walrus, dugong, and manatee. The informative text is accurate and written in an easy-to-follow style.

More than 1,000 attractive, full-color, accurate illustrations give clarity and immediacy to the text. The information-filled captions accompanying the illustrations have added appeal. In addition to showing the marine forms individually, there are numerous smaller pictures depicting development, habits, etc. Geographic-distribution maps accompany most of the entries.

In this generous-sized book the pages lie flat when the volume is opened. Scientific and common names are given for entries; measurements are in customary and metric. There is a full index. Relatively inexpensive, *The Great Book of the Sea* should prove a valuable, easy-to-use reference on a great variety of creatures who live in and around the oceans for junior high students to adults.

Animal Life: A Prentice Hall Illustrated Dictionary. By Martin Walters and others. Prentice Hall, 1992. 160p. illus. hardcover $19 (0-13-681719-X).
591'.03 Zoology—Dictionaries, Juvenile [CIP] 92-19466

This illustrated dictionary provides more than 800 entries covering microorganisms, insects, amphibians, reptiles, fish, prehistoric life-forms, and mammals. Entries are also included for body parts and processes, such as *spine* and *hibernation*. The book was first published in Great Britain as *The Illustrated Dictionary of Animal Life*. Targeted to nine- through fourteen-year-olds, this dictionary is one of a series; other titles include *Earth Sciences* and *Science and Technology*.

Information varies from entry to entry and may include facts about habitat, reproduction, communication, and survival strategies of the animal being described. Family and species information is sometimes given. Entries are generally concise and readable. Some topics, such as *metamorphosis*, are given one- or two-page coverage, but most have three to five sentences. The part of speech is given for each entry, boldface type designates cross-references, and guidewords are given for each page. As may be surmised, most entries are nouns, but some adjectives, such as *prehensile* or *aerial*, can be found. Each letter has its own color that is carried through the section by a bar at the tops of pages. Realistically drawn and colored illustrations are present for about 225 entries. The animals covered represent all parts of the world. Some of them, however, such as *addax* (a kind of antelope) or *lory* (a bird) seem esoteric for children. Although each page carries approximately seven entries, the layout does not appear cluttered.

The authors are identified by name only. It would have been helpful to know the areas of expertise of the contributors. Child consumers should be accorded the same respect as that provided for adult readers in the matter of giving the credentials and authority of the authors.

The Kingfisher Illustrated Encyclopedia of Animals [RBB O 15 92] covers more than 2,000 animals in a more consistent format. With more than 1,000 color drawings and photographs, it is the preferred title for reference collections. *Animal Life* is an attractive supplementary purchase for public and school libraries.

Endangered Wildlife of the World. 11v. Marshall Cavendish, 1993. bibliog. illus. indexes. maps. hardcover $399.95 (1-85435-489-2).
591.52'9 Endangered species—Juvenile literature ‖ Wildlife conservation—Juvenile literature [CIP] 92-14974

Animals labeled as endangered, threatened, or vulnerable by the "Endangered Species List" of the U.S. Fish and Wildlife Service or by the "Red List" of the International Union for the Conservation of Nature and Natural Resources are treated in this 11-volume set. The encyclopedia was compiled with the assistance of an 18-member editorial board composed of experts on the various categories of included animals (amphibians, birds, fish, insects, invertebrates, mammals, and reptiles) as well as experts on captive breeding and conservation. The 1,200 species and subspecies covered are indexed and cross-referenced in this work developed for school library media centers and public libraries.

The one- to three-page signed entries are arranged alphabetically by the English or common name of the creature, for example, *Alligators*, *Monkeys*, and *Woodpeckers*. The scientific name follows the common name in parentheses. The species' status in the wild is designated by one of the following: possibly extinct, endangered, threatened, in captivity, or rare. The taxonomic classification is given, including class, order, family, and, when appropriate, subfamily and tribe. A physical description of the animal follows and includes as much natural history (diet, habitat, reproduction, etc.) as is known. The narrative describes the creature's behavior, appearance, and habitat; explains why the population is declining; and summarizes conservation activities and strategies.

The format makes the set easy to use. Good-size, dark print in triple columns is easy on the eyes. The paper is shiny, and the use of color boxes to set off specific information is effective. Numerous color photographs range in size from one-quarter to one full page. However, some entries are not illustrated, while other creatures are represented by black-and-white drawings on a blue background. Most entries include a range map showing the current location of the species; especially helpful are those that include the former range, before the decline in population of the species.

The 1,536 pages are numbered consecutively through the 11 volumes of the set. Each volume contains a table of contents and a glossary of such common terms as *home range*, *gestation*, and *diurnal*. The entries for endangered species end in volume 10, and these are followed by 10 short essays about various habitats and conservation issues.

Volume 11 contains an animal-kingdom chart, indexes, appendixes, and a bibliography. The three indexes include a geographic index and one for scientific names. The comprehensive index lists creatures by type (e.g., turtles), common name, and scientific name. Appendix A provides addresses for North American wildlife organizations and U.S. government offices. Appendix B lists addresses for state offices and wildlife refuges in the U.S. by state, followed by those in Canada. Selected subscription publications appear in appendix C. The 18-page, double-columned bibliography is arranged by groups of animals (amphibians, birds, mammals) and features American and British books, journals, and government and organization publications.

The set is visually attractive, the information is as complete as possible, and the text is readable and well presented. Children in the upper intermediate grades will be able to use the work with assistance and guidance. It is helpful to have so much information on endangered species throughout the world available in one source. Often the information is scattered in many sources, if available at all. For instance, an excellent reference for high school, college, and public libraries is the *Official World Wildlife Fund Guide to Endangered Species of North America* [RBB My 15 90], and while it covers both plants and animals, its scope is limited to one continent.

Endangered Wildlife of the World is recommended as a beginning, reliable source for students in the upper intermediate grades, middle school, and high school. Since this set is a solid, easily used reference, it should be considered by public libraries as well.

Venomous Reptiles of North America. By Carl H. Ernst. Smithsonian, 1992. 216p. bibliog. illus. index. maps. hardcover $35 (1-56096-114-8).
597.96'0469 Poisonous snakes—North America ‖ Gila monster [CIP] 91-3535

Professor Ernst of George Mason University is an award-winning author of several books on animals. Despite widespread interest in the topic, the editors claim that this is the first comprehensive book on North American venomous reptiles in 30 years. It surveys some 20 snakes and one lizard. Articles range from 3½ pages to 19½ pages. There are 55 colorplates in the center of the book and 61 black-and-white drawings and photographs throughout the text. An interesting introduction provides useful information. This is followed by "Identification of Venomous Reptiles," a key to assist users in identification. Unfortunately, there is no explanation of the key's use.

Each entry has a physical description of the reptile, information on the karyotype (the morphological characteristics of the chromosomes in a cell), the fossil record, and distribution and geographic variation. These sections are frequently illustrated with line drawings and maps. Rounding out the articles are paragraphs habitat, behavior, reproduction, growth and longevity, food and feeding, venom and bites, predators and defense, and population. Within each article is profuse use of scientific names and citations to published research. Metric measurements are used throughout the text.

The text is accompanied by a 50-page bibliography with close to 1,000 listings of books and articles, some of them very current. This is followed by a glossary of 54 scientific terms with pronunciation and short definition. An index of subjects and both scientific and popular names concludes the volume.

Klauber's *Rattlesnakes* (Univ. of California, 1982) and Ditmar's *Reptiles of North America* (Doubleday, 1936) have been through numerous editions and are somewhat dated. The book under review has color photographs while the older ones have black-and-white ones. Users will still have to rely on regional books for identification purposes; for example, *The Great Outdoors Book of Florida Snakes* by Anderson (Great Outdoors Pub., 1989). *Venomous Reptiles of North America* is the most comprehensive and current book in the field and will be a valuable addition to academic and public libraries.

The Golden Concise Encyclopedia of Mammals. By David Lambert. Golden Books/Western Publishing, 1992. 96p. illus. index. hardcover $10.95 (0-307-16559-0).
599 Mammals [BKL]

This oversize British import from Ilex Publishers provides more than 350 illustrated entries for young readers ages 6–11. The book begins with an introduction that details the characteristics, evolution, family tree, and adaptation of mammals. The introduction does not contain instructions for the reader on how to locate information.

The author does not define the principle of organization of the book, but the contents page outlines the presentation of mammals by groups. For example, various carnivores appear in nine sections, and two are devoted to whales. A one-paragraph entry for each mammal provides brief information, such as that for *Crested Porcupine*: "This African porcupine is as heavy as a medium-sized dog. When threatened, it charges backward and drives its quills deep into an enemy." All entries are accompanied by illustrations, appearing in one of two patterns. In most sections, the print entries are on one page, and each is accompanied by a line drawing that corresponds to the realistic, colored, group illustration of the animals on the opposite page. A few sections present the information on two-page spreads, matching a small, colored illustration with each print entry. Special features include notes in the entries identifying threatened species of mammals and introductory comments in larger print about the group of animals under discussion. The volume concludes with an index of animal names.

While the colorful illustrations are an asset of this book, a disconcerting feature is the inclusion of a number of related mammals in the same illustration, irrespective of the fact that in real life the geographic areas vary. This is especially evident in the title-page illustration containing three South American anteaters and a tree pangolin from Africa or southeastern Asia. There is no glossary, and a number of entries do not specify where the mammal may be found. Indeed, it is necessary to read the introductory comments to "Monotremes and Marsupials" to determine that the numbat, for example, lives in or near Australia. Furthermore, younger readers will undoubtedly need assistance in reading entries and using the table of contents and the index to locate information.

Based on a sampling of entries, *The Golden Concise Encyclopedia of Mammals* checks for accuracy when compared to *World Book* (1992), as well as the *Encyclopedia of Mammals*. In evaluating this new book for purchase, it is important to keep in mind that brevity of entries is intended. But other works, such as the those in the Eyewitness family or *The Kingfisher Illustrated Encyclopedia of Animals* [RBB O 15 92], are needed in the reference collection to provide fuller information and definitions of such terms as *herbivores* and *migration*.

The Multimedia Encyclopedia of Mammalian Biology. CD-ROM. McGraw-Hill, 1992. bibliog. illus. maps. $995 to a single user (0-07-707700-8); $1,250 for up to 16 users (0-07-707701-6).
599 Mammals—Encyclopedias ‖ Mammals—Software [BKL]

The Multimedia Encyclopedia of Mammalian Biology (MEMB) on CD-ROM includes the full text, photographs (approximately 3,500), and nearly 500 maps from *Grzimek's Encyclopedia of Mammals* (McGraw-Hill, 1990). Additional articles, movies, and sound clips were added to supplement the printed volumes. Although the print source is often found in adult reference collections (but certainly used at times by children), it seemed reasonable to hope that the multimedia edition might draw a wider generational audience because of the attraction of live-movie and sound illustrations. However, perhaps because of the complexity of the program, McGraw-Hill lists an age range of high school through adult for this product.

HARDWARE, SOFTWARE, AND INSTALLATION. The program can be run on a stand-alone PC ($995), and two network versions are available. One network version allows up to 16 users ($1,250); the other, up to 100 (no price given). Basic hardware and software requirements are an IBM or compatible AT computer (a minimum of 386SX is highly recommended), an SVGA monitor, a floppy-disk drive (either size), 2 MB free hard-disk space, 2 MB RAM (4 MB recommended), DOS 3.3 or higher, a standard ISO 9660 CD-ROM drive compatible with Microsoft Multimedia Extensions, Microsoft Windows 3.x, and a Microsoft-compatible mouse. A sound card compatible with Microsoft Windows with Multimedia Extensions is required to hear the sound clips. To view the movie shorts, additional hardware and software are needed: a DVI (Digital Video Interactive) Action Media series 2 playback card and DVI Multimedia control interface software. MS DOS 5.0 and Microsoft Windows 3.1 also are required for this option.

Other CD-ROM encyclopedias manage to come close to movie clips without the DVI equipment, and this requirement may be a drawback for libraries that have not invested in this equipment. The use of Microsoft Windows may offer other problems to libraries using this product for public access. Unless some form of security software is installed, it is, of course, easy to exit to DOS and fiddle with the computer.

Installation is uncomplicated and done through the Windows environment from a floppy disk (3½- and 5¼-inch disks were included in the review package). Once installed, the program appears as an icon in the applications group of the Windows Program Manager. Starting the MEMB, then, is a simple matter of clicking on the icon.

SEARCHING AND DISPLAYING. From the opening screen, one can go directly into the encyclopedia or can choose from such other options as a guided tour, whether to use long or short menus, exiting, or seeing a list of the advisory board, which is reprinted in the documentation.

The guided tour was disappointing. It consists of screen after screen illustrating the various windows that can appear and buttons that can be clicked to change magnification, move around within the text, use hyperlink and hypertext, and display the current status of a search. However, none of the windows are active to allow any experimentation. The only options in the tour are to select a "continue" button that displays a new screen or to exit the tour. The screen display is unintuitive and far less useful than a two-page illustration found in the documentation. A narrative explanation through the sound board seems an obvious needed addition to the program.

Many different methods to access information are built into MEMB. For example, in the browse mode a user can order the information four different ways: according to the table of contents in the print version; in a taxonomic order; in a biogeographic order; or in a thematic (biological concept) order. A search mode allows simple, one-term searches or complicated Boolean searching. Other access points are provided, such as a thesaurus search, and it is possible to prioritize searching to focus on articles with sound or pictures. One can even create graphs—pie chart and line—from textual material retrieved.

Included are the usual helpful features found in most CD-ROM encyclopedias, such as the ability to save text to a file or print selected portions. The instant hyperlinks, allowing use in a nonlinear manner, work well. The index feature (selected by clicking on an icon representing index cards) is a bit puzzling; the display looks like an inverted file of Latin terms. However, when selecting a term and choosing the *go to* option, a message reading "no entries" sometimes appeared.

CONCLUSION. All in all, the multitude of choices makes MEMB at once the richest tool for complex research and the most difficult and frustrating program to pick up and use without extensive practice. Given the outstanding nature of the print source, the value of the information on this disc is certain. But with the complexity of searching and the use of Windows, one can expect a long learning curve to develop facility with the program.

Compared with *Mammals: A Multimedia Encyclopedia* from the National Geographic Society, which is easy for any age to use, MEMB will require a far higher level of staff support to explain to the public. The documentation, exclusive of appendixes, runs on for 91 pages. Expecting adult or children's reference departments—or even the public—to become familiar with this monumental explanation seems overly optimistic. If the user interface were considerably simplified, this would become a useful tool in all sorts of libraries. As it is, possibly only in an academic library environment could *The Multimedia Encyclopedia of Mammalian Biology* be used effectively. (By *Charles Anderson*, deputy librarian, King County Public Library, Seattle, Washington.)

Canine Lexicon. By Andrew De Prisco and James B. Johnson. T.F.H., 1993. 896p. bibliog. illus. hardcover $79.95 (0-86622-198-0).
599.74442 Dogs—Encyclopedias [BKL]

Although a cat now resides in the White House, the dog remains a loyal friend and a hardworking assistant. Whether herding sheep or cattle, searching for lost skiers, assisting disabled people, or providing unconditional friendship, dogs play important roles in everyday life. Selecting the right dog and caring for it are major commitments, and people often seek information about breeds and training at the library.

Canine Lexicon was prepared by the authors of *The Mini-Atlas of Dog Breeds*, which RBB evaluated as an especially useful pet-selection tool [RBB D 1 90]. This new title provides a one-volume overview of all topics relating to dogs. It offers an alphabetical listing of breeds (*Abyssinian Sand dog, Dogue de Bordeaux*), anatomical terms (*gay tail, heart*), articles on the dog world (*agility trials, choosing a dog*), organizations and abbreviations (A.V.M.A, *American Kennel Club*), and dog care (*grooming, nutrition*). Unlike most dog books, this one includes an article on mixed breeds (*mongrels*). Entries range in length from a few lines to several pages; *see* references appear when appropriate. The work is lavishly illustrated with 1,300 full-color photographs that enhance the text and illustrate the diversity of the species.

The *Canine Lexicon* is similar in scope to the American Kennel Club's *Complete Dog Book* [RBB O 15 92]. The latter has only a few full-color plates but offers detailed charts of such anatomical characteristics as tail and eye types and facial shapes. While its coverage emphasizes only the 134 purebreds recognized by the A.K.C. and the breed standards for competition, it costs less ($27.50) than the work under review. *The Ultimate Dog Book* by David Taylor (Simon & Schuster, 1992) offers greater detail on various aspects of dog care but less comprehensive coverage of different breeds. Another T.F.H. publication, the *Atlas of Dog Breeds of the World* [RBB S 15 89], covers all the breeds and includes full-page color pictures but does not provide information about care and training. Libraries with large collections or high demand for information about dogs may want all these books. Libraries with small budgets or more basic collections would do well to select either the *Canine Lexicon* or *The Complete Dog Book*, along with *The Dog Owner's Home Veterinary Handbook* by veterinarian Delbert G. Carson and medical doctor James M. Giffin (rev. ed., Howell, 1992).

MEDICINE, HEALTH, TECHNOLOGY, MANAGEMENT

Oxford Illustrated Encyclopedia of Invention and Technology. Ed. by Monty Finniston. Oxford, 1992. 391p. illus. tables. hardcover $49.95 (0-19-869138-6).
603 Inventions—Dictionaries ‖ Technology—Dictionaries [BKL]

This sixth volume in the eight-volume *Oxford Illustrated Encyclopedia* series covers technology and invention separately from science, which was covered in *The Physical World* and *The Natural World*, volumes 1 and 2 in the series. Technology is defined as the "application of science to useful ends." The purpose of the work is to give a broad and international view of technology, emphasizing both historical and modern aspects.

As with all volumes in this series, the work is arranged alphabetically. *See* and *see also* references are denoted by an asterisk. The length of articles ranges from a definition of a sentence or two to over a page for such subjects as *Flying, History of* and *Computer, History of*. Illustrations include color and black-and-white photographs, charts, graphs, time charts, and diagrams. Diagrams are clear and easy to understand. Those for *Fire Fighting Equipment, Genetic Engineering,* and *Harness and Saddlery* provide a visual understanding not possible with text. The photography is outstanding, as evidenced by the pictures of a diving bell and drilling rig. The subjects range from such highly technical ones as *Biotechnology* to the more mundane *Lawn-Mower*.

More than 150 important figures in technology and invention have approximately a paragraph devoted to their achievements. The inclusion of such geographically widespread individuals as Edward Jenner, Augusta Ada Lovelace, Alexandre Gustave Eiffel, Gottlieb Daimler, and Isaac Singer indicate the international flavor maintained throughout the work. There are a few curious omissions. For example, Robert Koch is mentioned in the articles on Kitasato Shibasaburo and Wilhelm Kolle, but he does not have his own entry.

This work has a distinctive British flavor due primarily to terms used (e.g., *lift* for elevator, *lorry* for truck, *petrol* for gasoline, *paraffin* for kerosene). The U.S. equivalents are given at the beginning of entries for these terms, but there are no cross-references from the U.S. terms to the British ones.

The Oxford Illustrated Encyclopedia of Invention and Technology is a necessary purchase for all libraries owning other volumes in the set. (Two more volumes remain to be published.) It is also an excellent one-volume reference for high school, public, and small academic libraries that cannot afford larger sets on science and technology. The illustrations in this work are worth the price alone.

Hazardous Substances Resource Guide. Ed. by Richard P. Pohanish and Stanley A. Greene. Gale, 1993. 510p. bibliog. indexes. tables. hardcover $175 (0-8103-8494-6).
604.7 Hazardous substances—Handbooks, manuals, etc. [OCLC] 93-105840

What is the connection between smoking and radon? Are there any health hazards associated with the cleaning product Pinesol? Is there a nontoxic alternative for removing ink stains from carpet? Phenol is used at work; is it dangerous? Questions about the chemicals used in homes and workplaces are frequently brought to the library. Until now, most comprehensive reference works dealing with hazardous chemicals have been written for government agencies, health professionals, and material-safety coordinators. Editors Pohanish and Greene have written this new directory for "citizens concerned with hazardous substances encountered in the home, community, and workplace . . . to help identify these toxic chemicals as well as organizations and references that can further provide information about the substance."

Beginning with 15 brief essays on common classes of hazardous chemicals, Pohanish and Greene describe substances like pesticides and solvents and discuss regulations and labeling of hazardous substances. This section ends with a brief list of references divided by subject. Unfortunately, these references are the only bibliography or documentation that allows the reader to easily identify additional information on his or her topic. The bulk of the work follows with 1,047 profiles of hazardous substances, listed in alphabetical order by chemical name. These entries include chemical abstract service number, synonyms, danger profile, uses, appearance, odor, effects of exposure, effects of long-term exposure, storage, and first-aid guide. Though clear and readable, patrons will find that the section on the effects of exposure lacks quantitative data and environmental specifics that could enable them to evaluate the effects of a chemical in a particular situation. Readers may find that their primary question remains, How dangerous is this substance to me?

For patrons wishing to pursue questions about various substances, "Resource Listings" includes information on more than 1,500 organizations, agencies, crisis services, publications, and information sources concerned with toxic chemicals and their effects on human health and the environment. These final pages are in a format similar to *Encyclopedia of Associations* and other Gale publications. With help, most patrons will be able to identify relevant information resources like asbestos hotlines, local poison-control centers, and cosmetic trade organizations.

Excellent indexing by chemical name and CAS number provide access to the profiles of substances, and a separate index is included for the titles and organizational names in "Resource Listings." Additional resource indexing by subject would have greatly enhanced the final sections. Missing from the work is an index by commercial-product name, such as Fantastik or Raid Bug Spray. However, patrons who know the active ingredients of such products will frequently be able to find relevant information in this book.

Hazardous Substances Resource Guide joins several other excellent reference titles found on library shelves. Its clear language and lack of technical data make it more readable to a general audience than *Dangerous Properties of Industrial Materials* (7th ed., 3v., Van Nostrand, 1988) or *Clinical Toxicology of Commercial Products* (5th ed., Williams & Wilkins, 1984). However, these titles cover a much larger number of substances; provide additional access points to chemical profiles, specific toxicity ratings, and exposure limits; and document the sources of their information with at least brief bibliographies. Libraries wishing to include this more technical information in their collections will want to look closely at the new edition of the *Handbook of Toxic and Hazardous Chemicals and Carcinogens* (3d ed., 2v., Noyes, 1992). Libraries already owning up-to-date versions of *The Hazardous Chemicals on File Collection* by Craig Norback (3v., Facts On File) already have much of the chemical profile information in the title under review. Keyword subject indexing in *Encyclopedia of Associations* and similar reference works provides superior access to resource listings than does this new Gale publication.

Hazardous Substances Resource Guide is especially valuable for its easy-to-comprehend language and clear, concise format. However, its omission of quantitative data, inadequate bibliographies, and lack of access by common product names limit its ability to stand alone as a valuable reference tool. It is an excellent title for public and academic libraries able to afford several expensive reference volumes on an increasingly timely topic.

Inventions and Discoveries, 1993: What's Happened, What's Coming, What's That? Ed. by Valérie-Anne Giscard d'Estaing and Mark Young. Facts On File, 1993. 248p. indexes. hardcover $24.95 (0-8160-2865-6; ISSN 1064-7600).
608 Inventions—History ‖ Technology—History [BKL]

This attractive book highlights thousands of inventions that have shaped the modern world—in the sciences, the arts, entertainment, sports, warfare, and everyday life. Inventions from "the historic to the contemporary, the outlandish to the practical, applications both simple and complex" are profiled chronologically within each discipline for the readers' enlightenment and entertainment. The more than 5,000 entries are about a paragraph in length and detail what the invention is, who invented it, how it is used, where it is used, and by whom. Many of the entries are accompanied by brilliant full-color photographs.

Inventions and Discoveries has been a European best-seller, published every year for 11 years in France, and translated into 13 languages. This first U.S. edition is edited by Mark Young, the editor of the U.S. edition of *The Guinness Book of Records*. The year 1993 in the title does not refer to the coverage of the book, which extends back to 4000 B.C.

On the contents pages, under each of the 12 chapter headings are subheadings. For example, the chapter "Media and Communication" includes "Language and Writing," "Publishing," "Mail Delivery," "Telephone," "Radio," "Video," and "Communication Cables." Additionally, each chapter features "What on Earth?"—an offbeat collection of such inventions as growing plastic trees in the desert and sand skiing; another feature is "Tomorrow's World," which offers a glimpse of inventions in the not-too-distant future, such as edible cotton and the confidential fax machine. A special feature within each chapter is the highlighting of inventors, such as Rachel Carson ("Humanity's Effect on Ecology," 1962) and Masaru Ibuka (Sony Walkman, 1979). The last chapter is a list of Nobel Prize winners (1901–92) in chemistry, physics, and physiology or medicine.

There are several other chronologies of inventions (e.g., *Asimov's Chronology of Science and Discovery* [RBB F 15 90]) that give more detail but lack the attractive illustrations of this book. *Inventions and Discoveries, 1993* will actively engage readers from junior high up, whether they are researchers, trivia buffs, or diehard technophiles.

America's Top Medical Jobs. Ed. by J. Michael Farr and Kathleen Martin. JIST Works; dist. by Career Press, 62 Beverly Rd., P.O. Box 34, Hawthorne, NJ 07507, 1992. 163p. tables. paper $9.95 (1-56370-046-8).
610.69 Medicine—Vocational guidance ‖ Health occupations ‖ Job application [CIP] 92-6270

America's Top Technical and Trade Jobs. Ed. by J. Michael Farr and Kathleen Martin. JIST Works; dist. by Career Press, 1992. 159p. tables. paper $9.95 (1-56370-041-7).
331.7'02 Labor market—U.S. ‖ Employment forecasting—U.S. ‖ Occupations—U.S. ‖ Vocational guidance—U.S. ‖ Job hunting—U.S. [CIP] 92-4660

Each of these two works selects about 50 jobs from the *Occupational Outlook Handbook* and reprints the OOH entries verbatim. This makes up more than half of each book. Additionally, labor market trends, a list of fastest-growing jobs, summary information on other jobs in the OOH, and a "quick job search" chapter are included. With a few very minor differences, these supplementary sections are identical in both works. Compiler Farr has written several works in this field, such as *A Young Person's Guide to Getting and Keeping a Good Job* and *The Work Book: Getting the Job You Want*.

The books begin with a short chapter by the respected authority Robert Wegman entitled "Labor Market and Career Planning Trends through the Year 2000." A second short chapter lists the 84 fastest-growing jobs and highlights the relevant (health-related or technical and trade) jobs in each book. After the alphabetically arranged job-description section (the one reprinting OOH entries) is a chapter with brief job outlook information on 200 other jobs. The last chapter, "Making Career Decisions and Getting a Good Job—in Less Time," is a focused, 21-page section based on Farr's *Quick Job Search*. Two appendixes chart "The Outlook for over 400 Occupations Employing More Than 25,000 People" and "Earnings, Education Required, Employment Rates and Other Details for Over 200 Jobs." The first appendix is based on information from the November 1989 *Monthly Labor Review*; the second, on the Department of Labor's 1990 Occupational Projections and Training Data.

The value of these works, compared with the *Occupational Outlook Handbook*, is that they allow readers to focus on jobs in two specific areas, if these are their interests. The biggest problem is datedness: the 1992–93 edition of OOH was available months before these works (based on the 1990–91 edition) were published. While the convenience of format and the focus on medical or trade and technical jobs could be useful for some job hunters, the datedness of the material and its exact duplication of the *Occupational Outlook Handbook* in some sections make these two works dispensable for most libraries.

Personal Health Reporter: Excerpts from Current Articles on 148 Medical Conditions and Treatments and Other Health Issues. Ed. by Alan M. Rees and Charlene Willey. Gale, 1993. 627p. bibliog. index. hardcover $95 (0-8103-8392-6; ISSN 1061-4125).
613'.03 Health—Encyclopedias ‖ Medicine, Popular—Encyclopedias ‖ Diseases—Popular works [BKL] 92-4114

Consumer health-information reference sources for the lay user occupy an important niche in reference collections, as documented in two RBB special lists [Ja 1 93, D 1 88]. *Personal Health Reporter* (PHR) joins this increasing array of sources aimed toward the general consumer. It strives to provide integrated and orderly access to current, authoritative medical information by excerpting significant articles concerning physical and mental health. The 148 topics covered by the PHR are treated in entries ranging in length from four to eight pages. Each contains extracts from several different sources and provides complete bibliographic citations. The editors compiled the information by scanning more than 250 sources, including government documents, newsletters, professional journals such as *Lancet*, and such popular magazines as *Prevention*.

The scope of PHR is broad, covering diseases and disorders, syndromes, health concerns of women, health problems of children, mental health, substance abuse, medical tests and diagnostic methods, medical and surgical procedures, nutritional topics, alternative medicine, new technology, consumer advocacy, and cost concerns. Subjects included range from acne to anabolic steroids, from back pain to breast-feeding, from endometriosis to exercise, and from sinusitis to sleep disorders. Topics are arranged alphabetically, and entries provide definitions and overviews and supply information on risks and alternatives. Entries conclude with a list of additional resources, including organizations, books, and articles. The volume concludes with a subject index.

It is unlikely that most libraries would own the wide variety of sources utilized in the articles in the *Personal Health Reporter*. By printing these excerpts, PHR saves time and energy compared with locating and obtaining the source documents. The intent of the publisher is to issue subsequent editions containing additional topics and updates to the previously covered subjects. With its encyclopedic format and readable text, PHR will satisfy many health consumers needing summary information. Its suggestions for further research can be utilized in obtaining more comprehensive materials when warranted. This new title will be of interest to academic, public, and special libraries that experience a large demand for consumer health information.

Complete Guide to Prescription & Non-Prescription Drugs. By H. Winter Griffith. Putnam/Perigee, 1992. 1,076p. index. paper $15.95 (0-399-51766-9).
615'.1 Drugs—Popular works ‖ Drugs, Non-prescription—Popular works [CIP] 92-21933

Questions about drugs are among the most common inquiries at the reference desk. Patients are often too timid to ask, and doctors and pharmacists are too busy to explain, so people turn to the library for information. The *Complete Guide to Prescription & Non-Prescription Drugs* is one of several current books available to answer these questions.

Organized in chart format like Griffith's *Complete Guide to Symptoms, Illness & Surgery for People over 50* [RBB My 15 92], this guide contains information on more than 5,000 brand-name and more than 700 generic drugs. The charts are arranged alphabetically by generic name or drug class—*Analgesics, Ephedrine*. Each chart contains brief information about brand names, uses, dosages, adverse reactions or side effects, overdose symptoms and treatment, and precautions with other drugs or foods. At the beginning of the book are detailed instructions for using the guide. A brand- and generic-name directory, charts of additional drug interactions, a glossary, and an index complete the work.

This book is written in nontechnical language for consumers rather than for medical professionals who would use works such as the *Physicians Desk Reference* or the *Physicians' Generix* [RBB Jl 92]. While this book is relatively easy to use, it has some disadvantages. A person taking a common drug and who is unsure of its name or type may have a problem locating it. The charts for acetaminophen, estrogen, and other frequently prescribed drugs refer the user to the brand-name directory to find the identity of the drug. There is no color drug-identification chart. Charts for drugs with long lists of possible interactions refer readers to the list of additional interactions, and people may miss important information if they fail to do this.

The Complete Drug Reference, published annually by Consumer Reports Books, contains more complete information in a layout that is easier to read. The articles include revision dates, so users know that they are current. The work has a drug-identification chart with color pictures, pictograms explaining use instructions, a section on combination chemotherapy for cancer patients, and lists of drugs contraindicated during pregnancy and breast-feeding. The general introductory material about medicines is outstanding. This is a better choice for reference collections. The *Complete Guide to Prescription & Non-Prescription Drugs* is an appropriate choice for circulating collections or for libraries with extreme budget constraints.

Zimmerman's Complete Guide to Nonprescription Drugs. 2d ed. By David R. Zimmerman. Visible Ink Press, 835 Penobscot Bldg., Detroit, MI 48226-4094, 1993. 1,125p. index. paper $19.95 (0-8103-9421-9).

615.1 Drugs, Nonprescription [OCLC] 92-32707

Americans spend $12 billion a year on nonprescription drugs. These readily available medications are useful for many common ailments. Used properly, they can save time and money by avoiding unnecessary trips to the doctor for expensive prescriptions. Choosing an appropriate nonprescription drug can be difficult. The numerous brand-name and generic preparations on the market vary in cost and effectiveness. *Zimmerman's Complete Guide to Nonprescription Drugs* provides extensive coverage of these products. This work is a revised edition of Zimmerman's 1983 work, *The Essential Guide to Nonprescription Drugs*.

The author compiled the information by monitoring the Food and Drug Administration's Over the Counter Drug Review, a multiple-step regulatory process used to evaluate safety and effectiveness. The FDA publishes several draft reports in *The Federal Register* and the final document on each group of drugs in the *Code of Federal Regulations*. Zimmerman's book summarizes and interprets this information on all currently available nonprescription drugs and presents it in an accessible form for lay readers.

The book is arranged in alphabetical chapters by type of drug—antacids, cold and cough medicines, etc. A symptoms index directs users to appropriate pages. Each chapter contains introductory material about the ailments that the drugs may treat and the ingredients used in them. The author then discusses the ingredients, the manufacturers' claims made about them and their accuracy, and warnings about their use. The chapters conclude with charts of the drug ingredients and the FDA assessment, whether in final or draft form, as safe and effective, conditionally safe and effective, or unsafe or ineffective. There are also tables with the drug name; dosage (adult and pediatric, where appropriate); author's rating of A, B, or C, corresponding to his interpretation of the FDA assessment, and comments about the drug's safety and efficacy. The author also stresses the necessity of seeking medical treatment for conditions that are too serious or those that do not respond to self-treatment. A detailed subject index completes the text.

Zimmerman's Complete Guide to Nonprescription Drugs has much more information than the *Physician's Desk Reference for Nonprescription Drugs*. The latter contains only the information from the manufacturer, while the former has objective information from scientific studies. *The Complete Drug Reference* has more extensive coverage of side effects and drug interactions, but it lists fewer nonprescription medicines. *Zimmerman's Complete Guide* is an inexpensive source that complements *The Complete Drug Reference*. It is easy to use and belongs in all public, health science, and consumer health library collections.

A Consumer's Dictionary of Household, Yard and Office Chemicals. By Ruth Winter. Crown, 1992. 329p. bibliog. paper $12 (0-517-58722-X).

615.9 Housing and health—Dictionaries ‖ Household supplies—Toxicology—Dictionaries [CIP] 91-33189

Toxic chemicals are a fact of modern life—we use them at home and at work. Minimizing the adverse effects of these substances is a concern, and finding current information about toxic substances that is accessible to laypeople can be a challenge. A *Consumer's Dictionary of Household, Yard and Office Chemicals* is a good introduction to this subject.

Winter, a science writer who also wrote the *Consumer's Dictionary of Food Additives* (3d ed., Crown, 1989) and the *Consumer's Dictionary of Cosmetic Ingredients* (3d ed., Crown, 1989), follows a similar format in this book. A general introduction covers the role of chemicals in both indoor and outdoor pollution, labels, means of exposure, and long- and short-term effects. Proper use of toxins and methods of protection are also included. The body of the book is an alphabetical list of terms. The entries range in length from a few words to several paragraphs. The subjects covered include specific substances (*acacia gum, asbestos, phenol*), classes of chemicals (*dry-cleaning fluid, jewelry cleaners, paints*), brand names (*Gain enzyme laundry detergent, Lysol brand disinfectant*), and miscellaneous terms (*dust mites, eye allergy, leukemia*). The entries describe the substances, their uses, and known effects of exposure. Some entries, like that for *pesticides*, provide detailed first-aid and decontamination protocols. The brief entries for medical conditions (*dermatitis, lymphoma*) would be more useful if they contained references to causative agents as well as definitions. The last section of the book contains lists of relevant agencies that have further information, poison control centers, Environmental Protection Agency regional offices, and a current bibliography of technical and lay material.

This useful introduction to the hazardous-materials field is reasonably priced and easy to read. *Toxics A to Z* by John Harte and others [RBB D 1 91] provides more detailed scientific information and complements Winter's book nicely. Annie Berthold Bond's *Clean and Green* (Ceres Press, 1990) provides nontoxic alternatives for housekeeping. All of these inexpensive sources are good additions to public library consumer-health collections.

Focus on Addictions: A Reference Handbook. By Kay Marie Porterfield. ABC-Clio, 1992. bibliog. index. hardcover $39 (0-87436-674-7).

616.85 Drug abuse—Handbooks, manuals, etc. ‖ Alcoholism—Handbooks, manuals, etc. ‖ Tobacco habit—Handbooks, manuals, etc. ‖ Eating disorders—Handbooks, manuals, etc. ‖ Compulsive behavior—Handbooks, manuals, etc. [OCLC] 92-26623

The newest addition to the Teenage Perspectives reference series, this handbook briefly describes common addictions and then provides annotated lists of publications, films, and organizations related to the topic. A general discussion of addictive behavior heads the book, followed by general resources. Subsequent chapters deal with alcoholism, drugs, tobacco, eating disorders, obsessive-compulsive and impulse-control disorders, and codependency (which largely treats alcoholic-affected families). Writing is clear and geared to the teenage reader.

The bibliographies are selective rather than comprehensive. The bases for selection are not noted. Entries appear useful, although some obvious titles, such as *When Food's a Foe*, were excluded. While some titles are classic, such as *Go Ask Alice* and *High and Outside*, most are items published within the last five years. A few titles are high/low entries, noted as quick reading. Disappointingly, no fiction titles are included in the obsessive-impulsive section. Most pamphlets are published by government agencies, and most films and videos are distributed by educational companies. Organizations listed are usually national, about half being governmental. A few hotlines are mentioned. Each entry includes full bibliographic citation and a one- to three-sentence description. Film and video entries include rental and purchase information. The index lists titles, authors, and broad topics. Access to distributors and more detailed indexing of the textual introductions would have been valuable.

The Best Years of Their Lives: A Resource Guide for Teenagers in Crisis (ALA, 1992) also provides good bibliographies on addiction for teenagers, and other publishers have offered lists of materials on substance abuse. Thus, this volume cannot be considered either unique or definitive. While *Focus on Addictions* stands as one possible reference tool for a subject much on the minds of teenagers, it is especially useful in a teen's hands and is recommended for school and public library collections.

Addictionary: A Primer of Recovery Terms and Concepts from Abstinence to Withdrawal. By Jan R. Wilson and Judith A. Wilson. Simon & Schuster/Fireside, 1992. 410p. bibliog. index. paper $13 (0-671-76696-1).

616.86'003 Compulsive behavior—Encyclopedias ‖ Twelve-step programs—Encyclopedias [CIP] 92-19070

Publishers have responded to the growth of the self-help movement with many books on recovering from various addictions and compulsions. *Addictionary*, written by certified addiction professionals who are in recovery themselves, provides an overview of 12-step programs for alcohol and drug dependency, eating disorders, codependency, and gambling, work, and sex addictions.

The book is arranged alphabetically by subject. The entries include psychological concepts (e.g., *Abstinence* and *Forgiveness*), specific substances (e.g., *Alcohol* and *Cocaine*), various recovery programs (e.g., *Debtors Anonymous*), and each of the 12 steps. Most entries are one to three pages in length. They summarize the subject, refer the reader to related entries in the book, and provide names, addresses, and telephone numbers of appropriate recovery groups. There is also a detailed subject index. A bibliography with brief annotations contains sources written between 1957 and 1991. An appendix lists the addresses and telephone numbers of all the programs mentioned throughout the book.

Addictionary is a useful introduction to the 12-step recovery method, but such sources as the *Encyclopedia of Alcoholism* (2d ed. [RBB N 1 91]) and the *Encyclopedia of Drug Abuse* (2d ed. [RBB F 15 92]) provide more comprehensive coverage of these areas. *The Recovery Resource Book* by Barbara Yoder [RBB Je 15 90] offers more complete information about the recovery field. *Addictionary* is a good addition to circulating collections in public and health-education libraries. The other sources cited here are preferable for reference collections.

The Cancer Dictionary. By Roberta Altman and Michael J. Sarg. Facts On File, 1992. 352p. hardcover $40 (0-8160-2608-4).
616.99'4 Cancer—Dictionaries [OCLC] 91-46941

Every year there are over 800,000 cases of cancer in the U.S. Cancer patients and their families need current information to understand their condition and make decisions about treatment. *The Cancer Dictionary* provides an overview of the field and is a good starting point for research.

Compiled by a medical writer (who is a cancer patient) and an oncologist, this dictionary contains more than 2,500 alphabetically arranged entries. It covers all aspects of cancer and its treatments. There are entries for individual cancers (*gastrointestinal carcinoid tumor*, *leukemia*); diagnostic tests (*CT scan*, *bone marrow aspiration*); symptoms (*anemia*); surgical procedures (*mastectomy*, *colectomy*); and the various types of chemotherapy and radiation therapy. The names of specific agents—*dibromodulcitol*—as well as general types—*antimetabolites* and *hormones*—are included. Information is provided about risk factors, prevention, carcinogens, and side effects. *See* and *see also* references facilitate access, and terms within an article that have their own entries are printed in small capitals.

Entries range in length from a few lines to several paragraphs. They explain the terms in language that an educated layperson can understand. The book also has four appendixes that list support organizations for cancer and AIDS, comprehensive cancer centers in the U.S., clinical trials and cooperative groups, and drugs used in the treatment of cancer and AIDS. The drug tables give chemical/generic name, brand name, and abbreviation. Chemotherapeutic agents, antiemetics, and pain medications are included.

The Cancer Dictionary is a useful starting point for information about this group of diseases. Patients and their families who want more detail can consult the *Cancer Source Book* by Franc C. Bair (1990) or the *American Cancer Society Cancer Book* (1986). For comprehensive information about treatment, *Everyone's Guide to Cancer Therapy* by Malin Dollinger (1992) is a current source. Marilyn J. Dodd's *Managing the Side Effects of Chemotherapy and Radiation* (1987) is also useful. This group of books belongs in all consumer health collections. *The Cancer Dictionary* would also be a useful ready-reference source for health science collections.

Encyclopedia of Childbearing: Critical Perspectives. Ed. by Barbara Katz Rothman. Oryx, 1993. 446p. bibliog. illus. index. tables. hardcover $74.50 (0-89774-648-1).
618.2'003 Pregnancy—Encyclopedias || Childbirth—Encyclopedias || Human reproduction—Social aspects—Encyclopedias [CIP] 92-14975

The subject of this encyclopedia is birth studies, a relatively new academic discipline growing out of feminist studies. Rather than focusing on the medical aspects of childbearing, the work's premise is that "pregnancy, childbirth, and motherhood are social constructions, and the practices, imagery, and technology a culture develops, or even in the case of science fiction, imagines developing, grow out of this cultural grounding." Contributors include scholars from such diverse fields as anthropology, art history, childbirth education, ethics, law, nursing, literature, women's studies, and medicine. The tone of the articles reflects the authors' areas of expertise; some entries demand a familiarity with the language of medicine and scholarship, while others are easily understood by the layperson.

A wide range of topics is covered in the 250 signed, alphabetically arranged entries that vary from one to three pages in length. Articles are included on such medical issues as *Ectopic Pregnancy* and *Shoulder Dystocia*, as well as on such practical topics as *Infant Feeding and Care* and *Shoes for Babies*. These are juxtaposed with articles on the treatment of pregnancy and childbirth in art and literature (*Creation Stories in Western Culture*, *Goddess Imagery*), legal issues (*Birth Certificates*, *Rights of the Pregnant Patient*), caregivers (*Labor Partners*, *Witch Midwives*), as well as the clinical and anthropological aspects of couvade (male symptoms of pregnancy). Among the many unique entries are *Childbearing in Prison*; *Amniocentesis, History of*; and *Diapers: Environmental Concerns*. Some entries are on specialized, narrow topics, for example, *The Pregnant Therapist* and *Midwives, Southern Black*. Several articles discuss childbirth practices in a small number of countries other than the U.S.; the editor selected to profile those that "contrast with American practices, systems, values, or beliefs."

A typical article is the three-page entry *Home Birth* that surveys the history of how the place of birth moved from the home to the hospital; explains why some women are again opting for home birth, most often assisted by a midwife; and advises that a lot of reading and thinking are needed before a mother chooses the option of home birth. All articles end with *see also* references and a "Resources" bibliography for further reading. The preliminaries of the book include a topical guide that organizes related articles under such subject headings as *Contraception*, *Infant Feeding*, and *New Procreative Technologies*. An appendix lists organizations and resources dealing with such issues as adoption and midwifery. A comprehensive index concludes the book.

Despite the wide-ranging scope of this interdisciplinary work, absent are some topics that one would expect to find in an encyclopedia of childbirth. For example, no entry discusses multiple births as a medical phenomenon, but twins are covered in *Twins: Myths and Legends*. Surprisingly, there is no overview article on abortion, but 10 separate entries on the subject are listed under *Abortion* in the topical guide. These range from a feminist, ethical analysis of the subject to coverage of RU486.

The *Encyclopedia of Childbearing* is an interesting compendium of diverse information that will be of use to students as well as general readers. Large public and academic libraries will find it useful as a quick-reference source, as well as a starting point for patron research.

The Naval Institute Guide to the Ships and Aircraft of the U.S. Fleet. 15th ed. By Norman Polmar. Naval Institute Press, 1993. 639p. illus. indexes. tables. hardcover $56.95 (1-55750-675-2).
623.825'0973 U.S. Navy—Lists of vessels || Warships—U.S. || Airplanes, Military—U.S. [BKL]

This fifteenth edition of *The Naval Institute Guide* is the first to be published since the end of the Cold War era. A new chapter on sealift ships, numerous photographs and descriptions reflecting Gulf War operations, and the initial chapter "State of the Fleet" all reflect the U.S. fleet of the early 1990s as well as ongoing naval programs and cancellations. This work provides detailed, comprehensive descriptions of all elements of the fleet, from organization, command structure, and personnel to ships, aircraft, weapon systems, and electronic systems.

Polmar is an author and adviser to secretaries of the Navy and others. He took over this work beginning with its eleventh edition in 1978. Contents are arranged in 34 chapters, from brief but key glossary and ship-classification chapters to the lengthy chapters on auxiliary ships and naval aviation. For example, "Amphibious Ships" gives the number of ships and their lift capacity (in numbers of troops, vehicle and cargo space, helicopter spots, and landing-craft spots) and provides numerous photographs and diagrams of ships and their features. Listings are given of individual ships; their builders; dates laid down, launched, and commissioned; and current status (active Atlantic or Pacific, reserve, etc.). Though the detail is complex and somewhat technical, it is accessible to a nonmilitary readership. There are chapters on the Fleet Marine Force, the Coast Guard, and the National Oceanic and Atmospheric Administration. Appendixes cover "Advanced Technology Ships," "Force Levels

1945–1990," "Navy Shipbuilding Programs, Fiscal 1947–1992," "Foreign Ship Transfers, 1987–1991," and "Navy and Coast Guard Ships Preserved as Memorials and Museums." A general index and a ship-name and class index aid access. An addendum briefly updates 16 of the chapters through October 1992.

There is no comparable guide to the U.S. fleet. Jane's, of course, publishes annual guides to fighting ships, naval weapon systems, and so on for all the world's military forces. *The Naval Institute Guide*, however, unifies the information for U.S. naval forces. For the most current information, Jane's volumes will be the best choice. But for comprehensive and unified coverage of the U.S. fleet and for the economy and convenience of purchasing just one volume, this work is recommended. Clientele of public and academic libraries will find it quite valuable.

American Automobile Collections and Museums: A Guide to U.S. Exhibits. By Michael Morlan. Bon A Tirer, P.O. Box 3480, Shawnee, KS 66203, 1992. 252p. bibliog. illus. index. paper $15.95 (1-878446-10-X).
629.209 Automobiles—U.S. ‖ Automobiles—Museums—U.S. ‖ Automobiles—Collectors and collecting—U.S. [OCLC] 92-70150

This guide to 139 vehicle exhibitions is Morlan's second museum guide. The first was *Kitty Hawk to NASA*, listing American museums dealing with flight. The arrangement of this new title is alphabetical by state and then by museum. *American Automobile Collections* is similar to the previous work in that it provides address; telephone number; directions; admission; description and history of the collection; hours of operation; notes regarding food services, gift shops, and film availability; and in most cases, a list of the vehicles on display. There are approximately 100 black-and-white photographs of different vehicles. These range from the famous, such as Sir Malcom Campbell's Bluebird or Elvis Presley's Stutz, to less-known but interesting cars, like a Hispano-Suiza or Thomas Flyer. A useful feature is the index of cars usually on display, which will be helpful to people interested in specific makes and models.

A worthwhile addition to libraries that serve not only automobile enthusiasts but also people interested in viewing important parts of this country's sociocultural history.

The Gardener's Reading Guide. By Jan Dean. Facts On File, 1993. indexes. hardcover $23.95 (0-8160-2754-4).
016.635 Gardening—Bibliography [CIP] 92-24321

This work is a labor of love by author Dean, who found armchair gardening as much fun as gardening in the dirt. Included in this annotated bibliography are more than 2,300 books that would be of interest to the average gardener. Excluded are nursery catalogs, newsletters, and highly technical or specialized works. The books listed are limited to those published in the last 15 years, except for classics and personal favorites of the author. A section on locating gardening books, complete with telephone numbers for mail-order houses and book clubs, is very useful, as is a list of publishers that specialize in gardening literature.

The work is organized into six topical chapters. "The Personal Side of Gardening" lists narratives and essays on gardening experiences, such as works by Beverley Nichols and *Thomas Jefferson's Garden Book*. This chapter also includes biographies of famous gardeners, adventures of plant hunters, and fictional works that feature gardens, for example, John Sherwood's mystery stories. "How-to Gardening" has sections covering numerous types of flowers, grasses, trees, and shrubs. It also lists books that focus on such topics as soil, watering methods, landscape design, and crafts from the garden. Organic gardening, xeriscape, and hydroponics are the subjects of "Specific Gardening Methods," while 16 different garden styles, such as oriental and topiary, comprise "Special Types of Gardens." "Regional Gardening" has sections covering four different regions of the U.S.; since the author lives in Fort Worth, Texas, that state is particulary well represented. Also listed are books focusing on gardens in other parts of the world, especially Europe, Japan, and China. Books that emphasize gardening for children, the disabled, and the elderly are listed in "Miscellaneous Gardening Topics." The book also has sections covering photography, botanical illustration, videos, and magazines.

Most entries consist of a bibliographic citation and a brief annotation. Since some of the listed works cover more than one topic, the author placed the citation in the most obvious category and cross-referenced it to other appropriate topics. These cross-references are provided through a list of "related books" that concludes most sections. Many of these lists have four to seven references, such as "Indoor Gardening" and "Food Gardening," while a few have more than 20, for example, "Herbs" and "Wildflowers." Concluding the book are subject and author indexes.

This work is similar in scope to Richard T. Isaacson's *Gardening: A Guide to the Literature* [RBB Je 15 86]), which was aimed at the general gardener and listed books, periodicals, and bulletins. While some overlap does exist between Isaacson and Dean, the former is now more than eight years old. Isaacson included 784 works ranked in order of usefulness; Dean has 2,300 annotated listings but does not rank them.

Gardener's Reading Guide is a work that truly has something for every type of gardener—young, elderly, disabled, city, country, indoor, outdoor, and armchair. Most library patrons interested in gardening will be able to find books of interest listed in this bibliography. In addition, it will be helpful to libraries building or updating gardening collections. It is a recommended purchase for public libraries.

Destructive and Useful Insects: Their Habits and Control. 5th ed. By Robert L. Metcalf and Robert A. Metcalf. McGraw-Hill, 1993. 1,072p. illus. index. tables. hardcover $85 (0-07-041692-3).
632'.7 Insect pests ‖ Beneficial insects ‖ Insect pests—Control [CIP] 92-18374

Originally published in 1928 by C. L. Metcalf and W. P. Flint, this book was intended as an introductory text and reference on North American entomology. Last revised in 1962 by Robert L. Metcalf, the monograph has been a classic reference in economic entomology and is intended for students, practicing farmers, gardeners, fruit growers, physicians, and general readers. The father-and-son authors—both distinguished scholars—have significantly revised *Destructive and Useful Insects* in this fifth edition.

This book covers more than 600 species of North American insects and claims to examine every economically and medically important species. The work is organized into 21 chapters on a variety of topics, such as "Insects as Enemies of Humans," "The Value of Insects to Humans," "Insects Injurious to Cotton," and "Insects Attacking Shade Trees and Shrubs." The work is profusely illustrated with black-and-white photographs, line drawings, and tables that are appropriately placed throughout the text.

New to this edition is information on 30 additional pests and pest complexes. The many tables, synopses, and outlines have been increased from 70 to 83. In addition, the index has been expanded by six pages. A random check determined that there have been a few changes in the illustrations by dropping some and adding others. The numerous footnotes have also been increased with the addition of new citations. Where appropriate, many of the tables have been updated; for instance, table 1.3, citing economic losses from insects, has been updated from 1957 data to that of 1988. Significantly, the text now incorporates many of the concepts of integrated pest management to control insects. This method is environmentally friendly and is now the preferred system for pest control.

The book uses common language in its explanations and descriptions. For instance, in the five pages devoted to the housefly, the authors first explain why it is considered a pest: "its disgusting habits of walking and feeding on garbage and excrement and also on the human person and food make it an ideal agent for the transfer of disease organisms." Following the discussion of the dangers of the insect are sections focusing on the housefly's "life history, appearance and habits" and finally on control measures. The entry ends with a bibliography of 16 citations to materials published from 1910 to 1973.

Unfortunately, this reference has a few flaws. The bulk of the illustrations within the text have not been updated—many are more than 30 years old. Citations to references more than 100 years old are also questionable.

Despite its shortcomings, this is a unique and useful reference. Where else could one find a history of the medfly, statistics on crop losses, detailed biological descriptions of insects, and professional pest-control measures? *Destructive and Useful Insect* serves its intended audience of agricultural workers and educated readers. If libraries own the previous version and found it useful, the new edition is recommended because of the revisions and additions to the text. This reference should be considered for academic and public library collections, as well as for those high schools where the technical information about insects is appropriate to the curriculum.

Garden Literature: An Index to Periodical Articles and Book Reviews. Garden Literature Press, 398 Columbus Ave., Ste. 181, Boston, MA 02116-6008, January–March 1992—. quarterly. paper $75/yr. (ISSN 1061-3722).
635 Gardening—Periodicals—Indexes || Plants—Periodicals—Indexes [BKL] 92-3974

This is an author-subject index to English-language periodical articles about plants and gardens. Published quarterly, the fourth issue will be an annual cumulation. Addressing itself to gardeners, garden designers and historians, growers, horticulturists, landscape architects, and conservationists, the index brings together in one place citations to articles otherwise scattered throughout several different indexes or not indexed at all.

Very easy to use, the index is arranged in two alphabetical sequences: part 1 is the main index of articles, and part 2 indexes book reviews. Full citations noting illustrations and bibliographies are given for all entries, and very short annotations for many. Subject headings range from *Acid Rain* and *Artists* to *Wetlands* and *Winter Gardens*. Cross-references to appropriate subject headings are used throughout. The subject headings generally use natural-language word order (i.e., *Edible Wild Plants* is listed under E). Individual plants are found under the scientific name with reference from the common name: "Daylily. See Hemerocallis." This first issue "contains articles indexed in January through March 1992 periodical issues, issues with 1991 imprints published in 1992 and new periodical titles published in Fall 1991."

Of the more than 100 publications indexed, 20 are also found in *Readers' Guide*; however, of the remaining titles, only about a dozen would be found in a medium-size public library. Several titles, including *Wilson Library Bulletin*, *Publishers Weekly*, and *Booklist*, are included for their book reviews. In addition to magazines, newsletters and newspapers are indexed. Publications are not all indexed cover to cover. Only feature articles on plants and gardening are indexed from such titles as *Gourmet* and *Smithsonian*.

With its comprehensive coverage, both laypeople and professionals will be interested in *Garden Literature*. In most academic and public libraries, however, this index will increase demand for interlibrary loan as the titles included are a mix of general, specialized, and scholarly, and few places will carry most of them.

The Gardener's Dictionary of Horticultural Terms. Comp. by Harold Bagust. Cassell; dist. by Sterling, 1992. 320p. illus. hardcover $29.95 (0-304-34106-1).
630'.03 Horticulture—Dictionaries || Gardening—Dictionaries [BKL]

This volume includes 2,900 entries, from *abatia* to *zymolsis*, and 1,200 explanatory diagrams that concisely define gardening and botanical terms in nontechnical language. Bagust, a recognized authority on pelargoniums (various herbs and shrubs of the genus *Pelargonium*, which includes the geraniums), is the author of many articles and six books, including *Miniature and Dwarf Geraniums* (Timber, 1988).

The preface states that the terms chosen for inclusion were culled from an extensive review of the literature from the last half-century. The headwords encompass historical references and obsolete terms (*cloche, hotbed, ha-ha*), pests and diseases (*black spot, collar rot, cribriform*), gardener's tools (*snead, thimbles and thumbs, besom*), and botanical terms (*bethos, polypodiaceae, pneumatophore*). Typical entries include a sentence or two and, frequently, a clear line drawing. The dictionary deliberately excludes most plant names and their origins, since comprehensive listings of plants are available in other sources. An appendix of illustrations details shapes, margins, tips, and bases of leaves; compound leaves; leaf lobing; and propagation and grafting techniques.

This dictionary, written for the layperson, is unique, especially for its inclusion of historical terminology. It will be especially appreciated by persons who are reading and writing nonspecialist works about the practice of gardening. *The Gardener's Dictionary of Horticultural Terms* is a handy compendium of concise definitions, with illustrations, that could supplement larger works in comprehensive collections.

North American Horticulture: A Reference Guide. 2d ed. Comp. by the American Horticultural Society; ed. by Thomas M. Barrett. Macmillan, 1992. 427p. index. hardcover $75 (0-02-897001-2).
635'.02573 Horticulture—U.S.—Societies, etc.—Directories || Gardening—U.S.—Societies, etc.—Directories || Conservation of natural resources—U.S.—Societies, etc.—Directories || Horticulture—Canada—Societies, etc.—Directories || Gardening—Canada—Societies, etc.—Directories [CIP] 90-20435

In his introduction to this latest edition of a work first published under this title in 1982, editor Barrett asserts that the intention here is to be as comprehensive as possible. With that goal in mind, this directory of more than 4,000 horticultural organizations and programs in the U.S. and Canada covers everything from native plant societies to community gardens.

Each chapter covers a different subject, beginning with national organizations and proceeding to more specific topics such as listings of horticultural and botanical libraries and organizations dealing with horticultural therapy. There is even a list of cemeteries with notable gardens. The section that covers U.S. and Canadian governmental programs relating to horticulture lists not only federal offices, but also governmental and university-sponsored programs in each state and province.

The state-by-state breakdown in some of the chapters is intended to include more local information than the previous edition. There is now a whole chapter on state and local horticultural groups. New to this edition are sections on native plant societies and botanical clubs and a brief chapter titled "Historical Horticulture and Museum Gardens" that lists historic and estate gardens, living historical farms and museums, historic landscape preservation societies, and other groups involved in the preservation or interpretation of the horticultural heritage of North America. For example, the Flower and Herb Exchange of Decorah, Iowa, is an organization dedicated to the preservation and exchange of heirloom herbs and flowers.

Comprehensive indexes by organizational name and by state will help guide users to the appropriate page. Adequate cross-references occur within the text. A few black-and-white photographs of gardens add interest.

For academic and public libraries with strong collections and/or programs in horticulture.

The New Royal Horticultural Society Dictionary of Gardening. 4v. Ed. by Anthony Huxley and others. Stockton Press, 1992. bibliog. illus. index. hardcover $795 (1-56159-001-0).
635'.03 Gardening—Dictionaries || Horticulture—Dictionaries [CIP] 92-3261

This work is a worthy successor to such illustrious gardening books as Liberty Hyde Bailey's *Standard Cyclopedia of Horticulture*, outlined in the "Historical Introduction" here. It is a total revision of the Royal Horticultural Society's 1951 *Dictionary of Gardening* and the first to be compiled on computer. The editors have incorporated more precise names, new species, and hybrids in this multivolume, multipurpose encyclopedia.

Taking the view outlined in the preface that gardening "combines craft and science, history and art," this work covers all aspects of growing plants, designing gardens, and conservation. The largest proportion of the work is devoted to descriptions of 3,983 genera of plants, which are accurately named and identified. These entries are as brief as a few paragraphs or as long as 10 pages for plants with many varieties. Some of the entries are accompanied by detailed black-and-white drawings. A fairly detailed explanation of the cultivation of the plant is included. Although these explanations are largely British in orientation, by reading how the plant grows in its natural environment—soil, water, maximum and minimum temperatures, pests, and fertilizer—gardeners can judge if it could be cultivated in their area.

In addition to plant descriptions, there are biographies of such people as growers, scientists, gardeners, and landscapers. Approximately 170 individuals are covered, including Luther Burbank, "Capability" Brown, Thomas Jefferson, Gertrude Jekyll, and Frederick Law Olmstead. The biographies concentrate on contributions to horticulture, landscaping, or gardening. Nearly 180 entries on general topics round out the work, ranging in length from 4 to 20 pages. They include *Arboriculture, Bonsai, Botanical Gardens, Indoor Plants, Orchids,* and *Water Gardening*. Particularly interesting and well written are the two articles on the history of gardening in the U.K. and the U.S.

A detailed explanation on using the set is included, with the parts of the plant entries labeled for identification. This is must reading for anyone unfamiliar with scientific dictionaries. A botanical glossary and a horticultural glossary are available in volumes 1 and 4, respectively, to help users with terminology. A glossary of biological epithets is useful in understanding scientific names. Volume 4 also contains the list "Pests, Diseases, and Disorders," an index of authors cited with pertinent dates, and an index of common names referenced to the scientific names. An extensive bibliography arranged by subject leads the user to more in-depth information on general topics.

Although written primarily by British gardeners and using British terms, American and other foreign contributors are included. All are experts in their fields and bring a high level of accuracy and enthusiasm to this work. These volumes will be useful to scientists, growers, botanists, agriculturalists, and gardeners. The set may be too advanced for the casual hobbyist who may find the scientific approach intimidating. The New York Botanical Garden Illustrated Encyclopedia of Horticulture [RBB S 15 83] was written for North American gardeners, takes a somewhat more popular approach, and is illustrated with photographs, rather than drawings. In 10 volumes, it is even more expensive than the set under review. Less-expensive works such as The American Horticulture Society Encyclopedia of Garden Plants [RBB Mr 15 90] (which, despite its title, is also British) or the Gardener's Companion [BKL My 1 91] might suffice where budgets are tight or detailed information is not in demand. For academic, special, and public libraries that can afford it, The New Royal Horticultural Society Dictionary of Gardening is an extremely useful addition to the gardening section.

Rodale's Illustrated Encyclopedia of Perennials. By Ellen Phillips and C. Colston Burrell. Rodale, 1993. 544p. bibliog. illus. index. hardcover $26.95 (0-87596-570-9).
635.9'32 Perennials || Perennials—Encyclopedias [OCLC] 92-30109

Does your garden consist of a couple of bedraggled rose plants and wilted petunias, while your neighbor's looks like the Longwood Gardens? Rodale's Illustrated Encyclopedia of Perennials is the latest offering for the green-thumbed and gardening wannabes. The book is divided into three major sections, focusing on designing gardens, growing perennials, and an A–Z dictionary of plant types.

The section on design covers choosing beds, borders, and islands to flatter the yard and selecting blooms to span or highlight seasons. The color-wheel technique for selecting complementary colors of plants is included. Height, arrangement, texture, degree of formality, light, and shade are discussed. Then the individual elements are pulled together into designs for the yard, including a variety of plans with suggested plants. Growing the perfect garden involves a number of elements. Knowing about climate, soil, soil preparation, diseases, and weeds figures strongly in a successful garden. Also included in this section are discussions and charts on the propagation and culture of a variety of plants.

The last half of the book is devoted to the individual perennials. One hundred sixty-one flowers, foliage plants, and ground covers are described. Besides descriptions, pointers are given on how to grow them and on their landscape uses. Entries for many popular plants, such as dianthus, are broken down into various varieties. For example, 14 varieties of hostas and 10 day lilies are included. Each entry has at least one color photograph of a variety of that plant.

The volume closes with a glossary, lists of sources and organizations, and suggested reading. The index allows access by popular and formal names. (The common name gives a see reference.) It also includes subject references to such topics as composting, flowers, and propagation.

Several guides to perennials have been published in recent years. Taylor's Guide to Perennials (rev. ed., H&M, 1986) and Perennials for American Gardens (Random, 1989) offer access to a large variety of plants. The Perennials volume in the Burpee American Gardening Series (Prentice Hall, 1991) gives a brief overview. Rodale's presentation is literally more from the ground up. It makes generous use of photographs, illustrations, charts, and special boxed segments to help pull the various concepts together. The information on designing gardens and growing plants contained in Rodale's Illustrated Encyclopedia of Perennials may make the book appropriate for circulating collections, with a second copy for reference. In either location, it will be a useful volume in public libraries.

Growing Beautiful Houseplants: An Illustrated Guide to the Selection and Care of over 1,000 Varieties. By Rob Herwig. Facts On File, 1992. 384p. bibliog. illus. index. hardcover $45 (0-8160-2454-5).
635.9'65 House plants—Dictionaries [OCLC] 89-77998

Incredible as it may sound, there are no such things as natural houseplants. Rather, they are cultivated indoor strains derived from wild outdoor varieties found in every corner of the earth. New plants are being developed continually through crossbreeding of existing varieties. Internationally reknowned horticulturist Herwig is quick to point this out in this latest reference work. Magnificently illustrated, this guide makes many previously published houseplant books obsolete. Coverage is as current and comprehensive as possible; included are a large percentage of the recently developed varieties not found in older plant guides.

Following the same format as his earlier work, the Good Housekeeping Encyclopedia of House Plants, this new reference begins with introductory chapters on the origin, naming, and cultivation of plants in general. These are followed by individual chapters devoted to nine specific types of plants—flowering, foliage, bromeliads, succulents, orchids, bulbs and tubers, container, bonsai, and disposables (seasonal potted throwaways). Attention is then devoted to growing conditions, detailing the types of plants that thrive in different indoor settings (offices, dark corners, windows, etc.). Dish gardens and terrariums are included in this discussion. Nothing is overlooked. Greenhouses, sun-rooms, winter gardens, and the like are all carefully covered. Building materials, light, ventilation, insulation, climate control, and more are examined in a clear and easy-to-understand text. Extensive instructional detail is devoted to the components of the plants themselves and their special needs, including dormancy periods, overwatering, underwatering, and feeding (fertilizing). The soil for each type of plant, repotting methods, rooting, pruning, growing from seeds, transplanting seedlings, advanced propagation methods (grafting), and diseases are covered in an equally thorough manner.

As expected, the plant descriptions comprise the bulk of the text. Exquisite photographs accompany 1,000 of the plants, and descriptions are provided for even more. Plants are arranged alphabetically by their scientific names, with common names appearing in the entries. In addition to the usual general care and propagation information, each entry includes specifics on light, temperature, water, humidity, and soil requirements. Information is complete, concise, and arranged in an easy-to-read format. Each plant appears in one or more categories in the appendixes, which group the plants by care requirements (light, location, temperature, and humidity) and by plant characteristics (foliage, flowering, cacti, etc.). The book concludes with an index that includes scientific and common plant names, as well as subjects.

Growing Beautiful Houseplants is truly as informative as it is stunning. Houseplant gardeners of all levels of experience will benefit from it. This coffee-table book is certain to be a popular and welcome addition to gardening collections.

The Photographic Encyclopedia of Wildflowers. By Teresa Farino. Smithmark, 1992. 224p. illus. index. hardcover $24.98 (0-8317-2806-X).
635.9676 Wild flowers—Encyclopedias [OCLC]

This stunningly beautiful book is distinguished from such similar-looking guides as Lady Bird Johnson's Wildflowers across America by its arrangement and breadth of coverage. Its detailed descriptions closely resemble those found in popular field guides such as the Audubon Society Field Guide to North American Wildflowers. Most guides on the subject limit themselves to one geographic area and are arranged by season and/or types of flora, often separating descriptions from photographs.

This encyclopedia, compiled in Britain, encompasses the world and is arranged by climatic and biogeographic zones. Divided into nine chapters—mountains, polar regions, boreal forests, temperate forests, grasslands, arid lands, tropical forests, freshwater wetlands, and coastlands—each zone's unique climate and flora are discussed separately. Flora are arranged alphabetically by scientific name.

Each entry contains detailed descriptions of the flowers with distinguishing physical features highlighted. This is followed by information on the flower's medicinal use—primarily indigenous or herbal remedies with occasional mention of modern medical use. Discussion also includes name origin, natural habitats, number of species, pollination methods, and any poisonous features. Where applicable, information is given on endangered species and national legal protection. The large color photographs that accompany each entry often show the flowers in a landscape setting. The index lists scientific names only, so there is no way to look up *jack-in-the-pulpit* or *lily-of-the-valley*.

Like most popular publications, this encyclopedia tends to emphasize the more commonly recognized wildflowers instead of the unusual and truly wild species. However, many of the flowers portrayed here are not found in North America and therefore will be new to American readers. Reasonably priced, most libraries, especially the small public ones on limited budgets, will want to acquire this gorgeous publication.

The Horse's Name Was . . . : A Dictionary of Famous Horses from History, Literature, Mythology, Television and Movies. By Terri A. Wear. Scarecrow, 1992. 211p. bibliog. index. hardcover $27.50 (0-8108-2599-6).

636.1 Horses—Dictionaries || Horses—Names—Dictionaries [CIP] 92-37724

Compiled by a librarian, this dictionary is aimed at horse lovers, crossword-puzzle enthusiasts, trivia buffs, and historians. It lists 1,307 horses famous in literature, mythology, history, television, radio, and film. The horses are listed alphabetically by name, with brief information on each. Each horse entry is numbered. The names of owners and other people associated with the horses, movie and book titles, and so on are integrated alphabetically and refer the reader to the appropriate animal. This helpful system enables one to look under *Queen Elizabeth* II, for example, to find a list of horses she has owned, or under *Oklahoma* to find the name of Curley's horse in the 1955 film.

Following the dictionary is a subject index, which provides entry numbers under such broad categories as *Comic Strip, Comic Book, and Cartoon Horses* and *Racehorses, Harness*. Some large categories, such as *Movie horses*, list too many entry numbers to be useful. The volume concludes with a bibliography, offering more than 70 titles for further reading.

Though much of the information here can be found scattered in a variety of other reference sources, there is no other work that brings it all together in a single volume. *The Horse's Name Was . . .* may not be a necessary purchase, but it's a trivia gold mine, and libraries should buy accordingly.

The Complete Dog Book. 18th ed. Howell Book House, 1992. 724p. illus. index. hardcover $27.50 (0-87605-464-5).

636.7088 Dogs [CIP] 91-42714

Published under the auspices of the American Kennel Club, this book includes information on 134 breeds of dogs, five of which have been added since the last edition. One hundred of the breed standards have been revised or reformatted. Updated sections on dog anatomy have been added; the health care section has been revised under the supervision of the University of Pennsylvania School of Veterinary Medicine.

Each section on an individual breed includes a black-and-white photograph, a brief history of the breed, characteristics, and the official standard used in judging at dog shows or field trials. Entries are arranged by type of dog (sporting, terriers, herding, etc.) and alphabetically by breed within these sections. Two inserts of color photographs of dogs supplement the black-and-white ones. Good basic information on selecting a puppy or dog, keeping a dog healthy, and training a dog follow the dog entries. A glossary of terms and a brief index conclude the volume.

For those wanting information on pure-bred dogs, at least the 134 recognized by the AKC, this is the most useful book available since it tells how an animal is judged and what disqualifies a dog from competition. Also, a section on types of competitions—dog shows, canine good citizens, obedience trials, field trials and hunting tests, herding, junior showmanship, and lure coursing—explains how dogs become champions. The sections on the individual breeds also provide some

guidance on personality and temperament. If a reader wants information on breeds not recognized by the AKC, *Mini Atlas of Dog Breeds* [RBB D 1 90] covers 400 breeds in 10 categories. *Mini Atlas* concentrates on dogs as pets rather than as show animals. For more affluent libraries, *Atlas of Dog Breeds* [RBB S 15 89] covers 400 breeds with 1,100 color illustrations. The original occupation of the breed with the characteristics that affect its behavior as a pet are stressed. This work also covers extinct breeds. But for those libraries that have found previous editions of *The Complete Dog Book* useful or that serve clients who breed and show dogs, this eighteenth edition is a necessary purchase.

The Reader's Digest Illustrated Book of Cats. Reader's Digest Press; dist. by Random, 1992. 256p. illus. index. hardcover $25 (0-88850-198-6).

636.8 Cats || Cat breeds [BKL]

Throughout history the popularity of cats has fluctuated dramatically. They were worshiped by the Egyptians, burned in medieval times, and today are the world's most popular pet and the subject of numerous books. This is one of the best general titles on the cat. It is divided into six sections covering the cat through history, feline anatomy, physiology, behavior, breeds, and care.

The first section reviews feline ancestry, related species, and the cat in art and literature. A time line shows the development of the species, and a family tree traces the origin of the domestic cat. Throughout the section are color photographs, reproductions of the cat in the art of the ancient and modern world, and side boxes containing interesting supplemental information, such as how cats were mummified in ancient Egypt.

The information in the anatomy and physiology sections is detailed. The physiology section, in addition to describing the functioning of major body systems, also includes a chapter on disorders of these systems and a description of infectuous diseases, their symptoms, and treatment. There is a separate index to the disorders, but they are also included in the general index.

The album of cats covers 44 breeds currently recognized by at least one cat association. The one- or two-page spread for each breed includes a beautiful artist's drawing of an ideal breed specimen. Other information provided includes the origin and history of the breed, a description of the ideal coat, and a chart showing how championship points are allocated for the breed. Small squares identify the countries where the breed is recognized by at least one cat association. Side boxes give information about the temperament of each breed. Five pages describe nine "exotic" breeds that have not yet gained widespread recognition. These are followed by a chapter on feline genetics and one reviewing the genetic combinations that effect color. The section ends with a glossary of terms used in breeding and showing.

Information about cat shows includes the history of international shows, details on entering a show, and how to organize a cat show. The judging system and disqualifying items are described. A list of organizations of cat fanciers and groups concerned with cat welfare conclude the book.

While similar in content to Gebhardt's *Complete Cat* (Macmillan, 1991), this title is broader in scope. Gebhardt focuses on showing cats with only cursory information on the evolution, physiology, and care of the animals. The comprehensive approach of this new title makes it not only an excellent reference source but an interesting and useful book for cat owners of both pedigreed and household pet varieties. Libraries may want copies for the circulating collection, too.

Consumer Product and Manufacturer Ratings, 1961–1990: A Worldwide Directory of about 1,800 Companies Rated Comparatively by the Quality, Price and Value of the Consumer Products They Manufacture or Market in Four Major Market Areas. 2v. Comp. by Intrep Data Corp. Gale, 1993. indexes. tables. hardcover $395 (0-8103-7707-1).

640'.73 Consumer goods—Evaluation || Manufacturers—Evaluation || Brand name products—Evaluation || Quality of products [CIP] 92-33181

Industry analysts, market researchers, consumer-protection agencies, trade associations, quality-control managers, and business students are among the intended audience for this monumental, unique new reference work. This 30-year retrospective look at how the products of thousands of the world's major manufacturers have been rated by independent testing groups offers unprecedented assistance in evaluating corporate performance. Included are manufacturers of a wide variety of consumer products in four world market areas: the U.S., Europe, Japan, and Australia.

The set is arranged in 14 consumer-product categories, such as automotive supplies and major appliances, and then by more than 300 product lines, including cookies, cough medicine, pasta, thermometers, etc. The range of products included is broad but not comprehensive; for example, neither toys nor CD players are included. The data are provided for a category of products, such as refrigerators from Sears or Whirlpool, but not for any individual models. The information about each manufacturer's product consists of a table called "Product Line Competitive Profile." This table gives numeric ratings for the quality position, price position, and value position for the manufacturer's product relative to the same product produced by all manufacturers in the same market area and in the same time period. These ratings range from 0 to 100, where 70 is average, and are derived from Thurstone's Law of Comparative Judgment. A technical appendix explains the methodology used for extracting data from product test studies and then converting the data to this numeric standard.

For some products, such as cereals from General Foods, ratings data are provided for all four world market areas. Reasonably, figures for some consumer goods are limited to one area, such as only the U.S. market for dairy products from Land O' Lakes. Sometimes, however, it is unexpected that U.S. figures are not provided for products sold here, such as Almay lipsticks, Braun toasters, and Nabisco snack foods. The user's guide discusses limitations of the data—including lack of information because no tests may have been performed on a particular product in a particular market—but maintains that the book provides the most comprehensive source available of objective data on product quality. An appendix lists the addresses for the four dozen testing agencies and publications that were the sources for the performance data utilized for the ratings.

Two indexes provide additional access points to the information. "Company Products and Addresses" gives alphabetic access to 1,800 firms and provides a list of the company's product lines. The "Market Area Index" provides alphabetic access by major product category for each of the four world market areas; each company entry includes address and product lines. A thorough user's guide is also included.

The intent is to make *Consumer Product and Manufacturer Ratings* into an ongoing research tool for this type of data. In addition to the 30-year retrospective edition, annual supplements are planned, and, currently, the volume covering 1991 ratings is available for $195, or for $100 if it is ordered with the retrospective edition. This source will prove valuable to specialized researchers and analysts, and comprehensive business collections may want to consider it for purchase.

The Directory of Food and Nutrition Information: For Professionals & Consumers. 2d ed. Ed. by Robyn C. Frank and Holly Berry Irving. Oryx, 1992. 332p. indexes. paper $55 (0-89774-689-9).
641'.02573 Food—Information services—Directories || Nutrition—U.S.—Information services—Directories [CIP] 92-23680

This directory is designed to assist nutrition professionals, librarians, and consumers in identifying resources useful in the fields of nutrition education, food science, food-service management, and other aspects of applied nutrition. This second edition, substantially expanded and updated since the title first appeared in 1984, lists an astounding number of sources in a wide variety of categories.

The directory is divided into two major parts, each having several chapters about different categories of resources. Part 1, compiled through questionnaire surveys, consists of 4 chapters covering 650 organizations, 230 academic programs, 150 software programs, and 70 nutrition-oriented databases. The scope of each chapter is broad, and the entries contain a substantial amount of information. For instance, the software listings range from specialized programs for nutrition professionals to educational programs for children. The entries identify host systems, program focus, intended audience, price, and documentation. The database entries, covering both CD-ROM products and online files, indicate subject strengths, update frequency, file size, print versions, scope of the source documents, search aids, and vendors.

Part 2 consists of 10 chapters and was compiled by the editors utilizing a variety of source documents and their specialized knowledge of the field of nutrition. The categories resources covered in part 2 empasize print sources, special collections, clearinghouses, and regional organizations. Each chapter begins with an introduction outlining the scope, audience, and evaluation methods used to select the resources listed. The entries include, when appropriate, useful annotations and full bibliographic citations. An illustration of the new food-guide pyramid and a chart listing recommended dietary allowances appear in an appendix.

The directory concludes with two subject indexes, one for each of the two main parts of the book, and both must be consulted for complete information retrieval. Alternative points of access are provided in many of the individual chapters. For example, consulting *meats* in the two subject indexes produces a combined total of 37 entries. If a user wanted only help lines, consulting *meats* in the index of the appropriate chapter yields 10 listings.

The editors of *The Directory of Food and Nutrition Information* are information specialists at the National Agricultural Library. Their collaboration has resulted in a unique, comprehensive, and authoritative work that will be useful in public, academic, and special libraries and will be invaluable to nutrition professionals.

The Low-Fat Supermarket. By Judith Scharman Smith and Scott D. Smith. Starburst, P.O. Box 4123, Lancaster, PA 17604, 1993. 300p. tables. paper $10.95 (0-914984-43-8).
641.14 Food—Fat content—Tables || Food—Cholesterol content—Tables [OCLC] 92-81392

A registered dietician and a medical doctor compiled this practical guide to cutting down on the consumption of fat. Brief narrative chapters cover the qualities and dangers of fat in the diet; the confusion over such terms as *lite* on food labels and the proposed government regulations; and tips for altering cooking methods to cut down on fat.

The bulk of the book consists of tables, organized into sections similar to those found in the supermarket (e.g., "Canned Goods," "Freezer Case," "Bakery"). These sections are further divided, first by type of food, then by product line, and then by brand. For instance, "Dairy Case" has sections covering cheese, cottage cheese, dairy desserts, milk, ricotta, sour cream, and yogurt. Nine different brands of yogurt are included, each with a table showing different varieties and flavors sold by that producer. For each variety, the table shows serving size, calories per serving, grams of fat, milligrams of sodium and cholesterol, and percentage of fat. Since the book is "designed to help you find lower fat foods," the only ones listed have less than 30 percent of their calories in fat. A final section provides similar tables for low-fat offerings from fast-food establishments.

More than 4,000 food items are said to be listed. The authors aimed to include information on national brands and some regional ones. They collected the data from manufacturers, government reports, and product labels. The explanations are succinct and clear and complement the tables well. Although early chapters provide enough information to interpret the significance of the amounts of fat, sodium, and cholesterol listed, a guide at the beginning of the tables (or even at the bottom of each page) would have added value, especially since there is no index.

The Low-Fat Supermarket is filled with tables having reference value, but it is a book that will be most useful when planning or making shopping trips. Thus, circulating copies may take precedence over reference. Although the public library is the logical home for this tool, libraries serving nutritionists and dieticians may also want to consider it.

Specialty Cookbooks: A Subject Guide. v. 1. By Harriet Ostroff and Tom Nichols. Garland, 1992. 659p. indexes. hardcover $90 (0-8240-6947-1).
016.6415 Cookery—Bibliography [CIP] 91-37398

This unannotated bibliography lists English-language cookbooks published from 1980 through 1990. The annual publishing output of cookbooks is so extensive that the compilers limited it to 4,500 specialized cookbooks divided into four categories: specific ingredients arranged from *Abalone* to *Zucchini*; specific dishes and courses arranged from *Appetizers* to *Turnovers*; specific meals, from *Breakfasts* to *Suppers*; and special techniques, from *Baking* to *Stir*

Frying. General, ethnic, and regional cookbooks were omitted, as were audiovisual materials. A second volume will cover the topics of equipment, special diets, and miscellaneous special conditions.

In the introduction, the compilers explain that each section contains entries arranged by date of publication and then alphabetically by title within a given year. Cookbooks written for children are listed last in each section. Each citation includes a full bibliographic description and notes the presence of illustrations. Addresses of some small presses are given with the citation. Many Canadian and British publishers are represented. The book concludes with separate author and title indexes. While the extent of this bibliography is impressive, it has a serious shortcoming—the absence of critical annotations. A chef who looked at it asked: Where are the evaluations of these books?

Several other bibliographies list historical cookbooks. The only other bibliography of current cookbooks is *Current Cookbooks: A Selected List of Methods and Cuisines* by Christine Bulson (CHOICE, 1990). It lists about 250 cookbooks by nationality, cooking techniques, courses and meals, ingredients, and special audiences and has annotations.

Specialty Cookbooks will be a welcome addition to schools training cooking professionals. While it is interesting to know that there are cookbooks devoted to earthworms, eels, and aloe vera, the high price of this book may serve to put it out of the reach of any but the largest public libraries.

The Directory of Business Information Resources 1992: Associations, Newsletters, Magazines, Trade Shows. Ed. by Leslie Mackenzie. Grey House Publishing, Pocket Knife Sq., Lakeville, CT 06039, 1992. 681p. bibliog. index. hardcover $135 (0-939300-11-7); paper $110 (0-939300-15-X).

650'.025 Trade and professional associations—U.S.—Directories ‖ Trade and professional associations—Canada—Directories ‖ Newsletters—U.S.—Directories ‖ Newsletters—Canada—Directories ‖ Business—Periodicals—Directories [CIP]

This resource directory aims to provide information "every business needs to stay current and competitive." Listing associations, newsletters, magazines, and trade shows for 95 major industry groups, the directory is arranged alphabetically by industry; a Standard Industrial Code (SIC) cross-reference table follows the table of contents.

Industry groups covered include amusement/entertainment, aviation, environment and conservation, garden supplies, jewelry, mining, travel, and water supply. Associations, newsletters, magazines, and trade shows are listed separately under each industry. Information given for the associations includes address, telephone and fax numbers, a brief description, executive director, year founded, and number of members. Usually listed for newsletters and magazines are publisher, address, telephone and fax numbers, description, editor, year founded, frequency, pages, and price. For trade shows, address, telephone and fax numbers, description, contact person, month, and number of attendees are provided. At the back of the book is a copy of the questionnaire used to gather the information; updates and additions are encouraged.

As the introduction states, this information can be found in other sources in libraries, such as the *Encyclopedia of Associations, Trade Shows Worldwide, Newsletters in Print,* and periodicals directories. However, having all this information in one volume arranged by industry is handy. *The Small Business Sourcebook* (4th ed., Gale, 1991) provides somewhat similar types of information, but the directory under review covers different industries, more trade shows, and adds newsletters. Public, academic, and business libraries will want to add this useful resource to their collections.

Who Knows What: The Essential Business Resource Book. By Daniel Starer. Holt, 1992. 1,239p. indexes. hardcover $45 (0-8050-1853-0).

016.65 Business information services—U.S.—Directories [CIP] 92-17132

This new reference provides lists of addresses and telephone numbers to contact business and government experts on a wide variety of topics. The work is arranged alphabetically by more than 500 subject categories, ranging from *Abrasives Industry* and *Barber and Beauty Shops* to *Foundations* and *Desktop Publishing.*

The section for each subject begins with a list of professional associations, including the name of the president, director, or chair. Next are listed titles of periodicals and their editors, libraries, and, finally, companies. Each address is followed by a single-sentence annotation describing either the membership or the focus of the business or institution. The entries for the federal government agencies tell who to ask for ("ask for the commodity analyst who is an expert in . . ."). *See also* connections are provided at the beginning of each section. For example, *Ships and Shipping Industry* includes *see also* references to *Container Industry, Freight Transportation,* and *Waterways and Ports.*

Each state has its own subject section, interfiled alphabetically with other topics in the book. Provided is the central telephone number to contact all state government offices, and then specific offices are listed, such as those for attorney general, banking, commerce, library services, ombudsperson, taxation, and unemployment. The appendix explains databases: their advantages, disadvantages, and how to use them. It includes a list of 12 major online companies, how to contact them, and what they do. Two indexes are included, one for subjects and another for associations, periodicals, and companies.

The author, a professional researcher, compiled this reference from his years of experience. Very useful to those new to research is the introductory material that not only explains the origin of this tome, but how best to approach research in general and the people one will contact when using this book. The section "Preparing for the Call" offers nine questions the researcher should consider. "Making the Call" has eight suggestions for telephone manners, getting past the secretary, and ending the conversation.

Who Knows What is intended as a desktop reference for the businessperson or professional who does not have immediate access to the wide range of directories typically owned by many libraries. It does not substitute for the larger number of listings or greater amounts of description found in standard directories with narrower scopes. However, the broad range of this work—listing contact information for industry, government, and the arts—makes it a useful and affordable one-volume tool for any reference desk, not just business as its subtitle indicates. High school librarians will find this a wonderful aid in teaching the research process to students. It should be considered by all libraries, regardless of size or area of specialization.

The Encyclopedia of Career Change and Work Issues. Ed. by Lawrence K. Jones. Oryx, 1992. 379p. bibliog. charts. illus. index. hardcover $67.50 (0-89774-610-4).

650.1 Vocational guidance—Encyclopedias ‖ Career changes—Encyclopedia ‖ Labor—Encyclopedias [CIP] 91-33913

This compilation treats varied issues and problems of the workplace from the point of view of the employee. Its purpose is to enable readers to deal effectively with these issues and problems. Among the more than 160 topics covered are the expected (such entries as *Résumé, Career Planning, Discrimination: People with Disabilities,* and *Law in the Workplace*) and the unexpected (*Low Back Pain, Fear of Flying, Nonstandard English,* and *Self-Esteem*). The authors of the signed articles are generally experts in their fields: Carol Tavris for *Anger,* Donald Super (professor emeritus of psychology and education at Columbia University) for *Career Roles,* and Roger Pearman (president of the Association for Psychological Type) for *Myers-Briggs Type Indicator,* to name a few. Each of the 151 contributors and 14 consulting editors is profiled in a section at the front of the book.

Arrangement is alphabetical by topic. Before the main body of the work, a "Guide to Related Topics" groups the articles under 21 general subjects, such as *Discrimination and Harassment, Pay and Benefits,* and *Women.* A 15-page index also aids access. Most articles are one to five pages in length, with a few as long as 17 pages. They are generally in three sections: information about the topic, practical application of the information, and annotated bibliographic references for further information. Even articles on technical topics such as *Benefits* are accessible to the layperson. Some entries are accompanied by charts or drawings. For example, the entry *Career Identity* includes a chart, "Career Involvement," reprinted from Donald T. Hall's book, *Careers in Organizations. Posture and Body Mechanics* has several drawings showing the safe way to lift and reach. *See also* references are listed at the end of most articles.

The quality of this work is generally excellent. The Board noted one minor problem; *Employee Information and Verification* is duplicated almost word for word in *Immigration*. This book is a unique contribution and will be useful in high school, college, and public libraries.

Professional Secretaries International Complete Office Handbook: The Secretary's Guide to Today's Electronic Office. Ed. by Susan W. Fenner. Random, 1992. 573p. bibliog. charts. illus. index. tables. hardcover $25 (0-679-40080-X).
651.8 Office practice—Automation [CIP] 91-43208

Computers, electronic mail, teleconferencing, and other information technologies have changed how businesses function and have placed new demands on administrative and office support personnel. This guide details office practices and procedures for today's electronic office while providing coverage of all traditional business areas.

Chapters deal with professional development and human relations, equipment and supplies, specialized office procedures, office communications, and grammar and punctuation. Each offers specific information. For example, the section on professional development and human relations is concerned with career advancement, time management and problem solving, organizational structures and office relationships, and business ethics and etiquette. In the equipment chapter, the telex and the mimeograph machine are mentioned, but more attention is given to the fax machine and the word processor. Various types of software are discussed, along with computer viruses and software copyright issues.

The "Specialized Office Procedures" section covers records management, accounting and bookkeeping, travel and meeting planning, and mail. "Office Communications" covers written correspondence and oral and electronic communication; the subsection "Office Publishing" points out features of typesetting versus desktop publishing, graphics, and printing methods. The final chapter is a review of grammar and punctuation.

While *Webster's Secretarial Handbook* (2d ed., 1983) has been a classic for office support personnel, time and technology have passed it by. *Webster's New World Secretarial Handbook*, fourth edition [RBB N 1 89], is more up-to-date, but *Professional Secretaries International Complete Office Handbook* has unique information on developing professionally and on desktop publishing. It offers guidelines for setting standards and developing and maintaining an effective electronic office; it belongs in all reference collections.

Codes and Ciphers. By Fred B. Wrixon. Prentice Hall, 1992. 288p. bibliog. illus. index. paper $18 (0-13-277047-4).
652'.8 Cryptography—Juvenile literature || Ciphers—Juvenile literature [CIP] 91-42848

This subject dictionary is intended for the interested layperson having no background in the science or art of cryptology. Its stated purpose is to provide an introduction to the "full scope of the art." The book includes entries for people, events, decoding equipment, titles of codes, names of ciphers, and general terminology of the field. Individual entries, ranging from two paragraphs to three pages in length, are listed alphabetically, and explanations are kept simple with minimal jargon. The codes discussed range from secret ones used by military and diplomatic personnel to the nonsecret codes used in science and industry (genetic code, bankcard code, etc.). Biographical entries focus on the person's significance to cryptology or his or her experiences with codes, rather than summarizing credentials or life's work (e.g., Marie Antoinette's method of concealment in her amatory notes; William Friedman's contributions as "the premier U.S. cryptanalyst").

The illustrations used to clarify how a particular concealment works are the most useful feature of *Codes and Ciphers*. Some are as simple as a key matched to plaintext; others show the operation of an entire code through multiple steps. An understanding of *fractionating ciphers* would be impossible were it not for the illustrations the author provides. Other objectives of the book are not as successful. There is no unified historical overview in an introduction or elsewhere, and the lack of adequate indexing makes it impossible to easily identify ancient codes, codes developed for specific wars, scandals, famous spies and agents, or notable successes or failures. For example, the entry *Maru Code* (the code used by Japanese supply ships during World War II) is not indexed under either Japan or World War II.

Codes and Ciphers serves a useful purpose by identifying and providing easily understood explanations for codes associated with cryptology and is recommended for high school and public libraries needing a basic introductory work. For more in-depth needs, users can consult David Shulman's *Annotated Bibliography of Cryptography* to identify articles on specific codes or a country's operations. Students interested in U.S. diplomatic history are well served by Ralph E. Weber's *United States Diplomatic Codes and Ciphers*, 1775–1938.

101 Business Ratios: A Manager's Handbook of Definitions, Equations, and Computer Algorithms. By Sheldon Gates. McLane Publications, P.O. Box 9-C, Scottsdale, AZ 85252, 1993. 288p. bibliog. charts. index. tables. hardcover $24.95 (1-881502-00-7).
658.151'1 Ratio analysis || Managerial accounting [CIP] 92-90816

This managerial reference book contains many different types of business ratios used to measure progress. The work is a personal anthology of well-known, little-known, and entirely new ratios compiled by Gates, who developed and used many of these ratios during his business career. Ratios are organized into six categories based on managerial need—sales, profit, debt/capital, efficiency, marketing, and investment. Each ratio is described five ways, starting with a succinct, written definition; an explanation of what the ratio measures; why it is important; who looks at it; and the meaning of the numbers. Managers of small and medium-size businesses, financial officers, lenders, management consultants, business investors, and students will find the ratios helpful in assessing a firm's financial health and relative value.

The book is organized in two parts. Chapters 1–7 introduce ratio analysis and then describe 101 specific measures as well as formulas for their computation. Chapters 8–11 are how-to sections concerned with practical application of the ratios; they explain finding the input numbers, calculating the ratios, and presenting the ratios in numerical and graphic formats. The reader is also introduced to the ways computers are used to process and report ratio information. Appendixes provide a list of ratios, a list of input statistics, a usage table, suggestions for acronymic naming of variables, stock market ratios, and miscellaneous tips for readers. In addition, a glossary defines many technical terms appearing in the text, and more than 40 graphs and tables of information are included. Many chapters also include a list of sources for the information presented.

While both *Industry Norms and Key Business Ratios* (Dun & Bradstreet, annual) and the *Almanac of Business and Industrial Financial Ratios* (20th ed., Prentice Hall, 1991) contain many financial ratios, no other title compiles these 101 ratios or cuts across the disciplines of accounting, economics, mathematics, and computer science. All business collections will want to add this small, inexpensive, but valuable, new resource.

Finance, Insurance, & Real Estate USA: Industry Analyses, Statistics, and Leading Organizations. Ed. Arsen J. Darnay. Gale, 1993. 750p. index. maps. tables. hardcover $169 (0-8103-8499-X; ISSN 1066-7350).
658.159330973 Finance—U.S.—Statistics || Insurance—U.S.—Statistics || Real estate—U.S.—Statistics [OCLC]

The purpose of this user-friendly resource is to provide, in one place, analyses of the U.S. industries of finance, insurance, and real estate. Synthesized here are data from the Federal Deposit Insurance Corporation, the Federal Reserve System, industry associations, *Ward's Business Directory*, and such government studies as *County Business Patterns, Benchmark Input-Output Accounts for the U.S. Economy,* and the *Industry-Occupation Matrix* prepared by the Bureau of Labor Statistics. Coverage includes national, state, and county ratios and data for 36 industries (12 at the three-digit SIC level; 24 at the four-digit SIC level), as well as information for more than 2,600 companies (address, telephone number, officers, sales/assets). Dates for the data series range from 1986 to 1990 (1986 to 1992 in some cases), and occupational data projections are provided through 2005.

Access to specific topics is provided by four indexes: 1987 SIC code (arranged numerically by code and alphabetically by industry name), keywords (including SIC codes that apply), company names, and occupations. Access within the main text is numerical by SIC code for national industry summaries (part 1 of the book) and alphabetical by state for state and 2,500 county industry summaries (part 2). The information is provided in tabular, graphic, and map formats and includes data regarding an industry's establishment counts (classified by employment and payroll), inputs and outputs, occupations employed by an industry (1990 data projected through 2005), and various rankings tables.

This resource will help to answer a broad range of questions from business and individuals, including queries about appropriate SIC codes, trends in various industries (e.g., size, income), where industries are geographically concentrated, the location and statistics of specific companies, and where a person with a specific occupation might be able to find a job.

Although many of the companies within the sectors of finance, industry, and real estate are covered in the Moody's manuals, *Standard & Poor's Corporation Records*, and the Dun & Bradstreet *Million Dollar Directory*, the summary statistics and analyses provided here cannot be found elsewhere. *Finance, Insurance, & Real Estate* USA will be a useful addition for academic, large public, and business libraries.

Research Guide to Corporate Acquisitions, Mergers, and Other Restructuring. By Michael Halperin and Steven J. Bell. Greenwood, 1992. 208p. bibliog. illus. index. hardcover $49.95 (0-313-27220-4).
016.65816 Consolidation and merger of corporations—Information services [CIP] 91-24199

Locating up-to-date information in the fast-changing realm of corporate acquisitions, mergers, divestitures, bankruptcies, stock filings, and other business changes is essential. Up to now, finding the right source for this information has been difficult, especially for librarians without large business collections or for those not doing much business reference work. Written by librarians at the Lippincott Library of the Wharton School at the University of Pennsylvania, this guide makes finding this information much easier.

The book explains the use of sources of information on a wide range of topics, such as monitoring corporate change, public disclosures of mergers and acquisitions (M&A), finding acquisition candidates, identifying corporate parents and their subsidiaries and divisions, and international M&A. Both print and electronic information sources are described, often with sample pages or screens. Two appendixes list the online databases and vendors described throughout the guide. A glossary defines about 50 terms, and a select bibliography lists more than 60 items.

The last chapter, "Information Checklist," ties all of the information from the previous eight chapters together and shows the kind of data one can find using this guide, such as financial, industry, and marketing information, and the sources used to find it. Under each section are typical facts one can locate (e.g., earning estimates, joint ventures, who owns whom, new product announcements) and the name of the source for that information. This chapter, by itself, is a valuable tool for any M&A or business researcher.

Many expensive online and CD-ROM databases exist today to find current information about companies. There are also cheaper alternatives like newspapers, newsletters, and magazines. Knowing which source to use to find specific information is now easier because of this excellent guide. Academic and public libraries answering questions about corporate acquisitions and mergers should purchase this book.

The ASTD Handbook of Instructional Technology. Ed. by George M. Piskurich. McGraw-Hill, 1993. 660p. bibliog. illus. index. tables. hardcover $59.95 (0-07-001531-7).
658.3'124 Employees—Training of—Data processing—Handbooks, manuals, etc. ‖ Employees—Training of—Audio-visual aids—Handbooks, manuals, etc. [CIP] 92-23142

The sponsor of this work, the American Society for Training and Development (ASTD), is the major professional association for persons engaged in the training and development of employees in business, industry, education, and government. This new handbook "is written by and for practitioners of instructional technology (IT)," who may include "trainer, educator, teacher, or instructional designer." The field of IT is broad, encompassing the machinery and methods used to convey knowledge. With an impressive list of many authoritative contributors from business and academia, the book fulfills its goal of gathering, in one volume, the current information on instructional technology.

Arranged around four major sections—media foundations, technology-based instruction, instructional design, and controversy and prophecy—this book is useful for the individual looking for information on specific aspects, such as "Authoring Systems Today," "Producing Video," "Designing Training Rooms," and "Self-Directed Learning." The scope of the work is broad. Coverage of training techniques that utilize state-of-the-art technology explains such topics as expert systems, hypermedia, teleconferencing, and interactive video. However, older techniques are not ignored: filmstrips, overhead transparencies, audiotapes, and graphics all appear in the discussion. The reader sees that, in all cases, the choice of the technology is related to the goals of the instruction. A complete index allows the reader to gather information on such applications as CAI (computer-assisted instruction) or CD-ROM, since they may be dealt with in several chapters.

This work is a textbook for the instructional technology practitioner, so each chapter clearly states learning objectives. Case studies, glossaries, and bibliographies make each chapter useful for the novice or experienced researcher. Good illustrative visuals, forms, and sample demonstrations complement the text. The chapter "How to Use Media Equipment," which includes terminology, description of basic techniques, and media management, should be mandatory reading for classroom teachers, salespersons, sales trainers, or architects who design rooms used for presentation. Part 4, "Controversy and Prophecy," explores the future of IT and places it in the context of new technological innovations and increased understanding of how people learn today.

The ASTD Handbook of Instructional Technology clearly is most appropriate for the IT practitioner in business and education. While the book's information is encyclopedic and readable for the general public, it may be of limited use in many general collections. On the other hand, since its focus is on technologies that best convey information, it will be valuable to library staff seriously engaged in training activities, bibliographic instruction, or design of learning aids for library patrons.

Business Week's Guide to the Best Executive Education Programs. By John A. Byrne and Cynthia Greene. McGraw-Hill, 1992. 248p. charts. index. hardcover $24.95 (0-07-009334-2); paper $14.95 (0-07-009335-0).
658.4'0071 Management—Study and teaching (Higher)—U.S.—Evaluation ‖ Master of business administration degree—U.S. ‖ Business schools—U.S.—Faculty—Attitudes ‖ Business students—U.S.—Attitudes [CIP] 92-26321

Business Week follows up on its rankings of graduate business schools with this look at nondegree executive education programs and MBA programs for executives. The magazine began its assessment by mailing more than 10,000 surveys to deans, companies, and participants in 56 of these programs. More than 3,000 questionnaires were returned, and the initial results were published, based on this data, in the October 28, 1991, issue. The current publication supplements this information by additional surveys of customer satisfaction and by interviewing "hundreds of students, alumni, recruiters, faculty members, and deans." Byrne, who directed this project, has reported on management education for 10 years for BW. An estimated 150 business schools now offer continuing education programs designed especially for executives; this guide profiles approximately one-third of these.

Interestingly, rankings of the best programs show disparities of several types. Many schools, rated at the top for traditional business education, do not perform as well in rankings of executive education programs. Corporate customers, executive alumni, and managers of executive education all have different opinions about the top schools. One institution may be best for general management programs, whereas it may be weak in financial education. The book discusses these differences and provides various graphs, lists, and appendixes to display the range of opinions.

Business Week averaged the ratings of programs from different categories of respondents to compile its list of the top 20 executive education programs, as well as a list of 10 runners-up. Approximately five pages are devoted to each of the top 20 schools. Following directory-type information (e.g., address, numbers of programs and participants, annual revenues) is a description of the "flagship general management course." Additional noteworthy programs are briefly described. One to two pages of quotations from participants conclude each entry. Identical information is provided for the 10 runners-up with the exception of the participant opinions. Another chapter describes the 10 most innovative programs (as opposed to schools), and a final chapter examines the top 20 executive MBA schools, providing information similar to that for the executive education programs.

Rankings are perennially useful and interesting. *Business Week's* process of choosing the best programs seems thorough for the 56 schools highlighted. For one who wants consumer information on other executive education programs, *Bricker's International Directory, Volume 2: Short-Term University Based Executive Programs* (1991) is a partial answer. For some readers, the original 1991 *Business Week* article may be adequate to satisfy curiosity. The *Guide to the Best Executive Education Programs* has far greater depth and breadth and should be considered for purchase by corporate and business school libraries and other libraries serving business or management clienteles.

The Competitive Intelligence Handbook. By Richard E. Combs and John D. Moorhead. Scarecrow, 1992. 196p. bibliog. index. hardcover $25 (0-8108-2606-2).

658.47 Business intelligence—Handbooks, manuals, etc. || Competition—Handbooks, manuals, etc. [CIP] 92-32740

The Desktop Business Intelligence Sourcebook: A Comprehensive Guidebook for the Information Age. By Kent R. Frantzve. Hyde Park Marketing Group, P.O. Box 8804, Cincinnati, OH 45208, 1992. 192p. bibliog. index. paper $16.95 (1-880186-00-4).

650.072 Business—Research—Handbooks, manuals, etc. || Business information services—U.S.—Handbooks, manuals, etc. || Reference books—Business—Bibliography || Business—Data bases—Directories [OCLC] 91-72603

These two titles appear on the surface to have similar objectives: describing sources of business information that will be useful to business people. *Competitive Intelligence Handbook* is not precisely suitable for reference collections but will be useful as professional reading for business librarians. With caveats to be noted below, *The Desktop Business Intelligence Sourcebook* could be used in small public libraries.

The Competitive Intelligence Handbook has two basic thrusts: to provide information on what the authors call the "discipline of competitive intelligence (CI) itself" and to list sources of information that CI professionals use. The authors define CI "as the selection, collection, interpretation, and distribution of publicly held information that has strategic importance." They note that "the job of CI is to understand the corporate world well enough to find the paper that company actions generate." They define "public" information; offer some general sources for such information, both domestic and international; list some books on CI and summarize their themes; and suggest online and hard-copy sources of information. Bibliographic citations are clear and complete, with brief annotations, and many online sources cited—particularly for Japanese information—include telephone numbers and gateway access points. A chapter on interviewing will be useful, particularly for the novice researcher. It is the how-to elements of *Competitive Intelligence Handbook* that will make it useful in professional reading collections.

Small libraries needing a bibliography of business information may be tempted by *The Desktop Business Intelligence Sourcebook.* The author says the book's purpose "is to provide general research guidance to all those who seek business related data and information, regardless of their skill level." He provides an extensive listing of hard-copy, online, and CD-ROM sources, which, he says, should be available in libraries. One helpful chapter lists the special issues of business periodicals that will assist those attempting to build a business collection. Another explains the Standard Industrial Classification.

However, there are some problems with this book. First, the author lists 14 public, academic, and special libraries with business collections. This list is so selective as to be of little use to those outside of New York, Boston, Chicago, and a few other cities. The author neglects to specify that many sources he cites as available in hardcopy are also accessible electronically online or on CD-ROM. In his section on electronic databases, he does not point out that some sources, such as *ABI/Inform, Business Dateline, Encyclopedia of Associations, Magazine Index,* and PAIS may be available both in CD-ROM and online. He notes the existence of information brokers but lists only the *Burwell Directory of Information Brokers* as a source for locating them. He suggests that entrepreneurs contact the Association of Independent Information Professionals but omits an address for that organization.

A small or medium-size public library needing an inexpensive research guide to assist business people in locating information sources may find *The Desktop Business Intelligence Sourcebook* useful. Large public and academic libraries or business libraries will want to add *The Competitive Intelligence Handbook* to their circulating collections.

Organization Charts: Structures of More Than 200 Businesses and Non-Profit Organizations. Ed. by Judith M. Nixon. Gale, 1992. 240p. charts. index. hardcover $129 (0-8103-8497-3).

658.402 Organization charts—Case studies [OCLC] 92-14166

A picture is worth a thousand words, and *Organization Charts* typifies that old adage with more than 200 graphic representations of corporate structures.

Both public and private, nonprofit and profit organizations are included, ranging from 3-M and Baltimore Gas and Electric Company to the University of Idaho Library and the Sycamore Girl Scout Council. Since this information is not readily available because many companies think of it as proprietary information, the editor scanned hundreds of annual reports, sent direct requests to companies, and searched major databases to present a representative sample of organization structures.

Each full-page entry includes an organization chart with its source and a date. Names of current position holders are not given. The foreword is helpful as a historical overview of organization charts and the way they are used in business. Some corporations—especially the Japanese—do not like to use traditional pyramid charts since they seem to reduce teamwork and give the implication that higher positions are more important than lower ones. Several interesting charts try to avoid these pitfalls by showing the structure in a concentric or circular chart (Chemed Corporation) or in a "sideways pyramid" that tends to de-emphasize the top-down authority relationships (Toshiba Corporation).

Charts are arranged in alphabetical order by company name. An index provides access by company name, parent organization and subsidiary, and subject access by industry or product line. Corporate address and telephone number in these entries would have been a helpful addition.

The preface states that this volume would be helpful to students, job seekers, researchers, and business people. Since the charts rarely show more than top management positions, it is hard to see how it would be of value to most job seekers. It will be useful in large academic business collections and corporate libraries.

The Seasons of Business: The Marketer's Guide to Consumer Behavior. By Judith Waldrop and Marcia Mogelonsky. American Demographics Books, 127 W. State St., Ithaca, NY 14850, 1992. 269p. index. maps. tables. hardcover $34.95 (0-936889-12-8); paper $27.50 (0-936889-13-6).

658.8'342 Consumer behavior—U.S. || Seasonal variations (Economics)—U.S. [OCLC] 91-58812

The purpose of this resource is to outline, month by month, the types of seasonal factors (events, weather patterns, and health-care issues) that influence customers' buying decisions. For each month, pivotal seasonally triggered consumer needs are identified and described in an informal narrative manner. Events in August include back-to-school shopping (with a discussion of which types of malls attract more customers), the need for working women to buy an executive wardrobe, crime's effect on shopping patterns, business travel, golf, and cultural events. In January, the factors are consumers' expectations that stores will have sales, dieting, the Super Bowl, winter sports, and New Year's resolutions. Each chapter begins with the month's weather summary for 40 cities throughout the U.S. and a chart listing items most likely to be on sale during that month. Dotted throughout the chapters are charts that graph patterns such as shipments of apples and oranges from California in 1990, jewelry-store sales versus total retail sales, tornado activities, and when during the year people tend to get married or divorced.

Sources for data (e.g., FBI, U.S. Chamber of Commerce, U.S. Department of Agriculture, Survey of Supermarket Floral Retailing) are cited at the bottom of all charts, and the index is detailed enough to allow access to the content of the book. Also, a great deal of peripheral information is usually included within categories. For example, under kosher foods, statistics are provided on the number of Jews who observe kosher dietary rules. For many libraries, accessing the statistical information provided here from nongovernment agencies such as Rodale Press or the National Sporting Goods Association is difficult or impossible.

The Seasons of Business will have utility as a reference tool because it gathers statistics from many different sources (including government agencies) into one handy place. It will also have appeal as a circulating item, since many customers will want to read it from cover to cover. People in small businesses, students doing papers for marketing classes, reference librarians trying to answer practical marketing questions, and consumers who want to have some perspective on the best times to buy certain items will find this book useful. As with resources such as *Famous First Facts*, *Guinness' Book of World Records*, and other eclectic almanac-like resources, this will find a place in the reference room of public and academic libraries. Many libraries will want to purchase a second copy for their cirulating collections.

The World Markets Desk Book: A Region-by-Region Survey of Global Trade Opportunities. By Lawrence W. Tuller. McGraw-Hill, 1993. 334p. index. tables. hardcover $29.95 (0-07-065478-6).
658.8'48 Export marketing—Handbooks, manuals, etc. ‖ International trade—Handbooks, manuals, etc. [CIP] 92-24542

Tuller is a leading international consultant and author of several books on business topics, including the *McGraw-Hill Handbook of Global Trade and Investment Financing* (1992). In this new title, he provides detailed, authoritative coverage of outstanding market opportunities in more than 50 countries and trading areas. He demonstrates how to take the guesswork out of selecting overseas markets for a company's products or services.

The World Markets Desk Book examines all areas of concern, including the country's political and economic stability, taxes and regulatory statutes, market-growth projections, and locating materials and labor with the lowest cost, highest quality, and best delivery schedules. For large countries, the book even identifies the best sites for establishing facilities and offers tips about specialized niche markets, disclosing which markets to attack now with which products. In addition, informal trade barriers as well as formal and cultural hurdles are discussed in detail.

Developed and developing countries are grouped together geographically in sections covering North and South America; Europe, Africa, and the Middle East; and Asia and the Pacific. Also, one chapter analyzes market opportunities and pitfalls in doing business in the U.S. Besides the table of contents, a country and subject index in the back adds more access points for information. Forty-eight tables provide graphic information as well.

This up-to-the-minute guide will help global executives open doors to worldwide market opportunities that may have been closed until now. International business students and investors will also find useful facts and expert analyses pointing to countries with trade possibilities and to those to avoid. While this well-written source has reference value with its summaries and statistics of trade and investment information, libraries might want to locate it in circulating collections so patrons can peruse it at their leisure.

Cracking Eastern Europe: Everything Marketers Must Know to Sell into the World's Newest Emerging Markets. By Allyn Enderlyn and Oliver C. Dziggel. Probus, 118 N. Clinton St., Chicago, IL 60606, 1992. 385p. index. maps. tables. hardcover $42.50 (1-55738-254-9).
658.8009497 Marketing—Europe, Eastern—Handbooks, manuals, etc. ‖ Europe, Eastern—Commerce ‖ Marketing—Europe, Eastern—Directories ‖ Europe, Eastern—Commerce—Directories [OCLC]

Dziggel and Enderlyn are cofounders of Enterprise Development International, a firm specializing in international business development and technology transfer. Their new trade guide is a gold mine of information for those interested in marketing, investing, or relocating to Eastern Europe. Eight countries (Albania, Bulgaria, Czechoslovakia, Germany, Hungary, Poland, Romania, and Yugoslavia) are discussed in individual chapters.

Each profile offers background information on the country's geography, history, and demographics. In addition, the authors provide tips on hot opportunities, descriptions of governmental business-development policies, advice on financial arrangements, requirements for licenses and trademarks, economic statistics, and key contact and information sources. Capsule descriptions of the countries in question are phrased in meaningful terms; for example, Romania is "slightly smaller than Oregon." Business information is of a practical nature: Poland offers a three-year tax holiday for companies with foreign investors; in Romania, foreigners may not own land or real estate but may lease from Romanian partners. Americans interested in moving into the Eastern European market will be encouraged to read that in Czechoslovakia "German is common, but English is preferred" and that Bulgaria has an Agency for the Encouragement of Foreign Investment. Potential travelers and investors will be less heartened to learn that eastern Germany's best hotel was $275 per night as of January 1992—and even more daunted by the best-hotel notation for Albania: "None."

Chapter 9, "Eastern Europe Key Contacts," directs readers to U.S. Department of Commerce sources, the U.S. Trade and Development Program, the Overseas Private Investment Corporation, private capital institutions active in East-West business, commercial offices of East European countries in the U.S., and U.S. commercial officers in Eastern Europe. Chapter 10 lists major sources of news and information about Eastern Europe, such as newsletters, directories, business bulletins, and handbooks. Also included is a description of the Consortia of American Businesses in Europe program that provides seed money for education, training, trade shows, and market research. The appendix includes useful tables and charts that compare Europe and Eastern Europe. Among the topics covered are population, higher education, western aid, inflation rates, military expenditures, imports, exports, energy output, per diem rates in late 1991, distances between cities in kilometers and in miles, and telecommunication infrastructure. Sources for the data are various government agencies and Runzheimer International.

Another recent title by the same authors, *Cracking the Pacific Rim* (Probus, 1992), provides similar information for nine additional countries (Hong Kong, Indonesia, Japan, Korea, Malaysia, Philippines, Singapore, Taiwan, and Thailand). Both titles are recommended for public, academic, and special libraries that serve clienteles interested in business opportunities in these emerging market areas. However, a word of caution is warranted: things change quickly today. When *Cracking Eastern Europe* went to press, Yugoslavia sounded like a great place to spend time and contemplate business ventures. The disclaimer on the verso of the title page advises readers that "Processes may have altered due to rapid changes in the industry."

FINE ARTS, DECORATIVE ARTS, MUSIC

A Guide to Art. Ed. by Sandro Sproccati. Abrams, 1992. 287p. illus. index. hardcover $29.95 (0-8109-3366-7).
709 Art—History [BKL] 91-77141

This chronologically arranged handbook covers art movements and major artists in Europe and North America from Giotto in the fourteenth century through the 1980s. Originally written in Italian under the editorship of a lecturer in modern art at the Venice Academy of Fine Arts, coverage is overwhelmingly on painters and paintings, although sculpture and architecture are included.

Intended for readers unfamiliar with the history of art, topics from the mid-nineteenth century to the present are given conscious emphasis because they are the "least familiar to the reader." Each chapter of the guide is a concise, straightforward historical essay supported by color illustrations of representative art works. The more than 600 illustrations are small but clear, and the color quality generally is good. In each chapter three features supplement the essays: brief biographical notes on the major artists mentioned in the text, a sidebar devoted to a pertinent theme or topic (theory of perspective, Gothic revival, tautology, etc.), and a synoptic chart relating contemporary happenings in art, political history, music, literature, religion, and philosophy.

Two appendixes and an index conclude the guide. The first appendix is a directory providing brief historical information on the basic collections of 26 great art museums in the Western world. (The five U.S. museums are the Metropolitan, the Museum of Modern Art, the Guggenheim, the National Gallery, and the Philadelphia Museum.) The second appendix is a small glossary of 27 miscellaneous terms (*catharsis, drip painting, koine,* etc.). While these two appendixes may aid the casual reader, reference librarians will turn to standard directories of museums and dictionaries of art terms. Of more value is the index of artists, where more than 800 artists are listed with references to the text and illustrations.

A Guide to Art is a clearly written handbook, but it is not a first-purchase item for reference collections. It will be a valuable title in the circulating collections of many public and college libraries serving museum goers and newcomers to the world of art.

The Visual Dictionary of Buildings. Dorling Kindersley; dist. by Houghton, 1992. 64p. illus. index. hardcover $14.95 (1-56458-102-0).
720'.3 Architecture—Dictionaries ǁ Decoration and ornament, Architectural—Dictionaries [CIP] 92-7673

The Visual Dictionary of Flight. Dorling Kindersley; dist. by Houghton, 1992. 64p. illus. index. hardcover $14.95 (1-56458-101-2).
629.133'014 Airplanes—Terminology—Juvenile literature ǁ Airplanes—Pictorial works—Juvenile literature ǁ Aeronautics—Terminology—Juvenile literature ǁ Aeronautics—Pictorial works—Juvenile literature ǁ Picture dictionaries, English—Juvenile literature [CIP] 92-7670

These two works are new titles in the Eyewitness Visual Dictionaries series and follow the previously established style for these books (see RBB [F 15 92] for a review of four of these dictionaries on the topics of animals, everyday things, the human body, and ships and sailing). Each volume offers strikingly visual and comprehensively informative material to provide instant access to the specialized vocabulary of its topic. Convinced that a picture will explain a subject more clearly than words, British publisher Dorling Kindersley presents vibrant, full-color photographs and illustrations that are identified and extensively labeled. Little textual explanation in the traditional dictionary style is included.

Buildings is a splendidly visual architectural journey through time, proceeding from the temples, tombs, and buildings of ancient Egypt, Greece, and Rome through medieval castles, houses, and churches; through the Renaissance, baroque, and neoclassical styles to the ceilings of the early sixteenth and seventeenth centuries; from the arches, vaults, domes, doors, and windows of earlier times to selectively spectacular modern buildings of the nineteenth and twentieth centuries, concluding with a time line of architectural styles. While the beauty of the photographic and illustrative history of *Buildings* is now expected from this series, a few surprising focuses must be noted. The two-page spread of a molded stucco ceiling (from the Banqueting House, Whitehall Palace, London, 1666–93) is not only presented in its elaborately ornamented beauty but is artfully analyzed and discussed in detail, as though for an art history class. Another visual wonder is the section on doors ranging from an Ionic doorway (Erechtheion, Athens, Greece, 421–405 B.C.) to art deco elevator doors (Chrysler Building, New York, 1928–30). This visual dictionary easily stands tall as an art history source as well as a reference for the structures, forms, and components of buildings.

Flight's pages range through time from the first sustained flight of balloons and airships through early monoplanes, biplanes, and triplanes; from World War I and World War II aircraft through jetliners, modern military aircraft, and helicopters; and from gliders to VTOL aircraft. The specialized vocabulary of 3,000 words used to identify and label the aircraft makes the dictionary read like a manufacturing or flight service manual. The uninitiated, for example, could never recognize the totally disassembled Kestrel V12 engine on page 25 as anything more than parts, yet the text on page 24 states, "One type [engine] had water-cooled cylinders arranged in a single line (in-line) or in a V-shape (like the V12 Kestrel shown here)." Also, the vocabulary uses many British terms. For instance, the book uses the word *fin*, which, in the U.S., would be identified as a vertical stabilizer or tail. An additional concern is that of inconsistencies or inaccuracies found in labeling. On page 22, for example, a part on the B17 Flying Fortress Bomber is labeled *plastic nose*. The term *plastic* was not used in 1939 and is not used now—the term should have been *plexiglass*. However, the flight service-manual style will appeal to young and old alike who have a passion for the mechanical and an understanding of the history of flight itself. All others may find this book engaging because of the photography and illustrations.

Both *Buildings* and *Flight* are eye-catching from cover to cover and include a detailed general index. While simple in presentation, they are rich in visual splendor. The visual dictionaries in this series have been described as appropriate for the entire family, and they will appeal to those age 10 through adult. Libraries, classrooms, and homes will find these inexpensive works sought after for both reference information and leisure reading.

Warren's Movie Poster Price Guide: 1993 Edition. By Jon R. Warren. American Collectors Exchange, 2401 Broad St., Chattanooga, TN 37408, 1992. 466p. illus. hardcover $29.95 (0-9634319-0-0).
741.43'029 Film posters, American—Catalogs ǁ Film posters, American—Collectors and collecting [BKL] 92-75822

The first edition of this price guide appeared in 1985, when the hobby of collecting movie posters was new. Prices have increased considerably in the last eight years, with those for rare movie posters skyrocketing. Both speculative investors and international art auction houses are now interested in these collectibles. Because of this volatile situation, annual editions of the guide are now planned.

The 60,000 entries in the guide cover poster prices from 1900 through 1992. The prices listed are those for "one sheet (27 x 41) movie posters of original release unless noted and are an average of retail prices by established dealers." The entries are listed by title of the movie; these appear alphabetically word by word, not letter by letter. For each poster, the entry includes the year the movie was released, studio, major stars, company code (auction house), month and year of the catalog or sale, lot number, size of the poster, actual sale price without buyer's premium if sold, and columns of suggested prices for posters in "VG" (very good) or "EX" (excellent) conditions.

Prices listed in this 1993 edition were those compiled during the summer of 1992; Warren maintains the auction-results database from which the information was generated. He also suggests how to start a collection; how to identify, date, and grade posters; and lists books and publications of interest.

Many other price guides for collectibles list only a few prices for movie posters. *Reel Art: Great Posters from the Golden Age of the Silver Screen,* by Stephen Rebello and Richard Allen (Abbeville, 1988), demonstrates the use and effectiveness of these posters and reproduces copies of many of them. However, no other resource lists the number of prices contained in *Warren's Movie Poster Price Guide*. As the hobby grows, public libraries will experience increased demand for the information contained in this resource.

Fun for Kids II: An Index to Children's Craft Books. By Marion F. Gallivan. Scarecrow, 1992. 482p. bibliog. hardcover $42.50 (0-8108-2546-5).
016.7455 Handicraft—Juvenile literature—Indexes [CIP] 92-16667

Considerably larger than the original volume published in 1981, *Fun for Kids* II indexes books published from 1981 to 1990. It blends the traditional and modern, both in kinds of crafts and in materials used.

The work indexes crafts for children pre-kindergarten through eighth grade. It is arranged in three parts. First is the list of more than 300 books indexed (the magazine *Pack-O-Fun* is also indexed from 1981 to 1991). Second is the subject index, with reference to the author of the original source and page numbers, appropriate grade level, and material used. Third is the index by type of craft material, which has similar citations under such headings as *Burlap*, *Leather*, *Seed Pods*, and *Yogurt Containers*.

This book will answer questions such as Where can I find information on making marbelized paper? or Where can I find information on making something from pine cones? This edition places great emphasis on crafts for Bible school projects and holiday and party ideas. Titles listed are all in print or listed in *Children's Catalog*. Subject headings are specific, with exhaustive subdivisions in many subject areas. For example, *Games* has seven pages devoted to kind and country subdivisions.

Children's librarians, youth leaders, and teachers will find this current craft index valuable.

Tuttle Dictionary of Antiques & Collectibles Terms. By Don Bingham and Joan Bingham. Tuttle, 1992. 243p. bibliog. paper $19.95 (0-8048-1756-1).
745'.03 Decorative arts—Dictionaries || Collectibles—Dictionaries [CIP] 91-67337

This handy guide provides much more than a pocketful of antiques and collectibles terms. The introduction consists of an essay not only explaining the concept of antique versus collectible but also advising the buyer about auctions and suggesting ways to detect reproductions and fakes. More than 4,000 entries identify objects, techniques, and famous names, from *Aalto, Alvar* (furniture) to *Zurich porcelain* (ceramics). Completing this quick-reference tool is a list of U.S. patent numbers and the years they were assigned from 1836 through 1964 and a bibliography of price guides, handbooks, and related titles.

Miller's Pocket Dictionary of Antiques (Mitchell Beazley Publishers, 1990) is a similar source. Like *Tuttle*, it has more than 4,000 entries and a bibliography. Unlike *Tuttle*, it includes illustrations, line drawings found at the rate of one on almost every other page. Another special feature in *Miller's* is a table of periods and styles (British, French, German, and American).

Although the *Tuttle Dictionary* costs twice as much as *Miller's*, several other points should be considered in choosing between the two. Although illustrations make for a more pleasing page layout, *Tuttle* offers more entries per page in its solid pages of print. The introductory essay is especially informative and will be of great interest to novice collectors. *Tuttle's* bibliography is broader in scope than *Miller's*, where the emphasis is decidedly British. One feature lacking in both titles is a pronunciation guide. If the budget allows for only one antiques and collectibles dictionary, *Tuttle* is a good choice.

Looking at Paintings: A Guide to Technical Terms. J. Paul Getty Museum, 179 Pacific Coast Hwy., Malibu, CA 90265-5799, 1992. 84p. bibliog. illus. paper $10.95 (0-89236-213-8).
750'.3 Painting—Dictionaries [CIP] 91-24329

Looking at Paintings is a slim paperback glossary of technical terms dealing with Western painting. Intended "for the museum visitor," the work will find use in libraries, although librarians may choose it for the circulating collection, preferring more comprehensive reference works, such as Mayer's *Handbook of Materials and Techniques* or Lucie-Smith's *Thames & Hudson Dictionary of Art Terms*, which cover architecture and sculpture as well. It should be noted that *Looking at Paintings* is one of a three-part series; the second volume covers prints, drawings, and watercolors; and the third, photographs.

Compiled by two curatorial staff members of the J. Paul Getty Museum, *Looking at Paintings* has been clearly written for the serious nonexpert, with sufficient detail to satisfy the targeted user. The alphabetically arranged entries are illustrated with good quality color and black-and-white reproductions of paintings or details of paintings. *See* references lead the reader to the preferred form of the term sought, and capitalized words within entries indicate a separate entry. The work concludes with a bibliography of 15 standard reference sources of definitions of technical art terms.

Looking at Paintings is not a first purchase for large art reference collections because it adds little information not found in other standard dictionaries of art terms. For its low price and clarity of presentation, it is worth consideration by public libraries that lack sources on this topic.

The World's Master Paintings: From the Early Renaissance to the Present Day. 2v. Comp. by Christopher Wright. Routledge, 1992. bibliog. illus. indexes. hardcover $350 (0-415-02240-1).
750.74 Painting—Catalogs || Painters—Catalogs [OCLC] 91-31694

Reference and art librarians are frequently called upon to identify locations of paintings, museums with the best collections of individual painters or periods, or the strength of a particular gallery. Such requests often involve lengthy searches through reference books such as Havlice's *World Painting Index*, museum directories, monographs and catalogues raisonnés, and periodical indexes. *The World's Master Paintings* is designed to identify the locations of more than 50,000 "publicly available" paintings from the Early Renaissance to the present day. Paintings that can be viewed by appointment or at "rare intervals" are usually considered publicly available for the purposes of this work. Paintings in private collections are omitted. Compiler Wright is the author of many books on European painting, including *Italian, French, and Spanish Painting of the Seventeenth Century* (1981).

Wright selected approximately 1,500 painters for inclusion based on three criteria: (1) those "universally acknowledged to be great," (2) painters "already known to informed people," and (3) "painters who ought to be included." Despite the book's title, almost all paintings included are the work of European or North American artists. Asian, African, and Islamic works are excluded; the Latin American painter Diego Rivera is here, but Frida Kahlo and Tamayo Rufino are not. While any selective compilation is bound to have some omissions, the Board was surprised to note the absence of contemporary painters Robert Indiana, Helen Frankenthaler, and Ivan Albright.

The first volume contains the most substantive part of the work, entitled "Painters and Paintings." It is arranged by century, further subdivided by specific movements during that century, then by country (except for the twentieth century, which is divided into early and late). Entries for each painter are arranged alphabetically and include alternate names and place and date of birth and death. A paragraph summarizes the painter's evolution of style, reputation, and issues surrounding attribution. A bibliography lists catalogues raisonnés or, if these do not exist, "any reasonably comprehensive book." A listing of major collections of the artist's work follows, arranged by city followed by the institutional name ("*Paris* Louvre"). Under each museum, paintings are listed alphabetically by the titles given to them by their owners; dates are provided, if known. This arrangement enables the reader to determine the distribution of an artist's works in the world's museums. For Monet, for example, more than 600 paintings are listed under the names of 170 museums in about 150 cities, from Aberdeen to Zurich. The countries in which cities are located are not usually noted, although states are given for cities in the U.S. Readers will have to check elsewhere to determine the locations of such cities as Vernon or Walsall.

The first volume also includes an index of painters for that volume. Painters whose identities are unknown are listed by their usual designations, such as "Master of the Legend of St. Lucy." *See* references are provided for alternate forms of names ("*Master of Flemalle* see under Campin, Robert").

Volume 2 lists all institutions mentioned in "Painters and Paintings" and the master painters represented in their collections.

Museums are arranged alphabetically by city so that museums in Toledo, Spain, are listed next to those in Toledo, Ohio, rather than with other Spanish institutions. This lack of access by country may be inconvenient for those planning to visit museums in particular countries. Again, Wright rarely provides country names. Museums listed are not limited to Europe and North America; institutions in Japan, Israel, South Africa, and Algeria are included. Entries for all but the smallest institutions include a few lines describing the painting collections, a list of key artists held, and a bibliography of museum catalogs that list the collection. Artists the museum owns are listed by nationality, sometimes with the number of paintings noted. Individual painting titles are not given.

The set concludes with a computer-generated index of painting titles, arranged by century. Each entry lists the title of the painting (in the case of the twentieth century, alphabetized under A, An, and The), the name of the artist, and its location. Because the original titles of paintings are often unknown, many of the titles listed here are purely descriptive, including about 600 entitled "Virgin and Child." The lack of an alphabetical list of paintings arranged by painter may be problematic for readers who know the name of an artist but not the exact title of a painting, and find that they must consult a long list of titles for the correct entry or go back to volume 1 and skim the whole list under the artist's name.

Sixty-three black-and-white, chronologically arranged plates at the end of the first volume provide examples of paintings listed in the book. However, there are no references to these plates within the listings of paintings under the artists' names, and their purpose is not clear.

The World's Master Paintings is a monumental work that will be essential for librarians and scholars who frequently have to identify the locations of paintings by well-known, mainstream artists. It will be invaluable for those needing to acquire slides or photographs of paintings. An alphabetical painting-title index by painter's name and an index by country would have improved access. Despite its cumbersome arrangement, large art collections will welcome this comprehensive tool for identifying painting locations and determining strengths of collections.

Themes in American Painting: A Reference Work to Common Styles and Genres. By Robert Henkes. McFarland, 1993. 260p. bibliog. illus. index. hardcover $39.95 (0-89950-734-4).
759.13 Painting, American—Themes, motives [CIP] 92-53599

Between 1965 and 1993, author Henkes produced three filmstrips and completed 12 books on art that included separate works on crucifixion and sport, two of the art themes selected for inclusion here. An additional 11 popular themes found in American paintings also are identified here—"Mother and Child," "Modes of Transportation," "The Clown," "The City," "Interiors," "Natural Disasters," "Wars and Aftermath," "Social Protest and Injustice," "Still Life," "Self-Portraits," and "Music."

Each theme is treated in a separate chapter that includes a narrative, 8–16 illustrations, and a bibliography. The art-criticism essays, written for the layperson and the beginning student, average 19 pages in length and help the user identify such schools as naturalism, realism, abstract expressionism, op art, and pop art. The articles on clown and sport themes are each 32 pages in length and seem out of proportion to the other topics. The discussions of still life and self-portraits add little of interest to art as social commentary. Included are 12 full-color illustrations printed on glossy paper and 139 halftone illustrations. These illustrations were carefully selected and contribute to the interest of the text. Too many of the paintings selected for discussion, however, are by such well-known artists as Reginald Marsh, Umberto Romano, Edward Hopper, Ben Shahn, and Mary Cassatt. This detracts from any freshness the book might have had.

The citations following each chapter are bibliographically complete but do not serve as end notes that could lead interested users to specific information. Indeed, many of the works cited are so general that it is difficult to understand their relationship to the subject under discussion. Another vexing feature of this work is the author's habit of discussing a certain painting but not including an illustration or, worse, not citing a printed source containing a reproduction. This failure is compounded by the author having carefully included in the index both the artist and the name of the work discussed. For example, Arshile Gorky, Lily Harmon, and Elizabeth Korn are included in the text and in the index, but reproductions of their paintings, which are discussed and indexed here, are not contained within the work, nor do citations lead to a printed source.

This new reference is not a necessary purchase for any library that includes art encyclopedias and several hundred titles on American art. Libraries selecting to purchase this work are advised to place it in the circulating collection because of the problems with its reference utility discussed here.

Leonard's Annual Price Index of Prints, Posters & Photographs. Ed. by Katheryn Acerbo. Auction Index, 30 Valentine Park, Newton, MA 02165, 1992. 731p. bibliog. hardcover $195 (0-918819-31-8).
760'.075 Arts—Prices ∥ Art—Collectors and collecting [BKL]

Announced as the first of an annual series, this volume lists prices paid in European, U.S., Canadian, and Australian auction houses for prints, posters, and photographs. It is a companion to Leonard's Annual Price Index of Art Auctions, which covers painting, drawing, and sculpture.

Alphabetically arranged by artist with dates and nationality, this edition provides auction prices of items sold between July 1, 1991, and June 30, 1992. Under each artist, individual works are entered by title, with a catalogue raisonné citation from the appropriate auction catalog. In the case of photographs, a citation is included for a book or journal where the image was reproduced. Prints and photographs by unknown artists are entered under "Anonymous," but unattributed posters are under "Posters."

Prices are cited in the currency in which the purchase was made and also in U.S. dollars, British pounds, French francs, deutsche marks, and yen. The U.S. price stands out prominently through placement in the margin adjacent to the auctioned item. All prices include the buyer's premium but exclude taxes. The buyer's premium charged by each auction house is cited in the directory of auction houses and sales dates, which immediately precede the main price index. Items that were "bought in" because they did not bring the reserve price set by the owner are indicated, and an estimated value is supplied.

Other prefatory material includes a 16-page glossary of terms, a key to abbreviations used throughout the volume, a two-page bibliography of basic biographical dictionaries and indexes found in most art reference collections, and a 13-page bibliography of material on photographers. Entries in both bibliographies are almost entirely English-language sources.

Although expensive, Leonard's Annual Price Index of Prints, Posters, & Photographs will be a useful reference source in specialized collections where current art sales prices are important to readers.

Lawrence's Dealer Print Prices 1992. Ed. by Lawrence L. Mehren and others. Long & Strider Press, 3104 E. Camelback Rd., Ste. 558, Phoenix, AZ 85016, 1992. 1,159p. bibliog. hardcover $79 (0-9631432-0-4; ISSN 1059-3187).
769 Prints—Catalogs [BKL] 91-4418

This new price guide is meant for "anyone who needs information on valuing fine prints." Lawrence's is to be an annual compilation of dealer catalogs and, for this first edition, the editor used 1991 price lists of dealers in the U.S., Canada, and Western Europe. Other sources such as Gordon's Print Price Annual list auction prices. Lawrence's lists more than 22,000 prints—old master, modern, and contemporary from obscure to popular artists—ranging in price from $5 to $450,000.

Data are presented in columnar form. Under each artist's name (dates and nationality provided), prints are listed alphabetically by title. Information includes size in inches and millimeters, condition, price in U.S. dollars and a foreign currency, medium, how signed, date of work, edition size, whether numbered, state, and catalogue raisonné number. Additional information may include rarity, watermark, and paper type. A sample entry, list of abbreviations, and a clear explanation of the data precedes the entries.

Many prints have multiple entries because they were listed in more than one dealer's catalog, but users will not know which dealer stocks which print. The preface notes that Lawrence's database is continually updated. To ascertain which dealer is selling a particular print, one should contact the publisher.

The editor notes that many more prints could have been included, but that he was selective. However, no criteria for his selections are stated. There does appear to be a significant number of landscape, bird, and animal prints and a much smaller representation of prominent contemporary artists. For instance, there are nine pages for Frank Weston Benson, five for Paul Hambleton Landacre, six pages each for David Young Cameron and John Taylor Arens but a half-page for Sol LeWitt, two entries for Louise Bougeois, three entries for Chuck Close and Alex Katz, and none for Julian Schnabel.

The novice collector will appreciate the helpful essay "Prints and How to Buy Them" and the bibliography of print reference literature. A bibliography of catalogues raisonnés and monographs is included along with an index to them by artist. It would be less cumbersome if this bibliography were arranged by artist. An international list of fine print dealers organized geographically and dealers' advertisements complete the volume.

Public libraries will find this new annual useful. Serious collectors will still need the *Print Price Annual* for auction prices and the *Print Collector's Newsletter*.

Print Price Index '93: 1991–1992 Auction Season. Ed. by Peter Hastings Falk. Sound View Press, 170 Boston Post Rd., Madison, CT 06443, 1993. annual. 1,470p. bibliog. hardcover $149 (ISSN 1058-2339).
769'.12 Prints—Prices—Periodicals [OCLC] 91-2902

Print Price Index '93 covers the 1991–92 season for original prints sold at more than 350 auctions in the U.S., Canada, Western Europe, and Japan. More than 40,000 entries are alphabetically arranged by artist. Among the data provided are the artist's nationality and birth and death dates; auction prices given in U.S. dollars, pounds, and generally deutsche marks; title of the work, medium, date of print, edition number, whether signed, and dimensions; reference to catalogues raisonnés; and auction house, date of sale, and lot number.

The prefatory pages are unusually lucid and provide the novice with an understanding of the important elements in the evaluation of prints. Sample entries are provided with clear instructions for identifying the data elements. The bulk of the book is the inclusive arrangement by artist. For the convenience of specialists, other sections of the book reprint the entries in full for eight categories of prints: books with original prints, botanical, Japanese and oriental, natural history, portfolios, posters, sporting, and topographical. Directories, geographically arranged, of both print dealers and auction houses (with auction dates) are provided. Researchers will appreciate the index to catalogues raisonnés and all users will find the well-organized bibliography helpful.

The foreword states that "in examining each catalogue, our service has been to go 'mining' for the selected facts, and then to organize and present those facts in a clear way so that collectors, dealers, appraisers, scholars, curators, and auctioneers may more accurately evaluate a print." The *Print Price Index '93* has attained this goal. Libraries serving collectors and art historians will want to place this annual on standing order because of its wealth of information and relatively reasonable price.

Film Annual, 1992. By Jim Fredrickson and Steve Stewart. Companion Publications, 27812 Glenhurst, Ste. 115, Aliso Viejo, CA 92656, 1992. 336p. indexes. paper $14.95 (0-9625277-2-6; ISSN 1061-4214).
778 [BKL] 92-4137

Film Annual, 1992 is the first volume of a new series highlighting "significant U.S. and foreign films" released in the U.S. during the previous year. Entries for 391 films released during 1991 are organized alphabetically and contain the following data: film distributor; a one- or two-paragraph synopsis of the plot and special features; major cast and characters, along with some supporting cast; production personnel; genre; country of origin, if different from the U.S.; MPAA movie rating; running time; and soundtrack recording label, if any. Each entry also includes a "critics rating" star system, based on the opinions expressed in at least 10 critical reviews.

A supplementary section lists the nominees and winners of the 1992 Academy Awards, the winners of the major Academy Awards between 1927 and 1990, and the winners of other film awards for 1991. A 22-page obituary appendix summarizes the lives and contributions of film industry people who died in 1991. Indexes include a listing of films in *Film Annual* by the number of stars they have been assigned in the book, a listing by film genre, and a complete name index accessing the filmographic information in the entries of the main body of the book.

The *Film Annual* series promises to be an inexpensive alternative to the *Film Review Annual*, which includes excerpts from film reviews. Little, if any, criticism is contained in the *Film Annual, 1992*, but, for small and medium-size public libraries and for academic libraries needing primarily filmographic information, this book is an ideal substitute for the more costly and comprehensive *Film Review Annual*.

Contemporary Composers. Ed. by Brian Morton and Pamela Collins. St. James Press, 1992. 1,019p. bibliog. hardcover $125 (1-55862-085-0).
780.922 Composers—Biography—Dictionaries || Music—Bio-bibliography [OCLC]

Contemporary Composers fills a void in the world of art (or serious) music. Edited by two English enthusiasts, this international directory is "a listener's guide to the broadest spectrum of contemporary composition." The nearly 600 living composers depicted were suggested by an advisory panel but profiled only if the potential entrants supplied essential information. No other work of this scope exists.

Each composer's entry consists of three parts. A brief paragraph of biographical basics in who's who style is first. The bulk of each alphabetically arranged entry is a chronological list (not a discography) of all known works classified in symphonic, chamber/instrumental, vocal/choral, operatic, and other categories. The dates of completion and initial performance are given for each work. Finally, a short assessment seeks to place each composer within the musical landscape of the times. The assessments are signed and are uniformly literate, succinct, and insightful. They are written mostly by academics who are as varied in nationality as the composers they describe. Not all are adorational, but no sharp axes gleam on these pages. As in all St. James Press directories, each entrant was invited to contribute a short personal statement introducing his or her work; while most preferred silence, those composers who did comment offer an invaluable perspective on their music.

Renowned composers known even outside musical circles appear here, for example, Leonard Bernstein, Aaron Copland, and Virgil Thompson (all three died during this book's preparation). Such eminent figures as Oliver Messiaen, John Cage, Philip Glass, Morton Gould, Lukas Foss, and Pierre Boulez are all represented, too. One might cavil that Stephen Sondheim is included, but not Andrew Lloyd Webber, and the 1991 Pulitzer Prize winner for music, Shulamit Ran, is also missing. The large majority of entrants, however, will be unknown to even the most avid concert-goer; many of them probably are unfamiliar to most professional musicians. As Brian Ferneyhough observes in the preface, the chief value of this directory may be in publicizing "unknowns" to those musical groups who have an interest in supporting serious composition. In an age where the gap between experimental musical forms and the still prevailing vehicles of expression (symphony orchestra, chamber ensemble, etc.) is in danger of becoming unbridgeable, such a directory is definitely worthwhile.

This work will be compared to *Baker's Biographical Dictionary of Musicians* [RBB F 1 92] and to *The New Grove Dictionary of Music and Musicians* (1980). Most of the composers found in *Contemporary Composers* are listed in *Baker's* but not in the *New Grove*. More specialized sources, such as *Contemporary American Composers: A Biographical Dictionary* (1982) and the *International Encyclopedia of Women Composers* (2d ed., 1987), do not have the broad coverage of the book under review. Also, those two books have no descriptive text.

This directory will be most useful for libraries associated with schools or conservatories of music, but any large public or academic library that collects musical reference works will wish to consider it.

The Rolling Stone Index: Twenty-Five Years of Popular Culture, 1967–1991. Comp. by Jeffrey N. Gatten. Popular Culture Ink, 1993. 1,112p. indexes. hardcover $85 (1-56075-030-8).

FINE ARTS, DECORATIVE ARTS, MUSIC

781.6'6 Rolling Stone—Indexes ‖ Rock music—Periodicals—Indexes [BKL] 92-81114

This index covers the first 25 years of *Rolling Stone* magazine. The publisher is not allied with the magazine but appears to have its approval for this project. Compiler Gatten is head of collection management at Kent State University Libraries; he considers RS "the premiere source of information on popular culture of the last twenty-five years." While the magazine's feature articles are indexed elsewhere, the compiler's objective was to produce a comprehensive index to all of RS's content. The only omissions from this volume are advertising, special lists that contain no annotations, and most illustrations. Annual updates are anticipated, as is a supplemental index to illustrations and their subjects, photographers, and illustrators.

The book is divided into nine major sections: "Articles & Columns," "Cover Appearances," "Letters to the Editor," "Poetry," "Random Notes," and four sections of reviews (books, concerts, movies, and records). Each citation consists of an entry ID, author (when known), title, issue, date, and page. Many of the sections have related point-of-use indexes; for example, the concert-review index lists concerts by performer, followed by separate indexes to reviewer and review title. Master indexes to author/reviewer and to titles complete the book.

The arrangement of the book is logical but complicated. Within each major section, items are arranged alphabetically and, when appropriate, then chronologically. Each item in the nine major indexes has been assigned a partially mnemonic entry ID. For example, the first entry in "Articles and Columns" is AR00001; that for "Book Reviews," BR00001. The point-of-use and master indexes both refer to that ID. In addition to access via the table of contents and the indexes in the back of the book, a "Letter Group Quick Reference" table is included. This can be used to search where an item should be found. For example, someone looking for reviews of Ivory Coast recordings could refer to this table to see where the record-review column intersects with the I row.

This complex source utilizes various conventions of reference books such as multiple types of arrangment, ID numbers, citations, etc. Users, including librarians, will need to read the directions for how to use the book, which are clearly written. But the complexity may be overwhelming to some users. Special libraries serving the entertainment industry as well as academic and public libraries with interest in popular culture, recent history, and the performing arts will probably want to include this volume in their collections. Any library with a full run of *Rolling Stone* should definitely consider purchase.

Best Rated CDs 1992: Jazz, Popular, Etc. Peri Press, Hemlock Ridge, P.O. Box 348, Voorheesville, NY 12186, 1992. 678p. index. paper $19.95 (1-879796-06-6).

781.63 Popular music—Compact disc catalogs [BKL]

Consisting of selections from the first five volumes of CD *Review Digest* [RBB Mr 15 89] covering the years 1983–1991, this compilation of CD music-review excerpts includes 2,094 entries covering blues, jazz, "pop/rock/roots," and show music. Inclusion in this guide is based on the fact that the CD "has been noticed by two or more reviewers [from the 41 American, Canadian, and British periodicals covered here] and received an award for excellence from at least one of these."

The guide is divided into four sections by type of music and organized alphabetically by the last name of the musical artist or the group's name. The information in each entry includes basic discographic data and a summary of awards won, with a star rating reflecting the number of awards. This is followed by excerpts from reviews, each of which notes the reviewer, the magazine volume and date, and the number of words in the original review. Each entry is given an accession number, which oddly appears after the discographic data, not before the entry where it would be more prominent; the range of accession numbers appearing on each page is noted at the top of the page.

All of the CDs that have a four- or five-star award rating are listed alphabetically at the beginning of the book. Following the main body of the book is an index of musical artists, citing entries by accession number. The index is unusually comprehensive because it includes not only the primary musicians, but also those mentioned as backup players in musical groups.

Best Rated CDs is a useful guide for consumers of popular-music CDs and therefore a valuable addition to most public and academic libraries. Libraries already subscribing to *CD Review Digest* may elect to circulate their copy of *Best Rated CDs*.

All-Music Guide: The Best CDs, Albums & Tapes. Ed. by Michael Erlewine. Miller Freeman; dist. by Publishers Group West, 1992. 1,176p. paper $19.95 (0-87930-264-X).

781.63 Music—Catalogs [BKL] 92-60948

All-Music is certainly an appropriate term to describe the scope of this massive selective guide to recorded music. It covers 27 music categories, ranging from rock/pop/soul to classical, and from rap to sound effects. Approximately 23,000 recordings (CDs, albums, and tapes) of more than 6,000 artists and composers are listed here. The book provides brief statements about the credentials of each of the 82 music reviewers, critics, and journalists who participated in selecting the artists and recordings and in writing the annotations, which are signed with the author's initials.

Each chapter deals with a different category of music and contains information that mixes history with advice on how to most effectively listen to the music genre covered. The entries within each chapter are organized alphabetically by musical artist or composer, and the listed recordings are preceded by a short overview of each musician's importance and brief biographical information. Each recording entry includes title, recording company, year of distribution, and a short annotation. Special symbols are used to indicate recordings that are "landmark," "representative of the best an artist has to offer," or ideal for introducing listeners to the work of the musical artist or composer. For classical music entries, the major works of each composer are represented by up to three recordings.

The editors state that in today's music scene—with recordings on more than one label, frequent changes in numbering, and the variety of formats—it is best to look up recordings by artist name and album title. Thus, the book does not include basic discographic information on the listed recordings; entries do not provide the label numbers or the recordings' lengths and sometimes do not mention the recording medium (tape, phonodisc, or CD). The indexing to the volume is minimal. An "Artist Index" is provided, and even this is incomplete; composers of classical music are included but not the performers.

Given the comprehensive coverage of the *All-Music Guide* and the mixture of opinions and judgments reflected in the book's commentary and annotations, it is inevitable that some readers will disagree with the choices of recordings that appear as entries. Despite this subjectivity and the incomplete discographic information, the *All-Music Guide*'s broad coverage, knowledgeable comments, and low cost make it a valuable reference resource for academic libraries as well as medium-size and large public libraries.

The Virgin Directory of World Music. By Philip Sweeney. Holt, 1992. 261p. discography. index. paper $14.95 (0-8050-2305-4).

781.63'09 Popular music—History and criticism ‖ Popular music—Developing countries—History and criticism ‖ Musicians—Developing countries [CIP] 92-9791

Popular music in America has generally been American music with few cross-cultural hits, unless the performers fit the American mold. However, those cultural boundaries have been changing in London, the author's home base, and they are loosening here as well. *The Virgin Directory of World Music* raises the question of what is world music, which, Sweeney admits, is not the perfect term nor is easy to define. He writes that it is music that is "not art or classical music, is in regular use by ordinary people to dance to, is listened to via radio or cassette."

The book is arranged by region and country; each region is introduced by a musician who has worked with at least one of the musical styles discussed. Essayists include Peter Gabriel, Maire Ni Bhraonain of Clannad, Manu Dibango, and Anthony Carter (the "Mighty Gabby"). The essays discuss both the region's music and the author's experience with it. Each of the 130-country entries cover the various styles of popular music, characteristic instruments, and key performers. These histories generally cover from the 1950s to the present, although many of the musical genres are adaptations of older traditional music. The essays vary in length from one to ten pages. While some performers like Ladysmith Black Mambazo, Bob Marley, and Clannad are well known, many will be unfamiliar names to readers. Performers and groups are highlighted in boldface type. The index includes performers, if more than the name is mentioned, musical styles, and instruments. A limited discography follows each country profile. There is no bibliography of sources.

This book will prove popular with those interested in the expanding world-music arena. It could also be useful in answering questions on the music of particular countries, assigned country papers being a seasonal phenomenon at many public and school libraries. *The Virgin Directory of World Music* will be a popular, inexpensive addition to either circulating or reference collections.

The Guinness Encyclopedia of Popular Music. 4v. Ed. by Colin Larkin. Guinness; dist. by New England Publishing Associates, P.O. Box 5, Chester, CT 06412, 1992. bibliog. index. hardcover $295 (1-882267-00-1).

781.64'03 Popular music—Encyclopedias [OCLC] 92-33209

This new Guinness encyclopedia, prepared with the assistance of 94 contributors and consultants, is a massive, four-volume, who's who of popular music. The book covers music of the entire twentieth century, with emphasis on the more recent rock era. The scope is international, and the majority of the 10,000 entries are biographical, focusing on the professional lives of performers, songwriters, producers, and promoters.

The profiles of soloists and groups range from such popular singers as Andy Williams to such less well known bands as Prefab Sprout, from older blues performers (Cow Cow Davenport) to country stars (Hank Williams). Also covered are artists from Latin countries (Celia Cruz), Africa (Stephen Osita Osadeve), and Japan (Ryuichi Sakamoto). The individual profiles are well written and interesting. While factual data are included (birth and death information, names of band members, titles of important recordings), the essays place the artist in context by discussing influences, controversies, disappointments, and successes. The profiles vary in length from 150 to more than 3,000 words for such musicians as Duke Ellington. Also included are entries for record companies, music festivals, organizations, and instruments. Some profiles conclude with suggestions for further reading; boldface type within the entries acts as a cross-reference to related articles. The articles are current, including Miles Davis' death in late 1991 and album releases in early 1992. The 101-page bibliography, with 4,000 listings, is alphabetically arranged by names of artists and genres. A 363-page index follows, with topics having an entry in the work shown in boldface type. Closing volume 4 is a quick-reference guide that lists all the essays.

In any such huge compendium as this new work, questions are raised about choice of topics, accuracy, and emphasis. For instance, Hank Williams died in Oak Hill, West Virginia, not in Virginia. The impetus for the Troggs' name change is attributed to Keith Altham in *Guinness* and to Larry Page in *The Penguin Encyclopedia of Popular Music*. While many less well known bands are included, Oingo Boingo is not, even though it has released several albums and has done soundtrack work on major motion pictures. Dexy's Midnight Runners' profile is approximately the same length as Neil Diamond's, who certainly has had a longer career and has been involved in important changes in popular music. However, *The Guinness Encyclopedia of Popular Music* is the most comprehensive reference work available on this topic. The range of coverage is broad, and the information provided is substantial. Libraries that have a large number of questions on popular music—and adequate funds—will want to give this title serious purchase consideration.

The Penguin Guide to Jazz on CD, LP and Cassette. By Richard Cook and Brian Morton. Penguin, 1992. 1,287p. index. paper $22.50 (0-14-015364-0).

016.781'65 Jazz—Discography [BKL]

In evaluating this new work, it is appropriate to begin with an overview of previous references on the topic. According to *The New Grove Dictionary of Jazz* [RBB Ap 15 89], jazz discography, since its beginnings in the 1930s, has been dominated by Europeans, including Charles Delaunay's *Hot Discography* (Paris, 1936), Hilton Schleman's *Rhythm on Records* (London, 1936), and Brian Rust's *Jazz Records, 1897–1942* (Chigwell, England, 1982). Important American contributions include Frederic Ramsey and Charles E. Smith's *Jazz Record Book* (1942), Orin Blackstone's *Index to Jazz* (1945–48), and Leonard Feather's biodiscographies: *Encyclopedia of Jazz* (reprinted 1984), *Encyclopedia of Jazz in the 60s* (reprinted 1986), and (with Ira Gitler) *Encyclopedia of Jazz in the '70s* (reprinted 1987). In the international New Grove title, two-thirds of the 4,500 entries are biographies, each accompanied by a discography and bibliography. Also, through the years, jazz discographers have produced specialized works dealing with specific aspects of the topic, for example, musical style (free jazz, bebop, swing), geographic area, record label, and the work of an individual performer.

The title under review, by two British writers and broadcasters, is a companion volume to one on classical music, *Penguin Guide to Compact Discs and Cassettes* (1992). Cook and Morton state in the introduction that "while a number of selective guides have appeared in the past, this is the first serious attempt to bring the whole spectrum of jazz recording within a single volume." To this end, the work attempts to be a comprehensive (though not exhaustive) critical guide to currently available recorded jazz from its beginning in 1917 to the present.

The book covers more than 1,300 jazz musicians and groups and is organized alphabetically by name. For each individual, information is provided about birth and death rates; instruments played and a note of other musical talents, such as "arranger"; and a list of record titles. The entry for each recording is preceded by a rating from one to five stars (five is the very best) and includes information about label and catalog number, formats in which available, performers and instrument credits, and date of recordings. Entries for musicians include critical annotations, sometimes of individual recordings, and often provide additional brief biographical information. Following this section of the book is a very selected list of recordings that include various artists, some listed by decade, others by instrument, and, lastly, one album featuring classic women jazz artists. The index lists the jazz musicians and every performer on every record, but there is no record title index.

This guide to recorded jazz is recommended for public, academic, and music libraries seeking to enrich their jazz collections and for amateur and professional jazz enthusiasts.

The Grove Press Guide to the Blues on CD. By Frank-John Hadley. Grove Press, 1993. 256p. index. paper $14.95 (0-8021-3328-2).

016.781643'026 Blues (Music)—Discography ‖ Compact discs—Reviews [CIP] 92-17305

Defining the blues as a "common language of virtually all American musics," this guide to compact-disc recordings includes not only traditional blues music, but also rhythm and blues, country and western, rock and roll, and jazz. The preface also makes clear that author Hadley, a frequent contributor to *Down Beat* and other music publications, has nothing against phonograph recordings—which he admits can be more authentic, if less clear, than the laser technology of compact discs. The work's publisher, Grove Press, should not be confused with the company that issues the family of New Grove music dictionaries.

Alphabetically arranged by performer, *The Grove Press Guide to the Blues* includes more than 700 entries for recent or reissued compact discs. Each entry consists of the album name, the recording company, a star rating (from one to five stars) by Hadley and three contributors, a two- to four-sentence descriptive and critical annotation, the running time, and the year of issue or a note that the recording is a reissue. The range of covered artists is great—from Bessie Smith and Muddy Waters to such current musical performers as Wynton Marsalis, Stevie Ray Vaughan, and even rock-and-roll performer Eric Clapton. The book also includes a 30-page section of compact disc–anthology entries, arranged alphabetically by title of compact disc. An index of album titles provides further access to all the guide's entries.

Intended as the first of a series of inexpensive books that highlight the best compact-disc recordings, this low-cost guide provides an informative, discerning, and reliable analysis of this increasingly popular and influential music genre. It is recommended for public libraries, academic libraries supporting music studies, and specialized music libraries. It is even appropriate for high school libraries serving students with blues-music interests. Public libraries should also consider a duplicate copy for their circulating collections.

Encyclopedia of the Blues. By Gérard Herzhaft. Tr. by Brigitte Debord. Univ. of Arkansas, 1992. 513p. bibliog. illus. index. hardcover $32 (1-55728-252-8); paper $16.95 (1-55728-253-6).
781.643'03 Blues (Music)—Dictionaries [CIP] 92-7386

Herzhaft's *Encyclopedia of the Blues* has been translated from the French for American audiences. It covers a wide variety of topics. Entries are mainly biographical but also include genres, festivals, instruments, and styles.

Biographical entries include dates of birth and death, if appropriate. They stress career influences, achievements, performances, and style rather than personal life. A limited number of recordings are noted in the sketches. Artists are listed under their popular names. For a performer like Barbecue Bob, there are no cross-references from his real name, nor is his real name in the index. Some people are discussed under such genres as *Blues Shouters, Female Blues Singers*, and *White Blues*. There are references from the names of those performers to the group entry. Some of these people deserve entries of their own, especially such performers as Alberta Hunter and Paul Butterfield.

Other entries range from *American Folk Blues Festival*, which was a part of the European revival of the blues, to histories of instruments (*Bass*), definitions of genres (*Delta Blues*), and histories of musical styles in famous blues cities (*Chicago*). The volume closes with a select bibliography arranged by subject. A discography of 200 important blues albums doesn't compare with the recent *Down Home Guide to the Blues* [RBB N 1 91]. There is also a list of 300 classic blues songs with a brief history of each and a list of musicians arranged by the instrument they played. Large black-and-white photographs add interest.

Blues Who's Who (1979) is perhaps the most comparable work. The *Encyclopedia of the Blues* presents biographical material in a narrative form as opposed to *Blues Who's Who*, which is a chronological listing of accomplishments. *Blues Who's Who* is only biographical. The two books don't always agree on facts. Texas Alexander, for example, was born variously in 1880 and 1890 and died in 1954 and 1955. The *Encyclopedia of the Blues* is, of course, more current and has broader coverage. Libraries owning *Blues Who's Who* and getting few blues-related questions may want to pass, but for libraries with an active blues audience, this will be a good addition.

International Dictionary of Opera. 2v. Ed. by C. Steven Larue. St. James Press, 1993. 1,500p. bibliog. illus. indexes. hardcover $250 (1-55862-081-8).
782.1'03 Opera—Dictionaries [CIP] 92-44271

Right in the wake of the four-volume *New Grove Dictionary of Opera* (NGDO) [RBB Ap 1 93] comes this two-volume *International Dictionary of Opera* (IDO) that can stand up proudly beside its competitor. IDO does not try to compete with NGDO in comprehensiveness, but what it does it does well. IDO provides biographical and critical analysis of almost 200 opera composers from John Blow to Philip Glass (compared with 2,900 in NGDO), more than 300 performers (compared with 2,500), more than 60 conductors (including Sarah Caldwell and James Levine), more than 30 librettists from Lorenzo da Ponte to W. H. Auden, as well as producers, directors, and designers such as Maurice Sendak and Franco Zeffirelli. For persons, each entry begins with a brief biographical sketch, bibliographic references to books or articles both by and about him or her, followed by a signed, critical essay written by a knowledgeable scholar or critic. For more than 400 operas (compared with 2,000 in NGDO), the set provides considerable detail on their composition and first performance, singers by voice, an evaluative essay, and a bibliography. The signed essay discusses the plot, its composition, and place in opera history.

Comparing this new work with NGDO, the biographies of performers are in most cases longer in IDO because of the addition of the essay assessing their careers and performances. These are not all positive comments, for example, "Few sopranos can match the passion and excitement that Varady brings to her performances.... [but] Sometimes she sings as if the dramatic situation and the meaning of the words have no importance for her." The article about Pavarotti in NGDO is not quite one-half page; in IDO the article is approximately 1½ pages, including is a half-page portrait of him as Nemorino (which also appears on the cover of each volume). For individual operas, space given can be more, equal, or less in IDO. The entry for Philip Glass includes mention of *Voyage*, his new opera that premiered in October 1992. NGDO mentions it under Glass' entry but also provides a separate entry. IDO lacks the topical articles (e.g., on dance, lighting, the orchestra) found in NGDO.

Numerous black-and-white illustrations further enhance the value of IDO. There is only one problem with these illustrations; they are not indexed. One can find a picture of Lily Pons as Cherubino with her biography and another as Lakme in the article about that opera, but one is not referred to it from the biography. In addition to portraits, illustrations include stage sets, posters, and scores; some are full page, some smaller.

All entries are categorized in listings at the front of each volume so one can see at a glance if a particular topic is included. At the end of volume 2 are several indexes. A title index lists all operas mentioned, whether in separate entries or in the article about the composer. A nationality index lists all persons by country; Americans and Italians predominate, but a Peruvian, a Latvian, and a Mexican are also listed. Notes on advisers and contributors provide documentation as to their occupations; most are music historians or academic faculty. Again, most are American, but a smattering of other nationalities were noted.

While some expected persons were not found (no Patrice Munsel or Fiorenza Cossotto), IDO includes the major forces from history and the present day. If one wants the totality of opera history, one must opt for NGDO. The *International Dictionary of Opera* is an excellent enhancement for the *New Grove Dictionary of Opera* for libraries that can afford them both. For libraries that cannot, the new work is a wonderful substitute at a more economical price. Its up-to-dateness and detailed entries for persons and operas should be useful in any library that has a clientele interested in the subject.

The New Grove Dictionary of Opera. 4v. Ed. by Stanley Sadie. Grove's Dictionaries of Music, 1992. bibliog. illus. index. hardcover $850 (0-935859-92-6).
782.1'03 Opera—Dictionaries [OCLC] 92-36276

The Grove Dictionary of Music and Musicians has been a dependable reference for music lovers since the first edition was published in London, in 1890. In the 20-volume sixth edition of *The New Grove Dictionary of Music and Musicians* (1980), higher standards of scholarship and a broader interpretation of modern musicology made the work more valuable to specialists while maintaining the readability of previous editions. Acclaim for this title led to the publication of three shorter multivolume works: *The New Grove Dictionary of Musical Instruments* [RBB Je 1 85], *The New Grove Dictionary of American Music* [RBB F 15 87], and *The New Grove Dictionary of Jazz* [RBB Ap 15 89]. *The New Grove Dictionary of Opera* is a superb addition to this Grove family of music reference sources.

Under the editorship of music scholar Sadie and with more than 1,000 contributors, this new title easily establishes itself as a comprehensive and definitive reference source in this field. In preparation since 1987, more than 80 percent of the entries have been rewritten, compared with those in the parent Grove publication. The set's four volumes, comprising more than 5,000 pages, include 10,000 articles, with 2,900 entries on composers, 2,500 on singers, and 2,000 on individual operas. More than 1,300 black-and-white illustrations of performers, sets, opera houses, and costumes give life to the text.

The preface gives a definition of opera for the purposes of this work: "the genre that arose in Italy about 1600 ... designed for performance in a theatre, embodying an element of continuing drama articulated through music, with words that are sung with instrumental support or punctuation." Nonwestern musical drama, such as Japanese No, is not covered. In the front matter such details as alphabetization, cross-references, dates, transliterations, bibliographies, and abbreviations are satisfactorily explained. Four appendixes conclude the work. "Role Names" gives character, voice type, opera, and composer ("Carmen, mezzo soprano, *Carmen*, Berlioz"). For characters appearing in multiple operas (Figaro, Faust, etc.), information for all operas is given. "Incipits of Arias, Ensembles, Etc." gives beginning phrase, character, opera, number of singers, and composer. The last two appendixes are "List of Contributors" and "Illustration Acknowledgments."

The thorough coverage of topics in this work is impressive. The definition and history of opera in all its forms (opera buffa, opera seria, operetta) covers 42 pages. Articles on opera in individual cities and countries give details about historical development, theaters and opera houses, opera companies, productions, conductors, and performers, as witness the 28-page article *Paris* with 25 striking illustrations of theaters (interior and exterior views), scenes, posters, etc. Articles on composers are also detailed. The article on Mozart gives biographical information and discusses his operatic career and his style, the latter with examples of musical notation. The article is followed by a seven-page bibliography. The article on Richard Wagner is followed by a 20-page bibliography. The inclusion of articles for individual operas is a departure from previous practice in Grove publications. Complete and leisurely description of an individual opera includes the history of the composer's creation and production, a list of characters with their voice parts, the opera's setting, an act-by-act summary of plot development and musical activity, as well as a critical evaluation of the opera. Illustrations of sets and scenes appear often. Those who wrote the works that were sources of operas are well covered, as are many other topics.

Opera is viewed broadly in this dictionary, as evidenced by such entries as *Stage Design*, which develops the topic historically in a 24-page article with 28 illustrations, many *see* references to individual designers, and a three-page bibliography. Costumes are similarly treated in detail as are machinery, dance, theater architecture, lighting, orchestra, traveling troupes, libretto, libraries and archives, and even tickets and opera glasses. A fascinating article on the sociology of opera discusses opera as a social statement and opera in society. Included are many entries on singers, past and present. Articles such as *Castrato*, *Soprano*, and *Ornamentation* describe what the singing was like and how it has changed over time.

Superlatives are lacking to describe this wonderful work. A feast for scholars, it can also be an education for opera lovers at any level of sophistication. *The New Grove Dictionary of Opera* can only enhance the academic or public library that purchases it. This new reference will be especially appreciated in cities where operas are regularly performed.

The Oxford Dictionary of Opera. By John Warrack and Ewan West. Oxford, 1992. 782p. bibliog. hardcover $40 (0-19-869164-5).
782.1'03 Opera—Dictionaries [CIP] 92-6730

Opera has been a popular form of entertainment for the last 400 years and shows no sign of going out of style. Today, exposure to this elaborate art form comes through television productions, videos, and recordings as well as live performances. Traditional favorites are joined by such new compositions as Dominik Argento's *Aspern Papers* (1988) and John Corigliano's *Ghosts of Versailles* (1991). Both standard and locally written operas are performed to enthusiastic audiences worldwide. *The Oxford Dictionary of Opera* appears at an opportune time to serve this interest. The authors are music scholars associated with Oxford University, and Warrack also wrote *The Concise Oxford Dictionary of Opera* (2d ed., 1979).

This new work has more than 4,500 entries and covers "all aspects of opera's historical development and present standing." Included are articles on approximately 750 individual composers, 600 operatic works with brief synopses and premier details, 900 singers, and 85 characters from literature and legend such as Antigone, Faust, and Don Juan who have been used in many operas. Opera in various countries and cities around the world, mentioning individual theaters, is covered. Also listed are authors of literary works that have inspired operas, conductors, opera companies, arias, and such topics as *Bel Canto* and *Medieval Liturgical Drama*. Entries range in length from a few lines to four pages for *Wagner, Richard*. Some items conclude with bibliographies, and "select worklists" are included for composers.

Two other recent one-volume opera dictionaries are *The Harper Dictionary of Opera and Operetta* [RBB Ja 15 91] and *A–Z of Opera* [RBB Mr 1 91]. The latter work, intended for opera novices, is much shorter than *Oxford* (at 223 pages) and excludes entries for opera characters and arias. The strengths of the *Harper Dictionary*, comparable in length to *Oxford*, are its coverage of operetta and its supplementary tables and lists. For topics covered by both works, *The Oxford Dictionary of Opera* provides more in-depth information, directed toward serious users and music lovers. It is a recommended purchase for public and academic libraries.

HeadBangers: The Worldwide MegaBook of Heavy Metal Bands. By Mark Hale. Popular Culture Ink, 1993. 542p. bibliog. illus. indexes. hardcover $65 (1-56075-029-4).
782.42 Heavy metal (Music)—Encyclopedias ‖ Rock music—Encyclopedias ‖ Rock groups—Encyclopedias [CIP] 92-81112

Anthrax, Slayer, Queensryche—if those names are meaningless to you, they won't be to many of your patrons ages 15 to 25. Today heavy metal is on the airwaves and MTV. However, once the media wouldn't touch music's bad boys, so they built their legions of fans record by record and tour by tour. This 3,458-entry who's who lists metal and metal influences, most of whom will not be found in other reference sources.

The introduction covers the history of metal's evolution from hard rock to speed metal to L.A. Glam and all the genres in between. The numbered entries vary in length from three or four lines for a minor band, such as Acrid, to more than 60 lines for Megadeth. Entries give place of origin, birth and death dates for bands, the various band lineups, and metal genre. Some include personnel notes, career notes, recordings, evaluations of live performances, and *see* references. Notes can discuss musical style throughout the band's life, personalities, and influences. The entries are wide ranging, from the Beatles as an influence to hard rock groups like Aerosmith and, of course, such metal bands as Metallica. The most important value of the book, however, is not the big names, who can be found elsewhere, but the short entries on minor and regional bands. The band information is current through 1989, with some updates through early 1992.

The closing material includes a description of such fanzines as *Kerrang*, which are the source of most metal information, a "Roots of Metal" discography, a bibliography, and a metal update. A number of indexes cover band name, performer, state and country of origin, style, album title, and album label and number. A few black-and-white photographs of bands add interest.

Hale fills a gap in dictionaries of musical biography. There are some older works on metal, such as *International Encyclopedia of Hard Rock and Heavy Metal* (1983), but they are dated and not as extensive. Libraries needing to round out their music collection will want to give *HeadBangers* serious consideration, and, as a side benefit, the library might even be seen as cool by some of its patrons.

American Women Songwriters: A Biographical Dictionary. By Virginia L. Grattan. Greenwood, 1993. 239p. bibliog. indexes. hardcover $39.95. (0-313-28510-1).
782.42'092 [B] Songs—U.S.—Bio-bibliography—Dictionaries ‖ Women composers—U.S.—Biography—Dictionaries [CIP] 92-32211

This book states that its purpose is not to provide a history or critical evaluation of contributions, but rather "to provide biographical information about the key American women who have written popular songs." The women range from Julia Ward Howe and the Hill sisters of the mid-1800s to such well-known entertainers of today as Aretha Franklin and Dolly Parton. Included are 181 "native-born American women" who have contributed to different types of popular music. The work is organized in 10 thematic chapters that cover pop rock, motion pictures, musicals, blues, jazz, folk, country, hymns, gospel, and early women songwriters. Each chapter opens with an introductory essay, followed by the alphabetically arranged biographies.

Entries range in length from a long paragraph or two (for Jean Kerr, Olive Duncan, and others) to six pages on Dorothy Fields, with most averaging 1 ½ pages. Personal background and career are usually described, along with major song titles. Sources are listed at the end of each article and are compiled in a bibliography at the end of the book. Periodical articles are as current as October 1991. Barbara Streisand's 1992 work in *Prince of Tides* is included, but Madonna's 1992 book, *Sex*, is not mentioned in her biography. A few photographs are included, as well as lyrics to nine random songs.

The inclusion of two indexes, one by song and one by name, are more useful access points than its arrangement by category. For example, Ella Fitzgerald and Katherine Dunham are both listed under "Pop Rock," along with Carole King and Tracy Chapman. Billie Holiday is in "Jazz," not "Blues."

As informative as this book is, the style is somewhat stilted, and inconsistencies in entries make its usefulness questionable. For instance, while many profiles include information about marital status, there is no mention of Dory Previn's divorce or Tracy Nelson's family. Roseanne Cash's entry notes that she is the half-sister of Carlene Carter, but this is not included in Carter's entry. Tin Pan Alley, the New York center of music publishing in the early part of this century, is somehow featured in the introduction to the pop rock chapter. Only after two pages on Bette Midler does the entry mention that "she also writes songs." Sylvia Fine is notable for having two songs nominated for Oscars, but she is not one of the women discussed in the chapter introduction to "Motion Pictures." Amy Grant, Gloria Estefan, and Valerie Simpson are not included among the biographees.

No other work of this specific scope is available, but Unsung: A History of Women in American Music (Greenwood, 1980) and the International Encyclopedia of Women Composers (2d ed., Books & Music, 1987) are both similar in their efforts to highlight women's compositions. High school and public libraries probably already have more current and complete information on today's popular singers than is contained in this new source. However, American Women Songwriters may be useful as a supplementary tool where music biography is in heavy demand.

Soul Music A–Z. By Hugh Gregory. Blandford; dist. by Sterling, 1992. 266p. bibliog. illus. hardcover $24.95 (0-7137-2179-0); paper $14.95 (0-7137-2183-9).
782.42'1644 Soul musicians ‖ Biography—Dictionaries [BKL]

British writer Gregory has compiled this biographical dictionary of almost 600 soul performers, songwriters, and producers. Entries run the gamut of soul's history. Producers from pioneer Ahmet Ertegun to today's Jimmy Jam and Terry Lewis are included. Performers also span time from Sam Cooke and his predecessors to new groups like the Fine Young Cannibals. In his introduction, Gregory acknowledges the difficulty in classifying soul singers. This problem is most obvious with contemporary performers and means that some "blue-eyed" soul singers like Michael Bolton have been omitted and rappers like L L Cool J included.

The biographical sketches focus on musical careers and associations with other artists. Entries include the year and place of birth, career background, and hit singles, with both U.S. and U.K. charting and year. For some performers there are brief discographies of albums likely to be available. Profiles range in length from one column to 1½ pages. Two inserts of black-and-white photographs spotlight big-name performers like Aretha Franklin, Ike and Tina Turner, and Mariah Carey. See and bold face see also references are used throughout the book, which has no index. A brief bibliography is appended.

Many of the big name contemporary performers will be found in works like The Penguin Encyclopedia of Popular Music and The Encyclopedia of Pop, Rock and Soul. As with so many genres of popular music, it is the early performers who sometimes fall between the cracks. Those libraries with a demand for information on early performers like Little Willie John will certainly want to consider Soul Music A–Z as an inexpensive addition to their music collection.

The Oxford Companion to Musical Instruments. By Anthony Baines. Oxford, 1992. 404p. bibliog. illus. hardcover $45 (0-19-311334-1).
784.19'03 Musical instruments—Dictionaries [CIP] 92-8635

Material from The New Oxford Companion to Music, bearing upon acoustical musical instruments, is the basis of this new one-volume work. Impeccably edited by Baines, this new companion celebrates in one alphabetic sequence the glory and range of instruments from around the world, from nose flutes to tabla, from the sitar to the oboe. Many of the entries in the work under review were rewritten from the earlier companion.

The individual entries cover specific instruments and families thereof (e.g., Wind Instruments) as well as their representation in different countries (e.g., Africa) and time periods (e.g., Baroque). Entries for western instruments provide a description, including details of their construction, often accompanied by a black-and-white photograph or a line drawing. Playing techniques, a brief history, and a list of the major repertory are sketched as well. Baines even deftly conveys the sound of many of the instruments. Cross-references and translated names of major instruments are also provided. Entries often include brief references to sources of more information, and full bibliographic citations are provided in an appendix. Another appendix is an alphabetical list of names of manufacturers and inventors of instruments.

While ostensibly written for the general reader, a musical background will definitely assist in gaining the full benefit of Baines' erudite depictions. The Oxford Companion to Musical Instruments is a well-produced, authoritative addition to any library serving adults, in particular to any library holding neither the aforementioned New Oxford Companion to Music nor the more comprehensive, three-volume New Grove Dictionary of Musical Instruments.

PERFORMING ARTS, RECREATION

Pick-up Games: The Rules, The Players, The Equipment. By D. W. Crisfield. Facts On File, 1992. 192p. bibliog. illus. index. hardcover $27.95 (0-8160-2700-5).
790.1'922 Games—Rules—Juvenile literature ‖ Games—Equipment and supplies—Juvenile literature ‖ Sports—Rules—Juvenile literature ‖ Sports—Equipment and supplies—Juvenile literature [CIP] 92-16296

Pick-up Games is a solid addition to the literature of recreation. The author, who has published several other sports books, has created an interesting catalog of more than 250 activities for the playground and backyard. The author defines a pick-up game as "an offshoot of an established sport" that has flexible boundaries and rules, adaptable to the players' needs.

The book is arranged alphabetically by 15 sports (badminton, baseball, basketball, etc.). The fifteenth category is a general one that lists games that are simply "a lot of fun to play." Here are listed such classics as Capture the Flag, Kick the Can, and Manhunt. Each chapter begins with a description of the base sport, followed by its offshoots. These games are arranged "developmentally" within a sport. That is, games that are derivatives of the original sport are listed first, followed by those that are variations on the derivative, and so on. All of the sports have diagrams of the regulation playing area as well as illustrations of how to play the derivatives. The descriptions of the games are clear and include number of players, equipment, playing area, and minimum age.

Several of the games are common variations on many of the base sports, and these are cross-referenced to the first alphabetical listing. For instance, Monkey in the Middle can be played in basketball, field hockey, lacrosse, and soccer; the complete description is given in the basketball chapter. Common names are used for the games, although there may be some geographic regions in which the games are known differently (e.g., Smear is known in various areas as Muckleball, Pile-on, Free for All, Pig Pile, Kill the Guy with the Ball, etc.). While these variant names are not referenced in the book, the organization by base sport enables the user to readily find this football derivative. Thus, regional peculiarities should not present a problem. The volume includes a glossary of terms and an index. A useful appendix is the chart that shows the minimum number of players needed for each game.

Although several good game books are available, few are as clear and concise as Pick-up Games. Also, this new title does an admirable job of relating the games to popular sports. This book should be popular in school and public libraries as well as in college libraries with sports and recreation studies.

Handel's National Directory for the Performing Arts. 2v. 5th ed. Bowker, 1992. 1,800p. indexes. hardcover $250 (0-8352-3250-6).
791'.02573 Performing arts—U.S.—Directories [BKL] 73-646635

Although it has a new publisher, the basic arrangement of this guide to performing arts institutions remains the same as in the last edition. The material is organized into two volumes. Volume 1 is concerned with organizations and facilities such as theaters and concert halls. Entries are arranged alphabetically by state, then by city, and, finally, by performing arts area—theater, dance, instrumental music, etc. Organization listings include relevant names, addresses, and telephone numbers; statistics for staff, budget, and attendance; and founding dates. Listings for facilities include stage dimensions and seating capacities, rental availability, resident groups, type of facility, etc. Additional points of access are provided by indexes for dance, instrumental music, vocal music, theater, and performing series. This last category covers entities concerned with more than one of the performing arts (e.g., festivals, community concerts, sponsoring organizations). There is also a facility index, an alphabetical listing of performing arts spaces.

Volume 2 covers educational institutions arranged alphabetically by state, city, and performing arts area. Specific information is provided on dance, music, and theater departments. Listed are contact persons, number of faculty and students, degrees offered, financial assistance offered, course offerings, and performing groups and resident artists, if any. Additional access points in this volume are provided by dance, music, and theater indexes. A general institution index lists alphabetically all the schools or institutions included.

Although this set provides a vast quantity of information, some of the flaws noted in RBB's review of the fourth edition [RBB Je 15 88] remain. One of eight such errors has been corrected in this fifth edition: Pick-Staiger Concert Hall in Evanston, Illinois, may now be found in volume 1. The problem with cross-references (or lack thereof) seems to remain in this edition. Once again, if one doesn't know that the Opera West Foundation is in San Francisco or is associated with the Lamplighters, one won't be able to find it in this directory.

Although it is disappointing to find some of the same omissions in this new edition, there is such a wealth of material in *Handel's* that they might be overlooked. The publisher states that of the more than 7,000 entries, over 1,000 are new to this edition. The hefty price tag may make this a choice for large libraries only, particularly those with performing arts collections.

Roller Coasters: An Illustrated Guide to the Rides in the United States and Canada, with a History. By Todd H. Throgmorton. McFarland, 1993. 154p. illus. index. hardcover $25.95 (0-89950-805-7).
791'.06 Roller coasters—U.S.—Directories ‖ Roller coasters—Canada—Directories ‖ Amusement parks—U.S.—Directories ‖ Amusement parks—Canada—Directories ‖ Roller coasters—History [CIP] 92-50939

For those people whose hearts thump with anticipation at the sight of a roller coaster, Throgmorton provides a helpful guide. Not only does he list the 196 roller coasters in the U.S. and Canada, but he also includes the addresses of the parks, the telephone numbers, brief statements about the parks, and details about each coaster. A self-described roller coaster addict, he has ridden on more than half the ones he describes.

The first chapter details the history of the roller coaster from its beginnings in the sixteenth century to its golden age in the 1920s. With the current popularity of theme parks, the rides are enjoying a revival. The bulk of the book is a geographically organized location guide to amusement parks and their coasters. Each coaster is described with its beginning year of operation, manufacturer, former location (if any), physical and technical information, length and time of the ride, and special features. Most of the entries are accompanied by a black-and-white photograph. The appendix contains a list of both wood and steel coasters operating in the U.S. and Canada; a comprehensive index concludes the work.

This title is likely to be the definitive guidebook to roller coasters. Since the author made no attempt to include current days and hours of operation, the book will retain its usefulness without becoming outdated. It is recommended for public libraries, as well as for specialized collections of popular-culture materials.

The Name Is Familiar: Who Played Who in the Movies: A Directory of Title Characters. By Robert Anthony Nowlan and Gwendolyn Wright Nowlan. Neal-Schuman, 1992. 1,014p. paper $75 (1-55570-054-3).
791.43'028 Characters and characteristics in motion pictures—Dictionaries ‖ Motion picture actors and actresses—Biography—Dictionaries [OCLC] 92-42877

Movie title characters and the actors who played them are the subject of this directory, which includes approximately 4,500 performers, 9,000 characters, and 9,000 films from the early silents to 1991. The criteria for selection are fraught with *buts* and *alsos*. For example, the film must be in English; the title must refer to one or more characters in the movie in some way (though the title doesn't have to explicitly name a character, as movies with titles that describe a character have also been included); films whose titles are questions—the answers to which identify particular characters—are listed, as are films in which pronouns suggest a character or characters; and occasionally a movie title names the performer who appears in the film. This still leaves the reader with a lot of questions about title inclusion. Even with an explanation in the three-page introduction, it is difficult to surmise how such titles as *Six Hours to Live* and *Sixteen Candles* were selected. The Nolans are the authors of *Movie Characters of Leading Performers of the Sound Era* [RBB Je 15 90], which describes 450 actors and the characters they played.

The arrangement here is simple. A 150-question trivia quiz, with answers, is prefatory to the actual directory. It will challenge the most confident and knowledgable of film afficionados. For example, "Name the film in which exotic beauty Maria Montez played twin sisters, good Tollea and evil Naja." The directory consists of three sections. The first is a list of performers who have appeared in title roles with the films in which they had these roles, the names of their title characters, the year of release, and the production company. The second section is a list of the title characters with the movie in which the character appeared, year of release, the production company, the actor who played the role, and an often amusing capsule description of the plot. The third section is a list of the films whose titles refer to a particular character or characters. Each entry in this section contains the year of release of the film, the studio or production company, the name of the title character and the performer who appeared in the role, the director, and other leading performers in the film.

There are many books that give film credits, so the information in the first and third sections is not unique. For the patron who knows the name of a film character but can't remember the name of the movie or the actor who played the part, the second part of this directory could be useful if the film falls within the guidelines mentioned above. For example, Freddie Clegg is the title character in *The Collector* and was played by Terence Stamp. However, this sort of question is not likely to be very common, and the "title character" twist isn't very useful. *The Name Is Familiar* provides 1,000 pages of amusing reading, but is not high-priority purchase for most libraries.

Film Noir: An Encyclopedic Reference to the American Style. 3d ed. Ed. by Alain Silver and Elizabeth Ward. Overlook; dist. by Viking, 1992. 479p. bibliog. illus. index. paper $22.95 (0-87951-479-5).
791.43'0909 Moving pictures—U.S. ‖ Moving picture plays—History and criticism ‖ Moving pictures—Plots, themes, etc. [CIP] 88-62182

The original edition of *Film Noir* (1979) was the first comprehensive English-language survey of American movies that reflect "noir sensibility"—the dark side of life. The introductory essay discusses the complexities of defining film noir, which, in this work, is seen as a cycle that incorporates aspects of both style and content to reflect American cultural preoccupations. These films were produced in a time of U.S. societal transition, from the end of World War II to 1960, which is now referred to as the period of "classic" film noir. This third edition reprints verbatim the contents of the 1979 book, updates appendixes that were added in the second edition of 1988, and provides a substantial amount of new material on recent films.

Completely new to the 1993 edition is extensive coverage, provided in appendix E, of the "neo-noir" period, defined here as beginning in the late 1970s and continuing until the present. This section of the book includes listings for 176 films, such as *Silence of the Lambs, Thelma and Louise,* and *Fatal Attraction.* The alphabetically listed entries include credits and release data but no critical appraisals. However, in a lengthy essay on neo-noir, the editors discuss the individual films, as well as various trends. They document a resurgence of interest in themes and protagonists of the noir films and attempts by filmmakers to recreate the noir mood. The editors view this conscious effort by filmmakers, who are "cognizant of a heritage and intent on placing their own interpretation on it," as the primary difference between films of the classic period and those they define as neo-noir.

The 1979 edition covered 300 individual films in entries that contain complete credits, plot summary, character analysis, and critical evaluation. New features in the second edition of *Film Noir* (1988) were two appendixes, both of which have been expanded and updated for the 1993 publication. Appendix C is a critical review of the literature on film noir. This lengthy revised essay provides in-depth discussion of contemporary studies that consider such issues as the portrayal of female characters as well as alienation, despair, love, and madness. Appendix D covers films from the classic period that were not listed in the first edition; new titles were added to this section in both the second and third editions of the work. Another appendix provides lists of the classic noir films indexed according to year of release, director, writer, composer, producer, featured actors, and releasing company.

The book is illustrated with several black-and-white publicity shots and movie stills. A three-page bibliography of books and periodical articles includes citations to general studies of film noir but not to works focusing on individual films or filmmakers. Additional features include a list of classic noir films available on videotape and a comprehensive index.

The editors of *Film Noir* state that the aim in creating the book "has always been to make it an accessible work, both as a specific reference and as an overview." They have succeeded in this objective. The book will be a welcome addition in large public libraries serving movie fans, as well as in specialized collections for scholars of the cinema and of popular culture.

The Great Hollywood Musical Pictures. By James Robert Parish and Michael R. Pitts. Scarecrow, 1992. 806p. illus. hardcover $79.50 (0-8108-2529-5).
791.43'6 Musical films—U.S.—History and criticism [CIP] 92-7483

Following on the heels of last year's *Hollywood Songsters* [RBB Ap 15 91], Parish and Pitts introduce *The Great Hollywood Musical Picture,* the latest in the "Great Picture" series. This book covers both the classics and newer musicals up to 1988. It is an *Annie* to *Ziegfield* compilation of about 340 musical films.

The essays range in length from two to more than three pages, depending on the importance of the film. Entries open with year, studio, and running time, followed by a comprehensive list of the behind-the-scenes staff, songs with performers, and cast list. The essays give the story line, any interesting history surrounding the film, and brief criticism. The book includes live-action and animated musicals, but a few are missing. For example, the animated *An American Tale* (1986) is omitted. The text is accompanied by 112 black-and-white photographs.

The authors' enthusiasm for musicals is evident, but they are critical of poor films and cite opinions from other sources about the films. For example, several sources are cited for *Night and Day,* including *The Melody Lingers On* by Roy Hemming and *Commonweal.* However, complete citations are not given in the text, and the book lacks a bibliography.

The book closes with a chronology of the movies included. An index by personal name or song would have been useful.

While the era of the musical has faded due to high production costs, this popular treatment will be welcome at libraries with musical fans, especially with cable movie channels reviving interest in the genre. The lengthy essays and comprehensive lists of credits will be helpful if the reader knows the name of the musical. Libraries owning works like the *Motion Picture Guide* and *Encyclopedia of the Musical Film* by Stanley Green may not need a book with entries on this scale.

Baseball in the Movies: A Comprehensive Reference, 1915–1991. By Hal Erickson. McFarland, 1992. 402p. bibliog. illus. index. hardcover $39.95 (0-89950-657-7).
791.43'655 Baseball films—History and criticism [CIP] 91-42875

Entries on 81 baseball films released through December 1991 are arranged here by title. Each contains a full cast list, production credits, production company, year of release, and a black-and-white still from the film. Readable essays of several pages give a synopsis and critique of the films with background and behind-the-scenes information. For instance, Erickson characterizes the conclusion of *Bull Durham* thus: "Crash Davis and Annie Savoy have come to realize that they're exactly the same, two seasoned players nearing the end of their rather ethereal careers, both in need of something that will last." Erickson owes much of his research to two prior sources: an April 1968 edition of *Films in Review* and the exhaustive baseball-film dictionary *Everything Baseball,* by James Mote (Prentice-Hall, 1989), which lists baseball films with brief credits and story line. *Baseball in the Movies'* complete survey of the literature is attested to by Erickson's bibliography of 120 plus items. His research included the American Film Institute and the Wisconsin Center for Film and Theatre Research collections. This volume also contains "Baseball Short Subjects," a review essay covering the most important short films, and "Baseball in Non-Baseball Films," which discusses other films in which the sport is depicted in some way. The index largely consists of film titles and personal names from the cast lists. There is no doubt that Ericson has written the definitive reference work on this film genre. A list of his picks of the best films and their availability in video format would have been helpful for the browser. Recommended for libraries with strong film collections.

Celluloid Wars: A Guide to Film and the American Experience of War. By Frank J. Wetta and Stephen J. Curley. Greenwood, 1992. 296p. bibliog. indexes. hardcover $45 (0-313-26099-0; ISSN 0899-0166).
791.43'658 War films—U.S.—History and criticism || U.S. in motion pictures || War films—U.S.—Catalogs || War films—U.S.—Bibliography [CIP] 92-8210

In a foreword, Roger Spiller of the U.S. Army Command and General Staff College writes, "Not only have Wetta and Curley cataloged the influence of war upon the history of filmmaking, but they have also examined the influence of films upon war making." These two ambitious goals are addressed largely in the two essays that begin the book.

In the first essay, war films are classified from four perspectives: mimetic (the subject of the film); pragmatic (the intended audience of the film); expressive (the filmmaker); and objective (work of art). These classifications provide readers with a context in which to discuss war films, but the essay is so wide-ranging that it barely touches the surface of its multifaceted subject. The seven pages of black-and-white movie stills add little to the essay. The second essay deals in part with how war films have influenced the fighting of wars, but its main focus is really on how war films affect the attitudes of film viewers—most of whom will never fight in a war. It stresses the vicarious element of viewing war films and the myths of heroism permeating them.

The succeeding nine chapters discuss American wars and how films have represented them. These are arranged in chronological order, beginning with the colonial wars of 1689–1763 and ending with the Vietnam War. Two other chapters cover "Banana Wars" in China, Morocco, Central America, the Caribbean, North Africa, and the Middle East (including the recent U.S. involvement in Iraq and Kuwait) and nuclear warfare. Each chapter is organized in the following sections: a brief chronology of war events; a two- to three-page commentary on how American cinema has treated the war, along with a short list of sources; and a filmography with asterisks indicating the editors' view of the film's appeal to the general public. The information for each film includes running time, color or black-and-white note, director, major actors, company, and date of release. Films that the editors rate as of the highest interest to the viewing public also contain a two-sentence annotation.

The last chapter of the book consists of an annotated bibliography listing "100 of the most important books and articles written about war films." Appendixes consist of two lists: "Top Ten War Films" and "Best Films for Each War." There is an index to the essays and the short filmography annotations. Unfortunately, basic information in the filmography, such as names of actors, is not indexed (except for the directors, who are listed in a separate index).

The *Encyclopedia of American War Films* (1989) covers many of the same films as those in *Celluloid Wars*, but the descriptive, analytic, and evaluative information for each film is more comprehensive and useful. *Celluloid Wars* is recommended for large academic libraries supporting film programs and large public libraries collecting comprehensively in this performing art. Other libraries should give priority to *The Encyclopedia of American War Films*.

A Cast of Thousands: A Compendium of Who Played What in Film. 3v. Comp. by Melinda Corey and George Ochoa. Facts On File, 1992. hardcover $245 (0-8160-2429-4).
791.43'75 Film credits ‖ Motion picture actors and actresses—Credits ‖ Motion picture producers and directors—Credits [CIP] 91-38115

Lists of motion pictures and their casts are hardly unique, although this comparatively moderately priced work is. Corey and Ochoa are a free-lance writing team and coauthors of *The Book of Answers* (1990) and the recently published *New York Public Library Book of Answers: Movies & TV* (1992). They have assembled in A *Cast of Thousands* "a book of nearly 10,000 movie casts . . . spanning 80 years, from *Queen Elizabeth* in 1912 to *The Silence of the Lambs* in 1991."

The three-volume set is divided into three parts. Part 1, *The Casts*, takes up the entire first volume with an alphabetical listing of movie titles with year of release, studio, director, and cast of actors with their roles. The second volume opens with part 2, *Index of Directors*, an alphabetical listing of directors followed by their films; part 3, *Index of Actors*, concludes the second volume and takes up the entire third volume with an alphabetical listing of all actors from the films featured in part 1.

The set is primarily one of lists: there are no annotations or critical commentaries whatsoever. There are, however, cross-references when appropriate. For example, the Cary Grant movie *The Bachelor and the Bobby Soxer* was released in the U.K. as *Bachelor Knight*. There is an appropriate *see* reference from the latter title to the former.

The authors point out in their introduction that "more than anything, A *Cast of Thousands* is a book about choices." Librarians looking for an all-inclusive list of absolutely every movie made will be disappointed, though the authors spell out some of their selection criteria in the introduction. The work features every Academy Award winner from a major category, plus cult favorites, major money-makers, and critical successes. American sound movies comprise the majority of the entries, though silent and foreign films appear, too. The authors admit that few of the movies listed "can boast 100% complete cast listings," as they purposely limited such works as costume dramas and musicals to about 15 cast members.

With so many caveats, why bother? Primarily because similar titles that are more comprehensive are much more expensive. The *Motion Picture Guide: 1927–1984* gives information on casts as well as plot synopsis and critical commentary for some 50,000 films but costs $750. The *American Film Institute Catalog of Motion Pictures* also gives cast analysis as well as plot summaries and citations to reviews but is not yet complete and is also costly. For instance, the latest volume, *Feature Films, 1911–1920*, costs $140. *Motion Picture Players' Credits: Worldwide Performers of 1967 through 1980 with Filmographies of Their Entire Careers* [RBB Je 1 91] lists 15,000 actors and costs only $145, but its scope means that favorites like Cary Grant and Clark Gable are too early for inclusion and others like Michelle Pfeiffer and Robin Williams are too late.

Large libraries with comprehensive film reference collections can likely pass on *A Cast of Thousands*. Small public and academic libraries looking for works similar to the above titles but that cannot justify the expenditure will want to consider this work.

The Slide Area: Film Book Reviews, 1989–1991. By Anthony Slide. Scarecrow, 1992. 260p. indexes. hardcover $29.50 (0-8108-2614-3).
791.43'75 Motion pictures—Book reviews ‖ Television—Book reviews [CIP] 92-32588

Slide has written or edited more than 40 books on film, including such titles as *International Film Industry: A Historical Dictionary* [RBB Je 15 89] and the many volumes of *Selected Film Criticism* [RBB F 15 85]. In January 1989, Slide began a monthly column in *Classic Images* where he attempts to review as many general books on film as possible, as well as major titles about television. *The Slide Area* is a compilation of more than 300 of these reviews published between 1989 and 1991. In his preface, Slide claims that many of the books he evaluates are not generally reviewed in the library media. This is an accurate statement regarding the bibliographic reference titles he covers, but it is inaccurate concerning the trade and non-bibliographic sources.

The reviews draw on the author's experience with the subject matter as well as his critical opinions. Arranged chronologically, the informative reviews are short (30–150 words) and are both descriptive and evaluative. Many of the reviews contain a statement of recommendation or a critique, such as "it has too many flaws to be acceptable as a reference work." Frequently, titles are compared with others on the topic. Slide states, "I make no excuse for my reviews being opinionated," and indeed they are, as well as, on occasion, sarcastic. But he also aims for them to be fair and entertaining. Following the compilation of reviews are a directory of publishers whose books are included, an author index, and a title index.

For large public and academic libraries doing retrospective collection development in the cinema and television, *The Slide Area* might be useful as a professional tool. For students of the cinema, it provides a single-volume bibliography of recent film books with the critical opinions of one expert in the field. Its reference use to the general reading public, however, is limited.

Variety Movie Guide. Ed. by Derek Elley and others. Prentice Hall Press, 1992. 704p. index. hardcover $40 (0-13-928359-5); paper $20 (0-13-928342-0).
791.43'75 Motion pictures—Reviews [CIP] 91-2164

Variety has long been known as the definitive entertainment newspaper. This book of 5,000 film reviews from 1914 to the present is a spin-off from the 21-volume *Variety Film Reviews* (1907–90) collection. These reviews capture the eyewitness opinion of contemporaneous film critics rather than the usual retrospective, secondhand musings.

Because of space limitations, much detail from the original reviews is lost, but the spirit and high quality of the writing has been kept. A glossary is provided to help today's reader decipher Variety's lingo, such as *megger* (director) and *b.f.* (boyfriend). The basics are included: plot, performance assessments, technical merits, and interesting background. Some historic prejudicial writing (e.g., during the world wars and the McCarthy era) has been toned down.

Each entry includes title, year of first public release, running time, country of origin (only English-language movies are included), color, sound, video form, director, producer, script, photography, editor, music, art director, cast list, production company, and Academy Award nominations. No rating symbols are used. An index lists directors and their movies reviewed in this volume.

The only reservation about this work is the lack of stated criteria for movies chosen. It appears that the best or seminal films were picked, but an explanation of the selection process would have helped. However, the incisive language and the feel of the firsthand critic more than compensate. This is just glorious reading!

Even though several good movie-review books are available, this one stands out as a fun addition to libraries that don't own the 21-volume set.

Fantastic Cinema Subject Guide: A Topical Index to 2,500 Horror, Science Fiction, and Fantasy Films. By Bryan Senn and John Johnson. McFarland, 1992. 682p. illus. index. hardcover $45 (0-89950-681-X).
016.79143'615 Fantastic films—Catalogs ‖ Horror films—Catalogs ‖ Science fiction films—Catalogs ‖ Fantasy—Film catalogs ‖ Horror—Film catalogs [CIP] 91-51230

Aimed at a special-interest adult audience, this work covers feature-length films available in English and released before May 1991. The authors are film enthusiasts by avocation, and the selections for their comprehensive listing of the cinema of the fantastic are those films from the "overlapping genres of horror, science fiction, and fantasy." Thus, comedies like *Topper* are excluded, and "only those ghost films with at least some brief element of horror or suspense are included."

The annotated survey of films is arranged by more than 100 subject headings, including such topics as *Bats, Fish-People, Mad Scientists*, and

Time Travel. At the beginning of each section is a brief introduction that discusses history, highlights, and trends. Some of the subject headings have several subdivisions, others are cross-referenced, and all are listed in the alphabetically arranged table of contents. Each entry contains information about the film production, the cast, and a plot synopsis. Some entries include a quotation from or about the film. For some films, trivia and gossip are included as "additional information," which the authors admit may not always be accurate. Titles that are entered under several subject headings contain different summaries for each entry, emphasizing the relationship to the specific genre. The information is clearly laid out on the page, but pages are cramped with double columns, single spacing, and small print. Stills from several of the films fare better in reproduction, and fantastic-film buffs—the book's intended audience—will enjoy them.

The book has appendixes that list 3-D films, films with a western setting, and films with black casts aimed at a black audience. The title index contains so much information that entries can be confusing. In addition to the page-number listing for each film, it indicates year of release and cross-references for applicable alternative titles. The index also includes, for 1,908 of the films, a critical rating from 1 to 10, based on the authors' opinion.

While this work has the disadvantages of any compendium that draws upon the knowledge and preferences of enthusiasts, it presents substantial filmographic information, useful genre listings, and the opinions of these hobbyists. *Fantastic Cinema Subject Guide* is a useful source for those looking for this highly specialized information.

From Page to Screen: Children's and Young Adult Books on Film and Video. Ed. by Joyce Moss and George Wilson. Gale, 1992. 429p. indexes. hardcover $35 (0-8103-7893-0).

016.79143/083 Children's literature—Film and video adaptations—Catalogs || Young adult literature—Film and video adaptations—Catalogs || Young adult literature—Bibliography || Children's literature—Bibliography || Young adult films—Catalogs [OCLC] 92-9781

From Page to Screen is a guide to 1,400 film, video, and laser disc adaptations of 750 literary works for children ages five through high school. Materials treated range from fairy tales and Shakespeare to the more contemporary works of Alex Haley and Dr. Seuss. The book will be useful for adults who want to select the best media for children; some items will appeal to adult viewers, too. School language arts or English departments will find this bibliography-filmography helpful in lesson planning.

Organized alphabetically by book title, each entry lists author, publisher and date, genre, and synopsis of the story. Following this is a listing of the cinematic adaptations giving film title, production information, description and brief evaluation of the work, review citations, film awards (if applicable), suggested audience age level, and distributor information, including price and format. The availability of public performance rights is noted, and two ratings follow each film citation: book symbols that rate how closely the film adaptation reflects the source and film reels for film strength independent of the book. These symbols allow a quick visual evaluation.

Abridged versions as well as complete works are listed: a 32-minute film version of Harry Mazer's *Snow Bound* is described as an "abridged version edited to accommodate classroom time.... It retains the basic plot and has lost none of the tension." But for those who want the full-length version (50 minutes), that is also listed. Nine cinema adaptations of Cinderella are described. Two of them closely follow the book and have high film ratings, such as *Rodgers and Hammerstein's Cinderella* (1964), three are high in film rating but have added or subtracted from the story, such as the Walt Disney adaptation, and the others have significantly weakened the story or the film is not of high quality. The evaluations note significant information, such as film location, actors, or character development to assist in the selection of a specific film.

Appendixes and indexes provide additional access to films for the hearing impaired, distributors' addresses and telephone numbers, awards, age levels, subjects, and author and film titles.

Some of these videos are included in sources like *Best Videos for Children & Young Adults* [RBBS 1591] and *Video Rating Guide for Libraries*. *From Page to Screen* is unique in that it includes only films and videos based on literary works and evaluates the media in terms of the books on which they are based. This work is highly recommended for the public and school library where it will help parents, teachers, and librarians find the best films and videos that transform the printed page to the screen.

The Laserdisc Film Guide: Complete Ratings for the Best and Worst Movies Available on Disc, 1993–1994. By Jeff Rovin. St. Martin's, 1993. 352p. paper $15.95 (0-312-08703-9).

016.79143'75 Videodiscs—Catalogs || Motion pictures—Catalogs || Videodisc—Evaluation [OCLC] 92-33340

According to author Rovin, a free-lance film critic, more than 3,000 feature films are currently available on laserdisc. Those who prefer films in this format will discover that this directory and rating guide is a helpful resource. Three hundred films are arranged here in alphabetical order. Each entry contains two parts: a rating of the audio and visual quality of the product and a review of the film itself. Additional product features, such as format, source, chapters, letterboxing, or supplemental material (trailers, cut scenes, interviews, etc.) are also indicated. Both the technical evaluations and the artistic ratings are based on a five-star system. The commentaries (some contributed by *San Francisco Examiner* columnist Bob Stephens) are witty and insightful. The introduction contains information on laserdisc suppliers, including ordering information and commentaries on service and reliability. A glossary of laserdisc terminology is also provided. Any consumer who purchases or rents feature films on laserdisc can benefit from the information in this inexpensive volume, and it is recommended for public library collections.

Les Brown's Encyclopedia of Television. 3d ed. Gale, 1992. 723p. bibliog. illus. index. tables. hardcover $39.95 (0-8103-8871-5); paper $22.95 (0-8103-9420-0).

791.45'03 Television broadcasting—Encyclopedias [CIP] 91-48157

On April 30, 1939, NBC began regular television service with a telecast of the opening of the New York World's Fair. There have been innumerable changes in the medium in the 50 years since that first flickering image of President Roosevelt appeared. The third edition of *Les Brown's Encyclopedia of Television* is a comprehensive chronicle of "the television that was, the television that is and the television that probably will be."

This updated edition, the first in 10 years, contains almost 3,000 entries on the people, programs, and companies as well as the legal and technological issues of the television industry. The coverage is both historical and current. Though the majority of entries cover U.S. television, information on major markets in Europe, Canada, and other places is included. Readers will find information on hit shows of the past and present, from "I Love Lucy" to "The Simpsons." All of the major networks are covered and many of the behind-the-scenes executives and producers. Such issues as *Family Viewing Time*, *Violence*, and *Children's Advertising* are also treated.

Of the entries, 900 are new to this edition and others have undergone revision or updating. Some of the new entries cover programs that have debuted in recent years such as "Murphy Brown," "L.A. Law," and "The Cosby Show." Entries for other series, such as "M*A*S*H" or "Little House on the Prairie," were expanded to reflect changes in the cast, etc. Information on cable television has been expanded with the new articles *Cable Labs*, *Cable Penetration*, and *Cable Networks*.

In addition to new and expanded entries, this edition of the encyclopedia has a general index and new and expanded tables in the appendix. Appendixes include tables on the top-rated network prime-time feature films, sports events, and programs; the Super Bowl rating history; television households in the U.S.; a list of FCC commissioners; and a list of European satellite broadcasters. A brief bibliography includes works from the last 20 years that deal with the television industry.

Brown as editor is aided by a notable list of contributors who can be found at the beginning of the volume. These include journalists and writers who have observed the industry for many years. Each contributor was responsible for certain sections of the encyclopedia. For example, Morton Silverstein, a producer of news documentaries for all three major networks, was responsible for the entries dealing with news and documentaries.

Libraries with earlier editions will want to add this new edition of the encyclopedia. Coverage of individual programs is not as extensive as in *The Complete Directory to Prime Time Network Shows 1946–Present* (5th ed., Ballantine, 1992), but *Les Brown's Encyclopedia* is an excellent and easy-to-use resource for information on all aspects of television.

The Soap Opera Book: Who's Who in Daytime Drama. Ed. by Nancy E. Rout and others. Todd Publications, P.O. Box 301, West Nyack, NY 10994, 1992. 311p. illus. index. paper $29.95 (0-915344-36-X; ISSN 1065-402X).
791.45'092 Soap operas—U.S.—Biography—Dictionaries || Television actors and actresses—U.S.—Biography—Dictionaries [BKL] 92-5618

Soap operas are the highly popular cash cows of the three major networks. More than 400 stars are profiled in this who's who. The entries, arranged alphabetically by the name of the actor or actress, include both long-established artists and current child stars. All entries are of living persons, but not all are currently working in daytime drama.

Most profiles include a black-and-white studio photograph. Basic opening facts encompass birthday (but usually not the year) and place, marital status, appearance, education, interests, awards, and daytime roles. The conversational narratives range from 200 to 750 words and cover the artists' personal lives, daytime and nighttime television roles, movies, and theater work. The sketches include a wide array of trivia; even Elaine Princi's infomercial for a 900-number psychic line is included. Sometimes the length devoted to an individual is misleading. Janine Turner of *Northern Exposure*, who spent one year on the soaps, has a longer profile than Genie Francis of Luke and Laura fame. The book includes lists of addresses for the networks and for fan clubs. A name index, which also lists the individual's daytime shows, concludes the volume.

Two other books profile soap stars, but both are 1985 imprints and include less than three dozen entries. Compared with the most recent editions of *Who's Who in Entertainment* and the *Television Almanac*, this new book covers many more popular stars not included in the other titles. The *Who's Who* volume, for the stars included, did a better job of listing facts such as year of birth and divorce information. Public libraries serving fans of daytime television may want to consider adding *The Soap Opera Book* to their collections.

Talk Shows and Hosts on Radio: A Directory Including Show Titles and Formats, Brief Biographical Sketches of Hosts, and Locators. By Annie M. Brewer and Donald E. Brewer. Whitefoord Press, 806 Oakwood Blvd., Dearborn, MI 48124, 1992. 199p. paper $24.95 (0-9632341-0-2).
791.44'09 Talk shows—United States—Directories [BKL]

The Radio Advertising Bureau reports that more than 15 million Americans listen to radio talk shows every day. This growing segment of the radio industry is represented by more than 700 network and locally produced talk shows across the dial and around the country.

The purpose of this directory is to assist radio-advertising time buyers in choosing programs compatible with their clients' products. Also, public relations people can use it to select hosts sympathetic to those they represent. The biographical sketches included are of interest to station managers in search of new talent as well as to listeners interested in information about their favorite "talk jock."

The title begins with a directory of radio stations and their locally produced shows, arranged by state and city. Each station's call letters, frequency, address, telephone and fax numbers, and owner's name and address are included in the entries. Each program produced by the station is then listed; among the items included are host name, schedule, format, and special show telephone or fax numbers. The next section is devoted to radio networks and shows produced at that level. Networks and shows are listed in alphabetical order, with the same type of information as in the first part of the book. The third section consists of about 100 biographical sketches of talk-show hosts. The information was provided by the stations and networks and is typical of promotional literature; that is, each sketch is short on personal data and long on "personality."

Indexes compromise the fourth section: an alphabetical list of local show hosts with program titles and station affiliations; a list of network program hosts, arranged in the same way; and two lists of programs arranged by subject (e.g., *Black*, *Farm*, *Medical/Health*), the first devoted to locally produced shows and the second to network offerings.

The nature of the radio industry is one of constant change—formats, hosts, and station ownership. Indeed, the reviewer noticed several changes in local radio programming that were not reflected in this directory. If the compilers update *Talk Shows and Hosts on Radio* with regularity, it should prove to be a useful reference tool. This seems likely, because the questionnaire used to gather information is included at the end of the book. The directory's modest price puts it within reach of many libraries, unlike most of the standard broadcasting reference works.

Quinlan's Illustrated Directory of Film Comedy Actors. By David Quinlan. Holt, 1992. 302p. bibliog. illus. hardcover $35 (0-8050-2394-1).
792'.028 [B] Comedians—U.S.—Biography—Dictionaries [CIP] 92-12512

Film historian and critic Quinlan has produced a biographical directory of almost 300 British and American film comedians. The personal profiles and career summations cover such stars from the silent era as Mabel Normand and Walter Forde and continue through such current performers as Whoopi Goldberg and Eric Idle. The accompanying filmographies list both shorts and features and include films released through 1992.

The entries range from a few paragraphs to a couple of pages in length and are much more detailed than those found in *Who Was Who on Screen* (1977), *The Encyclopedia of Film* (Perigee, 1991), or any of the Halliwell directories. The entries include the author's critique of individual films and discussion of each artist's influence on the field of comedy and are similar in style to the essays found in *A Biographical Dictionary of Film* (1981). All the entries include a black-and-white portrait of the individual. Additional photographs include movie stills and publicity shots. The entries are arranged alphabetically. There are no indexes—for film titles or characters, for example—that would aid research.

This directory includes many obscure comedians often ignored in other standard sources and provides insights into the comic works of actors better known for dramatic roles, such as Alec Guinness. Another positive feature is the inclusion of both American and British personalities in the same volume. Public and academic libraries with strong film collections will want to consider purchasing this new title.

The Concise Oxford Companion to the Theatre. Ed. by Phyllis Hartnoll and Peter Found. Oxford, 1992. 568p. bibliog. hardcover $35 (0-19-866136-3).
792'.03 Theater—Dictionaries || Drama—Dictionaries [CIP] 91-23749

An entire generation of new actors has emerged, and an earlier generation has passed since the first publication of *The Concise Oxford Companion to the Theatre* in 1972. Theaters have closed and opened; actors and directors have risen and fallen. It stands to reason then, that the entries in this second edition have been completely revised, expanded, updated, and, in some cases, deleted.

Compared with the fourth edition (1983) of the parent publication, *The Oxford Companion to the Theatre*, it is not unusual to find duplication of many entries, expansion of some, and abridgment of others in this new edition of *The Concise Oxford*. In an effort to contain the size of the current work, many of the entries on minor theaters and formerly popular actors and directors have been deleted. Others, such as George and Ira Gershwin, Irving Berlin, and Maurice Chevalier, who previously were omitted or merely named in a related entry in the parent edition, now have been included in their own right. Examples of expanded, updated biographies include those for Mike Nichols, Neil Simon, José Ferrer, Katharine Hepburn, and Albert Finney. Newcomers include Anthony Hopkins, Michael Bogdanov, the Fringe Theatre, and the Tokyo Globe. There had to be a cutoff point, and the editors opted for age 40; biographies for persons born after 1952 have been excluded. In an additional effort to save space and to avoid internal duplication, the editors have used numerous cross-references, asterisks, boldface type, and other similar devices to alert the reader to more information found elsewhere in the book. This can be somewhat confusing until the reader becomes accustomed to the system. For example, the continuation of Peter Brook's biography is found under *International Center of Theatre Research*, which he founded.

As with previous publications, the bias is decidedly toward British and American theater, although the actual coverage is worldwide and spans all eras, from the time of Plato and Euripedes to the present. Similarly, all aspects of the field are included, ranging from acting styles and techniques to staging, lighting, and costume design. All types of libraries will want the new edition of this classic reference work, whether they own the parent volume or the first edition of the concise version. Because of the deletions, it is advisable for libraries owning the original *Concise Oxford Companion to the Theatre* to use it along with the new edition.

Stage It with Music: An Encyclopedic Guide to the American Musical Theatre. By Thomas S. Hischak. Greenwood, 1993. 341p. bibliog. index. hardcover $45 (0-313-28708-2).
792.6'0973 Musicals—Encyclopedias [CIP] 92-35321

This volume highlights 300 or so important Broadway musical shows and the musical careers of scores of people involved in their production. Major performers, composers, lyricists and librettists, directors, producers, choreographers, and others appear in this fascinating look at more than 100 years of musicals, up to and including *Jelly's Last Jam* (1992). Also incorporated into the alphabetical flow are entries on musical genres and subjects (e.g., *Comic Strip Musicals*, *Flop Musicals*) and musical series, such as Ziegfield Follies. A list of these entries appears before the main A–Z section of the book. Cross-references are noted by upper-case letters. A chronological list of shows sketched (from *The Black Crook* in 1866), a selective bibliography, and a detailed index close the work.

Author Hischak has designed the work for the seeker of basic facts on specific shows and show people. Entries are brief but well written. For each show profiled, the year it opened and its main creators and performers are identified, hit songs named, and the number of performances in its original production reported. Sometimes the plot is briefly outlined. The personal sketches are rarely longer than three sentences and list only major credits with no biographical substance except birth and death dates.

There are several recent encyclopedic works on the American musical theater, and they are listed in Hischak's bibliography. In the preface, he acknowledges two predecessors in particular: Gerald Bordman and Stanley Green. The former compiled *American Musical Theatre*, 2d ed. [RBB Jl 92], and the latter edited *Broadway Musicals Show by Show* (1990). These works and others, such as Ken Bloom's *American Song: The Complete Musical Theatre Companion* [RBB N 1 85], are similar in scope but do not focus simultaneously upon shows and show people. Therefore, even though the current work is appropriate for all public libraries and worthy of consideration by high school or college libraries, each library must decide if its current holdings of guides to the American musical theater warrant purchasing another.

Who's Who in Comedy: Comedians, Comics and Clowns from Vaudeville to Today's Stand-Ups. By Ronald L. Smith. Facts On File, 1992. 512p. bibliog. illus. index. hardcover $50 (0-8160-2338-7).
792.7028 Comedians—Biography [CIP] 92-42881

Approximately 500 twentieth-century, English-speaking comedians are represented in this informative reference source. According to author Smith, *Who's Who in Comedy* is "not an encyclopedia in the purest sense of the word" because it does not include certain factual data—such as a chronology of personal events and marital status. Instead, the author states, "the book is designed to answer two basic questions: 'Who is the person?' and 'What makes this person funny?'"

Judged by these two criteria, the book succeeds admirably. Each entry begins with the stage name of the comedian, his or her real name, and dates of birth and death (if appropriate). The main body of each entry consists of a well-written narrative that sets the comedian in general historical context and briefly traces how the person (or group) got started and became successful. It points out the high and low points of each performer's professional career and then offers a capsule appraisal of his or her contributions to the art of comedy. Each entry also includes a list of the creative comic output of the comedian, encompassing a variety of media—audiocassettes, videos, books, films, Broadway shows, TV, and radio, along with the appropriate dates for each. Approximately 100 black-and-white photographs of performers add interest.

Three useful, though not comprehensive, indexes complete the book: "Nickname and Character Name Index;" "Catch-Phrase Index," which isolates a few expressions exclusively associated with a comedian (e.g., "And away we go" from Jackie Gleason and "Nyuk nyuk nyuk" from Curly Howard of the Three Stooges); and "Categorical Index," which tries to classify the comedy performed by each comedian in the book.

This is an entertaining information source on the wacky and wonderful world of American comedy (only nine of the entries are for British performers). Whereas some researchers may be disappointed at the lack of hard data, others will find this book a good starting point for research. Though arranged in a traditional alphabetical format, the work reads well as a browsing book. It highlights not only the lives of the comic artists included but also underscores the variety and richness of twentieth-century comedy. Recommended for most academic libraries (including community college libraries supporting programs in the performing arts) and medium-size and large public libraries.

The Recreation Handbook: 342 Games and Other Activities for Teams and Individuals. By Robert L. Loeffelbein. McFarland, 1992. 237p. illus. paper $24.95 (0-89950-744-1).
793'.01922 Games—Juvenile literature ‖ Sports for children—Juvenile literature [OCLC] 92-50310

This volume briefly describes hundreds of games and activities for teams and individuals. The author includes many traditional games along with modern variations and some newer pastimes for players age six and up.

Games are arranged under basic themes: aquatic, basketball, bat and ball, bowling, kickball, combative sports, throwing, mallet or stick games, paddle or racket games, table games, running, word play, games requiring special equipment, indoor activities, and crafts. The author assumes that the reader knows basic rules of standard tennis, basketball, pool, etc. Entries vary from a few lines to more than one page in length. Simple diagrams are included when appropriate. Most entries note age level, organizational level, number of players, supervision (referee, scorekeeper, or none), playing time, space, and equipment. Directions for playing, scoring, and variations complete each entry. Several entries include the game source (e.g., U.S. naval sources and various recreational districts).

The strength of this book is the inclusion of so many games, but it has limitations as a reference work. Arrangement is somewhat arbitrary; some games could go under two categories and are not cross-referenced (e.g., table pool). An index to the games by age level would have been useful. Directions, too, vary considerably; some give much heed to faults, while other games don't mention wrong plays at all. Variations for disabled players are rarely given; no mention is made of senior players. The author gives little attention to safety; in fact, for many games listed for children, the author states that no supervision is needed. (This is especially surprising since the author is a former parks and recreation district superintendent.)

Recreation is a growing topic, and good reference tools do exist. While not an all-inclusive volume, libraries wanting a supplemental book on games and other activities should consider this for the circulating collection.

The Pool Player's National Pocket Billiards Directory: The Directory of American Billiard Information with Billiard Parlor Yellow Pages and Billiard Books, Magazines, and Videos in Print! Que House, P.O. Box 2009, Manteca, CA 95336, 1992. annual. 262p. bibliog. paper $29.95 (0-945071-51-5; ISSN 1053-7236).
794.73 Pool (Game)—U.S.—Directories [OCLC] 91-662268

This book is definitely for a specialized clientele, and, in the words of the pool players themselves, it is a "superb guide," "worth its weight in gold," and "fills a gap as big as the Grand Canyon." Nearly half the directory is a list of billiard parlors by state and then by city, giving name, address, and telephone number for each, with notations about special features (arcade, bowling alley, college, lounge, league, tournament room, delicatessen/restaurant, etc.). Shorter lists, similarly organized, cover competitive play (leagues, tournaments, etc.). A second section of the book covers publications, including audio and videotapes, books, periodicals, and publishers, while a third section lists billiard supplies and services. Special features sprinkled throughout the book include pool etiquette and how to select a cue.

This book could be useful in a library at any level needing directories on various sports, but its best use seems to be as a reference book for dedicated pool players and people working in billiard establishments. Local telephone directory yellow pages give information about billiard parlors and sources of supplies adequate to meet usual demand.

Outstanding Women Athletes: Who They Are and How They Influenced Sports in America. By Janet Woolum. Oryx, 1992. 279p. bibliog. illus. index. hardcover $39.95.
796'.0194 [B] Women athletes—U.S.—Biography—Dictionaries || Sports for women—U.S.—History [CIP] 92-199

In addition to providing biographical sketches, *Outstanding Women Athletes* brings together a wealth of information on the history of women's sports. Woolum, an independent historian, focuses on women's sports from the late nineteenth century to 1991.

The heart of this book is one- to three-page biographies of 60 noted athletes, arranged from Tenley Albright to Babe Zaharias. While most of the athletes are Americans, a few, such as Olga Korbut and Grete Andersen Waitz, are included because of their impact on American sports. Some 19 sports are covered, including golf, swimming, and track and less well known ones such as sled-dog, auto, and horse racing.

Each easy-to-read biographical sketch begins with date and place of birth, and, if appropriate, death; most conclude by identifying books for further reading. The sketches cover early life, training, education, accomplishments, honors and awards, and contributions following active participation in athletics. A black-and-white photograph is provided for each woman. Forty-eight of these women are also covered in *Great Athletes* [RBB Jl 92].

Outstanding Women Athletes is more than just a collection of biographical sketches. The book begins with an informative chapter, "Women in American Sports," which covers changes in competition, dress reform, women's sports organizations, Title IX, and the impact of World War II and civil rights on women's athletics. This chapter concludes with a chronological summary, "Milestones in Women's Sports." Chapter 2, "Women in the Olympics," highlights women's significant achievements and identifies new women's events in each Olympics. Chapter 4 is an annotated bibliography of approximately 90 titles not identified in the individual biographies. Chapter 5 is a directory of 90 sports organizations; some focus on women, but most, such as the U.S. Volleyball Association, include both men and women.

The book contains four appendixes: "List of Olympic Medalists by Sport," "Awards and Championships," "Athletes Profiled in This Book, Arranged by Sport," and "List of Organization Acronyms." The comprehensive index includes sports, organizations, and names of athletes featured in the biographical sketches as well as those only mentioned within chapters.

Outstanding Women Athletes is well organized and contains a wealth of information on women's sports. It will be popular with young people and adults in public, academic, and middle school and high school libraries.

Sports Halls of Fame: A Directory of Over 100 Sports Museums in the United States. By Doug Gelbert. McFarland, 1992. 176p. illus. index. hardcover $34.50 (0-89950-660-7).
796'.06 Sports museums—U.S.—Directories || Halls of fame—U.S.—Directories [CIP] 92-53506

Most baseball enthusiasts are probably aware of the National Baseball Hall of Fame and Museum in Cooperstown, New York. They may be surprised to learn of the Original Baseball Hall of Fame Museum of Minnesota where 100,000 fans each year make the trek to see baseball memorabilia. *Sports Halls of Fame* presents 100 public halls of fame and sports museums in the U.S., organized in three sections. The first part lists 68 national sports museums, which include not only the obvious sports of baseball, basketball, and football, but also croquet, fishing, archery, jousting, and golf. Part 2 includes museums that highlight the achievement of sports heroes (e.g., the Roger Maris Museum) or are dedicated to a multisport concept (e.g., the National Art Museum of Sport). Part 3 lists sports museums, arranged by state, that have primarily a regional interest, such as the Rose Bowl Hall of Fame (open only two hours each week, February to August) and the Alabama Sports Hall of Fame (a 30,000-square-foot complex).

Each entry begins with several paragraphs on the history of the sport, followed by an explanation of the museum's location, with mailing address, telephone number, admission fee, and hours of operation. The description of the exhibits includes major highlights of the collection with mention of any notable special events or induction ceremonies. Black-and-white photographs of the museum accompany most entries. Other attractions, such as art museums or historic houses in the area, are also mentioned. An appendix lists all the entries by state. An index provides access by name, city, and subject.

Only about 50 sports museums are listed in the "Institutions by Category" index of the *Official Museum Directory*. *Sports Halls of Fame* will provide information on the most notable sports museums and certainly will enhance any public library's travel collection by providing information on these museums for vacationers.

The Historical Dictionary of Golfing Terms: From 1500 to the Present. By Peter Davies. Michael Kesend; dist. by Talman, 1992. 188p. illus. paper $14.95 (0-935576-44-4).
796.352'03 Golf—Dictionaries || Golf—History [CIP] 92-27571

Official USGA Record Book, 1895–1990: USGA Championships and International Events. By the United States Golf Association. Triumph Books, 644 S. Clark St., Ste. 2000, Chicago, IL 60605, 1992. 235p. illus. hardcover $59.95 (1-880141-39-6).
796.352'64 Golf—Tournaments—U.S.—Statistics [BKL] 92-64444

From the more widely known *ace* (a hole in one or to play a hole in one) to the obscure *yips* (a chronic nervousness in putting or other play)—these and more than 700 other terms were compiled from sample readings in the printed literature of golf. *The Historical Dictionary of Golfing Terms* provides readers with a source for the development of the rich language of the sport through five centuries of play. Beginning in the fifteenth century, when the Scots borrowed the Dutch term *colf* (club) and transformed it to *golf*, through the twentieth century in which the Americans have dominated the language of the sport with terms such as *birdie* and *eagle*, this dictionary presents both the archaic and current usages of golfing terms. Each entry provides part of speech, date of first use, etymologies (when appropriate), definitions, and dated citations. No attempt is made to cover slang, except that in widespread usage. Author Davies was executive editor of the first edition of the *American Heritage Dictionary of the English Language*. *The Historical Dictionary of Golfing Terms* is a revision of the 1980 *Davies' Dictionary of Golfing Terms*.

Official USGA Record Book, 1895–1990 provides facts and statistics from the U.S. Golf Association's 95-year history. Results from every USGA-sanctioned championship tournament are given. The book is arranged in three sections: 1895–1959, 1960–80, and 1981–90. Each section includes a history and tabulation for each of the tournaments, including the U.S. Open, Women's Open, Amateur Championships, Girls', Seniors', Walker Cup, Curtis Cup, etc. Narrative histories highlight major events of each year. The scores of every competitor, tournament sites and dates, yardage and par scores, and breakdowns of prize money are also provided for researchers and enthusiasts. A name index would have been helpful, since the only access is through the table of contents.

The Historical Dictionary of Golfing Terms is both a scholarly research tool and a browsable reference tome. It will be a welcome addition to any public library's or golfer's bookshelves. The *Official USGA Record Book* is a worthwhile acquisition for the more specialized sports reference collection.

The Great American Baseball Stat Book, 1993. By Gary Gillette. HarperPerennial, 1993. 502p. tables. paper $15 (0-06-273220-X; ISSN 1056-5116).
796.357 Baseball—U.S.—Statistics [OCLC]

Baseball, essentially, is a game of individual situations—right-hand batter vs. left-hand pitcher, runner on third, two out, late

PERFORMING ARTS, RECREATION

inning, in batter's home park—that, repeated over a period of time, can give rise to certain statistical tendencies. In publication since 1987, *The Great American Baseball Stat Book* seeks to record these "tendencies" to provide more information on active ball players and teams than does any other statistical source. The *Stat Book* goes beyond the traditional official statistics of at bats (AB), runs (R), hits (H), and runs batted in (RBI). It provides situational statistics (stats on the way a player performs in a specific situation) and special reports that analyze player and team performance.

The method used in the past to gather these statistics is impressive: it was a total volunteer effort. "Project Scoresheet" enlisted volunteer scorekeepers to record games and send the results to a clearinghouse for analysis and compilation. This project is no longer functioning, but a research and consulting company called the Baseball Workshop has taken its place. The process has become more systematic, and statistics now are gathered in the field by paid scorekeepers who fax the results, which are then fed into the database. The data are so fresh that the *Stat Book* is published before the official statistics of the season are released.

Like previous editions, the 1993 volume is divided into five parts. "Regular Players' Situational Statistics" provides data by batter and by pitcher, and debut batters and pitchers are covered in "Nonregular Players' Situational Statistics." "Team and League Statistics" includes situational data, statistics for the American and National Leagues, team batting by lineup order and by defensive position, and team and league starting and relief pitching statistics. "Special Reports" covers such topics as starting and relief pitching, base stealing, fielding, and park effects. Part 5 includes a batter and pitcher register with career records. A few changes from previous editions have been made, due to reader suggestions, such as providing lines for designated hitter and pinch hitters, as well as disabled-list information.

With this edition, the database of statistics is now nine years old. Since most of the players in the game today have careers that started after 1984, each annual edition of *The Great American Baseball Stat Book* increases in value as a retrospective statistical record book and predictor of players and teams. This compilation of statistics is one of many similar volumes issued each year, such as USA *Today Baseball Weekly Almanac* [RBB Je 1 92] and the *Elias Baseball Analyst* (Simon & Schuster/Fireside). However, the *Stat Book* offers more statistics, for a longer period of time, than either of these tools. It is recommended for the baseball-stat fanatic, comprehensive reference collections, and even the circulating stacks of public libraries.

Professional Baseball Franchises: From the Abbeville Athletics to the Zanesville Indians. By Peter Filichia. Facts On File, 1993. 288p. bibliog. index. hardcover $25.95 (0-8160-2647-5).
796.357'64 Baseball—U.S.—Clubs—Registers || Baseball—Clubs—Registers || Baseball—U.S.—Clubs—History || Baseball—Clubs—History [CIP] 92-12766

This book lists every city or town in which major- or minor-league baseball has been played professionally in an established league in the U.S., Canada, and Mexico since the beginning of the sport in 1869.

More than 1,100 entries are included in the "Team Listings by City," the major section of the book. Alphabetically arranged by city, each entry includes the team's name, nickname, any variant names, the league in which the team played, a designation whether it was a major or minor league, the years in which the team operated, and a brief note about what happened to the team. No statistics, such as won-loss records, are included, nor are any names of individuals provided. Other features enhance access to the main section of listings. An alphabetic list of teams whose names do not include city names provides a reference to the city where the team is listed in the book. An index of team nicknames lists the cities that have had teams with that name; 138 teams have been named *Indians*, but only one was named *Freaks*. Also included as an appendix is an alphabetical list of the names of leagues, including the Negro leagues, with their dates of existence.

To make this book truly international, Japanese cities and teams should have been included. Also, a one-page example entry with notes identifying parts of the entry would be more helpful to the user than the narrative explanatory material in the section "How to Use This Book." But as a resource for baseball history, especially on a regional or local level, this tool is unique and is recommended for sports reference collections.

Baseball: A Comprehensive Bibliography: Supplement 1 (1985–May 1992). Comp. by Myron J. Smith. McFarland, 1993. 422p. indexes. hardcover $45 (0-89950-799-9).
016.796357'0973 Baseball—U.S.—Bibliography || Baseball—Canada—Bibliography [CIP] 92-50892

Baseball claims to be America's game, and it is difficult to argue against that fact when presented with this bibliography of more than 8,000 sources relating to the sport. Covering books, journals, and documents, this work updates the author's first baseball bibliography published in 1986, which covered works published from the nineteenth century through 1984. Similar in format to the original, this supplement includes articles about a wide range of baseball topics, such as the history of the game, baseball in art and literature, rules, equipment, the business of baseball, little league and other youth organizations, and baseball in other nations. Nearly one-half of the work consists of references to biographical sources, both for individual players and for collections of baseball biographies. The work attempts to be comprehensive, citing sources as varied as *Baseball Card Monthly*, *Sports Illustrated*, *Architectural Digest*, and the *Journal of the American Podiatric Medical Association*. While the sources indexed have all been published since January 1985, they discuss topics and personalities throughout the history of the game. Because of this approach, a reader can identify sources relating to Bo Jackson, Shoeless Joe Jackson, and Reggie Jackson on successive pages.

This work will be essential for all baseball scholars and should be acquired by those libraries that make use of the original edition. Libraries that do not require a comprehensive bibliography on the sport may be able to make do with the other indexes already in their collections.

Black American Women in Olympic Track and Field: A Complete Illustrated Reference. By Michael D. Davis. McFarland, 1992. 170p. illus. index. tables. hardcover $24.95 (0-89950-692-5).
796.42'092 [B] Women track and field athletes—U.S.—Biography || Afro-American women athletes—Biography || Olympics—History [CIP] 91-50946

Journalist Davis has compiled a concise account of the accomplishments of black American women in Olympic track and field. Following a short introduction is an "Olympic Checklist," a seven-page summary of the participation of black American women from the 1932 through the 1988 games. The rest of the book is an alphabetically arranged biographical dictionary. Entries vary from 2 lines to 20 pages on Wilma Rudolph. Twenty of the more than 90 entries are based on first-person interviews. The interviews are particularly enlightening, not only for information about training and competition, but for the light they shed on race relations. Many of the women came from abject poverty and had to fight discrimination and misunderstanding every step of the way. The book is illustrated with a dozen black-and-white photographs, primarily of the athletes in competition. An appendix, "Sex, Chromosomes, and Gold Medals," discusses the problems of sexual identification in women's track and field. A detailed index concludes the book.

Black Olympian Medalists [RBB Jl 91] covers both male and female athletes through the 1988 games. Its bibliographies will help the student writing a paper, but its biographies are relatively brief. *Black American Women in Olympic Track and Field* provides extensive coverage of these athletes and is a long-overdue tribute to their contributions. It is recommended for reference shelves in public libraries, academic libraries, and school library media centers, where it will be an inspiration to aspiring young women athletes.

The National Hockey League Official Guide & Record Book, 1992–93. Comp. by NHL Communications Group and the 24 NHL club public relations directors. National Hockey League; dist. by Triumph Books, 644 S. Clark St., Ste. 2000, Chicago, IL 60605, 1992. 424p. illus. hardcover $39.95 (1-880141-18-3); paper $16.95 (1-880141-17-5).
796.96 National Hockey League—Statistics || Hockey players—Records [BKL]

The sixty-first edition of this annual is billed as the game's most comprehensive statistical annual, and it lives up to that pronouncement. The book is divided into seven sections: "Clubs," "Final Statistics 1991–92," "NHL Record Book," "Stanley Cup Guide & Record Book," "Player Register," "Goaltending Register," and "1991–92 Player Transactions." The team section (including expansion teams) provides the 1992–93 schedule, year-by-year record, list of players, club records, directory of executives, etc. The player register lists every skater who appeared in an NHL game in the 1991–92 season as well as those drafted or on reserve lists. Each player's lifetime record is covered season by season, not only in the NHL but college and other hockey league records as well. With all the new Russian players in the NHL, an interesting feature in the player register is a pronunciation guide to players' names, for example, "Hrkac (HUHR-kuhz)." Cumulative records for retired players are also included. All NHL records are covered, including scoring, assists, goaltending, games played, coaching records, play-off records, and most points in one period. Also listed are Hall-of-Fame inductees, play-off formats, lists of referees and linesmen, all-star teams, first-round draft choices, rule changes, historical chronology, and more.

The many lists of dates, players, games, and goals make this the best single source for NHL data. Although there are other good annual guides to the game and players (e.g., *Hockey Scouting Report* or *Sporting News Hockey Register*), this is the premier work for data on teams and players. It should be in all libraries that serve hockey fans.

The Sailing Dictionary. 2d. ed. By Joachim Schult. Tr. by Barbara Webb. Rev. by Jeremy Howard-Williams. Sheridan House, 1992. 331p. illus. hardcover $29.95 (0-924486-37-6).
797.1'2403 Sailing—Dictionaries—English [OCLC] 92-19757

Since the introduction of fiberglass-reinforced plastics 20 years ago, a host of revolutionary changes have come to the sport of sailing, including new technology and new technical terms relating to methods and building materials. *The Sailing Dictionary* is an attempt to keep those who buy, equip, and sail boats abreast of the specialized jargon so they can better communicate.

The dictionary has more than 4,000 terms, including definitions of well-established words and phrases as well as new terms resulting from modern navigation electronics, grand prix racing, and other developments since the first edition was published in 1981. The entries vary in length from a single sentence to paragraphs of 10 sentences or more. Many are accompanied by line drawings, which, in many instances, make the definitions clearer (e.g., drawings of knots and various pieces of nautical hardware, a chart of the Beaufort Scale of wind speeds).

Author Schult is a well-known German seaman who has written several books on sailing. Howard-Williams is a sailor of 50 year's experience who has written eight books on sailing.

The dictionary has three features that enhance its reference use: a list of abbreviations of frequently used terms in the text, drawings of flags of the International Code of Signals, and drawings of International Association of Lighthouse Authority marks on channel markers, the latter two on the endpapers. *The Sailing Dictionary* is an essential purpose for libraries building strong sailing collections.

LITERATURE

Gale's Literary Index: CD-ROM. IBM version 1.0. Gale, 1993. semiannual. $149; networked version, $225 (ISSN 1066-7709).
800 Literature—Indexes ‖ Authors—Indexes ‖ Criticism—Indexes [BKL] 92-6740

With the number of multivolume literature sources published by Gale growing almost every year, determining in which series a given author and/or title will be included can often mean going to several indexes. Although the *Contemporary Authors Cumulative Index* indexes most (but not all) of the Gale series, it is strictly an author index; those users wishing to search for specific titles in the various series must look in the separate cumulative title indexes for each. *Gale's Literary Index* on CD-ROM attempts to solve this problem, allowing one to locate authors and titles in the 32 literary series published by Gale. The user's guide claims the work "combines and cross-references more than 110,000 author names including pseudonyms and variant names and over 120,000 titles into one source."

Gale's Literary Index requires an IBM XT, AT, PS/2, or compatible (80286 or faster processor is recommended), MS-DOS or PC-DOS version 3.1 or higher, MS-DOS CD-ROM Extensions 2.0 or higher, 640K of RAM (512K available), and a hard drive with 1MB available space, although more space is necessary for temporary storage of information downloaded or saved. A color monitor is recommended, although not required. During the setup procedure, options for printing and downloading (to floppies or the hard drive) may be set, including a limit on the number of pages that may be printed. (There does not, however, appear to be a way to alter these settings after installation, short of deleting the program entirely and reinstalling it.) There is also a "Collection Tagging" option, where one can select from a list those Gale series that are held in the library. A message of up to 70 characters may be entered for each title, or one may accept the default message: "Available in this library." Unlike the printing/downloading options, this feature may be altered after installation.

Gale's Literary Index is similar in appearance to Gale's most recent literary CD-ROM, DISC*overing Authors* [RBB My 1 93]. Both have software provided by Metatec/Discovery Systems, and both offer the same menu-driven ease of use as well as occasional quirkiness. One may search the *Literary Index* by author or title. There is also an extended-search option where Boolean searching and field searching are allowed. When selecting either the author or title search, a window opens at the beginning of an alphabetically arranged listing. The user may either scroll down the list or simply begin typing a word, with the list scrolling down as letters are typed.

The author search retrieves an entry that lists all Gale series in which the author appears (though not specific page numbers), with a red letter A (on color monitors) appearing to the left of those titles that the library holds (assuming the collection-tagging feature was enabled). Following this is a listing of specific titles written by that author that appear in Gale series with the Gale volume(s) and page numbers on which the title is covered, again with a red A appearing to the left of those titles in the library.

The title search retrieves a list of the various Gale series covering a specific title; the user may press J to jump to the entry for the author of the requested work. The title search appears to be limited primarily to the critical—rather than biographical—Gale series and, therefore, does not represent any new indexing. For example, although Gale's Dictionary of Literary Biography (DLB) series mentions many specific titles within the essays on each author, the printed work has no title index so these volumes are not found in a title search of the disc. Title searches for *Dracula* and *The Mayor of Casterbridge* failed to bring up one citation to DLB, though each work is mentioned in their respective author's entries in the set.

The extended-search option allows one to search by keywords in an author's name, keywords in a title, nationality, and a range of birth and/or death years. With the first three options, pressing F4 opens a word list that allows the user to check if a word is indexed before actually initiating the search. Boolean operators and truncation may be used in the extended search. Thus, one may search the author field for "MAZO AND ROCHE" to find Mazo de la Roche, rather than guessing how the name is indexed in the regular author search.

Gale's Literary Index is easy to use, and few users will need to use the context-sensitive help screens (at the press of F1) or the help card included. (Unfortunately, as was the case with DISC*overing Authors*, the help card is two-sided, making it impossible to post at the terminal.) Nevertheless, the program has some odd features that not every user will catch. For example, the title-search screen revealed two separate entries for *Great Expectations* by Dickens—each bringing up different entries. A nice feature is that the titles in the title-search window are listed several ways, including with and without initial articles and with alternative or non-English titles. The help screen indicates that *The Adventure of Huckleberry Finn* will be listed in three ways: *Adventures of Huckleberry Finn, The, Huckleberry Finn,* and *The Adventures of . . .*, with any of the three retrieving the same record. Unfortunately, this is not the case, as *Huckleberry Finn* retrieves an entry citing *World Literature Criticism*, whereas the other two retrieve an entry citing *Twentieth-Century Literary Criticism*. Performing an author search would not have solved this problem either, as the titles listing in the Mark Twain entry lists the title under Huckleberry Finn and, 20 titles (four screens) later, under The Adventures of Huckleberry Finn, with different citations for each.

This latter point brings up another oddity: initial articles are alphabetized in the title listings under an author's name. This would be forgivable if the same title were listed both with and without the initial article (as is true in the title-search screen), but this is not the case. Thus, there are nine entries listed before Absalom, Absalom in Faulkner's entry, such as "A Courtship" and "A Fable."

The collection-tagging feature also presents some annoyances. If the user performs a title search that reveals the title is included in one specific volume owned by the library, pressing A brings up an "availability list" that lists all of the Gale titles tagged in the collection-tagging program—not just the one cited on the screen. Therefore, the user may have to scroll through several screens of Gale titles just to find, for example, the library's call number for Twentieth-Century Literary Criticism. This is irritating, particularly given how other CD-ROM programs have context-sensitive collection tagging. Even worse, however, is the fact that the entire availability list will print out (or download) when a user chooses to print or download a citation.

Gale's Literary Index will prove most valuable in those libraries that have the majority of the 32 series indexed. Depending upon the type of search involved and the amount of use the printed volumes receive at a library, the disc can be a valuable time-saver. Best of all, the software is easy to use, so most patrons should have no difficulty finding what they need. Gale should, however, work on the integrity of some of the data on the disc, as well as improve the collection-tagging feature.

DISCovering Authors: Biographies & Criticism on 300 Most-Studied Writers. IBM Version 1.0. CD-ROM. Gale, 1992. $500 (0-8103-5058-0).
800 Authors—Biography ‖ Literature—Bio-bibliography ‖ Literature—History and Criticism [OCLC] 92-6735

This product marks Gale's first foray into publishing parts of its various literature series on CD-ROM. The user's manual states that the disc contains "biographical, bibliographical, and critical information on the most-studied authors from ancient times to the present." The disc covers 305 authors, representing some 35 nationalities and spanning from the time of Aristotle to the present. The disc is strictly textual, with no illustrations.

HARDWARE, SOFTWARE, AND INSTALLATION. DISCovering Authors may be used with an IBM or compatible PC (80286 processor or faster is recommended) with MS-DOS or PC-DOS 3.1 or higher, MS-DOS CD-ROM extensions 2.0 or higher, 640K RAM (500K available), and a hard disk with 1 MB of free space. The program can be run from a floppy disk, but with slower performance. A color monitor is recommended but not required. A multiuser network version is also available.

The user's manual gives full information on how to install the program, at which time one may also specify the maximum number of pages to allow for printing, whether downloading may be performed, and other items for configuring the system. The manual does not indicate how to alter any of these settings, however, so it appears that the settings cannot be changed once made, short of deleting the program entirely and reinstalling it from scratch. All the material on the disc can be easily printed or downloaded by the user; the program also allows for specific lines to be marked so an entire entry does not have to be printed or downloaded.

SEARCHING AND DISPLAYING. The program is quite easy to use, with all instructions clearly explained on the screen. Online help is available with the press of the F1 key. A help card is also provided, although it is unfortunately two-sided, preventing libraries from posting it on the terminal.

One may search by author, title, subject term/character, and personal data on authors. There is also an "advanced search mode," which allows Boolean and proximity (NEAR) searching with words or phrases. With the author, title, and subject term/character searches, a window opens and allows the user to type in letters, with the system scrolling through the list as each letter is typed, which allows the user to see if a term is in the database before actually executing the search.

An author search will retrieve a biographical essay as well as a list of writings, media adaptations, and a relatively lengthy bibliography of further readings. Whenever a screen is pulled up, the user has the option to "jump" to other sections of the entry by pressing the J key; this prevents the user from having to scroll through the entire biographical section to find, for example, the list of media adaptations. This ability to jump through various parts of entries or lists appears throughout the program and makes it fast to use. Finally, the user can also bring up criticism about the writer. These critical excerpts are similar to those found in other Gale works, such as Contemporary Literary Criticism, and feature information on the author of the critical essay as well as a full bibliographic citation to where the essay originally appeared. Typically, four to seven essays on each author are included.

The "personal data" search allows one to retrieve a list of authors based on various criteria, such as birth date, death date, nationality, genre, etc., and then go to their biographies. Rather than trying to guess what term Gale used for each of these criteria, the user may press the F4 key to scroll through a word list of terms used in that field. These word lists—which appear throughout the program at various points—also indicate some weaknesses in the indexing. The genre word list, for example, includes both poems and poetry as searchable terms. The subject/character name search is particularly frustrating, as one must search by the first element of a character's name rather than the last name. Thus, one encounters Doctor Zhivago and Dr. Pangloss in the same search. It is obvious that little editing was employed and that the word lists were compiled directly from the text being indexed. For instance, Donna Elvira appears twice—once with two spaces after the first element of the name.

This type of indexing is especially evident in title searches. For example, in the list of titles one sees 1911–1925 and 1926–1950, both authored by George Bernard Shaw. It is only after going to Shaw's bibliography that one notices these two "titles" are volumes listed under his Collected Letters. Fortunately, both the subject/character and title searches allow the user to type in keywords with the press of the F3 key, thereby allowing one to simply type in a word like native and retrieve all titles with that word in it.

The advanced search mode allows retrieval of text anywhere in a record and, therefore, has some advantages over the other search modes. For instance, searching for Wuthering Heights in the title search mode retrieves six critical essays—all taken from the Brontë entry. Searching for the phrase Wuthering Heights in the advanced search mode, however, results in 16 hits—including mention of the title within criticisms of William Golding and Thomas Hardy. The advanced search mode is also useful for tracing literary themes. One can search fate* NEAR trag* (the * is the truncation symbol) and retrieve 25 hits with those words appearing within 30 characters of each other anywhere in an entry. (The 30-character proximity window may be changed by the user.)

COMPARABILITY TO PRINT SOURCES. DISCovering Authors overlaps with several other Gale works, though the user's guide states that "many of the entries . . . have been specially revised and extensively updated from information found in Gale's acclaimed literary and biography series" and that "the remaining entries have been created exclusively for this CD." Advertisements from Gale have indicated that about 30 percent of the entries are original to this work, and this figure is generally confirmed by a sampling conducted by the Board. In an examination of critical excerpts for 15 authors, it was found that approximately 75 percent were reprinted from volumes in Gale's various literary-criticism series. Many of the new essays are unsigned critical overviews written just for this CD-ROM product. The vast majority of entries that came from other sources were pulled from Gale's six-volume World Literature Criticism [RBB D 1 92]. Many authors on the CD, however, have not yet appeared in any of the Gale literary-criticism series, including Aeschylus, Aristotle, Benjamin Franklin, and Daniel Keyes. Also, it was noted that virtually every author on the disc has appeared in at least one Gale biographical work, such as Contemporary Authors or Dictionary of Literary Biography.

CONCLUSION. DISCovering Authors is a good first effort for Gale in placing biographical and critical information on a CD-ROM. Updates are implied in the documentation, and the user does not have to return the disc if a new one comes out. The $500 price tag is quite reasonable, considering that the recently released World Literature Criticism, which the present disc most closely resembles in scope (although DISCovering Authors contains more authors), costs $360.

This easy-to-use program is not without its quirks, but the interface bodes well for the future of CD-ROM publishing by Gale and, if nothing else, certainly saves on shelf space. Public, high school, and academic libraries that cater to an endless stream of literary-criticism queries should seriously consider this product.

The Cassell Dictionary of Literary and Language Terms. By Christina Ruse and Marilyn Hopton. Cassell; dist. by Sterling, 1992. 320p. hardcover $17.95 (0-304-31927-9).
808'.042 English language—Dictionaries || Literature—Terminology || Criticism—Terminology || English language—Terms and phrases [BKL]

Joining an already crowded field of dictionaries of literary terms, this compilation by two British teachers is intended as an introductory guide for "students who are studying English at an advanced level." Many of the 1,600 entries are devoted to grammatical, rhetorical, or other language terms, including parts of speech, punctuation marks, and verb forms. In addition, the work includes a varied assortment of terms pertaining to journalism, publishing, printing, and related fields (e.g., *archivist, dust jacket, tie-in,* ISBN, *leaflet*). Pronunciation is indicated for foreign terms and other words that might be problematic. Definitions are generous in length, clear, and well written and frequently provide examples or illustrative quotations.

Although the authors include many of the basic literary terms, they also omit some significant ones, among them *deus ex machina, reader-response criticism,* and *semiotics.* In addition, several concepts particularly important to the study of American literature are missing, for instance, *Harlem Renaissance, local color,* and *transcendentalism.* Some terms or their meanings are commonly used only in the U.K. (e.g., *agony column, D-notice, flannel, knocking copy*). Following the dictionary entries is a concise chronology of British and international literature through the early 1920s. The compilers' explanation for not extending the outline beyond that point is that the brief format would require eliminating so many writers that the chart would be meaningless.

The wide-ranging choice of entries for this volume results in somewhat of a hodgepodge and gives the impression that the work may have been designed to complement a particular course being taught in the U.K. Certainly, various other compilations, among them Beckson and Ganz's *Literary Terms: A Dictionary* and Holman and Harmon's *a Handbook to Literature* (6th ed., Macmillan, 1992) provide more substantial coverage of literary terms. Although this dictionary has some commendable features, its lack of focus and British slant may limit its value in the U.S. However, because it provides excellent definitions for language terms, it might be useful as a supplemental purchase for libraries serving high school students and undergraduates.

Science and Technical Writing: A Manual of Style. Ed. by Philip Rubens. Holt, 1992. 513p. bibliog. illus. index. hardcover $40 (0-8050-1831-X).
808'.0666 Technical writing [CIP] 91-36422

Similar in concept to *The Chicago Manual of Style,* this book is aimed at the scientific and technical writer or editor. It is organized in outline form with a listing of topics at the beginning of each chapter. Chapters include such subjects as audience analysis and document planning, paragraph and sentence construction, punctuation, scientific terminology, quotations, indexing, and design. Much of the advice here is not specific to science and technical writing. For instance, rules on plurals, possessives, and suffixes and prefixes are similar to those found in other style manuals. Other chapters, however, do contain unique material: "Specialized Terminology" gives lists of sci/tech terms, and "Numbers and Symbols" covers scientific notation and tells how to compare powers of 10.

Useful chapters include those on creating indexes, illustrations, tables, charts, and page layout. Another addresses writing for audiences that include nonnative readers of English, since the scientific community is an international one. A major drawback, particularly in the sciences, is that this manual includes nothing on writing for electronic media, such as electronic newsletters, journals, and discussion groups, nor is mention made of the use of electronic-publishing software. A bibliography is arranged by chapter but doesn't have a list of specific style manuals in the sciences, such as the one from the American Chemical Society, nor is any reference made to the style requirements of major sci/tech journals such as *Science* and *Nature.* Little space is devoted to citation practices in the sciences. The index at the back of the book is not as detailed as the one in *The Chicago Manual of Style.*

For the advantages noted above, this manual can be a very useful guide for individual purchase or as a reference item in an office, but academic libraries will want to continue to rely on the style manuals published by the specific scientific disciplines. Public libraries will want to consider purchase for science and technical journalists.

Masterplots II CD-ROM. CD-ROM. EBSCO, 1992 (1-882248-00-7).
808.8 Literature—Stories, plots, etc. [BKL]

Since Masterplots first appeared in 1949, teachers and librarians have debated its merits versus its potential for misuse and abuse. When the Masterplots II series was initiated in 1986, it augmented the traditional plot summaries with critical and contextual analysis, and the controversy over the work's legitimate place in the reference collection became less intense. Now the full texts of seven of the Masterplots II series are available on CD-ROM: *American Fiction* [RBB O 15 86], *British and Commonwealth Fiction* [RBB Ja 15 88], *Drama* [RBB S 1 90], *Juvenile and Young Adult Fiction* [RBB Ag 91], *Nonfiction* [RBB N 1 89], *Short Story* [RBB S 1 87], and *World Fiction* (1988). In addition, the disc contains the contents of *Cyclopedia of Literary Characters* II [RBB Ja 1 91] and *Cyclopedia of World Authors* II [RBB Mr 1 90]. Although the documentation indicates that the text of *Cyclopedia of World Authors* (rev. ed., Salem Press, 1974) is also on the disc, trial-and-error searching revealed that only those biographical sketches for authors whose works are treated in a Masterplots II set are included. While the disc does not contain the six-volume *Masterplots II: Poetry Series* [RBB N 1 92], EBSCO indicates that it plans to add that series at a later date and will offer the revised disc to purchasers of the original version for a small update charge.

Thus, *Masterplots* II CD-ROM includes the full texts of essays on more than 2,900 literary works. In addition, it provides profiles of the principal characters in approximately 1,400 of the works and biographical sketches of more than 800 of the authors. The bibliographic references that accompany the essays and biographies are also included. With the exception of some of the titles covered in *Juvenile and Young Adult Fiction,* the works covered in these Masterplots II series do not repeat the titles treated in the original Masterplots series, which was issued in a definitive 12-volume edition in 1976 [RSBR D 15 77].

HARDWARE, SOFTWARE, AND INSTALLATION. *Masterplots* II CD-ROM requires an IBM PC, XT, or compatible computer with 640K RAM and 5MB of hard disk space available; a CD-ROM player with interface card; and a double-sided floppy-disk drive. It operates under DOS 3.2 or higher and Microsoft Extensions 2.1. Installation is a simple procedure that takes only a few minutes to complete. Setting up such local options as print features and color combinations will, of course, take longer. The disc can also be installed on a LAN for no additional charge, regardless of the number of workstations.

SEARCHING AND DISPLAYING. *Masterplots* II CD-ROM uses the same search and retrieval software as other EBSCO CD-ROM products, for instance, *Magazine Article Summaries* [RBB Ap 1 93]. It offers basic and advanced search modes, both of which can be mastered fairly easily and quickly due to straightforward screen layouts, judicious use of on-screen prompts, and an elaborate network of help screens.

A library can choose which of three query screens will display for patrons who use the basic search level. The basic screen that displays by default provides a variety of search options in a simple format. The user can choose to search for a name, term, or phrase anywhere in the database; use Boolean logic to include or exclude other terms; search only within a specific field or fields (author heading, title heading, subject, or locale); or combine the above types of searches. In addition, the basic mode offers the option of browsing the author, title, subject, and genre indexes and selecting terms and headings to be searched from the lists provided. This is a valuable feature, since the subject and genre lists provide cross-references to related headings.

The advanced search mode features all the capabilities of the basic search while adding categories for searching the genre field and bibliographic references and the ability to combine results of previous queries. Thus, the user can conduct a very general or extremely specific search depending on which and how many categories on the query screen are utilized. For example, an ALL search for the term *mysterious stranger* produces a list of 20 essays that treat or mention works that incorporate such a character, while searching the author field for *Twain* and the title field for *Mysterious Stranger* results in a single match for Twain's work by this title. Similarly, a subject search for *World War II* produces a list of 175 works on that topic, while adding *Wouk* in the author field narrows the results list to six.

The list of results produced by a search notes the author and title treated by the essay and the title of the print series in which it appeared. The user can go directly to the full essay from the results list or to an abbreviated entry that provides key information from the essay. In the full essay, the user has a variety of options, including viewing the highlighted terms that matched the inquiry, searching for additional words or phrases within the essay, or moving to hypertext links that provide access to related essays, author biographies, and character profiles.

Surprisingly, the software does not provide for a time-of-plot search, which would have been a useful feature, particularly when combined with a locale search. However, since the time-of-plot field appears directly before the locale field, users can compensate for this lack by entering a date or period with a geographic location in the ALL field and surrounding the terms with brackets. This instructs the software to conduct a proximity search, which will search for matching terms within 50 characters of each other. (The number-of-characters default can be changed by the user.) For example, the search "[1940's London]" produced 17 matches for titles set in London during the 1940s. Searches can also be expanded by using an asterisk to truncate terms and a question mark as a wild card to replace a letter.

An unfortunate software problem was discovered when a search for *O'Connor* yielded no results when entered in either the ALL or the AUTHOR field. Since a search for *Flannery* did produce results, a call was made to the EBSCO technical-assistance line to determine whether the problem was unique to the review disc. The courteous and helpful representative called back within two hours to report that the system was incorrectly treating terms ending with *or* that are not followed by another word as searches using OR as a Boolean operator. He indicated that this would be corrected in the next version of the disc and that, in the meantime, typing an asterisk at the end of terms ending with *or* would enable such searches to run correctly.

DOCUMENTATION. Accompanying *Masterplots II* CD-ROM are three printed guides: a general reference manual for EBSCO-CD products, a supplement covering EBSCO-CD version 3.41, and a 13-page "What's Inside Guide" to the *Masterplots II* CD-ROM. Due to its excellent online tutorial (which is divided into components covering such topics as searching, displaying, and downloading), on-screen prompts for function keys, and a network of help screens, most users will be able to search this database successfully without using any of these sources. However, more sophisticated users will find it frustrating to have to consult multiple sources to find instructions for a particular procedure. EBSCO should provide a single, up-to-date, product-specific manual.

PRINTING AND DOWNLOADING. The system makes it easy to print or download text to a disk. Options include printing the entire results list or selecting specific items in the list to be printed, printing the current screen, printing an entire essay, or marking specific lines of text to be printed.

CONCLUSION. Because the *Masterplots II* series contained on this disc supplement the basic *Masterplots* set, many of the standard authors frequently studied by high school students and undergraduates do not appear in this product. For instance, users will not find essays on, or biographies of, such authors as Austen, Chaucer, Dickinson, Eliot, Frost, Hardy, Shakespeare, Whitman, or Wordsworth. Often, a major writer is included, but his or her principal works are not, as is the case with Hawthorne's *The Scarlet Letter*, Faulkner's *The Sound and the Fury*, and Williams' *A Streetcar Named Desire*.

High school, public, and academic libraries in which the printed *Masterplots* series are a mainstay will want to consider this electronic version, which offers a wide variety of searching options in a simple and easy-to-use format. Not only does the CD-ROM serve as a highly sophisticated and detailed index to the *Masterplots II* series, it also offers an effective deterrent to the mutilation problems that are prevalent with the printed volumes. Libraries that own only a few of these sets can realize a substantial savings by purchasing the CD-ROM version at $1,295, since the total cost of the print sets exceeds $3,000.

Fiction Index for Readers 10 to 16: Subject Access to Over 8200 Books (1960–1990). By Vicki Anderson. McFarland, 1992. 477p. indexes. hardcover $35 (0-89950-703-4).
016.80883'0835 Young adult fiction—Stories, plots, etc.—Indexes ‖ Children's stories—Stories, plots, etc.—Indexes ‖ Young adult fiction—Bibliography ‖ Children's stories—Bibliography [CIP] 91-50954

The author states in her introduction that "The purpose of this reference book is to help the library staff identify fiction books by specific subjects." Anderson, who has previously compiled an annotated bibliography of sequels for the same age group [RBB Ag 90], relied on the recommendations of working librarians for titles to be included in this volume. She has noted Newbery Medal winners, but she does not otherwise indicate literary excellence, nor does she note which titles are out-of-print. Reading or interest levels are not indicated for individual titles.

The book is divided into two major sections: a subject index and an annotated bibliography. Some of the more than 200 subject headings are too specific (e.g., *Birds, Tame* and *Birds, Wild*) while others are repetitive (e.g., *Brothers; Sisters; Brothers and Sisters*). The more general headings (e.g., *Adventure*) have cross-references to related headings. Each of the titles in the annotated bibliography appears under at least one subject heading, some under three or four. The number of titles listed under each heading vary from several hundred for the general subjects to four or five for the more specific.

The bibliography is arranged alphabetically by author and includes publisher, date, and a brief, general annotation that often does not capture the essence of the book. For example, the annotation for *Watership Down*—"Lots of harrowing adventures, warm humor and memorable animals"—is confusing as to its content and reading level. It is also difficult to locate a title in the subject index based solely on the annotation. This limits its use in finding books with themes similar to a specific title. The book also has several specialized lists (books with fewer than 100 pages, books with more than 300 pages, and books that are translations) and a title index to the bibliography.

Olderr's Young Adult Fiction Index [RBB Ap 1 90] is an annual publication that has more intensive subject indexing and also lists characters and series. However, so far it covers only the years 1988–1990. Librarians working with teens will often find themselves using *Fiction Index for Readers 10 to 16* when creating their own bibliographies or helping children, teachers, or parents find fiction titles with specific themes. But they should realize that they will have to consult other sources for reading or interest levels, availability, and detailed descriptions of titles.

Science Fiction and Fantasy Literature, 1975–1991: A Bibliography of Science Fiction, Fantasy, and Horror Fiction Books and Nonfiction Monographs. By Robert Reginald. Gale, 1992. 1,512p. hardcover $199 (0-8103-1825-3).
016.80883'876 Science fiction—Bio-bibliography ‖ Fantasic fiction—Bio-bibliography ‖ Horror tales—Bio-bibliography ‖ Authors—20th century—Biography [CIP] 92-28219

Following the same format as Reginald's *Science Fiction and Fantasy Literature: A Checklist, 1700–1974*, this hefty supplement identifies almost 22,000 English-language works of science fiction, fantasy, and horror issued for the first time between 1975 and 1991. Nonfiction relating to these genres is also covered. In addition, the compiler includes titles that he omitted from his first bibliography and provides additional information for some of the original entries. Although the previous compilation included a biographical volume, that component has been dropped from the supplement.

The primary portion of this bibliography is arranged alphabetically by author and then by title. In addition to basic bibliographic information and pagination, each entry indicates whether the title was hardbound or paperback and categorizes the work by type (e.g., novel, story, anthology, nonfiction). Series, limited printings, and awards are also noted when appropriate. Cross-references are provided between variant forms of an author's name. While the author arrangement is certainly appropriate for fictional works, a subject approach would have been a much more useful way to treat the listings for nonfiction. The compiler's failure to provide subject access to bibliographic, biographical, critical, and other nonfiction works is a serious flaw and significantly detracts from the potential usefulness of the volume.

Entry numbering in this volume begins where the earlier volume left off. Entries that correct or add to information that appeared in the previous checklist retain their original numbering, and jointly authored works receive one number that is then repeated under the listing for each coauthor. Consequently, entry numbers cannot be used as a reliable means of locating entries since the numbers are frequently not in sequence. Therefore, the title index provides references to authors rather than to item numbers.

A particularly useful feature of this work is an alphabetical guide (by both author and publisher) to science fiction, fantasy, and horror series, with works within each series appearing in sequential order. Other supplementary sections list publishers' doubles and recipients of major science fiction, fantasy, and horror awards.

More monographs pertaining to fantastic literature were published within the 17-year period covered by this volume than during the entire 274 years represented in Reginald's original checklist. Keeping up with this flood of materials must be a Sisyphean task, but it is obviously a labor of love for Reginald, who estimates that he has identified at least 98 percent of the titles in the genres he is attempting to document.

A librarian at California State University at San Bernardino, Reginald has written or compiled numerous works relating to science fiction. One of his most recent contributions to the literature of this field, *Reference Guide to Science Fiction, Fantasy and Horror* [RBB N 15 92] was published under his real name, Michael Burgess. In that guide, and without acknowledging his authorship, Burgess describes his bibliography covering the years 1700–1974 as "a necessary purchase for all academic and large public libraries and for any serious SF researcher." Although that conclusion is an overstatement, there is no doubt that this work and its companion volume form the most comprehensive bibliography of English-language fantastic literature available. Academic and public libraries in need of such thorough coverage of these genres will welcome this compilation, although some institutions may find the price prohibitive.

Portraying Persons with Disabilities: An Annotated Bibliography of Fiction for Children and Teenagers. 3d ed. By Debra E. J. Robertson. Bowker, 1992. 482p. bibliog. indexes. hardcover $39.95 (0-8352-3023-6).
016.80883'93520816 Children's stories—Bibliography || Young adult fiction—Bibliography || Handicapped—Juvenile literature—Bibliography || Handicapped in literature—Bibliography [CIP] 91-39177

This volume updates Bowker's prior lists of fiction on this topic, *Notes from a Different Drummer* (1977) and *More Notes from a Different Drummer* (1984). An accompanying volume to be published this fall, *Portraying Persons with Disabilities: An Annotated Bibliography of Nonfiction for Children and Teenagers* will update *Accept Me as I Am* (1985).

In the first chapter of this book, the author includes a list of the most highly recommended titles from *Notes from a Different Drummer* and *More Notes*. In another chapter, she summarizes media and curriculum trends in the 1980s.

The main body of the book is arranged like *Accept Me as I Am*. The annotated titles are divided into four categories: physical problems, sensory problems, cognitive and behavior problems, and multiple/severe problems. Cross-references are provided for those titles that cover two different categories. Each entry includes a full citation; approximate reading level (more by interest level than by vocabulary); a reference to a review in BOOKLIST, *Horn Book*, or one of four other journals; specific disability; and an annotation (plot and analysis). Length varies from one-third page to one and one-half pages and usually correlates to the significance of the book. The editor includes books where disabilities are matter-of-factly included in the story and are not necessarily the focus of the work. Effort has also been made to include a variety of genres: sf, mystery, romance—although westerns seem slighted. Preteen and teen titles seem to dominate.

A bibliography of professional writing about disabilities follows the main list. Three indexes access material by title, author, and subject. The author and title indexes include books from *Notes from a Different Drummer* and *More Notes*. An index by reading level would have been useful.

Writing is clear, and titles that librarians would expect to find are included. Books listed were published between 1982 and 1991 and include such current topics as AIDS, attention-deficit disorder, and anorexia. The editor notes correctly that professionals, more than youth, will be the prime users of this volume.

Particularly because of the Americans with Disabilities Act and the awareness of people's differences, this annotated bibliography of fictional portrayals of persons with disabilities is a timely addition for school and public libraries and academic libraries that support an education major.

Supernatural Fiction for Teens: More Than 1300 Good Paperbacks to Read for Wonderment, Fear, and Fun. 2d ed. By Cosette Kies. Libraries Unlimited, 1992. 267p. indexes. paper $24.95 (0-87287-940-2).
016.80883'937 Bibliography—Best books—Young adult fiction || Bibliography—Best books—Fantastic fiction || Supernatural in literature—Bibliography || Young adult fiction—Bibliography || Fantastic fiction—Bibliography [CIP] 91-45469

This bibliography of good reads for teens annotates 1,300 supernatural fiction paperbacks. Updating the 1987 edition (which listed 500 titles), it includes books through 1991.

The author selected titles based on personal examination of available paperbacks, which accounts for some of the uneven coverage. For instance, Joan Lowery Nixon has only one title listed, while Peter Straub has three. Bram Stoker is included, but Jane Austen is not. *The Silver Kiss* is not listed. Titles fit one of three categories: parapsychology/psychic phenomena, horror, or tales including magical and occult elements such as Arthurian legend (the weakest group). Entries are arranged alphabetically by author and include a two- to three-sentence annotation. For those titles made into movies (or vice versa), information on the film(s) is included. The author also categorizes each title by main reader audience: teen, younger teen, adult, classic. Some designations seem arbitrary, but they can be useful for selection purposes.

Title and subject indexes complete the volume. Subjects are broad, such as *evil* and *vampires*. Having age-group and movie indexes would have been handy, especially since these features are unique to this volume.

Overall, this bibliography is a useful addition to the YA collection. It cannot be used alone, and the author acknowledges this by listing other, sometimes complementary, related selection guides. That only paperbacks are included may be a drawback—or a plus—as a selection aid, depending on the library's needs.

Familiar Quotations: A Collection of Passages, Phrases, and Proverbs Traced to Their Sources in Ancient and Modern Literature. 16th ed. By John Bartlett; ed. by Justin Kaplan. Little, Brown, 1992. 1,405p. indexes. hardcover $40 (0-316-08277-5).
808.88'2 Quotations, English [CIP] 91-21170

This new edition of *Bartlett's* is not just updated, it is extensively revised as well. It contains 22,500 quotations arranged chronologically from ancient Egypt to "Me want cookie" from "Sesame Street." Of the 2,550 people quoted, 340 are new to this edition; 245 people from the fifteenth edition have been dropped. Among the people added are Chinua Achebe, Russell Baker, Mel Brooks, Joseph Campbell, Jesse Jackson, Garrison Keillor, Toni Morrison, and Bruce Springsteen. Not all the new names are recent ones, though. Nancy Astor, Aulus Gellius (c. 123–165), David Ben-Gurion, St. Bonaventure, and Walter Winchell all appear for the first time in this edition. Most of the people dropped would be unfamiliar to today's reader. A few exceptions are John Ciardi, Rutherford Hayes, and Sir Anthony Eden.

Some changes in coverage obviously reflect the taste of a new compiler. For instance, this edition contains far fewer quotations from modern poets like Richard Wilbur and George Seferis and more from contemporary novelists like Saul Bellow and Norman Mailer.

Sometimes people from the last edition are represented here with totally different quotes—John Updike, for example. Even the Shakespeare section has been slightly revised. In some cases, attributions have been changed. For example, a quotation attributed to Spencer Tracy in the last edition is now ascribed to Noël Coward. One of *Bartlett's* strengths is that it gives printed sources for quotations whenever possible. Some quotations that lacked a printed source in the previous edition now have one. For instance, a source is provided for Jack Kerouac's remark, "We're a *beat* generation." Even birth dates, such as the one for Tennessee Williams, have been corrected.

Bartlett's concludes with a keyword-in-context index that is identical in format to previous editions. The size of the book has remained fairly constant by the use of wider pages and the dropping of some notes.

In an interview with RBB [F 1 91], compiler Justin Kaplan, a Pulitzer-Prize–winning biographer, said that this sixteenth edition would contain some well-known advertising slogans like "Where's the beef?" He apparently thought better of this because they aren't here. *Bartlett's* emphasis is still very literary. Few quotable business leaders are found—there's no Malcolm Forbes or Warren Buffet. More extensive quotations from poetry can be found in *The Columbia Granger's Dictionary of Poetry Quotations* [RBB S 15 92], but, surprisingly, there is poetry in *Bartlett's* not listed in *Columbia Granger's*. While many women have been added to this edition of *Bartlett's*, libraries will still need *The Beacon Book of Quotations by Women* and/or *The New Quotable Woman* [RBB O 15 92].

The sixteenth edition of Bartlett's *Familiar Quotations* is a real bargain and is an essential purchase for all libraries, high school and up. —Sandy Whiteley

The Columbia Granger's Dictionary of Poetry Quotations. Ed. by Edith P. Hazen. Columbia, 1992. 1,132p. indexes. hardcover $99 (0-231-07546-4).

808.881 Quotations, English [CIP] 91-42240

Librarians have long relied on *Columbia Granger's Index to Poetry* for a listing of titles and first lines of famous poems. More recently, Virginia Kline's useful *Last Lines* [RBB Ja 15 91] indexed the conclusions of well-known poems. Now librarians have a reference work that deals with those inevitable situations when a patron remembers some other part of a poem. *The Columbia Granger's Dictionary of Poetry Quotations*, edited by a coeditor of the ninth edition of *Columbia Granger's Index to Poetry* [RBB Ag 90], is described in the introduction as "a logical extension of *Granger's*." It is based on the same list of anthologies as the ninth edition. Quotations were selected by eight members of the Department of English at Columbia University "from the 4,000 poems that have been most anthologized, as shown by *The Columbia Granger's Index to Poetry*." The introduction also notes that these consultants "added quotations from the long works of such poets as Chaucer, Shakespeare, Pope, Byron, and Whitman, who would otherwise have been under-represented, because anthologists do not always select the same passages from long works."

Arranged alphabetically by poet's name, entries include the poet's birth and death dates and quotation(s) from specific poems, arranged alphabetically by the name of the poem. Line numbers are given for quotations except for those from long poems or where differing versions of a poem exist. The entries conclude with a listing of the codes for the anthologies that contain the poem. The only criticism the Board has of the quotations is that there is no indication when the entire poem has been quoted. Many of Shakespeare's sonnets, for example, are reprinted in their entirety. In other cases, one wonders why an entire stanza or poem was not simply reprinted. Gelett Burgess' famous "The Purple Cow," for example, has lines 1 and 2 as one quote, and then line 4 as another, skipping the third line entirely.

The work concludes with a 106-page subject index and a 498-page keyword index that lists words in context. Both give the poet's name and quotation number, making the task of finding the actual quotation easy. Both are comprehensive, although it is odd that the subject index spells out the poet's name in full under each subject heading, whereas the keyword index truncates the name; Ezra Pound, for example, appears as "POUN" everywhere in the index.

This was obviously done to save space, and it in no way lessens the reader's ability to find the proper quotation, but it nevertheless appears a bit peculiar to a reader unacquainted with the poet's name. There is no title index.

Libraries already owning *Columbia Granger's World of Poetry* on CD-ROM [RBB Mr 1 92] will not find this volume a necessary purchase. A random sampling of 50 quotations from *Dictionary of Poetry Quotations* revealed that all were included on the CD-ROM, sometimes with lengthier quotations. This is not surprising, in that *World of Poetry* lists this volume as a source. It should be pointed out, however, that the CD-ROM version does not indicate the line numbers of quoted material, whereas this work usually does.

No quotation book will have every possible passage a patron is looking for, but *Dictionary of Poetry Quotations* will certainly be a valuable addition for public, academic, and high school libraries and is a worthwhile addition to the *Columbia Granger's* family.

The Oxford Dictionary of Quotations. 4th. ed. Ed. by Angela Partington. Oxford, 1992. 1,061p. index. hardcover $35 (0-19-866185-1).

808.881 Quoatations—English [BKL]

Of making many quotation dictionaries there is no end. Fresh on the heels of the new edition of *Bartlett's* [RBB N 1 92] comes this revision of *The Oxford Dictionary of Quotations*, last published in 1979. It contains 17,500 quotations from 2,500 authors. Some of the new quotations were taken from *The Oxford Dictionary of Modern Quotations* [RBB My 1 91].

The work is still alphabetically arranged so that Samuel Pepys precedes S. J. Perelman who is followed by Pericles. For each author are provided not only the dates of birth and death but an identifying tag. For instance, Francis Crick is described as "British molecular biologist." A source is given for each quotation, sometimes with even chapter and page number. A keyword-in-context index enables readers to find a known quotation.

How different is *Oxford* from *Bartlett's*? While British in origin, *Oxford* contains quotations from many Americans. In fact, Americans are found here who are not in *Bartlett's*: Goodman Ace on TV ("we call it a medium because nothing's well done"), Dean Acheson, Polly Adler, Buzz Aldrin, Robert Altman, to name just a few. But *Bartlett's* has British stuff not in *Oxford*: Monty Python's Flying Circus, Simon Gray, Salman Rushdie. *Bartlett's* is unique in having many quotations from non-Western sources: the *Book of the Dead*, Confucius, the *Bhagavad Gita*, the Koran. Even when the same people are found in both books, there is often a different selection of quotations. For instance, while both books have several quotations from Norman Mailer, only one is found in both. While both books print quotations in the original language as well as English for French and German writers, *Oxford* provides, when appropriate, the original Latin, Greek, or Russian as well.

The Oxford Dictionary of Quotations does not take the place of *Bartlett's* for Americans. There is not as much Emerson, Longfellow, Lincoln, or Twain, for instance. But it shouldn't be seen as just a British complement to *Bartlett's*. Both these books have wide scopes and little overlap with each other. Fortunately, their reasonable prices mean that libraries will be able to buy them both. —Sandy Whiteley

Magill's Survey of World Literature. 6v. Ed. by Frank N. Magill. Marshall Cavendish, 1992. bibliog. illus. indexes. hardcover $389.95 (1-85435-482-5).

809 Literature—History and criticism ‖ Literature—Stories, plots, etc. ‖ Literature—Bio-bibliography ‖ Authors—Biography—Dictionaries [CIP] 92-11198

This survey combines elements of both the Critical Survey and Masterplots series published by Salem Press and is similar to *Magill's Survey of American Literature* [RBB Mr 15 92]. Articles on 215 writers from antiquity to the present day are arranged alphabetically by name. Writers range from the classical, such as Aristotle and Plato, to contemporary figures, including Nobel Prize winners such as Czeslaw Milosz and more popular writers such as P. D. James and John le Carré. Coverage is given to novelists, poets, dramatists, and masters of nonfiction and the short story, including the Asians Yukio Mishima and Skikibu Muraski. Americans are excluded since they are covered in a separate set. The result is an eclectic and highly selective mix. The brief "Publisher's Note" sheds little light on why authors were chosen (which seems to be typical of Magill sets). There are entries for Oliver Goldsmith but not Richard Brinsley Sheridan, the Brothers Grimm but not Hans Christian Andersen, Katherine Mansfield but not Patrick White, Victor Hugo but not Alexandre Dumas.

Each entry begins with brief top matter giving place and date of birth and death (if relevant) and principal literary achievement. The articles consist of one to two pages of biography, followed by one to two pages of analysis. After the analysis is discussion of individual works; the average number of works included for each author is three. The section on each work covers a page or two and is introduced by capsule information giving the date of first publication, type of work, and brief summary. Following is a summary of the writer's principal themes and achievements and a selected bibliography of secondary sources. There are no bibliographies of writers' works. As in other Magill productions, the essays are written in a style accessible to high school and college students. Each author is represented by a full-page portrait or photograph.

At the end of each volume is a list of all the authors included in the set and the same glossary. The last volume concludes with author and title indexes. Each author entry includes a listing of the individual works discussed.

There is a great deal of duplication between this set and other reference tools published by Salem Press. Yukio Mishima, for instance, is also included in *Critical Survey of Long Fiction: Foreign Language Series* and *Critical Survey of Short Fiction*. There is overlap with the individual Mishima titles discussed in *Masterplots Revised Edition* and *Masterplots II World Fiction Series*. All of the entries have been rewritten, however, instead of simply being reprinted from other sets.

Magill's Survey of World Literature brings together in a single convenient set the biographical and analytical elements found in the Critical Surveys and the individual title treatment that characterizes Masterplots. Like those other series, it presents information in an accessible way. It should help introduce students to a few of the major writers from other cultures. For these reasons, it is a good choice for small public and high school libraries. Because it is so selective, and because it duplicates coverage in other sources, libraries that already own a good selection of Salem Press/Magill sets can skip this one.

World Literature Criticism: 1500 to the Present: A Selection of Major Authors from Gale's Literary Criticism Series. 6v. Ed. by James P. Draper. Gale, 1992. bibliog. illus. indexes. hardcover $360 (0-8103-8361-6).
809 Literature—History and criticism [OCLC] 92-25007

Presented as a "one-stop, authoritative guide to the whole spectrum of world literature," *World Literature Criticism* (WLC) presents critical commentary from other Gale reference works. As such, it is similar in concept to the recently released *Shakespeare for Students* [RBB Jl 92], which largely reprints material available in other open-ended Gale series.

WLC is arranged in a manner quite similar to volumes in Gale's Literary Criticism series, from which 95 percent of the entries were selected. The introduction claims the entries were "completely updated for publication . . . ranging from new author introductions to wide changes in the selection of criticism," with the remaining 5 percent prepared especially for WLC. The Board examined the entries for six authors and found that all of the critical commentary on them had appeared in previous volumes in the Literary Criticism series, with the exception of two excerpts that had a few sentences added. The most extensive revisions appeared to be in the introductions about the authors' lives and work.

WLC contains entries for 231 authors, ranging from Miguel de Cervantes and William Shakespeare to John Updike and Wole Soyinka. Many literary forms are represented, including poetry and drama. Thirty-three of the writers are women, and thirteen are black. Authors selected for inclusion were based on recommendations from an advisory panel of high school teachers and high school and public librarians. This probably explains the inclusion of relatively minor authors such as Hans Christian Andersen, Anne Frank, and Bram Stoker.

Arranged by author name, each entry begins with an introduction that tends to run three pages or so covering the author's life and principal works, concluding with a list of other Gale volumes where information on the author may be found. This is followed by anywhere from four to seven critical excerpts in chronological order, each of which is fully cited. The entry concludes with a bibliography that (by Gale standards) is relatively brief—usually featuring only about six citations. The introduction notes, however, that "these lists were specially compiled to meet the needs of high school and college students . . . [and] most of the sources cited are available in typical small and medium-sized libraries." The entries also feature a "List of Principal Works" for each author. Some entries feature a listing of "Major Media Adaptations," which were specially conceived for WLC. Unfortunately, there appears to be no rationale for the inclusion of this list in an entry. The entry for Thomas Hardy, for example, lists two adaptations, while the Nathaniel Hawthorne and Herman Melville entries do not have these lists. The set concludes with author, nationality, and title indexes. The nationality index shows that 28 countries are represented. More than half the entries, however, are for British and American authors.

For libraries that cannot afford to maintain ongoing subscriptions to the many Gale Literary Criticism series, this set presents a reasonably priced alternative.

Caribbean Women Novelists: An Annotated Critical Bibliography. Comp. by Lizabeth Paravisini-Gebert and Olga Torres-Seda. Greenwood, 1993. 428p. indexes. hardcover $69.95 (0-313-28342-7; ISSN 0742-6801).
809'.89287 Caribbean fiction—Women authors—Bibliography ‖ Caribbean fiction—Women authors—History and criticism—Bibliography [CIP] 92-37915

Out of the depths of silence is an emerging interest in women writers, including those from all spectra of the African diaspora. In this work—a title in the Bibliographies and Indexes in World Literature series—female writers of the Caribbean are the focus of scholarship. For the purpose of this book, the Caribbean represents the geographic area encompassing the islands of the Caribbean Sea, Belize, Guyana, and Surinam. Entries include "both writers born and raised in the region and those who, regardless of their place of residence or birth, have identified themselves as Caribbean." In this ambitious and painstaking study, women writers who have composed at least one novel since 1950 are treated. Included is a critical bibliographic review of the works by and about 149 women writers such as Rosa Guy, Jamaica Kincaid, Paule Marshall, Miriam Zito, Jean D'Costa, Beatrice Archer, and many more.

Writers are arranged alphabetically, and the entries range in length from less than one page (*Gladys "Marel" Garcia*) to more than 50 (*Jean Rhys*). Each profiled author is briefly identified with basic biographical information. The compilers' objective was to prepare as comprehensive a list as possible of each writer's works as well as all relative critical reactions from journals, newspapers, occasional papers, and such academic studies as theses and conference papers. The listings of the works authored by the profiled individuals include not only their novels, but also short stories, poetry, essays, translations they prepared, interviews they conducted, stage adaptations, and any other types of literary endeavors that could be identified. The compilers obtained copies of every item cited except in a few cases noted as "unavailable." A few items have annotations, primarily the entries for novels. The citations reflect the complex linguistic traditions of the area, with many of the titles written in languages other than English, but works available in translation are clearly noted.

Opening the book is a list of general reference works that feature various aspects of the subject, and an appendix discusses resources available for literature in the Netherlands Antilles. Closing the study are a list of authors by country and three indexes: titles of novels, names of critics, and one for themes and keywords. It would have been useful for quick lookups had an alphabetical list of the profiled authors been included, either as an index or on a contents page. This is especially true since no cross-references are provided in the work for individuals with compound surnames.

Even though the Caribbean region has common historical experiences, it is marked by fragmentation produced by colonial control. This led to four distinct linguistic traditions (French, Spanish, English, Dutch), and most previous research has focused on one of these languages or a particular nationality. Likewise, most previous reference tools have focused on the literature of one specific tradition. One title that includes brief listings for more than 400 writers of the entire region, regardless of language or time period, is *Caribbean Writers: Bio-Bibliographical Critical Encyclopedia* [RSBR Mr 1 81]. However, that book is now more than 12 years old, and most of the citations in the work under review are to materials published since that date.

The challenge for the compilers of *Caribbean Women Novelists* was to produce a comprehensive and up-to-date resource on its subject, encompassing the diversity of languages and traditions, in order "to provide a useful tool for the comparative study of women's literature." They have succeeded with this comprehensive critical bibliographic study. In large public libraries and in academic institutions, this resource will help fill an information void. It is recommended for specialized collections in literary, ethnic, and women's studies.

Masterplots II: Poetry Series. 6v. Ed. by Frank N. Magill. Salem Press, 1992. bibliog. indexes. hardcover $425 (0-89356-584-9).
809.1 Poetry—Themes, motives [CIP] 91-44341

Critical Survey of Poetry: English Language Series. 8v. Rev. ed. Ed. by Frank N. Magill. Salem Press, 1992. bibliog. index. hardcover $475 (0-89356-834-1).
821.009'03 English poetry—Dictionaries || American poetry—Dictionaries || English poetry—Bio-bibliography || American poetry—Bio-bibliography || Poets, English—Biography—Dictionaries [CIP] 92-3727

Of these two sets in the Salem Press family of literary reference tools, *Masterplots II: Poetry Series* is new, while *Critical Survey* is a revision of a set published in 1982.

Masterplots follows the example of other titles in the series by discussing individual works. Its six volumes examine more than 750 poems, arranged alphabetically from "A" by Louis Zukofsky to "Zone" by Guillaume Apollinaire. Most poems are from the sixteenth through the twentieth centuries, though there are a few by eighth-century Chinese masters Tu Fu and Li Po. More than 270 poets are represented. Yeats is the most frequently represented poet, with 16 poems, followed by Shakespeare, Wordsworth, and Wallace Stevens. While the emphasis is on poetry in English, the set also examines poetry in other languages. The most frequently represented non-English-language poet is Baudelaire. The brief publisher's note provides few clues as to how poems were chosen. Some familiar works, such as Pope's "The Rape of the Lock" and Coleridge's "The Rime of the Ancient Mariner," are not included because they are in another Masterplots series. The publisher points out that an effort was made to present "a range of ethnic voices" in the selection of twentieth-century American poetry, including works by Nikki Giovanni, Leslie Marmon Silko, Alberto Rios, and Cathy Song.

Essays, which are seldom more than four pages in length, follow the same format. At the beginning of each entry is the author's full name, birth and death dates, the type of poem (e.g., lyric, dramatic monologue, ode), and the year of the poem's first publication. In the case of poems not originally written in English, information on an English-language collection in which the poem can be found is also provided. Following this information is an overview of the poem, a discussion of the forms and devices employed in it, and a brief examination of the poem's themes and meaning. The essays, all of which are signed, were written by 240 contributors, listed at the beginning of volume 1. Nearly all are affiliated with U.S. colleges and universities. All of the essays are clearly written and generally accessible, though they vary somewhat in approach. Some provide background information on the poem and author, while others focus entirely on the text. Some provide more explanation, while others assume familiarity with concepts and terms.

Following the essays, volume 6 contains a bibliography and several indexes. The first section of the bibliography is an annotated list of general critical and theoretical works. The second section is a list of monographs on approximately 90 individual poets. Just as the essays focus on the poem rather than on the author, the bibliography emphasizes critical rather than biographical sources. An author index, a type-of-poem index, and a title index complete the set.

Masterplots' focus makes it a complement to *Critical Survey of Poetry*. In that work 368 essays are arranged alphabetically by poet rather than by poem. Following dates and locations of each poet's birth and death, an essay provides information and interpretation in a consistent format: principal poetry, other literary forms, achievements, biography, analysis, other major works, and a bibliography of secondary sources. Essays average around 16 pages in length. All are signed, although unlike *Masterplots*, no affiliations are provided in the list of contributors. The two sets differ in scope, since *Critical Survey* covers only English-language poets. (A separate set, *Critical Survey of Poetry: Foreign Language Series*, covers non-English languages.) Nevertheless, a great majority of the poets represented in *Masterplots* are also discussed in *Critical Survey*.

Compared to the 1982 edition, the revised *Critical Survey* contains 91 essays that have been revised, 44 completely rewritten, and 27 that introduce new poets. In addition, all the English-language poets contained in the 1987 *Supplement to the Critical Survey* have been incorporated into the new set. Among the 27 new poets are Raymond Carver, Carolyn Forche, Jorie Graham, and Audre Lord. Approximately an equal number of poets have been dropped, including G. K. Chesterton, William Dean Howells, and Bret Harte, individuals no longer considered primarily in terms of their poetry. Revision involves mostly updated biographical information and expanded and updated lists of authors' works. In some cases, analysis has also been updated to reflect more recent aspects of a poet's career. Twenty-two essays follow the author essays and deal with various aspects of the genre. The one on the twentieth century has been revised in light of developments since the late 1970s, and new essays on Asian American poetry, Chicano poetry, native American poetry, Commonwealth poetry, and feminist criticism replace five of the essays from the 1982 edition. All of the bibliographies of secondary sources have been updated. The set concludes with an author-title index that provides good access to the individual poems discussed in the author essays. The amount of revision probably does warrant purchase of the new edition, even for those libraries already owning the previous set.

Both the Masterplots and the Critical Survey series are familiar to librarians as useful, if somewhat formulaic, tools for students of literature at the upper high school and college levels. To apply the Masterplots' concept to poetry is an interesting approach that provides more detailed discussion of individual works than can be found in the Critical Survey series. Some students may be frustrated by the fact that *Masterplots* provides little background information, often not even nationality, to help them put the poems in context. For this reason, *Masterplots* works best as a companion to a resource like *Critical Survey*, which provides a greater range of information and discusses individual poems in relation to a poet's entire body of work. Both works are recommended for high school, undergraduate, and medium-sized to large public libraries.

Reference Guide to Science Fiction, Fantasy, and Horror. By Michael Burgess. Libraries Unlimited, 1992. 403p. indexes. hardcover $45 (0-87287-611-X).
016.8093'876 Reference books—Science fiction—Bibliography || Science fiction—History and criticism—Bibliography || Reference books—Fantastic fiction—Bibliography || Fantastic fiction—History and criticism—Bibliography || Reference books—Horror tales—Bibliography [CIP] 91-44853

This is one of the best and most complete works to be published on the three popular genres of science fiction, fantasy, and horror. It is designed to guide librarians, researchers, and fans to reference works dealing with some of the most popular literature of the twentieth century. Burgess, a science fiction critic and librarian, brings a unique perspective to his annotations. For example, he decries a lack of indexing where it is necessary and abhors the overuse of abbreviations.

The book is divided into 29 sections, including "Encyclopedias and Dictionaries," "Awards Lists," "Biographical and Literary Directories," and "Magazine and Anthology Indexes." Each section begins with a scope note explaining what is included and why. A complete bibliographic citation is followed by an annotation that varies from a brief note indicating that the item was not available for examination to three or four lengthy paragraphs. A description of the work is followed by a critique of its strengths and weaknesses. For example, for James Gunn's *New Encyclopedia of Science Fiction*, Burgess points out "typographical and textual errors, with which the book overflows in profusion, and the lack of cross- and see-also references (or index)." He recommends Nicholls' *Encyclopedia of Science Fiction* as a much superior work.

Following the 551 annotations is an extremely useful section,

"Core Collections," that lists by annotation number the works Burgess recommends for research university collections, state university collections, small private and community college collections, large city public libraries, medium-size county and city libraries, small public and county libraries, and personal research libraries. This will be an invaluable starting point for libraries working to build or evaluate a collection. The work ends with author, title, and subject indexes.

The *Reference Guide to Science Fiction, Fantasy, and Horror* is such an excellent example of how to organize and analyze materials that it should serve as a model. Comprehensive, easy to use, and reasonably priced, this work belongs in every library that has patrons interested in science fiction, fantasy, or horror.

The Bloomsbury Guide to Women's Literature. Ed. by Claire Buck. Prentice Hall, 1992. 1,171p. bibliog. illus. hardcover $40 (0-13-689621-9); paper $20 (0-13-089665-9).
809'.89287 Women authors—Dictionaries || Women authors || Women in literature—Dictionaries || Women in literature [CIP] 92-10415

The editor's intention was "to bring together for the first time information about writing by women from all periods and from the whole world in a form that was accessible and affordable for as many readers as possible." This aim is admirably accomplished in this new work, with 5,000 dictionary entries and 37 essays on women's writing in various cultures and time periods. Forty scholars from various countries contributed to the volume, and their individual, signed essays act as introductions and pointers to the dictionary entries for the writers, works, and genres listed in the guide.

The book has a point of view: to represent the volume and range of women's literary production, especially those "writers and kinds of writing that have hitherto been marginalized." Thus, the user of this readable work can find not only such well-known figures as Virginia Woolf, Abigail Adams, and Hannah Arendt, but also writers of science fiction, children's literature, diaries, romance novels, and other categories often excluded from critical attention.

The historical scope of the work begins with writers of Greek and Roman antiquity. The reader learns, for example, of Telesilla, a poet of the fifth century B.C., although only fragments of her writings have survived. The guide has a broad international sweep, ranging from Nawal El Sa'dawi of Egypt to Margaret Atwood of Canada. The individual entries range in length from a few sentences to two pages and provide factual data, historical analysis, and literary critique. The tone of the entries may be illustrated by the conclusion to the three-paragraph profile for Sara Parton (1811–72), who wrote under the pseudonym Fanny Fern: "For directness, humour, forthright support of women and blunt assessment of their harassers, Parton was and is hard to match."

In addition to the profiles of people, the large dictionary section has entries for places, works, and definitions of terms, both literary and cultural (e.g., *gothic, arranged marriages*). Supplementing the text are 150 black-and-white photographs and portraits. The entries and essays are abundantly filled with cross-references. Although the editor gave preference to writers whose works are available in English, authors who have untranslated works are included in order to provide adequate representation for each area of the world.

From a librarian's perspective, one problem with this work is its partial bibliographic information. Some entries conclude with short bibliographies of secondary sources, but many do not. Some entries list all works by the writer, but the comprehensiveness is unclear in others. The citations provided include titles, but not publishers, and, in some cases, years of publication are missing (e.g., *Anne of Bohemia*).

The *Bloomsbury Guide to Women's Literature* provides a much needed one-volume reader's companion to women's literature of the world. While it will not substitute for reference works with more in-depth coverage of individual genres or national literatures, it will be a first choice for students of women's writing and for information about the literary endeavors of hundreds, if not thousands, of women excluded by the "patriarchal tradition." This work is recommended for purchase by public and academic libraries and those high schools offering advanced literary studies.

Characters in 19th–Century Literature. By Kelly King Howes. Gale, 1993. 500p. bibliog. index. hardcover $49.95 (0-8103-8398-5).
809.927 Characters and characteristics in literature || Literature, Modern—19th century—History and criticism [OCLC]

This compilation, aimed at high school and college students, was prepared with the assistance of an advisory board of librarians and teachers. It provides brief plot summations and detailed character analyses for approximately 200 novels, plays, and short stories by 100 nineteenth-century writers who are currently studied in U.S. classrooms. An effort was made to include women and ethnic writers, but the emphasis is on major authors of the period. Individuals listed range from Fanny Burney (1725–1840) to Rudyard Kipling (1865–1936) and from Harriet Wilson (1828–1863) to Fernán Caballero (1796–1877).

This volume was patterned after the earlier title *Characters in Twentieth Century Literature* [RBB Mr 1 90], and approximately 10 authors who wrote at the turn of the century appear in both volumes (Chekhov, Crane, O. Henry, Hardy, etc.), but the articles have been revised and expanded here. The book is arranged alphabetically by author and provides the individual's dates, nationality, and principal genres. Then the various works are considered in individual essays that analyze how the characters develop the author's themes. A list of further readings is provided for each author, including, but not limited to, such other Gale publications as the *Dictionary of Literary Biography*. The volume concludes with an index of titles and characters.

Compared with this new work, more comprehensive listings of characters, with less detail for each, are available in other reference tools, such as Magill's *Cyclopedia of Literary Characters* (1963) and the *Dictionary of American Literary Characters* [RBB Mr 1 90]. Libraries owning the various Masterplots series may find they already have adequate coverage of the authors and works included in this volume. While not an essential purchase for libraries owning these other tools, this new work will be helpful in public, high school, and academic library collections where there is high demand for compilations of brief literary analysis.

A Dictionary of Biblical Tradition in English Literature. Ed. by Lyle Jeffrey. Eerdmans, 1992. 976p. bibliog. hardcover $79.95 (0-8028-3634-8).
809.938203 Religion and literature—Dictionaries || Bible in literature—Dictionaries [BKL] 92-30468

This work—designed for serious general readers, students, and scholars—aims to "help the modern reader understand how biblical motifs, concepts, names, quotations, and allusions have been transmitted through exegetical tradition and used by authors of English literature from the Middle Ages to the present." Jeffrey, a professor of English literature at the University of Ottawa, worked with 160 contributors for 16 years to produce this dictionary. It contains approximately 1,000 articles, arranged alphabetically. Subjects include persons (*Eve, Methuselah*), places (*Ur, Gethsemane*), real and mythical animals (*Sheep, Unicorn*), quotations (*Fought the Good Fight, Get Thee behind Me*), common allusions (*Swords into Plowshares, Filthy Lucre*), parables (*Prodigal Son, Unprofitable Servant*), concepts (*Theocracy, Holy Spirit*), and familiar terms in Greek, Hebrew, and Latin (*Agnus Dei, Kyrie Eleison*). *See* and *see also* references are liberal but not always effective. For example, there is no *see* reference from *Milk* or *Honey* to *Land of Milk and Honey*, or from *Cross* or *Cruxifixion* to *Passion, Cross*.

Some articles provide short identification only ("*Hermon*: assumed by some to be the mount of the transfiguration of Jesus"); others vary in length from several paragraphs to multiple pages. Longer articles are signed and consist of three parts: (1) appearances of the term in the Bible, citing books, chapters, and verses; (2) interpretation of the term by early writers, such as Jewish commentators and church fathers, followed by later exegetical writers by period; and (3) the tracing of "significant strands in literary development through exemplary representations from the Middle Ages to the twentieth century." Essays conclude with short bibliographies of books, articles, dissertations, and citations to other reference sources such as *Encyclopaedia Judaica* or the *Catholic Encyclopedia*. The book ends with an extensive section of specialized bibliographies, accompanied by explanatory text that will be especially valuable to students of English literature who need a concise introduction to biblical scholarship.

The articles are scholarly and rich with detail. A typical entry, *Swords into Plowshares* refers to the Book of Joel, in which the image is reversed (plowshares beaten into swords); discusses types of swords and farm implements used at the time the Old Testament was written; cites early commentary on the passages (e.g., Tertullian, St. Jerome, St. Bonaventure); and outlines usage of the allusion in literature from William Langland's *Pier Plowman* to William Blake's *Jerusalem* and D. H. Lawrence's *The Man Who Died*. The dictionary's strength is the identification of writers throughout history who have made use of biblical themes. For example, the entry *Fire and Brimstone* includes discussion of this allusion in Dante's *Divine Comedy*, Middle English Corpus Christi plays, Brontë's *Jane Eyre*, Crane's *Red Badge of Courage*, and Maugham's *Of Human Bondage*. Shakespeare, Chaucer, Spenser, and Blake are, of course, among the most frequently cited authors, but readers may be pleasantly surprised to also find references to the works of Tennessee Williams (*Unicorn*), Margaret Atwood (*Election, Handmaid*), Mark Twain (*Spare the Rod*), Norman Mailer (*Judas Iscariot*), and Annie Dillard (*Bridge, Bridegroom*). There is no index by author name.

While several dictionaries of general and literary allusions have been published recently, none approaches the scope of the work under review. The only other dictionary to focus exclusively on biblical allusions in literature is *A Dictionary of Biblical Allusions in English Literature* by Walter B. Fulghum (1965). That dictionary contains approximately 300 entries, most of which are much shorter than those in Jeffrey and do not address commentary by early writers. Because both dictionaries are selective, each contains unique articles and literary references. Jeffrey's more scholarly and comprehensive *Dictionary of Biblical Tradition in English Literature* will be a valuable addition to the collections of academic and theological libraries.

The Vietnam War in Literature: An Annotated Bibliography of Criticism. By Philip K. Jason. Salem Press, 1992. 175p. bibliog. index. hardcover $40 (0-89356-679-9).
016.8108'0358 American literature—20th century—History and criticism—Bibliography || Vietnamese Conflict, 1961–1975—Literature and the conflict—Bibliography || American literature—20th century—Bibliography || Vietamese Conflict, 1961–1975—Bibliography || War stories—American —Bibliography [CIP] 92-12898

This new title, in the Magill Bibliographies series, begins with an introduction by the author on the imaginative literature of the Vietnam War. He explains the scope of the work, which includes listings for works of criticism on the genres of literary nonfiction as well as novels, poetry, drama, and film. Criticism on specific films, play productions, commentaries in foreign languages, theses, and dissertations are excluded. An especially informative description of the major special collections of Vietnam War material is helpful.

The bibliography is divided into four main sections. "General Studies—Background" contains annotations of representative studies from various disciplines that give the context of the war. "Criticism—General" includes works that cross genre lines. The third section consists of works of literary criticism on particular genres, such as fiction and drama. The fourth section, comprising more than one-half of the book, is "Authors and Works," which treats 69 writers of imaginative works by selectively listing criticism of their most important titles.

The works of criticism listed date from the 1970s to 1991, with most having publication dates in the 1980s. Included are citations to book-length studies, subsections of monographs, essays in collections, and scholarly periodicals. Full bibliographic details are provided for each of the approximately 500 entries. The annotations are informative, each having about 6–10 lines that give a synopsis of the work as well as the seminal points raised in each criticism.

The Vietnam War Bibliography [RBB Je 1 84] listed 4,000 items, in a variety of languages, covering the U.S. involvement from the mid-1940s through 1975, but very few listings for fiction were included. *Vietnam War Literature* [RBB Ja 15 89] provided a bibliography of more than 700 imaginative works about the Vietnam War but did not include works of commentary. Thus, an annotation could be located for Larry Heinemann's *Paco's Story*, while the work under review can be consulted to locate four works of criticism about the book. All four of these citations are for materials published as sections within monographs or annuals and would therefore be impossible to locate through periodical indexes. Due to the specialized nature of *The Vietnam War in Literature*, public and academic libraries must assess their needs for surveys of literary criticism in this area before purchasing this unique and reasonably priced compilation.

American Ethnic Literatures: Native American, African American, Chicano/Latino, and Asian American Writers and Their Backgrounds. By David R. Peck. Salem Press, 1992. 218p. index. hardcover $40 (0-89356-684-5).
016.81 09'920693 American literature—Minority authors—Bibliography || Hispanic Americans in literature—Bibliography || Asian Americans in literature—Bibliography || Afro-Americans in literature—Bibliography || Ethnic groups in literature—Bibliography [CIP] 92-12897

This new title in the Magill Bibliographies series is a scholarly endeavor to provide a guide to the array of creative and scholarly works in the four major American ethnic literatures. Focusing on Native Americans, African Americans, Hispanic Americans, and Asian Americans, Peck has prepared a bibliographic survey of these ethnic traditions that enhances literary, ethnic, and American studies.

The opening chapter of the work is an annotated listing of reference sources, bibliographies, and key journals for ethnic studies. Included here are both general titles, such as *We the People: An Atlas of America's Ethnic Diversity*, and works on specific groups, such as *Bibliographic Guide to Black Studies*. The second chapter is a presentation of major studies that address the social and historical records for these groups in American society, beginning with general works on theories of race, immigration history, textbooks, and collections of essays and concluding with major historical studies of each specific group. The third chapter is devoted to "Teaching Ethnic Literature" and lists journals, teaching guides, anthologies of comparative ethnic literatures, and guides to audiovisual materials. The fourth chapter lists general studies of ethnic literature and is subdivided into sections on such topics as biography, fiction, and theater.

The largest portion of the book is devoted to separate chapters for the literature of each ethnic minority. These include a brief narrative history of the literary tradition, a selected list of primary works, and a bibliography of the major critical studies. These chapters provide short annotations for full-length works, including general sources, major anthologies, and secondary studies. Also included are unannotated lists of works by ethnic minority writers. The volume concludes with an index that is an excellent aid to its usefulness.

American Ethnic Literatures provides a bibliography, in a single volume, where instructors, students, and librarians can glean listings of the major primary literature in the four ethnic traditions, as well as sources for literary criticism and background studies. The volume reflects not only primary sources, but also the historical and social context for each group's literary tradition. Not only is this an important reference tool for all secondary and undergraduate literature collections, it is a timely resource that addresses a need in this multicultural society. Education and librarianship are responsive to the subject of ethnic diversity, and this new title is a welcome volume that can enhance the study of America's multiethnic traditions.

Twins in Children's and Adolescent Literature: An Annotated Bibliography. By Dee Storey. Scarecrow, 1992. 400p. indexes. hardcover $42.50 (0-8108-2641-0).
016.8109'9282 Children's stories, American—Bibliography || Young adult fiction, American—Bibliography || Twins—Juvenile fiction—Bibliography [CIP] 92-40560

The 366 entries in this bibliography demonstrate the complexity and completeness of Storey's research. Citing her own fascination with everything from the Bobbsey Twins to the twins in her family, Storey has developed a bibliography spanning the multitude of literature that mentions this subject matter. This book is written for the person fascinated with twins. The duos listed are identical, fraternal, facsimiles, clones, robots, doppelgangers, wannabe's, and mistaken-for's. Their literary roles may be as main, secondary, or minor characters. This tome even lists books where the mother is pregnant with twins.

Listing literature published from 1904 to 1992, the entries may be either in print, out of print, or reissued as paperbacks. Sequels, trilogies, and updates are listed to encourage further reading and character development. The author, who teaches children's literature, explains in the preface that twins from multicultural traditions are misrepresented in the available literature. She concludes, "Basically, the average story about twins in children's and adolescent literature was about a white, middle class family with a. every day concerns or b. mysteries to solve. By far realistic fiction was the genre most used by authors to tell their stories."

The entries are arranged alphabetically by author within literary-role headings. Standard annotated bibliographic citations include appropriate grade level for each title. Background notes contain information on the family, the twins, and the topics related to the story and to the issues for the twins. A highlight in some entries is the remarks of authors on why they wrote about twins. The annotations are succinct and at times may be difficult to understand until the user is able to adjust to the format of the entries. This is especially the case where the numbering and ages of children within a family are given, or when multiple books are listed. Indexes for author/illustrator, title, and subject are useful for locating entries, especially when looking for themes of the literature.

The popularity of twins and the reissuing of many books, as noted in this bibliography, may make *Twins in Children's and Adolescent Literature* a good purchase for some large public libraries that collect specialized reading lists, but most will find that titles like *The Bookfinder* adequately fill the needs of their patrons.

Masterpieces of African-American Literature. Ed. by Frank N. Magill. HarperCollins, 1992. 593p. indexes. hardcover $40 (0-06-270066-9).
810.9'896073 American literature—Afro-American authors—Dictionaries ‖ American literature—Afro-American authors—Stories, plots, etc. ‖ Afro-Americans in literature—Dictionaries [CIP] 92-52542

About 150 works of literature by more than 90 African American authors are described in this new work, a companion to *Masterpieces of World Literature*. Coverage ranges more than 200 years, including both early literature, such as *Our Nig* by Harriet Jacob and *Clotel* by William Wells Brown, and such contemporary works as *Mama* by best-selling novelist Terry McMillan, Shelby Steele's controversial *The Content of Our Character*, and Charles Johnson's *Middle Passage*, winner of the 1990 National Book Award. In addition to novels, the volume discusses autobiographies, poetry, plays, essays, speeches, and short stories.

Arranged alphabetically by title, each entry follows a standard format. For a work of fiction or drama, an entry begins with brief ready-reference information giving author's name and dates, type of work, type of plot, time of plot, locale, and date of first publication. This information is followed by a description of the principal characters, a summary of the plot, some critical analysis, and a concluding section called "Critical Context." Nonfiction receives similar treatment, except that the ready-reference summaries introducing each entry are briefer, and the sections on literary characters are omitted. For autobiographical treatments, there are short descriptions of the principal personages that figure in the work. In some cases, works are grouped together by literary genre instead of being discussed individually by title. Thus, there are the essays for "The Poetry of Ai," "The Poetry of Amiri Baraka," and "The Speeches of Martin Luther King, Jr." In all, 30 authors and their works are presented this way. Entries average 2,500 words in length and—as one has come to expect from a Frank N. Magill production—are written in a clear and accessible style. Each entry is signed. No affiliations are provided in the list of contributors that follows the brief preface. The volume concludes with author and title indexes.

There is no shortage of information about most of the authors discussed here. Many of them can be found in volumes of Gale's *Dictionary of Literary Biography*, such as *Afro-American Writers before the Harlem Renaissance* and *Afro-American Writers from the Harlem Renaissance to 1940*. The DLB covers more writers and provides more information about their lives and careers. Information about newer writers can be found in Gale's *Black Writers*, a spin-off of *Contemporary Authors*. Many of the writers are also discussed in various other sets edited by Magill, including the Critical Survey and Masterplots series. A number of the titles analyzed in *Masterpieces of African-American Literature* are also included in one or another Masterplots set. However, the volume under review adds a number of titles, especially newer ones, not found elsewhere and also offers the advantage of a convenient format. It is extremely useful to have these works presented in a single volume. Libraries that need information on African American literature but cannot afford to invest heavily in the large sets from Salem Press or Gale will welcome this volume. Even those libraries that do own the larger sets will want to consider this volume as a convenient, accessible way to help support a multicultural curriculum. Recommended for high school, public, and undergraduate libraries.

Dictionary of Literary Biography: Twentieth-Century Caribbean and Black African Writers: First Series. v.117. Ed. by Bernth Lindfors and Reinhard Sander. Gale, 1992. 406p. bibliog. illus. index. hardcover $113 (0-8103-7594-X).
810.9'9729 Caribbean literature (English)—Biobibliography ‖ African literature (English)—Black authors—Biobibliography ‖ African literature (English)—Black authors—Dictionaries ‖ Caribbean literature (English)—Dictionaries ‖ Authors, Caribbean—Biography—Dictionaries [OCLC] 92-8972

This recent DLB volume profiles 18 African and 12 Carribean authors, only 3 of whom have been written about in this series before. Included is Derek Walcott, winner of the Nobel Prize for Literature for 1992; other familiar names are Chinua Achebe, Buchi Emecheta, and Jean Rhys. Nigeria (7 authors), South Africa (5), Ghana (5), and Guyana (5) are the most-represented countries. The Caribbean authors included are also of African heritage or are closely identified with it; Caribbean authors of Hispanic descent are covered in other DLB volumes.

As in other DLB volumes, each article begins with a list of the author's writings and ends with a bibliography of relevant critical writings. Articles trace the development of each writer's career and vary in length from 4 to 23 pages. All are interesting reading. Photographs, representations of book jackets and manuscript pages, quotations from works, etc., are used by way of illustration. The book ends with an appended article about autobiographical slave narratives and a bibliography on the larger subject of the volume. Articles are signed, and contributors' affiliations are given. There is a series index. A second volume on Caribbean and African writers is planned.

This volume is for all libraries that have made a commitment to the DLB series and for those whose patrons would be interested in these authors.

A Reader's Guide to the American Novel of Detection. By Marvin Lachman. G. K. Hall, 1993. 435p. bibliog. indexes. hardcover $45 (0-8161-1803-5).
813'.08720924 Detective and mystery stories, American—Stories, plots, etc. ‖ Detective and mystery stories, American—Bibliography [CIP] 92-25726

Covering 1,314 titles of American detective fiction by 166 North American authors published through 1991, this second book in the Reader's Guide series focuses on amateur detectives such as Amanda Cross's Kate Fansler and Harry Kemelman's Rabbi David Small. The author, an Edgar Award winner and a reviewer for several detective-fiction journals, has excluded titles that have as their protagonist a police officer, private investigator, or professional detective. He does make some exceptions, such as Nero Wolfe, who even though his profession was that of private investigation, proceeded as an amateur. This book follows the same format as the first title in the series, *A Reader's Guide to the Classic British Mystery* [RBB S 1 88], and is designed for the mystery buff.

In the main section of the book, entries are arranged alphabetically by author and chronologically by series character, followed by non-series books. Annotations are limited to plot descriptions, not critical reviews, and, of course, do not reveal the identities of any murderers. Included are lists of pseudonyms, creators, and series characters and indexes by occupation of series character, location, setting, subject, period of the story (1670–1979), and holiday, making this a quick-reference source for readers. The author concludes with his personal recommendation of "One Hundred Notable Novels of Detection." There is no title index.

Several guides provide more comprehensive coverage of mysteries but are not annotated, for example, Hubin's *Crime Fiction*. The armchair detective may want to browse through *A Reader's Guide* for titles by a favorite author or use it to find a new author based on the reader's interests. Libraries that need another guide to this genre should keep a copy next to the fiction section for easy reference.

Contemporary Gay American Novelists: A Bio-bibliographical Critical Sourcebook. Ed. by Emmanuel S. Nelson. Greenwood, 1993. bibliog. index. hardcover $69.50 (0-313-28019-3).
813'.54099206642 Novelists, American—20th century—Biography—Dictionaries ‖ Homosexuality and literature—U.S.—History—20th century ‖ American fiction—20th century—Bio-bibliography ‖ American fiction—Men authors—Bio-bibliography ‖ Gay men—U.S.—Biography—Dictionaries [CIP] 92-25762

Gay and lesbian studies is emerging as a serious area of study at many universities, resulting in an increase in the publication of scholarly works on the topic. Nelson has done an excellent job in editing this book about gay novelists, which should be a welcome addition in all research libraries as well as other libraries where there is an interest in gay and lesbian culture.

Contemporary Gay American Novelists profiles 57 serious and widely read male writers who were selected by the editor as representative of the variety of gay literature. These individuals are authors of detective stories, science fiction, personal histories, and novels that portray various aspects of gay life and culture. Authors who write only pulp novels and erotic fiction are not included, nor are those who asked not to be publicly identified as gay. Biographees range from the famous, such as James Baldwin and Christopher Isherwood, to lesser-known novelists whose "works deserve wider attention," such as John Fox and Peter Weltner.

Most of the biobibliographies were written by gay scholars, giving an insightful and empathic tone to the essays. The profiles vary in length from 4 to 19 pages, and all open with biographical information about the novelist. This is followed by a discussion of major works and themes, pointing out the role of gender identity in the writings, as well as ideas living novelists may be interested in pursuing in the future. The "Critical Reception" section of the essay discusses the significance of the author's works, as well as providing information about how the writings have been received by gay and mainstream media and audiences. The essays conclude with two bibliographies, one of works by the novelist and the other of selected studies about him.

This new work is well written and fascinating to read. Scholars and general readers, as well as closeted gays, will find it an enlightening book to both consult and browse. It fills a need in the area of gay and lesbian studies and is recommended for academic and large public libraries.

The Oxford Illustrated Literary Guide to Great Britain and Ireland. 2d. ed. Ed. by Dorothy Eagle and Hilary Carnell. Oxford, 1992. 335p. bibliog. illus. maps. hardcover $45 (0-19-212988-0).
820.9 Literary landmarks—Great Britain—Guide-books ‖ Literary landmarks—Ireland—Guide-books ‖ Authors, English—Homes and haunts—Guide-books ‖ Authors, Irish—Homes and haunts—Guide-books ‖ Great Britain—Description and travel—1971—Guide-books [CIP] 91-20240

Intended for the "literary pilgrim," this work features place-names "which have associations with writers and their work" from England, Scotland, Wales, and Ireland. This edition adds 137 authors to the 1981 edition, bringing the total to 1,050. As in that edition, living authors are excluded.

The main body of this work is 1,337 place-names arranged A–Z. Entries include "cities, towns, villages, districts, and houses where writers have been born, educated, or buried, or where they have lived, worked, and drawn inspiration for their writing." Entries range from a few lines to some 50 pages devoted to London. Each entry begins with a grid position on one of the 13 maps that end the volume and notes the nearest highway. The preface claims 105 places were added to this edition; a sampling by the Board revealed this to be accurate. Somewhat distressing is the fact that virtually all references to visiting hours for various landmarks have been removed from this edition. It is likely the editors may have simply forgone the difficulty of keeping up with them.

The work concludes with an index of authors. The index gives brief biographical information on the authors, with page-number references listed after the names of works that are mentioned within entries in the guide. Some omissions are evident. Anyone attempting to find information about Thomas Hardy's "Egdon Heath"—which figures so prominently in his *The Return of the Native*—will not find it under that novel's name but only by skimming through page references to his other works.

This volume features numerous black-and-white illustrations and 32 colorplates. All of the colorplates have been changed for this edition; although some black-and-white illustrations have been added, most remain the same.

The arrangement of this work supposes a certain amount of knowledge on the part of the reader. Our previous review of this work pointed out that unless the reader knows certain places are in London, he or she may not find the entry since there are few cross-references. This continues to hold true for the new edition. Places like Bloomsbury, Chelsea, and Kingsbury—all districts of London—are gathered within that city's entry with no cross-references elsewhere.

The only major reference work at all similar to this volume is Lois Fisher's *Literary Gazetteer of England* (1980), which features some 1,200 localities and 500 authors. Now a little dated, it is restricted solely to England but remains useful for general information and nicely complements the present volume.

Public and academic libraries that have a large clientele of Anglophiles will no doubt find this new edition of the guide useful. Others that already own the first edition will have to consider if the number of revisions is sufficient to make this a necessary purchase. Those who do not own the first edition at all, however, should certainly consider purchasing this reasonably priced, attractive work.

Modern Irish Literature and Culture: A Chronology. By James M. Cahalan. G. K. Hall, 1993. 374p. bibliog. index. hardcover $45 (0-8161-7264-1).
820.9'9415 English literature—Irish authors—Chronology ‖ Ireland—History—18th century—Chronology ‖ Ireland—History—19th century—Chronology ‖ Ireland—History—20th century—Chronology ‖ Northern Ireland—History—Chronology [CIP] 92-15105

This scholarly work is a unique guide to significant literary events in Ireland from 1601 to 1992. The book utilizes a chronological structure to present developments in Irish drama, fiction, poetry, and prose nonfiction. Irish literature is defined here more broadly than "Anglo-Irish," and works written in Irish Gaelic are covered, as well as those written in English. Cahalan, author of several books on Irish literature, believes that history is not merely "background," but an "arena in which writers participate and make their mark." Thus, the work is interdisciplinary and interrelates political and historical events with literary and cultural endeavors.

While the chronology begins with the seventeenth century—when the Irish first aspired to a national identity—the emphasis is on the period from 1800 to the present. Only the most significant events are covered for the earlier centuries, while every year since 1858 has its own entry. For each year, an opening paragraph summarizes political, economic, and historical events in order to place the literary endeavors in context; these are grouped together and listed under such headings as "Drama," "Fiction," and "Poetry." Developments in Irish culture are highlighted in such categories as "Architecture," "Art," "Cultural Institutions," "Education," and "Irish Language." An important feature of the chronology is its inclusion of important events in the development of Irish journals and newspapers; the author believes they constitute a major interdisciplinary cultural arena and claims that this work presents the "most comprehensive chronology of Irish periodicals available."

The reader will find such names as Samuel Beckett, Austin Clarke, and Charles Lever, as well as such lesser-known personalities as Máirtín ó Cadhain and Pádraic Pearse. The entries for each year include the authors and titles of important works but offer more than a dated list of bibliographic citations or events. Brief narratives frequently discuss a work's theme, its critical reception, or its political significance. A typical annual entry, such as that for 1960, includes information about the advent of Irish television, the first annual gathering of the Yeats Summer School, the novels of Edna O'Brien and Benedict Kiely, the short stories of Aidan Higgins, and the career of *Kilkenny Magazine*. Other features of the book include a section of 37 brief biographical sketches for major personalities that appear frequently in the chronology, a bibliography of secondary works used in the preparation of the text, and a comprehensive index.

Modern Irish Literature and Culture will complement such reference works as *Dictionary of Irish Literature*, by Robert Hogan (1980), *A Biographical Dictionary of Irish Writers* [RBB Ap 15 86], and *Dictionary of Irish Biography* [RBB Je 1 89]. It is recommended for literature collections in academic and large public libraries, as well as those emphasizing Irish and British history.

The Top 500 Poems. Ed. by William Harmon. Columbia, 1992. 1,132p. indexes. hardcover $29.95 (0-231-08028-X).
821.008 English poetry ‖ American poetry [CIP] 91-42239

In the introduction, Harmon boldly proclaims, "This is it!" He is right. The task he set for himself was to compile an anthology with which anyone could start to gain a familiarity with poetry in English. He has nobly done yeoman's work in selecting and commenting upon the 500 poems that have been anthologized most often, based on the 400 collections indexed in the ninth edition of *The Columbia Granger's Index to Poetry*. Harmon is a professor of English at the University of North Carolina and edited *The Concise Columbia Book of Poetry* and the *Oxford Book of American Light Verse*. He also coedited the fifth edition of *A Handbook to Literature*.

Represented in *The Top 500 Poems* are 160 poets. Shakespeare has 29 entries. Anonymous has 21, Donne has 19, Blake has 18, and Dickinson and Yeats each have 14. Harmon justifies the fact that "three-quarters of the poems are British . . . because British poetry has been with us three times as along as American poetry." Coverage spans six centuries, ranging from Chaucer in the Middle Ages to Allen Ginsberg and Sylvia Plath. The nineteenth century contributed the greatest number of poems (169), with the twentieth century second with 122.

The format is attractive. The paper is of high quality, margins are wide, and the poetry is in dark, readable print. Each poet is introduced with a short paragraph in small print with just enough data to pique curiosity. Comments by Harmon, in yet a different font, follow the selections. He writes with a sly sense of humor, describing alliteration as "sliding along the slippery slope of selfsame sounds." The entries for poets are in chronological order, and a detailed table of contents and a name index provide additional access points. An index of titles and first lines is included, as well as an appendix that ranks the poems according to the number of times they have been anthologized.

All types of libraries will be interested in this volume as a basic anthology of poetry in English. It will be welcome in elementary and secondary school library media centers, public library poetry and reference collections, home libraries, and as a gift. If your library can buy only one volume of poetry, let this be it.

Shakespeare's Characters: A Players Press Guide. By Kenneth McLeish. Players Press, 1992. 252p. hardcover $39.95 (0-88734-608-1).

822.3'3 Shakespeare, William—Characters ‖ Characters and characteristics in literature [CIP] 90-53234

McLeish, well known in Great Britain as a free lance writer, broadcaster, and reviewer, has been associated with a number of books on the arts, including music and drama. This book is a revision of a title first published in Essex, England, in 1985, as the *Longman Guide to Shakespeare's Characters: A Who's Who of Shakespeare*, although this is not mentioned anywhere in the volume. This does not detract from the value of the book; however, libraries should check catalogs before purchase.

The book is useful for actors, directors, and those unfamiliar with Shakespeare's plays. The reader can use this who's who to get to know the bard's characters as real human personalities. Almost all major and minor characters are included. They are arranged alphabetically; the italicized name of the play appears in parentheses after each. According to McLeish, no two characters are exactly alike. Readers coming to the plays for the first time will find informal, meaningful descriptions in a few lines for minor characters ("*Taborer* [*The Two Noble Kinsmen*]: Drummer for the morris-dance. He does not speak") and in several paragraphs for such major roles as "Richard (*Richard II*)." In some entries quotations from Shakespeare help define the character. Summaries of 38 plays (*The Rape of Lucrece* is not included) are also treated. There are cross-references to name variations ("Hotspur, see Percy, Harry"), but the volume does not have an index.

Quennell and Johnson's *Who's Who in Shakespeare* (1973) treats the characters in a similar but slightly more formal way and includes excellent photographs and illustrations of scenes from the productions. Magill's *Cyclopedia of Literary Characters* (1963) includes a helpful index and brief descriptions. Both of these volumes include *Lucrece*. Libraries not owning one of the above, or the original edition of this work, will want to purchase this handy compendium.

Dictionary of Mexican Literature. Ed. by Eladio Cortés. Greenwood, 1992. 768p. bibliog. index. hardcover $85 (0-313-26271-3).

860.9'972 Mexican literature—Dictionaries ‖ Mexican literature—20th century—Dictionaries [CIP] 91-10529

This volume represents the first major work in the English language devoted exclusively to Mexican authors. Cortés, a professor of Spanish at Rutgers University and author of numerous books and articles, and his 40 contributors have assembled a work that contains entries "covering the most important writers, literary schools, and cultural movements in Mexican literary history," noting that "there is an emphasis on figures in the twentieth century."

After the preface and tables of abbreviations, the work opens with the 19-page essay "Overview of Mexican Letters and Literature," which provides an excellent summary, noting with asterisks those names in the essay that have entries in the dictionary. Following this essay are the entries proper. The volume has 545 entries total, 534 of which are biographical entries. The remaining 11 are topical entries, such as *Magical Realism* and *Theater in Colonial Mexico*. The emphasis of this dictionary is biographical, rather than topical, and more than 80 percent of the individuals profiled are writers still living or who died during the twentieth century. There are cross-references within the work from popular pen names ("*Finisterre*. See CAMPOS Ramirez, Alejandro") and from Spanish phrases for movements ("*Contemporaneos*. See VANGUARDIST Prose Fiction in Mexico"). One blind cross-reference was spotted: "*Teodoro de Ortontobolo*. See BASILIO, Librado," though there is no entry for Basilio.

The signed entries vary in length from less than one page to 16 pages for Emilio Carballido. The biographies present an overview of the author's life and works. The essays are careful to translate into English most Spanish titles cited, even when no printed English translation of the work in question exists. The longest entries feature biographies of only a couple of pages, at best, and devote the rest of the space to bibliographies, which are perhaps the most noteworthy aspect of this dictionary. Bibliographies are divided into two sections: one lists works by the author; and a second cites works about the writer. The preface notes that the bibliographic entries selected "are usually those which are most easily available in the United States" and that they are not comprehensive. Nevertheless, these lists will be of tremendous benefit, and this work is as valuable for bibliographic references as for biographical information. Carballido's entry, for example, lists five pages of works by him and almost 10 pages of work about him. All entries include original title, translation of the title into English, place of publication, publisher, date of publication, and page numbers. Works that have been published in English are also noted. The work concludes with a 13-page bibliography citing general works on Mexican literature and an index.

Compared with another new reference title, *Spanish American Authors*, the work under review covers many more authors of Mexican origin and a broader time period and includes those who wrote plays, as well as novels and poetry. The *Dictionary of Mexican Literature* is a unique work that deserves a place in any academic or public library with an interest in Mexican literature. A sampling of writers included in this new source revealed that only about 15 percent are in Gale's *Contemporary Authors* or its companion work, *Hispanic Writers* [RBB Ja 1 91], indicating that this volume contains many unique entries. Even if there were a more substantial overlap, however, the bibliographies alone would justify the purchase of this highly recommended book.

Spanish American Authors: The Twentieth Century. By Angel Flores. Wilson, 1992. 915p. bibliog. hardcover $100 (0-8242-0806-4).

860.9'868 [B] Authors, Spanish American—20th century—Biography—Dictionaries [CIP] 92-7591

This addition to the Wilson author series includes profiles of 331 major twentieth-century novelists and poets from Puerto Rico, the Caribbean, and Central and South America. The noted Hispanist Flores selected the authors for inclusion in this work, not only to exemplify the literatures of all the Latin American countries, but also because each individual is an "important literary creator." Flores knew many of the authors personally and invited them to write sketches discussing their lives and works. These autobiographical statements are abundant in this work, although most are accompanied by additional narrative from either the editor or one of the contributors. Much of the biographical and critical material was originally written in Spanish and then translated into English for this publication. The list of 100 contributors reflects a varied and impressive range of expertise.

The book is arranged alphabetically by the writer's surname, and a complete list of biographees appears in the front matter. Entries

GEOGRAPHY, BIOGRAPHY

Man-Made Catastrophies: From the Burning of Rome to the Lockerbie Crash. By Lee Davis. Facts On File, 1992. 352p. bibliog. illus. index. hardcover $40 (0-8160-2035-3).
904 Disasters [CIP] 91-41859

Natural Disasters: From the Black Plague to the Eruption of Mt. Pinatubo. By Lee Davis. Facts On File, 1992. 352p. bibliog. illus. index. hardcover $40 (0-8160-2034-5).
904 Natural disasters [OCLC] 91-38395

Journalist Davis is the author of several biographical works on Broadway composers. In these two new books, he documents calamities from the time of ancient Rome to 1991.

In *Man-Made Catastrophies* he acknowledges that while there are natural disasters of epoch proportions, he believes the element of tragedy is greater when a human element can be held responsible. This book has sections on air crashes, civil unrest and terrorism, explosions, fires, maritime disasters, nuclear accidents, railway disasters, and space disasters—284 incidents in all. The format for each section is uniform. First is a list of incidents organized by country, followed by a chronology listing them by year. The number of disasters listed in these sections exceeds the number actually discussed in the text. For example, under "Air Crashes" 129 accidents are listed, but only 60 are discussed; these are noted with an asterisk. Within each section, entries are arranged by place. The date of the accident is noted followed by an abstract detailing the event and casualties. Essays of one-half to one and one-half pages describe the incidents. The sections "Air Crashes" and "Nuclear and Industrial Accidents" each have a short glossary of technical terms. The "Civil Unrest and Terrorism" section has a "Key to Major Terrorist Organizations."

Natural Disasters has sections on avalanches, earthquakes, famines and droughts, floods, epidemics, hurricanes, snowstorms, tornadoes, typhoons, and volcanic eruptions. The arrangement and format are the same as in *Man-Made Catastrophes*. Each book has more than 100 black-and-white illustrations (both photographs and drawings), a bibliography, and an index.

The Great International Disaster Book (1976) and *Great Disasters* (1989) both cover ancient to modern times. *The Great International Disaster Book* covers more than 100 natural and man-made disasters while *Great Disasters* describes approximately 80 natural events. The former has only 24 illustrations while the latter has 300, many of them color. *The Great International Disaster Book* has the most scholarly analysis, citing costs, trends, etc. The new books by Davis provide more coverage of catastrophes caused by man and are more up-to-date.

Whenever there is a catastrophe, the public and media display a macabre interest in recalling and comparing past events with the present. These two readable books from Facts On File will make this easy to do. Public, academic, and high school libraries will want to consider purchase.

Warfare and Armed Conflicts: A Statistical Reference to Casualty and Other Figures, 1618–1991. 2v. By Michael Clodfelter. McFarland, 1992. 1,414p. bibliog. index. hardcover $125 (0-89950-544-9).
904'.7 Military history, Modern—Encyclopedias || Military history, Modern—Statistics [CIP] 91-52632

This new subject encyclopedia, in two volumes and containing more than 1,400 pages, presents an unrelenting account of warfare and its cost in human lives. Costs of war materials and animal deaths are covered in detail, but it is the death and wounded-in-action figures that serve to make this one of the grimmest books to ever take its place in a reference collection. The author has described, for the last four centuries, the "method, manner, and moment of the deaths and disablements of the millions claimed by modern warfare." Important military engagements are described in enough detail for users to understand the intended purpose and effectiveness of the weapons used. Users will appreciate the author's summary of important battles that account for the ultimate impact of the soldiers killed in action.

Eight hundred twenty significant battles—including riots—are included, ranging over time from the Japanese Civil War and the Polish-Swedish War, both initiated in 1600, to the Persian Gulf War of 1990–91. Important conflicts such as the Gordon Riots, the Detroit Riots of 1943, Night of the Long Knives, and the Babi Yar Massacre are also included. The organization of the book is clearly indicated in the detailed table of contents. Entries are arranged first by century (the seventeenth through the twentieth), then by geographic region or major conflict (Western Europe, Africa, Caribbean, World War II Pacific Theater, etc.), and then by specific battle or topic (*Zulu Rebellion 1906*, *Aleutian Islands 1942–43*, *The American Soldier in Vietnam*, etc.). The comprehensive index identifies the names of major personalities, weapons, ships, and individual battles. The bibliography is keyed to parts of the text, making it easy to identify secondary source materials.

The author's carefully worded introduction on the use of war-related statistics reflects the care he exercised in evaluating primary sources and archival documents to compile the casualty figures. Nevertheless, many users will be disappointed to not find citations to sources used to glean statistics. For example, there is no readily identified source cited to help verify that 20,000 people died of heart attacks and 6,000 committed suicide during the Battle of Berlin in 1945. The author's coverage of the strategic bombing of Germany during World War II is excellent, but no official U.S., U.K., or German government sources are cited, nor is there a reference in the bibliography to any part of the Strategic Bombing Survey documents completed after the war. In the opinion of the Board, the lack of specific source citations in *Warfare and Armed Conflicts* is a serious omission that detracts from the authoritativeness and reference value of this otherwise excellent work. Nevertheless, the author's careful and detailed presentation of a vast amount of information about four centuries of conflict warrants purchase consideration of this volume by large public and academic libraries.

Facts On File News Digest CD-ROM. Facts On File, 1992. annual. $595 for current *Facts On File* print subscribers; $695 for nonsubscribers.
905'.2 History, Modern—20th century—Data bases [OCLC] 92-644388

Three years ago, Facts On File produced a CD-ROM version of its popular weekly news digest. In its review [RBB D 15 89], the Board praised the easy access it offered to a nine-year cumulation of news summaries, the flexibility of Boolean operators, the visual appeal of its Microsoft Windows menus, and its reasonable price. The Board found problematic its lack of proximity searching, its unsatisfactory on-screen prompts, the cumbersome maps database, limited downloading capabilities, and infrequent updating (yearly).

This new version of *Facts On File News Digest* CD-ROM is a more tempting purchase because it covers a greater span of years (1980–1991), provides excellent on-screen prompts and content-specific help, allows proximity searching, installs easily, is networkable, has complete downloading capability, and enables users to tailor printouts or downloaded information to fit their needs. EBSCO hypertext software, designed especially for *Facts On File*, provides a more understandable user interface than Windows' pull-down menus and dialog boxes. The lower price tag ($595 for *Facts On File* subscribers, down from $670 for the earlier version) increases its appeal. Annual cumulative updates are available for $295 per year; in 1993, a quarterly cumulative edition will be available for $795.

HARDWARE, SOFTWARE, AND INSTALLATION. *Facts On File* requires an IBM PC, XT, AT, PS/2, or compatible with a hard disk, MS-DOS version 3.1 or higher, a minimum of 640K memory, a CD-ROM drive, and Microsoft Extensions version 2.1 or higher. While these requirements seem modest, *Facts On File* needs at least two million bytes of free space in order to be installed. Installation was simple and clearly described in the manual. Instructions for networking are also provided there.

Facts On File enables libraries to tailor some features of the package to meet their own needs. By accessing a "Tailor" menu, librarians can establish security measures that require user identification for access to menus with the most complex searching strategies, set "inactivity time-out" periods, and specify the number of hits that can be printed at one time. Also through this menu, librarians can compile and print such statistical reports as the number of new searches, total hits, average number of queries per search, and number of articles and article pages printed.

SEARCHING AND DISPLAYING. Users are given the option of a "basic" or "advanced" search. They construct searches by typing words and phrases in fill-in-the-blank forms. Basic searches allow users to type phrases up to three lines in length, which are linked with the Boolean AND operator. For example, the Board used a simple search of *libertarian* on one line and *candidate* on the next in order to identify the Libertarian Party's presidential candidate. Words or phrases for concepts to be excluded can be typed on a fourth line, labeled "But NOT." Synonyms or alternate words or phrases are separated by commas—the equivalent of the Boolean OR. Proximity searching is done by typing the words within brackets. Articles are retrieved if these words appear within 50 characters of one another in any order. The number of characters can be changed for a single search or permanently changed by changing the default in the tailor menu. We found the number of barrels of oil spilled by the Exxon *Valdez* by typing [Exxon Valdez] on the first line of the query profile and *barrels* on the second. Truncation is automatic for plurals; a question mark replaces a single unkown letter; and an asterisk retrieves all variants of a word stem.

While the availability of proximity searching alleviates some of the frustration encountered with the first version of *Facts On File*, there are still problems here that perhaps are inherent in searching long news summaries that cover many subjects. In a search for information on conventions or conferences of Green Party members, *green party, greens* was typed on one line, and *conference, convention* on the next line. *Facts On File* retrieved the desired information but also a summary article discussing the colors of the African National Congress (including *green*) and an item about a rally at a Washington *convention* center. Typing words describing all concepts within brackets in order to establish proximity excluded relevant citations.

The advanced searching option offers two query profiles on the same screen—one for keyword searching in all fields and a second for subject searching. Both can be used in a single search. For example, in a search on the Green Party convention, we typed *sports* in the "But NOT" field under subject searching in order to eliminate articles about the *Green* Bay Packers in the National Football *Conference*. Subjects are usually very broad, corresponding to the categories given in the headlines of the paper *Facts On File*, not in its index. An "expert" searching system enables users to save their search queries, display them as a numbered "Query History List," and combine set numbers in more complex searches.

An index feature offered by *Facts On File* is not as valuable as free-text searching. The index is a hierarchical list of 300,000 "headings, subheadings, and article descriptions." When we searched for index entries about the Exxon *Valdez*, two articles plus cross-references to *Alaska—Exxon* and *Exxon Corp.* were listed. One of the articles turned out to be about an unrelated subject (the death of Nikolaas Tinbergen, a British zoologist). A free-text search of [Exxon Valdez] retrieved 41 items.

When articles are displayed, many of them contain highlighted *see* references; *Facts On File's* hypertext capability allows users to move directly to the referenced article by moving the cursor to the cross-reference and pressing ENTER.

As with the earlier version of *Facts On File News Digest* CD-ROM, the maps are the least attractive feature. The 300 general and specialized maps are retrieved by highlighting the name of a region or country mentioned in an article and selecting the maps database. An alphabetical list of maps can also be browsed. When the Board tried to display certain maps (e.g., Antarctica, California, Idaho), the system displayed the message "no map to display." Maps lack clarity and detail. When we selected the map of counties and county seats in Arkansas, *Facts On File* displayed only the northwest corner of the state. Even at this scale, the names of county seats could not be read. The map "Alaska—Glaciers and Icefields" included shaded and numbered features (presumably glaciers and icefields), but there was no key to the numbers. Displaying a full map took about 30–45 seconds on our IBM PS/2. The user must leave the article to view the maps, so the map cannot be consulted while reading the article. Facts On File might better serve users by providing a paper atlas, similar to that in the print version of *Facts On File*, with each CD-ROM package.

Printing with *Facts On File News Digest* CD-ROM is flexible. Users can print out the entire text of an article, a single screen, or sections of an article that they have marked. They can also download to a floppy disk.

DOCUMENTATION. The *Facts On File* "welcome" screen offers users the option of running a tutorial, which takes about an hour to complete. Online context-sensitive help can be obtained anywhere in the search process. It guides new users through the search process, requiring some response from them. A 74-page manual and a reference card that can be attached to a monitor or keyboard come with the CD. The manual is well organized, clear, and concise. It includes examples of search screens, a good description of Boolean operators, a list of stop words, a troubleshooting guide, and a glossary. Toll-free telephone customer support is available during weekday business hours.

CONCLUSION. *Facts On File News Digest* CD-ROM is the only CD-ROM system that offers the full text of news summaries. Large public and academic libraries that have newspaper indexes on CD-ROM and the newspapers themselves on microfilm, or full-text newspapers on CD-ROM, may want to skip *Facts On File*, especially if they have a subscription to the paper copy, which is more frequently updated. However, *Facts On File* would be a good purchase for a library with a limited budget and no electronic access to news files. As library users become more comfortable with electronic databases and less willing to search several years' worth of indexes to find information, demand for such sources as *Facts On File News Digest* CD-ROM will increase. Improvements in searching and printing features make this CD-ROM a solid purchase for high school, public, and small academic libraries.

The New Standard Jewish Encyclopedia. 7th ed. Ed. by Geoffrey Wigoder. Facts On File, 1992. 1,001p. illus. hardcover $59.95 (0-8160-2690-4).
909'.04924 Jews—Encyclopedias [CIP] 92-18351

Many of the 8,000 articles in this one-volume encyclopedia have been updated since the last edition in 1977, and several new ones have been added (e.g., a biography of Saul Bellow). It covers all aspects of Jewish life, including religion, traditions, culture, events, places, and people important in Jewish history. A significant proportion of the entries are biographical (non-Jews are indicated by an asterisk). The unsigned articles were written by Judaic scholars and staff members of other Judaic reference works.

Articles range in length from two sentences to three pages; cross-references are noted in the body of an article in small capital letters. Some of the shorter articles will leave users wanting more information, but there are no references to further reading. The newly revised articles are up-to-date and include information about the Commonwealth of Independent States (USSR is included as a cross-reference only) and Yitzhak Rabin's reelection. Statistics on the number of Jews in countries and U.S. cities have been updated. The entry *Aliyyah* has been updated with statistics on immigration of Jews to Israel through 1991. Many of the articles are accompanied by black-and-white photographs or drawings. Only a handful are new to this edition. Some photographs are dated, for instance, a portrait of Leonard Bernstein and a photograph of Tel Aviv from the air. This edition has about 1,000 fewer pages than the last one. The publisher seems to have accomplished this by using narrower margins on pages; a significant amount of information has not been dropped.

Editor Wigoder is a prolific writer on Jewish topics. He also edited the *Encyclopedia of Judaism* [RBB Mr 1 90], which concentrates on religion without trying to cover all aspects of Jewish life. Its illustrations are much more attractive. High school, college, and public libraries that need a quick-reference source for a variety of Jewish topics will want *The New Standard Jewish Encyclopedia* for their collections. It may even be used for answers to questions that do not deal directly with Judaism.

Statesmen Who Changed the World: A Bio-Bibliographical Dictionary of Diplomacy. Ed. by Frank W. Thackeray and John E. Findling. Greenwood, 1993. 696p. bibliog. index. hardcover $85 (0-313-27380-4).
909.08'0922 [B] Statesmen—Biography ‖ Diplomats—Biography ‖ Kings and rulers—Biography ‖ World politics—Bio-bibliography [CIP] 92-14616

This work comprises a set of essays on more than 60 heads of state or diplomats who have made a mark upon Western history since the fifteenth century. In this project, the editors have enlisted contributions from nearly that many American-based historians. Each statesman (only two are women) is sketched biographically, with emphasis given to the figure's role in international affairs. Each sketch is coupled with a bibliographic essay (or annotated bibliography) in which the contributor highlights major archival and secondary sources. A selective bibliography of works by and about each subject closes each entry.

Invariably, the bibliographic segments are more useful than the biographical sketches. The latter do not seem to fill a void, especially for such well known figures as Napoleon I, Metternich, de Gaulle, and Franklin Delano Roosevelt. However, the essays summarizing contemporary scholarship serve as useful pathfinders to current thought on these figures. Further, the bibliographies serve the librarian as checklists with which to assess a library's holdings.

Entries for the personages in the dictionary are arranged alphabetically. Historically, they range from Machiavelli, Charles V, Phillip II, and Elizabeth I to the only living entrants: Castro, Gorbachev, Nixon, and Kissinger (the last two are paired in one entry). Seventeen of those profiled are Americans: from Franklin, Jefferson, and Madison through J. William Fulbright. Many of these statesmen are unfamiliar names—Adam Czartoryski, Carlos Tabor, William II, Alexander Pavlovich I, and Luis María Drago—and doubtless might not have been selected in another editor's compilation. One might also note that the significance of events in the Far East and Africa seems underplayed in this volume, perhaps understandable in a work that focuses upon Western statesmen.

Five appendixes conclude this work. Appendix A lists other historical figures mentioned in the main entries; appendix B is a list of conferences and treaties similarly mentioned; appendix C defines major diplomatic, political, and military events; appendix D names important organizations and terms; and appendix E gives chronologies of heads of states for Austria, the British Isles, France, Germany, the Holy Roman Empire, Italy, Russia/USSR, Spain, and the U.S.

Most of the persons covered in this work are also profiled in various sets of *Great Lives from History* (American series [RBB O 15 87], British and Commonwealth series [RBB Je 1 88], and Renaissance to 1900 series). *Books for College Libraries* and the *Reader's Advisor* serve much of the same advisory function as this dictionary for most of the figures as well. Smaller academic and public libraries owning these tools might forego purchase of this new work. Still, the coverage of *Statesmen Who Changed the World* is comprehensive, and the treatments, on the whole, are balanced. Its key strength may lie in its singling out for attention lesser-known statesmen for beginning historians and other scholars. It is an appropriate selection for university and other research libraries.

The Cold War, 1945–1991. 3v. Ed. by Benjamin Frankel. Gale, 1992. bibliog. illus. index. hardcover $250 (0-8103-8927-4).
909.82 Cold War ‖ World politics—1945– [OCLC] 92-30486

With *The Cold War, 1945–1991*, Gale has pulled off a coup. The Cold War has dominated the international scene in the last half of the twentieth century but has never received quite the attention in reference sources given here. Due to the threat of mutual annihilation by nuclear weapons, the grim rivalry of two vast political, economic, and social systems shaped world events for more than 40 years following World War II. With the recent collapse of the Soviet Union and its Eastern European satellites, a review of the period, although too early to be definitive, is certainly in order. This encyclopedic guide seeks to illuminate the Cold War by its focus upon Western and communist country participants in the struggle and by an analysis of the major themes and events that marked the era.

Volume 1 depicts 149 important figures in the U.S. and Western Europe involved in some manner in this conflict. Ranging in length from two to twelve pages, the sketches are uniformly well written. The subjects are familiar (e.g., Acheson, Dulles, DeGaulle, Kennedy, and Thatcher) and less so (e.g., Rab Butler, Dick Clark, Robert W. Komer, Richard Perle, and Albert J. Wohlsetter). Military, scholarly, and journalistic figures are mingled alphabetically with political luminaries. Each biography emphasizes the entrant's role in the Cold War and includes lists of recommended works by and about the person along with a few selected general works. Related entries in other volumes are noted. Each of the entries' authors is named, but unfortunately no further infomation is given about them.

Volume 2 similarly sketches 134 important leaders from the Soviet Union, Eastern Europe, China, and Third World nations who comprised the communist-world counterparts of those featured in volume 1. A few foreign names appear as contributors to volume 2, but most appear to be researchers based in the West (on the premise that the winners of a war write its history). Both volumes 1 and 2 have black-and-white photographs for selected entries and their own indexes.

Volume 3, subtitled *Resources: Chronology, History, Concepts, Events, Organizations, Bibliography, Archives,* examines "the major events and themes that dominated the period." Among the concepts, events, organizations covered in this volume are Brinkmanship, Cuban Missile Crisis, and National Security Council. Also included are a 120-page narrative history of the conflict written by general editor Frankel and a cumulative index to all three volumes in the set. The work also has black-and-white photographs.

The set should prove of value to all who seek information on the events and the participants most deeply engaged on the postwar international stage. The entries are essentially factual and objective in tone. Editor Frankel is an acknowledged expert on national security issues. He has done a superb job of overseeing the project. The work's cachet is further enhanced by a concise foreword written by Townsend Hoopes, a Defense Department official in the Truman and Johnson administrations and himself a scholar. The entire set is intended to serve as a one-stop reference resource for students ranging from high school age to Ph.D. candidates, as well as for interested citizens. Scholars will eventually produce more definitive treatments of the Cold War, aided by the availability of information only now being declassified and by the benefits of a more remote stance from which to assay those anxious decades. But for the time being, this set will prove useful in academic and public libraries.

Great Events. 10v. Salem Press, 1992. illus. indexes. hardcover $250 (0-89356-796-5).
909.82 History, Modern—20th century—Juvenile literature [CIP] 92-28671

Aimed at students in the middle grades and up, *Great Events* is the second set in the Twentieth Century series (see RBB [Jl 92] for a review of *Great Athletes*, the first set in the series). Subsequent publications are planned that will address milestones of science and technology and of the arts and popular culture.

In this new title, the major political, economic, and social developments of the last 100 years are presented in 472 well-written, easy-to-understand articles. The material is organized chronologically, with the first half-century covered in four volumes and the second half in six. The selections are well chosen and wide ranging. In the first volume alone, covering the years 1900–16, events include the Boxer Rebellion in China, the U.S. miners' strikes, the Panama Canal, the independence of Norway, the Second Hague Peace Conference, the Belgian annexation of the Congo, dollar diplomacy, the establishment of the U.S. Health Service, the establishment of the income tax in the U.S., the Mexican Revolution, the assassination of Archduke Ferdinand, the Balkan Wars, and Henry Ford's development of the assembly line.

In the choice of great events to be profiled, the publisher's aim was to chronicle the "movements that have affected the course of civilization at the level of nations as well as of individuals." The broad scope of the first volume continues throughout the set, and the reader can learn of important developments over the last century in civil rights, social reform, independence movements, international relations, and national politics, as well as economic successes and problems. While much attention is given to U.S. history, the work profiles important events in every corner of the globe. The developments profiled are as recent as 1992, as demonstrated in the three articles that conclude volume 10: "The War in El Salvador Ends," "Economic Woes Plague the Commonwealth of Independent States," and "The European Economic Community Attempts to Create a Single Market."

The format is consistent throughout the set. Most articles are three pages in length, including a clearly reproduced black-and-white illustration. The event is named in a newspaper-banner headline, and a double-column gray box below the title provides a one-sentence synopsis of the event. At the beginning of the article is a ready-reference box, in gray shading, that announces the what, when, where, and who of the event. The text of each entry is divided into three parts: a description of the event itself, its background, and its consequences and importance.

In the back matter of each of the 10 volumes are a chronological list of events and four indexes covering the material in the entire set. Included are an alphabetical keyword index and a personal-name index. The category index uses broad topics such as *Civil Rights*, *Economics and Economic Reform*, *International Relations*, and *Military Conflicts*, with *see* and *see also* references. The geographic index is as current as possible; for example, it uses a *see also* reference from *Commonwealth of Independent States* to *Soviet Union*. The lack of a general index does not appear to be a problem since the event can be accessed easily through the separate indexes. Also, in volume 10, an additional feature is a "Time Line" that provides, in four columns, the date, the event, the category, and the country or the region.

Great Events is tailor-made for students from grade 6 through high school. The information is concise and accurately presented in an interesting manner. Students will find it a good starting place for identification of historical and international topics. The publisher has fulfilled its promise of "a comprehensive overview of its topic in a format that combines texts and photographs to present subject matter that is both inviting to the eye and engaging to readers from the middle-school level on up." The set is recommended for middle and high school library media centers and juvenile reference collections of public libraries. Adult collections and community college libraries might also want to consider this very readable source with its coverage of topics having wide appeal and interest.

Culturgrams: The Nations around Us. 2v. By the David M. Kennedy Center for International Studies. Brigham Young Univ.; dist. by Garrett Park Press, 1992. maps. paper $40 (v.1: 0-912048-86-7; v.2: 0-912048-87-5).
909.82'8 Manners and customs || Intercultural communication [CIP] 90-49834

Begun in 1977, these "people maps" present the unique customs, beliefs, and traditions for a country's people in a four-page summary. Fifty-one countries in the Americas and Europe were covered in the first compilation of *Culturgrams* [RBB Ja 1 86]. This newest compendium profiles more than 100 countries, with volume 1 covering the Americas and Europe and volume 2 including many of the nations of Africa, Asia, and Oceania. The Kennedy Center for International Studies at Brigham Young University updates the existing profiles annually, prepares new ones, and sells them individually or in batches. The work under review is the bound compilation of all the currently available *Culturgrams*.

Each country summary includes details on how to visit in private homes, explaining gestures, customs, and courtesies. For example, showing the bottom of one's foot is derogatory in some traditions, so crossing one's legs is inappropriate in many Middle Eastern cultures. Information about business conditions, common languages, diets, holidays, and polite and impolite actions are complete enough to assist the reader in contacting people from the various countries. Also included for each nation are brief descriptions of the land and climate, history, government, economy, education, health, transportation, and communication. Profiles conclude with information for the traveler, the address of the country's embassy in the U.S., and a suggestion to "consult your local library" for more detailed information.

This work does not claim to produce country experts; it is intended as an introduction to each country and its people. Many other sources present more detailed textual and statistical information about the economies, governments, and demographics of various countries. The strengths of *Culturgrams* include its discussion of life-styles and its presentation of the differences among the cultures of the world in an easily understood manner. The work gives the reader a better understanding of the difficulties that a foreign visitor or student may have in adjusting to our culture, just as it provides U.S. natives with an introduction to customs that would be encountered when visiting other cultures or nations. This source is especially useful as a multicultural teaching aid in junior or senior high schools, as well as in colleges. The work provides practical and quick information for the teacher, traveler, overseas worker or developer, and libraries where patrons search for such knowledge. Although not covering all countries of the world, its affordability and possible uses recommend this new edition for public, school, and undergraduate collections.

The Traveler's Reading Guide: Ready-Made Reading Lists for the Armchair Traveler. Rev. ed. Ed. by Maggy Simony. Facts On File, 1993. 510p. index. hardcover. $50 (0-8160-2648-3).
016.91 Travel—Bibliography [OCLC] 92-8175

Inspired by an interest in armchair travel and convinced that learning about a geographic place enhances the travel experience, Simony compiled reading lists of guides and fiction and nonfiction works about various locales around the world. These annotated bibliographies, with the same title as this new edition, were first published in three paperback volumes between 1981 and 1984 [RBB Mr 1 83; N 15 83; N 1 84]; they were subsequently issued in a single-volume hardcover edition (for a synopsis of the 1987 book, see the omnibus review of travel guides in RBB [Ja 1 88]). *The Traveler's Reading Guide* became a standard reference and a popular bibliography "intended for the reasonably literate traveler."

The new edition maintains the same purpose and arrangement as the earlier version. It is organized into seven parts arranged by continent, and these are further subdivided by country and, in some cases, by state or province. The reading lists for each area are subdivided by type of material. Short one- to three-sentence annotations accompany the entries, sometimes including quotations from book-reviewing media. The listings are entered under authors' names and typically provide information about other travel writings of the person or earlier editions of the work. The number of listings for each area varies, and the preface indicates that this reflects the trends in the volume of publishing covering that particular destination.

Appendixes give additional guidebook information sources, offer reading lists about travel literature, note collections of travel writings, and contain a list of authors of novels with English settings. An author index concludes the volume. The guide excludes outdoor-travel books and guides, biographies and autobiographies, mysteries, classic literature, privately published materials, local histories, and works published by tourist organizations.

The 1993 edition is billed as "completely revised and updated," although the only sentence addressing specific changes in the new edition states that "there are more series guides listed, fewer annotated guidebooks and no travel articles." However, in the listings for most destinations, titles from the late 1980s and early 1990s predominate, indicating that the book is composed of substantially new material.

For instance, the Japan section begins with a list of 15 guidebooks from various series; these citations do not provide dates of publication. Annotations are included for an additional seven separately published guidebooks: two are dated 1990, three are from 1985–89, and the remaining two are from 1980–84. Of the 30 entries in the two sections listing background readings (24 titles) and history (6 titles), nine items are dated 1990 or 1991, 12 were published 1985–89, seven are dated 1980–84, and two entries are for older, classic works. A broader time span appears in the section for novels: of the 27 entries, 10 are for authors writing in the 1950s to 1970s; three are from the early 1980s, while 14 are from 1985–90. Based on a sampling of other places listed in the book, this chronological pattern is typical, even though most destinations do not have as many listings as Japan. Although the entries are relatively current, readers will not find lists for some newly independent countries (e.g., works are entered under "Soviet Union"), and no words of caution are included about travel to such currently dangerous locales as the former Yugoslavia.

As with the earlier edition of *The Traveler's Reading Guide*, this book enables the user to identify available handbooks for many countries, including those like Sardinia that are not covered by the standard series, and compiles in one volume citations to materials that enable the reader to capture the flavor of the culture and history of the destination. The guide is a recommended purchase for collections of travel materials, but its ready-made reading lists will need to be supplemented with current travel articles and the purchase of current guidebooks.

Who Was Who in World Exploration. By Carl Waldman and Alan Wexler. Facts On File, 1992. 712p. bibliog. illus. maps. hardcover $65 (0-8160-2172-4).
910'.922 [B] Explorers—Biography—Dictionaires [CIP] 92-21277

The Columbian quincentenary has stimulated the examination of world exploration. This volume helps the reader identify more than 800 figures throughout history. The term *explorer* is used very broadly: numerous artists and writers such as Audubon and T. E. Lawrence are listed along with more traditional figures such as Magellan. No specific criteria for inclusion are mentioned.

Entries are in A–Z order by name and vary in length from a couple sentences to several pages. A tag at the beginning of the entry characterizes the person; for instance, Kit Carson is described as an "American frontiersman and guide in the West." The dates of the person's important trips are listed before the essay that describes his or her life and significant achievements. Figures are usually presented in a positive light, and controversial issues are few. Cross-references are used for variant forms of names, and names within entries printed in small capital letters indicate a separate entry for that person. About 100 black-and-white reproductions of prints and photographs are scattered throughout the book.

In an appendix, the explorers are listed by the geographic area they explored. This partially makes up for the lack of an index. However, readers looking for the explorer of a specific country will have to look up all the names listed under the region in which that country is located. Line drawings of the continents and present-day countries comprise another appendix. The routes of important explorations are not shown on these maps, so their value is questionable. An extensive bibliography arranged by geographic area concludes the book.

This volume resembles Macmillan's *World Explorers and Discoverers* [RBB Je 1 92]. That volume uses a narrower definition of the term *explorer* and has only 300 entries, but they are longer and deal more with the controversial nature of exploration. It also includes some portraits and extensive indexes. Both books have surprising omissions: Macmillan doesn't include Mercator, and Facts On File omits Osa and Martin Johnson. Most of the extra coverage in the Facts On File book is of Western pioneers such as Marcus Whitman and Brigham Young who usually aren't thought of as explorers.

Libraries needing comprehensive coverage of this topic will want both these books; either one is satisfactory for most libraries, though the Macmillan book provides more depth of coverage.

The World Book Encyclopedia of People and Places. 6v. World Book, 1992. charts. illus. index. maps. hardcover $149.50 (0-7166-3492-9).
910.3 Geography—Encyclopedias [OCLC] 91-68041

A joint project of World Book and British and German publishing firms, this set is not a spin off of *World Book Encyclopedia* but is an entirely new work for upper elementary and middle school children. Entries for 215 countries and territories are arranged alphabetically from *Afghanistan* to *Zimbabwe*. They range from two pages each for *Benin*, *Bermuda*, and *Brunei* to 46 for *United States*, 38 for *China*, and 40 for *Germany*. There is the two-page entry *Commonwealth of Independent States* and separate entries for its 11 independent countries. Most of these are also just two pages; *Russia* is 22. Coverage of the world's nations seems based on their size and relative importance. Unlike many sets for children, European countries are not emphasized at the expense of the rest of the world. The entry *Mexico*, for instance, is longer than *Belgium*.

Coverage is standardized, but there is provision for special features when appropriate. Fact boxes for each country give statistics; describe the form of government; list exports, imports, and trading partners; and show health, employment, and education data graphically. A small four-color map is also provided. Larger countries are given two-page spreads on history (sometimes divided by period), environment (really geographic information), the people and the economy, and often the arts or wildlife. For the largest nations, there is usually a spread on an important city. Special features accompany longer entries. For instance, in *Mexico* there are spreads on tourism and forces of nature (earthquakes and volcanoes), in *New Zealand* on the Maoris, and in *Burma* on festivals. Coverage is current as of early 1992. *Yugoslavia* acknowledges the breakup of that nation.

Some 2,000 attractive color photographs illustrate important facts about the countries, not just the picturesque, and have appropriate captions. Some entries have thematic or locator maps or time lines. About half of each page is taken up with illustrations; the other half is text set in a relatively large typeface that will be easy for children to read. The detailed index in volume 6 notes illustrations and maps. While many of the index entries are for specific places or people, general subject entries help readers trace a topic throughout the set. For example, under *pollution* are almost 20 references: in Australia, in Canada, etc.

There are many series for children that cover individual countries. They are usually written to a standard length, regardless of the importance of the nation, and do not cover as many countries as this new set. The *World Book Encyclopedia of People and Places* is highly recommended for school and public libraries for its attractive balanced coverage of the world's nations.—*Sandy Whiteley*

Explorers and Discoverers of the World. Ed. by Daniel B. Baker. Gale, 1993. 675p. illus. indexes. maps. hardcover $59.95 (0-8103-5421-7).
910.92 Explorers—Biography ‖ Discoverers in geography [OCLC] 92-055094

Many libraries, especially after the 1992 recognition of Columbus' voyages, might pass up new titles about explorers, but here is a biographical source that deserves consideration. More than 300 explorers and discoverers are profiled, ranging from Pytheas and Nearchus of ancient Greece to Will Steger, who was part of an international team that crossed Antarctica in 1990. Biographies range in length from one-half to three pages, many with portraits or maps, and all with bibliographies.

Selection criteria in the preface make it clear that "one aim of this book was to include women and non-Europeans." Comparing this volume with other standard titles on explorers shows that this aim was accomplished. Few other sources for nonspecialists even mention Isabella Bird, Cheng Ho, Ibn Battuta, or Nain Singh. This book, written for high school students and general readers, not only provides personal information where available (warts and all), but also puts discoveries into historical perspective.

The well-written introduction outlines "exploration as a reflection of society" and explains that the book's goal is to objectively present "what the explorers did, with a minimum of judgment on the consequences." Information on Arab, Australian, and Asian explorers will be especially welcome for students' geography reports in junior high and up, and the many cross-references make it easy to compare exploration in a particular region. For example, John Byron and Louis Antoine de Bougainville established claims on the Falkland Islands in 1765. Richard Burton, John Hanning Speke, Ludwig Krapf, and Samuel and Florence Baker all looked for the Nile's source. Several indexes provide access by area explored, time period, and explorer's place of birth. A comprehensive index concludes the text.

Remarkable in a work of this type is what interesting reading it makes. People may actually browse this for its unusual stories. Imagine reading how Willem Barents' 1596–97 winter quarters were discovered, undisturbed, 274 years after his voyage, or about the Canadian Susie Carson Rijnhart whose year-old baby died traveling with her through Tibet. Unfortunately, this work is not perfect. There are a few spelling errors, and no cross-references for maiden names. The maps at the beginning of the book are not particularly helpful, perhaps because too many modern place-names are crowded in. These shortcomings are minor, however, compared with the valuable features of Explorers and Discoverers of the World. High school and public libraries that don't own World Explorers and Discoverers [RBB Je 1 92] or Who Was Who in World Exploration [RBB O 15 92] will want to purchase.

The Atlas of the Ancient World: Charting the Great Civilizations of the Past. By Margaret Oliphant. Simon & Schuster, 1992. 220p. bibliog. illus. index. maps. hardcover $40 (0-671-75103-4).
911 Geography, Ancient—Maps [CIP] 91-38075

This lavishly illustrated book treats nine ancient civilizations, beginning in Mesopotamia, Egypt, and Persia and culminating in the Roman world. Other chapters are devoted to China, India, and the Americas. The chapter "Greece and the Aegean," for example, discusses the Minoans, the Mycenaeans, the rise of the city-state, Alexander the Great, and the Hellenistic world. Boxed inserts cover topics such as famous archaeologists, the Gods of Olympus, the Elgin Marbles, and drama.

Each civilization is presented in text, attractive photographs and drawings (many in color), site plans, and maps. The latter are minimal, however, and this atlas will get more use in the circulating collections of libraries than as a reference book. The chronology and bibliography at the end of this handsome book are both arranged by civilization. —Sandy Whiteley

Biographical Dictionary of Geography. By Robert P. Larkin and Gary L. Peters. Greenwood, 1993. 384p. bibliog. index. hardcover $69.50 (0-313-27622-6).
910.922 Geographers—Biography—Dictionaries [CIP] 92-18364

Starting in 625 B.C. with Thales of Miletus and continuing to David W. Harvey, born in 1935, this collection of brief biographical sketches covers more than 70 individuals who have contributed to the evolution of the modern discipline of geography. The editors chose to profile those who represent a cross section of the subfields within the discipline, ancient to modern. Larkin and Peters are both geography professors, the former at the University of Colorado, the latter at California State University. They have also published Dictionary of Concepts in Human Geography (Greenwood, 1983) and Dictionary of Concepts in Physical Geography [RBB N 1 88].

Along with figures familiarly associated with geography, such as Amundsen, Darwin, and Copernicus, this work also covers contributions to the discipline by such persons as John Muir, Aristotle, and Immanuel Kant. While the majority of biographees are deceased, a dozen profiles are included for living individuals. The entries, presented alphabetically by surname, are typically two pages of text followed by a selected bibliography of writings by the individual, a chronology of important events in the person's life, and citations to other biographical references. The narrative portion focuses on how the individual's career contributed to the field. For instance, for Alexander von Humboldt, the text concludes, "What has not been so generally recognized among English-speaking scholars is Humboldt's insistence on the areal associations of diverse categories of physical and human phenomena. This is his contribution to geographic knowledge and the discipline of geography." Asterisks are used to indicate internal cross-referencing among geographers.

The appendix includes an arrangement of names by nationality and a chronological list. Seventy-five percent of the biographies are listed under the U.S., U.K., or Germany. The remainder represent such nations as Turkey, China, and Greece. The chronological list is particularly useful because it allows the reader to get a quick sense of how an individual fit into the overall development of ideas in the field. Following the appendix is a brief subject index.

Many of the people included in this new title will be found in such standard sources as Dictionary of Scientific Biography and Biographical Encyclopedia of Scientists. However, the Biographical Dictionary of Geography is unique because of its focus on contributions to the discipline of geography and the connections it makes among the work of scientists in this field. It is a recommended purchase for academic libraries supporting research in geography.

The Children's Atlas of Exploration: Follow in the Footsteps of the Great Explorers. By Antony Mason. Millbrook, 1993. 96p. illus. index. hardcover $18.90 (1-56294-256-5).
911 Discoveries in geography—Maps ‖ Voyages and travels—Maps ‖ Explorers—History—Maps [CIP] 92-28856

The Children's Atlas of People & Places: Travel the World and Visit People in Far-off Lands. By Jenny Wood. Millbrook, 1993. 96p. illus. index. hardcover $18.90 (1-56294-257-3).
912 Atlases [CIP] 92-28857

These attractive atlases were both prepared in Britain.

The Children's Atlas of People & Places is an oversize atlas for children in grades 2–6. It reflects current political changes as of its publication date. The atlas is divided up by continent and includes an introduction about the planet and sections on the poles, oceans, and the changing world. Maps usually cover more than half of each page, and scale is given in both miles and kilometers. Pages also have text and color photographs; each country's flag, capital, and population is listed to the side of each page. Essays in each of the sections discuss ever so briefly the role of the people, climate, and resources on that particular continent. Both place-names on maps and the text are indexed.

Coverage of Europe is quite extensive, taking up more than one-third of the 96 pages. The U.S. is presented in two parts: eastern and western, on two separate pages divided along the Mississippi, which may be confusing for a young researcher. This is an attractive, inexpensive resource similar to Rand McNally's Chidlren's World Atlas [RBB D 15 89] but more current. It is a worthwhile purchase for elementary school and public libraries.

The Children's Atlas of Exploration covers from 2000 B.C. through 1989 and has double-page spreads emphasizing text and pictures; the maps occupy one-half page or less. A brief introduction about explorers and exploring is followed by six sections: Europe, Asia, Africa, the Americas, the South Seas and Australia, and the "final frontier" (the oceans, poles, and space). A great deal of information is condensed in the brief essays. A time line highlighting landmarks of exploration can be found at the end of the volume prior to the index. Routes of explorers are shown on each map by color codes; however, scale is not provided, and the small maps give few clues for actual locations. Meriwether Lewis is mentioned briefly and the route of his expedition is shown on a map, but Clark is not mentioned at all.

This atlas falls short of its goal as a reference tool to provide young researchers with an understanding of exploration. Children will find the maps confusing and too small to grasp the actual distances traveled by the explorers. They would be better off going directly to an encyclopedia or resources on individual explorers, such as Milton Lomask's Great Lives: Exploration. For children grades 4–6, The Atlas of North American Exploration [RBB D 15 92] would be more useful for this part of the world.

The Atlas of North American Exploration: From the Norse Voyages to the Race to the Pole. By William H. Goetzmann and Glyndwr Williams. Prentice Hall, 1992. 222p. bibliog. illus. index. hardcover $40 (0-13-297128-3).
911.7 North America—Discovery and exploration—Maps ‖ Explorers—North America—History—Maps [CIP] 92-8573

This colorful atlas covers 500 years of exploration. In double-page spreads, it summarizes more than 80 quests and features maps used by the explorers as well as modern renditions.

Early "mythical" journeys from Europe begin the book. Then five parts chronicle early voyages to the North American continent, early settlements, frontier work, continental exploration, and northern trips. A selective bibliography and extensive index to both text and maps follow.

Four-color maps detail journeys and settlements and include points where significant events occurred. Sometimes a single explorer is featured; sometimes the route of a group of like explorers is traced. The reader needs to know geography, because scale is not given and the tight cropping of maps gives few contextual clues as to location. Text explains the significance of each voyage, and attractive illustrations are found on each page. While covering famous explorers like Drake and Lewis and Clark as well as such lesser-known men as Pierre and Paul Mallet, the authors do point out that other cultures explored and inhabited the continent prior to the Europeans.

The Times Atlas of World Exploration [RBB Ap 15 92] covers 3,000 years of exploration around the world and thus doesn't give as detailed information about North America. The Board has also reviewed several collections of biographies of explorers recently, but *The Atlas of North American Exploration* stresses the routes taken (as shown on maps) rather than biographical information on the explorers. It will be a useful, attractive addition to public, academic, and middle and high school libraries.

Atlas of the World. Oxford, 1992. 288p. charts. illus. index. hardcover $65 (0-19-520955-9).
912 Atlases [CIP] 92-14534

Oxford commissioned the internationally known cartographic firm of George Philip & Son to compile this splendid new world atlas. This company was one of the pioneers in the use of multicolored maps, and its expertise is clearly evident in the beautiful design here, especially in the 160-page section of maps showing all regions of the world. The topographic maps have as many as 14 shades of color to highlight their geography (e.g., "South America—West"). Color scales along the edge of the page denote the altitude of land areas in feet and meters. At the top of each map is a distance scale giving units in miles and kilometers. Small black-and-white insert maps show latitude and longitude. Excellent scale of size is most obvious in the coverage of island groups in the Southwest Pacific, Central America, and West Indies areas. Topography is clear, and map scales are appropriate so landmarks can be distinguished. Also included are a few political maps, primarily for continents.

While the world maps comprise the largest portion of this atlas, three additional parts add value. "World Statistics" is six pages of tables comparing countries, cities, distances, climates, and physical dimensions of geographic areas. Most units of measurement are given in both the metric and English systems. Throughout the text all monetary values are converted to U.S. dollars. The 48-page "Introduction to World Geography" surveys 23 topics, including the environment, agriculture, energy, trade, and health. These short essays are abundantly illustrated with pie and bar graphs, maps, charts, tables, and diagrams in a variety of colors. In the "City Maps" section, 66 major cities from each region of the world are represented, with maps drawn to the scale of 1:200,000. These are in four colors, show most major landmarks, and vary in size from two pages for New York City to one-quarter page for Istanbul.

This atlas lies flat for ease of reading and copying. The maps do not bleed into the gutter of the book but leave varying widths of margin. Some maps are placed horizontally within the text, necessitating the rotation of the atlas for reading by the user. All maps have letters and numbers running along the edge of the page to assist the user in locating specific areas from the references in the indexes. Each of the four sections of this work has its own pagination, and two separate indexes are included. Accompanying the city maps section is a 25-page index, listing more than 11,000 entries for names of places and such major landmarks as airports and universities. The index following the world maps section is 127 pages in length, four columns per page, totaling 62,000 entries for names of places and features. For each entry, both indexes provide latitude and longitude as well as the alphanumeric citations to the location on the most detailed map.

With the vast number and rapidity of changes taking place in the political world today, many publishers are having difficulty in keeping up with events. This atlas is no different. The many changes in the Commonwealth of Independent States and Germany are all noted. The recent changes in Czechoslovakia and Ethiopia obviously occurred past the publication deadline. Some of the changes in Yugoslavia are noted. Despite these forgivable flaws, this is still one of the most current atlases available today. For a moderately priced atlas, this work has extensive indexing. Its well-designed format and superior use of map colors make Oxford's *Atlas of the World* an appropriate selection for junior and senior high schools as well as public and academic libraries.

Hammond Atlas of the World. Hammond, 1992. 303p. illus. index. tables. $65 (0-8437-1175-2).
912 Atlases [CIP] 92-675635

The maps in this new atlas have been computer generated from a digital cartographic database developed by Hammond over the last several years. The core "Maps of the World" section consists of 160 pages (measuring 10¾ inches by 14 inches and printed on acid-free stock) arranged by continent. More than 60 of the maps are double pages, and all are printed upright, with north at the top of the page. Since the atlas opens flat, these maps display across the two pages, without gutter margins. Comparable scales are employed; the regions of North America are covered in a set of 11 double-page maps at 1:3M (million). The maps for Africa and Latin America are mainly 1:6M. A two-page political map of the world opens the core section, followed by political maps of the continents, with countries appearing in muted, contrasting, pastel shades. For the maps of the continents, a new projection developed by Hammond has been employed (called "optimal conformal") to reduce distortion to the minimum. The physical-political maps, constituting the bulk of the core atlas section, indicate relief by brown shading; political boundaries are clearly indicated and marked. A series of muted hues designates special land uses such as national parks, urbanized areas, or native reserves. Main highways appear in red, and railroads in gray. The map margins include a small locator map; projection and scale, given as both a fraction and by a mile and kilometer bar; the set of symbols used to designate cities in different size classes; and a brief descriptive text. Capital cities are underlined, and select cultural landmarks are indicated by small red squares. A proprietary, computerized type-placement program has been employed to position place-names and point names. The last five pages of the core section are devoted to maps of eight U.S. metropolitan areas at 1:1M; here and elsewhere throughout the core section are small inset maps of metropolitan areas at larger scales, indicated by a bar but not as a fraction.

Several other sections supplement the core set of maps. Thirteen physical maps of the continents are actual photographs of three-dimensional models and depict the relief of the ocean floor as well as the land masses. An introductory section contains attractively illustrated discussions of the evolution of cartography and map projections and a user's guide to the atlas. The section "Global Relationships" presents basic information by means of thematic maps and other well-designed graphics on such topics as the environment, population, languages, religions, standards of living, economic resources, and climate. Two sections give tabular information: a quick-reference listing of countries, states, and territories, giving area, population, capital city, and atlas page and grid reference; and a set of tables giving data on major natural features of the world, such as principal mountains and lakes, and population of major cities, by country. U.S. population figures are 1990 census totals or more recent estimates.

A 115,000-entry name index refers by atlas page and alphanumeric grid reference (in red) to the largest scale map on which the name occurs. This red reference column is placed, somewhat misleadingly, immediately to the left of the associated name column, contrary to the reader's natural tendency to refer to the red column to the right. In an unusual typographical error, Mount Godwin-Austen is incorrectly spelled in parentheses alongside the index entry K2 but appears correctly in its own spot in the G listings. The front and back endpapers contain, respectively, a world locator map guide to the atlas and a world time-zone map. The atlas reflects recent changes in the former Soviet Union, Czechoslovakia, and Yugoslavia.

The Pentagram Design group implemented the overall graphic

look of the atlas and has achieved a high standard of clarity and visual appeal. Utilizing advanced technology and other innovations and a fresh and unified design conception, Hammond has produced a superb world atlas. It is balanced and very current in its geographic coverage, employs comparable map scales, and is legible and attractive to the eye. The supplementary material is judiciously selected and concisely and beautifully presented. The digital cartographic database Hammond has developed will enable it to generate new map and atlas products expeditiously. The system's first product, this outstanding general world atlas, is a landmark in U.S. atlas publishing and is a highly recommended purchase.

The New York Times Atlas of the World. 3d rev. concise ed. Times Books, 1992. 244p. illus. index. hardcover $75 (0-8129-2076-7).
912 Atlases [CIP] 92-53668

The New York Times Atlas of the World. New family ed. Times Books, 1992. 156p. charts. index. hardcover $37.50 (0-8129-2075-9).
912 Atlases [CIP] 92-53666

National Geographic Atlas of the World. Rev. 6th ed. National Geographic Society, 1992. 136p. illus. index. hardcover $89 (0-87044-834-X); paper $73 (0-87044-915-X).
912 Atlases [CIP] 92-27845

The political face of the world has undergone considerable upheaval since the publication of the "World Atlas Survey" [RBB D 1 90]. The demand for an atlas that reflects the way the world looks today—never mind tomorrow—is a publisher's nightmare during this time of turmoil and change. We are now seeing the newest wave of atlas revisions. In recent months RBB has reviewed the Hammond Atlas of the World [RBB Ja 15 93], Today's World [RBB F 1 93], and Atlas of the World [RBB F 15 93]. This review will look at three additional atlases.

The British cartographic firm of John C. Bartholomew & Son prepared the ninth comprehensive edition of The Times Atlas of the World, which is the basis for the maps contained in the two versions of The New York Times Atlas of the World under review here. The third revised concise edition, originally published in Great Britain as The Times Atlas of the World (concise 6th ed., 1992), is a well-made, large-format, general world atlas. Its layout is similar to the revised edition of 1988 [RBB D 1 90], but it reflects the numerous political changes that have occurred in recent years. All former Soviet republics, Slovenia, Bosnia-Herzegovina, and Croatia are shown as independent nations. A united Germany and a united Yemen are indicated. New settlements in Israel and the West Bank are listed. The revision of name forms and spelling occurs throughout, especially in the former Soviet republics and Eastern Europe.

The atlas uses four basic scales (1:12M, 1:6M, 1:3M, and 1:1M), with smaller scales for maps of the oceans, the poles, and the hemispheres (e.g., 1:24M, 1:48M) and larger scales for cities (e.g., 1:300,000, 1:500,000). The coverage is balanced, with Europe and North America getting a slight edge in the 146 pages of maps. Most of the maps are physical maps and cover two pages. The atlas begins with 44 pages of introductory material (e.g., geographic comparisons, map projections, and a world view/distribution of climate, energy, vegetation, and food), and it concludes with a "completely revised 100,000-entry index."

The New York Times Atlas of the World, new family edition, offers less extensive coverage than the third revised edition discussed above. The maps are not as detailed, and, generally, the principal scales are smaller (e.g., 1:5M, 1:7.5M, 1:10M, and 1:20M). The new family edition incorporates the same updates as the third revised edition, and it also contains geographic comparisons. However, the new family edition's states and territories section provides more information, albeit brief, for each country, including a picture of the nation's flag. The new family edition also provides a six-page geographic dictionary. Revised maps include a united Germany and a united Yemen and the former Soviet republics and Slovenia, Bosnia-Herzegovina, Croatia, and Namibia as independent nations.

The new version of the National Geographic Atlas of the World revises the sixth edition that was published in 1990—a year that atlas publishers wish to forget. The atlas begins with a series of thematic and world maps, accompanied by text, that cover such topics as food, minerals, climate, energy, and population. The back of the atlas includes a section that provides brief profiles, including flags, of U.S. states, Canadian provinces, and the nations of the world. Other sections focus on geographic comparisons, climate, and population of selected places around the world. The concluding item for the atlas is the 150,000-entry index, which includes 14,000 changes since the atlas was last published in 1990.

It is the middle portion of this atlas that people recognize and associate with the National Geographic Society. These colorful pages are arranged by continent, followed by sections on the oceans and the heavens. The coverage of each geographic area begins with a satellite image and a physical map of the continent or ocean floor. The information for populated continents includes text and maps on its geography and a series of maps of selected urban regions. The maps are two-page spreads that lie open and flat. A variety of scales are used throughout the atlas. The National Geographic Atlas contains the same basic changes as noted in the two versions of The New York Times Atlas.

All three works under review are as current and complete as can be any atlas with a 1992 publication date. The New York Times Atlas of the World, third revised concise edition, and the National Geographic Atlas of the World are more comprehensive and detailed than the new family edition of The New York Times Atlas. Either of these two larger works could be a small library's only atlas purchase if budgets are limited. However, most libraries will want to acquire both of these general-purpose atlases. Libraries with large atlas collections and circulating atlases will also want to consider the new family edition of The New York Times Atlas of the World.

Reader's Digest Atlas of the World. 3d ed. Reader's Digest; dist. by Random, 1992. 240p. illus. index. hardcover $39.95 (0-89577-264-7).
912 Atlases [CIP] 87-675016

The Times Atlas of the World: Ninth Comprehensive Edition. Times Books, 1992. [514p.]. index. hardcover $175 (0-8129-2077-5).
912 Atlases [CIP] 92-53672

Since December 1992, no fewer than seven world-atlas reviews have appeared in RBB. This is an obvious indication of the world's constantly changing face. Not since the end of World War II have the political boundaries of nations experienced such a transformation. This review looks at two more world atlases, the Reader's Digest Atlas of the World and The Times Atlas of the World. The previous editions of both these atlases had the very recent imprint date of 1990 (see "World Atlas Survey" [RBB D 1 90]). In normal times, an atlas that is just two years old would still be considered current. Not so today.

The Reader's Digest Atlas of the World consists of maps from the New International Atlas, which is published by Rand McNally. Almost half of the maps cover two pages. The atlas emphasizes North America, Europe, and Asia, in that order, with Africa, South America, and Australia all tied for fourth place. Each continent begins with an environments map that shows urbanized areas and nine different land types (e.g., cropland, forest, swamp, tundra). The atlas uses a limited number of scales: continent maps are 1:24 million, and regional maps are primarily 1:3M, 1:6M, and 1:12M. This consistency makes comparisons from one region to another very easy. The atlas reflects the recent political changes of the world: united Germany and Yemen, independent Namibia, and former Soviet republics as independent nations. However, Yugoslavia is still shown as one country.

The introductory section, "A World of Wonders," consists of 30 two-page profiles that cover a variety of topics on the solar system, the oceans, evolution, the climate, and the physical earth. The atlas concludes with a 40,000-plus place-name index. The Reader's Digest Atlas of the World is not a substitute for The Times Atlas of the World or the National Geographic Atlas of the World [RBB Ap 15 93], nor does it claim to be. However, it is a very good atlas for its size and purpose. The Rand McNally maps are quality maps—clear and easy to read. It is an excellent and affordable atlas that will meet the needs of small libraries and will serve as an alternate atlas source in large libraries.

If atlases were compared with automobiles, The Times Atlas of the World would be a Rolls Royce. This is the most comprehensive world atlas currently available. It is a collaborative effort between the Times of London and the prestigious cartographic firm of Bartholomew and Son. This atlas is the basis for the new family edition and the third revised concise edition of the *New York Times Atlas of the World* [RBB Ap 15 93].

The atlas contains 129 double-page maps and uses a variety of map scales, with the majority falling between 1:1M and 1:5M. As is the case with most atlases, it has a European and U.S. emphasis, but all other parts of the world are adequately covered. Numerous large-scale (e.g., 1:75,000, 1:100,000, 1:250,00) city and island maps are located throughout the atlas. The maps reflect all of the political changes of recent years for Germany, Yemen, the former Soviet Union, and war-torn Yugoslavia (Slovenia, Croatia, Bosnia-Herzegovina). It also shows the boundary between the new nations of Slovakia and the Czech Republic. These are changes that everyone now expects to see in a current source, and the *Times Atlas* includes these and more.

The ninth edition contains extensive revisions of international boundaries, national administrative areas and divisions, roads and railways, and place-names and name forms. The 210,000 place-name index is the most comprehensive of any atlas. It has undergone a considerable revision and has been completely reset. The introductory part of the atlas contains a statistical guide to the states and territories of the world; an illustrated list of geographic comparisons (e.g., oceans, lakes, continents); sections on the universe and solar system, map projections, and earth sciences; and seven two-page physical maps of the world that cover different continents and hemispheres.

The Times Atlas of the World is an essential purchase for any medium to large public or academic library. Small libraries will also want to consider it, in spite of its price, because it is three sources in one: a mini-geographic-reference source (introductory material), a thorough gazetteer (place-name index), and a detailed, comprehensive world atlas.

Reader's Digest Bartholomew Illustrated Atlas of the World. Rev. ed. Reader's Digest Press; dist. by Random, 1992. 124p. illus. index. hardcover $22 (0-89577-422-4).
912 Atlases [OCLC]

The great virtue of this updated atlas is its recognition of the new nations created by the breakup of the Soviet Union. Both the political and physical maps show the former republics as countries. However, all the maps do not yet recognize the similar situation in Yugoslavia. The separate republics of that former nation are shown only on the physical map.

Introductory materials include profiles of each continent, including population and other statistics for selected countries on a particular continent. Unfortunately, neither the profile of Europe nor that of Asia includes information about the aforementioned new countries.

A continent-by-continent approach is used to lay out the various areas of the world. This results in maps of small scale that cannot contain a great amount of detail. The editors claim that cities and towns with populations as small as 10,000 are shown. This is the case with the maps of the U.S. and Russia, but smaller countries, such as Japan and Great Britain, do not have this kind of detail. The use of color on both political and physical maps is excellent and easy to interpret. The index of more than 30,000 place-names is fairly comprehensive for an atlas of this size, but it does not contain population figures.

Several new atlases will be published this fall, but this one can be recommended for school and public libraries where an inexpensive revised atlas is needed.

Today's World: A New World Atlas from the Cartographers of Rand McNally. Rand McNally, 1992. 192p. index. hardcover $24.95 (0-528-83500-9).
912 Atlases [CIP] 92-16250

Librarians who have been waiting for a reasonably priced atlas that includes all the recent changes in countries and boundaries around the world should order a copy of this large-format volume and keep their fingers crossed that no more changes will occur for a while. In this atlas, readers will find the united Germany, divided Soviet Union, and volatile former Yugoslavia, clearly shown with borders marked in bright colors. Special markings are provided for boundaries that are disputed and for those that are indefinite or undefined.

Maps appear in a continental sequence, beginning with Europe. Following the map of the entire continent, a series of more detailed maps show geographic subareas of the continent in sequence as pages are turned. Maps are clearly marked with topographic, political, and natural features (e.g., cities, roads, rivers, mountain ranges, deserts) as well as latitude and longitude. Size and style of print vary to show the political importance of cities and capitals. Alternate names of cities are given when appropriate (Moskva, Moscow), as are historical names (Volgograd, Stalingrad). The atlas includes a map of the world, a time-zone map, and maps of the Atlantic, Pacific, and Indian Oceans. The scale for each map is given, as are bars for measuring distances in both miles and kilometers. Instructions on using the atlas are clear, succinct, and well illustrated. The index, containing 69,000 names, is easy to use; each entry includes the name, the nature of the feature (peninsula, state, etc.), country, map reference key, and page number.

Today's World does an admirable job of portraying the countries of the world with current boundaries. Purchase of the book includes a "Rand McNally Guarantee" for a free, updated, world wall map should the maps in the atlas become outdated because of world changes before December 31, 1993. This atlas is appropriate for public, school, and academic libraries and for users from middle through graduate school.

Atlas of the Third World. 2d ed. Ed. by George Kurian. Facts On File, 1992. 384p. charts. index. hardcover $125 (0-8160-1930-4).
912'.19724 Natural resources—Developing countries—Maps ‖ Developing countries—Economic conditions—Maps ‖ Developing countries—Social conditions—Maps [CIP] 88-675259

The first edition of *Atlas of the Third World* [RBB Ag 84] contained more than 1,000 maps and statistical charts describing the economic, political, demographic, and geographic aspects of the world's developing countries. The second edition continues the purpose and format, updating some charts and maps, adding some, and dropping a few. The resulting work is larger, with 600 maps and more than 2,000 charts. Maps added in the second edition include "Third World in 1914" and "English in the Third World." There is more emphasis on environment, debt, agriculture, and the role of women. Although name changes are reflected, the list of countries included has changed little. Vietnam, excluded from the original work because of lack of information, is included in the new edition, bringing the total of country profiles to 81.

The arrangement is the same, with the first section organized thematically and covering such topics as population, industry, and defense. This is followed by the country-profiles section, arranged alphabetically by country name. In both editions, the maps are well spaced with adequate margins and not too much detail for map size. The new edition is more attractive, dropping the squared-off appearance of the maps in the first edition and making greater use of color. Another improvement is the inclusion of source citations in the thematic section. The introduction lists eight sources used to compile the country profiles, such as *International Financial Statistics*, 1990 and *Britannica World Data*, 1991.

Atlas of the Third World, second edition, is recommended for academic and large public libraries. Libraries that puchased the 1984 edition should consider acquiring the 1992 edition, both for updated material and for maps and charts not included in the original work. Libraries should consider retaining the original work because of the maps that were dropped and for the benefit of scholars who may want to compare the newer and older material.

The Young People's Atlas of the United States. By James Harrisson and Eleanor Van Zandt. Kingfisher Books, 1992. 128p. illus. index. hardcover $16.95 (1-85697-804-4).
912.73 U.S.—Maps [CIP] 92-53116

This book consists of double-page spreads showing the U.S., six regions of the country, and each individual state. Oversize pages emphasize text and pictures; the relief maps occupy one-half page or less. The maps show interstate highways, major rivers, large cities, and significant natural features. The distance scale of each map is given in miles and kilometers; no map projections are provided. A small relief map of the U.S. shows the featured state in red. State birds, trees, and flowers are pictured, and the fact box lists such items as capitol, area, population, statehood date, highest point, motto, and title of state song. State nicknames are used as running heads on the pages of the book.

A brief essay of two or three paragraphs in length discusses the state's location, history, economy, natural phenomena, and cities. Also included for each state are captioned pictures or drawings of persons, events, or features important to the area. For instance, the New Jersey entry highlights the Atlantic City boardwalk, the Delaware River, Bell Telephone Laboratories, the opossum, the Meadowlands, Batsto Mill, and Princeton University. The captioned features sometimes duplicate information provided in the main text. The index includes entries for the place-names from the maps, as well as for some of the information in the text.

This is an attractive, browsable source, with inviting page layouts that will appeal to students from the fifth grade up. Maps are easy to read because of the lack of detail. The authors are writers and editors, rather than geographers, and the text would be challenging for young readers. Much of the information typically available in atlases is not here, for example, maps of population, climate, economy, products, natural resources, or an overview of geography.

The Young People's Atlas is similar in format and price to both the Rand McNally Children's Atlas of the United States (1989) and the Doubleday Atlas of the United States of America (1990), although the title under review contains more information than Rand McNally, more pictures than Doubleday, and is written for a somewhat older audience than either of those. All the information in these sources can be found in encyclopedias, but school and public libraries needing an atlas for the middle grades and up that they can circulate will want to consider The Young People's Atlas.

Parks Directory of the United States. Ed. by Darren L. Smith. Omnigraphics, 1992. 525p. indexes. hardcover $85 (1-55888-765-2).
917.304 Parks—U.S.—Directories || Recreation areas—U.S.—Directories || Historic sites—U.S.—Directories || U.S.—Directories | Forests and forestry—U.S.—Directories [CIP] 91-45072

This comprehensive guide to our public parks is divided into three sections: national parks, state parks, and park-related organizations and agencies.

The first section provides descriptions of the 358 parks that comprise our National Park System, including the huge Katmai National Park and Preserve in Alaska, and the tiny (one-half acre) Federal Hall National Memorial on Wall Street in New York City. National battlefields, historic sites, lakeshores, monuments, scenic rivers, and other units are arranged alphabetically by name. Entries include address, telephone number, size, date authorized, entrance fee, facilities, activities, and special features. The descriptions indicate wheelchair accessibility of campgrounds and restrooms and, in some instances, suggest the relative comfort of same ("winterized cabins," "flush toilets," "outhouses").

The second section provides similar information about 3,324 park and recreation areas administered by state park agencies in the 50 states. Helpful information about the sites' locations (general directions, accessibility from major highways, distances from nearby towns) is included. If a state's park agency also administers forests, fish and wildlife areas, and historic sites, these are included. The address and telephone number of each state park division and its regional offices are provided at the beginning of each state chapter.

Part 3 lists national and regional offices of parks-related groups, such as the American Camping Association and the National Audubon Society, and agencies like the U.S. Fish and Wildlife Service. The address and telephone number of the travel and tourism office of each state are also listed.

A master index provides access to the parks by name. The classification index lists parks by category, such as National Military Park and State Recreational Area.

Future editions of this useful book would be enhanced by an index to the special features so that readers can identify "the largest all-masonry fortification in the Western world" (Fort Jefferson National Monument in Florida) or "the home of the daughter of an ex-house slave who became a bank president" (Maggie L. Walker National Historic Site in Virginia). Also useful would be a geographic index to the national parks and outline maps at the beginning of the state chapters to help locate lesser-known parks and to assist travelers planning park-related stops.

Public and academic libraries should consider this well-conceived and executed directory.

America's Top Rated Cities: A Statistical Handbook. v.1: Southern Region. Ed. by Rhoda Garoogian and others. Universal Reference Publications, 1355 W. Palmetto Park Rd., Ste. 315, Boca Raton, FL 33486, 1992. 279p. paper $29.95 (1-881220-01-X); $129.95 for 5v. set (1-881220-00-1).
917.5 Cities and towns Southern States Statistics [BKL] 92-80903

Statistical profiles of 15 southern cities are contained in this guide to "the best cities for business and living." The basis for this designation is that the cities have been cited as choice spots in various magazine surveys over the past three years. Excerpts from these surveys are included in the overview of each city. This volume is one of a five-volume set. The others cover western, central, eastern, and northeastern cities, with 10–12 cities in each volume.

This volume is arranged alphabetically by city from Atlanta to West Palm Beach and divided into two sections: business environment and living environment. Covered under business are such things as state finances, demographics, employment, taxes, commercial real estate, transportation, business headquarters, and hotels and convention centers. The living section includes cost of living, housing costs, utilities, health care, education, public safety, culture and recreation, media, climate, and air and water quality. In most cases, the city statistics are shown in relation to national figures. Statistics appear to be the most current available (many from the 1990 census), and sources are provided for each piece of data. A useful section of comparative statistics and a list of chambers of commerce follow the city entries.

All of the 15 cities appear in Places Rated Almanac, which covers the same information but approaches it in a different manner, using a mathematical scoring system to rank the cities in relation to nine factors. America's Top Rated Cities has the advantage of arrangement by city rather than rating factor, making it easier to access information. In addition, the comparative statistics chart is in actual numbers; for example, the tax rate is given in dollars rather than as a numerical score. Gale's four-volume Cities of the United States [RBB Ap 1 89] gives comparable information on twice as many cities and is twice as expensive. Omnigraphics' Moving and Relocation Sourcebook [RBB Jl 92] provides similar information for 100 metropolitan areas and also covers component parts of these areas. But both the Gale and Omnigraphics titles cover the largest cities, which are not necessarily the most desirable places to live or do business.

This up-to-date set will prove a useful addition to reference collections. Spiral-bound volumes covering individual cities are also available for $7.95.

Daily Celebrity Almanac, 1993. By Bob Barry. B & B Publishing, P.O. Box 393, Fontana, WI 53125, 1992. 442p. annual. illus. index. paper $29.95 (1-880190-01-X; ISSN 1041-9616).
920 Celebrities—Miscellanea || Birthdays || Chronology, Historical || Calendars [OCLC]

This oversize paperback, published annually, is designed for the serious trivia buff and the dedicated browser of all ages. Arranged chronologically, it devotes one page to each month, and one page to each day, of 1993. The monthly page highlights dates of national interest, including contests and festivals, with contact telephone numbers. The daily pages list birthdays of celebrities from all walks of life and give trivia about the person. These pages also list, by year, historic events that occurred on that date, ranging from the important to the obscure. Some months are preceded by a page of celebrity photos, and some dates are noted with an asterisk that refers the reader back to the month page. The author has met many of the subjects in his work as a radio personality, and this book is the source for many radio announcers who include birthdays and other trivia in their on-air commentaries.

The book is of minimal use for research but does contain an index, which is arranged alphabetically by name and gives every date where the person is mentioned. Names in the text appear in boldface, large capital letters, which makes it easier to find an entry. School and public libraries, especially those that experience tremendous use of such books as the Guinness Book of Records, would find an audience for this title. It is fun to browse, and teachers or librarians could use the trivia for displays and bulletin boards. But its poor binding and the need to update it yearly make it an extra purchase.

The Kid's Address Book: Over 1,500 Addresses of Celebrities, Athletes, Entertainers and More... By Michael Levine. Putnam, 1992. 192p. paper $8.95 (0-399-51783-9).
920'.0025 Celebrities—Directories—Juvenile literature || Celebrities—U.S.—Directories—Juvenile literature || Letter-writing—Juvenile literature [CIP] 92-6815

Levine, author of *The Address Book: How to Reach Anyone Who Is Anyone*, *The Corporate Address Book*, and *The Environmental Address Book* [RBB O 15 91], has compiled one especially for young people, although adults will use it as well. Believing that it is important for children to voice their opinions about products, events, and decisions that directly affect their future, Levine provides addresses for manufacturers and organizations as well as for rock stars and sports figures. More than 1,500 addresses are arranged in nine chapters roughly by type, such as television and movie stars, sports figures, publishers, government agencies, and manufacturers. There is some overlap, such as singers who appear in the chapters entitled "Fan Mail" and "Music Makers."

The range is very broad. There are addresses for support groups such as Let's Face It (for the facially disfigured), for royalty, youth religious groups, cartoon characters, and fast-food chains. On one page alone, one can find addresses for Luke Perry, costar of *Beverly Hills 90210*, and Queen Beatrix of the Netherlands. One error in identification was noted. Ms. Elizabeth is identified as a professional wrestler. Her young fans know she is a wrestling manager and wife of wrestling champion "Macho Man."

The author's intent is to motivate children to write letters, and he gives them some handy tips. In a separate chapter, he tells parents why young people should use letter writing as a means of empowerment. There is no index, so locating a particular address is not easy. However, the price is right, and where else could you find the addresses of the Simpsons, Dan Quayle, Captain America, the Youth Section of the Democratic Socialists of America, the American Junior Hereford Association, the Nasty Boys, the Arizona Condors, and Tom Cruise? Recommended for browsing and reference in children and young adult departments of public libraries and school library media collections.

Icons: An A–Z Guide to the People Who Shaped Our Time. By James Park. Macmillan/Collier, 1992. 508p. index. paper $12.95 (0-02-047100-9).
920'.009 Celebrities—Biography—Dictionaries || Biography—20th century—Dictionaries [CIP] 91-36769

Icons profiles some 1,000 men and women of varying nationalities and professions who, by standards not made clear by author Park, "justify some claim to fame." Since he does not define the criteria for inclusion, there are some glaring omissions: Eleanor Roosevelt, Rudolph Nureyev (although Baryshnikov is listed), and the Grateful Dead.

The profiles give the best-known name of the subject, usually—but not always—birth and death dates, an arbitrary characterization ("German novelist, poet, playwright" [Günter Grass]; "American victim" [Patty Hearst, Alger Hiss], "French politician" [Jean Monnet]), and, frequently, a symbol designating the person as, for example, "of global impact, postmodern, superrich, necromantic love-icon." Park lists the symbols in the front of the book; it would be useful to have them as running heads or footers, so the reader is not forced to flip back and forth to determine what the large ampersand stands for. The index includes names (but not all the subjects profiled), terms, organizations, and book and film titles referred to in the text; however, there is no listing by category. Cross-references in the text lead from variant forms of names (e.g., from *Smith, John Maynard* to *Maynard Smith, John*). There is neither a bibliography nor bibliographic references, although titles and dates of books and films (in translation, where necessary) are provided.

The profiles are subjective. Patty Hearst's begins, "Patty Hearst was the American dream turned American victim, her media profile going from innocent heroine to rich-bitch slut faster than that of the average American rape victim. Heiress to the Hearst newspaper fortune, her kidnap on February 4, 1974, by a group of disaffected middle-class wackos calling themselves the Symbionese Liberation Army, who were already responsible for numerous acts of ill-planned and more-than-slightly psychotic violence, turned her into front-page news."

For librarians needing an objective source of brief biographic information, *The International Dictionary of 20th Century Biography* (1987) is a better choice. It has more biographies (more than 5,600, compared with the 1,000 in *Icons*), a subject index, and, in many cases, brief bibliographic notes. With the caveat of subjectivity, however, *Icons* is an interesting choice for public and high school libraries.

Faces In the News: An Index to Photographic Portraits, 1987–1991. comp. by Herbert H. Hoffman. Scarecrow, 1992. 480p. hardcover $42.50 (0-8108-2530-9).
016.92'0009 Biography—20th century—Portraits—Periodicals—Indexes [OCLC] 91-45152

Where do you turn if you need to locate a photograph of a contemporary personality? This unique index features approximately 6,000 people who have been pictured in four widely read periodicals (*Time, Newsweek, U.S. News & World Report*, and *People*) and in *Current Biography*. The time period covered is January 1987 to June 1991. The author, a librarian, has compiled other indexes. Entries are arranged alphabetically by last name or first name if this is the customary usage. Each name is given a one- to two-word descriptor such as "TV pers." or "Soybean spec." The photograph size—designated as small, medium, or large—precedes the citation information. Color or the lack of it is noted at the end of each citation. It appears that not all photographs in the periodicals for the time period covered were included. In a spot check of the July 4, 1988, *Newsweek*, photographs of many newsworthy persons such as Martha Clarke, Magic Johnson, and Kristin Ries were not listed. The preface should have indicated if photographs were chosen selectively, and if so, what criteria were used for the selections. Moreover, this book has some limitations. Many descriptors are inconsistent or ambiguous as, for example, in labeling Paul Castellano as "Gangster" and John Gotti as "Mafioso." Saddam Hussein is described as "Iraq [sic] politician," and Aung San Sun Kyi as a "Burma [sic] polit." rather than a dissident. Additionally, some abbreviations are difficult to decipher. David Lange, for example, is described as "NZ prem.," and Greg Withrow as a "Neonazi pers." Greg Lemond is listed twice, described as "Byciclist [sic]" and "Cyclist." Finally, a number of deceased figures, some from the previous century, are listed. While this is not a problem for those with a mature historical sense, younger readers may be confused. The time period covered is too short and the four sources selected for indexing too circumscribed for *Faces in the News* to be of broad reference value. It is hoped that future editions will carry more consistent descriptors, an abbreviations key, an index by descriptor, and information on selection policy.

Research Guide to European Historical Biography: 1450–Present. v. 1–4. Beacham Publishing, 1992. index. hardcover $299 (0-933833-28-8).
016.92004 Celebrities—Europe—Biography || Celebrities—Europe—Biography—Bibliography || Europe—History—Bio-bibliography [OCLC] 88-19316

This set, projected to be eight volumes (only the first four are reviewed here), fills a gap for many libraries. It provides brief biographic sketches of "four hundred prominent men and women who shaped European civilization since 1450," with nearly 200 subjects covered in the initial set. The first four volumes include explorers, heads of state, diplomats, military leaders, and social reformers. A few living people (Margaret Thatcher, Lech Walesa) are profiled. Subjects in volumes 5 through 8 will consist of scientists, philosophers, political theorists, theologians, artists, writers, and musicians; they are listed in an index in volume 4 of the present work.

This set is similar in arrangement to *Research Guide to American Historical Biography* (1988). Each entry includes a chronology, listing important events in the subject's life; an essay describing activities of historical significance; an overview of biographies of the person; an evaluation of those biographies (essentially a brief annotated bibliography); an overview of writings by the person; fictional and film biographies, if any; a roster of museums, historical landmarks, and societies relevant to the subject; and an annotated list of other sources about the general period in which the subject lived. Each article is signed, and the author's affiliation provided; it would be useful to note the authors' credentials for writing on the subject in the list of contributors.

The primary criteria for including subjects in the guide were whether materials are available in English and generally accessible in libraries. Biographies cited are frequently designated with A, G, or Y, suggesting academic, general, or young audiences, based on subject matter and readability. Where works for children and young adults are available on the subject, these are listed in a separate section and annotated.

The appendixes list major events in modern European history; rulers of selected European empires; and lines of succession for various royal families. Subjects are grouped by periods and areas of historical activity, contributions to history (e.g., *Deposed Monarch, Treason*), and wars and treaties in which they participated.

There are minor quibbles; proofreading seems lax (e.g., in one case "sight" is used where "site" is meant). The maps in the front of volume 1 that depict Europe's boundaries in various years are muddy.

Biographical sketches of many subjects covered here may not be readily available in small libraries. *St. James Guide to Biography* [RBB S 1 91] also evaluates biographies but has no time or geographic limits. People treated range from Jesus to John Lennon. About 70 of the people in the *Research Guide* are also in the *St. James Guide*. Despite its price, academic, public, and even high school libraries should consider *Research Guide to European Historical Biography*. It will be useful both as a reference tool and as a resource for collection development.

A Dictionary of Twentieth Century World Biography. Rev. ed. Ed. by Asa Briggs. Oxford, 1992. 615p. hardcover $30 (0-19-211679-7).
920.00904 [B] Biography—20th century—Dictionaries [BKL] 92-26938

First published in 1985 under the title *Longman Dictionary of 20th Century Biography*, this work provides brief biographies of 1,750 people considered important in recent history. A wide variety of fields is represented, from politics and sports to the arts. While some current people such as Michael Jackson are included, the majority of the biographees are deceased. Entries are arranged in a single alphabetical sequence, and their length ranges from a single paragraph to a full page for Winston Churchill. Year of birth (and death, when appropriate) is given after the name, followed by a brief characterization (i.e., "British engineer and inventor," "South African writer and politician"). Although entrants' book, film, or composition titles are noted, further sources of biographical information are not.

A better selection for a one-volume biographical dictionary for this period is Edward Vernoff and Rima Shore's *The International Dictionary of 20th Century Biography* (1987), which is still in print. It includes 5,650 alphabetically arranged entries. Besides the obvious difference in breadth of coverage, some special features in Vernoff and Shore should be highlighted. Many of the entries include references to biographies or autobiographies. There is a classified index in which broad fields like *Business and Finance* and *Politics and Law* are further subdivided by country of origin.

Some interesting observations may be made with the aid of this index. Under *Politics and Law*, only 10 percent of the over 300 entries identified under U.S. are also listed in *A Dictionary of 20th Century World Biography*. Names identified under U.K. are included at the rate of 65 percent. In the field of *Business and Finance*, only 5 percent of the Americans in Vernoff and Shore are found in *A Dictionary of 20th Century World Biography*, while 19 percent of those identified as Europeans are represented. Naturally, editorial choices have to be made in selecting names for a biographical dictionary, but if a work aims to be international in scope, these percentages should probably be more evenly distributed.

Not a first choice for U.S. libraries.

Political Parties of Asia and the Pacific: A Reference Guide. Ed. by D. S. Lewis and D. J. Sagar. Longman; dist. by Gale, 1992. 369p. indexes. maps. hardcover $145 (0-582-09811-4).
324.2'5 Political parties—Asia || Political parties—Islands of the Pacific [BKL]

This new work is a country-by-country directory of political parties now active in Asia and the Pacific. The publisher is issuing a number of similar books on various regions of the world, such as *Political Parties of Eastern Europe and the Soviet Union* (Longman, 1992). This series emerged from three editions of *Political Parties of the World* issued in the 1980s, the final one from St. James Press in 1988 (see RBB [D 1 85] for a review of the second edition). These works, including the title under review, draw upon the resources of CIRCA Research and Reference Information, which also produces *Keesing's Record of World Events*. For the current volume, the editors relied not only upon data supplied by political parties themselves but also upon myriad other sources.

The intent of *Political Parties of Asia and the Pacific* is to provide a profile of the electoral and party landscape of 44 Asiatic nations and 18 territories, as of July 1992. For each nation, a précis of political background is given first, covering its capital city, constitutional structure, electoral system, and evolution of suffrage. A black-and-white map is included, as well as charts listing the number of seats held by various parties as a result of recent general elections. This section is followed by sketches of essential facts about each country's major and minor parties, respectively. The editors exclude protest groups but not major guerrilla organizations; this leads to difficult judgments, as they freely admit. The major parties receive fuller depictions, including a historical gloss, descriptions of their orientation and structure, number of members, and lists of any publications. Also included for all active, legal parties are addresses, names of leaders, and number of seats won in recent elections. The volume concludes with indexes of personal names and party names, both vital for its utility as a reference tool.

Some limits in coverage must be noted: no states in the strife-ridden Middle East are included. Neither is Russia. No nation west of Kazakhstan and Afghanistan is profiled. Even so, countries representing about one-half of the population of the globe are here.

A check of factual authenticity was attempted with any comparable work. Due to constant flux in most Asian countries' party alignments (splits, mergers, etc.), a fair comparison required finding an equally recently published work. None were identified. Facts On File's most recent *World Encyclopedia of Political Systems and Parties* was issued in 1987 (2d ed. [RBB O 1 87]). Greenwood's *Political Parties of Asia and the Pacific* appeared in 1985. Nevertheless, entries for India in the former work and in the Longman title were inspected, and no clearly disparate items were seen. No other work in the 1990s covers this ground for India, China, Japan, Indonesia, and Australia, not to mention the 50-odd other states included here.

The volume's appeal will be limited to those libraries with clientele interested in present-day Asian studies. For specialists, this is an important reference with current directory information. But at the price of $145, most other libraries holding any of the aforementioned titles issued in the 1980s might decide to pass on this one.

Who's Who in Africa: Leaders for the 1990s. By Alan Rake. Scarecrow, 1992. 448p. index. hardcover $59.50 (0-8108-2557-0).
920.067 Statesmen—Africa, Sub-Saharan—Biography || Africa, Sub-Saharan—Politics and government [OCLC] 92-8166

Filling a gap in current African biography, this book provides profiles of more than 300 political figures in the 47 African countries south of the Sahara. Persons included are "those in power, those recently in office, and those most likely to succeed, whether from the ranks of the opposition or from relatively minor positions in the ruling structure." It has been 10 years since *Who's Who in Africa* was last published as a section of Europa Publications' *Africa South of the Sahara*. A previous book by Rake and John Dickie, *Who's Who in Africa: The Political, Military and Business Leaders of Africa*, was published in 1973 (African Development). According to Rake, three-quarters of the persons covered in the old book are not included in this new one.

Entries here are arranged by country, and then alphabetically by name. Each country section begins with a list of facts: population (mostly from 1990 World Bank figures), date of independence, head of state, a description of the type of government, and a list of active political parties, including underground groups. The section on Sudan, for example, describes the government as "military rule by the Revolutionary Command Council for National Salvation," states that political parties have been banned since June 1989, and lists four parties that exist underground. Information for most countries is current as of the summer of 1991.

Numbers of persons listed within each country section range from one (Equatorial Guinea) to 21 (South Africa). Entries vary in length from one-half page to two or three pages for major figures. The variety and depth of information contained in each entry is the strength of this book. Rake is managing editor of the London-based *African Business* and *New African* magazines. In his preface, he states that he has attempted to "produce a book which includes insight, anecdote and comment and a general assessment as well as a list of dates and events." He has achieved his goal admirably. Each entry is rich in fascinating inside information and packed with facts and dates that would be time-consuming to compile from other sources. Each begins with a brief, italicized paragraph summarizing points covered in the main body of the entry plus fairly subjective information about the person's physical appearance, personality, habits, and other characteristics. For example, Frederik De Klerk is "a worrier and chain smoker who conceals a nervous disposition behind a bland exterior and perfect manners."

The body of each entry includes the person's date of birth, tribal membership (if appropriate), education, military training (for example, Prince Johnson of Liberia was trained in military police tactics at Fort Jackson, South Carolina), career history, political alliances and positions over the years, party affiliations, and current position. Entries are usually limited to the person's professional and political life; personal information, such as names of spouses or other family members, is not included unless it is politically significant. Although concise, the entries contain a number of surprises. For example, Amos Sawyer, interim president of Liberia, holds a Ph.D. from Northwestern University. The Marxist Leninist League of Tigre Province, Ethiopia, is modeled on the Albanian version of socialism. Relevant political movements within African countries are discussed within the context of each person's entry. For example, the entry for Legesse Zenawi of Ethiopia explains briefly the difference between the Tigre People's Liberation Front and the Tigre Liberation Front.

An alphabetical index of persons is included in the back of the book. It includes only those people who have entries, not those mentioned within entries.

It is difficult to find concise, up-to-date information on many the of the political figures covered in *Who's Who in Africa*. This book will be a valuable complement to *Dictionary of African Historical Biography* [RBB Ap 1 87]. Although the latter book contains a "Supplement of Post-1960 Political Figures," *Who's Who in Africa* provides more extensive coverage of current leaders. It is an essential purchase for academic and large public libraries and will be useful in any library that serves a clientele interested in Africa.

Black Women in America: An Historical Encyclopedia. 2v. Ed. by Darlene Clark Hine and others. Carlson, 1993. 1,530p. bibliog. illus. index. hardcover $195 (0-926019-61-9).
920.72'08996073 Afro-American women—Encyclopedias [CIP] 92-39947

Black Women in America: An Historical Encyclopedia was initiated in order "to reclaim and to create heightened awareness about individuals, contributions, and struggles that have made African-American survival and progress possible." The encyclopedia is the work of dedicated scholars of black women's history. Editor Hine is a professor of American history at Michigan State University, founder of the Black Women in the Middle West Project at Purdue University, and editor of Carlson Publishing's Black Women in United States History series (1990). Associate editors are Elsa Barkley Brown of the University of Michigan's Department of History and Center for Afro-American and African Studies and Rosalyn Terborg-Penn, professor of history at Morgan State University. Many of the women on the 21-member editorial advisory board belong to the Association of Black Women Historians. In the work under review, all essays are signed by contributors whose credentials are listed in the back of the encyclopedia, along with those of the editors and the advisory board.

Approximately three-quarters of *Black Women in America*'s 804 entries are biographies of individual black women who "played a role on the national stage or in national news" or who were "prominent only in their local communities but were typical of women throughout the country." While the encyclopedia dutifully includes all the best-known black female historical figures (e.g., Harriet Tubman, and Sojourner Truth), its importance for reference collections is its emphasis on such lesser known women as cartoonist Zelda Jackson Ormes, quiltmaker Harriet Powers, and Civil War–spy Mary Elizabeth Bowser. Entries for four black men—W. E. B. Du Bois, Frederick Douglass, Booker T. Washington, and Marcus Garvey—were included because "the encyclopedia would have been incomplete without the presentation of their ideas."

One-quarter of the book's entries are on black women's organizations (*Housewives' League of Detroit*, *Colored Women's Progressive Franchise Association*), educational institutions and organizations (*United Negro College Fund*, *Spelman College*), and broad topics relevant to black women's history (*Slave Narratives*, *Harlem Renaissance*). Broad topics are always addressed from the perspective of black women's history. The article *Slavery*, for example, emphasizes trade of women and girls, gender issues, marriage, childbearing and child care, sexual abuse, and rape. Articles range in length from several paragraphs to more than 20 pages.

Historical scope extends from 1619, when three black women were brought to Jamestown, Virginia, by a Dutch ship, to 1992, when astronaut Mae Jemison became the first black woman to travel in space, when Lusia Harris-Stewart was inducted into the Basketball Hall of Fame, and Carol Moseley-Braun was nominated for the U.S. Senate. Although a few entries describe black women who lived or worked in Canada (e.g., *Cary, Mary Ann Shadd*), the encyclopedia concentrates on the U.S. rather than the Americas.

Most articles include bibliographies of sources the author used to write the entry or provide additional information. The level of materials cited varies with the subject of the article. Essays on contemporary entertainers (e.g., *Winfrey, Oprah* and *Turner, Tina*) cite such popular publications as *Cosmopolitan*, *Jet*, *Ebony*, *Essence*, and *Time*; articles on historical figures and topics include more scholarly bibliographies. For example, the bibliography for *Slavery* is divided into sections on documents, books, and articles and includes many references to legal materials, nineteenth-century periodicals, and slave narratives. Contributors of articles on less-studied women or topics often consulted such unpublished materials as typescripts (e.g., *Young Women's Christian Association*) or personal interviews (e.g., *Wallace, Sippie* and *Sweet Honey in the Rock*). Articles on musicians either include or cite discographies.

Bibliographies are up-to-date, including many sources from the 1990s. Although the bibliographies are not intended to be exhaustive, a few are surprisingly sparse. For example, *Parks, Rosa* cites several books and articles in *Ebony* and *Essence* but lists no scholarly journal articles or even the citation to the Supreme Court's ruling on bus desegregation. Also, the bibliography for *Tyson, Cicely* lists one monograph and two reference books, but no articles.

A chronology of black women's history includes such landmark events as the first published slave narrative by a black woman (1831), Sara E. Goode's 1885 patent for her "Folding Cabinet Bed," and JoAnne Little's 1975 acquittal of the murder of her prison guard. A thoughtfully annotated bibliography prepared by Janet Sims-Wood, a reader-services librarian at Howard University's Moorland-Springarn Research Center, lists major reference works, general histories, and research collections housing primary materials. A classified list of biographical entries identifies black women according to occupation or activity, such as athlete, librarian, nun, bandleader, or temperance activist.

The carefully constructed 150-page index lists "tens of thousands" of access points to topics and individuals. Because the biographical articles are limited to black women, readers will find the index useful for locating discussions on the impact of males (Robert Gould Shaw, Alvin Ailey) and white women (Harriet Beecher Stowe) on black women's history and culture. Also included in the index are black women not covered in their own entries (e.g., Iman, Sister Souljah, and Lt. Phoebe Jeter, who shot down the first Scud missile in the Persian Gulf War), book titles (*The Color Purple*), television shows ("The Jeffersons," "Star Trek"), and individual cities. *See* references enhance the index's usefulness.

A "Reader's Guide," a list of abbreviations, and an alphabetical list of topical entries are special features that increase the usefulness of the encyclopedia. Many of the excellent photographs are from the Moorland-Springarn Research Center and the Schomburg Center of the New York Public Library.

Black Women in America is a labor of love and a joy to read. It is stunningly detailed and comprehensive, pulling together research from manuscript collections as well as the popular press, yet engagingly written so that it will be as fascinating and accessible to the high school student and the general reader as it is to the historian. Articles such as *Fashion Industry* and *Beauty Culture* provide unique perspectives on general topics. Citations to primary sources suggest possiblities for further research.

The closest competitor to *Black Women in America* is *Notable Black American Women*, edited by Jessie Carney Smith [RBB Ap 15 92], but the latter is a strictly biographical source, providing articles on 500 women. The biographical information for each individual is comparable in the two works, but the new title has a broader scope—it covers more people, includes articles on topics and organizations, and provides more extensive indexing. While small libraries that already own *Notable Black American Women* will need to evaluate whether they can afford the additional coverage in the work under review, *Black Women in America: An Historical Encyclopedia* is highly recommended for high school, public, and academic libraries.

Major Authors and Illustrators for Children and Young Adults: A Selection of Sketches from Something about the Author. 6v. By Laurie Collier and Joyce Nakamura. Gale, 1992. bibliog. illus. hardcover $265 (0-8103-7702-0).
928 Children's literature—Biobibliography || Authors, American—Biobibliography [OCLC] 92-73849

This six-volume biographical directory includes 800 sketches of well-known authors and illustrators of children's books. They range from Kenneth Grahame and Wanda Gag to Graeme Base and the Babysitter's Club's Ann Martin. The individual selections have been adapted from Gale's *Something about the Author* (SATA) and feature separate sections on personal data, career summaries, awards and honors, writings, adaptions in other media, works in progress, and additional information sources. An important feature is the "Sidelights" section, which provides a critical narrative on the individual's life and career. Entries have not been just reprinted from SATA but have been updated when appropriate, and the "Sidelights" essays have been rewritten. Entries are arranged in alphabetical order and include current black-and-white photographs of the subjects. Some entries include sample illustrations, book jackets, or movie stills. However, there are fewer illustrations than in the parent set, and they are often smaller.

Authors were chosen for inclusion through a selection process that surveyed 1,500 school and public librarians. The responses were then reviewed by an advisory board of six professionals currently active in children's library services. The authors and illustrators included cover the spectrum of children's literature, including all genres in levels from preschool through young adult.

Wilson's Junior Authors and Illustrators series is now in six volumes and covers more than 1,500 people. There is a considerable amount of overlap in the people covered with the Gale set. However, *Major Authors and Illustrators* includes more nineteenth-century authors such as Louisa May Alcott and J. M. Barrie. Its entries are longer and have more illustrations.

Major Authors and Illustrators will be helpful to students doing reports. The format is easily accessible, and the vocabulary level is suitable for upper-elementary grades. Students will especially respond to the personal insights and reminiscences included in the "Sidelights" sections. Libraries that serve student populations and that do not have a standing order for *Something about the Author* (now in 70 volumes) or its companion *Authors and Artists for Young Adults* (now in 9 volumes) should consider purchase.

State Census Records. By Ann S. Lainhart. Genealogical Publishing, 1992. 116p. hardcover $17.95 (0-8063-1362-5).
929 Genealogy—Archival resources—Bibliography [BKL]

Genealogists, demographers, and social historians will welcome the publication of *State Census Records*, which systematically inventories censuses conducted by the states and the prestatehood territories. These records were compiled at various times for different reasons; some are voter-registration lists, some are tax rolls, and some are simple enumerations to justify defense measures or granting statehood. Their value has long been recognized for their usefulness in filling gaps left by missing federal censuses and for information that complements federal censuses. State censuses often asked different questions than the federal censuses regarding naturalization, education, parents' place of marriage, and details of military service. Local census takers occasionally added notes of personal interest, such as "Oldest person in town" and "Born at sea." In addition, state censuses are opened to the public more quickly than allowed by the federal census' 72-year moratorium.

Preparing for a speech at the 1988 convention of the Federation of Genealogical Societies, the author discovered that earlier attempts to describe state censuses were incomplete and sometimes inaccurate. She surveyed state archives, libraries, and historical societies and compiled an inventory for the convention. Lainhart subsequently contacted genealogists and local historians in each state to update, revise, and expand the 1988 booklet to its present format.

Arranged alphabetically by state, the entries begin with the current location(s) of manuscript copies of the censuses and then detail the kinds of information found in each. When appropriate, entries are divided county by county and sometimes district by district. Reference is made to published sources of the data, extant indexes and indexes in progress, and sources and procedures for research assistance offered by state and local agencies. Credit is given to local experts who provided information for the survey, offering yet another lead for persistent researchers.

Information is provided for 44 states. The author asserts that no state or territorial censuses exist for Connecticut, Idaho, Kentucky, Montana, New Hampshire, Ohio, Pennsylvania, and Vermont; however, she includes entries for Kentucky, Montana, and Ohio that describe potentially useful demographic records such as school, tax, and voter lists. A curious omission is West Virginia, which has no entry and is not listed among the states without such records. While it is logical to examine Virginia's records for pre–1863 information, West Virginia later produced its own tax lists and rosters of veterans and veterans' widows.

This volume offers pragmatic information about accessing valuable data and should be part of every collection that supports research in American genealogy and history.

Italians to America: Lists of Passengers Arriving at U.S. Ports, 1880–1899. v.2: Passengers Arriving at New York, January 1885–June 1887. Ed. by Ira A. Glazier and P. William Filby. Scholarly Resources, 1992. 644p. index. hardcover $75 (0-8420-2465-4).
929'.3 Italian Americans—Genealogy || Ships—U.S.—Passenger lists || Registers of births, etc.—U.S. || U.S.—Genealogy [CIP] 92-24504

This is a multivolume computer-produced listing of Italian immigrants to the U.S. during the period of maximum immigration, 1880 to the end of the century. Twelve volumes are planned, of which volumes 1, 2 (the volume under review), 3, and 4 have already appeared; volumes 5 and 6 are promised for late fall.

Arrangement is by date of arrival of ships, nearly always docking at New York. Information given is precise day of arrival, name of ship, and port or ports of departure. Then follows a list of passengers, by family name, but not in any order. Each entry gives surname, first name, age, sex, the destination (nearly always New York), occupation, and occasionally the Italian city or village of origin. The last two categories are largely not present or unreliable. Few ships' agents were careful to record this information. In most cases the occupation, if given at all, is listed as "farmer," while on other ships the term for the entire manifest is "laborer." Still, some lists of occupations are quite detailed, though "peasant" does occur regularly, along with "cultivator." Codes or abbreviations are used for occupations, and codes for the Italian villages; a listing of these codes is given at the front, as well as a list of abbreviations for cities of destination.

The total number of names in this volume is not given, but a flyer states that the 12 projected volumes will include about 900,000 names. It is not known whether the estimate of 900,000 means persons or families. The name index at the end of volume 2 runs to nearly 300 pages.

It would be useful if the publisher, who presumably has all the data in computerized form, would offer a reference service or would make the data available on disk. For example, the question may arise as to how many people, or what families, emigrated from, say, Palermo or a smaller place like Mondello. Even though most arriving shiploads did not have this information listed, perhaps enough do to enable scholars to establish emigration patterns and genealogists to trace families when only place origin is known. Such a disk would also serve as a cumulative name index to the set.

This entire work is a great service to genealogists and to librarians working in areas with large Italian immigrant populations. For all such it is a must buy.

African Names: Names from the African Continent for Children and Adults. By Julia Stewart. Citadel, 1993. 171p. paper $9.95 (0-8065-1386-1).

929.4'096 Names, Personal—African—Dictionaries—English ‖ Names, Personal—Africa—Dictionaries—English [OCLC] 93-9441

Naming a newborn or changing an adult's name to an African one can be a simple matter—the legal process is straightforward—or it can be complex, as the family considers many factors. This source will make the process more meaningful, as it contains a tremendous amount of helpful information.

The author has a deep feeling for and familiarity with African heritage, from the long history of the continent to the wide array of languages. The introduction discusses changing traditional personal and family names to African names, family-naming practices in the continent, major languages, Muslim names, gender considerations, and converting a present name to an African variation. A map shows locations of the main languages of Africa.

The bulk of the work is an alphabetical list of more than 1,000 names divided into female and male sections with pronunciation and definition for each. In many instances, the name is also that of an important person, organization, or object, and this significance is explained. When appropriate, the meaning of a name in nations outside Africa is noted. Between the alphabetical sections, the author has interspersed pertinent quotations that both enliven use and provide a deeper appreciation for African heritage.

Several appendixes will also prove helpful—African names used as surnames, modern leaders (arranged by country and including years as head of the country), suggested reading, and a bibliography. Neither *The Dictionary of African Historical Biography* (2d ed., 1986) nor *The Book of African Names* (1991) are listed here.

Nearly every public library, as well as many academic and secondary school libraries, will want to purchase a copy of *African Names* for reference and consider a copy for circulation, so the enrichment can continue at home.

The Perfect Name for the Perfect Baby. By Joan Wilen and Lydia Wilen. Ballantine, 1993. 307p. paper $8 (0-449-90654-X).

929.44 Names, Personal [OCLC] 92-90401

Wit and novelty all combine here to produce a delightful dictionary of first names. Uniquely organized, the first half of *The Perfect Name* presents first names in such categories as "Names from the Bible," "Names of Your Favorite Soap Stars," and "The Way the Wind Blows: Names of Hurricanes." The second half of the book consists of two extensive lists: one of girls' names and one of boys'.

The helpful introductory section on important considerations in the naming game discusses such questions as, Will a nickname really work? Should you use a unique spelling? Should you use "Junior"? Among the categories that follow, the reader finds a list of saints' names, their feast days, and substantial biographical statements. An interesting list of gemstones that can be used as first names includes family/origin, colors, and an interesting historical statement on the gem's traditional meaning. A surprising bit of information included in the names-of-hurricanes section is the history and practice of the National Weather Service in naming storms.

The Wilens confess to selectivity in this book. Indeed, in the section "Names of Fictional Characters," they note that they don't aim for comprehensiveness; they simply include names from their favorite books, plays, and movies and hope that the reader finds them helpful. With this in mind, it is not fair to compare *The Perfect Name* to such works as Alfred Kolatch's *New Name Dictionary* (Jonathan David, 1989) or Hanks and Hodges' *Dictionary of First Names* (Oxford, 1990). But such comparisons do reveal that *The Perfect Name* is much more fun. At the price, *The Perfect Name for the Perfect Baby* is money well spent in any public library collection. Once received, the decision to place it in the circulating or reference collection will be a tough one.

Lines of Succession: Heraldry of the Royal Families of Europe. By Jiří Louda and Michael Maclagan. Macmillan, 1992. 308p. charts. illus. index. maps. hardcover $75 (0-02-897255-4).

929.7 Heraldry—Europe ‖ Europe—Kings and rulers [OCLC] 91-35681

Originally published in England in 1981 and in a 1991 revision, this is the first American edition of a work combining history, genealogy, and heraldry. Louda depicts European royalty's genealogy and its heraldic representations in more than 100 charts. These display more than 2,000 four-color coats of arms and illustrate the often complex lineage of ruling families from over 30 countries and kingdoms, ranging from Great Britain to Russia and Greece. Historical background is provided by Maclagan's narrative text, which presents an account of the people and events that resulted in particular royal family trees and patterns of succession. An introduction to heraldry, covering some basic terms and styles, as well as notes to the abbreviations found in the charts, is helpful to the reader unfamiliar with the subject. The text is further enhanced by a number of black-and-white illustrations, photographs, and maps. The index covers text, charts, and illustrations.

Even a cursory reading of the chapters devoted to specific countries or kingdoms gives one a taste of the richness of European history. The accompanying family trees, emblazoned with coats of arms, neatly summarize the lines of descent. Two of the many charts are particularly compelling: "Relationships of European Monarchs before and at the Time of the First World War" illustrates the intrinsic complexities some would say contributed to that conflict; "Common Descent of the Present European Sovereigns since William the Conqueror" shows quite clearly the numerous family ties shared by the crowned heads of Europe.

This is not a tool for quick-reference use; however, it will fill the need for a basic sourcebook for European history.

HISTORY

Magill's History of Europe. 6v. Rev. ed. Ed. by Frank N. Magill. Grolier, 1993. bibliog. indexes. hardcover $219 (0-7172-7173-0).

940 Europe—History [OCLC] 92-54832

This six-volume set is a compilation and revision of the Great Events from History series, previously published by Salem Press. This new set contains 288 articles pertaining to events that shaped the Western world from 1750 B.C. to 1992, whereas the previous *Ancient & Medieval* set (1972) and *Modern European* set (1973) covered events from 4000 B.C. to 1969. The format for each article remains the same and includes type of event, time, locale, principal personages, summary of the event, pertinent literature, and additional recommended readings.

Every signed article and literature critique is written by a history professor and contains a summary that runs two to three pages. Each article also contains summaries of two important books on the topic that run 600–800 words each. Many of these articles are unchanged from the original series and do not include any recent literature in the bibliographies. Several events were dropped from the original series, some new articles covering events before 1969 were added, and all events from 1970 to 1992 are new to this series. Some of the new events include the Chernobyl disaster, the reuniting of East and West Germany, the dissolution of the Soviet Union, and civil war in Yugoslavia.

The print is smaller than in the earlier edition, but the layout is still easy to read, and information easy to find. Volume 6 contains the cumulative indexes listing the events alphabetically, by keywords, by categories (diplomatic, political, military, etc.), and by principal personages, and each volume contains a chronological index for the entire set.

The concept of summarizing historical events and making them understandable to high school and undergraduate students by placing them in a chronological context gives value to these books as research tools. The easily read summaries give students necessary background information, and the lists of principal personages are a good starting point for further research.

The World War One Source Book. By Philip J. Haythornthwaite. Arms & Armour; dist. by Sterling, 1992. 416p. bibliog. illus. index. hardcover $29.95 (0-85409-102-6).
940.3' World War, 1914–1918—Sources [BKL]

The author's aim is to "compress the largest amount of information into the smallest possible space, and to insert . . . some of the most surprising and interesting events" from World War I or the Great War. In the same series as the *Napoleonic Source Book* [RBB My 1 91] and the *American Civil War Source Book*, this encyclopedia is packed with details for the student and interested reader.

In the first section, "History of War," the 1914 war effort on the Western, Eastern, Balkan, and Turkish fronts is covered as well as the eventual action in Italy, Palestine, Mesopotamia, Africa, and the war at sea from 1915–1918. Subsections on casualties and chronologies of each front complete this section. Covered in other major sections are "Weapons and Tactics," which are surveyed through their development, method of use, and strategies; "Warring Nations," which includes individual colony involvement where applicable; and biographies of major personalities. Reference lists facilitate exploration beyond this book.

Two final sections are "Sources," an annotated list of further readings, and "Miscellanea," which gathers such items as place-names, currencies, rations, national statistics, aces, and more. A glossary and index complete the compilation.

Appealingly punctuated with maps, photographs, cartoons, and information boxes with quotations, *The World War One Source Book* invites inquiry. Recommended for small libraries, especially public and high school collections, this book is a wealth of information at an affordable price. Large collections will find it useful as a point of relational reading to the many other resources in their collections.

A Dictionary of Twentieth Century History: 1914–1990. By Peter Teed. Oxford, 1992. 520p. hardcover $30 (0-19-211676-2); paper $9.95 (0-19-285207-8).
940.5 History, Modern—20th century—Dictionaries [OCLC] 92-218815

More than 2,000 entries are included in this eclectic international survey of the twentieth century. Typical entries are 75 to 100 words, with some, especially the biographies, running a bit longer. These are in no way intended to be in-depth analyses. Entries are alphabetically arranged, beginning with *Abboud, Ibrahim* (a little-known Sudanese general) and ending with *Zulu*. Most of the subjects covered are easily recognizable and well known (e.g., *Stalingrad, Lusitania*), but lesser-known events are also covered, such as *Invergordon Mutiny*, a 1931 protest among Royal Navy personnel. Virtually every country in the world has an entry (including such newer ones as *Slovenia* and *Estonia*), as do many obscure places that are vestigial colonial possessions or outposts. Coverage is current as of the end of 1990. Cross-references are noted with asterisks.

Works such as *The Facts On File Encyclopedia of the 20th Century* [RBB D 15 91] and the *Dictionary of 20th Century History* [RBB N 15 90] provide more comprehensive coverage for libraries. The *Dictionary of 20th Century History* is suitable for home reference use.

Encyclopedia of Romanticism: Culture in Britain, 1780s–1830s. Ed. by Laura Dabundo. Garland, 1992. 662p. bibliog. index. hardcover $95 (0-8240-6997-8).
941.07'3 Great Britain—Civilization—19th century—Encyclopedias || Great Britain—Civilization—18th century—Encyclopedias || Romanticism—Great Britain—Encyclopedias [CIP] 92-2682

With its emphasis on the individual, the imagination, and a return to nature, the romantic movement in England has long struck a responsive chord in twentieth-century readers, and it has inspired a large body of critical scholarship. Thus, it is surprising that this is the first work to attempt to provide encyclopedic coverage of the era. Roughly spanning the period from the 1780s to the mid-1830s, the *Encyclopedia of Romanticism* complements Garland's *Victorian Britain: An Encyclopedia*, which covers the years 1837–1901.

In surveying the "social, cultural, and intellectual climate of English Romanticism," the encyclopedia focuses on individuals, ideas, historical events, technological innovations, and social and economic issues that influenced and shaped the time. While the emphasis is on the romantic period in England, separate articles are devoted to American, French, German, Russian, and Spanish romanticism. The majority of the 345 alphabetically arranged entries were contributed by individuals associated with academic institutions. Varying in quality and authority, articles range in length from 500 to 2,500 words. Each signed entry is followed by a brief bibliography. Although conventional *see also* references are used generously both within and at the end of articles, many users will miss the statement in the preface that the use of only the last name of an individual from the period indicates that he or she has a separate entry in the encyclopedia. The use of boldface type would have been a better means of providing such cross-references.

Almost 60 percent of the entries are devoted to individuals, ranging from major and minor literary figures (e.g., William Wordsworth, Agnes Maria Bennett) to artists, philosophers, and scientists (e.g., Joseph Turner, Jeremy Bentham, Joseph Priestley). The encyclopedia also provides extensive coverage of literary forms, movements, themes, and concepts, for example, the articles *Byronic Hero, Gothicism, Reconciliation of Opposites,* and *Willing Suspension of Disbelief*. In addition, the volume treats a diversity of other subjects, such as *Criminality, Domestic Architecture, Food and Culinary Habits,* and *Opium and Laudanum*. Amazingly, for a source devoted to a movement that celebrated nature, there are no articles on nature or natural history, except for *Geological Sciences*. Other topics that one would have expected to merit articles include agriculture, fashion, transportation, and women. Also conspicuously lacking are an introductory essay providing an overview of the romantic period in England and a selective bibliography of general sources for the period.

Another of the encyclopedia's flaws is its index, which provides pagination only for the titles of entries and for some names of individuals. The majority of the index entries refer the user only to titles of pertinent articles. Thus, the user looking for information on Edward Young is referred to *Blake, William* and *Sentimentalism* and must skim those articles to find mention of Young. Such an index obviously simplified the editor's task since no effort was required to group subentries into meaningful categories. However, the result is inefficient for the user. Anyone seeking references to Wordsworth's *The Prelude*, for example, has the formidable task of reading more than 80 articles in pursuit of such allusions. Secondly, the index provides insufficient cross-references between topics. For instance, there is no cross-reference from *Mental Illness* to the article *Insanity and Eccentric Genius*. In addition, a more detailed index would have increased the value of the work. For example, a number of the periodicals discussed in *Journalism* are not found in the index.

Although the unevenness of its coverage and the inadequacies of the index diminish the quality of this volume, at present this is the only work of its type for the romantic era. However, St. Martin's has announced its intention to publish a similar compendium, *A Handbook to English Romanticism*, later this year. While it does not measure up to the calibre of *Victorian Britain*, the *Encyclopedia of Romanticism* will be a useful companion for students and scholars of the romantic period.

German Reunification: A Reference Guide and Commentary. By Jonathan Osmond. Longman; dist. by Gale, 1992. 312p. bibliog. index. hardcover $85 (0-582-09650-2).
[943.0879 Germany—History—Unification, 1990 BKL]

This work is divided into three major sections. Part 1 begins with a chronology of events from January 1989, when "Erich Honecker declares Berlin Wall will last another 100 years," to May 1992, when "Public service workers' strikes intensify." The chronology is followed by a three-page summary of changes in the borders of Germany before 1949, a brief history of the German Democratic Republic (GDR) from 1949 to the mid-1980s, and a detailed account of developments in the GDR from the origins of its collapse in 1989 through the situation in a united Germany in spring 1992. Most of this account is political, with some reference to economic and social matters.

Part 2 contains six signed essays on East Germany covering integration into the European Community, electoral volatility in the united Germany, politicians and parties, the economy, trade unions, and the impact of unification on women.

HISTORY

Part 3, "Reference Section," begins with the alphabetical directory of people, parties, organizations, places, and terms relating to the events of 1989–92. The majority relate to the former GDR. Lists of officials, tables of election results and economic indicators, and the text of four major treaties (in full or abbreviated form) complete this section.

Access is said to be facilitated by the use of boldface type on the first mention of a topic in part 1 to indicate an entry in the directory. However, users dipping into the work after the first mention get no help with initialisms, parties, persons, etc. An accurate index is provided.

Compiler Osmond and most of the contributors are lecturers specializing in Eastern European affairs at British universities. Osmond explains in the preface that published materials were their main sources: East and West German newspapers, official publications from Bonn and Berlin, reports by research institutes, written accounts by and interviews with prominent participants in the events, and eyewitness and personal accounts of ordinary people in East and West Germany. He explains that while no detailed source references are given in the text, the bibliography provides the "main and most easily accessible published works in English and in German which were used in the compilation of the book." The bibliography provides complete citations to books and journal articles under such headings as *Political Memoirs*, *The Stasi*, and *Women*.

Lacking is a portrayal of the "often devastating problems of personal and family adjustment" referred to in the preface. Perhaps the "increase in attacks on foreign refugees" listed in the chronology for September through October 1991 would have been covered in such a chapter. In addition, the maps promised in the contents were not in the volume reviewed by the Board. They are missed.

The book's title would more accurately have been *East Germany and Reunification*. However, *German Reunification* is a well-organized fact-filled study of political and economic changes in Germany between 1989 and 1992. The volume's intended audience is "scholars, students, and all seeking to understand the new Germany." Scholars will probably find the work too superficial, and the interested public will find it dry and narrow. Nevertheless, academic libraries supporting strong European or modern history studies will want to consider it for purchase.

Eastern Europe and the Commonwealth of Independent States 1992. Europa; dist by Gale, 1992. 583p. bibliog. maps. tables. hardcover $375 (0-946653-77-1; ISSN 0962-1040).
947′.0854 Europe, Eastern—Economic conditions, 1989- ‖ Europea, Eastern—Politics and government, 1989- ‖ Former soviet republics—Economic conditions ‖ Former soviet republics—Politics and government [BKL]

This latest release completes Europa's Regional Surveys of the World series. The other titles in the series are *Africa South of the Sahara*; *The Middle East and North Africa*; *The Far East and Australasia*; *South America, Central America, and the Caribbean*; *Western Europe* [RBB Je 1 89]; and *The USA and Canada* [RBB My 15 90]. Anyone familiar with them will know what to expect here. The fact that it was prepared during a time of dramatic changes in Eastern Europe makes this book's timely appearance all the more impressive. Coverage is current through late summer-early fall of 1991.

Eastern Europe and the Commonwealth of Independent States aims to provide a "comprehensive description and analysis of the countries of the region, placing them in their international and historical context." Prepared by 30 specialist writers, predominantly British academics, the work is arranged in four parts. First are 10 signed essays that describe and assess broad regional issues such as "Nationalism and National Minorities," "Eastern European Economies," and "The Environment in the Region." For example, the environment essay explains the legacy of environmental damage left by an inefficient industrial system patterned after the Soviet smokestack industries of the 1950s. These introductory essays are 5–10 pages in length.

Surveys of Albania, Bulgaria, Czechoslovakia, Hungary, Poland, Rumania, and Yugoslavia make up part 2 of this title. Typical is the Poland survey with sections on geography, history and economics, a map, a chronology (966 to September 1991), a statistical survey, and a directory. These last two sections cover, for example, births, deaths, emigration, livestock products, tourism, political parties, courts, radio stations, trade organizations, opera houses, and welfare organizations. Many of the statistical tables are identical to those in the 1991 *Europa World Year Book*. A 20-item bibliography completes each survey; 1991 citations are included. The Czechoslovakia and Yugoslavia surveys include "minisurveys" on each republic.

Part 3 covers the USSR and successor states. Twelve signed essays deal with the former Soviet Union (e.g., "Nationalism in the USSR," "The Energy Industries," "The August Revolution and Its Consequences"), followed by surveys on each of the 15 republics.

More than 170 biographical profiles of political figures such as Vaclav Havel, Ion Iliescu, and Lech Walesa make up the fourth and last part of the book. These are brief and will serve merely to identify individuals prominent in political events.

The daily news is dominated by events in Eastern Europe, and it's hard to imagine any library in which this source would not see heavy use. It provides more detailed and, in some cases, more up-to-date information than the 1991 *Europa World Year Book*. (The 1992 *World Year Book* is now available from Gale.) Its price will probably limit purchase to academic and large public libraries.

Russia and the Commonwealth A to Z. By Andrew Wilson and Nina Bachkatov. HarperCollins, 1992. 258p. bibliog. index. hardcover $30 (0-06-271551-8); paper $15 (0-06-273145-9).
947.085′4 Soviet Union—Politics and government—1985–1991—Dictionaries ‖ Commonwealth of Independent States—Dictionaries ‖ Russia (Federation)—Politics and government—Dictionaries [CIP] 92-52547

This engaging book and the timeliness of its subject will no doubt draw readers like flies to sweet buns. However, acquisitions librarians should make sure they note the description on its cover before purchase: "An informative, illuminating and often irreverent guide to the history, politics, culture, personalities and society of modern Russia." The book looks and feels like a dictionary, but it is not going to compete for shelf space with any of the conventional sources.

Wilson is Moscow correspondant for the *London Observer*, and Bachkatov is a free-lance journalist. Both have covered Soviet happenings since 1986. *Russia and the Commonwealth A to Z* grew out of their research for a more conventional book, projected as a comprehensive review and analysis of the changes they were witnessing. Three criteria were used to select the 1,000-plus entries presented here. First, was the subject an essential part of current events? Second, was it a "significant or commonly used reference point from the recent past?" Third, was it likely to be referred to in the future?

Much of the information comes from firsthand observations. Other sources used include BBC broadcasts and various publications of the International Institute for Strategic Studies. The entries range in length from one sentence to 200 words and include people (e.g., "*Bovin, Aleksandr Yevgenyevich.* Leading Izvestia political columnist . . . ambassador to Israel"); places (e.g., "*North Korea.* Neighbour dramatically down in affection since Moscow discovered the South Korean economy"); and concepts (e.g., "*De-politicization.* Word coined by radicals to suggest the un-making of the Soviet Union"). Although generally readable, some of the entries seem a little disjointed. For example *Germany* begins with the following two sentences: "Historic enemy reunified in October 1990. Like real capitalists, the Soviets turned their agreement into cash: $10 billion just for withdrawing their troops, $29 billion of aid and credits." The reader may feel that he or she has caught only a snippet of a longer conversation.

Typical of the entries that give this book its irreverent and highly entertaining flavor is *Jogging*: "Way to impress neighbours with one's Western-style fitness training, boosted in 1990 when Jane Fonda, followed by cameras, led 500 Moscow joggers on a traipse along the river." Or *Eroticism*: "Notion alien to Russian, and subsequently to Soviet, culture." This is not to imply that *Russia and the Commonwealth A to Z* has no entries with solid descriptions and data. It does. But it is not always easy to tell when the authors are trying to entertain or trying to inform. Internal cross-references are indicated by asterisks, and a thematic index has been provided.

This enjoyable, inexpensive (in paperback) book is recommended for the browsing section of any library with patrons interested in Soviet culture. However, it should not be purchased as a competitor to more solid works of reference, such as Stephen White's *Political and Economic Encyclopedia of the Soviet Union and Eastern Europe* (St. James,

1990) or an updated *Soviet and East European Political Dictionary* (ABC-Clio, 1984).

Historical Dictionary of Revolutionary China 1839–1976. Ed. by Edwin Pak-wah Leung. Greenwood, 1992. 566p. bibliog. index. hardcover $85 (0-313-26457-0).
951 Revolutions—China—History—Dictionaries || China—History—19th century—Dictionaries || China—History—20th century—Dictionaries [CIP] 91-15990

Beginning with the Opium War, when China's loss set the stage for various revolutionary movements that followed, and continuing through the end of the Cultural Revolution, when the Gang of Four was arrested, the *Historical Dictionary of Revolutionary China 1839–1976* treats persons, incidents, organizations, movements, and policies. More than 70 scholars from around the world contributed signed articles to this work, edited by Pak-wah Leung of Seton Hall University. Articles range from one to five pages in length, and most contain references for further reading. Of course, Sun Yat-sen, Mao Tse-tung, and Chiang Kai-shek are included, but so are Ch'iu Chin ("martyr of the 1911 Revolution; forerunner of the Chinese feminist movement"); Tz'u-hsi, the Empress Dowager; scholars such as Yen Fu ("Translator and interpreter of Charles Darwin . . . and other Western thinkers"); and such Americans as Edgar Snow and General Joseph Stilwell. Topical entries include *Boxer Rebellion, Taiping Revolution, Iron and Blood Society, Quotations from Chairman Mao, Hundred Flowers*—a broad collection that gives a good picture of these years.

Internal cross-references are noted with an asterisk. Most entries are given in English (e.g., *New Tide Society*), but a few are in Chinese (*Ko-lao Hui* [Elder Brother Society]). Romanization is basically Wade-Giles "because scholars in the China field have used it widely since the nineteenth century," but the index uses both the Wade-Giles and pinyin systems to accommodate present practice. Additional helps are a 25-page chronology of events, a 23-page bibliography of materials in English and Chinese, a glossary showing romanized terms with their Chinese characters, and an index.

The only major problem encountered in using this volume was finding the Cultural Revolution (certainly an important event), which was referred to many times by an asterisk in other entries but which is not where it is expected under C. Instead, it is found in G as *Great Proletarian Cultural Revolution* and is located only by using a *see* reference in the index.

While other biographical references cover this period in China, this dictionary provides coverage of both persons and subjects. The authoritative but readable text of the *Historical Dictionary of Revolutionary China* will be a valuable resource for public and academic libraries and may also be of use in some high school libraries.

The Middle East: A Political Dictionary. By Lawrence Ziring. ABC-Clio, 1992. 410p. index. tables. hardcover $56.50 (0-87436-612-7); paper $29.95 (0-87436-697-6).
956'.003 Middle East—Politics and government—Dictionaries || Middle East—Dictionaries [OCLC] 92-15379

Essentially an updated and expanded version of the author's *Middle East Political Dictionary* (ABC-Clio, 1984), this work uses the same arrangement, organizing material under seven major topics (e.g., "Diplomacy," "Israelis and Palestinians," "Conflict"). Alphabetically arranged articles under each topic are composed of two parts: a general history and/or description (with cross-references) followed by an analytic or interpretive essay entitled "Significance."

Defining the Middle East as all the countries from Morocco on the Atlantic Ocean to Pakistan in the east and from Turkey in the north to the Sudan in the south, Ziring provides a guide to recent history and current events in 22 sovereign states. Topics as recent as Operation Desert Storm and the Madrid Peace Conference and as varied as *The Satanic Verses*, the Hizbollah, and the Polisario Front are addressed with a view toward placing them in perspective with the recent history of this volatile region. A subject index using entry rather than page numbers, tables of current statistics, and a reference map add to this book's value.

The Middle East: A Political Dictionary generally compares favorably with its predecessor. Unfortunately, there is no bibliography, and this is the one area in which the new edition does not improve upon the earlier one. Academic and public libraries needing current information on this part of the world will want to consider purchase.

Historical Dictionary of Israel. By Bernard Reich. Scarecrow, 1992. 351p. bibliog. hardcover $47.50 (0-8108-2535-X).
956.94'003 Israel—History—Dictionaries || Israel—Politics and government—Dictionaries [CIP] 92-5324

This is number 8 in Scarecrow's Asian Historical Dictionaries series. Additional titles cover Indonesia, Jordan, Vietnam, and other nations. The compiler is a professor of international affairs at George Washington University and has written previously about the Middle East and Israel. His *Political Leaders of the Contemporary Middle East and North Africa: A Biographical Dictionary* was favorably reviewed here [RBB My 15 90].

The new work aims to provide a comprehensive reference source on the people, places, and events that contributed to the modern Jewish state. The book begins with a 19-page chronology from Abraham through January 1992, including the current peace conference. It relates directly to the dictionary by capitalizing words that are entries. A list of tables follows, providing the years, who presidents, prime ministers, and other leaders were in office; statistics on immigration to Palestine/Israel each year from 1882 through 1989; the population of the new state by religion; and the text of the 1948 Declaration of the Establishment of the State of Israel.

A 22-page introduction provides an overview of the contents. The bulk of the work is a dictionary of clearly written entries, ranging from a few sentences to a few pages, depending on the topic. Running heads at the top of each page and *see also* references assist the reader. Years of birth and death are given in biographies. Representative entries include *Arabs in Israel, Balfour Declaration, Six Day War,* and *World Zionist Organization.*

The work's strength is in enabling users to gain a good understanding of the political aspects of the state. Information is balanced, such as in the entry *Intifada*, which describes the five-year-old Palestinian uprising. At the end of the work is a 65-page bibliography arranged by subject, from general works to Zionism and anti-Zionism.

The *Historical Dictionary of Israel* is a thorough, solid reference source on the modern nation. It is also helpful in gaining an understanding of why the past is so important to the country. Placing the extensive bibliography at the back of the work increases the work's value to librarians and advanced students. General users, however, may have found short bibliographic references after the entries more helpful for immediate follow-up. The work will be useful in a wide range of public and academic libraries. While the information can be found in other sources, bringing it together in one source is helpful.

The Vietnam War: Handbook of the Literature and Research. By James S. Olson. Greenwood, 1993. 498p. bibliog. indexes. hardcover $85 (0-313-27422-3).
959.704 Vietnamese Conflict, 1961–1975 [OCLC] 92-25626

The Vietnam War has been over for 17 years, and a tremendous number of books on the conflict have been published during that time. This handbook provides a discussion by various scholars of the major works. It is divided into 23 chapters, each an extended bibliographic essay that treats one of a variety of topics, such as military strategy, air power, peace negotiations, Indo-Chinese refugees, prisoners of war, and women's and blacks' participation in the war. The essays emphasize the scholarly rather than the popular literature, although some popular books like David Halberstam's are included. Only English-language works are discussed, with an emphasis on those published in the U.S. A valuable part of each chapter is the extensive bibliographies. A filmography in an appendix gives film title, year of release, and director, but no other information. Certain films listed, such as *Star Wars, Invasion of the Body Snatchers,* and *The Fountainhead,* have a tenuous connection to the Vietnam War. The book concludes with author and subject indexes.

There are several bibliographies of fiction on the Vietnam War (e.g., *The Vietnam War in Literature* [RBB My 1 93]), but this work stresses nonfiction. Academic and public libraries that need a work that summarizes and evaluates the most important writings on the war will want to purchase *The Vietnam War: Handbook of the Literature and Research.*

HISTORY

Political Leaders of Contemporary Africa South of the Sahara: A Biographical Dictionary. Ed. by Harvey Glickman. Greenwood, 1992. 361p. bibliog. index. hardcover $65 (0-313-26781-2).

967.03'2 Politicians—Africa, Sub-Saharan—Biography—Dictionaries ‖ Statesmen—Africa, Sub-Saharan—Biography—Dictionaries ‖ Africa, Sub-Saharan—Biography ‖ Africa, Sub-Saharan—Politics and government—1960– [CIP] 91-39641

This work profiles 54 leaders from sub-Saharan Africa since 1945. Chosen for inclusion were individuals who shaped events in the emerging countries and/or governments of Africa. Among those covered are Idi Amin, Hastings Banda, Félix Houphouët-Boigny, Kenneth Kaunda, Julius Nyerere, and Desmond Mpilo Tutu.

All of the entries have been penned by social scientists who work in the field of African studies. The introduction discusses the lack of female participants in leadership roles on this continent. Profiles are arranged alphabetically and average six pages in length. Each begins with a tag that notes the offices held by the person (with dates) and concludes with a bibliography of works by and about him. The essays briefly cover childhood and education but stress the political careers of these men. Appendixes include a listing of subjects by country from Angola to Zimbabwe, a chronology of the twentieth century, bibliographic notes, and a detailed index that lists political parties as well as personal names.

Who's Who in Africa [RBB S 1 92] profiles only current African leaders; 25 of the people in *Political Leaders* are also found in *Who's Who*. The 29 people in *Political Leaders* who are not in *Who's Who*, such as Milton Obote and Jomo Kenyatta, are either no longer in power or deceased.

Political Leaders in Contemporary Africa South of the Sahara is a well-written resource that will be of value for reference service in academic, public, and secondary school libraries.

The Young People's Encyclopedia of the United States. 10v. Ed. by William E. Shapiro. Millbrook, 1992. illus. index. maps. hardcover $239.50 (1-56294-151-8).

970'.003 U.S.—Encyclopedias, Juvenile ‖ North America—Encyclopedias, Juvenile [OCLC] 91-4141

This set is designed to provide basic information for children ages 9–12 about the U.S. and its neighbors. With over 1,200 entries, the encyclopedia covers such topics as history, geography, the performing arts, scientific discoveries, industry, sports, religion, and nature as they are reflected in American life. Mexico and Canada are given entries but not European countries. This is not intended to be a comprehensive encyclopedia for children but a specialized work that will assist them in "understanding our nation's place in the world today."

Entries are arranged alphabetically in 10 volumes. The first three letters of the first and last entry in each volume are shown on the spine under the volume number. Volume 4, for example, shows FER–HER on the spine, the first entry being *Fermi* and the last *Heron*. The full entry title for the first and last entry is shown on the front cover of each volume. Pages are numbered sequentially, but page numbers are not shown on the cover.

Articles in the encyclopedia are brief, usually one to two paragraphs. Information is presented in a noncontroversial way. The entry *Ku Klux Klan* gives the basic facts about the Klan in a dozen or so lines and says only that the Klan would "threaten and attack black people." Each of the 50 states is given a two-page spread. In addition to historical information, the state entry includes a fact box listing the capital, area, population, date of statehood, principal rivers, highest points, motto, and state song. A second box lists places of interest in the state. Also included are a picture of the state flag, flower, bird, and tree, and a map. There are brief entries for major cities.

U.S. presidents are each given a full-page article. Date of birth, education, political party, term of office, and marital status are shown in a box. Each entry is illustrated by a small portrait. Topics of special interest are highlighted by a two-page spread and color margins; examples are *Exploration of North America*, *Jazz*, and *The Space Program*. Articles appear for ethnic groups, and among the biographical entries are many for minority-group members. Many boxed features accompany articles; for example, lists of the top 20 newspapers by circulation and the 10 largest advertisers. All articles are accompanied by one of 12 symbols that identify a subject area, such as science and space or sports. Articles are not signed. A list of consultants and their affiliations is found at the beginning of volume 1. The encyclopedia does a good job covering the various aspects of American life.

The encyclopedia is heavily illustrated, with almost 2,000 full-color illustrations, often two or more to a two-page spread. Photographs, which are uniformly good, are supplemented by drawings, maps, and charts. While the majority of these visual aids are of high quality (e.g., the plan of the Hartsfield International Airport or the drawing of Paul Bunyan), some are poor. The portraits of the presidents are a good example of this inconsistency. Lyndon Johnson's portrait is a bad likeness, but Jefferson's is satisfactory. Drawings accompanying biographies are also sometimes poorly done. The ones for Charles Lindbergh, Margaret Mead, and Robert Peary look grainy, almost as if they were done on a low-quality computer printer. However, despite this problem, the set is visually appealing, and the illustrations supplement the text in valuable ways.

An index to the entire set is included in volume 10. Main entries are highlighted by boldface type. Page numbers for illustrations are in italics. Volume numbers are not cited in the index, only page numbers. This may make its use difficult for young children. Though a boxed legend on each page of the index lists volume numbers and the pages found in each, it is easy to miss. The same is true for any page that has more than one entry, as is common in this set. A reader looking up something other than a main entry would not know which entry to read to find the topic. Following the main index is a topical index divided into 12 areas corresponding to the symbols used throughout the encyclopedia. A legend defining each of the symbols is at the front of each volume. An explanation of how to use the encyclopedia is found in volume 1. Within each entry, small capital letters are used to designate articles of related interest.

The Young People's Encyclopedia of the United States is similar in coverage to older sets, such as the *American Heritage New Illustrated History of the United States*. However, the information in this set is more current and more limited. Entries are brief; while the editors state the set is written at a fourth- to fifth-grade reading level it may not provide enough information on any one topic for children that old. This encyclopedia would be a useful companion to other works on American history and life but cannot stand as the sole source for children on either topic. School libraries and large public libraries will want to consider this set in light of curriculum demands and collection needs. It is an attractive and appealing place to begin the study of our nation.

The Hispanic-American Almanac: A Reference Work on Hispanics in the United States. By Nicolás Kanellos. Gale, 1993. 900p. bibliog. illus. index. hardcover $99.50 (0-8103-7944-9).

973 Hispanic Americans—Encyclopedias ‖ Hispanic Americans—Biography ‖ Hispanic Americans—Social life and customs ‖ Almanacs, American [OCLC] 92-75003

A parallel publication to *The Negro Almanac* (5th ed. [RBB Ap 15 90]), this resource brings together information from diverse disciplines concerning the background, history, and contributions of Hispanic Americans. During the four years it took to research and compile the almanac, the renowned Hispanic scholar Kanellos was assisted by a distinguished panel of advisors and contributors whose essays in the almanac are signed. The expressed intention of the work is to serve as "a one-stop source for information on people of the U.S. whose ancestors—or they themselves—originated in Spain, the Spanish-speaking countries of South and Central America, Mexico, Puerto Rico, or Cuba." The book carefully notes throughout the text that while the Spanish language acts as a unifying factor, great diversity exists within the Hispanic American community.

The almanac is organized in 25 chapters on such topics as population, language, education, music, media, business, women, film, art, and scholarship. Early chapters focus on background and history, and one provides reprints of important documents, such as presidential messages enunciating the Monroe Doctrine, resolutions approved by the Constitutional Convention of Puerto Rico in 1952, and an English translation of "Our America" by José Martí.

A typical narrative chapter is the one devoted to the family, which is 22 pages in length and illustrated with seven photographs of family activities. It opens with a general discussion about the cultural diversity of the Hispanic community and the institution of the family in a societal context. A section on the institutions of the Hispanic family clearly describes the importance of *la familia* (the greater family) and the roles of *parentesco* (the concept of familism), *compadrazgo* (godparenthood), *confianza* (trust), and family ideology. Attention is then directed to the historical background and current situation of these familial institutions for specific groups of Hispanic Americans, including Puerto Ricans, Dominicans, Cubans, and Mexican Americans. The chapter concludes with a list of 21 references to books and articles, most of which were published in the 1980s.

One chapter is devoted to Hispanic American organizations, profiling 44 associations that have a broad, national scope. Other chapters list additional organizations that focus on narrower concerns, such as religion, labor, or politics. Similarly, one chapter is devoted to profiles of 50 "Prominent Hispanics" and their accomplishments in a variety of fields, while many additional brief biographical sketches are included in most topical chapters. The amount of information included for individuals varies substantially from chapter to chapter, but in all cases, year of birth and summary of achievements are included.

More than 400 photographs, maps, and charts enhance the text, including, for example, a table of the 30 largest Hispanic businesses and others showing television stations that are owned by or affiliated with Telemundo. Generally, statistics are presented within the narrative, rather than in tables, and the demographics are as recent as the figures released by the U.S. Census Bureau in 1991. Other features of the work include a general bibliography, a glossary of frequently used Spanish terms, and a keyword index of people, places, and events.

The front matter does not include instructions for using the book or definitions of terms for beginners, such as *Latino* or *Chicano*. It would have been helpful if the book included an explanation of its organization. For instance, biographical sketches appear throughout the work, and the table of contents is inconsistent in noting whether a particular chapter includes such profiles. Nor is it clear why some profiles are included in a separate section and others are in a topical chapter.

More than 22 million Hispanics live in the U.S., making it one of the largest Spanish-speaking countries in the world. *The Hispanic-American Almanac* is a unique and important compendium of information about the history, culture, and accomplishments of this diverse population. It is an essential purchase for high school, public, and academic libraries.

The United States. 3v. Ed. by Godfrey Hodgson. Facts On File, 1992. bibliog. index. tables. maps. hardcover $150 (0-8160-1621-6).
973 U.S. [CIP] 91-494

This is the latest addition to Facts On File's regional series, Handbooks to the Modern World. A volume on Canada is also due to be published this fall. The Board gave generally positive recommendations to previous titles in the series, *The Soviet Union and Eastern Europe* and *Western Europe* [RBB Ag 86]. As with all sources of this type, the statistics will soon be out-of-date. However, the articles are of high quality and will be useful for many years. Hodgson is foreign editor of the London's *Independent* newspaper and has published other books on American affairs, including *America in Our Time*. The 55 contributors are English and American academics and writers. For example, theologian Martin Marty wrote "The American Ethical Condition and Prospect." All essays are signed.

Volume 1 profiles the 50 states plus the District of Columbia. The profiles, uniformly arranged, cover history, geography, population, employment, agriculture, education, health, social services, crime, media, and government. For example, the Arkansas entry describes the 1957 Little Rock school integration crisis and gives statistics on marriage rate, ethnic composition, housing starts, crop production, teacher salaries, criminal justice expenditures, and voting. All population data are from the 1990 census. Each profile begins with a black-and-white map of the state and concludes with brief biographical sketches of elected officials and a telephone and address list of state information sources (e.g., chamber of commerce, board of tourism). A series of state-by-state comparative statistics completes this volume (e.g., population, employment, personal income).

Volumes 2 and 3 consist of several dozen essays grouped into five broad categories: post–World War I history, demography, politics, economics, and social affairs. Often 5,000 to 10,000 words in length, they offer a well-balanced mix of background explanation, detail, and analysis. For example, the essay "Crime and Punishment" begins with a discussion of the measurement of crime (police statistics, victimization surveys, self-report studies) and its social dimensions (region, community size, sex, race, age, and class). Substantial statistical evidence is cited ("In 1988, 28% of all people arrested for serious crimes were under the age of 18 and 57% were under the age of 25"). Following is a clear overview of types of crimes, reasons for criminal activity, methods of treatment (e.g., retribution versus rehabilitation), and the issue of capital punishment. Some essays conclude with bibliographies. The index at the back of volume 3 covers the whole set.

This is a recommended purchase for large public libraries and to support undergraduate work in academic libraries. While the first volume belongs in the reference collection, volumes 2 and 3 should probably be circulated. Europa's *The USA and Canada* [My 15 90] does not treat individual states, and it is less current and more expensive. However, it does include more directory information than *The United States*.

African American Encyclopedia. 6v. Ed. by Michael W. Williams. Marshall Cavendish, 1993. bibliog. indexes. hardcover $479.95 (1-85435-545-7).
973'.0496073 Afro-Americans—Encyclopedias [OCLC] 93-141

With 2,900 entries in six volumes, this new set encompasses several thousand years and a wide range of topics. Most of the 150 contributors are professors of African American studies at colleges and universities throughout the U.S. A list of their names and academic affiliations appears in volume 1, and the articles each authored are signed. The text is written in easily understood language, and technical topics are avoided. The emphasis is on the experiences, history, and contributions of African Americans in the U.S.

Entries are arranged alphabetically in two columns per page and range from A. *Philip Randolph Institute* to *Zydeco*. Coverage includes individuals, institutions, literary works, films, plays, television series, musical groups and styles, sports, legal decisions, events, places, movements, and organizations. Three levels of entries—varying in length—are included. Short, dictionary-type entries range in length from a few lines to a column or two. Signed articles of two or three pages, or approximately 500 words, conclude with lists of suggested readings. Examples of this kind of entry are the articles *Folklore*, *Football*, *Harlem Renaissance*, *Detective Fiction by African American Writers*, *Judges*, and *Jazz*. Also in this category are articles on more important individuals: Frederick Douglass, Ida B. Wells, Carter G. Woodson, Martin Luther King, Aretha Franklin, Barbara Jordan, Jesse Jackson, Michael Jackson, and Spike Lee, to name a few. The third type of entry generally continues for 5,000 words and covers five to seven pages. These lengthy articles focus on more general topics, such as *Affirmative Action*, *Family Life*, *Health*, and *Religion*, all dealt with in an African American context. The lists of suggested readings appended to the longer articles are annotated with a few sentences that describe the content of each work.

In general, the set is well balanced between contemporary and historical issues and individuals. Some coverage reflects events that occurred as recently as the elections of November 1992. Carol Moseley Braun's successful run for the U.S. Senate is noted, although no mention is made in the article on Al Sharpton of his unsuccessful bid for the Senate in the New York primary. There is good coverage of contemporary popular culture, with entries for such people as actresses Halle Berry and Jasmine Guy and musical groups Public Enemy and En Vogue.

Access is enhanced by a comprehensive index in volume 6 and also by capitalizing within articles those names or terms that have entries of their own. However, no *see* references are included in the main body of the book, and those in the index cover alternate forms of names and acronyms, not subjects. This means the reader has to do some second-guessing. For example, runaway slaves are entered as *slave runaways*, not necessarily the first place one might look.

A brief editorial note at the beginning of the set states that it is the goal of the encyclopedia to provide objective information. In fact, there is an admirable lack of bias in articles on controversial issues, such as *Amos 'n' Andy* and *Farrakhan, Louis*. Nevertheless, some might argue whether, as stated in the article *African Heritage*, Europe really was "in the throes of the so-called Dark Ages" as late as 1324; or whether, as stated in *Afrocentricity*, Black History Month is "largely ineffective." The Board did notice some inconsistencies. Virginia Hamilton, the noted children's author, has no entry of her own, though she is discussed at some length in *Juvenile and Young Adult Fiction by African Americans*. Walter Dean Myers, on the other hand, does have his own brief entry but is not mentioned in the juvenile and young adult fiction survey article.

Enhancing the text are more than 1,500 black-and-white illustrations. Most frequently, these are pictures of individuals featured in the biographical entries. Reproductions of photographs on various aspects of black life and culture, often from the collections of the Library of Congress and the National Archives, are used effectively. For example, pictures of an African American military band, volunteers in an office of the segregated Navy, and black women railroad workers illustrate *World War II and African Americans*. Maps, tables, and graphs are also included to illustrate such topics as the current country boundaries in Africa and the 10 largest black U.S. metropolitan populations of 1988.

Volume 6 of the set, following the encyclopedic entries, includes six special lists and a bibliography. The list of the 100 most profitable black-owned businesses of 1992 includes name, founding date, name of the chief officer, and headquarters address. Addresses are also included in the list of research centers and libraries that focus on the study of African American life. Names of predominantly African American colleges and universities are organized by state, as are the lists of periodicals and newspapers and of radio and television stations. The names of persons who are featured in the encyclopedia's biographical entries appear in a list organized by profession. A 14-page bibliography of recent books and periodical articles is topically arranged into such broad categories as "Black Nationalism," "Health," and "Performing Arts."

In terms of scope, the only comparable work is the *Negro Almanac*. While the encyclopedia is arranged alphabetically, the *Negro Almanac* is arranged thematically. This provides a different perspective by putting some of the people, issues, and events it covers in context instead of presenting them in isolation. Also, the *Negro Almanac* has a number of valuable features, such as a chronology of African American participation in the American Revolution and a list of inventions by African Americans, that cannot be found in the encyclopedia. By virtue of its greater length, however, the encyclopedia is much more comprehensive. Depending on the community served, some small libraries may continue to rely on the *Negro Almanac* alone. However, the *African American Encyclopedia* will be extremely useful in public, high school, and college libraries and is highly recommended.

The Black 100: A Ranking of the Most Influential African-Americans, Past and Present. By Columbus Salley. Citadel, 1993. 320p. bibliog. illus. index. hardcover $21.95 (0-8065-1299-7).
973'.0496073 Afro-Americans—Biography ‖ Afro-Americans—History [OCLC] 92-39545

This work is not a traditional biographical reference source, although sketches are included for 81 men and 21 women of African-American descent, ranging in time from 1619 to individuals living today. The author has selected persons who are the "collective giant on whose shoulders African-Americans stand in their unending quest for full economic, political and social equality" and then has ranked these individuals, from 1 to 100, based on the contribution of each to the "ongoing struggle to realize full citizenship." The rankings were not formulated in a scientific or quantitative mode but were based on the author's evaluation of the impact each profiled individual has had on "the struggle of Blacks to be whatever they choose." Salley is an entrepreneur, a former government official, a superintendent emeritus of the Newark (New Jersey) public school system, and the author of *What Color is Your God? Black Consciousness and the Christian Faith* (1988).

The individuals profiled here come from all periods of American history, worked in a multiplicity of professions, and represent a wide variety of viewpoints. Featured personalities are famous, ranging from Martin Luther King (#1) to Rosa Parks (#100), from Hank Aaron (#87) to Phyllis Wheatley (#19), and from Clarence Thomas (#98) to Harriet Tubman (#12). Each entry opens with a portrait, followed by a two- to six-page biographical sketch, including both factual data and the rationale for the ranking of the subject. Typically, the narrative features quotations both by and about the person and an explanation of how the individual relates to other featured subjects. For instance, the entry for James Baldwin (#49) opens with a quote from Maya Angelou on his significance as a black writer who dared "to confront this racist nation," and this theme is explored through the remainder of the vignette. Salley explains how Baldwin was an author-activist who avoided taking sides with the tactics of either Martin Luther King or Malcolm X, but rather, "he always saw his role as a writer to give blacks a superior moral and spiritual sense, which would keep them from becoming as debased as racist whites in America." No full citations to references are included in the profiles, but some entries provide a selected list of works by the profiled individual. The volume concludes with a selected bibliography and an index.

For the vast majority of the subjects profiled in *The Black 100*, a host of biographical reference sources exist, such as *The Negro Almanac* [RBB Ap 15 90], *Notable Black American Women* [RBB Ap 15 92], *African American Biographies* [RBB Ag 1 92], and *Contemporary Black Biography* [RBB Ap 1 92], and any of these more comprehensive and traditional sources are preferred for the reference collection. However, *The Black 100* is written in a readable style and is sure to create controversy, as any book of rankings does. Public, high school, and undergraduate libraries may want to consider purchasing this work for circulating collections because of the unique perspective provided by the author.

The Kaiser Index to Black Resources, 1948–1986. 5v. Carlson Publishing, 1992. hardcover $995 (0-926019-60-0).
016.973'0496073 Afro-Americans—Indexes ‖ Blacks—Indexes [CIP] 92-11493

In 1948, the reference staff of the Schomburg Library branch of the New York Public Library, the nation's preeminent research collection on the African American experience, began a practice common to reference departments: a card file of citations to sources they had found useful in answering questions. The file grew to include systematic indexing of periodicals and newspapers. All of this was done—growing to more than 100,000 cards bearing 174,000 citations through 1986—during staff members' spare time; it was never anyone's assigned duty. It was, instead, a labor of love, undertaken of necessity in response to the dearth in 1948 of reference works dealing with blacks.

Even though reference publishing since then has taken note of the need to cover black studies, the Kaiser File, named after Ernest Kaiser (the librarian who contributed the most to its development), remains an important reference tool for researchers and staff at the Schomburg. *The Kaiser Index* makes the file available to a wider audience in improved form over its p-slip original. During the process of transcribing the thousands of handwritten entries to machine-readable form, subject headings were revised to conform with current Library of Congress headings, and the categories and order of information in each citation were standardized.

The 174,000 citations are arranged by LC subject headings. Under each heading, items appear in annual blocks in reverse chronological order and, within each annual block, alphabetically by title. Although many citations include authors' names, this information was not recorded consistently as the file developed over the years, and thus there is no author index to the citations. One hundred sixty-six periodicals and newspapers provided most of those citations. Mingled among citations to these sources are entries for books (whose citations include their Schomburg call number) and pamphlets and other ephemera. Many citations include brief annotations summarizing content and noting the presence of illustrations.

Inconsistencies in the content of entries are a result of both the manner in which many staff members worked on this in spare moments and the inability to do a major retrospective cleanup of the index to add authors' names and annotations to citations lacking these features. Adding such information would have required returning to the original sources and, in effect, redoing much of a 28-year project from scratch.

Despite the effort to edit every entry for consistency, if not completeness, some problems linger. For example, under the heading *Authors*,

West Indian is an entry reading "Has 2,000 authors; Caribbean Writers: A Bio-bibliographical Critical Encyclopedia...." In this case, the annotation noting that the encyclopedia covers 2,000 authors incorrectly precedes the title of Donald Herdeck's *Caribbean Writers*. Such problems, especially considering the size and home-grown genesis of this database, are few and far between. If a user is stumped by such a citation, the introduction invites librarians to call the reference desk at the Schomburg Library for assistance. Through its interlibrary loan department, the library also offers photocopies of articles indexed.

The other major index to periodical literature in this field, G. K. Hall's *Index to Black Periodicals*, formerly *Index to Periodical Articles by and about Blacks* and earlier *Index to Periodical Articles by and about Negroes*, began its coverage with 1950. (Its predecessor during the 1940s was A. P. Marshall's *Guide to Negro Periodical Literature*.) This serial's selection of journals indexed has ebbed and flowed over the years. The overlap of coverage between it and the *Kaiser Index* is such that neither source is sufficient by itself; the two complement one another, and any library with a serious interest in African American studies needs both. Because it covers the period leading up to the landmark years and wake of the civil rights struggle, *The Kaiser Index* is a significant complement to general-purpose magazine and newspaper indexes and specialized indexes in American history. Academic and large public libraries should consider purchase.

The Presidents of the United States. By Samuel Crompton. Smithmark, 1992. 80p. illus. index. hardcover $7.98 (0-8317-7074-0).
973.0992 [B] Presidents—United States—Biography [OCLC]

This slender book by historian Samuel Crompton summarizes the basic personal, social, and political events that shaped each presidential term of office. Individual articles are arranged in chronological order, beginning with George Washington and ending with George Bush.

Each article provides a brief description of the individual's public persona and a summary of his life and career. The entries vary in length from one to four pages; each article includes at least two illustrations, so some articles consist of only four or five paragraphs of text. Each entry includes a portrait or photograph of the subject. Additional illustrations, sometimes as many as three per page, feature reproductions in various mediums. Approximately 20 percent are in color.

While this book provides no information that can't be found in a general encyclopedia, its articles provide a basic overview of each administration, and its numerous illustrations complement the text. Designed for home use, it will also be suitable for middle and high school libraries and public libraries.

Sanitary Fairs: A Philatelic and Historical Study of Civil War Benevolences. By Alvin Robert Kantor and Marjorie Sered Kantor. SF Publishing, 1088 Bluff Rd., Glencoe, IL 60022, 1992. 304p. bibliog. illus. index. hardcover $60 (0-9632603-0-8).
973.7'77 U.S. Sanitary Commission ‖ U.S.—History—Civil War, 1861–1865—Hospitals, charities, etc. ‖ Covers (Philately) [BKL] 92-61024

This unique reference and lavishly illustrated volume deals with Civil War envelopes rather than the U.S. postage stamps that were affixed to them and will have an appeal far beyond the interests of stamp collectors. Under the aegis of philately, the work is also a study of the manner in which the U.S. Sanitary Commission—predecessor of the Red Cross and of the Veterans Administration—was organized and financially supported. The authors spent 14 years preparing this title, following a lifetime of collecting the envelopes, photographs, and letters that are reproduced here.

The Sanitary Commission originated during the Civil War and, without federal funding, depended on the general public for financial support. Sanitary fairs were gatherings where speeches were made, but also where volunteers undertook to raise money for hospitals, ambulances, care of the wounded, and even medical care of veterans. They did this by selling the usual type of souvenirs, but among them were envelopes, called *covers* in the world of philately today. These were preprinted, usually in the upper-left corners, with the name and date of the fair and acted both as a souvenir and as a medium of postal communication. Initially, regular U.S. postage stamps had to be affixed, but after a while the fairs issued their own stamps that could be used as well as, or even instead of, the regular postage. Many of these covers and stamps are rare and are of much interest to collectors today. The book is painstaking in identifying and describing the materials depicted, citing any previous commentary about them, relating the historical context of their issue, providing a "rarity code" from 1 to 5 for each of the philatelic items, and including Scott numbers whenever appropriate.

The preprinted covers took on elaborate proportions, and some of the halftone illustrations in this book show great ingenuity, with coats of arms, patriotic emblems, state seals, pictures of hospitals, other buildings, and the like being quite common. These ornamental covers enable historians to reconstruct many details of life during the Civil War era that would otherwise be unknown. The book also gives details on how Civil War soldiers were allowed to frank their mail, as well as a separate chapter on prisoner-of-war mail and even on mail from hospital inmates who were also POWs. Also described are women's relief organizations, which sprang up in areas where the U.S. commission did not reach. The book ends with a useful appendix that lists all known hospitals, both Union and Confederate, as of 1864, with the number of beds in each. Also included are a glossary of philatelic terms, a six-page bibliography, and an excellent index.

Sanitary Fairs, with its approximately 500 illustrations, serves as a work of history and will be useful in any library that has a clientele interested in this period of time. With its emphasis on the covers and stamps related to the operation of the U.S. Sanitary Commission, it is also a specialized reference for libraries serving philatelic enthusiasts.

The Union Army, 1861–1865: Organizations and Operations, Volume II: The Western Theater. By Frank J. Welcher. Indiana Univ., 1993. 990p. indexes. hardcover $75 (0-253-36454-X).
973.7'41 U.S. Army—History—Civil War, 1861–1865 ‖ U.S. Army—Organization—History—19th century ‖ U.S.—History—Civil War, 1861–1865—Campaigns [CIP]

Like the first volume published in 1989, this volume consists largely of accounts of the organization of the various units of the Union Army, arranged by departments, armies, army corps, and other minor organizations of fighting men, followed by a long section narrating the battles and campaigns fought against the confederacy during the Civil War. Volume 1 covered the eastern theater; this one covers battles in the western theater, which included Tennessee, Mississippi, western Virginia, and other states.

Reviewers of the first volume criticized the lack of an index, pointing out that it was difficult to follow the career of any individual officer, particularly a senior one, unless he happened to remain with the same unit throughout, which was not common. The promised index appears in volume 2 and covers both volumes. Though each has separate pagination, the volumes are easily distinguished in the two indexes—one of personal names and the other of Union army units—by the typeface used, roman for volume 1 and boldface for volume 2. Although each unit commander's name is given in full in the text, his rank is not. The lack of this information may be excused on the grounds that military rank changed often, especially in time of combat. Even so, some indication of rank might have been included in the name index; thus, William T. Sherman might have been listed as "Col., 1861; Brig. Gen., Aug. 1861; Maj. Gen., May 1862; Lt. Gen., 1866; Gen., 1869." Admittedly this would have greatly increased the amount of work required and extended the pagination of the index well beyond its present 64 pages. But for historical and genealogical purposes, it would have greatly enhanced the value of the book.

This work, like its earlier volume, is sound, scholarly, thorough, and trustworthy. It is a monument in the field of Civil War research, and no library that serves those with an interest in Civil War history can afford to be without it.

The Gay Nineties in America: A Cultural Dictionary of the 1890s. By Robert L. Gale. Greenwood, 1992. 457p. bibliog. index. hardcover $75 (0-313-27819-9).
973.8 U.S.—Civilization—1865–1918—Dictionaries [CIP] 91-47061

The publication of this volume is timely as we begin to celebrate various centennials of the 1890s in America. Interesting parallels from the 1890s to our age abound: the rise of conservative religious leaders, the presence of robber barons making fortunes arrogantly, the economic downturn and financial scandals, the significant progress of blacks, and, at the same time, a troublesome worsening of race relations.

Professor Gale's purpose is to give readers "a more thoughtful understanding of the excitement and ferment of that turbulent decade" and to provide a brief overview for persons interested in a topic, a person, or a specific literary work.

Divided into six main sections, *Gay Nineties* consists of a chronology of events from 1888 to 1901, an alphabetical list of the approximately 500 entries, the dictionary itself, a bibliography, a classified appendix listing the biographical entries by occupation, and finally a subject index.

The main entries consist of biographical essays on approximately 95 writers, journalists, critics, and a number of other important personalities in the arts, politics, social work, industry, and sports. Reformer Jane Addams is found along with inventor Alexander Graham Bell, businessman Marshall Field, and labor-leader Samuel Gompers. There are entries for 140 individual books (*How the Other Half Lives*, *Sister Carrie*) and 30 magazines such as *Collier's* and *Scribner's*. The remainder of the entries are topical essays on landmark events (e.g., *Panic of 1893*, *Spanish-American War*) and essays on crime, immigration, sports, and radio, among others.

The biographical and literary entries are strong, with ample cross-references (denoted with an asterisk) to other people who also have entries. The topical essays, however, seem uneven in their length and treatment. For example, the essay *Alcoholism* simply refers the reader to the biographies in the dictionary of people who had alcohol problems, whereas the entry *Sports* is 2½ pages long.

The question that presents itself to the reference librarian is whether other literary, biographical, or historical sources already in the reference collection can provide the same information as *The Gay Nineties*. Libraries owning the *Dictionary of American History* and *The Oxford Companion to American Literature* may find this work is not a high-priority purchase. However, it provides direct access to the time period for students who may not know enough about the 1890s to look up people and events in those other sources.

The Writer's Guide to Everyday Life in the 1800s. By Marc McCutcheon. Writer's Digest, 1993. 304p. hardcover $18.95 (0-89879-541-9).
973.8′4 U.S.—Social life and customs—19th century—Miscellanea [OCLC] 92-43336

This compendium of details about daily life in the U.S. was written as a reference for authors of westerns, romances, mysteries, and historical dramas so that they can readily add "color and credibility" to their stories set in the nineteenth century. The information is presented in 14 topical chapters covering such subjects as "Around the House," "Occupations," "Amusements," "Courtship and Marriage," and "Out on the Range." A number of the chapters have topical subdivisions as well. For instance, "Getting Around" is divided into sections covering carriages, coaches, and wagons; stage lines; railroads; and water travel.

Chapters briefly introduce the topic and contain a listing of short definitions that usually indicate the time period of usage. The terms used as entry words are listed alphabetically within each chapter or subsection. About one-third of the definitions include quotations from writings of the period; brief bibliographic citations are provided in the text with complete publication details included in the "References" section in the back of the book. Also included in each chapter are sidebars and special lists on such topics as medical treatments, the price of tailoring, and a chronology of hairstyles. Following the topical chapters are five separate chronologies that range in length from three to seven pages: events, noted books and novels, selected magazines, innovations, and popular songs.

The details in the book are often interesting. One can learn that the fee for a medical house call could often be reduced if the doctor's horse was fed; that in the 1880s almost every town had a roller-skating rink; and that oysters were so popular that they were not only sold in the streets and in special rooms in saloons, but they were the central attraction of many parties. However, the information provided is also selective, and often sources are not clearly cited. For instance, the list of traveling amusements is based on the 1845 *Annals of Salem* (Massachusetts), while information on this topic is not discernible about other areas of the country. The list of drinks served at a fashionable barroom in the 1840s was "taken from an advertisement," with no additional information about this source.

This book will be of interest to its intended readership of writers, but it would probably be best used by browsers or those experts looking for specific definitions or facts. Although it contains a wealth of details, the lack of indexing limits its reference usefulness for quick access to the information. This is not a definitive volume, so it is recommended for large collections or those with appropriate specialties.

Awesome Almanac of Illinois. By Jean F. Blashfield. B&B Publishing, P.O. Box 393, Fontana, WI 53125, 1993. 199p. illus. index. paper $12.95 (1-880190-04-4).
977.3 Illinois—History—Miscellanea ‖ Almanacs, American—Illinois [OCLC] 92-74707

Awesome Almanac of Indiana. By Nancy Jacobson. B & B Publishing, 1993. 151p. illus. index. paper $12.95 (1-880190-04-4).
977.2 Indiana—History—Miscellanea ‖ Almanacs, American—Indiana [BKL]

This new series of almanacs highlights facts and myths, celebrities and celebrations of the states. Each covers "the best, the worst, the most, the least, the famous, the infamous" of each state. The first five titles cover Illinois, Indiana, Wisconsin, Michigan, and Minnesota. Upcoming volumes will be on Ohio, Florida, Massachusetts, and northern and southern California.

The arrangement of the first two volumes is similar (e.g., sections on "Creative Indiana" and "The Sporting Life" compared with "The Arts" and "The Illinois Athlete)." Other sections treat business, natural resources, education, and entertainment. The table of contents and additional sections at the end—a chronology of state history—and an accurate index of people, places, and organizations—make each volume accessible for reference use. Information is current, and the writing style is lively. Layout, graphics, black-and-white photographs, and charts make the books enjoyable to use. There is no separate bibliography.

While librarians will find the books useful for a variety of reference needs, the general public will enjoy browsing through them for facts and legends, whether at home or while traveling. Although the softbound books may need reinforcing, they are reasonably priced and attractive. Public and high school libraries will want the volume for their state; they may want the books for surrounding states as well.

Latin America and the Caribbean: A Critical Guide to Research Sources. Ed. by Paula H. Covington. Greenwood, 1992. 924p. bibliog. indexes. hardcover $115 (0-313-26403-1; ISSN 1054-9102).
016.98 Latin America—Bibliography ‖ Caribbean Area—Bibliography [CIP] 91-34622

This guide to the growing field of Latin American studies provides essays on research trends, lists over 6,000 reference sources, and identifies specialized collections in U.S. research libraries. Given its multidisciplinary focus and easy-to-use format, it will be of value to a variety of users, including not only students, librarians, and scholars in Latin American studies, but also those seeking important sources in areas beyond their specialization and non–Latin Americanists engaged in comparative studies.

The book is divided into 15 chapters, beginning with a general bibliography of interdisciplinary sources, followed by chapters covering broad disciplines in the social sciences and the humanities, such as sociology and literature. Some chapters are divided into subfields (e.g. "Performing Arts" into "Dance" and "Theater"), regions ("Caribbean Literature"), or different time periods ("History"). Each chapter has an introductory essay highlighting the state of research within the discipline and its subfields, one or more sections listing reference sources for scholarly research, and a section describing relevant special collections, such as clipping files, primary-source material, and film resources. Almost all entries have annotations that are evaluative as well as descriptive, which should help users identify those works most useful in their fields of interest. Materials in Spanish and Portuguese are listed, but the majority of the works cited are in English. Generally, the scholarly essays are well written and well documented. The essay on the history of Brazil, for example, contains footnotes citing 250 books and articles. Author, title, and subject indexes complete the volume.

One of the book's most interesting features is a chapter on databases, which will appeal to researchers seeking sophisticated access to the most current information. The chapter describes the five databases established in the past decade that are specifically tailored for Latin American studies, reports on the fledging electronic information industry in Latin America, and speculates on the impact of technology on Latin American scholarship.

The book's 51 contributors come from a broad range of specialties and include bibliographers, curators, librarians, and faculty members. Editor Covington is Latin American and Iberian bibliographer at Vanderbilt University.

Used with other specialized sources like the annual *Handbook of Latin American Studies*, this timely guide will provide improved access for those interested in this part of the world.

The Western Reader's Guide: A Selected Bibliography of Nonfiction Magazines, 1953–91. By James A. Browning. Western Publications, Inc./Barbed Wire Press, P.O. Box 2107, Stillwater, OK 74076, 1992. 344p. hardcover $29.95 (0-935269-09-6).
016.978 West (U.S.)—History—Bibliography || West (U.S.)—Biography—Bibliography [CIP] 92-35419

This work is only a personal-name index, suggesting that the book is mistitled. More specifically, it is an index to approximately 2,000 names of persons who were the subject of articles in nonfiction western magazines published 1953–91. The author does not give a list of the "more than two dozen" magazines from which the bibliography is compiled. However, a random selection of 100 titles found that 18 different periodicals were included, ranked as follows by the number of citations: *Real West*, 15 percent; *True West*, 14 percent; *Frontier Times*, 12 percent; *Great West*, 7 percent; and then 14 other titles, in decreasing order, down to *Big West*, with only one percent. Only three titles of this genre are still published today: *True West* (the grandparent of the genre), *Old West*, and *Wild West*.

The author explains his use of personal names by stating that this was "the most practical alternative to the impossibility of keeping index cards on every topic of every article ever published." Consequently, the work is only of value when a name is known. Popular topics such as camels in the West, barbed wire, guns and ammo, or even such a specific location or event as the Rock Creek Massacre cannot be located. This objection is weakened somewhat by the argument that anyone who wanted to look up the Rock Creek Massacre would probably know that Wild Bill Hickok was associated with it. But it is unlikely that the reader would also know that a less-famous individual, Herman Good, was also connected, and so would miss a second article listed only under that name. No biographical data are provided about the individuals listed in the book, but the title of the citation is often a clue to the person's identity. For example, under the entry *Battey, Thomas C.* is a citation to the *Real West* article "A Quaker Missionary among the Kiowas." Pseudonyms are cross-referenced to the real names (e.g., "*Buntline, Ned* see Judson, Edward Z. C.").

Even though this work provides only access by name, it is the only source that indexes this genre of post-1950 western nonfiction magazines. Since these magazines were considered pulp or ephemeral in many instances, the articles cited will be difficult to locate. However, the book is recommended for libraries whose clientele includes serious western-history buffs, as well as for extensive special collections of popular literature and culture.

Encyclopedia of Western Lawmen & Outlaws. By Jay Robert Nash. Paragon House, 1992. 571p. bibliog. illus. index. hardcover $49.95 (1-55778-507-4).
978'.00992 [B] West (U.S.)—Biography—Encyclopedias | Peace officers—West (U.S.)—Biography—Encyclopedias || Outlaws—West (U.S.)—Biography—Encyclopedias [CIP] 91-46116

This work is largely excerpted from the six-volume *Encyclopedia of World Crime* [RBB O 1 90]. The largest section is an alphabetical listing, with many black-and-white illustrations, of both lawmen and bad men, most of them from the second half of the nineteenth century. Each entry is about one-third to a full page or more. Some women are included—Poker Alice, Belle Starr, Calamity Jane.

Following is a section of briefer entries for less important lawmen (only three or four lines each), and then a similar section for minor outlaw gang members, sidekicks, and those about whom nothing is known except that they killed and were captured. Next is a section of mostly full-page illustrations, arranged by the name of the locality or occasionally by well-known personal name—Billy the Kid, etc.

Many of these pictures are not found in the usual books dealing the West. Unfortunately, the index doesn't include these illustrations. For example, it has about 50 references to the Lincoln County War, yet the fine illustration showing masked men cutting a farmer's barbed-wire fence, in connection with this war, is not listed.

Preceding the index is an extensive but unannotated bibliography of about 40 pages. This is not very useful, as there is no tie-in with the text. There are dozens of nondescriptive titles listed, such as *Shutters West* or *Rice and Salt*, without indication as to why they are included. And there are some surprising omissions even in this extensive bibliography. Ramon Adams' 1964 classic, *Burs under the Saddle*, is not listed, though its index has 124 references to Billy the Kid. No cutoff date is given for the bibliography, but a random search turned up only one title published in 1981, one in 1979, and the vast majority—aside from contemporary nineteenth- century accounts—published between 1940 and 1970. Finally, it is necessary to make frequent use of the general index that concludes the book because of the three separate listings of names in the text—the full sketches, the shorter entries for lesser lawmen, and the same for lesser bandidos.

Despite these problems, the work has some value for reference librarians. It is probably the most extensive listing of outlaws and lawmen of the Wild West ever compiled. The narrative is well done, often with bits of dialog taken from contemporary sources. Libraries that regularly purchase "gunslinger" type books by Ramon Adams, Dane Coolidge, or Bill O'Neal will want to add this one to their collection, if they don't already own the *Encyclopedia of World Crime*.

Historical Dictionary of Australia. By James C. Docherty. Scarecrow, 1992. 300p. bibliog. tables. hardcover $35 (0-8108-2613-5).
994'.003 Australia—History—Dictionaries [CIP] 92-32339

This dictionary is the first in the new Oceanian Historical Dictionaries series, following Scarecrow's series of historical dictionaries for other areas of the world. The current work is intended to introduce the reader to the history and culture of Australia, ranging in time from the first human settlement thousands of years ago to 1992. The emphasis is on the modern period, and in the alphabetic dictionary section are entries for states and territories, large urban centers, major commodities, and biographies of such individuals as John Thomas Lang and Robert Gordon Menzies. Entries range from a few sentences to more than two pages; *see* and *see also* references are interspersed appropriately.

History is provided in the broad topical entries for such subjects as *Sheep and Wool*, *Diamonds*, *Convicts*, and *Irish*. In the two-page entry *Women*, the book relates how, until the 1830s, most European female settlers were convicts; how a shortage of women persisted until after the passing of the frontier society; and how women have pressured for such changes in the twentieth century as equality in employment opportunities, concluding with the Affirmative Action Act of 1986.

Approximately one-half of the book is the dictionary portion; the remainder consists of other materials to introduce Australian history. Preceding the dictionary are outline maps and an introductory essay about the continent's physical features, peoples, economy, and politics. In the back of the book are several appendixes, beginning with a chronology ranging in time from 60,000 B.C., with the migration of aborigines from Southeast Asia to Australia, to 1992 election results. Names of all governors-general and prime ministers are listed, and several tables of historical statistics are included. A substantial appendix is devoted to the bibliography, beginning with an essay providing an overview of the literature, and then citations are organized into 15 topical sections (e.g., political biographies, travel accounts, industry histories).

Compared with this new title, more comprehensive and expensive tools exist, such as the 11-volume *Australians: A Historical Library*. The work under review supplements ready-reference tools such as *The Far East and Australasia* (23d ed.), the *Australian Reference Dictionary* (Oxford, 1991), and the *Australian Encyclopedia* (1984). The *Historical Dictionary of Australia*, with its readable format, is moderately priced, up-to-date, convenient to use, and appropriate for all undergraduate academic libraries as well as public libraries serving patrons interested in this continent.

Index to Type of Material

ALMANACS

Almanac of Anniversaries, The, 80
Awesome Almanac of Illinois, 164
Awesome Almanac of Indiana, 164
Daily Celebrity Almanac, 1993, 151
European Women's Almanac, The, 49
Hispanic-American Almanac, The, 160
Information Please Kids' Almanac, The, 34
Social Work Almanac, 70
Washington Almanac, The, 52
Webster's II New Riverside Desk Reference, 36

ANNUALS

Amnesty International, 53
Film Annual, 1992, 115

ANTHOLOGIES

New Book of Popular Science, The, 89
Top 500 Poems, The, 140
Treasury of the Encyclopaedia Britannica, The, 34

ATLASES

Atlas of Endangered Animals, The, 47
Atlas of Endangered Places, The, 47
Atlas of North American Exploration, The, 147
Atlas of World Political Flashpoints, An, 54
Atlas of the 1990 Census, 48
Atlas of the Ancient World, The, 147
Atlas of the Third World, 150
Atlas of the World, 148
Children's Atlas of Exploration, The, 147
Children's Atlas of People & Places, The, 147
Hammond Atlas of the World, 148
National Geographic Atlas of the World, 149
New York Times Atlas of the World, The, 149
New York Times Atlas of the World, The New family ed., 149
Rand McNally Picture Atlas of Prehistoric Life, 94
Reader's Digest Atlas of the World, 149
Reader's Digest Bartholomew Illustrated Atlas of the World, 150
Times Atlas of the World, The, 149
Today's World, 150
Young People's Atlas of the United States, The, 150

BIBLIOGRAPHIES

AIDS Crisis in America, 72
American Ethnic Literatures, 138
Atomic Bomb, The, 69
Baseball, 128
Best Books for Public Libraries, 31
Books for You, 29
CD-ROM 1992, 29
Caribbean Women Novelists, 135
From Page to Screen, 124
Gemology, 94
How to Research the Supreme Court, 66
Latin America and the Caribbean, 164
Lesbian Sources, 47
Lesbianism, 47
Magazines for Libraries, 37
Major Authors and Illustrators for Children and Young Adults, 155
More Exciting, Funny, Scary, Short, Different, and Sad Books Kids Like about Animals, Science, Sports, Families, Songs and Other Things, 28
Newbery and Caldecott Medalists and Honor Book Winners, 27
Newbery and Caldecott medal and Honor Books in Other Media, 27
Nuclear Present, The, 69
Play, Learn, and Grow, 33
Portraying Persons with Disabilities, 133
Reader's Guide to the American Novel of Detection, A, 139
Recommended Reference Books in Paperback, 28
Reference Books for Children, xx
Reference Guide to Afro-American Publications and Editors, 1827-1946, A, 29
Reference Guide to Science, Fiction, Fantasy, and Horror, xx
Reference Sources for Small and Medium-Sized Libraries, 26
Religious Information Sources, 40
Research Guide to European Historical Biography, 152
Science Fiction and Fantasy Literature, 1975-1991, 132
Sensitive Issues, 28
Specialty Cookbooks, 106
State Census Records, 155
Supernatural Fiction for Teens, 133
Traveler's Reading Guide, The, 145
Twins in Children's and Adolescent Literature, 138
Vietnam War in Literature, The, 138
Western Reader's Guide, The, 165

BIOGRAPHICAL DICTIONARIES

African American Generals and Flag Officers, 68
American Women Songwriters, 119
Biographical Dictionary of Geography, 147
Black 100, The, 162
Black American Women in Olympic Track and Field, 128
Contemporary Composers, 115
Contemporary Entrepreneurs, 60
Contemporary Gay American Novelists, 139
Corporate Eponymy, 61
Dictionary of Literary Biography: Twentieth-Century Caribbean and Black African Writers, 139
Dictionary of Twentieth Century World Biography, A, 153
Explorers and Discoverers of the World, 146
Icons, 152
Masterpieces of African-American Literature, 139
Outstanding Women Athletes, 127
Political Leaders in Weimar Germany, xx
Political Leaders of Contemporary Africa South of the Sahara, 160
Presidents of the United States, The, 163
Quinlan's Illustrated Directory of Film Comedy Actors, 125
Soap Opera Book, The, 125
Soul Music A-Z, 120
Spanish American Authors, 141
Statesmen Who Changed the World, 144
Who Was Who in World Exploration, 146
Who's Who in Africa, 153
Who's Who in Comedy, 126
Who's Who in Science and Engineering, 1992-1993, 92
Who's Who in the United Nations and Related Agencies, 64

CATALOGS

Best Rated CDs 1992, 116
Laserdisc Film Guide, The, 124
Leonard's Annual Price Index of Prints, Posters & Photographs, 114
Official Guide to U.S. Stamps, The, 79
Warren's Movie Poster Price Guide, 112
World's Master Paintings, The, 113

CHRONOLOGIES

Chronology and Fact Book of the United Nations, 1941-1991, 64
Great Events, 144
Inventions and Discoveries, 1993, 98
Modern Irish Literature and Culture, 140
Soldier's Chronology, The, 69

CRITICISMS

Characters in 19th-Century Literature, 137
Critical Survey of Poetry, 136
Film Noir, 121
Magill's Survey of World Literature, 134
Masterplots II, 136
Slide Area, The, 123
Variety Music Guide, 123
World Literature Criticism, 135

INDEX TO TYPE OF MATERIAL

DATABASES

Children's Reference Plus, 27
DISCovering Authors, 130
Facts On File News Digest CD-ROM, 142
Magazine Article Summaries Full Text Elite on CD-ROM, 37
Masterplots II CD-ROM, 131
Oxford English Dictionary: Second Edition on Compact Disc, The, 82

DATABASES / INDEXES

Gale's Literary Index, 129

DICTIONARIES

Academic Press Dictionary of Science and Technology, 90
African Names, 156
American Heritage Dictionary of the English Language, The, 84
Anchor Bible Dictionary, The, 41
Animal Life, 95
Beacon Book of Quotations by Women, The, 39
Blackwell Dictionary of Judaica, The, 44
Blackwell Dictionary of Twentieth-Century Social Thought, The, 45
Bloomsbury Guide to Women's Literature, The, 137
Brewer's Book of Myth and Legend, 43
British English for American Readers, 84
Cancer Dictionary, The, 101
Cassell Dictionary of Literary and Language Terms, The, 131
Children's Writer's Word Book, 88
Codes and Ciphers, 108
Columbia Granger's Dictioanry of Poetry Quotations, The, 134
Computer Dictionary, 26
Concise Illustrated Dictionary of Science and Technology, The, 90
Concise Oxford Companion to the Theatre, The, 125
Concise Oxford Dictionary of Proverbs, The, 81
Consumer's Dictionary of Household, Yard and Office Chemicals, A, 100
Contemporary Thesaurus of Social Science Terms and Synonyms, The, 32
Dictionary of AIDS-Related Terminology, 72
Dictionary of Banking, 57
Dictionary of Biblical Tradition in English Literature, A, 137
Dictionary of Business and Management, 57
Dictionary of Cults, Sects, Religions and the Occult, 41
Dictionary of Environmental Quotation, A, 58
Dictionary of Investing, 57
Dictionary of Mexican Literature, 141
Dictionary of Mysticism and the Esoteric Traditions, 39
Dictionary of Politics, 52
Dictionary of Quotations from Shakespeare, 58
Dictionary of Sacred and Magical Plants, The, 80
Dictionary of Symbolism, 46
Dictionary of the American West, 87
Dictionary of Twentieth Century History, A, 157
Dictionary of United States Economic History, 56
Encyclopedic Dictionary of Language and Languages, An, 81
Familiar Quotations, 133
From Archetype to Zeitgeist, 35
Gardener's Dictionary of Horticultural Terms, The, 103
Gay Nineties in America, The, 163
Gods and Symbols of Ancient Mexico and the Maya, 45
Growing Beautiful Houseplants, 104
Historical Dictionary of Australia, 165
Historical Dictionary of Golfing Terms, The, 127
Historical Dictionary of Israel, 159
Historical Dictionary of Revolutionary China 1839-1976, 159
Horse's Name Was . . ., The, 105
Illustrated Computer Graphics Dictionary, 26
International Dictionary of Opera, 118
Joys of Hebrew, The, 81
Kingfisher Book of Words, The, 88
Library, Media, and Archival Preservation Glossary, A, 32
Link's International Dictionary of Business Economics, 55
Looking at Paintings, 113
Macmillan Visual Dictionary, The, 86
Middle East, The, 159
Name Is Familiar, The, 121
New Grove Dictionary of Opera, The, 118
New Palgrave Dictionary of Money and Finance, The, 57
New Quotable Woman, The, 39
New York Public Library Book of Twentieth-Century American Quotations, The, 38
Oxford Companion to Musical Instruments, The, 120
Oxford Dictionary of Modern Slang, The, 87
Oxford Dictionary of Opera, The, 119
Oxford Dictionary of Quotations, The, 134
Oxford Thesaurus, The, 86
Perfect Name for the Perfect Baby, The, 156
Random House Word Menu, 86
Reader's Digest Illustrated Book of Cats, The, 105
Religious Radio and Television in the United States, 1921-1991, 42
Reverse Symbolism Dictionary, 46
Roget's International Thesaurus, 85
Roget's 21st Century Thesaurus in Dictionary Form, 85
Russia and the Commonwealth A to Z, 158
Sailing Dictionary, The, 129
Tuttle Dictionary of Antiques and Collectibles Terms, 113
Visual Dictionary of Buildings, The, 112
Visual Dictionary of Flight, The, 112
Warriors' Words, 68
Webster's New World Dictionary for Young Adults, 84
Webster's II New Riverside Desk Quotations, 58
Whistlin' Dixie, 87

DIRECTORIES

AIDS Directory, The, 71
Alternative Health Care Resources, 72
American Directory of Organized Labor, 56
American Wholesalers and Distributors Directory, 59
Assistance & Benefits Information Directory, 69
Big Outside, The, 58
Caring for Kids with Special Needs, 73
Children's Book Awards International, 33
Directory of Business Information Resources, 1992, The, 107
Directory of European Business, 61
Directory of Food and Nutrition Information, 106
Directory of Multinationals, 62
Directory of Russian MPs, 55
Election Results Directory, 55
Environmental Industries Marketplace, 60
European Business Services Directory, 61
Federal Regional Yellow Book, 67
Fifth Directory of Periodicals, The, 82
Fund Raiser's Guide to Religious Philanthropy, 70
Gale Directory of Databases, 30
Government Directory of Addresses and Telephone Numbers, The, 59
Handel's National Directory for the Performing Arts, 121
Harris Manufacturers Directory, 1993, 59
Indoor Air Quality Directory, The, 74
International Organizations, 63
Job Seeker's Guide to Private and Public Companies, 61
Kid's Address Book, The, 152
Legal Resource Directory, 65
Martindale-Hubbell Bar Register of Preeminent Lawyers, 63
Mexico Company Handbook, 1992, 62
National Housing Directory for People with Disabilities, 1993, The, 72
National Trade and Professional Associations of the United States, 1993, 30
Native Americans Information Directory, 71
North American Horticulture, 103
Online Inc.'s Top 500 Library Microcomputer Software Application Programs, 31
Parks Directory of the United States, 151
Pool Player's National Pocket Billard Directory, The, 126
Professional Baseball Franchises, 128
Register of North American Hospitals, 1993, 72
Register of North American Insurance Companies, 1993, 76
Right Guide, The, 53
Roller Coasters, 121
Senior Citizen Services, 48
Spiritual Seeker's Guide, The, 43
Sports Halls of Fame, 127
Talk Shows and Hosts on Radio, 125
U.S.-Mexico Trade Pages, The, 62
Virgin Directory of World Music, The, 116
Which MBA?, 78
Who Knows What, 107
Who Owns Corporate America, 57
Who's Who in the Peace Corps, 70
Wilderness U, 77
Women's Information Directory, 74
World Business Directory, 60

DISCOGRAPHIES

Grove Press Guide to the Blues on CD, The, 117
Lawrence's Dealer Print Prices 1992, 114
Penguin Guide to Jazz on CD, LP and Cassette, The, 117

ENCYCLOPEDIAS

Addictionry, 100
African American Encyclopedia, 161
Black Women in America, 154

INDEX TO TYPE OF MATERIAL

Cambridge Encyclopedia of Human Evolution, The, 95
Canine Lexicon, 97
Cold War, 1945-1992, The, 144
Contemporary Religions, 42
Encyclopedia of American Social History, 46
Encyclopedia of Career Change and Work Issues, The, 107
Encyclopedia of Childbearing, 101
Encyclopedia of Early Childhood Education, 77
Encyclopedia of Ethics, 40
Encyclopedia of Ghosts and Spirits, The, 39
Encyclopedia of Heresies and Heretics, 42
Encyclopedia of Learning and Memory, 40
Encyclopedia of Romanticism, 157
Encyclopedia of Western Lawmen & Outlaws, 165
Encyclopedia of the Blues, 118
Encyclopedia of the British Press, 1422-1992, The, 38
Endangered Wildlife of the World, 95
Evolving Constitution, The, 65
Factfinder, 35
Golden Concise Encyclopedia of Mammals, The, 96
Greek and Roman Mythology A to Z, 44
Green Encyclopedia, The, 75
Guinness Encyclopedia of Popular Music, The, 117
Harper Encyclopedia of Military Biography, 68
HeadBangers, 119
International Military and Defense Encyclopedia, 67
Kingfisher Children's Encyclopedia, The, 88
Kingfisher Illustrated Encyclopedia of Animals, The, 88
Les Brown's Encyclopedia of Television, 124
Macmillan Encyclopedia of Computers, 26
Magill's History of Europe, 156
McGraw-Hill Encyclopedia of Science & Technology, 90
Multimedia Encyclopedia of Mammalian Biology, The, 96
My First Encyclopedia, 36
New Royal Horticultural Society Dictionary of Gardening, The, 103
New Standard Jewish Encyclopedia, The, 143
Oxford Companion to Politics of the World, The, 52
Oxford Companion to the English Language, The, 82
Oxford Companion to the Supreme Court of the United States, The, 66
Oxford Illustrated Encyclopedia of Invention and Technology, 98
Oxford Illustrated Encyclopedia of Peoples and Cultures, 50
Personal Health Reporter, 99
Photographic Encyclopedia of Wildflowers, The, 104
Presidency A to Z, The, 67
Random House Library of Knowledge First Encyclopedia, The, 88
Rodale's Illustrated Encyclopedia of Perennials, 104
Spies and Provocateurs, 54
Stage It with Music, 126
Warfare and Armed Conflicts, 142
Way Nature Works, The, 92
Webster's New World Encyclopedia, 37
World Book Encyclopedia of People and Places, The, 146
Young People's Encyclopedia of the United States, The, 160
Young World, 36

ENCYCLOPEDIAS / DATABASES

Microsoft Encarta Multimedia Encyclopedia, 34

FILMOGRAPHIES

Baseball in the Movies, 122
Cast of Thousands, A, 123
Celluloid Wars, 122
Fantastic Cinema Subject Guide, 123
Great Hollywood Musical Pictures, The, 122

GUIDEBOOKS

50 Fabulous Places to Raise Your Family, 50
All-Music Guide, 116
American Automobile Collections and Museums, 102
American Military Cemeteries, xx
Business Week's Guide to the Best Executive Education Programs, 109
Complete Guide to College Visits, The, 79
Complete Guide to Prescription & Non-Prescription Drugs, 99
Education for the Earth, 75
Festival Europe!, 80
Fund Your Way through College, 79
Gardener's Reading Guide, The, 102
German Reunification, 157
Great Book of the Sea, The, 95
Guide to Art, A, 112
Guide to the National Wildlife Refuges, 59
Hazardous Substances Resource Guide, 98
How to Pick a Perfect Private School, 77
Illustrative Guide to Rocks & Minerals, An, 94
International Affairs Directory of Organizations, 68
Islam and Islamic Groups, 44
National Hockey League Official Guide & Record Book, 1992-93, The, 128
Naval Institute Guide to the Ships and Aircraft of the U.S. Fleet, The, 101
Official USGA Record Book, 1895-1990, 127
Oxford Illustrated Literary Guide to Great Britain and Ireland, The, 140
Reference Guide to Science Fiction, Fantasy, and Horror, 136
Research Guide to Corporate Acquisitions, Mergers, and Other Restructuring, 109
Shakespeare's Characters, 141
Tapping the Government Grapevine, 31
Themes in American Painting, 114
World Class Business, 63
Zimmerman's Complete Guide to Nonprescription Drugs, 100

HANDBOOKS

ASTD Handbook of Instructional Technology, The, 109
America's Top Medical Jobs, 99
America's Top Rated Cities, 151
America's Top Technical and Trade Jobs, 99
Competitive Intelligence Handbook, The, 110
Complete Dog Book, The, 105
Cracking Eastern Europe, 111
Culturgrams, 145
Destructive and Useful Insects, 102
Developments and Research on Aging, 49
Economic Indicators Handbook, 55
Focus on Addictions, 100
Handbook of Campaign Spending, 53
Henry Holt Handbook of Current Science & Technology, The, 89
Importers Manual USA, 80
Islam in North America, 44
Loving Journeys Guide to Adoption, 73
McGraw-Hill Recycling Handbook, The, 75
Minerals of the World, 93
Numbers You Need, The, 92
101 Business Ratios, 108
Open Secrets, 53
Pick-up Games, 120
Professional Secretaries International Complete Office Handbook, 108
Recreation Handbook, The, 126
Recycling in America, 76
Science and Technical Writing, 131
Science and Technology Desk Reference, 89
Statistical Handbook on the American Family, 50
Student Contact Book, 78
Tuttle Guide to the Single European Market, 64
United States, The, 161
Vietnam War, The, 159
Water Quality and Availability, 58
World Markets Desk Book, The, 111

INDEXES

CD-ROM Periodical Index, 31
Charts, Graphs & Stats Index, 51
Faces in the News, 152
Fiction Index for Readers 10 to 16, 132
Fun for Kids II, 113
Garden Literature, 103
Kaiser Index to Black Resources, 1948-1986, The, 162
Multicultural Projects Index, 76
Print Price Index '93, 115
Rolling Stone Index, The, 115
Today's Science on File, 89

PERIODICALS

Health Care State Rankings, 1993, 74

POLITICS, ASIA

Political Parties of Asia and the Pacific, 153

SOURCEBOOKS

American Curriculum, The, 78
Black Americans, 49
Caregiving of Older Adults, 73
Census Snapshot for All U.S. Places, 1990, 51
Child Care Crisis, 73
Consumer Product and Manufacturer Ratings, 1961-1990, 105
Desktop Business Intelligence Sourcebook, The, 110
Eastern Europe and the Commonwealth of Independent States, 158
Economist Desk Companion, The, 93
European Business Rankings, 62
Finance, Insurance, & Real Estate USA, 108
Great American Baseball Stat Book, 1993, The, 127

INDEX TO TYPE OF MATERIAL

Great Thinkers of the Western World, 40
Guinness Book of Records 1492, The, 36
Hispanic Americans, 49
International Marketing Data and Statistics, 1993, 51
Italians to America, 155
Legal Issues and Older Adults, 66
Lines of Succession, 156
Low-Fat Supermarket, The, 106
Man-Made Catastrophies, 142
Markets of the U.S. for Business Planners, 56
Natural Disasters, 142
Nature Projects On File, 91
Organization Charts, 110
Primer on Sexual Harassment, 65
Recycling Sourcebook, 76
Religious Holidays and Calendars, 93
Sanitary Fairs, 163
Seasons of Business, The, 110
Union Army, 1861-1865, The, 163
Unlocking the Files of the FBI, 33
UpClose 1990 Census Sourcebook, 48
Venomous Reptiles of North America, 96
World War One Source Book, The, 157
Writer's Guide to Everyday Life in the 1800s, 164

Subject Index

AIDS (Disease)
  AIDS Crisis in America, 72
  AIDS Directory, The, 71
  Dictionary of AIDS-Related Terminology, 72

Administrative agencies
  Federal Regional Yellow Book, 67

Adoption
  Loving Journeys Guide to Adoption, 73

Afro-American generals
  African American Generals and Flag Officers, 68

Afro-American periodicals
  Reference Guide to Afro-American Publications and Editors, 1827-1946, A, 29

Afro-American women
  Black Women in America, 154

Afro-Americans
  African American Encyclopedia, 161
  Black 100, The, 162
  Black Americans, 49
  Kaiser Index to Black Resources, 1948-1986, The, 162

Aged
  Caregiving of Older Adults, 73
  Legal Issues and Older Adults, 66
  Senior Citizen Services, 48

Airplanes
  Visual Dictionary of Flight, The, 112

Almanacs, children's
  Information Please Kids' Almanac, The, 34

Alternative medicine
  Alternative Health Care Resources, 72

American literature
  American Ethnic Literatures, 138
  Masterpieces of African-American Literature, 139
  Vietnam War in Literature, The, 138

Animal, Fossil
  Rand McNally Picture Atlas of Prehistoric Life, 94

Animals
  Kingfisher Illustrated Encyclopedia of Animals, The, 88

Anniversaries
  Almanac of Anniversaries, The, 80

Architecture
  Visual Dictionary of Buildings, The, 112

Art
  Guide to Art, A, 112

Leonard's Annual Price Index of Prints, Posters & Photographs, 114

Atlases
  Atlas of the World, 148
  Children's Atlas of People & Places, The, 147
  Hammond Atlas of the World, 148
  National Geographic Atlas of the World, 149
  New York Times Atlas of the World, The, 149
  New York Times Atlas of the World, The New family ed., 149
  Reader's Digest Atlas of the World, 149
  Reader's Digest Bartholomew Illustrated Atlas of the World, 150
  Times Atlas of the World, The, 149
  Today's World, 150

Atomic bomb
  Atomic Bomb, The, 69

Audio-visual materials
  Library, Media, and Archival Preservation Glossary, A, 32

Australia
  Historical Dictionary of Australia, 165

Authors
  DISCovering Authors, 130

Authors, Spanish American
  Spanish American Authors, 141

Automobiles
  American Automobile Collections and Museums, 102

Banks and banking
  Dictionary of Banking, 57

Baseball
  Baseball, 128
  Great American Baseball Stat Book, 1993, The, 127
  Professional Baseball Franchises, 128

Baseball films
  Baseball in the Movies, 122

Bible
  Anchor Bible Dictionary, The, 41
  Dictionary of Biblical Tradition in English Literature, A, 137

Bibliography
  Play, Learn, and Grow, 33
  Recommended Reference Books in Paperback, 28
  Supernatural Fiction for Teens, 133

Biography
  Dictionary of Twentieth Century World Biography, A, 153
  Faces in the News, 152

Blues (Music)
  Encyclopedia of the Blues, 118

Blues (Music)
  Grove Press Guide to the Blues on CD, The, 117

Business
  Desktop Business Intelligence Sourcebook, The, 110
  Dictionary of Business and Management, 57

Business enterprises
  European Business Services Directory, 61
  Job Seeker's Guide to Private and Public Companies, 61
  World Business Directory, 60

Business information services
  Who Knows What, 107

Business intelligence
  Competitive Intelligence Handbook, The, 110

Businessmen
  Contemporary Entrepreneurs, 60
  Corporate Eponymy, 61

CD-ROM
  CD-ROM 1992, 29

Calendars
  Religious Holidays and Calendars, 93

Campaign funds
  Handbook of Campaign Spending, 53
  Open Secrets, 53

Cancer
  Cancer Dictionary, The, 101

Caribbean fiction
  Caribbean Women Novelists, 135

Caribbean literature (English)
  Dictionary of Literary Biography: Twentieth-Century Caribbean and Black African Writers, 139

Cats
  Reader's Digest Illustrated Book of Cats, The, 105

Celebrities
  Daily Celebrity Almanac, 1993, 151
  Icons, 152
  Kid's Address Book, The, 152
  Research Guide to European Historical Biography, 152

Characters and characteristics
  Characters in 19th-Century Literature, 137
  Name Is Familiar, The, 121

SUBJECT INDEX

Charts, diagrams, etc.
  Charts, Graphs & Stats Index, 51
Child care services
  Child Care Crisis, 73
Children
  Caring for Kids with Special Needs, 73
Children's encyclopedias
  Factfinder, 35
  Kingfisher Children's Encyclopedia, The, 88
  My First Encyclopedia, 36
  Random House Library of Knowledge First Encyclopedia, The, 88
  Young World, 36
Children's literature
  Children's Book Awards International, 33
  Children's Reference Plus, 27
  From Page to Screen, 124
  Major Authors and Illustrators for Children and Young Adults, 155
  More Exciting, Funny, Scary, Short, Different, and Sad Books Kids Like about Animals, Science, Sports, Families, Songs and Other Things, 28
  Sensitive Issues, 28
Children's literature, America
  Newbery and Caldecott Medalists and Honor Book Winners, 27
Children's reference books
  Reference Books for Children, xx
Children's stories
  Portraying Persons with Disabilities, 133
Children's stories, American
  Twins in Children's and Adolescent Literature, 138
Cities and towns
  America's Top Rated Cities, 151
Civil rights
  Amnesty International, 53
Cold War
  Cold War, 1945-1992, The, 144
College, Choice of
  Complete Guide to College Visits, The, 79
Comedians
  Quinlan's Illustrated Directory of Film Comedy Actors, 125
  Who's Who in Comedy, 126
Composers
  Contemporary Composers, 115
Compulsive Behavior
  Addictionary, 100
Computer graphics
  Illustrated Computer Graphics Dictionary, 26
Computers
  Computer Dictionary, 26
  Macmillan Encyclopedia of Computers, 26
Conservatism
  Right Guide, The, 53
Consolidation and merger
  Research Guide to Corporate Acquisitions, Mergers, and Other Restructuring, 109
Consumer behavior
  Seasons of Business, The, 110
Consumer goods
  Consumer Product and Manufacturer Ratings, 1961-1990, 105
Cookery
  Specialty Cookbooks, 106
Corporations
  European Business Rankings, 62
  Mexico Company Handbook, 1992, 62
Cryptography
  Codes and Ciphers, 108
Curiosities and wonders
  Guinness Book of Records 1492, The, 36
Databases
  Gale Directory of Databases, 30
Decorative arts
  Tuttle Dictionary of Antiques and Collectibles Terms, 113
Demography
  UpClose 1990 Census Sourcebook, 48
Detective and mystery stories
  Reader's Guide to the American Novel of Detection, A, 139
Disasters
  Man-Made Catastrophies, 142
  Natural Disasters, 142
Discoveries in geography
  Children's Atlas of Exploration, The, 147
Dogs
  Canine Lexicon, 97
  Complete Dog Book, The, 105
Drug abuse
  Focus on Addictions, 100
Drugs
  Complete Guide to Prescription & Non-Prescription Drugs, 99
Drugs, Nonprescription
  Zimmerman's Complete Guide to Nonprescription Drugs, 100
Early childhood education
  Encyclopedia of Early Childhood Education, 77
Economic assistance, Domestic
  Assistance & Benefits Information Directory, 69
Economic history
  International Marketing Data and Statistics, 1993, 51
Economic indicators
  Economic Indicators Handbook, 55
Economics
  Link's International Dictionary of Business Economics, 55
Education
  American Curriculum, The, 78
Employees
  ASTD Handbook of Instructional Technology, The, 109
Encyclopedias and dictionaries
  From Archetype to Zeitgeist, 35
  Microsoft Encarta Multimedia Encyclopedia, 34
  Treasury of the Encyclopaedia Britannica, The, 34
  Webster's II New Riverside Desk Reference, 36
  Webster's New World Encyclopedia, 37
Endangered species
  Atlas of Endangered Animals, The, 47
  Endangered Wildlife of the World, 95
Endowments
  Fund Raiser's Guide to Religious Philanthropy, 70
English language
  American Heritage Dictionary of the English Language, The, 84
  British English for American Readers, 84
  Cassell Dictionary of Literary and Language Terms, The, 131
  Children's Writer's Word Book, 88
  Dictionary of the American West, 87
  Oxford Companion to the English Language, The, 82
  Oxford Dictionary of Modern Slang, The, 87
  Oxford English Dictionary: Second Edition on Compact Disc, The, 82
  Oxford Thesaurus, The, 86
  Random House Word Menu, 86
  Roget's 21st Century Thesaurus in Dictionary Form, 85
  Roget's International Thesaurus, 85
  Webster' New World Dictionary for Young Adults, 84
  Whistlin' Dixie, 87
English literature
  Modern Irish Literature and Culture, 140
English philology
  Fifth Directory of Periodicals, The, 82
English poetry
  Critical Survey of Poetry, 136
  Top 500 Poems, The, 140
Environmental protection
  Green Encyclopedia, The, 75
  Indoor Air Quality Directory, The, 74
Environmental science
  Education for the Earth, 75
Ethics
  Encyclopedia of Ethics, 40
Europe
  Directory of European Business, 61
  Magill's History of Europe, 156
Europe 1992
  Tuttle Guide to the Single European Market, 64
Europe, Eastern
  Eastern Europe and the Commonwealth of Independent States, 158
Explorers
  Explorers and Discoverers of the World, 146
  Who Was Who in World Exploration, 146
Export marketing
  World Markets Desk Book, The, 111
Family
  Statistical Handbook on the American

SUBJECT INDEX

Family, 50
Fantastic films
: Fantastic Cinema Subject Guide, 123

Festivals
: Festival Europe!, 80

Film credits
: Cast of Thousands, A, 123

Film posters, American
: Warren's Movie Poster Price Guide, 112

Finance
: Finance, Insurance, & Real Estate USA, 108
: New Palgrave Dictionary of Money and Finance, The, 57

Food
: Directory of Food and Nutrition Information, 106
: Low-Fat Supermarket, The, 106

Games
: Pick-up Games, 120
: Recreation Handbook, The, 126

Gardening
: Garden Literature, 103
: Gardener's Reading Guide, The, 102
: New Royal Horticultural Society Dictionary of Gardening, The, 103

Gems
: Gemology, 94

Genealogy
: State Census Records, 155

Geographers
: Biographical Dictionary of Geography, 147
: Atlas of the Ancient World, The, 147

Geography
: Oxford Illustrated Encyclopedia of Peoples and Cultures, 50
: World Book Encyclopedia of People and Places, The, 146

Geopolitics
: Atlas of World Political Flashpoints, An, 54

Germany
: German Reunification, 157

Gerontology
: Developments and Research on Aging, 49

Ghosts
: Encyclopedia of Ghosts and Spirits, The, 39

Golf
: Historical Dictionary of Golfing Terms, The, 127
: Official USGA Record Book, 1895-1990, 127

Government publications
: Tapping the Government Grapevine, 31

Great Britain
: Encyclopedia of Romanticism, 157

Handicapped
: National Housing Directory for People with Disabilities, 1993, The, 72

Handicraft
: Fun for Kids II, 113

Hazardous substances
: Hazardous Substances Resource Guide, 98

Health
: Personal Health Reporter, 99

Health status indicators
: Health Care State Rankings, 1993, 74

Heavy metal (Music)
: HeadBangers, 119

Heraldry
: Lines of Succession, 156

Heresies, Christian
: Encyclopedia of Heresies and Heretics, 42

Hispanic Americans
: Hispanic Americans, 49
: Hispanic-American Almanac, The, 160

History, Modern
: Dictionary of Twentieth Century History, A, 157
: Facts On File News Digest CD-ROM, 142
: Great Events, 144

Horses
: Horse's Name Was . . . , The, 105

Horticulture
: Gardener's Dictionary of Horticultural Terms, The, 103
: North American Horticulture, 103

Hospitals
: Register of North American Hospitals, 1993, 72

House plants
: Growing Beautiful Houseplants, 104

Housing and health
: Consumer's Dictionary of Household, Yard and Office Chemicals, A, 100

Human evolution
: Cambridge Encyclopedia of Human Evolution, The, 95

Illinois
: Awesome Almanac of Illinois, 164

Imports
: Importers Manual USA, 80

Indiana
: Awesome Almanac of Indiana, 164

Indians of Mexico
: Gods and Symbols of Ancient Mexico and the Maya, 45

Indians of North America
: Native Americans Information Directory, 71

Insect pests
: Destructive and Useful Insects, 102

Insurance companies
: Register of North American Insurance Companies, 1993, 76

Intelligence officers
: Spies and Provocateurs, 54

Intercultural education
: Multicultural Projects Index, 76

International agencies
: International Organizations, 63

International business
: World Class Business, 63

International business enterpr
: Directory of Multinationals, 62

Inventions
: Inventions and Discoveries, 1993, 98

Inventions
: Oxford Illustrated Encyclopedia of Invention and Technology, 98

Investments
: Dictionary of Investing, 57

Islam
: Islam in North America, 44

Islam and state
: Islam and Islamic Groups, 44

Israel
: Historical Dictionary of Israel, 159

Italian Americans
: Italians to America, 155

Jazz
: Penguin Guide to Jazz on CD, LP and Cassette, The, 117

Jews
: New Standard Jewish Encyclopedia, The, 143

Judaism
: Blackwell Dictionary of Judaica, The, 44

Labor market
: America's Top Technical and Trade Jobs, 99

Language and languages
: Encyclopedic Dictionary of Language and Languages, An, 81

Latin America
: Latin America and the Caribbean, 164

Lawyers
: Martindale-Hubbell Bar Register of Preeminent Lawyers, 63

Learning, Psychology of
: Encyclopedia of Learning and Memory, 40

Legal aid
: Legal Resource Directory, 65

Legislators
: Directory of Russian MPs, 55

Lesbianism
: Lesbian Sources, 47

Lesbianism
: Lesbianism, 47

Literary landmarks
: Oxford Illustrated Literary Guide to Great Britain and Ireland, The, 140

Literature
: Gale's Literary Index, 129
: Magill's Survey of World Literature, 134
: Masterplots II CD-ROM, 131
: World Literature Criticism, 135

Mammals
: Golden Concise Encyclopedia of Mammals, The, 96

SUBJECT INDEX

Multimedia Encyclopedia of Mammalian Biology, The, 96

Man
Atlas of Endangered Places, The, 47

Management
Business Week's Guide to the Best Executive Education Programs, 109

Manners and customs
Culturgrams, 145

Manufactures
Harris Manufacturers Directory, 1993, 59

Marine fauna
Great Book of the Sea, The, 95

Marketing
Cracking Eastern Europe, 111

Master of business administrat
Which MBA?, 78

Mathematics
Numbers You Need, The, 92

Medicine
America's Top Medical Jobs, 99

Mexican literature
Dictionary of Mexican Literature, 141

Middle East
Middle East, The, 159

Military art and science
International Military and Defense Encyclopedia, 67
Warriors' Words, 68

Military biography
Harper Encyclopedia of Military Biography, 68

Military history, Modern
Warfare and Armed Conflicts, 142

Mineralogy
Illustrative Guide to Rocks & Minerals, An, 94

Minerals
Minerals of the World, 93

Motion pictures
Film Annual, 1992, 115
Slide Area, The, 123
Variety Music Guide, 123

Moving pictures
Film Noir, 121

Music
All-Music Guide, 116

Musical films
Great Hollywood Musical Pictures, The, 122

Musical instruments
Oxford Companion to Musical Instruments, The, 120

Musicals
Stage It with Music, 126

Mythology
Brewer's Book of Myth and Legend, 43

Mythology, Classical
Greek and Roman Mythology A to Z, 44

Names, Personal
African Names, 156

Names, Personal
Perfect Name for the Perfect Baby, The, 156

National Hockey League
National Hockey League Official Guide & Record Book, 1992-93, The, 128

National cemeteries
American Military Cemeteries, xx

Natural history
Nature Projects On File, 91
Way Nature Works, The, 92

Natural resources
Atlas of the Third World, 150

Nature
Dictionary of Environmental Quotation, A, 58

Newbery Medal books
Newbery and Caldecott medal and Honor Books in Other Media, 27

North America
Atlas of North American Exploration, The, 147

Novelists, American
Contemporary Gay American Novelists, 139

Nuclear arms control
Nuclear Present, The, 69

Occultism
Dictionary of Mysticism and the Esoteric Traditions, 39

Office practice
Professional Secretaries International Complete Office Handbook, 108

On-line data processing
Online Inc.'s Top 500 Library Microcomputer Software Application Programs, 31

Opera
International Dictionary of Opera, 118
New Grove Dictionary of Opera, The, 118
Oxford Dictionary of Opera, The, 119

Organization charts
Organization Charts, 110

Outdoor education
Wilderness U, 77

Painting
Looking at Paintings, 113

Painting
World's Master Paintings, The, 113

Painting, American
Themes in American Painting, 114

Parks
Parks Directory of the United States, 151

Peace Corps (U.S.)
Who's Who in the Peace Corps, 70

Perennials
Rodale's Illustrated Encyclopedia of Perennials, 104

Performing arts
Handel's National Directory for the Performing Arts, 121

Periodicals
CD-ROM Periodical Index, 31
Magazine Article Summaries Full Text Elite on CD-ROM, 37
Magazines for Libraries, 37

Philosophy
Great Thinkers of the Western World, 40

Picture dictionaries, English
Macmillan Visual Dictionary, The, 86

Plants
Dictionary of Sacred and Magical Plants, The, 80

Poetry
Masterplots II, 136

Poisonous snakes
Venomous Reptiles of North America, 96

Political parties
Political Parties of Asia and the Pacific, 153

Political science
Dictionary of Politics, 52
Oxford Companion to Politics of the World, The, 52

Politicians
Political Leaders in Weimar Germany, xx
Political Leaders of Contemporary Africa South of the Sahara, 160

Pool (Game)
Pool Player's National Pocket Billard Directory, The, 126

Popular music
Best Rated CDs 1992, 116
Guinness Encyclopedia of Popular Music, The, 117
Virgin Directory of World Music, The, 116

Postage stamps
Official Guide to U.S. Stamps, The, 79

Pregnancy
Encyclopedia of Childbearing, 101

Presidents
Presidency A to Z, The, 67

Presidents
Presidents of the United States, The, 163

Press
Encyclopedia of the British Press, 1422-1992, The, 38

Prints
Lawrence's Dealer Print Prices 1992, 114
Print Price Index '93, 115

Private schools
How to Pick a Perfect Private School, 77

Proverbs, English
Concise Oxford Dictionary of Proverbs, The, 81

Proverbs, Hebrew
Joys of Hebrew, The, 81

Public libraries
Best Books for Public Libraries, 31

SUBJECT INDEX

Quality of life
  50 Fabulous Places to Raise Your Family, 50

Quotations
  Oxford Dictionary of Quotations, The, 134

Quotations, American
  New York Public Library Book of Twentieth-Century American Quotations, The, 38
  Quotations, English
  Columbia Granger's Dictioanry of Poetry Quotations, The, 134
  Familiar Quotations, 133
  Webster's II New Riverside Desk Quotations, 58

Radio in religion
  Religious Radio and Television in the United States, 1921-1991, 42

Ratio analysis
  101 Business Ratios, 108

Recycling (Waste, etc.)
  McGraw-Hill Recycling Handbook, The, 75
  Recycling Sourcebook, 76
  Recycling in America, 76

Reference books
  Reference Guide to Science Fiction, Fantasy, and Horror, 136
  Reference Guide to Science, Fiction, Fantasy, and Horror, xx
  Reference Sources for Small and Medium-Sized Libraries, 26

Religion
  Religious Information Sources, 40

Religions
  Contemporary Religions, 42
  Dictionary of Cults, Sects, Religions and the Occult, 41
  Spiritual Seeker's Guide, The, 43

Research
  Student Contact Book, 78

Revolutions
  Historical Dictionary of Revolutionary China 1839-1976, 159

Roller coasters
  Roller Coasters, 121

Rolling Stone
  Rolling Stone Index, The, 115

Sailing
  Sailing Dictionary, The, 129

Science
  Academic Press Dictionary of Science and Technology, 90
  Concise Illustrated Dictionary of Science and Technology, The, 90
  Henry Holt Handbook of Current Science & Technology, The, 89
  McGraw-Hill Encyclopedia of Science & Technology, 90
  New Book of Popular Science, The, 89
  Science and Technology Desk Reference, 89
  Today's Science on File, 89

Science fiction
  Science Fiction and Fantasy Literature, 1975-1991, 132

Scientists
  Who's Who in Science and Engineering, 1992-1993, 92

Sexual harassment of women
  Primer on Sexual Harassment, 65

Shakespeare, William
  Dictionary of Quotations from Shakespeare, 58
  Shakespeare's Characters, 141

Signs and symbols
  Dictionary of Symbolism, 46

Soap operas
  Soap Opera Book, The, 125

Social sciences
  Blackwell Dictionary of Twentieth-Century Social Thought, The, 45
  Contemporary Thesaurus of Social Science Terms and Synonyms, The, 32

Social service
  Social Work Almanac, 70

Songs
  American Women Songwriters, 119

Soul musicians
  Soul Music A-Z, 120

Soviet Union
  Russia and the Commonwealth A to Z, 158

Sports museums
  Sports Halls of Fame, 127

Statesmen
  Statesmen Who Changed the World, 144
  Who's Who in Africa, 153

Stockholders
  Who Owns Corporate America, 57

Student aid
  Fund Your Way through College, 79

Symbolism
  Reverse Symbolism Dictionary, 46

Talk shows
  Talk Shows and Hosts on Radio, 125

Technical writing
  Science and Technical Writing, 131

Television broadcasting
  Les Brown's Encyclopedia of Television, 124

Theater
  Concise Oxford Companion to the Theatre, The, 125

Trade and professional assns
  National Trade and Professional Associations of the United States, 1993, 30
  Directory of Business Information Resources, 1992, The, 107

Trade-unions
  American Directory of Organized Labor, 56

Travel
  Traveler's Reading Guide, The, 145

U.S.
  Atlas of the 1990 Census, 48
  Census Snapshot for All U.S. Places, 1990, 51
  Dictionary of United States Economic History, 56
  Election Results Directory, 55
  Encyclopedia of American Social History, 46
  Environmental Industries Marketplace, 60
  Evolving Constitution, The, 65
  Gay Nineties in America, The, 163
  Government Directory of Addresses and Telephone Numbers, The, 59
  Markets of the U.S. for Business Planners, 56
  Soldier's Chronology, The, 69
  U.S.-Mexico Trade Pages, The, 62
  United States, The, 161
  Washington Almanac, The, 52
  Writer's Guide to Everyday Life in the 1800s, 164
  Young People's Atlas of the United States, The, 150
  Young People's Encyclopedia of the United States, The, 160

U.S. Army
  Union Army, 1861-1865, The, 163

U.S. Federal Bureau of Investigation
  Unlocking the Files of the FBI, 33

U.S. Navy
  Naval Institute Guide to the Ships and Aircraft of the U.S. Fleet, The, 101

U.S. Sanitary Commission
  Sanitary Fairs, 163

U.S. Supreme Court
  How to Research the Supreme Court, 66
  Oxford Companion to the Supreme Court of the United States, The, 66

United Nations
  Chronology and Fact Book of the United Nations, 1941-1991, 64
  Who's Who in the United Nations and Related Agencies, 64

Videodiscs
  Laserdisc Film Guide, The, 124

Vietnamese Conflict, 1961-1975
  Vietnam War, The, 159

Vocabulary
  Kingfisher Book of Words, The, 88

Vocational guidance
  Encyclopedia of Career Change and Work Issues, The, 107

War
  International Affairs Directory of Organizations, 68

War films
  Celluloid Wars, 122

Water quality
  Water Quality and Availability, 58

Weights and measures
  Economist Desk Companion, The, 93

West (U.S.)
  Encyclopedia of Western Lawmen & Outlaws, 165
  Western Reader's Guide, The, 165

Wholesale trade
  American Wholesalers and Distributors Directory, 59

Wild flowers
  Photographic Encyclopedia of Wildflowers, The, 104
Wilderness
  Big Outside, The, 58
Wildlife refuges
  Guide to the National Wildlife Refuges, 59
Women
  Beacon Book of Quotations by Women, The, 39
  European Women's Almanac, The, 49
  New Quotable Woman, The, 39
Women athletes
  Outstanding Women Athletes, 127
Women authors
  Bloomsbury Guide to Women's Literature, The, 137
Women track and field athletes
  Black American Women in Olympic Track and Field, 128
Women's institutes
  Women's Information Directory, 74
World War, 1914-1918
  World War One Source Book, The, 157
Young adult fiction
  Fiction Index for Readers 10 to 16, 132
Young adult literature
  Books for You, 29
Zoology
  Animal Life, 95

Title Index

AIDS Crisis in America, 72
AIDS Directory, The, 71
ASTD Handbook of Instructional Technology, The, 109
Academic Press Dictionary of Science and Technology, 90
Addictionary, 100
African American Encyclopedia, 161
African American Generals and Flag Officers, 68
African Names, 156
All-Music Guide, 116
Almanac of Anniversaries, The, 80
Alternative Health Care Resources, 72
America's Top Medical Jobs, 99
America's Top Rated Cities, 151
America's Top Technical and Trade Jobs, 99
American Automobile Collections and Museums, 102
American Curriculum, The, 78
American Directory of Organized Labor, 56
American Ethnic Literatures, 138
American Heritage Dictionary of the English Language, The, 84
American Military Cemeteries, xx
American Wholesalers and Distributors Directory, 59
American Women Songwriters, 119
Amnesty International, 53
Anchor Bible Dictionary, The, 41
Animal Life, 95
Assistance & Benefits Information Directory, 69
Atlas of Endangered Animals, The, 47
Atlas of Endangered Places, The, 47
Atlas of North American Exploration, The, 147
Atlas of World Political Flashpoints, An, 54
Atlas of the 1990 Census, 48
Atlas of the Ancient World, The, 147
Atlas of the Third World, 150
Atlas of the World, 148
Atomic Bomb, The, 69
Awesome Almanac of Illinois, 164
Awesome Almanac of Indiana, 164
Baseball, 128
Baseball in the Movies, 122
Beacon Book of Quotations by Women, The, 39
Best Books for Public Libraries, 31
Best Rated CDs 1992, 116
Big Outside, The, 58
Biographical Dictionary of Geography, 147
Black 100, The, 162
Black American Women in Olympic Track and Field, 128
Black Americans, 49
Black Women in America, 154
Blackwell Dictionary of Judaica, The, 44
Blackwell Dictionary of Twentieth-Century Social Thought, The, 45
Bloomsbury Guide to Women's Literature, The, 137
Books for You, 29
Brewer's Book of Myth and Legend, 43

British English for American Readers, 84
Business Week's Guide to the Best Executive Education Programs, 109
CD-ROM 1992, 29
CD-ROM Periodical Index, 31
Cambridge Encyclopedia of Human Evolution, The, 95
Cancer Dictionary, The, 101
Canine Lexicon, 97
Caregiving of Older Adults, 73
Caribbean Women Novelists, 135
Caring for Kids with Special Needs, 73
Cassell Dictionary of Literary and Language Terms, The, 131
Cast of Thousands, A, 123
Celluloid Wars, 122
Census Snapshot for All U.S. Places, 1990, 51
Characters in 19th-Century Literature, 137
Charts, Graphs & Stats Index, 51
Child Care Crisis, 73
Children's Atlas of Exploration, The, 147
Children's Atlas of People & Places, The, 147
Children's Book Awards International, 33
Children's Reference Plus, 27
Children's Writer's Word Book, 88
Chronology and Fact Book of the United Nations, 1941-1991, 64
Codes and Ciphers, 108
Cold War, 1945-1992, The, 144
Columbia Granger's Dictioanry of Poetry Quotations, The, 134
Competitive Intelligence Handbook, The, 110
Complete Dog Book, The, 105
Complete Guide to College Visits, The, 79
Complete Guide to Prescription & Non-Prescription Drugs, 99
Computer Dictionary, 26
Concise Illustrated Dictionary of Science and Technology, The, 90
Concise Oxford Companion to the Theatre, The, 125
Concise Oxford Dictionary of Proverbs, The, 81
Consumer Product and Manufacturer Ratings, 1961-1990, 105
Consumer's Dictionary of Household, Yard and Office Chemicals, A, 100
Contemporary Composers, 115
Contemporary Entrepreneurs, 60
Contemporary Gay American Novelists, 139
Contemporary Religions, 42
Contemporary Thesaurus of Social Science Terms and Synonyms, The, 32
Corporate Eponymy, 61
Cracking Eastern Europe, 111
Critical Survey of Poetry, 136
Culturgrams, 145
DISCovering Authors, 130
Daily Celebrity Almanac, 1993, 151
Desktop Business Intelligence Sourcebook, The, 110
Destructive and Useful Insects, 102
Developments and Research on Aging, 49
Dictionary of AIDS-Related Terminology, 72

Dictionary of Banking, 57
Dictionary of Biblical Tradition in English Literature, A, 137
Dictionary of Business and Management, 57
Dictionary of Cults, Sects, Religions and the Occult, 41
Dictionary of Environmental Quotation, A, 58
Dictionary of Investing, 57
Dictionary of Literary Biography: Twentieth-Century Caribbean and Black African Writers, 139
Dictionary of Mexican Literature, 141
Dictionary of Mysticism and the Esoteric Traditions, 39
Dictionary of Politics, 52
Dictionary of Quotations from Shakespeare, 58
Dictionary of Sacred and Magical Plants, The, 80
Dictionary of Symbolism, 46
Dictionary of Twentieth Century History, A, 157
Dictionary of Twentieth Century World Biography, A, 153
Dictionary of United States Economic History, 56
Dictionary of the American West, 87
Directory of Business Information Resources, 1992, The, 107
Directory of European Business, 61
Directory of Food and Nutrition Information, 106
Directory of Multinationals, 62
Directory of Russian MPs, 55
Eastern Europe and the Commonwealth of Independent States, 158
Economic Indicators Handbook, 55
Economist Desk Companion, The, 93
Education for the Earth, 75
Election Results Directory, 55
Encyclopedia of American Social History, 46
Encyclopedia of Career Change and Work Issues, The, 107
Encyclopedia of Childbearing, 101
Encyclopedia of Early Childhood Education, 77
Encyclopedia of Ethics, 40
Encyclopedia of Ghosts and Spirits, The, 39
Encyclopedia of Heresies and Heretics, 42
Encyclopedia of Learning and Memory, 40
Encyclopedia of Romanticism, 157
Encyclopedia of Western Lawmen & Outlaws, 165
Encyclopedia of the Blues, 118
Encyclopedia of the British Press, 1422-1992, The, 38
Encyclopedic Dictionary of Language and Languages, An, 81
Endangered Wildlife of the World, 95
Environmental Industries Marketplace, 60
European Business Rankings, 62
European Business Services Directory, 61
European Women's Almanac, The, 49
Evolving Constitution, The, 65
Explorers and Discoverers of the World, 146
Faces in the News, 152

Factfinder, 35
Facts On File News Digest CD-ROM, 142
Familiar Quotations, 133
Fantastic Cinema Subject Guide, 123
Federal Regional Yellow Book, 67
Festival Europe!, 80
Fiction Index for Readers 10 to 16, 132
Fifth Directory of Periodicals, The, 82
50 Fabulous Places to Raise Your Family, 50
Film Annual, 1992, 115
Film Noir, 121
Finance, Insurance, & Real Estate USA, 108
Focus on Addictions, 100
From Archetype to Zeitgeist, 35
From Page to Screen, 124
Fun for Kids II, 113
Fund Raiser's Guide to Religious Philanthropy, 70
Fund Your Way through College, 79
Gale Directory of Databases, 30
Gale's Literary Index, 129
Garden Literature, 103
Gardener's Dictionary of Horticultural Terms, The, 103
Gardener's Reading Guide, The, 102
Gay Nineties in America, The, 163
Gemology, 94
German Reunification, 157
Gods and Symbols of Ancient Mexico and the Maya, 45
Golden Concise Encyclopedia of Mammals, The, 96
Government Directory of Addresses and Telephone Numbers, The, 59
Great American Baseball Stat Book, 1993, The, 127
Great Book of the Sea, The, 95
Great Events, 144
Great Hollywood Musical Pictures, The, 122
Great Thinkers of the Western World, 40
Greek and Roman Mythology A to Z, 44
Green Encyclopedia, The, 75
Grove Press Guide to the Blues on CD, The, 117
Growing Beautiful Houseplants, 104
Guide to Art, A, 112
Guide to the National Wildlife Refuges, 59
Guinness Book of Records 1492, The, 36
Guinness Encyclopedia of Popular Music, The, 117
Hammond Atlas of the World, 148
Handbook of Campaign Spending, 53
Handel's National Directory for the Performing Arts, 121
Harper Encyclopedia of Military Biography, 68
Harris Manufacturers Directory, 1993, 59
Hazardous Substances Resource Guide, 98
HeadBangers, 119
Health Care State Rankings, 1993, 74
Henry Holt Handbook of Current Science & Technology, The, 89
Hispanic Americans, 49
Hispanic-American Almanac, The, 160
Historical Dictionary of Australia, 165
Historical Dictionary of Golfing Terms, The, 127
Historical Dictionary of Israel, 159
Historical Dictionary of Revolutionary China 1839-1976, 159
Horse's Name Was . . . , The, 105
How to Pick a Perfect Private School, 77
How to Research the Supreme Court, 66
Icons, 152
Illustrated Computer Graphics Dictionary, 26
Illustrative Guide to Rocks & Minerals, An, 94
Importers Manual USA, 80
Indoor Air Quality Directory, The, 74
Information Please Kids' Almanac, The, 34

International Affairs Directory of Organizations, 68
International Dictionary of Opera, 118
International Marketing Data and Statistics, 1993, 51
International Military and Defense Encyclopedia, 67
International Organizations, 63
Inventions and Discoveries, 1993, 98
Islam and Islamic Groups, 44
Islam in North America, 44
Italians to America, 155
Job Seeker's Guide to Private and Public Companies, 61
Joys of Hebrew, The, 81
Kaiser Index to Black Resources, 1948-1986, The, 162
Kid's Address Book, The, 152
Kingfisher Book of Words, The, 88
Kingfisher Children's Encyclopedia, The, 88
Kingfisher Illustrated Encyclopedia of Animals, The, 88
Laserdisc Film Guide, The, 124
Latin America and the Caribbean, 164
Lawrence's Dealer Print Prices 1992, 114
Legal Issues and Older Adults, 66
Legal Resource Directory, 65
Leonard's Annual Price Index of Prints, Posters & Photographs, 114
Les Brown's Encyclopedia of Television, 124
Lesbian Sources, 47
Lesbianism, 47
Library, Media, and Archival Preservation Glossary, A, 32
Lines of Succession, 156
Link's International Dictionary of Business Economics, 55
Looking at Paintings, 113
Loving Journeys Guide to Adoption, 73
Low-Fat Supermarket, The, 106
Macmillan Encyclopedia of Computers, 26
Macmillan Visual Dictionary, The, 86
Magazine Article Summaries Full Text Elite on CD-ROM, 37
Magazines for Libraries, 37
Magill's History of Europe, 156
Magill's Survey of World Literature, 134
Major Authors and Illustrators for Children and Young Adults, 155
Man-Made Catastrophies, 142
Markets of the U.S. for Business Planners, 56
Martindale-Hubbell Bar Register of Preeminent Lawyers, 65
Masterpieces of African-American Literature, 139
Masterplots II, 136
Masterplots II CD-ROM, 131
McGraw-Hill Encyclopedia of Science & Technology, 90
McGraw-Hill Recycling Handbook, The, 75
Mexico Company Handbook, 1992, 62
Microsoft Encarta Multimedia Encyclopedia, 34
Middle East, The, 159
Minerals of the World, 93
Modern Irish Literature and Culture, 140
More Exciting, Funny, Scary, Short, Different, and Sad Books Kids Like about Animals, Science, Sports, Families, Songs and Other Things, 28
Multicultural Projects Index, 76
Multimedia Encyclopedia of Mammalian Biology, The, 96
My First Encyclopedia, 36
Name Is Familiar, The, 121
National Geographic Atlas of the World, 149
National Hockey League Official Guide & Record Book, 1992-93, The, 128

National Housing Directory for People with Disabilities, 1993, The, 72
National Trade and Professional Associations of the United States, 1993, 30
Native Americans Information Directory, 71
Natural Disasters, 142
Nature Projects On File, 91
Naval Institute Guide to the Ships and Aircraft of the U.S. Fleet, The, 101
New Book of Popular Science, The, 89
New Grove Dictionary of Opera, The, 118
New Palgrave Dictionary of Money and Finance, The, 57
New Quotable Woman, The, 39
New Royal Horticultural Society Dictionary of Gardening, The, 103
New Standard Jewish Encyclopedia, The, 143
New York Public Library Book of Twentieth-Century American Quotations, The, 38
New York Times Atlas of the World, The, 149
New York Times Atlas of the World, The New family ed., 149
Newbery and Caldecott Medalists and Honor Book Winners, 27
Newbery and Caldecott medal and Honor Books in Other Media, 27
North American Horticulture, 103
Nuclear Present, The, 69
Numbers You Need, The, 92
Official Guide to U.S. Stamps, The, 79
Official USGA Record Book, 1895-1990, 127
101 Business Ratios, 108
Online Inc.'s Top 500 Library Microcomputer Software Application Programs, 31
Open Secrets, 53
Organization Charts, 110
Outstanding Women Athletes, 127
Oxford Companion to Musical Instruments, The, 120
Oxford Companion to Politics of the World, The, 52
Oxford Companion to the English Language, The, 82
Oxford Companion to the Supreme Court of the United States, The, 66
Oxford Dictionary of Modern Slang, The, 87
Oxford Dictionary of Opera, The, 119
Oxford Dictionary of Quotations, The, 134
Oxford English Dictionary: Second Edition on Compact Disc, The, 82
Oxford Illustrated Encyclopedia of Invention and Technology, 98
Oxford Illustrated Encyclopedia of Peoples and Cultures, 50
Oxford Illustrated Literary Guide to Great Britain and Ireland, The, 140
Oxford Thesaurus, The, 86
Parks Directory of the United States, 151
Penguin Guide to Jazz on CD, LP and Cassette, The, 117
Perfect Name for the Perfect Baby, The, 156
Personal Health Reporter, 99
Photographic Encyclopedia of Wildflowers, The, 104
Pick-up Games, 120
Play, Learn, and Grow, 33
Political Leaders in Weimar Germany, xx
Political Leaders of Contemporary Africa South of the Sahara, 160
Political Parties of Asia and the Pacific, 153
Pool Player's National Pocket Billard Directory, The, 126
Portraying Persons with Disabilities, 133
Presidency A to Z, The, 67
Presidents of the United States, The, 163
Primer on Sexual Harassment, 65
Print Price Index '93, 115

TITLE INDEX

Professional Baseball Franchises, 128
Professional Secretaries International Complete Office Handbook, 108
Quinlan's Illustrated Directory of Film Comedy Actors, 125
Rand McNally Picture Atlas of Prehistoric Life, 94
Random House Library of Knowledge First Encyclopedia, The, 88
Random House Word Menu, 86
Reader's Digest Atlas of the World, 149
Reader's Digest Bartholomew Illustrated Atlas of the World, 150
Reader's Digest Illustrated Book of Cats, The, 105
Reader's Guide to the American Novel of Detection, A, 139
Recommended Reference Books in Paperback, 28
Recreation Handbook, The, 126
Recycling Sourcebook, 76
Recycling in America, 76
Reference Books for Children, xx
Reference Guide to Afro-American Publications and Editors, 1827-1946, A, 29
Reference Guide to Science Fiction, Fantasy, and Horror, 136
Reference Guide to Science, Fiction, Fantasy, and Horror, xx
Reference Sources for Small and Medium-Sized Libraries, 26
Register of North American Hospitals, 1993, 72
Register of North American Insurance Companies, 1993, 76
Religious Holidays and Calendars, 93
Religious Information Sources, 40
Religious Radio and Television in the United States, 1921-1991, 42
Research Guide to Corporate Acquisitions, Mergers, and Other Restructuring, 109
Research Guide to European Historical Biography, 152
Reverse Symbolism Dictionary, 46
Right Guide, The, 53
Rodale's Illustrated Encyclopedia of Perennials, 104
Roget's 21st Century Thesaurus in Dictionary Form, 85
Roget's International Thesaurus, 85
Roller Coasters, 121
Rolling Stone Index, The, 115

Russia and the Commonwealth A to Z, 158
Sailing Dictionary, The, 129
Sanitary Fairs, 163
Science Fiction and Fantasy Literature, 1975-1991, 132
Science and Technical Writing, 131
Science and Technology Desk Reference, 89
Seasons of Business, The, 110
Senior Citizen Services, 48
Sensitive Issues, 28
Shakespeare's Characters, 141
Slide Area, The, 123
Soap Opera Book, The, 125
Social Work Almanac, 70
Soldier's Chronology, The, 69
Soul Music A-Z, 120
Spanish American Authors, 141
Specialty Cookbooks, 106
Spies and Provocateurs, 54
Spiritual Seeker's Guide, The, 43
Sports Halls of Fame, 127
Stage It with Music, 126
State Census Records, 155
Statesmen Who Changed the World, 144
Statistical Handbook on the American Family, 50
Student Contact Book, 78
Supernatural Fiction for Teens, 133
Talk Shows and Hosts on Radio, 125
Tapping the Government Grapevine, 31
Themes in American Painting, 114
Times Atlas of the World, The, 149
Today's Science on File, 89
Today's World, 150
Top 500 Poems, The, 140
Traveler's Reading Guide, The, 145
Treasury of the Encyclopaedia Britannica, The, 34
Tuttle Dictionary of Antiques and Collectibles Terms, 113
Tuttle Guide to the Single European Market, 64
Twins in Children's and Adolescent Literature, 138
U.S.-Mexico Trade Pages, The, 62
Union Army, 1861-1865, The, 163
United States, The, 161
Unlocking the Files of the FBI, 33
UpClose 1990 Census Sourcebook, 48
Variety Music Guide, 123
Venomous Reptiles of North America, 96
Vietnam War in Literature, The, 138

Vietnam War, The, 159
Virgin Directory of World Music, The, 116
Visual Dictionary of Buildings, The, 112
Visual Dictionary of Flight, The, 112
Warfare and Armed Conflicts, 142
Warren's Movie Poster Price Guide, 112
Warriors' Words, 68
Washington Almanac, The, 52
Water Quality and Availability, 58
Way Nature Works, The, 92
Webster' New World Dictionary for Young Adults, 84
Webster's II New Riverside Desk Quotations, 58
Webster's II New Riverside Desk Reference, 36
Webster's New World Encyclopedia, 37
Western Reader's Guide, The, 165
Which MBA? , 78
Whistlin' Dixie, 87
Who Knows What, 107
Who Owns Corporate America, 57
Who Was Who in World Exploration, 146
Who's Who in Africa, 153
Who's Who in Comedy, 126
Who's Who in Science and Engineering, 1992-1993, 92
Who's Who in the Peace Corps, 70
Who's Who in the United Nations and Related Agencies, 64
Wilderness U, 77
Women's Information Directory, 74
World Book Encyclopedia of People and Places, The, 146
World Business Directory, 60
World Class Business, 63
World Literature Criticism, 135
World Markets Desk Book, The, 111
World War One Source Book, The, 157
World's Master Paintings, The, 113
Writer's Guide to Everyday Life in the 1800s, 164
Young People's Atlas of the United States, The, 150
Young People's Encyclopedia of the United States, The, 160
Young World, 36
Zimmerman's Complete Guide to Nonprescription Drugs, 100